THE LIKENESS OF VENICE

DENNIS ROMANO

THE LIKENESS
OF VENICE

A Life of
Doge Francesco Foscari
1373–1457

YALE UNIVERSITY PRESS ∾ NEW HAVEN AND LONDON

Designed by Emily Lees

Printed in China

Library of Congress Cataloging-in-Publication Data
Romano, Dennis, 1951–
The likeness of Venice : a life of Doge Francesco Foscari,
1373–1457 / Dennis Romano.
p. cm.
Includes bibliographical references and index.
ISBN 978-0-300-11202-3 (cl : alk. paper)
1. Foscari, Francesco, 1373–1457. 2. Heads of state—Italy—Venice
—Biography. 3. Venice (Italy)—History—697–1508.   I. Title.
DG677.94.R65 2007
945'.3105092—dc22
[B]
2006020350

A catalogue record for this book is available from
The British Library

Endpapers: Detail of fig. 29

Magistris optimis

Laurie Williams
Robert C. Wallace
(*In memoriam*)

John Andronica
Katherine Fischer Drew
Stanley Chojnacki

Dominus dux sit illa Imago, qu(a)e representat dominium venetiarum.

(The lord doge is that likeness which represents the government of the Venetians.)

The Council of Ten, 5 July 1447

CONTENTS

ACKNOWLEDGEMENTS

While researching and writing this book I accumulated numerous debts which I now happily acknowledge. First, I would like to thank the institutions whose generous financial support made it possible for me to travel to Venice and elsewhere for research and to have periods of uninterrupted time in which to write. The Cesare Barbieri Prize, awarded by the Society for Italian Historical Studies and administered by Trinity College, Hartford, supported my initial work on Foscari's career as procurator of San Marco. I am especially grateful to John Alcorn for the hospitality extended to me during my visit to Trinity. The vast bulk of the research on Foscari's life and career and the initial stages of writing were carried out during two consecutive years of sabbatical leave. During the first, I was fortunate to be in the welcoming environment of the National Humanities Center, on a fellowship funded by the National Endowment for the Humanities. The second year, which I spent working at the Library of Congress, was supported by a fellowship from the John Simon Guggenheim Memorial Foundation. I also wish to thank the Office of the Dean of the Maxwell School of Citizenship and Public Affairs at Syracuse University for making those two years of sabbatical leave possible.

My work would not have been accomplished either at home or abroad without the unfailing assistance of dedicated librarians and archivists. I wish to thank the staffs of the Archivio Apostolico Vaticano, the Biblioteca Apostolica Vaticana, the Archivio di Stato of Milan and that of Florence, the Folger Shakespeare Library, the Library of Congress, and the library of Syracuse University. Thanks are especially owed to Jean Houston and Eliza Robertson, the two amazingly efficient librarians at the National Humanities Center and to the staff of the Inter-library loan office at Syracuse University. I also wish to thank the library at the University of Pennsylvania for its long-term loan of microfilms of the records of the Venetian Senate. In Venice I am especially grateful to the staffs of the Museo Civico Correr and the Biblioteca Nazionale Marciana. I also wish to thank Don Gianni Bernardo at the library of the Seminario Patriarcale. I extend hearty thanks to Madile Gambier, Dennis Cecchin, and Francesco Turio Böhm for assistance with the photographs, as well as a special acknowledgement to the late Umberto LoCascio in the photo archive at the Correr. My biggest research debt as usual is to the expert staff of the Archivio di Stato of Venice. After so many years working there, walking into the reading room has the feel of arriving "a casa." I wish to thank especially Edoardo Giuffrida, Franco Rossi, Claudia Salmini, Sandra Sambo, and Alessandra Schiavon for their assistance. My deepest appreciation goes to both Michela dal Borgo and her husband Sandro Bosato for help that extends far beyond the archives to encompass an enduring friendship.

Many other individuals have also assisted me in important ways. I am grateful to John Martin and Edward Muir for their early support of this project and to the late Patricia Labalme for the same. Patsy was especially generous in sharing materials regarding Bernardo Giustinian. I regret that I cannot present her with a copy of this book. The same is true for Vittore Branca who showed great interest in this project. And I continue to feel the loss of Irene Alm. Dieter Girgensohn and Giuseppe Gullino have been helpful and good-natured as we have worked simultaneously on various aspects of Foscari and his reign. And Antonio Foscari has kindly sent me various published materials regarding his distinguished ancestor. Gillian Malpass at Yale University Press offered encouragement for this project, and Ruth Thackeray provided extremely smart copy-editing.

Still others have offered assistance, friendship, hospitality or all three. I wish to thank Patricia Fortini Brown, Paula Clarke, Tracy Cooper, Anna Distefano, Marcello Fantoni, Wayne and Linnea Franits, James Grubb, Wendy Heller, Deborah Howard, Holly Hurlburt, Kate Jansen, Ben and Judy Kohl, Marion Kuntz, George Labalme, Jack Levison, Pam Long and Bob Korn, Kate Lowe and Eugene McLaughlin, Sarah Blake McHam, Maureen Miller, Carlo Montanaro, Tom Nixon and Dan Sherbo, Sergio Perini, David Peterson, Susan Ritterpusch, Michael Rocke, Don and Betty Romano, Elaine Ruffolo, Anne Markham Schulz, Alan Stahl, David Stam, and Helena Szepe. I am indebted to Craige Champion and especially to Robert Ulery for their assistance with the translation of various Latin passages, epigrams, and epitaphs and to Gary Radke, one of my colleagues at Syracuse, for his careful reading of the manuscript. Special thanks are due to Debra and Joe Pincus. Throughout this project Debra has been a source of encouragement and knowledge as I have tried to understand the large literature on fifteenth-century Venetian art and architecture. Both she and Joe have been the sounding board for many of the ideas in this book as they developed. Those invigorating conversations often took place in their kitchen over a bottle of wine and a meal. I am for ever grateful to my parents, Dante and Mary Romano, for their support and excitement as this project has developed. And finally recognition must be paid to the Labrador retrievers: the extraordinary Abby with whom this project began and the exuberant Zachary with whom it has come to a conclusion.

I dedicate this book to five distinguished teachers with whom I was privileged to study. Robert C. Wallace and Laurie Williams taught history and French respectively at George C. Marshall High School in Falls Church, Virginia. The force of their personalities opened my eyes to the possibilities of studying worlds far removed in time and place. It is a deep sadness that the dedication to them must be posthumous. I had the good fortune while an undergraduate at Wake Forest University to study in Venice with John Andronica. His commitment, steadfastness, and good humor are all examples of what a teacher should be. At Rice University, I was fortunate to find in Katherine Fischer Drew a perfect model for how to be a professional historian. Finally, Stanley Chojnacki has been a mentor and friend for over thirty years now. I could not have found a better guide into the world of Venetian scholarship. Far too often the influence of teachers goes unrecognized. I hope this dedication repays at least some of the debts I owe them all.

ILLUSTRATIONS

27. Palazzo Medici, Florence. Photo courtesy of Scala/Art Resource, NY.

28. Cà Foscari. Photo courtesy of Böhm.

29. Cà Foscari, third-floor frieze. Photo courtesy of Böhm.

FIGURES 30–45 (Between p. 310 and p. 311)

30. Cà Foscari, sculpture over rear courtyard gate, from Jan Grevembroch, "Saggi di familiari magnificenze" (MCC, MS. Gradenigo-Dolfin 229, fig. 45). Photo courtesy of Museo Civico Correr.

31. Island monastery of San Cristoforo della Pace, from Vincenzo Coronelli, *Le singolarità di Venezia,* 1697. Photo courtesy of Museo Civico Correr.

32. Cà del Duca. Photo courtesy of Böhm.

33. Memorial plaque commemorating the Peace of Lodi at San Cristoforo della Pace, from Jan Grevembroch, "Varie venete curiostà sacre e profane" (MCC, MS. Gradenigo-Dolfin, 65/I, fig. 100). Photo courtesy of Museo Civico Correr.

34. The Council of Ten's deliberation of 22 October 1457 (ASV, Consiglio dei Dieci, Deliberazioni misti, reg. 15, fol. 140r). Photo courtesy of Archivio di Stato di Venezia, Atto di concessione n. 25/2005.

35. Scala dei Giganti, Ducal Palace. Photo courtesy of Museo Civico Correr.

36. Tomb of Doge Foscari, sarcophagus, Santa Maria Gloriosa dei Frari. Photo courtesy of Böhm.

37. Tomb of Doge Foscari, effigy, Santa Maria Gloriosa dei Frari. Photo courtesy of Böhm.

38. Etching of Foscari tomb by Marco Sebastiano Giampiccoli (1777). (MCC, Stampe Gherro 290). Photo courtesy of Museo Civico Correr.

39. Tomb of Doge Foscari, epitaph. Photo by Dino Zanella, courtesy of Debra Pincus.

40. Tomb of Doge Foscari, inscription on base of left column. Photo courtesy of Böhm.

MAPS (p. xvii)

AUTHOR'S NOTE

Most names is this book are rendered in their Italian or Venetian forms rather than in Latin. Thus Iacobus becomes Giacomo, with the notable exception of both the doge's son and Pietro Loredan's son whose names are commonly rendered as Jacopo. Such variants as Bernardo Giustinian(o) and Marin(o) Sanudo/Sanuto similarly reflect spellings as they appear in archival and printed sources. Works of art, libraries, and buildings are in Venice unless otherwise stated. The Venetian calendar year in this period began on 1 March. All dates in the text have been converted to the calendar year beginning 1 January, but retained according to Venetian usage in the notes with the abbreviation mv (*more veneto*). For example 15 January 1442 mv is rendered in the text as 15 January 1443.

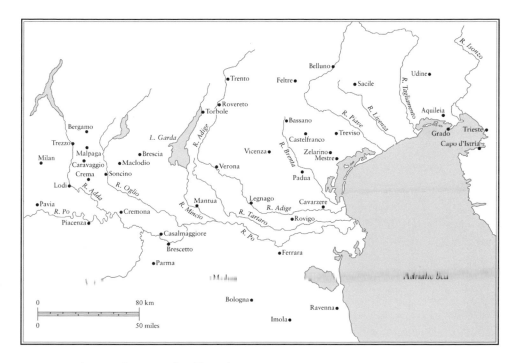

1   The terraferma in the fifteenth century.

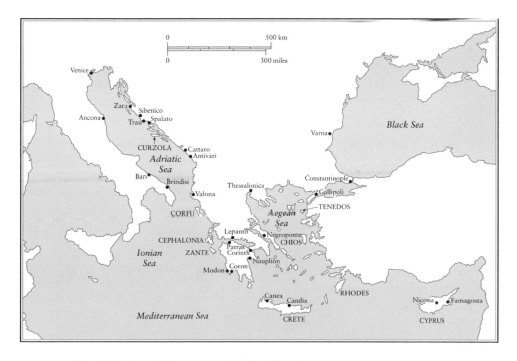

2   The Adriatic and Aegean seas in the fifteenth century.

PREFACE

Eodem anno Veneti deposuerunt ducem suum, qui in ducatu
manserat per annos xxxv cum magna prudentia regens et affabilitate.

(In that same year [1457] the Venetians deposed their doge
[Foscari], who had been on the ducal throne for 35 years
ruling with great prudence and affability.)

Archbishop Antoninus of Florence[1]

"Men know as little of the state's real acts as of the grave's
unfathomed mysteries."

Lord Byron, The Two Foscari[2]

"One cannot write history without dealing with the history
of images."

Thomas F. Mathews[3]

Thanks in large measure to the play by Lord Byron and the opera by
Giuseppe Verdi, Francesco Foscari, the Doge of Venice from 1423 to
1457, stands as one of the great tragic figures in history. A man of
extraordinary intellect, pride, and ability, he was forced, some say on
account of the implacable enmity of members of the rival Loredan

family, to banish his only surviving son Jacopo not once but twice. And then only months after Jacopo died in exile, he himself suffered the disgrace of being forced from the ducal throne at age eighty-four. Humiliated and in poor health, Foscari died just days after his successor Pasquale Malipiero was elected. His is a tragic story to be sure, and one that has been told many times before. But the story of Francesco Foscari is much more than a personal tragedy, more than simply another example of a great man brought low. For the events of his life, especially the incidents surrounding Jacopo's exile and Foscari's deposition, amounted to a crisis of governance in the Venetian Republic, one that centered on the nature of ducal power. That crisis was itself precipitated in no small measure by the radical transformations taking place across the Italian peninsula in the Renaissance and by the need for the Venetian government to adjust to those changes.

Throughout its five hundred year history as an independent state, the Republic of Venice produced surprisingly few individuals whose names still resonate today. Among those whose fame resists oblivion are Marco Polo, Titian, Antonio Vivaldi, and Giacomo Casanova – none of whom made his name in the arena of politics, the realm for which while it flourished the Republic was most renowned. Especially between the fourteenth and seventeenth centuries, as the European state system took shape and matured under the tutelage of kings seeking to fulfill their dynastic ambitions, Venice served as the model or template for an alternative pathway to political development, one based upon republican rather than monarchical principles, and in so doing garnered great admiration for the stability and constancy of its regime. As the bishop, church reformer, and Venetian nobleman Gasparo Contarini argued in his treatise *De magistratibus et republica venetorum* (1543), the key to the Republic's political success lay in its inspired combination of Aristotle's three forms of ideal rule, with the doge offering the monarchic element, the Senate the aristocratic, and the Great Council the democratic.[4] By the seventeenth and eighteenth centuries, however, as new republican regimes took shape in Holland and North America and as democratic sentiments awakened elsewhere, the Republic of Venice took on a new cast. No longer did observers regard it as a model of right rule, but instead as a closed, aristocratic, and secretive regime enforcing its will through fear and terror, often by means of the Council of Ten. This view gained even wider currency once Napoleon swept the Venetian Repub-

lic from the political map of Europe and as historians and others including Byron set about ruminating on the Republic's meaning.

Given the manifest importance of Venice in "the political education
of Europe," the absence of doges among its famous native sons is surprising.[5] Specialists in Venetian history, however, are likely to cite as
examples – in addition to Foscari – Enrico Dandolo, the blind octoge-
narian who conquered Constantinople in 1204; Marino Falier, the doge-
turned-conspirator who sought to overthrow the Republic in 1355;
Andrea Gritti, the soldier-spy who orchestrated a resurgence of the city
following the disastrous League of Cambrai in the early sixteenth
century; and Leonardo Donà, the pious bureaucrat, who nonetheless
defied a papal interdict in 1607.[6] And yet this paucity of renowned doges
was largely the fulfillment of a calculated strategy on the part of Venice's
ruling elite, for the regime was first and foremost a corporate one, in
which that elite, defined as those who enjoyed a hereditary right to
membership in the Great Council and who styled themselves as noble,
sought to present a unified front to outside observers, to inculcate
among themselves the ideal of unanimity, and to discourage overt displays of individualism. Where these political ideals most clearly clashed
with countervailing forces was in the figure of the doge for he was
simultaneously Venice's chief republican magistrate, its duke or prince,
and the earthly representative of Venice's patron Saint Mark.

The doge was and remained a "paradoxical" figure.[7] At first as a
Byzantine military official, then as an independent ruler, the doge
enjoyed an extraordinary degree of power and authority over the
Venetian community. But as the city grew in wealth and prestige and
the cadre of wealthy merchants increased, he found himself increasingly
under pressure to take the concerns of those men into account. By 1032
they had imposed on him the requirement that he appoint two ducal
councilors; a century later the precedent was established that he could
not contravene his councilors' opinions. Over the course of these centuries, as Venice evolved from a dukedom into a commune – that is, from
a princely state into a republican one – the doge saw his power gradually diminish, especially as it was codified in his *promissione* or oath of
office. Nevertheless, he retained vast reservoirs of authority and prestige
upon which to draw.[8]

One of the most bountiful founts of ducal power was symbolic since
the doge was believed to be the very embodiment of the Republic. The

Council of Ten made this clear during Foscari's reign when in July 1447 they had to determine whether or not the doge should excuse himself from council meetings when matters regarding Venice's relations with the papacy were being debated. Foscari's presence was at issue since members of the council with close relatives who enjoyed important clerical benefices were required to leave during such debates in order to avoid possible conflicts of interest. Foscari's nephew held just such a benefice. In the end the Ten decided that Foscari should attend but should not vote or make a speech. What is significant is the reasoning behind this decision: they argued that it was essential for the doge to preside at the meeting since he was "that *Imago* which represents the government [*dominium*] of the Venetians [...] and by whose means the entire government of our state is administered." They held that their ancestors had not intended the doge to fall under this specific prohibition, since "they [the ancestors] reserved the presence of the prince on account of the dignity of the dogeship and his symbolic function [*representationem*]."[9]

The term that the members of the Ten applied to the doge – *imago* – defies easy translation into English. In its most literal sense, it means a picture or statue and was commonly used to refer to what would today be considered works of art. Indeed, Foscari's son Jacopo once imported to Venice an *imago lapidea*, in other words, a piece of sculpture. But just as many works of art in the Renaissance were thought to have special properties as transmitters of saintly or divine power and were venerated for those powers, so in this context the term *imago* carried similar connotations – the doge was like an icon, transmitting the power of Saint Mark to his people. Many of the governmental palaces in Renaissance Italy were decorated with religious paintings which had an almost totemic significance and which in a real sense legitimated and consecrated the proceedings that took place within them. One thinks of the *Maestà* – the image of the Virgin painted for the Sala del Consiglio in the Palazzo Pubblico in Siena. So in a similar way, the Ten believed that Foscari's presence was required to give the council's actions legitimacy. More figuratively, the term *imago* suggests an idea, a semblance, a ghost. Accordingly, the doge was understood to embody or make visible the spirit or essence of the Republic. However, the word that best captures the meaning the members of the Ten meant to convey is "likeness" for it suggests both a physical and spiritual resemblance. The doge, in this case Foscari, was the very likeness of Venice. This does not mean that there was an identity of the two as in the famous phrase supposedly uttered by Louis XIV – *l'état c'est moi* – but rather a resemblance, the doge represented or personified the Republic.[10]

The debate over Foscari's attendance at the meeting of the Ten encapsulated the dilemmas facing the regime, ones that to a very great extent had to do with the dogeship itself. The first of these concerned the role of kinship in the Venetian political system. In essence, the Venetian Republic rested on family principles since political enfranchisement, defined as the right to sit in the Great Council, depended upon membership in a specific set of lineages, most of which had been set in place since the beginning of the fourteenth century. For this reason, Venetian politics can profitably be viewed as a constant struggle among those constituent families to control the levers of power. The conflict between the Foscari and the Loredans provides an excellent example of just such inter-familial competition.[11]

At the same time, the government had constantly to be on guard that kinship interests not overwhelm the state, that private interests not supersede the public good. Precisely such concerns prompted the original ruling regarding kinsmen who enjoyed clerical benefices. But it was around the office of doge where family interests proved most threatening. At the least the Venetians feared that doges would use their reservoir of power to reward their kinsmen and promote their families' interests. More ominously, they worried that doges would attempt to make the office hereditary, that they would try – as happened several times in the central Middle Ages – to have their sons succeed them in office and thereby turn Venice, like most other states of Renaissance Europe, into a hereditary monarchy. Kinship allegiances remained both the solid foundation and the principal threat to the stability of the regime.[12]

The second dilemma the Venetians faced was manifest in the sphere of foreign relations. Over the course of the fourteenth century many of the smaller Italian city-states had been absorbed into the larger ones so that Venice found itself in the fifteenth century confronting a new set of political realities on the peninsula. This presented the Venetians with another problem, for while in terms of domestic policy they wished to limit the power of the doge, in foreign affairs they faced a new imperative – the need to move away from the slow-moving deliberative processes of the larger governmental councils and toward the more rapid and secretive decision-making procedures characteristic of princely states.[13] In other words, they needed stronger executive authority to match that of their rivals. In his funeral oration for Foscari, the humanist Bernardo Giustinian acknowledged that whereas many of the great leaders of antiquity such as Alexander, Hannibal, and Julius Caesar could act on their own, doges were required to consult with various bodies. Nevertheless, the question remained whether Venice's new more effective executive would center on the doge or perhaps on one of the smaller councils such as the Council of Ten, which had been established in the fourteenth century to handle state emergencies.[14]

Venice was not alone in facing this predicament. Indeed, as the processes of territorial consolidation proceeded peninsula-wide, there was a marked trend away from republican regimes and toward princely rule. This is most famously the case in Florence where, during the fifteenth century, the Medici family, first under the banker Cosimo, known as il Vecchio, and then under his son Piero and his grandson Lorenzo, known as il Magnifico, slowly gutted the Florentine Republic until by the sixteenth century the Medici had transformed themselves with the help of wider European powers into the Grand Dukes of Tuscany.[15] Some historians believe they detect a similar trend in Venice, beginning with Foscari and culminating in doges Marco and Agostino Barbarigo, brothers who reigned in succession at the very end of the fifteenth century. But with the death of Agostino in 1501, the analysis suggests, Venice's republican impulses reasserted themselves as new and more decisive limits were placed on ducal power so that in the sixteenth century the doge was rendered a mere figurehead, much like the constitutional monarchs of later periods, and a fixture in Contarini's vision of Venice's tripartite regime.[16]

What is clear is that during Foscari's reign new territorial realities and the scandals involving his kinsmen conjoined to create a crisis for Venetian republicanism as the Council of Ten, driven in large measure by the hatred of the Loredans and by the ambitions of other men, forced Foscari from the ducal office. The institutional aspects of this struggle need to be emphasized since from the seventeenth through the nineteenth centuries, historians and other writers attributed Foscari's deposition to the relentless animosity of the Loredans to the exclusion of all other considerations. In their hands the story of Foscari's reign was reduced to a tale of vendetta without larger political significance. Then beginning in the nineteenth century the pendulum swung in the opposite direction as a group of historians, including Samuele Romanin and Francesco Berlan, utilizing the records of the Council of Ten itself, reevaluated the events of Foscari's reign and concluded that the Ten acted, as the Ten themselves stated, not out of a desire to destroy Foscari but simply because old age had rendered him incompetent. These historians too saw no crisis, just a measured governmental response to a system facing paralysis.[17] Given the significance of the issue and especially in light of the advances that have been made in recent decades in understanding the familial and social bases of Venetian politics, it is time to take a fresh look at the life and reign of Francesco Foscari, to assess the man and the times in which he lived, his achievements and failures, and the role the vendetta narrative has played in shaping opinions of his reign.

And yet while those more general considerations about Venetian politics weigh heavily, it is important to emphasize that this is first and foremost a biography, an account of one of the most fascinating and complex men ever to occupy the ducal throne and a formidable figure even by the daunting standards of Renaissance Italy. What I have sought to do in this study is to restore Foscari to the full complexity of his life and times, to capture the varied facets of his personality: his piety and pragmatism, his bouts of what might be labeled depression and his moments of great triumph, his fatherly instincts and indulgence toward his son, his love of pomp and his regard for the law. What I have tried not to do is to reduce him and his reign to a solitary theme such as a single-minded quest for greater ducal power or to turn the ultimate tragedy of his reign into a predetermined, if emotionally compelling, story of revenge. Foscari was complex and self-contradictory, consistent and inconstant, steadfast and wavering; in other words he lived his life as a vital human being, not simply an *imago*, although symbols, especially when they applied to the dogeship, counted for much.

Trying to get at Foscari is not easy given the sources from which one must work. There is, of course, the usual panoply of chronicles, histories, and governmental records; the latter are particularly useful since they include the bills that Foscari sponsored or co-sponsored, making it possible to trace his views on specific issues as well as his more general ideological orientation. With a few exceptions, such as Foscari's last will and testament, the kinds of document that biographers naturally prefer are lacking – personal letters, diaries, and the like – what might be considered the records of the private man, those sources that give special insight into the individual. What survives is a series of building projects with which Foscari was involved and for which in some cases he was the principal patron. These include a chapel dedicated to the Madonna in the basilica of San Marco, the great ceremonial entryway into the Ducal Palace known as the Porta della Carta, Cà Foscari (the doge's private palace on the Grand Canal), and Foscari's magnificent tomb in the Franciscan church of Santa Maria Gloriosa dei Frari. Through these building and sculptural programs Foscari (or in the case of his tomb, his heirs) revealed his vision of the dogeship as well as his aspirations for his family and for Venice. And so, despite their very public nature, these monuments provide an intimate glimpse into the man himself. For that reason, they are central to this study and stand, alongside several painted portraits of Foscari, at the thematic center of the following chapters just as they stood at the center of different phases of his life. They are as valuable for understanding the man and the changing nature of the dogeship during his reign as any written source.

Since the publication of Jacob Burckhardt's pioneering study in 1860, one of the great contributions of Italian Renaissance studies to history in general has been its demonstration of the interplay between art and power, between rulers' patronage of artists and the creation and manipulation of images of authority.[18] For this reason, I owe a special debt to the many art historians who have examined and explicated the iconography behind the various architectural projects that Foscari undertook. At the same time, I have tried to make my own contribution to an understanding of these monuments by embedding them even more fully into the historical context whence they emerged.

This book then is an account of one man's life, a consideration of Venetian politics during the Italian Renaissance, and an examination of the architectural monuments and portraits created during one ducal reign. I have chosen to present Foscari's life chronologically since I believe that a sustained narrative is the best manner in which to convey the full confluence of forces and events culminating in the final dramatic years of Foscari's reign. My hope is that the various themes meld gracefully together and that readers will pursue them in the light of their own interests. Even more, I hope I have not done a disservice to

Foscari, who had no say in this, yet another portrait of him. The biographer's task is a daunting one, riddled with ethical dilemmas and an overriding responsibility to try to do justice to the subject. Foscari himself would have been astonished to know that his image continues to exert power and influence in lands unknown to him five and a half centuries after his death.

I

Becoming Doge
1373–1423

Non magni commodi est ducatus Venetiarum, sed
maxime seruitutus; est enim organum ciuitatis.

(The dogeship of Venice does not provide its
incumbent with great reward but demands
service; indeed it is an instrument of the city.)
Aeneas Silvius Piccolomini[1]

On the night of 15 April 1423, the vigil of the feast day of Saint Isidore,
a committee of forty-one electors meeting in conclave selected
Francesco Foscari as the sixty-eighth Doge of Venice.[2] The outcome of
the election was a surprise, even to the electors, for Foscari was the
youngest member of the forty-one. Among the more distinguished candidates likely to succeed the recently deceased Tommaso Mocenigo were
the popular naval hero Pietro Loredan and the venerable Marino Caravello. Yet a number of factors had brought Foscari and Venice to this
point. Although only fifty years old, Foscari had gained vast experience
in both domestic and international affairs, holding many of the most
important posts in government and serving on sensitive embassies. What
is more, he and his closest relatives, that is his father Niccolò but espe-

cially his uncle – also named Francesco but known as Franzi – had accumulated the personal wealth and social connections necessary to aspire to the highest offices in the Venetian Republic. Foscari rode the wave of a generational shift in Venetian politics, as the cohort that had come of age during one of Venice's gravest crises, the War of Chioggia (1379–81), in which the city almost succumbed to its maritime rival Genoa, began to pass from the scene. Additionally, Foscari had shown himself to be an advocate of new policies that favored Venetian expansion onto the Italian terraferma, some argued at the expense of maritime interests. Finally, Foscari demonstrated the personal drive and individual attributes necessary to pursue his goal of attaining the dogeship.

With his election, Foscari joined the long line of doges whose portraits ringed the upper part of the walls of the recently refurbished Great Council Hall, each portrait inscribed with a motto proclaiming the doge's accomplishments. In 1577 a fire destroyed the original series, as well as the narrative painting cycles by such artists as Giovanni Bellini and Vittore Carpaccio depicting events in Venice's history on the lower walls.[3] The portrait of Foscari now found on the right side of the wall opposite Tintoretto's *Paradiso* is a work of the late sixteenth century from the school of Tintoretto (fig. 1). Paired with a portrait of his predecessor Tommaso Mocenigo, it depicts Foscari in three-quarter view. He holds in one hand the end of a banderole which unfurls around his left shoulder and behind his back. It is inscribed with the legend "POST MARE PERDOMITUM, POST URBES MARTE SUBACTAS / FLORENTEM PATRIAM LONGAVUS PACE RELIQUI" (After subjugating the sea, after conquering the cities by war, in my old age, I bequeathed a flourishing Fatherland at peace). The motto refers to the many decades of war that consumed Foscari's dogeship and to the Peace of Lodi (1454) and the formation of the Italian League which brought an end to those wars. The portrait conforms to the conventions of the later sixteenth century in pose and costume.

What the original portrait of Foscari looked like is unknown, although a fragment from the fifteenth century depicting doges Antonio Venier and Michele Steno shows them in three-quarter view as well. Some suggest that a more likely reflection of the original is a small panel painting usually attributed to the painter Lazzaro Bastiani (plate 1).[4] It shows Foscari in profile against a dark background. The gold and crimson brocade robes of state envelop his body, making it difficult to delineate the curve of his shoulder and creating the awkward impression that he has turned his back slightly to the viewer. The elaborate buttons of the cape stand out against the background. Foscari wears the ducal *corno* or beret, a style of headdress adapted from the Byzantine court and under it the white skullcap or *camauro*, secured by the string which ties under his neck.[5] The top part of the *corno* is sheathed in the same brocaded fabric as the cape while the lower section is decorated with a wide band of richly embroidered gold cloth with lozenges and studs resembling mounted jewels. The face is rendered with precision, depicting the doge with sagging jowls, a thick neck, and bags under his eyes. The overall impression is one of intelligence tinged with skepticism or bemusement as Foscari appears to arch an eyebrow and to turn up his lips in the faintest of smiles. It is not difficult to imagine it as the expression of a hard-nosed realist calmly listening to the rhetorical flourishes of a particularly sycophantic subject petitioning for a favor.

But it is risky to hazard such insights from this picture for its purpose, like that of most fifteenth-century portraits, was not to capture the sitter's personality. It was intended instead to celebrate the ducal office and commemorate Foscari's attainment of it. As such it provides telling clues to the way the Venetians wished to imagine their rulers and what it meant for an individual to ascend to the dogeship. And so this chapter examines the ducal office as well as the events and factors which brought Foscari to the throne on that April night in 1423.

Francesco Foscari was born in 1373, the eldest son of Niccolò di Giovanni Foscari and Cateruzia Michiel, probably in the family palace in the parish of San Simeon Apostolo, across the Grand Canal from the present-day railroad station.[6] The Foscari were a moderately important family within Venice's ruling elite. Tradition claimed that they had immigrated to Venice from the countryside around Mestre in the late tenth century. Certainly individuals bearing that name began to appear in documents shortly after the year 1000.[7] But it was the family's inclusion in the legislative and social process known as the *Serrata* or Closing of the Great Council in the period from 1297 to 1323 that paved the way for their future prestige, for it guaranteed them as well as the one hundred and fifty or so other families included in the *Serrata*, the exclusive and hereditary right to sit in the council and thereby the exclusive opportunity to be elected to various offices of state, including the dogeship.[8] And although the

Foscari were not counted among the *case vecchie*, the oldest and most distinguished families within the Venetian patriciate, they were numbered among a second distinguished subset of patrician clans, the *case nuove*.[9]

In the closed world of Venetian politics, based as it was on membership in a patrilineage, family counted for a great deal; and for all intents and purposes, the Foscari family's rise to political and social prominence began with the doge's great-grandfather Niccolò.[10] Niccolò, who married three times, owned a great deal of property, both in the city of Venice, much of it at Rialto, and on the terraferma, at Zellarino in the district around Treviso and at Noventa in the area around Padua. Niccolò's possession of these terraferma properties, as well perhaps as his second marriage (to Balzanella da Peraga), drew him into the orbit of the mainland Italian princes, especially the Carrara lords of Padua and the Scaligeri of Verona.[11] In 1328 Cangrande I della Scala knighted him. And three years later, in 1331, John, Count of Luxembourg and King of Bohemia and Poland, son of the late Holy Roman Emperor Henry VII, invested him and his heirs with the estates of Zellarino and Noventa as well as some other property at Sant'Ambrogio (San Bruson) as honorary fiefs which carried with them the title of count.[12]

In January 1341 Niccolò Foscari dictated his last will and testament to the notary Felice de Merlis. He named as his executors his wife Isabeta, his sons, and the procurators of San Marco, special officials in charge of the basilica who gradually came also to assume a variety of fiduciary responsibilities. In his will he provided dowries for his daughters Agnesina and Maria and named his sons Giovanni and Jacobello as his universal heirs. He also made a number of important charitable bequests, asking, for example, that the hospital or hospice which he had begun constructing for twelve poor inmates on the island of Murano be completed. In order to secure its financial future he endowed it with a number of properties, including several on Murano and on the terraferma near Mestre. He reserved for the family the right to name the hospital's prior as well as the rest of the staff. Niccolò's home parish, San Simeon Apostolo, was also the recipient of several bequests. He left funds for the construction and outfitting of a chapel dedicated to the Virgin, repair of the campanile, and a house for one of the parish clergy. He also left money for the building of a *cavana* or hut between the monastery of San Segondo and San Zulian, which could serve as a way-station for boats traveling in the lagoon.[13]

Niccolò's elder son Giovanni, the doge's grandfather, who flourished during the middle decades of the fourteenth century, enjoyed a fairly distinguished political career which included terms as podesta or chief administrator in Padua and Treviso, as well as several diplomatic missions. But he twice ran foul of the government: in 1356, when he abandoned the town of Asolo to enemy Hungarian troops; and again in 1372, during a failed attempt to mediate between the government and his son Paolo, who was then the Bishop of Venice (Castello), in a conflict over the death tax. In his will, dated 1366, Giovanni bequeathed money for perpetual masses in "our chapel in San Simeon Apostolo" and increased the endowment for "our hospital on Murano." Although he bequeathed to his wife her clothing, he asked that a particularly beautiful gem as well as his Bible remain in the patriline. He made various provisions for his several sons, noting in particular that he had spent a great deal of time, money, and effort seeking to advance Paolo's ecclesiastical career, which he ended as Archbishop of Patras in Greece.[14]

In addition to the churchman Paolo, Giovanni had at least five other sons, including the doge's father Niccolò and his uncle Franzi. Only in this generation, at least as far as can be judged from the surviving documents, did the family begin to demonstrate more than a passing interest in Venice's overseas dominions and maritime trade; until this point, much of its wealth appears to have been tied up in property.[15] In this, they differed from many Venetian noble families who had long looked to trade with the east but came late to an interest in the terraferma. Around 1372 Niccolò married Cateruzia Michiel, who brought to the marriage a dowry of 3000 ducats, a very large sum. This may have provided the liquid capital needed for business ventures. Certainly in the 1390s Niccolò was involved in trade at Bari and Trani. His political career began in 1379 and continued without long interruption until his death in 1412. During this time he held a series of important posts, including *avogador di comun* (state attorney), ducal councilor, governor of Corfu, captain of Verona, and member of the Council of Ten. He also served on the committee of forty-one that elected Michele Steno doge in 1400.[16]

Niccolò in turn had six children, three sons and three daughters. The eldest son Francesco is the subject of this study, while the youngest son, Marco (b. 1394) became a procurator of San Marco.[17] In 1418 Marco acknowledged receipt of a dowry of 1000 ducats and a *corredo* (a gift by the bride's family to the couple) of 600 ducats from his wife Margarita, daughter of nobleman Francesco Marcello.[18] Donato, the middle son, had died by 1421.[19] As for Niccolò's daughters, the future doge's sisters, Franceschina married nobleman Santo Venier, while Elena became a nun and eventually abbess of the venerable and influential Benedictine convent San Zaccaria, located not far from San Marco. Nothing is known about a third daughter named Brexeida. In his will, Niccolò named as his executors his wife, sons, and brother Franzi along with his son-in-law Santo Venier and nobleman Marco Loredan. Niccolò asked to be buried at San Simeon Apostolo and that his fellow members of the confraternity of San Marco and the priests of the parish church attend his funeral. Niccolò named Cateruzia his universal heir and advised her to divide his estate as equitably as possible among his children, noting, however, that Francesco had already received much at the time of his marriage.[20] In her own will, dated June 1412, Niccolò's widow and Foscari's mother Cateruzia made various bequests to her male and female children, but left the residue of her estate to her sons equally. She asked as well that her daughter Franceschina take her little brother Marco into her home. She bequeathed money for the building fund of the church of San Silvestro (likely her natal parish), for the redemption of imprisoned debtors, and for the poor of Crete. She also disposed of three female slaves: Marta she gave to her son Marco, who was required to free her after an additional ten years of service; Caterina she freed entirely; Anastasia she bequeathed to her daughter Elena, the nun at San Zaccaria.[21]

The future doge's uncle Franzi was significantly younger than his half-brother Niccolò. In 1386 he was betrothed to Sterina, daughter of the Greek despot or lord of Lepanto Giovanni Bua Spatas, although the marriage did not take place until 1395. Sterina brought a dowry of 11,000 hyperpers (about 3300 ducats) and the castle of Dragameston. However, the territory was eventually lost to the lord of Cephalonia, Carlo Tocco.[22] Franzi began his political career with a term in 1394 as the *capo di sestiere* or neighborhood supervisor for the Santa Croce section of the city, while continuing to engage in trade in such places as Cyprus, Beirut, and Damascus. From the late 1390s until his death in late 1424 or early 1425, Franzi devoted much of his energy to politics and governance of the state, but these activities are best recounted in the context of his nephew's career. Franzi and Sterina produced six sons, Filippo, Urbano, Giovanni, Paolo, Polidoro, and Sgurus, and at least two daughters: Patavia and Samaritana.[23] Franzi appears to have abandoned the family's traditional base in San Simeon Apostolo, apparently taking up residence in various parishes, including Sant'Aponal and San Canciano. In spite of the physical separation, members of the family continued to cooperate, aid one another, and in some instances to own property in common.[24] In 1425 Doge Foscari named his cousin Polidoro *primicerio* or vicar of the basilica of San Marco. Polidoro went on to become Bishop of Bergamo and Archbishop of Zara. Franzi's branch of the Foscari family became extinct in 1607.[25]

In many respects, the Foscari family was typical of those within the Venetian patriciate. In terms of size, they were small in relation to such patrilineages as the Contarini and Morosini, but substantial when compared with any of the families represented in the Great Council by a single adult individual.[26] Like many – perhaps most – Venetian noble families, the Foscari engaged in trade with the eastern Mediterranean, although they were not among the city's great merchant families. There is no evidence, for example, that they owned private merchant vessels or purchased the rights to state-owned galleys in this period.[27] Much of their wealth was tied up instead in property, both in the city, including buildings in the red-light district known as the Castelleto and a tavern called the Stella, and on the terraferma.[28] Their precocious involvement with the mainland did distinguish them from many other families. And certainly their title as counts set them apart. But the family's political interests lay solidly in Venice; and many of the men in the generations leading up to the doge enjoyed successful if not particularly distinguished careers. None, in the generations before Francesco, became a procurator of San Marco – the most prestigious post in the government after the dogeship. The family did, however, show an interest in ecclesiastical careers and in charitable institutions such as confraternities and hospitals. And like other families within the patriciate, the Foscari forged connections and alliances to other patrilines through marriages. These included ties to such ancient and distinguished Venetian houses as the Michiels, as well as to the Bua Spatas, feudatories in Greece.

Into this family Francesco Foscari was born in 1373. Virtually nothing is known about his birth or upbringing. A story recounted by Pope Pius II can be discounted as fantastically apocryphal. According to that account, when Foscari's father and the father of future pope Eugenius IV, a fellow Venetian, were trading together in Egypt, a hermit or prophet

(Pius uses the two terms in different versions of the story) predicted that their sons would reach the summits of power in the secular and ecclesiastical spheres. Like the story of Moses found in the bulrushes of the River Nile by the pharaoh's daughter, this legend sought to account for the future greatness of both men. It may as well provide some evidence of the family's commercial interests in the eastern Mediterranean.[29] Almost certainly, the young Francesco would have begun his schooling at a fairly early age, either with a private family tutor or more likely at a school. He would have learned basic literacy skills in Latin and Venetian, as well as enough arithmetic to manage his personal and business affairs.[30] Yet there is evidence to suggest that Foscari's education extended well beyond this rudimentary level. Antonio Morosini, who was certainly knowledgeable about if not an intimate of Foscari and whose chronicle serves as an important source for the first decade of Foscari's reign, wrote in 1430 that as doge Foscari responded to ambassadors from Genoa in "bon Latin" and on another occasion to an embassy from Florence with eloquence and "sweetness" of speech; others commented on his eloquence as well.[31] These notices suggest that Francesco's father Niccolò had his son schooled in rhetorical skills, which were rapidly becoming the backbone of the educational program advocated by the early humanists. Certainly Foscari's own son Jacopo moved in learned circles, corresponding with the humanists Francesco Barbaro, Poggio Bracciolini, and Leonardo Bruni among others. The family thus appears to have emphasized the value of a good education.[32]

It also seems likely that Foscari, like many young Venetian patrician males of the period, was sent overseas not only to gain practical knowledge of the lands and peoples of the eastern Mediterranean and experience in mercantile affairs, but also to bolster the family's fortune.[33] He might, for example, have accompanied his father on some of his merchant ventures to southern Italy. But the first sure indication of Foscari's involvement in trade activities comes from a case brought in 1411 before the *giudici di petizion*, a court with jurisdiction over debts and commercial disputes, in which he was seeking to recover 1893 ducats from Ermolao da Patras as payment for some pearls which he had shipped from Beirut in 1407. The case also indicates that Foscari had been in Damascus.[34] As described below, after a brief period of office-holding in 1403 and 1404, Foscari disappears from politics until 1408, so it seems likely that he spent part of those years in the east as a merchant.

The one event of his early life about which there is no doubt is his marriage. In 1395 at age twenty-two, Foscari married Maria, daughter of the wealthy banker Andrea di Lorenzo Priuli.[35] Foscari entered marriage fairly young: it was common for patrician males to wait until their late twenties or even early thirties to marry. The Priuli were another of the *case nuove*. The size of Maria's dowry is unknown. As the Foscari had not yet shown themselves to be among the city's leading power brokers, they might have accepted a relatively small dowry in return for an alliance with the influential banking family. They might even have had to put up a good deal of money in the form of gifts to the bride. As noted above, Foscari's father Niccolò stated in his will that his wife Cateruzia should take into consideration that Francesco had already received a healthy share of the patrimony in marriage expenses. What the marriage did offer the groom was an immediate if indirect connection to the clients of his father-in-law's bank – a valuable asset for an aspiring politician. Francesco and Maria Priuli went on to produce four children: sons Giovanni and Lorenzo and daughters Camilla and Bianca.

Apart from the fortunate marriage, then, there was nothing in either Francesco's upbringing or in the family's past to suggest that he was about to move into the highest circles of power. The historian Giuseppe Gullino attributes this success to a concerted effort by Niccolò, Franzi, and Francesco, what he calls a "unique political strategy" to position themselves at the summit of power. That strategy played out against the backdrop of the critical choices facing Venice at the beginning of the fifteenth century concerning the future direction of the city's foreign policy and economic interests. In order to understand further Foscari's catapulting into power, it is important to know where the fortunes of Venice stood *circa* 1400.

Writing in the 1380s, the chronicler and ducal chancellor Rafaino Caresini penned words that in retrospect seem prophetic. He wrote that while the sea was the source of Venice's "honors and riches," the mainland or terraferma brought nothing but "scandals and mistakes."[36] In this Caresini was giving voice to a commonly held and long-accepted view among the Venetian ruling elite. Over the centuries, especially after the Venetian-led conquest of Constantinople by Western crusaders in 1204, trade with the eastern Mediterranean had made the city fabulously wealthy and bolstered the fortunes of innumerable Venetian families. While some families, especially the *case vecchie*, could trace their trade interests to the eleventh century or even earlier, many others saw their fortunes rise as a direct consequence of Venice's expansion in the post-conquest boom. These same new families then secured their political power in the *Serrata* of the Great Council.[37]

Not surprisingly, Venetian foreign policy was geared to the protection of trade and hence of merchant family interests. This entailed first and foremost hegemony over the Adriatic Sea. While Venice maintained fairly firm control over the northern part of the sea (dubbed the Gulf of Venice), its effort to dominate the rest of the basin faced constant competition from such southern Italian cities as Bari (under the control of Naples) and from various towns along the Dalmatian coast. Venice's most dangerous competitor in the region, however, was the Kingdom of Hungary, which claimed control of Dalmatia as well as the troublesome region of Friuli.[38]

Beyond the Adriatic, Venetian policy aimed at the maintenance of strategically situated islands and coastal towns along the trade routes to Constantinople, Beirut, and Alexandria. In the division of spoils following the conquest of Constantinople in 1204, Venice had taken as its three-eighths (or as the expression of the time put it, "a quarter and a half a quarter") share of the Byzantine empire, those parts that furthered its maritime interests, namely the wharves and warehouses of Constantinople itself, as well as various towns and islands in or near the Greek archipelago, including Negroponte in the western Aegean Sea, Modon and Coron in the Ionian Sea, and the large and prosperous island of Crete.[39] These locales provided resupply stations for Venetian merchant ships traveling to the east to secure silks and spices, as well as markets for the purchase of local trade goods, such as olive oil, wine, raisins, cheese, and sheepskins. In this period the Venetians' chief competitors in the eastern Mediterranean were not the Byzantines or the Turks but the Genoese. During the thirteenth and fourteenth centuries, the two maritime republics fought four wars, the last of which, the War of Chioggia (1379–81), proved nearly fatal to the Venetians. In alliance with the Carrara lords of Padua and the King of Hungary, the Genoese succeeded in capturing Chioggia at the southern end of the lagoon and blockading Venice.[40] As a boy of six when the war started, Foscari would have been too young to understand it fully, but he certainly would have been cognizant of the crisis and felt the tension that gripped the city. Indeed, the experience of seeing his native city surrounded on both land and sea might have contributed in some measure to his later advocacy of terraferma expansion.

In addition to maintaining colonies in the east, the government found other ways to benefit the mercantile interests of the ruling elite as well. First and foremost, it managed and funded the Arsenal, a massive public shipyard, where a large and highly skilled workforce built the vessels which plied the seas and protected Venetian interests. The Arsenal specialized in the construction of both great or merchant galleys and light galleys, whose large crews of combat-ready oarsmen made these vessels maneuverable, hence suitable for warfare. State ownership of the great galleys amounted to a governmental subsidy for merchants who were relieved thus of the cost of building and maintaining their own ships and hence able to invest more of their capital in goods. The Venetian Senate supervised these vessels, auctioning the great galleys to the highest bidder, setting the schedules and itineraries for their convoy voyages, and requiring the equitable distribution of cargo space.[41]

By contrast, Venetian policy toward the terraferma in the period before 1400 was decidedly non-interventionist, a stance with deep ideological roots. The whole of northern and central Italy was theoretically under the jurisdiction of the Holy Roman Emperor. But in the twelfth and thirteenth centuries the emerging communes or city-states took advantage of the chaos and confusion generated by the Investiture Controversy and the subsequent conflicts between the popes and emperors Frederick Barbarossa and Frederick II to wrest concessions from the competing powers and secure their liberties. Venice, isolated from the mainland by the waters of the lagoon, asserted that it lay outside imperial jurisdiction. It even claimed a kind of parity with the papal and imperial powers, celebrating Doge Sebastiano Ziani's mediating role in the peace forged between Pope Alexander III and the Emperor Frederick Barbarossa in 1177 through paintings in the Ducal Palace.[42]

On the whole, Venice successfully avoided entanglement in terraferma affairs, largely escaping the clashes between the papal Guelfs and the rival faction of imperial Ghibellines which dominated the politics of most of the city-states. To minimize possible conflicts of interest, the government tried unsuccessfully in the late thirteenth century to restrict the purchase of land by Venetian nobles in the March of Treviso and the area around Ferrara. In fact, just three years before Niccolò Foscari's enfeoffment by the King of Bohemia in 1331, the government prohibited (obviously without much effect) just such actions.[43]

But while Venice sought to maintain political distance from Italian affairs, it also worked to secure its economic interests on the terraferma. This involved first and foremost measures to guarantee the unfettered movement of goods along the roadways and especially the rivers leading into the Italian hinterland and through the Alpine passes into Germany and Austria. It also entailed a policy of coercion by which Venice forced a number of smaller cities to accept its role as the staple port of the Adriatic. This policy particularly affected Ferrara, strategically located near the mouth of the Po. At the beginning of the fourteenth century Venice made a play for political control of Ferrara. This resulted in the pope, Ferrara's overlord, placing Venice under interdict. But even though Venice lost the subsequent war, the eventual peace treaty reconfirmed the requirement that goods traveling to Ferrara via the Adriatic first pass through Venice.[44]

Gradually, however, threats to Venetian economic interests from the signorial or princely states of the Po valley forced the Republic to adopt a more interventionist policy toward the terraferma. Efforts by the Scaligeri lords of Verona to extend their authority eastward led to a war which resulted in Venice's annexation of the towns of Treviso and Conegliano in 1339. But for the rest of the fourteenth century Venice was content to return to its former stance, especially as its energies were diverted elsewhere by revolts in Crete in 1342 and 1363, the on-going struggle with Genoa for dominance on the seas, and Turkish incursions into the Balkans.[45] But by the turn of the fifteenth century it was becoming clear that the old policy was inadequate to meet the new pressures being exerted by the Carrara of Padua and the Visconti of Milan. It was in the unfolding of these events that the growing influence of the Foscari family made itself felt.

In 1402 Giangaleazzo Visconti, the Duke of Milan who had absorbed the lands of the Scaligeri as part of his effort to create a huge north Italian dominion, died. Francesco Novello da Carrara, ruler of Padua and heretofore a dependent of Venice, stepped in to fill the vacuum. In August 1403, over Venetian protestations, Carrara, who was allied with Milan's archrival Florence as well as with the Marquess of Ferrara, declared war on

Milan, at that moment under the control of Giangaleazzo's widow Caterina. Carrara hoped to create a state extending from the River Mincio in the west to Friuli in the east – a prospect that threatened Venice's vital trade routes into the hinterland. In the spring of 1404, with the last members of the Scaligeri or Della Scala family in tow, he set out to wrest Verona and Vicenza from the Milanese. Verona quickly succumbed, but Vicenza, seeking to avoid Carrara rule, surrendered itself to Venice, while for her part Caterina, the Duchess of Milan, agreed to cede Bassano, Feltre, and Cividale to the Venetians in an effort to gain their support against Carrara. Despite Florentine efforts at mediation, Venice declared war on Padua on 25 June 1404; and for the rest of the year, Padua and its ally Ferrara successfully resisted the Venetian forces. But in early 1405 the tide turned. In March, Niccolò III, the ruler of Ferrara, deserted his Paduan ally and reached a peace accord with Venice. Venice's brutal policy toward Verona began to show results as well. [46]

The primary advocate of that policy was Foscari's uncle Franzi who at the beginning of the year assumed office as one of the six ducal councilors. On 5 May Franzi proposed that the Veronese, given their "evil and perverse disposition," receive an ultimatum – either surrender the city within five days or else the besieging forces would be allowed to take the city and sack it. [47] Verona capitulated in June. As Carrara's position grew more precarious, he began negotiations to sell Padua to Venice while retaining certain property rights and other privileges for his family, but some in the Senate, including Niccolò Foscari, one of the *savi del consiglio* (the six "sages" who formed the Senate's steering committee), were intransigent and called for what amounted to unconditional surrender. [48] By the fall, still more Carrarese towns, including Monselice and Cittadella, fell under Venetian dominion; and finally in November Padua surrendered. Carrara and his sons were taken to Venice where they were condemned by the Council of Ten, which handled the most sensitive cases of state security, and strangled. [49]

In the space of a few short years then, Venice had emerged as a terraferma power in possession of a dominion extending from the Mincio in the west, almost to the Po in the south, and including the March of Treviso and the towns of Padua, Vicenza, and Verona. [50] This represented a momentous shift in Venetian affairs, one whose repercussions would be felt to the end of the Republic's history in 1797 and beyond. It was not a premeditated step but rather an *ad hoc* response to decisions on

the part of Carrara, coupled with a growing recognition by the Venetians that the old policy of relying on satellite signorial states was inadequate to the threat posed by the process of consolidation which was
leading to the creation of a few large states on the Italian peninsula.
Venice's action was not, as far as can be determined, the product of a
restricted group within the ruling class whose interests were tied to the
land.[51] Rather it drew on broad-based support within the patriciate.

As far as the Foscari family is concerned, the half-brothers Franzi and
Niccolò had revealed themselves to be hardliners unwilling to make
compromises with the rebel Carraresi. What is more, throughout the war
they were deeply involved on both the administrative and diplomatic
fronts, although not in the actual fighting.[52] In 1404 and again in early
1405 Franzi undertook diplomatic missions to Bologna. And later in 1405
he was a member of the board of advisors on the war (the *savi alla
guerra*) and then in 1406 captain and podesta of Feltre.[53] Niccolò served
on missions to Mantua and was among the signatories to the peace with
the lord of Ferrara Niccolò d'Este in March 1405.[54] Even if the family
was not pursuing the war out of narrow economic interests, it seems
likely that their properties and heritage on the mainland gave them a
certain authority as experts in terraferma affairs.

The young Francesco played a supporting role in these events. His
political career had begun modestly enough in 1395 with his election
as the *capo di sestiere* for Santa Croce, the section of the city in which
the family palace was located.[55] But in August 1403, just when Padua
declared war on Milan, he was selected as one of the *savi agli ordini* concerned with maritime matters.[56] The position of *savio agli ordini* was the
ultimate fast-track job for it granted young men entry into the Senate
as well as the right to sit in the Pien Collegio (Full College), the committee comprising both the Signoria and the Collegio which essentially
ran the government.[57] In that position, Foscari supported the Venetian
decision to prosecute the war.[58] In 1404 he was elected to the Council
of Forty, which served as Venice's court of appeals. He served as one of
its heads (*capi*) from the end of March until the end of April, and in
that position advocated that the city press Caterina Visconti to recognize Venice's right to all lands east of the River Mincio, especially
Vicenza and Verona.[59] But Foscari's whereabouts during the decisive later
phases of the war are unknown: as noted above, he disappears from the
record of office holders until 1408. In historical memory, however,

Foscari is intimately associated with the Paduan conquest.[60] This was at least partly a result of confusion with his uncle Franzi, often called Francesco in the sources.[61] But it has to do as well with subsequent events which transformed Foscari into the symbol of Venetian expansion. Indeed, it took some time for the Venetians to displace their mistrust of the terraferma and accept their new dominion, time for it to become a part of their consciousness and self-image. This is readily apparent in the epitaph on the tomb of Michele Steno (1400–1413), the doge who ruled in these years (fig. 2). It reads as follows:

IACET IN HOC TVMVLO SERENISSIMVS / PRINCEPS ET DOMINVS DOMINVS MICHAEL / STENO OLIM DVX VENETIARVM AMATOR / IVSTITIE PACIS ET VBERTATIS ANIMA / CVIVS REQVIESCAT IN PACE OBIIT / MILLESIMO QVADRIGENTESIMO TER / TIODECIMO DIE VIGESIMOSEXTO DECEMBRIS.

(In this tomb lies most serene prince and lord, Lord Michele Steno formerly Doge of the Venetians, lover of justice, peace, and plenty, may his soul rest in peace. He died 26 December 1413.)

The epitaph contains no reference to Venice's expansion onto the terraferma, in many ways the highlight of Steno's reign. The only commemoration of these events on the monument was the display of the keys to Padua, which delegates from the city presented to the doge at the time of the city's submission.[62] *Imperium* (empire) had not yet become a component of the ducal mystique.

During the next two decades leading up to Foscari's election as doge, Venetian foreign affairs centered on three different but interconnected arenas. The first involved the eastern frontier region of Friuli and control of the eastern Adriatic coast. Venice's chief rival for influence over this area was Sigismund, King of Hungary. And while Venice had an ally in the noble Savorgnan family of Friuli, the king relied on support from the nominal head of the region, the Patriarch of Aquileia. The Venetians scored a major victory when in 1409 Ladislaus of Naples, a rival to Sigismund, renounced his claims to Dalmatia and ceded Zara to Venice. This set Venice and Sigismund, who became King of the Romans and hence Holy Roman Emperor-elect in 1410, on a collision course. In the fall of 1411 the Hungarians invaded Friuli. A Venetian counterattack in 1412 was only partly successful. Fortunately for them, more urgent problems – among them a renewed Turkish threat, the schism within the Catholic Church involving rival claimants to the papal throne, and the heretical movement of John Huss in Bohemia – led Sigismund to agree to a five-year peace in April 1413, according to which Venice relinquished Feltre and Belluno, towns north of Venice.[63]

The second problem area centered on the Duchy of Milan and the status of the smaller princely states on Venice's western and southern borders, such as Brescia, under the control of the Terzi family, rulers of Parma and Reggio. By the second decade of the century, Filippo Maria Visconti had begun to reconstitute the duchy as it had existed under his father Giangaleazzo. But any immediate danger of Milanese expansion eastward was put on hold when in 1414 Venice and Milan signed a treaty by which Visconti gave up claims to territory in the March of Treviso, implicitly recognizing that area as being within Venice's zone of influence. Moreover, the two powers agreed to aid one another if attacked by a third party.[64]

The third area of concern was the eastern Mediterranean, where Venice maintained an uneasy relationship with the Ottoman Turks. Although the Venetians were content to pay tribute to the sultan for the territories they had gained in Albania (including Scutari, Drivasto, and Dulcigno) and Greece (Patras and Lepanto), they made no compromises with regard to sea lanes. In a treaty signed in 1411 between the Republic and the contender for the sultanate Musa, the Turks agreed not to send warships south or west of the island of Tenedos. However, the new sultan Mehmed I (1413–21) renewed raids on Venetian interests including the town of Negroponte. When in 1416 a fleet under the command of the Captain of the Gulf Pietro Loredan entered the Dardanelles, the Turks attacked it near Gallipoli. Loredan scored a stunning victory. A treaty similar to the one of 1411 was reached in 1419. And for the next few years, Venice sought to hold the line against the Turks by propping up the power of the Byzantine Paleologue family in the Morea, the region known in classical times as the Peloponnesus.[65]

When Foscari reemerges in the historical record, it is first as a diplomat engaged in negotiations on the Italian peninsula. In 1408–09 he was sent on several missions in an effort to stabilize the hold of the Terzi family over Parma and Reggio from possible incursions by the Este of Ferrara.[66] On 1 July 1409 the Senate ordered him to secure Brescello, a strategic site on the Po.[67] This is one of the few instances in Foscari's career when he had any direct military responsibilities. During his service there, he surely gained a better understanding of the geography of the Po valley at a point where several political entities converged. In late July the Senate charged Foscari with a mission to Cabrino Fondulo, ruler of Cremona, who was threatening Pandolfo Malatesta's control of Brescia.[68]

In September 1409, having for unknown reasons refused the post of proveditor (or commissioner) of Verona, Foscari went to Ferrara to persuade the Este to join the effort to drive the French marshall, Jean Le Meingre, known as Boucicault, who had designs on Milan, out of Lombardy.[69] And in April 1410 Foscari was elected for a second time as a *savio agli ordini*. But he refused the post and instead took up office as one of the *provveditori di comun*, magistrates with jurisdiction over certain industries, including wool and silk cloth.[70] In the summer of 1410 he and his two colleagues in the office (Giovanni Morosini and Pietro Venier) proposed measures to assist the silk industry; and in September 1411 he and Venier recommended taxing imported English cloth in an effort to bolster local manufacturing.[71] Otherwise he was inactive for the rest of the year. But two events around this time set Foscari on track to reach the highest echelons of power. First, in the spring of 1411 his uncle Franzi was elected for a two-year term as the Venetian governor of Crete. And then Foscari's father Niccolò died during the spring of 1412. Franzi's absence from Venice and Niccolò's death made it possible for Foscari to assume offices without violating the rules prohibiting more than one member of a patriline from sitting in the same council.[72]

And so began Foscari's real rise to prominence. In March 1412 he was elected to a term as one of the *savi alla guerra*.[73] These men supervised the war effort on the mainland, an office that eventually evolved into that of the *savi della terraferma*. While in this post, Foscari inspected the readiness of Venetian troops stationed against the Hungarian assault in Friuli, worked to combat fraud among the troops, and advocated the creation of a special committee to take up residence in the Ducal Palace during emergencies.[74] During Foscari's own reign as doge, members of the Signoria were required in several crises to remain in the Ducal Palace.[75]

In July 1412 Foscari and Pietro Loredan got into an altercation which may have been the beginning of their long-standing rivalry. At the urging of the new Council of One Hundred of War, Foscari and Barbono Morosini were selected to consult with Carlo Malatesta, the captain-general of Venice's troops, about the military campaign against Sigismund. But Loredan, already recognized as a military expert and something of a war hero even before his victory at Gallipoli, volunteered for the job, preempting (and in Giuseppe Gullino's view very likely offending) Foscari and Morosini. The two also disagreed on the efficacy of Malatesta's tactics.[76]

During the next year Foscari's career took a very different direction. In September 1412 he began a term as one of the *avogadori di comun*, actually taking up the post just months after his father's death while serving in that same office.[77] The *avogadori* served as state prosecutors, bringing both criminal and civil cases before the Council of Forty. As such they enjoyed a reputation as defenders of the law and advocates of judicial and legal equity. In the sixteenth century they represented the interests of the minor nobles of the Great Council against the more influential members who controlled the Senate and Council of Ten.[78] But by the beginning of the fifteenth century the Venetian nobility had begun to bifurcate, with poorer members depending on minor government offices for a living, resenting their more prepotent brethren, and looking to the *avogadori* for protection.[79] From all indications, Foscari took the job of *avogador* extremely seriously. In his funeral oration for Foscari, Bernardo Giustinian attached special significance to Foscari's term as state attorney, noting how he used the position to defend justice, attack avaricious and embezzling office-holders, and punish those who neglected their duty. Giustinian cited in particular Foscari's condemnation of an unnamed but particularly rich and powerful citizen.[80] Giustinian's use of the term *civis* (citizen) to describe this individual is, in the Venetian context, particularly ambiguous since he may have been referring generically to a member of the nobility or more technically to one of the *cittadini*, a kind of secondary Venetian elite made up of merchants and bureaucrats. The only case in the *avogadori* records that seems to match even remotely Giustinian's description concerns a certain Bondi di Lazzara, a shopkeeper on the street of spice-dealers. He was accused of falsifying a claim against the estate of a doctor and persuading various persons to commit perjury. Misdeeds like these threatened property rights and indeed the integrity of the entire legal system. Bondi, who was tried in absentia, was banished in perpetuity: if captured, he would have his hand amputated and be imprisoned.[81] As state attorney Foscari also advocated for admission to the nobility for members of cadet branches of patrician clans living in Crete.[82] In neither of these ways, however zealous he might have been in fulfilling his obligations, does it appear that Foscari was acting unusually. But what his term as state attorney, like the earlier one as *provveditore di comun*, did provide for Foscari was an opportunity to demonstrate his concern for two important constituencies: the lesser members of the ruling elite and those representing the city's guild or manufacturing interests. Thus while he was advancing into the inner circles of power, he was simultaneously creating for himself a reputation as an advocate for the less powerful members of Venetian society.

During the summer of 1413 Foscari served on a diplomatic mission to Sigismund.[83] And in that year he was elected one of the six *savi del consiglio*, also known as the *savi grandi*, and enjoyed his first term on the Council of Ten.[84] In December 1413 he was elected along with Antonio Contarini and Tommaso Mocenigo to serve on a diplomatic mission to Pope John XXIII and Sigismund who were negotiating at Lodi regarding the upcoming church council to be held at Constance.[85] The death of Doge Michele Steno that same month set in motion the elaborate ducal election procedures. On 7 January 1414 Foscari's fellow emissary, the bachelor Tommaso Mocenigo, was elected to the dogeship. He immediately quit Lodi and returned to Venice. Foscari remained on the diplomatic mission until March.

During the next two years Foscari served almost continuously as a *savio del consiglio*, although he did undertake an embassy to Florence in the summer of 1415, the purpose of which was to turn the Florentines against Sigismund.[86] Then in early 1416 Foscari married for a second time.[87] It is uncertain when his first wife, Maria Priuli, died; but it would have been unusual for a patrician male like Foscari to remain a widower for long. And so with the assistance of the intermediary Lorenzo Zambon, an arrangement was made for Foscari to take as his new bride Marina, daughter of nobleman Bartolomeo Nani. Part of the marriage ceremony is documented as taking place on 12 February 1416; Marina then transferred to Foscari's home on the 27th, bringing a dowry of 1000 ducats and an additional 400 ducats in the form of the *corredo*. These sums were perfectly in keeping with the norms for noble marriages of the time.[88] There was a significant age gap between Marina, who was perhaps only in her early to mid-teens, and the forty-two-year-old Foscari. During the electoral campaign for doge eight years later, Foscari's opponents commented specifically on his wife's youth and potential fecundity. As will become clear, the nobles were especially wary of doges with many children, fearing filial influence and the potential dynastic implications of ducal sons.[89] And indeed Marina did bear six children: three boys (Jacopo, Donato, and Domenico) and three girls (Benedetta, Paola, and Maria).[90] In 1418, like many well-to-do men of the period, Foscari purchased a slave, a Tartar woman named Anastasia, for the sum of 75 ducats.[91] Her duties almost certainly included helping with this growing brood of children.

In January 1416 Foscari pulled off an extraordinary political coup by managing to get himself elected to the post of procurator of San Marco at a time when there was no vacancy in the office.[92] Procuratorships were, as noted above, the most prestigious offices in the government after the dogeship. The procurators were among the few officials in Venice elected for life, and generally speaking only the most prominent and respected members of the patrician regime attained this post. As the diarist and chronicler Marino Sanudo put it, the office was the "stepping stone" to the dogeship.[93] At this time there were six procurators: two, known as the procurators *de supra*, were responsible for the maintenance and supervision of the basilica, especially the treasury. This had been the procurators' original mission and obligation. But testators, having great trust in the men who held this important office, began to name them as executors of their estates. The position thus expanded to assume a fiduciary role, including administering estates and managing charitable endowments for hospitals, orphans, and other needy groups. Four procurators handled these responsibilities. Two, the procurators *de citra*, were responsible for estates of testators who lived on "this side," that is the San Marco side of the Grand Canal; the other two, the procurators *de ultra*, were in charge of estates on the "other" side of the waterway.[94]

According to the chronicler Pietro Dolfin, who is not to be confused with the more frequently cited Giorgio, Foscari saw a chance to advance his own fortunes while serving as *savio del consiglio*. He recognized that the procurator *de citra* Giovanni Barbo was no longer able to discharge his duties on account of old age. Seizing the opportunity, Foscari somehow or another saw to it that a proposal was made in the Great Council by five of the ducal councilors that another procurator be elected to execute the office for Barbo. Then, again according to Dolfin, Foscari set about "making deals with relatives and friends" to ensure that they would select him. Accordingly, on 17 January 1416 the Great Council voted to create a third procurator *de citra* and elected Foscari to the post. Apparently, Foscari's electioneering was so effective that he was nominated by both nominating committees in the Great Council and hence ran unchallenged.[95]

The law itself, which was likely drafted by Foscari or his closest allies, was a model of tact and diplomacy. The preamble paid homage to Barbo, acknowledging his many years of service to the Republic, but then went on to state that because of his "infirmity and illness" he needed some respite from the post. According to the law, he would remain in office and continue to enjoy his salary and other perquisites, but a third procurator would be elected to the procuratorship *de citra*, as had happened twice before, in 1355 and 1361. Additionally, Barbo would continue to reside in the procurators' apartments in Piazza San Marco, while the new procurator would be given a housing allowance of 40 ducats per annum. Upon the death of one of the two procurators *de citra* living in the assigned apartments, the third would move into his place. The law explicitly stated that at that point no successor would be elected; instead the office would revert to its traditional two occupants. The proposal passed overwhelmingly, with 432 votes in favor, 14 votes opposed, and 5 abstentions. Foscari was elected on the same day by a vote of 319 to 110.[96]

In this effort Foscari showed extraordinary skill and finesse. He created an opportunity where none had existed before by highlighting Barbo's incapacity, a cruel irony given that Foscari was to be removed from the dogeship for the same purported reason more than forty years later. Normally, the office would have muddled along until death removed Barbo from the scene. It was only logical that Foscari, having orchestrated the opening, would be a prime candidate for the post, yet he apparently spared no effort in making sure that he had the necessary support for his candidacy, cultivating his "parenti et amici."

"Parenti, amici, e vicini" (relatives, friends, and neighbors) played a crucial role in the politics of Italian Renaissance cities.[97] The Medici of Florence relied upon a network of friends and relatives that had its geographical center in the family's home parish of San Lorenzo and the gonfalon or precinct of the city known as Lion d'Oro in order to pave the way for their rise to prominence.[98] But the term *vicini* or neighbors is conspicuously missing in Dolfin's description of Foscari's network; he refers only to kin and friends. This likely reflects certain peculiarities of Venetian urban life for it appears that the cultivation of neighborhood ties was less politically useful to members of the Venetian ruling class than it was to men in other urban settings such as Florence and Genoa.[99] Although active neighborhood support was not discouraged and might indeed provide some basis for a popular following, it was not critical when it came time to garner votes in the councils of government. Following the *Serrata* and the closure of the ruling elite, it was more important for politically ambitious men to develop citywide networks through friendship and marriage. What is most noteworthy in this regard is that Foscari sought election as one of the procurators *de citra*, the procurators responsible for estates of those who had lived on the San Marco side of the Grand Canal, even though the family home was in San Simeon Apostolo on the "other" side. Apparently Foscari did not see any need to use the procuratorship to consolidate a local power base. In fact, the opposite may have been true: he may have used it to broaden his citywide base of support. Also telling were Foscari's efforts to ensure that his maneuvers would not offend members of the Barbo family and their allies. He did this by making sure that Barbo continued to enjoy the office and its benefits until his death. In addition, he apparently tried to downplay the novelty of his action by emphasizing that similar elections had occurred twice before during the Trecento.

In his *Vite dei dogi* (Lives of the doges), written in the last years of the fifteenth century, Marino Sanudo recounts that once in office Foscari used its patronage powers to advance his candidacy for Venice's highest post. According to Sanudo, Foscari had his "eye on the dogeship," and when he became procurator he found the accounts of various estates entrusted to Barbo in disorder and the bags in which the proceeds of these accounts were kept "full of money." Unlike a modern-day bank in which assets are pooled and invested, the procurators themselves kept the money for each estate in separate bags.[100] Foscari began to dispense those monies to poor noblemen and to help noble daughters marry. Sanudo reports that Foscari distributed more than 30,000 ducats in all and that this largesse made many partial to him.[101] Written more than a century and a half after Foscari's death, Francesco Sansovino's guidebook-cum-treatise *Venetia città nobilissima* provides a slightly more detailed account of Foscari's procuratorial activities.

According to Sansovino, Foscari won the "grace and favor of all" by dowering young women, favoring various nobles and *cittadini*, restoring churches and hospitals, and spending in "joyous, praiseworthy, and good" works many thousands of ducats.[102]

Unfortunately, almost all of the central administrative records of the procurators' archives have been lost, making an audit of the office's financial activities virtually impossible. All that remain are account books for some of the individual estates for which the procurators were responsible. Judging from these records, it is difficult to imagine that the procurators' accounts had fallen into chaos, at least not the kind that would have yielded 30,000 ducats in unused funds, but perhaps they had since the procurators were responsible for the administration of approximately one thousand perpetual trusts.[103] Moreover, a relatively primitive accounting system made it extremely difficult even for the procurators to get an overview of the office's financial status.[104] Although there is no direct evidence for this, it is possible that Giovanni Barbo and his fellow procurator Alvise Loredan (elected in 1382) had been less than thorough in their supervision of the office or that their zeal for administration had waned with time. This was not the case with Foscari. In 1420, after both Barbo and Loredan had died, Foscari got a new colleague in the person of Bertuccio Querini, and the two seem to have undertaken a thorough audit.[105]

Foscari did, as Sanudo claimed, use estate funds to dower noble girls and help poor nobles. Some records for an endowment established by nobleman Giorgio Morosini in his will of May 1377, for example, show that between February 1416 and February 1419 Barbo, Loredan, and Foscari distributed 1500 ducats to eighty-seven girls, although only eight of them were noble.[106] Of the eight, at least three were selected by Foscari, and two of them were related to him in one way or another. One of the payments was made to help dower Maria, daughter of the late Giacomo Priuli of San Stae. Foscari's first wife was a Priuli, and in fact the payment appears to have been made to Foscari's former father-in-law Andrea.[107] The second payment was made to the dowry fund of Cristina Nani, daughter of the late Costantino Nani. Foscari's second wife was a Nani. The third was to help dower Morosina Morosini, daughter of the late Leonardo Morosini. Of the eight bequests to noble girls, Foscari selected three, Barbo and Loredan each selected two; the eighth case is indecipherable. Among the dowry distributions made by

Foscari and Bertuccio Querini from another estate, that of the late procurator of San Marco Pietro Corner, one was made to subvent the marriage of Foscari's half-cousin Samaritana, daughter of his uncle Franzi.[108] Based on this extremely limited evidence, three points can be made. First, Foscari was not acting differently from his colleagues; certainly he was not rewarding noble girls at a much more frequent rate than they were. Second, Foscari used the funds primarily to help patricians to whom he was related by blood or marriage and who, at least in the case of his half-cousin, were not poor. Third, the continued involvement of Giovanni Barbo in distributing funds raises the intriguing possibility that, with or without Barbo's complicity, Foscari exaggerated the former's incapacity in order to advance to the procuratorship.

In addition to endowing noble daughters, Foscari used trust funds to help poor nobles. One such fund was that of nobleman Leonardo Vitturi, who in his will of 1305 established a perpetual trust to assist his poor relations. The records of this estate suggest that payments had not fallen radically into arrears and that preceding procurators had faithfully discharged their duty. One of the account books records distributions made in September 1415 and March 1416. It shows that the procurators divided the available funds into 120 shares worth the small sum of 1 *soldo*, 16 *piccoli* apiece and distributed those shares to ninety-eight individuals. At least thirty of them bore the name Vitturi. But sixty-eight individuals with other noble surnames also received shares, although the notary did not record how they were related to the Vitturi. They came from at least sixteen other patrician families: Gradenigo, Soranzo, Cocco, Falier, Pisani, Loredan, Marcello, Gabriel, Pasqualigo, Lando, Boldu, Bollani, Papacizza, Salomon, Buora, and Querini.[109] These families represented a broad spectrum of the Venetian patriciate, ranging from those with little prestige or clout, for example the Buoras, to *case vecchie* such as the Soranzos and Querini. The Vitturi endowment is significant because it demonstrates yet again how the myriad ties linking members of the patriciate created at least the possibility for Foscari to advance politically by expanding his network of ties and obligations through the strategic distribution of charity, although again there is no 'smoking gun' to prove that this was the case. But it does perhaps give some credence to Sanudo's claim that Foscari made many partial to him by dispensing funds to "poveri gientelomeni."

But nobles were not the only ones to benefit. Records from Foscari's years as procurator show that the procurators assisted individuals from all levels and grades of society, lay and religious, noble and non-noble, male and female. One such beneficiary was Giovanni Caldiera, a young man of *cittadino* status, who received payments from an endowment founded by *magister* Andrea di Ausimo to help students. Caldiera was given money to help pay for his studies at the University of Padua.[110] He went on to become an important humanist and a leading apologist for Venice's patrician regime; his *De concordantia poetarum, philosophorum et theologorum*, for example, includes a passage that portrays Foscari as the very embodiment of the regime.[111] More humble members of society also received support from the procurators' funds while Foscari was in office. He directed dowry subventions from Giorgio Morosini's estate to Gasparina, daughter of a sailor; Margarita, wife of a fisherman named Raffaele; and Cristina, a cobbler's daughter who married a furrier.[112] There is no way of finding out why Foscari selected these particular recipients. However, while he used some of the funds to advance his network, he clearly took his responsibility to the poor and to non-nobles equally seriously.

On the basis of the available evidence, it is impossible to prove or disprove Sanudo's claim regarding Foscari's use of the 30,000 ducats in unused funds in order to build a clientele. It may have been part and parcel of an attempt by Sanudo to cast Foscari in an unfavorable light, as described below. Several of Foscari's rivals for the dogeship in 1423, including Marino Caravello, Antonio Contarini, and Leonardo Mocenigo, were themselves procurators and therefore could presumably call upon similar networks of friends and clients for support.

According to Sansovino, Foscari did more than build a clientele: he also won favor by, among other things, restoring churches and hospitals. There does appear to be some justification for these claims. The first effort occurred in May 1419, when a question arose about the government's use of the procurators' funds. As was customary, the commune had borrowed money from trust funds administered by the procurators for its own purposes. In this instance, it had borrowed 700 ducats from the estate of Verde della Scala, who in her will dated 1393 had bequeathed the balance of her estate for the repair of churches in Venice. "As was manifest to all," a fire in March 1419 had destroyed much of San Marco's roof, and now the basilica itself was in need of repairs.[113]

Accordingly, the Senate decided, perhaps at the urging of the procurators, to take 700 ducats from the governmental fund designated for littoral defenses and return the money to the procurators *de citra*, who were authorized to transfer it to the procurators *de supra* for the repair of San Marco. The vote was 58 in favor and 25 against, with 9 abstentions.[114] In this instance, intentionally or not, Foscari became associated with a major restoration of Venice's main church.

The second effort occurred in October 1420 when Foscari and Querini complained to the Great Council that many of the hospitals endowed and erected for the maintenance of aged sailors and others sacrificed in the city's defense were so badly administered that the intended beneficiaries were not receiving the assistance they required or deserved. On the advice of the procurators themselves, the Great Council authorized them to restructure the hospitals so that those who had shed blood for the city would be given individual houses as well as an annual subsidy of 20 ducats. By so doing they would end abuse and reward the deserving poor.[115] More than a year earlier the Council of Ten had had to curb Foscari's effort to sell property in order to benefit the sailors' hospital.[116] In his zeal to assist the poor, Foscari burnished his image as one who took his obligations as procurator seriously.

In his terms as *avogador* and *provveditore di comun* Foscari had shown a certain genius for administration, for understanding and shaping the work of the Venetian bureaucracy, and for protecting the interests of the less powerful in Venetian society. These qualities are also evident in his role as procurator of San Marco. His efforts at hospital reform and his vigorous pursuit of criminals as *avogador*, prove that he was a strong proponent of the law. He thus certainly earned Sansovino's accolade of meriting the "grace and favor of all." In pursuing the dogeship, Foscari chose an administrative route, and in the process mastered the intricacies of Venice's council-based politics.

In the meantime Foscari's future rival for the dogeship, Pietro Loredan, was following a very different path to power and position. He had already served as captain of the Gulf and proveditor in Dalmatia when in February 1416 he was named captain-general of the sea: his mission was to escort Delfino Venier on an embassy to the sultan Mehmed, whose forces had been assaulting Negroponte. He was also given permission to harass Turkish maritime interests.[117] Quite unexpectedly the Turkish and Venetian fleets came upon one another in the waters off Gallipoli and on 29 May joined battle. Loredan and the Venetian forces scored a stunning victory, capturing fifteen Turkish vessels and taking more than a thousand prisoners. Loredan reported the victory in a long and detailed letter to the Signoria. The news was received with joy and celebrated with a solemn procession in Piazza San Marco. Venice and the sultan reached a peace in August; and further celebrations greeted Loredan's return to Venice in December.[118]

The letter that Loredan sent to the Senate announcing the victory was in its way an attempt at personal publicity and self-promotion. In it he described how he and his troops "virilly" met the "vigorous Turks who fought like dragons." Despite wounds to his jaw, nose, and left hand, he was able "with the grace of God" to kill a great number of Turks. Loredan took special pleasure in the capture and execution of Giorgio Calergi, who had participated in a Cretan revolt against Venice: Loredan found it his "greatest honor" to have had Calergi "cut to pieces on the poop of my galley." He claimed that the Venetians owed the victory to God, "whose most blessed name should be glorified and always magnified and to San Marco our protector Evangelist and most blessed intercessor." Loredan's letter circulated widely and was copied into chronicles and other histories.[119] Thus while Foscari was cultivating a reputation for energetic administration and defense of the poor, Loredan was portraying himself as a dashing military hero. Juxtaposed were two very different visions of Venetian manhood and leadership.

Over the next several years, in addition to performing his procuratorial duties, Foscari engaged in business ventures and continued to serve in various offices. Documents recently brought to light indicate that in the early 1420s Foscari was actively engaged in trade. He was involved in a business partnership with an unspecified number of associates, one of whom was nobleman Maffeo Zane of the parish of Santa Maria Mater Domini. Among the activities in which the company participated was trade in Alexandria.[120] As far as governmental service is concerned, Foscari served as a *savio del consiglio* and undertook several more diplomatic missions for the Republic. He thus found himself more than ever at the center of discussions and debates regarding Venetian foreign policy, especially those concerning the terraferma. In July 1416 and again in March 1417 he undertook embassies to renew alliances with the King of Naples and the Duke of Austria aimed against the emperor-elect Sigismund.[121] And in December 1417 he was sent with

Marino Caravello, Antonio Contarini, and Fantin Michiel on an embassy to congratulate Martin V on his election to the papacy, the election that ended the Great Schism. The ambassadors were also charged with seeking papal intercession in renewing the peace between Venice and Sigismund.[122]

Sigismund remained Venice's main preoccupation. In 1418 the Venetians seized the strategically important town of Rovereto on the River Adige from its overlord Aldrigetto de Lizana in order to protect Veronese territory from possible imperial incursion.[123] Then in 1419 Sigismund's forces invaded Friuli. But with the emperor still distracted by the Hussites, events went dramatically in Venice's favor as Sacile, Cividale, Prata, Portogruaro, Belluno, Feltre, Udine, Cadore, and Aquileia came under its control. From here Venice extended its conquest to Istria and down the Dalmatian and Albanian coasts. Venetian forces under the command of Loredan, now in the role of captain of the gulf, took possession of the islands Brazza, Lesina, and Curzola and various towns including Traù, Spalato, Cattaro, Scutari, Antivari, and Dulcigno. And the Patriarch of Aquileia was forced to recognize the loss of Friuli to Venice in return for an annual tribute of 3000 ducats and retention of San Vito, San Daniele, and Aquileia itself.[124]

With the Turks temporarily thwarted by their defeat at Gallipoli and with Sigismund's efforts rebuffed, it appeared that Venice had finally achieved its foreign policy goals: dominance over the Adriatic, protection of trade routes in the eastern Mediterranean, and establishment of a terraferma buffer zone. By 1420, however, a new threat was looming on the horizon, one that would dominate Venetian affairs for the next forty years, arguably for the next century, namely Venice's western neighbor, the Duchy of Milan.

Over the past several years Filippo Maria Visconti, Duke of Milan, had consolidated his power within the duchy and now seemed intent on extending his dominion on the model of his father Giangaleazzo. In 1421 he seized the eastern Lombard city of Brescia from Pandolfo Malatesta and wrested Parma from the Este of Ferrara. Even more ominously he fomented a revolt in Genoa which led to the city's reabsorption into the Visconti dominion. Then in 1422 he occupied Forlì. These actions particularly alarmed the Florentines, who remembered only too well Giangaleazzo Visconti's attempts to encircle their state. But his advances also worried the Venetians, who "could take nothing for granted when it came to their dominion on the terraferma."[125]

According to the standard accounts, the election that brought Foscari to the dogeship in April 1423 was played out against the backdrop of a furious debate within the patriciate over the future direction of Venetian foreign policy. This debate purportedly pitted the Foscari party, which favored an alliance with Florence as part of an aggressive approach to the terraferma against Doge Mocenigo's party, which advocated adherence to Venice's traditional focus on the eastern Mediterranean while warning of the dangers of further terraferma expansion. The dispute reportedly mirrored the economic interests of the two parties since the poorer nobles who supported Foscari were likely to benefit from salaried administrative jobs on the terraferma, while the supporters of Mocenigo wished to protect their lucrative trade interests in the east.[126]

This highly persuasive account of a rift within the patriciate (which not coincidentally serves a critical narrative function as a prelude to later events in Foscari's reign) is based on the evidence of three speeches that Doge Mocenigo purportedly gave in the final years of his reign, including one made on his deathbed. All three are found in Sanudo's *Vite dei dogi*, where they are placed after the narrative describing Mocenigo's life and reign and before the life of Foscari.[127] Sanudo reports that the speeches came from the "Libro dell'Illustre Messer Tommaso Mocenigo Doge di Venezia." A small manuscript that begins with similar wording and with brief annotations in Sanudo's handwriting is now housed at the Biblioteca Nazionale Marciana.[128] Mocenigo supposedly made the first two speeches in response to requests from Florence to enter into a league aimed against Milan, the first in January 1420, the second in July 1421, an alliance Foscari is said to have favored. In the second speech Mocenigo urges the patricians to remain on good terms with Visconti, with whose lands the Venetians benefit by way of a rich and prosperous trade. He compares the current terraferma dominions to a garden which produces much and costs little; and he presents an impressive set of statistics demonstrating the economic benefits of trade with Visconti territories. By contrast, he calls Florence "the vilest commune in Italy" and notes how the Florentines have bankrupted themselves waging war.[129] Throughout Mocenigo sarcastically addresses Foscari as "young procurator" and ends the speech with a vow to maintain peace.

The best known of these speeches is the third, which Mocenigo is supposed to have delivered to the Signoria from his deathbed in late March or early April 1423. Aware that he is dying, Mocenigo begins with a kind of state of the union address. He gives a glowing, statistic-filled account of Venice's current economic prosperity. He cites the healthy state of the funded debt, the impressive reach of Venetian trade, the strength of the navy, and the prosperous real-estate market. The city is home to over a thousand noblemen whose annual income is between 700 and 4000 ducats and a skilled workforce of sailors and artisans who maintain the fleets. He concludes this section by urging yet again his countrymen to keep the peace, noting that God destroys those who wage unjust war.

Mindful of the imminent ducal election Mocenigo then assesses the leading candidates. The first man he names is the procurator Marino Car-avello, whom he describes as "a worthy man" and one whose intellect and goodness merit consideration. Francesco Bembo, Pietro Loredan, Giacomo Trevisan, Antonio Contarini, Fantin Michiel, and Albano Badoer follow in rapid succession and are similarly recommended. Mocenigo says of them, "they are all wise and capable men who are worthy of the position." He then launches into a devastating attack on Foscari:

> [There are] those who say they wish to elect mister Francesco Foscari, but I don't understand why, because the said mister Francesco Foscari speaks lies and says many other things which are without foundation; he soars and flies [in his rhetoric] more than falcons. And God does not wish it. If you make him doge, in no time you will be at war. And he who has ten thousand ducats will not have even one thousand; he who has ten houses, will not have but one; he who has ten coats will not find one; and he who has ten vests or stockings or shirts, will be hard pressed to retain one. And so it will be with everything else in such manner that you will lose your gold and silver as well as your honor and reputation. And you who are now lords of lords, will be vassals to soldiers.[130]

In the final section Mocenigo returns to his praise of Venice's prosperity and reputation and prays that God will help his successor to govern the city well.

Despite the appeal of the speeches, both for their purported insights into divisions within the ruling elite and for their help in explaining subsequent events, there are good reasons for doubting their authenticity. In an essay published in 1955 Hans Baron convincingly demonstrated that the chronology of the speeches which is reportedly tied to Florentine diplomatic missions is fatally flawed. He concluded that the first speech was "a totally fictitious product, composed after Mocenigo's death, and forged in order to set the stage for the subsequent address."[131] As for the second speech, he showed that it contained an interpolation entirely out of keeping with the conventions of contemporary political oratory, although he did believe that it contained "an economic and statistical refutation of the soundness of Foscari's plea for helping Florence."[132] The third speech he accepted as essentially authentic except for an obvious interpolation by a Franciscan redactor. Baron argued that the three speeches had been edited some time between September 1433 and August 1434, a period during which Venice again felt threatened – this time by Florence's bellicose stance in its war against Lucca.[133]

But there are reasons to question the authenticity of all three speeches. First, there is no mention of the speeches in either the chronicle of Giorgio Dolfin or that of Antonio Morosini, although both men were alive and writing during Foscari's reign.[134] It seems unlikely that neither would have recorded such goings-on. Morosini in particular was finely attuned to Venice's maritime affairs and is likely to have responded with enthusiasm to Mocenigo's conservative policy. Second, Sanudo states (as does his original source) that the speeches come from Mocenigo's *Libro*, perhaps his copybook or *ricordanza*.[135] Their awkward position in his text (after Mocenigo's life and before Foscari's election) suggests that it was his sole source for the speeches. That is, when Sanudo used them, they had not yet entered the tradition by which the Venetians remembered the history of their city.[136] Third, as noted shortly, Sanudo claims in his account of the actual election that Foscari's victory was a great surprise given that many older and more distinguished men were in competition. If this is the case, then one wonders why Mocenigo went out of his way to criticize so ferociously a candidate who had little prospect of victory.[137]

At the same time, a number of economic historians have accepted the statistics reported in Mocenigo's deathbed oration as substantially reliable.[138] But as head of the state, Mocenigo would naturally have kept himself informed about Venice's current state of affairs. Such statistics easily could have been incorporated into these "speeches," perhaps from an authentic speech made by the doge. Mocenigo had many opportunities to recount such figures. In fact, one of the best occurred just about the time of the first purported speech. In 1421 the Venetians celebrated what they took to be the one-thousandth anniversary of the founding of the city in March 421. It was an occasion for orations in praise of the city, including one by the chronicler Lorenzo de Monacis.[139] The celebration of Venetian prosperity contained in the Mocenigo speeches is entirely in keeping with the kind of information that might have been compiled for such an event. However, a recent examination of the sections of the speech dealing with Venetian coinage suggests that those sections are not in fact reliable and that they too were composed some time after 1429.[140]

The Mocenigo speeches were almost certainly composed or redacted well after the events they purport to represent. My own suspicion is that they were reworked many times, first perhaps – as Baron noted – in the 1430s but then again some time after Foscari's reign, for they appear to reflect controversies in the late fifteenth century about Venice's role vis-à-vis the terraferma and the Turks. As Frederic Lane has observed, "most of the manuscripts at the Marciana in which the [third] speech is to be found are party pamphlets containing other less reliable tracts opposing an adventuresome Italian policy and advocating vigorous maritime action."[141] The Mocenigo family produced two more doges in the fifteenth century, including Pietro Mocenigo (doge 1474–76), who had served before his election as the commander of the fleet battling the Turks.[142] Sanudo's speeches may reflect an on-going Mocenigo family preoccupation with eastern maritime affairs – one that they intentionally backdated to Doge Tommaso.[143]

Stripping away the speeches is painful since it leaves one with a much less colorful account of the final years of Mocenigo's reign. Several historians have acknowledged the dubious authenticity of the orations, but then gone on to retell the events anyway. Unfortunately, excising myth from history is something that has to be performed repeatedly when recounting the life of Foscari. The final chapter of this study examines how and to what ends the various legends have been used.

What can be said here with some certitude is that toward the end of Mocenigo's reign Venice was again facing challenges on both the eastern Mediterranean and terraferma fronts, which certainly prompted a good deal of debate. It is also clear that the Florentines were attempting to mediate the dispute between Venice and Sigismund in the hope that by

helping to pacify the situation on Venice's northern and eastern frontiers, the Republic of Saint Mark would pay more attention to Visconti's
actions in the south and west, even though the Venetians had reconfirmed their alliance with Visconti in February 1422.[144] The Florentines
sent ambassadors to Venice at the end of March 1423 to act as go-
betweens with Sigismund. But, according to the secret deliberations of
the Senate, there was no discussion of actually forming a league with
Florence against Milan, and the patriciate was not as sharply divided as
the speeches would seem to indicate.[145] Various members did develop
expertise in particular spheres and no doubt promoted those interests.
The Loredans, as already noted, were known for their maritime skill,
whereas the Foscari were specialists in mainland affairs. Foscari's uncle
Franzi was very active on the terraferma front in this period: he served
as a *savio della guerra* in 1419 and 1420 and as a member of its successor body the *savi della terraferma* in 1421 and 1422. He also acted for a
time in 1421–22 as captain of Verona.[146] But many members of the patriciate, including the Foscari themselves, had financial assets and interests
in both regions, and in 1425 the ducal councilor Francesco Loredan was
pushing for greater access to church benefices on the terraferma for
native Venetians.[147] The debates of the period likely reflected generational differences in outlook: those of Doge Mocenigo's age, who had
experienced the War of Chioggia, remembered all too well the dangers
that lay on the mainland, whereas younger men like Foscari, who had
come of political age during the period in which Venice fairly effort-
lessly had taken control of Padua, Vicenza, and Verona, were much less
wary of terraferma entanglements.[148] The memory of this generational
conflict was perhaps preserved in the speeches, specifically in Mocenigo's
attacks on the "young procurator." Finally, subsequent events provide a
further indication that the speeches exaggerate the rift for it was not
until December 1425 that Venice accomplished its diplomatic volte-face
and agreed to a league with Florence. If indeed Foscari hankered for
this alliance, then it is difficult to explain why he waited more than two
and a half years after his election to bring it about.[149]

A comparison of the epitaphs on the tombs of Doge Mocenigo (d.
1423) and Steno (d. 1413) provides a good measure of just how much
Venice had changed in the intervening years. As noted above, Steno's
made no mention of the terraferma conquests that had marked his reign
but concentrated instead on his personal qualities as doge. By contrast,

Mocenigo's epitaph highlighted his accomplishments, in particular the humbling of the Turks as well as the addition of various territories to the Venetian realm, including Friuli and the towns of Feltre, Spalato, Cattaro, Traù, and Pola (fig. 3). It reads:

HEC BREVIS ILLVSTRI MOCENIGA AB ORIGINE THOMAM / MAGNANIMVM TENET VRNA DVCEM GRAVIS ISTE MODESTVS / IVSTICIE PRINCEPS QVE FVIT DECVS IPSE SENATVS / ETERNOS VENETVM TITVLOS SVPER ASTRA LOCHAVIT / HIC TEVCRVM TVMIDAM DELEVIT IN EQVORE CLASSEM / OPIDA TARVISI CENETE FELTRI QVE REDEMIT / VNGARIAM DOMVIT RABIEM PATRIAM QVE SVBEGIT / INDE FORI IVLLI CATARVM SPALATVM QVE TARGVRAM / EQVORA PIRRATIS PATEFECIT CLAVSA PEREMPTIS / DIGNA POLVM SVBIIT PATRIIS MENS FESSA TRIVMPHIS.

(This small urn holds the magnanimous doge Tommaso, from the illustrious Mocenigo stock. He was a solemn and modest prince of justice and the jewel of the Senate. He placed the eternal glories of Venice above the stars. He destroyed the arrogant fleet of the Turks on the seas. He redeemed the towns of Treviso, Ceneda, and Feltre. He tamed the Hungarian wrath and subdued the country, whence Friuli, Cattaro, Spalato, and Traù. He cleared the closed sea by destroying the pirates. His worthy mind approaches heaven, wearied by his country's triumphs.)[150]

As his epitaph indicates, the Venetians had come to accept their dominion and its responsibilities. Mocenigo's generation believed that it had, in the words of historian Roberto Cessi, "assured the stability and greatness of the country's maritime power, resolved the crisis of the hinterland with the annexation of the adjacent provinces and [that Venice] would be able to confine the extent of its continental engagement to that restricted area."[151] While this may have been true, Venice had not yet made the institutional and political adjustments necessary to rule its terraferma realm and compete with other territorial powers, nor had it yet found a way to incorporate the mainland culturally into its vision of itself.[152] These were projects for Foscari's reign, and ones that would ultimately claim Foscari as their victim.

Institutional adaptation began immediately after Mocenigo's death with changes to the *promissione*, the ducal oath of office. At the death of each

doge, the Great Council elected a committee of five men to examine
the oath. In general the correctors, as they came to be known, identified abuses of the last incumbent and potential future concerns and recommended revisions to the oath which the council then voted to accept
or reject. By examining changes made to the *promissioni* over the centuries, historians are able to trace the evolution of the ducal office.[153]

Doge Mocenigo died on Easter Sunday, 4 April 1423. Two days later,
on the 6th, the Great Council met to begin the process of choosing his
successor. On that day, the council approved the electoral procedures to
be followed and selected as the five correctors Marino Caravello, Rosso
Marino, Fantin Michiel, Antonio Contarini, and Foscari.[154] The following day the correctors made their recommendations to the Great
Council. The first was by far the most important since it represented a
significant step in the constitutional transformation of Venice. On the
recommendation of Michiel, Contarini, and Foscari (presumably Caravello and Marino were not in favor), the Great Council approved a
measure that stripped the Arengo of the last vestiges of its authority. The
Arengo was the assembly of the entire Venetian community. In the early
centuries of the city's existence, this meeting, which took place either
on boats or in San Marco, elected the doge and had at least theoretically ultimate authority.[155] Now the Great Council approved a measure
abolishing the Arengo's legislative powers. Furthermore it decided that
the Arengo would no longer be assembled, except to be informed of
(but not to confirm) the results of ducal elections. This represented the
final suppression of Venice's "ancient communal democracy."[156] It can
also be viewed as the last stage of the *Serrata*, the process by which the
nobles in the Great Council concentrated power in their hands. The fact
that Foscari recommended this change when two of his fellow correctors did not suggests that he did not want to accord non-nobles even a
nominal role in government, despite his obligation to assist the poor and
powerless in his position as procurator.

The correctors recommended and the Great Council approved nine
other amendments to the oath. Several dealt with administrative issues
concerning the ducal stewards (*gastaldi*) and secretaries and the salaries
of ducal servants. Another required the doge and his councilors to meet
with judges once a month to remind them to render justice swiftly and
equitably. Two concerned the doge's obligation to host meals for various
groups, including the chaplains of San Marco. And two others sought

to elevate further the dignity of the ducal office: one made it illegal for the insignia of San Marco to be displayed upside-down during ducal funerals, although it did allow for the deceased doge's personal arms to be displayed in that manner; the other required the doge to obtain an ermine cape (*bavero*) and wear it at least ten times a year. Finally, a new provision decreed that the future doge should, like everyone else, make forced loans to the state on the basis of his total wealth, although he was granted an exemption for up to 2000 ducats' worth of silver plate.[157]

The oath that Foscari eventually vowed to observe included a prologue and 116 clauses. He swore to preserve the state, uphold justice, punish wrongdoers, promote commerce, and protect Venice's currency. Many of the clauses were prescriptive. Among other responsibilities, he was required to have his wife swear an oath upon entering the Ducal Palace, present a golden cloth to the church of San Marco, support a chaplain, maintain six trumpeters, preside over council meetings everyday except holidays, and root out heresy. But other clauses were proscriptive; they placed significant limits on ducal authority. Several were designed to control the doge's contact with foreign governments. So, for example, he was forbidden to receive ambassadors and nuncios except in the presence of his councilors and the heads of the Forty, to open letters from the emperor or pope or kings without showing them to his councilors, to accept any fiefs, to purchase lands outside the *dogado* (the area between Grado and Cavarzere), or to take a foreign wife without first getting the government's approval. He was even forbidden to leave the *dogado* or to go beyond the port of Malamocco without permission. Other clauses sought to guarantee the doge's impartiality and immunity from undue influence. To this end, he swore not to aid or maintain any party, push for the revocation of punishments meted out to the descendants of the Querini-Tiepolo conspirators of 1310, intervene in judicial cases, or meddle in elections. The doge was also forbidden to engage in trade.[158]

The *promissione* also sought to limit what might be construed as prerogatives traditionally associated with monarchy. Several clauses placed restrictions on the doge's power to grant pardons or to receive or give presents except those prescribed by custom.[159] In addition, he could not spend more than 100 lire of governmental money in work on the Ducal Palace. Members of the doge's family were a major concern. The doge had to inform his councilors when his sons came of age. Moreover, members of his family, including his sons, daughters-in-law, and grand-children, were forbidden to accept any gifts. And like the doge himself, his sons and grandsons were prohibited from serving as pledges to the commune.

Finally, the *promissione* included provisions regarding the doge's possible incapacity, abdication, or removal from office. Clause 54 stated that if the doge became incapable of exercising his office on account of illness or for any other reason, then the ducal councilors should select one of their number to serve in his place (as vice-doge) until the doge could resume his duties. With regard to removal from office, the oath provided that if all six ducal councilors were in agreement along with a majority in the Great Council, then the doge could be removed and required to vacate the Ducal Palace within three days. At the same time, if the doge wished to abdicate, he could do so only with the consent of all six councilors as well as a majority of the Great Council. The last clause made the doge swear to observe everything in the oath.[160]

Having revised the *promissione*, the Great Council next proceeded to the election, which followed an elaborate, long-standing procedure. First, the Great Council dismissed all members under thirty years of age. Then with the assistance of the *ballotino* (ballot boy), a prepubescent boy chosen at random whose job it was to draw the ballots from the electoral urns, a committee of thirty was selected by lot from the remaining council members. The thirty were in turn reduced by lot to nine. The nine then nominated a committee of forty (one had to get at least seven votes in the nine to be elected), which was reduced by lot to twelve. The twelve nominated a committee of twenty-five (nine of twelve votes were required to be selected), which was reduced by lot to nine. The nine nominated forty-five (again, seven votes were required), reduced by lot to eleven. The eleven nominated a committee of forty-one (nine votes required); those forty-one had the task of electing the doge.[161]

This remarkable procedure was not a perverse joke or a mere flight of fancy; it was carefully designed to reduce the danger of factional interference in elections by incorporating a generous element of chance.[162] The several rounds of lottery made it difficult for anyone to guarantee that he or even his allies would have a place in the nominating committees. Chance served to underscore the essential equality of all members of the Great Council. As Gasparo Contarini observed, the procedure created the impression that "the whole multitude [of the Great

Council] might seem to have a part in this creation and election of their prince."[163] There may have been an additional reason for relying on the *ballotino* to draw the ballots: the element of chance involved the belief that the will of God would influence the election.[164]

In order to reduce family influence, no more than one member of any patriline could sit in any of the electoral committees. As commentators have remarked, however, the Venetians were careful to balance simple sortition with nomination as a way of assuring the "dominance of the rich and powerful once the election was in motion."[165] But they have failed to note another requirement of the electoral procedure, namely a rule prohibiting members of the committees of nine and of twelve from nominating themselves or indeed of participating at any further stage of the election except as members of the forty-one. Furthermore, members of the final nominating committee of eleven were ineligible to participate in the forty-one.[166] These rules were intended to prevent the members of the nominating committees from forming pacts to nominate and elect one another. It also meant that any man hoping to have an overwhelming number of supporters in the final committee of forty-one would have to have a huge (one might even say an impossibly large) network of friends and relations within the patriciate to pull this off.

The electoral procedure began on 7 April with the selection of the first committee of thirty, which was quickly reduced by lot to nine. However, only two of the six men whom Sanudo later identified as the leading contenders were then elected to the forty; they were the procurators Antonio Contarini and Marino Caravello. But two of Foscari's supporters (Albano Badoer and Bulgaro Vitturi) were members of that committee, and both were fortunate enough to survive the next lottery and sit in the twelve. Accordingly, the committee of twenty-five nominated by the twelve included Foscari and his former father-in-law Andrea Priuli, but also rivals Contarini and Pietro Loredan. On 8 April Priuli, Contarini, and Loredan won the lottery to sit in the nine, while Foscari did not. The resulting forty-five included two men with strong ties to Foscari (his brother-in-law Santo Venier and his current father-in-law Bartolomeo Nani). Although no men instantly recognizable as Foscari supporters survived the lottery to serve in the eleven, there must have been several since the forty-one included at least eleven of them. The committee of forty-one that would elect the doge was constituted on 10 April. According to Sanudo, Foscari was its youngest member.[167]

Once the forty-one had been selected, they were sequestered in the Ducal Palace and not allowed to have any contact with the outside world. They then elected three of their members to serve as the heads of the committee. The election itself began when each of the forty-one was asked to write the name of his nominee on a piece of paper and deposit it in an urn. The three heads then drew up a list of the nominees but did not reveal how many among the forty-one had nominated the same person. Then the nominees were scrutinized as members of the forty-one spoke to both their strengths and weaknesses as candidates. The nominee under discussion was required to leave the room, but upon returning was informed of any criticism and allowed to defend himself. After this examination was complete, a vote was taken. If no candidate received the required 25 votes, the process of nomination, scrutiny, and voting was repeated until a winner emerged.[168]

In his life of Foscari, Sanudo gives two very different versions of Foscari's election, another sign that his account was based on various sources that he failed to meld into a seamless narrative. He must have taken the second and much more cryptic account directly from the records of the Great Council for in it he reviewed the changes to the *promissione* and then listed the members of the forty-one in the exact order in which they appear in the council's records.[169] Like the council records, he noted that Foscari was elected at the 22nd hour on 15 April and, again quoting the Great Council deliberations, that he "happily" entered office the following day. But he added three points not contained in the council records: first that Paolo Orio was opposed to Foscari, second that Foscari was elected on the feast of Saint Isidore, and third that Foscari was fifty-one years of age.[170]

Sanudo's first account gives more detail.[171] It states that six candidates emerged in the forty-one: Marino Caravello, Francesco Bembo, Antonio Contarini, Leonardo Mocenigo, Pietro Loredan, and Foscari. Loredan was the early favorite, but Foscari knew that he had several sure votes in the committee. And he had a twofold strategy to secure his own election: first, to criticize the other candidates, and second, to make sure that only three of his partisans would reveal their preference while the others would keep their choice secret. During the scrutiny that followed, Foscari made sure that the weaknesses of the various candidates were discussed. The debate as recorded by Sanudo reveals a good deal about the qualities the Venetians sought in a doge. For example, Marino Caravello's candidacy was undercut by his age and health. According to Sanudo, he was criticized for being "most aged and infirm." This is surprising since it was common for the Venetians to elect very aged men to the city's highest office. Indeed, one modern historian has characterized the Venetian Republic as a gerontocracy on the grounds that the average age of doges at election in this period was seventy-two. The electors usually preferred older men since they were less prone than younger ones to act rashly or in haste. What is more, older men were likely to have long experience in government and to have honed the consensus-building skills that council-based republican government required. And electors may have selected older men in the hope that their reigns would be short and hence that their own chances of future election improved.[172] In Caravello's case, it was probably his infirmity that mattered.

Another of the contenders was Leonardo Mocenigo, brother of the recently deceased doge Tommaso. Mocenigo's greatest disadvantage was the electors' sentiment that he ought not to succeed his brother in the dogeship. As noted above, members of the patriciate were very concerned about familial influence over the office and the dynastic implications of fraternal or filial succession.[173] This clearly diminished Mocenigo's chances. Two other candidates also had serious drawbacks, at least as presented by Foscari's supporters. Sanudo's description of Francesco Bembo's situation is extremely cryptic. He says, "Il Benbo [*sic*] era impedimentà, zotto e mal condicionatto." The exact meaning is uncertain, although it can probably be translated "Bembo had his impediments [to office], he was lame and not up to the post." Apparently the electors thought that the ducal office required dignity and a certain physical presence, a concern with image that was increasing, as implied by the new requirement for the doge to wear an ermine cape. As the head of state, the doge had a prominent place in official ceremonies, receiving ambassadors and other visiting dignitaries. Foscari's supporters played on the fear that Bembo's physical disabilities and general unsuitability would tarnish the reputation of the Republic. (Apparently like today, candidates had to look the part.) The complaints against Antonio Contarini are easier to grasp. He was criticized for having too many sons, daughters, and sons-in-law. As in the case of Mocenigo, this concern played on fears that the Contarini kinsmen would insinuate themselves into the office.

Pietro Loredan, the favorite, posed special problems for Foscari and his supporters since they did not want to be seen as undermining a popular war hero. And so the task of criticizing Loredan fell to Albano Badoer, the oldest member of the committee of forty-one and, according to Sanudo, a friend (*amicho*) of Foscari. Rather than attack Loredan personally, Badoer noted that Loredan was an experienced general and popular with the sailors. If Venice should go to war, he would be needed as captain-general. In other words, the city could not spare him from the navy. Loredan defended himself by reciting his war record and, if the chronicle of Agostino Agostini written in the 1570s is to be believed, by displaying his battle scars.[174] Nevertheless, he lost his lead in subsequent rounds of voting.

Foscari was the last of the major contenders. Loredan commissioned one of his partisans, Pietro Orio, to speak against him. Orio's criticism of Foscari's candidacy was two-edged. His first line of attack was personal. He claimed that Foscari was too young for the position, that he had too many sons, and that because he had married a second time, he would produce even more sons, since his wife was giving birth every year. Sanudo does not record how Foscari responded to this charge, but clearly his opponents were using the same tactics that Foscari's partisans had used against Antonio Contarini – namely playing on fears of undue family influence. The age issue was unavoidable since Foscari was only fifty. Precocity had marked his entire career. On the other hand, Loredan cannot have been much older than that. Indeed, according to the Agostini chronicle, after criticizing Loredan during his scrutiny, Albano Badoer reminded him that he was still young and could run for doge again in the future. For his part, Foscari may intentionally have selected the elderly Badoer as his advocate as a way of defusing the age issue and preventing the election from turning into a contest between generations.

Orio's second line of attack was to highlight policy differences and to try to frighten the electors with the prospect of a Foscari dogeship. He called Foscari an enemy of peace and reminded the electors of Doge Mocenigo's deathbed warning (remember that this is as in Sanudo). At this point, another Foscari partisan, Bulgaro Vitturi, spoke in Foscari's defense, noting among other things that Foscari was not poor, indeed that he was worth 150,000 ducats.[175] It is unclear why his wealth was an issue unless Foscari was perceived as being too closely allied with the poorer members of the patriciate. When he was criticized in a later scrutiny by Bernardo Pisani and Paolo Correr, Foscari defended himself.[176]

Sanudo's report of the balloting is so cryptic as to be almost undecipherable. It is best to quote the revelant passage in its entirety.

> He [Foscari] was astute. And in the first scrutiny he got 11 votes. And his friends did not reveal themselves, and with great finesse he pulled in a few more votes, begging them to vote for him so that he would have some votes. And so they did it, not imagining that he might win. He gained two votes and got 12, and on the 8th ballot, he had 16. On the ninth he had 12. On the tenth at the nomination of ser Bernardo Pisani, ser Fantino Pizzamano revealed his preference for Foscari and spoke in his favor. Ser Leonardo Mocenigo had more votes than the others. But Foscari's [hidden] eight came out and voted for him so that he jumped to 26 votes and was elected on the 15th of April at the twelfth hour.[177]

The Agostini chronicle, which clearly draws either on Sanudo or on Sanudo's original source, fills in some crucial gaps and clarifies some points. It says that on the ninth ballot, Foscari got 17 votes – a more credible number than the 12 given by Sanudo, since at that point Foscari would have realized that with 17 open votes and 8 hidden ones, he had victory in hand. But before that could transpire, a bit of horse-trading took place. Mocenigo, who was until then the frontrunner (and did not know about the 8 hidden votes), decided to vote for Foscari, as the Agostini chronicle says, "in order to garner his favor." And so Foscari won the election with 26 votes, one more than the 25 necessary.[178]

The Agostini chronicle also states that Foscari took advantage of a procedural technicality. As one of the two youngest members of the committee of forty-one, Foscari was designated *portonaro* (doorkeeper) – a job that appears to have entailed the reading of the ballot results. What this perhaps means is that Foscari had a clearer picture of what was happening than most of the other electors. According to another account, as the youngest members of the forty-one, the *portonari* also assisted the eldest members with their personal needs; this duty may have offered Foscari the opportunity to circulate more freely among the electors and solicit their votes.[179] The reason the youngest members of the committee were assigned this task is that – given the preference for the elderly – they were the men least likely to be elected and could therefore be entrusted with this responsibility. Apparently the rule-makers did not count on a man like Foscari.

Sanudo's account of the election has further anomalies. For instance, in one version he says Foscari was fifty, in the other fifty-one. More significantly, at the beginning of the fuller account, he says: "And the rumor came out of the forty-one for ser Bernardo Pisani son of the late Pietro, who had 27 votes. He was nominated doge by 14 of the forty-one." But, as noted above, in his subsequent discussion of the electoral scrutinies, there is no mention of Pisani as one of the frontrunners. Additionally, in the debate over abolition of the Arengo, Sanudo attributes an important role to the Grand Chancellor Francesco della Siega. However he was not elected Grand Chancellor until 1439.[180] Sanudo may have used as his source for the fuller version a diary of one of the members of the forty one, for at the point in the account where the reasons for not electing Loredan are presented, the text says, "thus it would not do *for us* to do it (i.e. elect him)" [emphasis mine].[181] Given the confusion of della Siega with an earlier Grand Chancellor, this source too was likely to have been written in hindsight and thus was subject to the influence of subsequent events. This would also explain the brief reference during the debate to Mocenigo's deathbed oration.

Thus Sanudo's account begs the question of whether it can be accepted as an accurate description of what happened or as a later interpretation based on sources that were biased against Foscari. The two more contemporary chronicles are of little help in solving the issue. Dolfin notes only that Foscari was elected on 15 April, while Morosini says that Foscari had 14 sure votes and that his election was a great surprise. He also notes that after his election Foscari was "confirmed by the Arengo." Evidently even some members of the patriciate did not yet fully understand the constitutional change that had been made, namely that the Arengo no longer confirmed but was simply informed of the ducal election.[182] While Sanudo's account is probably generally correct in outline, it seems to present Foscari in a deliberately unflattering light. This might have been at least in part a result of trying to explain how a man who seemed to have little chance of success did indeed become doge.

However, when examined together, Foscari's elections as procurator of San Marco and as doge do reveal a great deal about the man and how he emerged victorious. They show that Foscari had mastered the intricacies and procedural subtleties of Venice's council-based government. As described above, in his election as procurator he created a vacancy where none had existed before and then got himself elected to it. And in the ducal election, he apparently took advantage of his purely fortuitous selection as *portonaro* to guide his bloc of partisans and lobby for votes. In an electoral system as complex as the Venetian one, mastery of parliamentary rules of order and appointment to even minor administrative positions could make the difference between success and failure. The contrast with Loredan is particularly informative. While the naval hero relied on histrionics, showing his battle scars and touting his war record, the bureaucrat Foscari went about methodically buttonholing electors and bargaining for individual votes.

In this task, Foscari was clearly aided by the network of friends and relations that he, his father, and his uncle had built over the past twenty years; but it would be wrong to exaggerate the importance of this. Sanudo for one attributed Foscari's election to the network of dependents that he had cultivated while procurator of San Marco. This could have been a slur designed to suggest that Foscari had won the election not on merit and support for his policies but merely through the workings of intrigue or lobbying. Sanudo might well have been commenting on electoral corruption in his own day. Clearly Foscari did employ the office's patronage power, but his network was not so extensive that he could guarantee an electoral victory; he had to work for it. He did manage to place eleven of his partisans in the forty-one, but in the early rounds Loredan had even more.

What Foscari's election suggests is an equivocal relationship between kinship, patronage networks, and advancement to office. As the criticisms leveled against Contarini and Foscari and the fear of Leonardo Mocenigo's possible succession to his brother indicate, family connections could actually hinder candidates in their quest for office. And candidates could not assume (as historians looking back often do) automatic support from kin and friends since in the relatively closed world of the Venetian elite, almost everyone was related in one way or another. Marriage alliances and other ties were no guarantee of political support.[183] The evidence from Foscari's term as procurator shows that he used the office as much to reinforce ties to men who were already allied to him as to extend his connections further afield, an indication of just how fragile those ties really were. As today, men in the Renaissance based their support of candidates on a variety of factors, including agreement with their policies, an assessment of their suitability for the particular office, and the promise of future benefits, not simply the recollection of past ones.

Part of Foscari's success has to be attributed to his powers of persuasion and to his dexterity at the kind of deal-making that elections required. He showed consummate political skill when he managed to orchestrate the procuratorial opening without offending the Barbo family. In the ducal election, he played the game even better, gradually accumulating more and more votes. As mentioned above, Leonardo Mocenigo agreed to vote for Foscari "in order to win his favor," not realizing that this would be the final round of votes. In this instance, however, it appears that Foscari did make some enemies. Later writers attributed the origins of the animosity between Foscari and Loredan to the unforeseen outcome of the election.

Thus even if he intended it as a slur, Sanudo was correct in portraying Foscari as someone who had his eye on the dogeship, as a man in a hurry. Only one so driven could have marshaled his knowledge of the system, his network of relatives and friends, and his talent at political deal-making to manage election to the dogeship at so young an age. Where Sanudo may lead one astray is in eliding Foscari the man with Venice itself and its program of territorial expansion, in making Foscari the scapegoat for Venice's subsequent foreign policy disasters. It is not clear that Venice had yet emerged as it would in the sixteenth century as the ambitious power which the League of Cambrai set about to humble.

Since Foscari was elected late on the night of 15 April, the installation ceremonies were delayed until the next day. Accordingly, on the morning of the 16th, as the bells of San Marco rang out, Foscari was led to the great pulpit in the church of San Marco made of porphyry and other marbles, known as the *bigonzo*, where he was presented to the community by the eldest member of the forty-one, his friend and supporter Albano Badoer. He then proceeded to the high altar where he swore to protect the church and received one of the most potent symbols of ducal sovereignty, the *vexillum* or banner of San Marco. The banner conferral "introduced into the [installation] rituals the idea that there was an eternal, mystical source for the doge's authority," namely, Saint Mark.

The flag functioned, much like the keys presented by Christ to Peter did in papal ideology, as the sign of an unbreakable relationship: in this case between Venice and its patron as mediated through the person of the doge.[184] The gold ducat, another powerful symbol of Venetian might, memorialized this moment. Foscari's coin, like that of his predecessors and successors, depicted him on its obverse receiving the banner from the saint (fig. 4).[185]

In the next stage of the installation ceremony, a special honor-guard of sailors from the Arsenal carried the doge and other members of the Signoria on a specially built platform around Piazza San Marco which was filled, according to the chronicler Giorgio Dolfin, "with all the people of Venice." As the procession made its way through the square, the men on the platform tossed coins to the jubilant throng. Illustrations of sixteenth-century investitures suggest a near riot as people in the crowd scrambled to catch the coins. Eventually the procession wound its way to the Ducal Palace where Foscari swore to uphold the *promissione* and was crowned with the ducal *corno*. He then gave a brief speech from a balcony of the palace, which the populace greeted with the words "So be it, so be it!"[186]

Foscari's installation included the three stages characteristic of later ducal installation ceremonies although in less elaborate and carefully delineated form: presentation; procession; and finally oath-taking and coronation.[187] These rituals emphasized and made visible the many different facets or aspects of the ducal office. The flag conferral ceremony conveyed the message that the doge was the vicar of Mark, the intercessor between the saint and his people, as well as the vehicle of divine illumination. At the same time, the doge retained a degree of monarchic authority as symbolized by the crown or ducal beret. But he was also the very human head of the republican regime. And like other members of the government, his power was limited – in his case by the *promissione*. It was the republican aspect that most struck foreign observers: they found the authority of the doge very meagre indeed compared with that held by rulers of other states. As revealed in the epigraph which begins this chapter, Aeneas Silvius Piccolomini, Pope Pius II, saw the ducal office as burdensome and viewed the doge as simply an "instrument of the city."[188] What outsiders did not understand was that a doge's strength lay precisely in his ability to manipulate the office, to emphasize one aspect of the position at one time and a different aspect at another. Even before assuming the ducal office Foscari had proven himself a master at working in just such interstices of power.

Bastiani's portrait of Foscari (plate 1) also sought to emphasize the republican aspects of the office. It presented Foscari not as an individual but as a type, namely the doge. As noted before, the painter did not intend to convey the personality of the man but to place him instead in a long line of doges stretching back to the earliest incumbents. For this reason the depiction of the robes and *corno* was nearly as important as capturing the likeness of the man. In Renaissance Italy election to the post of abbess allowed nuns, who were supposed to cultivate humility and anonymity, the "possibility of personality," namely the chance to be portrayed as individuals rather than as a type, namely religious women.[189] Exactly the opposite was true for the doges of Venice. Upon election, they were supposed to shed their personality or individuality, assume the ducal persona, and become icons of the state. It is perhaps for this reason that Bastiani chose to depict the ducal robes as enveloping Foscari's body, just as ideally the office was supposed to subsume the man.

But the portrait also conveys other meanings which complicate that central message. Foscari is depicted with his right shoulder facing the viewer. Contemporary theories regarding the body claimed that the right was morally superior to the left or "sinister" side.[190] Thus the portrait pays subtle tribute to the idea of the doge as a divinely protected figure, the representative of Mark. But there is another layer of meaning in that profile portraits drew their inspiration from ancient portrait medals and coins depicting the Roman emperors. In this way, the profile portrait also conveyed "connotations of far-flung empire as well as legitimacy of governance for the ruler who sought not only to preserve, but also to enlarge, his state."[191] Such allusions, however, could be dangerous, especially in Venice where the doge's power was carefully circumscribed.

At least six other contemporary or near contemporary portraits of Foscari exist (none is securely datable) and a seventh, not counting the sculptural ones on Foscari's tomb and on the Porta della Carta, is known to have existed. The extant portraits convey the range of possibilities inherent in the ducal office. The first is a panel attributed by some to Gentile Bellini and by others to the workshop of Michele Giambono. It bears a remarkable resemblance to the Bastiani portrait except that

Foscari is shown facing left. It may even have served as the model for Bastiani's portrayal.[192] The second is found in one of the illuminated initials on the first page of text of a copy of Foscari's *promissione*, a copy likely produced by the workshop of the miniaturist Cristoforo Cortese for Foscari family consumption a decade or more after his election (plates 2 and 3).[193] The initial shows a kneeling Foscari, dressed in full ducal regalia, receiving a book, likely the *promissione* itself, and a benediction from a seated Saint Mark who is dressed in red and pink. Saints Nicholas and Francis present Foscari to the city's patron saint. Saint Francis, who holds a small cross in his hand, was clearly chosen in his capacity as Foscari's name-saint. The selection of Nicholas is a bit more surprising. In this image he is dressed in green and wears a bishop's mitre and carries a crozier. As the patron of sailors, Saint Nicholas held a special place of honor in Venice. A church dedicated to him on the Lido housed, according to the Venetians, his relics and was the focus of the ceremony held each Ascension Day, when the doge performed the city's marriage to the sea. There was also a chapel dedicated to Nicholas within the Ducal Palace itself. Especially popular among the lower orders of Venetian society, his inclusion may have been meant to suggest that Foscari represented the entire community before Mark.[194] Additionally, Saint Nicholas was known for his charitable acts, especially for his assistance in helping dower poor girls. Thus his inclusion may also have been a reference to Foscari's charitable activities especially during his time as a procurator of San Marco. However, Nicholas may have been included because he had more personal associations for Foscari in being his father's name-saint. In a sense then, Foscari is presented by his biological father (Nicholas) and his spiritual father (Francis) to the father of the state (Mark). The Foscari coat of arms held by an angel at the bottom of the page further emphasizes these familial associations, associations especially appropriate for this family copy of the *promissione*. In any case, this image shows the doge in a position of fealty, and so the primary message is clear. The doge's authority derives from Mark. Presented to the lord by his pledges, Foscari swears his allegiance to the saint. The image emphasizes the dogeship's sacral qualities as Mark's vicar on earth.

The third and fourth painted depictions of Foscari are, in many respects, the mirror images of the *promissione* portrait since Foscari is now shown in the position of patron or lord, as is Mark in the *promissione* portrayal. The third image is a tempera portrait on vellum, the torn-away first illuminated page of a capitulary or statute book of one of Venice's many confraternities (fig. 6). It shows Foscari in full ducal robes including the *corno*, sitting on a throne inside the Ducal Palace. The portrait is much cruder than the Bastiani portrait, but Foscari is clearly identifiable by the family coat of arms over the door in the background. The Foscari emblem was one of the few in Venice to include the winged lion of Saint Mark as an element.[195] The doge is pictured in the act of receiving from one of the members of the confraternity a copy of the group's statutes. The overall impression is princely rather than republican as the enthroned doge receives one of his subjects within the restricted confines of the Ducal Palace.

The fourth image also shows Foscari in the position of patron (fig. 5). As in the *promissione* miniature, it too appears as an illumination, in this case in a copy of a treatise entitled *Commentariorum secundi anni de gestis Scipionis Picinini exercitus Venetorum imperatoris in Hannibalem Sforciam Mediolanensium ducem*; written by the Neapolitan humanist Porcellio Pandoni; it is an account of military affairs near the end of Foscari's reign which the author dedicated to the doge.[196] In the text, the mercenary captain Jacopo Piccinino is portrayed in the guise of Scipio and Francesco Sforza as Hannibal. The illumination shows Foscari seated under a tent receiving the treatise from the author with the armored Piccinino by his side. But the portrait of Foscari bears little resemblance to other images of him; and it seems likely that the artist based his image on a generic type, perhaps a doge on a Venetian ducat. The portrayal of Foscari in a tent presumably near the field of battle likewise suggests that the unknown miniaturist had little knowledge of the ducal office or its incumbent and was simply carrying out the commission of producing a luxurious gift that Pandoni could present to the doge.[197] By contrast, someone as well known as Jacopo Bellini included a portrait of Foscari in a book of drawings (now in the Louvre, Paris): according to the late fifteenth-century index, one of the images depicted "an architectural setting with Doge Foscari and others;" since the compilation of the index, however, ten pages of the volume have been lost, this drawing among them.[198]

The fifth surviving image is, like the Bastiani portrait, a profile view of the doge. It appears, as in miniature, in a copy of the ducal *promissione* to which has been appended the capitulary of the ducal councilors (plate 4). Attributed to Leonardo Bellini, nephew of Jacopo and an accomplished miniaturist, this finely rendered portrait shows what appears to be a young Doge Foscari, depicted in republican guise.[199] The sixth extant portrait is also of small dimension. Attributed by some to Antonio Gambello and by others to Antonello Griffo, the chief engraver at the Venetian mint, it is a profile medal of copper alloy (fig. 7).[200] Like the Bastiani and Bellini portraits, the medal depicts Foscari in his robes of state. In fact the three images bear such a striking resemblance to one another that any two might have been copies of the third or all three copies of another unidentified prototype.[201] But the reverse of the medal amplifies and complicates the message of the painted images for it reproduces a statue personifying Venice, as it appears in one of the quatrefoil openings on the second-floor loggia of the Ducal Palace (fig. 9).[202] There are significant differences between the images however. In the Ducal Palace rendition, the figure of Venice (labeled "VENEÇIA") holds a sword in one hand and a scroll in the other on which are inscribed the words "FORTIS IUSTA TRONO FURIAS MARE SUB PEDE PONO" (Brave, just, I put the furies under my throne, the sea under my foot). She trounces under her feet figures of discord and sedition or perhaps discord and war.[203] Venice appears even more militant in the Foscari medal version, for the scroll has been replaced with a shield. Furthermore, the legend has been amplified to read "VENETIA MAGNA." The medal thus creates an even stronger identity of doge and Venice, ruler and state, than the Bastiani or Bellini portraits. And more than the painted portrait, it calls to mind the world of the Roman emperors and the medals which they had struck. As the first in a line of dogal medals, it also introduces into Venice a vogue for medals depicting rulers hitherto confined to the princely courts of the terraferma.[204] Republican magistrate, princely ruler, Mark's vicar, Roman emperor, personification of Venice – these were some of the meanings of the dogeship that were available to Foscari and that he would skillfully draw upon during his tenure in office.

And so to everyone's surprise – except perhaps his own – Francesco Foscari became Doge of Venice on 15 April 1423, the vigil of the feast of Saint Isidore. What Sanudo and others failed to mention was the irony of Foscari's election on that date. For on that same day in 1355, the Council of Ten had arrested an earlier doge, Marino Falier, for attempting to overthrow the Republic and to establish himself as the Signore or lord of Venice. The Ten beheaded Falier two days later. Thereafter, in commemoration of its triumph over the conspiracy, the government required the sitting doge to make a pilgrimage to the chapel of Saint Isidore in San Marco every 16 April.[205] This ducal *andata* or official visit, just one of several required annually of the doge, celebrated the Republic's survival. At the same time it served as a powerful warning to the doge to be mindful not only of his place within Venice's system of republican government but also not coincidentally of the power of the Ten.[206] The Great Council Hall contained another reminder of this event: in the frieze of ducal portraits, Falier's likeness had been blackened and in its stead had been placed the words "HIC EST LOCUS/MARINI FALETRI/DECAPITATI PRO CRIMINIBUS" (Here is the spot of Marino Falier who was decapitated for his crimes) (fig. 10).[207] These were lessons Francesco Foscari would have done well to heed.

2

Tribute to the Virgin
1423–1433

Plaude, decus mundi, Venetum clarisima turba,
sorte ducem solita sacra cum feceris altum
Ytalie sydus, cui munera magna dedere
Jupiter ipse, Venus florens, dulcisque Minerva;
utque tibi, princeps, magno luceret Olimpo
vim dedit et gratiam populo Mercurius almam.

Neque minus generosa domus tu Fuscara gaude
cum nunc lucescas, Francisco principe facto.
Felices patriae quas temperat urbs Venetorum.

Plaudite, nam populis successit dux ius equus
mille quadrigentis domini currentibus annis
vigenisque tribus cum sol ter quinque per orbem
inerat et thauri lustrabat cornua fortis.

Cristoforo di Monte

(Applaud, o jewel of the world, o famous crowd
of Venice, since, with the accustomed sacred lot,
you have made the high doge Italy's star, to whom
Jupiter himself, flowering Venus, and sweet
Minerva give great gifts; and so that for you the
prince would shine from great Olympus,

Mercury gave him strength and fostering grace
to the people.

Nor should you rejoice less, eminent house of
Foscari, since now you shine, Francesco having
been made prince. Happy are the countries that
the city of the Venetians governs.

Applaud, for a just and pious doge has come to
the people, in fourteen hundred and twenty-
three, anno domini, when the sun had been
thrice five times through the heavens and was
shining upon the horns of the strong bull.)[1]

Both Venice and Foscari's kinsmen greeted the news of his ascension to
the ducal throne with, as the words of Cristoforo di Monte's motet
attest, jubilation. The very stars had had a hand in the election of a man
to whom the gods had given the greatest gifts. And the people could
rejoice that a "just and pious" man, had, following the customary electoral procedures (sorte ducem solita sacra), ascended to the ducal throne.
Born in Feltre and active in Padua, the center of a rich musical tradition, Cristoforo almost certainly composed the piece for the festivities
celebrating Foscari's election since he embedded the date of the doge's
victory into the text of the motet itself.[2]

Cristoforo di Monte was not the only musician to compose works in
honor of Foscari's installation. Antonio Romano, master of the choir
school at San Marco, also composed a piece for Foscari. The first cantus
of Romano's motet, Carminibus festos, addresses Foscari directly, hailing him
as "great father, only ornament of our age, you are our secure peace, with
fostering laws you piously give justice to the people." Seeking to convey
that a new age has dawned for Venice, the cantus continues: "No longer
shall the fearful arms of the tyrant clash [. . .] with you as doge the scene
will change and a golden race will arise in the world." O requies populi,
the second cantus, focuses on the twin bases of ducal power. Foscari is at
once the "repose of the people" and the specially favored of Saint Mark.
Indeed, the final section underscores that relationship: "But to you, o great
parent, in whose possession is the city's greatest power, Mark, jewel of the
Venetians, we pray, that he [Foscari] may go exaltedly among the people
for many long years; may the gods prolong the journey."[3]

The festivities celebrating Foscari's election included numerous processions and receptions at which these motets were likely sung. They also involved more militant celebrations in the form of jousts in Piazza San Marco.[4] Jousts were nothing new in Venice, for even though horses were legally banned from normal use in the streets, tournaments had been held in the city since at least the thirteenth century. Their staging in this most mercantile of all Italian cities testifies to the lure that northern European chivalric traditions had for merchants not only in Venice but throughout Italy. In fact, most of the participants in these military contests were not native Venetians, few of whom were skilled horsemen, but rather foreign princes and mercenary captains (often one and the same) who took part in order to display their prowess and advertise their availability for hire.

But the most significant of the festivities was the formal transfer of Foscari's wife Marina Nani to the Ducal Palace. It is uncertain when her entrance ceremony took place. On 20 May, a little over a month after Foscari's election, nobleman Vittore Bragadin, who was serving at the time as Venice's captain in Vicenza, requested permission to remain in Venice in order to honor the doge and dogaressa during her entry. He was granted an eight-day extension of his leave. However, at this very moment plague began to sweep the city, and the entry seems to have been postponed. Sanudo reports that the transfer did not take place until the beginning of the new year.[5] In several important respects the dogaressa's entrance ceremony mimicked Italian wedding customs. Specifically, the dogaressa was formally transferred, like a new bride, to the Ducal Palace, the home of her husband, in the *bucintoro* or state barge.[6] Whether she was transported from Foscari's home or, as was customary for a wedding, from her father's home, is unclear. If it followed the pattern of later dogaressal entries, then before departing her home, Marina Foscari swore an oath, pledging to uphold the rules contained in the ducal *promissione* pertaining to her position. In general these clauses regulated family matters, limiting the dogaressa's ability to exercise influence or seek favors for her kin or friends.[7] The dogaressa and an escort of women attendants were then conducted to the Ducal Palace where a lavish meal was served.

Another important component of the dogaressa's formal entry into the palace served to incorporate the disenfranchised guild community into the body politic. Since the mid-thirteenth century the guilds of

Venice, in marked contrast to those of Florence, had been legally excluded from exercising a role in the governance of the city and were, in fact, placed under the legal jurisdiction of a magistracy known as the *giustizieri vecchi* (old justices). Also, since at least the thirteenth century, the guilds had staged elaborate processions honoring the doge and his wife upon his election. In Foscari's case these celebrations continued for some time. In June 1425, more than two years after his election, the Council of Ten authorized the guilds that had not yet had a chance to honor the doge to do so. At the same time it sanctioned yet another joust in Piazza San Marco which the city of Padua wished to sponsor "for the honor and joy at the creation of the most serene lord doge."[8]

Most significantly of all, however, with Marina Nani Foscari's formal entry into the Ducal Palace, the Venetian Republic now had at its helm a vigorous ducal couple with numerous sons and daughters and the prospect of more to come. The contrast with Foscari's predecessor, the elderly bachelor Tommaso Mocenigo, could not have been greater. Of course the presence of those same ducal sons raised anew the unsettling prospect of influence-peddling and dynastic ambitions which the ducal *promissione* sought to hold at bay and which had been a point of contention during the electoral scrutinies. But for now at least those fears were set aside as the city celebrated its new leader.

In his first official pronouncement as doge, Foscari ordered that a solemn procession be held on Friday 23 April, the feast day of Saint George, attended by the clergy and the *scuole*, followed by a mass in San Marco.[9] It may well have been for just such an occasion that another motet honoring Foscari, the *Christus vincit*, was composed by Hugo de Lantins, a Franco-Flemish musician at the time in the employ of the Malatesta family, the ruling house of the city of Pesaro. Set as a cantilena, the text of this laudatory political motet reads simply: "Christ conquers, Christ reigns, Christ commands. To our lord Francesco Foscari, by the grace of God, the renowned Doge of Venice, Dalmatia, and Croatia, and ruler of a quarter part and half a quarter of the empire of Romania, health, honor, life, and victory. Amen." Since "the text of *Christus vincit* already existed as a Venetian acclamation, or *laus*," all the composer had to do was insert the name of the appropriate doge into it. But its "cantilena texture was associated in particular with preexistent texts for the Virgin Mary."[10] And so in this way the motet, the third extant in honor of Foscari, called to mind Venice's special associations with the Virgin.

Those Marian associations would have been abundantly clear after the procession on 23 April, when the Great Council met for the first time under Foscari's rule.[11] The meeting was held, as several chronicles note, in the "sala nuova" or as Sanudo says, the "salla nuova fabrichata," that is in the recently renovated Great Council Hall, the main focus of which was the ducal throne situated along the eastern wall.[12] The throne itself stood directly under Guariento's great fresco *The Coronation of the Virgin* (fig. 8), in the place where Tintoretto's gigantic canvas *Paradiso* now stands. (The fresco was damaged beyond repair in the fire of 1577.) The coronation of the Virgin was an especially popular theme in Venetian art of the fourteenth and fifteenth centuries, alluding as it did to Venice's special relationship with the Virgin (the Venetians placed the city's foundation on 25 March, the feast of the Annunciation) and eliding Venice and the Virgin into one symbolic entity. It reflected as well the Venetians' deep Marian devotion.[13] As discussed above, in the early fourteenth century Foscari's own great-grandfather Niccolò commissioned a chapel dedicated to Mary in the family's home parish of San Simeon Apostolo. The composition of Guariento's painting, with the saints seated in rows at right angles to the heavenly throne, appeared to mirror the arrangement of the ducal throne and the rows of benches on which council members sat, creating a "visual parallel" between the celestial court and the "relationship of the Great Council to its own prince."[14] As such it was part of a rich iconographic tradition by which Venice figured itself as a mirror of the heavenly city.

Two foreign princes, Obizzo da Polenta, the lord of Ravenna, and Gianfrancesco Gonzaga, the Marquess of Mantua, graced that first meeting with their attendance while letters congratulating Foscari on his election arrived from other states.[15] From time to time the Venetian Republic rewarded foreign princes for their loyalty and service to Venice with honorary membership in the Great Council. The first meeting of Foscari's reign had one important piece of business on its agenda, to fill the empty post of procurator of San Marco *de citra* created by Foscari's election as doge. According to Antonio Morosini's chronicle, two candidates emerged from the nominating committees: Pietro Minoto and Albano Badoer of Sant'Angelo, the man who had played such an important role in Foscari's election to the dogeship. Badoer defeated Minoto decisively, receiving 850 of the 970 votes cast. The Marquess of Mantua received the honor of formally placing Badoer's name forward, although

Sanudo indicates that it was the doge who actually promoted Badoer's election.[16] Clearly Foscari wanted to keep the procurators' pool of charitable funds securely in the hands of one of his strongest partisans. By more or less selecting his own successor as procurator the very first time he presided over the Great Council, Foscari thus once again demonstrated his skill at manipulating political processes.

But while the celebrations that greeted Foscari's election proceeded apace, the realities of rule also quickly began to make themselves felt. Within a month of the election Venice faced a major foreign policy challenge, and by early summer the city was suffering a devastating out-break of the plague. These were just the first in a series of political and personal crises that the doge would confront during his first decade of rule. Partly in response to these events, Foscari and the procurators *de supra* would take the decision to construct in the basilica of San Marco a major new chapel to honor the Virgin and seek her favor. Yet given the events that lay ahead during these difficult years, there must have been times when Foscari felt that the Queen of Heaven had turned her back on the man whose throne she symbolically and pictorially protected.

Foscari's first foreign policy crisis occurred not on the Italian mainland, as one might expect given the supposedly contentious debate preced-ing Foscari's election, but in the city's traditional center of interest in the eastern Mediterranean. In early May 1423 news reached Venice via nobleman Delfino Venier, the proveditor of the Morea, of the death of the Byzantine emperor Manuel, who had recently weathered a Turkish siege of his capital at Constantinople. Manuel was in fact still alive, although he had been severely incapacitated by a stroke, leaving his son John (VIII) as emperor and his youngest son, Andronicus, Despot of Thessalonica.[17] But even more troubling news followed when the Vene-tians learned that Sultan Murad II's Turkish troops were laying siege to the city of Thessalonica and invading the Morea. The Turks had easily overrun the Hexamilion, the wall 6 miles in length that Manuel had constructed in 1415 across the Isthmus of Corinth, in order to "turn the Morea into a Byzantine island."[18] More than 20,000 Turkish troops invaded the peninsula, devastating the land and taking numerous Greek inhabitants as slaves. The Venetians were especially concerned with the security of Modon and Coron, their two outposts on the southwestern tip of the peninsula, often referred to as the "eyes" of the Republic given their strategic significance at the mouth of the Adriatic.[19]

It was in these increasingly desparate circumstances that the despot Andronicus decided, with the consent of the city's inhabitants, to offer Thessalonica to Venice, on condition that the Venetians observe Thessalonica's customs and statutes.[20] Andronicus saw this as the only way to safeguard the city from the Turks. Before the Venetian Senate agreed to the takeover, however, it sought the advice of Albano Badoer, Pietro Zeno, Pietro Querini, Francesco Trevisan, and Giorgio Valaresso, men it described as experts, "in the facts of Thessalonica and of other places in those parts." On 7 July the Senate voted to accept the offer, although it also agreed to send an envoy to Manuel informing him of their decision and seeking his consent.[21] A few days later the Senate elected the knights (*milites*) Niccolò Zorzi and Foscari's brother-in-law Santo Venier to serve as the proveditors of Thessalonica. On 27 July the two received their commission. Among their charges they were ordered to reinforce the city's defenses, congratulate Andronicus on the cession, and guarantee the rights of the inhabitants of the city, including the Greek clergy. In addition, one of the two was to make his way to the sultan's court in order to inform him that the Venetians had accepted the city only in order to prevent it from falling into rival Christian hands.[22]

The real motives behind the Senate's decision were certainly more complicated. The historian Donald Nicol attributes Venice's annexation of Thessalonica to the "new and more adventurous" Doge Foscari, who "was intent on taking more vigorous action against the Turks," and who recognized the city's strategic importance.[23] The sources make it difficult, however, to attribute much personal responsibility to Foscari, although they do show that the doge and some of his closest allies (Santo Venier and Albano Badoer) were deeply engaged in the decision-making process. But so were many others. This was after all a senatorial not a ducal decision, for many patricians had interests in the region; and Thessalonica could indeed provide a possible bulwark against further Turkish moves against Venetian possessions, especially Negroponte. But clearly the Venetians were concerned about how this action would be perceived, especially by other western powers. When the Senate voted to accept Andronicus's offer on 7 July, they wanted to emphasize that they had agreed to it "for the honor of the Christian faith and not out of ambition for dominion."[24] The senators were reacting to a common perception in Latin Christian Europe that Venice was slow to act against the Turks and not willing to risk its commercial ventures for Christian solidarity. For their part, the Venetians felt that they were already bearing most of the burden of the Christian defense against the Turkish threat.

News reached Venice in October that the proveditors Zorzi and Venier had taken possession of Thessalonica on 14 September and raised the standard of San Marco in the city.[25] But they wrote that they had found the city in dire straits and that they needed more men for the city's defense, and food to relieve the inhabitants' starvation. The Senate responded that it would send both food and reinforcements. But none of this was sufficient to alleviate the desperate situation created by the Turkish siege of the city.[26] In the winter of 1424 Niccolò Zorzi fulfilled the proveditors' commission by going to the sultan's court to explain Venice's actions. But his efforts were rebuffed, and he was arrested at Adrianople.[27] Venice responded decisively to this diplomatic affront. On 17 April it authorized the captain-general of the sea, Pietro Loredan, Foscari's former rival for the dogeship, to sail to Thessalonica where Santo Venier would bring him up to date on the situation. As a conciliatory gesture, the Senate authorized Loredan to offer the sultan an annual tribute of between one and two thousand ducats, money which would come from the revenues of Thessalonica. If the sultan rejected his proposal, then the Senate licensed Loredan to take military action by moving his ships to the area around Gallipoli, the site of his dramatic victory over the Turks in 1416, and inflict maximum damage on the enemy's forces. If possible, he was to reiterate to the Turks that Venetian possession of Thessalonica was undertaken first and foremost to prevent it from falling into the possession of rival Christian powers.[28] In May 1424 the Senate elected two new proveditors to Thessalonica to relieve Zorzi and Venier: Bernardo Loredan was designated duke; Giacomo Dandolo, captain of the city.[29]

But the Venetian annexation of Thessalonica did little to relieve the pressure on the much-reduced Byzantine empire. Consequently in the fall of 1423 the emperor John decided to travel to the west in order to seek support for the defense of Constantinople. Diplomatic visits and in particular entrance ceremonies were delicate affairs, carefully scrutinized by observers and participants alike.[30] For this reason, the Venetians decided to give John a grand show. On 11 December the Great Council authorized the expenditure of up to 200 ducats to honor him.[31] The emperor had taken passage on the Venetian merchant galleys returning from Tana and Constantinople and arrived in Venice on 15 December. As a sign of respect, Foscari and the entire Signoria as well as many nobles traveled to San Niccolò on the Lido to greet the emperor and conduct him on the *bucintoro*, first to San Marco and then to his accommodations at the Benedictine monastery on the island of San Giorgio Maggiore. They also presented John and his escort with gifts of various sorts.[32]

John's visit was only the first of many important diplomatic visits that Foscari would host as doge. Under Foscari's reign pomp and display became increasingly important aspects of Venetian politics and diplomacy. On 10 June 1423, for example, the Great Council passed a law requiring the ducal councilors as well as the heads of the Forty to wear "vestes de colore," that is bright red robes, rather than the black robes that patricians normally wore when they were seated at the tribune, the row of seats flanking the ducal throne, and "in every other place where they represent the Signoria." Such outfits increased the "honor and reputation" of Venice, added solemnity to the proceedings, and at the same time reinforced hierarchies and divisions within the patriciate by marking off high officials from rank and file members.[33]

The emperor's plan was to try to reconcile Venice and Sigismund, the King of Hungary and emperor-elect, the two western powers most directly threatened by the Turks and hence most likely to respond to his appeal for aid. But the Venetians, as they often did, equivocated, expressing their reluctance to go it alone. Furthermore, they rebuffed his effort to raise money by offering them as surety two rubies, which he valued at 40,000 ducats. But they did agree to pay up to 8 ducats a day to subsidize his maintenance. On 17 January 1424 John departed Venice, traveling to Milan, Mantua, and elsewhere. On his arrival in Hungary he similarly received little concrete support from Sigismund and returned to Constantinople within the year.[34] Shortly after his departure from Venice, news arrived that his father Manuel had signed a new treaty with the sultan in which Manuel agreed to pay the Turks an annual tribute for the Morea of 100,000 hyperpers. Sanudo judged this agreement harshly, stating "Thus the Morea was turned into a tax farm of the Turk."[35]

As John's abortive mission demonstrates, the Venetian decision to annex Thessalonica had little to do with Christian solidarity and everything to do with Venice's desire to protect its Aegean outposts as well

as the sea lanes leading to Constantinople and the Black Sea. Foscari
and Venice played a double game, offering encouragement (but little
else) to the Byzantines, while trying not to antagonize the Turks. The
Venetian takeover of Thessalonica undoubtedly bought the Byzantines
some time, but it could not stem the Turkish tide. Venice managed to
hold the city until 1430, all the while engaging in skirmishes with the
Turks. At the same time Venice tried to solidify its position in the
Balkans.[36] This first foreign policy crisis, the Thessalonica annexation,
certainly makes a lie of claims that Foscari was interested only in terraferma affairs. But it reveals little else about the man. By contrast, his
first domestic crisis tells much about him and about his initial concep-
tion of the dogeship.

That crisis was the plague, which made its terrible return to the lagoon
city in May 1423. By July much of the government was virtually shut
down as nobles fled the city for their villas on the mainland or to other
islands of the lagoon in order to escape the congestion and contagion
of the city. The Great Council passed only one minor bill during the
month of July, and the Council of Ten undertook no action at all except
for the routine business of electing its presiding officers. The Senate too
was in such crisis that in August the Great Council voted to reduce the
number of men required for a Senate quorum from seventy to sixty.
Still the plague continued to rage. Morosini records that between six
and eight people were dying every day at the beginning of the outbreak, but by August and September the number had risen to forty. The
final death toll, according to the *signori di notte* (lords of the nightwatch),
was 15,300 – this out of a population of approximately 85,000.[37]
    After its initial paralysis, the government eventually began to react.
On 11 August the Council of Ten ordered the *signori di notte* to double
the number of police patrols since those fleeing the city had left their
houses and goods unattended.[38] Then on 29 August Foscari and the
ducal councilors proposed a broad plan to the Senate. First, as a way of
reducing the chance of new outbreaks, they would restrict access to the
city for those coming from areas already infected by the plague. Anyone
breaking this ban would be subject to six months in jail and a fine of
100 lire. More importantly, they proposed that the government build a
hospital on the Lido or nearby island for the care of plague victims.
They asked that between one and two thousand ducats be authorized

for the hospital and that it be staffed with a prior or prioress, one or more physicians, and three female assistants who would serve as nurses. All the expenses were to be paid by the Salt Office, which as its name indicates controlled the lucrative trade in salt. Finally, they proposed that anyone infected with the plague in the city or the surrounding islands or anyone arriving by ship be immediately tranferred to the hospital for care. The Senate passed the bill by a surprisingly close vote with 53 in favor, 31 opposed, and 12 abstentions.[39]

Having received senatorial authorization for the hospital, Foscari and his councilors next set about finding a suitable location for it. They settled on the island of Santa Maria di Nazareth, close to the Lido, which housed an order of Augustinian friars. The friars agreed to swap it for another island near Chioggia at the southern end of the lagoon. The Great Council approved this exchange on 10 October and charged the Signoria to seek papal approval. So began the Lazzaretto, Venice's plague hospital.[40]

The proposal to create the Lazzaretto originated with Foscari and his six ducal councilors. Given his vast experience with the administration of hospitals while procurator of San Marco, however, it seems likely that the main driving force was Foscari himself. And as already noted, his family were patrons of a hospital on the island of Murano: in the 1440s the doge, his brother Marco, and his cousin Filippo had joint patronage rights there.[41] By taking the lead in the establishment of the plague hospital, Foscari assumed a familiar role and played to his administrative strengths. And he could again demonstrate his concern for the poor and most vulnerable members of Venetian society. On the same day that the bill regarding the Lazzaretto was put forward, Foscari and his councilors placed before the Senate a separate bill seeking authorization to repair wells and build new ones throughout the city. The preamble to the bill observed that "our people" (*populus noster*) often suffered from shortages of water brought about by drought during the summer months. Foscari was tapping into a traditional political alliance between doges and the *popolo*, one which accorded well with the idea of the doge as prince. Unlike the bill to create the Lazzaretto, this one passed overwhelmingly.[42]

The plague of 1423 was a defining moment for Foscari personally: his actions during the late summer that year helped to shape his image of the ducal office, with an emphasis on its beneficent and paternal aspects. Foscari became in this moment of crisis a father to the larger community, just as the text of Romano's motet called him, a father looking after those who were suffering. But the notion of the doge as father was highly charged and potentially divisive for it drew attention to the princely attributes of the office and tended to run counter to visions of the doge as republican magistrate. The symbolic representation of the doge as father also ran up against the real-life family politics of doges and their sons.

Among several other public works projects undertaken during the first year of Foscari's reign were three construction programs, all of which the Senate approved in July. The first authorized the expenditure of funds for the repair of the cathedral of Torcello in the northern lagoon, once a thriving settlement but now in serious decline.[43] The second approved use of proceeds from the tax on wine to pay for dredging the Grand Canal. And the third ordered the dismantling of all unauthorized wooden stands or stalls surrounding the San Marco and Ducal Palace complex. A variety of motives prompted these measures, including concerns for the free movement of commercial traffic and decorum, as well as the desire to honor God.[44]

But the two most important projects undertaken at this time focused on the governmental and commercial centers at San Marco and Rialto. The Great Council had decided during the final year of Doge Mocenigo's reign to undertake a major addition to the Ducal Palace. On 27 September 1422 it observed that the "palace dedicated to rendering the law" was in a state of ruin. Evidently, this law court stood between the basilica of San Marco and the wing of the palace housing the Great Council Hall which faced the water. Accordingly, the council voted to build a new wing running along the Piazzetta which would match architecturally the Great Council wing. (The third wing, which housed the ducal family, also met the Great Council wing at a right angle so that the entire complex formed a kind of U-shaped structure.) The council ordered the Salt Office to pay for the construction, authorizing 6000 ducats in the first year; and between two and four thousand in subsequent years. The funds were to be transferred to the procurators of San Marco. The council also made clear that decisions regarding the palace were to be made by what amounted to the Pien Collegio minus the *savi agli ordini*.[45] But work on the palace was delayed, first perhaps by Mocenigo's death and then by the plague. According to

Morosini, construction did not begin until March 1424. On the 27th of that month, workmen began to tear down the old courthouse building.[46] Work on the new wing (which even today bears Foscari's name) would take several years to complete (fig. 11). Architecturally, the extension was conservative; it was designed to match the fourteenth-century Great Council Hall wing.

At the same time the Senate decided to rebuild another important governmental structure, the loggia at Rialto. The loggia stood at the Rialto market, on the far side of the wooden bridge. As a poem of 1442 by the Florentine Jacopo d'Albizzotto Guidi indicates, it served as a gathering spot for nobles, a place where "news on the Rialto," to quote Shakespeare's *Merchant of Venice*, could be shared and exchanged.[47] On 11 March 1424 a bill to rebuild the loggia failed to pass. But twelve days later, on the 23rd, the Senate approved the measure and authorized the expenditure of up to 600 ducats, as well as the recycling of columns from the soon-to-be-torn-down courthouse for the loggia.[48] The loggia no longer stands. It was demolished in the sixteenth century during a major renovation of the Rialto market complex. But it is visible in Jacopo de' Barbari's 1500 bird's-eye-view map of Venice and one small section of the porch is depicted as well in Carpaccio's *Healing of the Possessed Man*, one of a large cycle of paintings done for the Scuola di San Giovanni Evangelista. The painting shows the structure supported by tall columns capped with Gothic capitals. Neither of these building projects can be directly attributed to Foscari, although he must have supported them. What is noteworthy is that both of these projects from early in his reign look to the past: in the case of the Ducal Palace through the replication of the already existing wing's architecture; and in the loggia through the recycling of architectural elements from the old courthouse.[49] Only a year into the reign, Foscari was not yet ready to put his personal stamp on the city; both projects celebrate instead Venice itself and its long history. They attest as well to the city's great wealth at the beginning of his rule and to an ever-growing concern with civic magnificence and splendor.[50]

Affairs on the terraferma, events that would forever define Foscari's reign, began to heat up at the beginning of 1424. The problem centered on the aggressive actions toward Florence of Venice's ally Filippo Maria Visconti, Duke of Milan. Already in control of Brescia and Genoa,

Visconti's troops entered Imola in the Romagna in February, taking as prisoner the city's lord, Ludovico degli Alidosi.[51] Next Visconti conquered Faenza. All of this worried the Florentines, who sent Rinaldo degli Albizzi on an embassy to Venice to make the Florentine case for common action against Milan. He warned the Venetians of the danger that Visconti posed, sought their alliance, and at a minimum requested that Venice inhibit Visconti's use of the River Po.[52] But in its response of 13 May, the Senate gave Albizzi an answer he did not want to hear. While sympathizing with the Florentine situation, it reminded the Florentines that Venice was in league with Milan against possible aggression by the Holy Roman Emperor and that Venice was powerless to shut off access to the Po. Florentine efforts to enlist the aid of the emperor and the Duke of Savoy similarly failed.[53]

The situation grew significantly worse for Florence when in late July its army under the command of Carlo Malatesta, lord of Rimini, was routed at Zagonara north of Faenza and Malatesta taken prisoner. This prompted a new embassy to Venice in September, led by two of the Tuscan city's most important citizens, Palla Strozzi and Giovanni de' Medici. But the Senate responded much as it had to the earlier Florentine mission.[54] According to Sanudo, these same Florentine ambassadors were present when Count Estorlet of Gorizia and Tyrol and his henchmen arrived in Venice in October to pledge their homage and fealty to the doge, as they had formerly done to the Patriarch of Aquileia. For the occasion, a large platform was constructed in Piazza San Marco and a public ceremony held in which the count received a baton and flags and Foscari made "a most notable speech." The formal submission of the count further secured Venice's eastern and northern frontiers against incursions by the emperor, and helped clear the way for possible action in the west. The day was, in Giorgio Dolfin's opinion, "a great triumph."[55]

Throughout the rest of the fall of 1424 and early winter of 1425 diplomats scurried across Italy, trying to find a solution to the growing Milanese threat, a situation made worse by yet another Milanese victory over the Florentines in the Val di Lamona in February.[56] The Venetians were particularly concerned for the security of the buffer states under the control of the rulers of Mantua, Ferrara, and Ravenna.[57] But Visconti's suspicion that Venice was favoring the Florentines grew when the mercenary captain Francesco Bussone, known as Carmagnola, who had recently fallen out with Visconti and who was the object of a Milanese murder plot, arrived in Venice in February. According to Morosini, Carmagnola arrived in disguise (*travvestidio*) – most likely a precaution as he was said also to be carrying large sums of money. The Signoria received him with great honor and granted him the right to travel about the city with armed bodyguards. Following negotiations conducted by nobleman Andrea Contarini, the Senate agreed, in early March, to accept Carmagnola into Venetian service, with an initial *condotta* or contract for 200 lances (a lance comprised three men: a heavily armed mounted soldier, a more lightly armed sergeant, and a page or servant) and a monthly stipend of 500 ducats. Yet many senators remained suspicious of the condottiere. The proposal authorizing his contract finally passed on a third vote with 84 in favor, 62 opposed, and 10 abstentions.[58]

Count Carmagnola was but the most recent of the many mercenary captains who over the course of the past century had come to play a pivotal role in the politics of the Italian states and who helped bring about, in Niccolò Machiavelli's estimation, Italy's eventual ruin. Venice had made its first significant use of mercenary forces in the 1330s during its contest with Mastino della Scala, lord of Verona, although it continued to rely on native troops as well. It was the Republic's expansion onto the terraferma at the beginning of the fifteenth century that necessitated changes in Venetian military organization, changes that included "a much larger permanent force with an accepted system of rapid expansion," lengthier contracts for mercenary captains, and the designation of "a permanent captain-general." But many Venetian patricians also continued to undertake active military service on both land and sea. And the government, always distrustful of the mercenary captains who had a well-deserved reputation for looking out for their own interests rather than those of their employers, continued to supervise military operations through the appointment of civilian proveditors.[59]

Carmagnola, who was born about 1385, arrived in Venice in a position of strength for he was, as one historian has put it, "victorious in war, married to a noblewoman, immensely rich, and honored even by the pope." Since 1412 he had been in the service of Visconti, rising by 1416 to the post of captain-general. He played a major role in reestablishing Milanese preeminence over Lombardy and neighboring areas by conquering among other places Monza in 1413, Trezzo in 1417, Bergamo in 1419, and Brescia and Genoa in 1421. Filippo Maria Visconti rewarded him with fiefs and a marriage in 1417 to Antonia Visconti, one of his relatives. During his governorship of Genoa, however, Carmagnola's relations with Visconti began to sour. And so he abandoned Milanese service and made his way to Venice.[60]

With an initial contract in hand, Carmagnola quickly began to make more demands of his Venetian employers, presenting them with a list of twenty-one requests which Foscari read to the Senate, including that he be designated captain-general, that his contract be increased to 500 lances, and that the government advance him a loan. The Senate resisted these requests; and in one particularly telling clause reiterated that while prisoners and all moveable goods taken in war would become the property of Carmagnola and his associates, all "towns, lands, castles, outposts, and forts and munitions" would come under the purview of the "lord doge Signoria, and the commune of the Venetians." Carmagnola accepted the Venetian conditions and, according to Dolfin, "swore his fidelity to the most illustrious Signoria of Venice in the hands of the most Serene prince doge of Venice."[61]

In the meantime, Visconti continued to put pressure on the Florentines, defeating them at Rapallo in April 1425 and twice in October, at Anghiari and at Faggiuola. This prompted further Florentine pleas for an alliance which the Venetians continued to rebuff, although they did attempt to mediate between the two powers. But on 23 November the Senate voted to form a league with the Florentines. Foscari informed the Milanese ambassadors of the decision and asked that they too reach an accord with the Florentines.[62] On 3 December the Senate approved, in the name of Christ, the Virgin, and Saints Mark and John the Baptist (the patron saint of Florence), the provisions of the league by a vote of 130 to 8 with 9 abstentions. The ten-year alliance provided among other things that Venice could negotiate for the league. Both republics agreed to mount armies of 8000 cavalry and 3000 footsoldiers, while Venice also promised to outfit a Po fleet, the expenses of which would be shared. And they agreed to divide the spoils of war as follows: Florence would get any lands wrested from Visconti in Tuscany or the Romagna, except for Lugo and Parma, which would be given to the Marquess of Ferrara, while all lands captured in Lombardy would devolve to Venice. Genoa and its territories would be restored to independence; to this end, a fleet under Venetian control but with joint financial backing of both republics would pursue the liberation of Genoa. The fate of the Malestesta lands adhering to Milan was to be determined by Venice.[63]

It is clear that the vast majority of the patriciate (as evidenced by the lopsidedness of the votes) supported Foscari's regime in this momentous decision to ally with Florence against Milan. Apparently any previous opposition to further mainland expansion had melted away, and the ruling class was ready to commit itself to territorial expansion beyond its traditional sphere in the Veneto and toward Lombardy. This was due no doubt to a growing realization that Milan constituted not a temporary but a permanent threat to Venetian interests. It was this recognition plus the need for some sort of political equilibrium in northern Italy that propelled Venice to ally with Florence, a state whose economic interests often conflicted with its own, but with whom it shared an ideological and rhetorical commitment to republicanism. As the official announcement of the league in January 1426 proclaimed, the allies pledged themselves to the "free and peaceful state of all Italy." The Florentine alliance marked another significant step in the Venetians' reimagining of themselves and their state.[64]

Venice moved quickly to prepare for war. Francesco Bembo was placed in charge of the Po fleet after Pietro Loredan refused the post, and Carmagnola was elected captain of the land forces. On 15 February he swore loyalty to the doge in San Marco.[65] The Venetians undertook an important governmental adjustment as well. In December 1425 the Great Council approved by a vote of 342 to 171 with 64 abstentions a motion put forward by Foscari and four of the ducal councilors to establish a Council of One Hundred which would handle the war effort and have essentially the same powers as the Senate. Such a council had been created before, in 1412, to supervise the war against the Hungarians. According to Dolfin, the One Hundred was created "in order that the affairs of the said war might be governed by better means and order and more maturely." This constitutional innovation, however, threatened in significant ways both the power of the Senate and of the Great Council and also testifies, as the large number of opposing and abstaining votes indicates, to a growing bifurcation within the ranks of the noble class.[66]

Events in the First Venetian/Visconti War moved rapidly.[67] Carmagnola, the recently designated captain-general, moved his troops against Brescia, while the Marquess of Ferrara Niccolò d'Este, captain-general of the Florentine troops and lieutenant-general of the Venetian ones, concentrated his efforts in the region beyond the Po. In March Brescia's Guelf party opened the city gates to the Venetians who quickly occupied the lower city. But they met stiff resistance from the Milanese who had retreated to the upper city, forcing the invading Venetians to set up a siege. Word of the entry into Brescia led the One Hundred on 23 March to order a distribution of alms to the poor and to monasteries in thanksgiving.[68] While Carmagnola carried on the siege of the upper city of Brescia, Pietro Bembo used Venice's Po fleet to carry the war further into Milanese territory by moving on Cremona and threatening Pavia. And in April Amedeo, Duke of Savoy, agreed to league with Venice, thereby creating problems for Visconti on his western front; while for their part the Malatestas sided with Milan.[69]

In May Venice made several new awards or concessions to Carmagnola. He was granted membership in the Great Council, and the Senate promised him a state – or, as they colorfully called it, "a nest" – on either side of the River Adda. Furthermore, the Senate gave him a great deal of authority over on-going negotiations and the territories recently taken. On 25 May, for example, the One Hundred gave its approval to several promises he had made to the Brescians.[70] At the same time, it remained wary of his precise intentions. In June the One Hundred decided that it was essential to have a "loyal person" at his side and in July voted on the recommendation of Foscari and the *savi del consiglio* to send Tommaso Malipiero back to the army as proveditor. Carmagnola had asked specifically for Malipiero. The One Hundred's justification is especially revealing. They noted that Carmagnola held their mainland state "in his hands."[71]

In September the Venetian army gained control over more strongholds within the city of Brescia. In November the last holdouts gave up, and the proveditors Fantin Michiel and Pietro Loredan occupied the entire city.[72] Throughout the fall Pope Martin V searched for a peace through his representative Niccolò Albergati, the Cardinal of Santa Croce in Jerusalem; and in December all sides sent representatives to Venice for negotiations. Finally, on 30 December they arranged the Peace of Venice. For its part, Venice got possession of Brescia and of the territory it had conquered on the riviera of Lake Garda, including the town of Salò. Florence got the restitution of lands taken by Visconti (with the exception of Imola and Forlì), but was unable to secure the freedom of Genoa from Visconti rule. Visconti further agreed not to interfere in Bologna or the Romagna or Tuscany, to recognize the rights of Savoy, to release Carmagnola's wife and daughters whom he had been holding hostage, and to restore Carmagnola's lands and wealth to him.[73] Thus at the end of the first mainland adventure of his reign, Foscari had added the important city of Brescia to the Venetian dominion. Venice had successfully expanded beyond its traditional sphere of mainland influence into Lombardy.

But the Peace of Venice turned out to be little more than a mid-winter pause in the conflict for its terms dissatisfied Visconti who almost immediately began preparing for what can be termed the Second Venetian/Visconti War. In March Carmagnola arrived in Venice for consultations. He was followed by his wife, who was splendidly received by the dogaressa and presented with jewels and gifts of cloth valued at 1000 ducats.[74] Visconti soon undertook military action in the Parmigiano and Mantovano, scoring victories at Torricella and Casalmaggiore on the Po, and then moving against Brescello further down the river. For his part, Carmagnola refused to come to the aid of the besieged Venetian forces in these places, despite repeated pleas from the Senate to do so. He claimed that his army was not yet ready for battle.[75] The reasons for Carmagnola's delay are unclear. Writing in 1889, his biographer Antonio Battistella gave him the benefit of the doubt, accepting the captain-general's explanation that he did not want to enter the field of battle without his forces in order; but others have condemned him for his inaction and argued that it helped sow doubts in Venetian minds regarding his reliability.[76] Regardless of the interpretation attached to it, his inaction clearly illustrates the extent to which Venice had placed itself at the mercy of its military captain.

But while Carmagnola dithered, the Venetians' Po fleet under the command of Francesco Bembo took the offensive, besting the Milanese squadron and retaking Brescello. Eventually Carmagnola got his massive army in order and during the summer undertook operations in the Bresciano and the Cremonese. The One Hundred urged him to cross the River Adda and take the fight to Visconti but to be on guard against Visconti's overtures for peace. By September it was clearly losing patience with Carmagnola's relative inaction, especially given the size and expense of his army.[77] But on 12 October the captain-general put

Venetian doubts temporarily to rest when he scored a victory over the Milanese at Maclodio, southwest of Brescia. It is estimated that a combined Venetian force of 18,000 cavalry and 8000 footsoldiers met a Visconti force of 12,000 cavalry and 6000 infantry under such captains as Francesco Sforza. The Venetians took thousands of Milanese soldiers prisoner, including their top commander, Carlo Malatesta.[78]

News of this spectacular victory reached Venice on 15 October and was met with jubilant celebrations and offerings to God. In his chronicle Morosini hoped that God would "destroy this tyrant [Visconti] for the good of all Italy."[79] The One Hundred elected Giorgio Corner and Santo Venier to undertake a mission to Carmagnola on behalf of the Republic and offer him rewards, including a palace in Venice as well as the villa of Castenedolo in the Bresciano. The Venetians also offered a palace in Venice to the vice-commander of the Venetian forces, Gianfrancesco Gonzaga.[80] The gift of a house in Venice was a special honor reserved for the Republic's most distinguished friends. The palace the government granted to Carmagnola stood in the parish of San Stae and had originally belonged to the Lion family, from whom the government had purchased the house in 1415 as a reward for another military commander, Pandolfo Malatesta. It took until 1430 for Gonzaga to get his palace; it happened when the government bought the Palace of the Two Towers in the parish of San Pantalon from the Giustinian family.[81] Unlike the largely honorific offering of these urban palaces, the awarding of rural fiefs, such as Castenedolo, provided condottieri with more tangible benefits, including additional sources of income (it was estimated that Castenedolo generated an annual revenue of 600 ducats), country seats for themselves and their families, as well as the administrative and judicial rights that went with these feudal enclaves. Some have argued that the granting of such fiefs was "the most effective way of retaining the services of a condottiere;" but this opinion underplays the threat that such grants represented to the Republic's sovereignty.[82] In fact, these concessions represented a partitioning of territory and the establishment of independent power bases for the captains. They also illustrate that men in the Renaissance did not yet see territorial or administrative integrity as identical with governmental authority.

Like generals throughout history, Carmagnola wanted to commemorate his victory at Maclodio and decided to do so by means of architecture. He let his Venetian masters know via his confidante Tommaso

Malipiero that he wished to build at Maclodio "unum turatum in volto," inside of which was to be a chapel dedicated to Saint Mark. As the Latin phrase suggests, the monument was intended to be a tower structure supported by a vault, perhaps similar to a city gate; and Carmagnola wanted it to be known as the "Victory Tower." Foscari and two of the councilors put the captain-general's plan to the One Hundred which approved the measure by a vote of 55 to 19 and ordered the provedi-tors of Brescia to supervise and pay for the project. The structure was never built, but it may have remained on Foscari's mind as his own later building projects demonstrate (see chapter 3 below).[83]

Following the victory at Maclodio, Venice once again encouraged Carmagnola to seize the opportunity and carry the war further into Visconti territory toward Milan itself. Instead, the captain-general engaged in mopping-up operations in the Bresciano and then went into winter quarters.[84] The preceding September the pope had tried to restart peace talks through his representative the Cardinal of Santa Croce. But it was not until the late fall that representatives of the various parties gathered in Ferrara for negotiations. They finally worked out an agree-ment in April 1428. This treaty, known as the Peace of Ferrara, was pub-lished or proclaimed on 10 May.[85] For the most part it reiterated the terms of the earlier Peace of Venice, with one important difference: it required Visconti to cede the important town of Bergamo and the sur-rounding Bergamasco to Venice.[86] This represented yet another signifi-cant addition to the Venetian state. The Republic's domain now extended to within a mere 60 kilometers of Visconti's capital.

The Peace of Ferrara, like the earlier Peace of Venice, was met with lavish celebrations; and Carmagnola was grandly received in the city. With the restoration of peace, the Senate ordered him to return the battle flags of both Venice and the League which Foscari had presented him at the time of his commission. Accordingly, on 9 May Carmagnola ceremonially returned the banners. But their disposition soon became a matter of controversy. The ducal councilor Ermolao Valaresso proposed that the flag of Saint Mark be placed in the basilica, "according to custom," but that that of the League be displayed in the offices of the procurators of San Marco, a less prestigious venue. That bill failed in face of another which authorized the placement of both banners in the church.[87] The issue, which might now seem trivial, was delicate because it posed a choice: if Venice did not place the League's flag in a place of great honor, the city's allies would be offended; alternatively, as the city's patron, Saint Mark himself might be affronted if he were forced to share his honor with that of the League. The latter path was chosen, no doubt in the hope that Mark would understand.

In July representatives from Bergamo arrived to solemnize that city's cession to Venice. They presented Foscari with the banner of their city. According to Dolfin, this purple and yellow flag was inscribed with the words *Civitas Bergomi* (the City of Bergamo). It too was placed in San Marco, where it served to commemorate Foscari's extension of the realm. The representatives also gave Foscari the keys to the city gates. According to Morosini, this ritual act signified Venice's "solemn dominion" over Bergamo, since the Bergamaschi no longer controlled access to their town.[88]

The lasting effects of the Peace of Ferrara are hard to assess. The treaty was a product of economic and political exhaustion on all sides. At the same time, it exposed the contrasting interests and objectives of Florence and Venice and did little to generate the kind of equilibrium that would have allowed Venice and Milan to enjoy a solid and secure peace. It also left both sides with reasons to resume the struggle, as the occasion warranted. Furthermore, it produced a situation in which both Milan and Venice were compelled to maintain large standing armies along their common border. The establishment of these "permanent billets" changed the nature of the Venetian army and had far-reaching fiscal and budgetary consequences.[89]

While the peace occasioned public festivities and celebrations, it also prompted personal reflections from Morosini, who interrupted the conclusion to his narrative of these events with a record of his hopes for the future. He prayed that all Venetians from the doge to the *popolo* would now look "to the common good" (*al ben comun*) and not to their particular interests. He further wished that they might remain united and deal fairly with one another, not giving in to friendships or hatred, to special pleadings or bribes. He asked that Venice remain renowned in riches and honor. Finally, he prayed that God would continue to favor the city, and that its citizens would not give sway to pride but rather live together in charity.[90] Morosini's reflections provide an insight into the mindset of the men who ruled Venice in this period, men who mixed their concern for worldly success with a usually sincere reverence for God. His plea that the Venetians not look to their individual interests is particularly telling in the context of the huge financial and administrative strain on the Venetian polity caused by the first two Venetian/Visconti wars. As described below, this opened rifts that would be difficult to repair.

Most historians agree that during the first half of the fifteenth century Venice was at the height of its economic might, might built first and foremost on trade. By the 1430s the Republic was sending out as many as twenty-four state-owned merchant galleys on various shipping routes or lines. The Romania line took ships to Constantinople and then on to Tana and Trebizond in the Black Sea; the Beirut line to Rhodes, Beirut, and Tripoli; the Alexandria line to Crete and Egypt; the Cyprus line to Crete, Rhodes, and Cyprus; the Flanders line to Lisbon, London, and Bruges; and the Aigues-Mortes galleys to Naples, Pisa, and ports on the southern coast of France and eastern coast of Spain. In the late 1430s the Venetians added a route to the Barbary coast with ships carrying cargo to Tunis, Granada, and Valencia. Depending on the route, these ships carried in their holds and on their decks precious cargo including silks and spices such as cinnamon, pepper, and frankincense. One galley on the Alexandria line alone might carry as much as 100,000 ducats' worth of goods. In addition as many as 300 privately owned Venetian merchant vessels plied the seas, carrying a variety of cargoes of greater bulk and lesser value such as wheat, wine, raisins, and furs.[91] But despite the great wealth pouring into private hands as a result of this trade, the necessity of fielding huge armies of mercenary soldiers placed enormous financial strain on the public finances of the Republic.

The government of Venice relied for its financial resources on three main revenue streams: taxes in the form of forced loans to the state; *dazii* or customs fees and indirect imposts on various products; and revenues generated by the subject territories both on the terraferma and in the east. The revenues from customs fees, while substantial, obviously depended on and varied with the overall health of the economy and the volume of trade passing through the city. Venice expected the terraferma dominions not only to pay their own administrative and defense costs, but also to send surpluses to the *dominante* (capital). The provincial cities along with their rural districts and clergy were required to make various kinds of financial contribution. In October 1427, for instance, the Senate ordered the rectors of Verona and Vicenza to exhort the bishops of those cities to lend 6000 and 4000 ducats respectively to Venice. On the same day it ordered the levy of a 4000-ducat loan from the Jews of Padua, Treviso, and Mestre.[92] But the primary source of revenue to finance the extraordinary expenses of Venice's terraferma wars derived from forced loans on individuals.

The Venetian state's reliance on forced loans dated from at least 1207. The system worked in the following way. An *estimo* or assessment of both moveable and immoveable property was made (and periodically revised) and those surveyed were required to make loans to the state on the basis of their assessment. So, for example, in any particular levy, an individual might be forced to pay to the state some percentage (generally 1 percent or less) of his assessed wealth. Only about 12 percent of the city's population had enough wealth to meet the qualifications of the *estimo* of 1379. In other words, forced loans fell on the wealthiest members of society. But it is important to note that since these imposts were not technically taxes but rather loans to the state, shares in this funded debt, known as the Monte, paid interest and came to be treated much like other forms of property; they were bought and sold, bequeathed in wills, even included in dowries. For a time, the government sought to amortize the debt by purchasing outstanding shares. The War of Chioggia, however, put a terrible strain on the system: in just four years citizens were taxed for approximately one quarter of their total wealth, and interest payments had to be suspended. Interest payments resumed in 1383, but at a lower rate, and shares continued to sell at a deep discount. The system weathered the Chioggian storm, but only after revealing many structural weaknesses.[93]

The first two Visconti wars put renewed financial pressure on the Monte. Only one levy was made between 1423 and 1425, but the outbreak of hostilities quickly changed that. Thirteen levies were assessed in 1426 and twelve more in 1427. Total receipts amounted to 500,000 ducats in 1426 and 570,000 ducats in 1427. At the same time interest payments on shares of the funded debt were cut in half, with the government retaining the balance as a tax or crediting it to the taxpayer's account.[94] In the preamble to this decision the One Hundred noted that it was not "just or useful that only those who make loans feel and bear the entire burden of the exactions" brought on by the present war.[95] In other words, those who garnered interest on Monte shares should share the pain as well. The financial strain was such that the One Hundred decided in April 1426 to appoint a fifteen-member board of sages to review and revise the assessments.[96] But the unrelenting imposition of levies was apparently more than some could bear. In October 1426 the Council of Ten considered whether or not to prosecute nobleman Pietro Contarini for an angry outburst he had made in the Loan Office. In the end the Ten decided by a vote of 12 to 1 that Contarini had spoken foolishly but not maliciously and determined that he should be reprimanded by "the most serene lord doge."[97]

Contarini's injudicious outburst was symptomatic of the growing tension within the patriciate brought on by the Visconti wars, tension that would eventually touch Foscari himself. As noted above, many in the Great Council were strongly opposed to the decision to create the Council of One Hundred. One consequence of the wars with Milan, as of all wars, was to increase the need for swift and efficient governmental action. This wartime necessity accelerated the trend, already apparent over the past several decades, of concentrating power in the Senate and the smaller councils (the Collegio and the Ten) and conversely diminishing the power of the Great Council. The decision to abolish the Arengo, taken at the time of Foscari's election, was similarly symptomatic of the trend away from what might be termed Venice's communal or communitarian period.[98]

Opposition to the One Hundred appears to have diminished during the first year of its existence. Thus when the council was up for renewal in September 1426, the Great Council approved its extension with only five opposing votes.[99] A little more than a year later, however, the Great Council's will had changed considerably. In December a bill was put before the Great Council to regularize the procedures for electing the One Hundred. Some were concerned that no term of office had been established for members of the One Hundred; in other words some in the Great Council feared that it might become a standing, permanent council rather than a regularly elected rotating one. The prologue to the Great Council law observed that Venice's ancestors had never intended that any council be permanent, "except for the Great Council, which is the principal regime of this city." And so in order to preserve "equality" (equalitas), the Great Council decided that the One Hundred should have a set term and that new elections to it should be held. The bill, proposed by the heads of the Council of Forty which had approved the measure the day before, passed overwhelmingly with 336 votes in favor,

16 opposed, and 9 abstentions. It clearly reveals the Great Council's concern to defend its standing as the only body with a permanent membership, as well as the desire to preserve what it perceived as parity within the nobility.[100] What in the end led to the demise of the One Hundred was peace. A day after the official proclamation of the Peace of Ferrara in May 1428, a bill to renew the One Hundred came before the Great Council which defeated it by a vote of 170 to 320 with 49 abstentions. The secretary who recorded the Senate's secret deliberations broke with his usual script and wrote in capital letters: "EXPIRATIO CONSILII CENTUM."[101]

The status of the Council of One Hundred in these years was not the only source of tension between those powerful members of the patriciate who participated in the Senate and the rank and file members of the Great Council. Both bodies also jealously sought to protect their right to elect officials to various posts. So, for instance, the Senate debated in March 1426 how to elect a new fleet commander. Francesco Loredan and Antonio Gradenigo proposed that they elect someone to the position of captain-general of the sea and that he be elected from among three candidates: one proposed by the Senate through its own process of nomination known as scrutiny; the others selected by the Great Council through two nominating committees. This proposal failed to pass. The winning proposal put forward by Foscari and by Bulgaro and Daniele Vitturi stipulated that a captain of the Gulf be elected by the traditional four nominating committees of the Great Council.[102] Similarly, in April 1424 the Great Council determined that it rather than the Senate ought to elect the lieutenant of Friuli, noting that in 1421 it had decided that several other administrative posts should be its electoral responsibility. These included all posts in the Polesine of Rovigo, the proveditor of Rovereto, and the officials of the silver division of the Mint. They justified their decision by arguing that elections by the Great Council contributed to the "contentment of all" and greater "equality" of participation.[103]

These decisions reveal more than mere bureaucratic competition and jostling for position: the tension was symptomatic of growing social division within the ranks of the patriciate, between those nobles who participated in the highest circles of government and enjoyed great wealth and the poorer nobles who depended on the salaries provided by minor administrative posts for their livelihood. As already emphasized, Foscari often made it his job to protect the poorer nobles. Some historians have even argued that Venice's terraferma expansion was driven by the desire to create a new cache of positions for minor nobles. In fact, terraferma expansion was driven by the need to protect strategic trade routes and counteract the expansionist policies of Milan. Nevertheless, an unintended consequence was the creation of a pool of salaried jobs which profited many in the nobility.[104]

Certainly a number of laws of this period underscore noble preoccupation with jobs. In September 1425, for instance, the Great Council debated whether nobles who for one reason or another were perpetually banned from holding office should be eligible for offices normally reserved for *populares* or non-nobles. The Great Council decided that they were not, although the original proposal to allow nobles to occupy such posts got 215 votes.[105] This proposal illustrates the strong sense of class consciousness that pervaded the nobility. One law of August 1425 is particularly revealing of Foscari's own attitudes in this regard. According to the preamble, the climate in the subject town of Durazzo in Albania was so unhealthy that a posting there amounted to a death sentence for nobles. On that occasion, Foscari alone proposed that *populares* be sent in their stead. The bill failed, but it shows that, despite his solicitous attitude toward the poor, Foscari was a man who also harbored a strong sense of noble superiority.[106] His charitable impulses were motivated by a sense of *noblesse oblige*, rather than any belief in the inherent equality of all men. He believed that the great had an obligation to take care of the poor but not to share power with them.

But within the ranks of the nobility the competition for offices continued unabated. One way to guarantee the widest possible circulation of offices was to establish a prescribed period of ineligibility for those who had recently held posts. And so in August 1425 the Great Council reaffirmed a law of 1422 declaring rectors who earned a salary of 400 ducats or more ineligible for election for a period of time equal to their term of office.[107] In November 1428 this rule was extended to a variety of offices in Venetian outposts earning less than 400 ducats per year. The Great Council justified this move by arguing that it was "just and decent" that all have the opportunity to participate equally. But a surprisingly large number of men voted against this change. The bill passed with 381 votes in favor, 119 opposed, and 17 abstentions.[108]

The regime also had to grapple with other concerns raised by office-holding in the overseas realms and especially in the newly acquired terraferma dominions. By far the most serious issue that the Republic had to confront was guaranteeing that public offices remain just that – public – that they not become personal sinecures or arenas for the establishment of private spheres of influence. The concern was that individual noblemen or even particular noble families might monopolize particular offices and use those posts or territories to establish their personal authority. The impulse to do so is evident in the sculptures and other commemorative plaques that noble office-holders erected in subject cities as a means of memorializing their regimes. In 1452 Bertuccio Grimani, for example, placed a memorial on the campanile of San Lorenzo del Pasenatico on the Istrian peninsula: the sculpture included his personal arms. But in this instance, as in most others, the Venetian state was careful to assert its equal or greater authority by including a lion of San Marco, the symbol of the Republic, and Foscari's arms as well.[109]

At least twice in the 1420s the Senate felt compelled to reaffirm the public nature of office-holding. In March 1425 it noted that rectors and others were in the habit of giving speeches on taking up and relinquishing office. These orations must have been self-aggrandizing, intended to draw attention to the merits of the individual incumbents rather than to the Venetian regime. Accordingly, the Senate voted 66 to 31 with 3 abstentions that henceforth those entering and leaving office were to say only that they consigned or accepted the office, "in the name of the most illustrious Signoria of Venice."[110] And in August 1427 it ruled that rectors were not to wear mourning clothes but instead to dress in bright and "cheerful" colors; although it granted exceptions for the deaths of fathers, mothers, brothers, wives, or children, even then office-holders were not to wear mourning clothes for more than eight days. Those breaking the law were subject to a 100-ducat fine.[111] In both these instances the Republic was trying to reinforce the principle that office-holders were representatives of the state rather than of particular families.

While poorer nobles engaged in a constant battle to win minor offices as a source of revenue, the Republic's most powerful men faced a different set of problems associated with office-holding. On the one hand, there was the simple problem of overwork. Especially during the war years, the leading figures were called on time and time again to shoulder a heavy burden of administrative responsibilities. On the other, they faced the equally alarming threat that their political rivals would try to remove them from the center of power in Venice by electing them to distant administrative posts or ruin their careers by electing them to particularly onerous and problematic offices. Both of these issues came dramatically to the fore in March 1427. On the 9th of that month the Great Council debated a proposal put forward by Foscari and his ducal councilors. Apparently when elections for such wartime posts as captaincies, ambassadorships, proveditorships, and other important positions arose, candidates appealed against being selected by calling out, "Don't elect me" and "Don't vote for me." The council ruled that anyone who made such protestations would be fined 100 lire and deprived of all offices for a year. The measure passed with only 27 nays and 15 abstentions. A second proposal by Foscari and two of his six councilors passed much more narrowly with 404 in favor, 223 opposed, and 71 abstentions. Noting the "arduous and ponderous facts of the present war," it revoked many of the usual excuses for refusing offices.[112] The wartime demands of office-holding were clearly straining the civic-mindedness and goodwill of many in the patriciate.

The second issue touched Foscari's long-time rival Pietro Loredan. Throughout the wars Loredan had shown himself to be a loyal member of the regime. Elected a procurator of San Marco *de ultra* in June 1426, he had borne more than his fair share of offices, including service as the podesta of Brescia.[113] When in March 1427 Foscari and his councilors elected him and Fantin Michiel to serve for an unspecified period of time as the proveditors of Brescia in Carmagnola's absence, the two agreed to serve, according to Morosini, most "graciously and willingly."[114] However, on the 26th of that same month, when the One Hundred elected them to serve as proveditors to Carmagnola, they refused the posts. Furthermore, they let it be known in the Senate that they wished to consult with their "kinsmen and friends" regarding this matter.[115] This convocation of kin and friends suggests that the wounds inflicted by Foscari's victory over Loredan in 1423 had not healed and that the strains brought on by the terraferma wars were serving to coalesce or reinforce preexisting interest groups (factions is too strong a word at this point) within the patriciate. Although it is not entirely clear what had provoked this new electoral contretemps, it provides further evidence that Brescia and Bergamo were acquired at a heavy cost that extended beyond the financial and the budgetary. Their annexation to the Venetian state cannot be considered an unalloyed success for they brought in their wake serious tensions within the patriciate which ran along economic, bureaucratic, and kinship lines.

Several deaths during these first years of Foscari's reign took their toll on the doge's personal life as well. Some time between mid-November 1424 and early January 1425 his uncle and close political ally Franzi died, thereby thrusting Foscari into the role of family patriarch.[116] As discussed above, the two had often worked closely together. Then in 1425 Foscari lost his son Donato, who, according to Sanudo, died "in Palazo [sic]."[117] Donato, who had been named after Foscari's deceased middle brother, can have been no more than ten years old as he was among the offspring of Foscari's second wife. And in December 1428 came the death of the venerable Albano Badoer.[118] In the space of three years, Foscari had lost two of his closest advisors as well as one of his sons. Perhaps the doge's grief was to some extent relieved when his youngest brother Marco embarked on a political career. In the summer of 1429 Marco held the post of *savio della terraferma*.[119] Foscari would come to rely heavily on him throughout the rest of his reign.

Albano Badoer's death created a vacancy in Foscari's old post as procurator *de citra*. The ducal councilor Natale Donato and Santo Venier (Foscari's brother-in-law, husband of his sister Franceschina) were nominated to fill it, but unspecified *disordine* led the state attorneys to declare the contest null and void. On 28 December a new election was held between candidates Paolo Correr and Fantin Michiel, which Michiel won.[120] While the existing records do not explain what happened, it is not unreasonable to speculate that Foscari and his supporters pursued irregular methods to get Venier elected. Alternatively, Foscari's enemies might have invented their own irregularities in order to thwart the doge's efforts to keep this post in friendly hands. Regardless, it represented a major defeat for the doge, one which came on the heels of a number of personal tragedies. It also provides yet another indication of growing discord within the ruling elite.

The next two years were relatively quiet, at least on the terraferma front. 1429 began with important negotiations in the Ten and Senate regarding a request by Carmagnola to be released from Venetian service, a request which may have been prompted by efforts on the part of

Visconti to reengage Carmagnola in his service. But the Venetians were not willing to let this happen and after a series of negotiations, including efforts by Foscari to gain a bit more flexibility for the Collegio in treating with the mercenary captain, the two sides eventually reached a new accord.[121]

The terms were very generous: Carmagnola was granted supreme authority over the troops, including civil and criminal jurisdiction except in lands where there was a Venetian governor; provision was made for him to maintain a force of 500 lances in addition to his personal followers; and he was offered a monthly stipend of 1000 ducats. Further, he could do as he pleased with prisoners taken in battle, but all lands he captured would come under the jurisdiction of Venice. The contract was to last two years with the option of a two-year renewal.[122] Early in the negotiations the Venetians decided to confer on Carmagnola more territory, specifically the towns of Chiari and Roccafranca in the Bresciano, both close by the River Oglio, and to guarantee his other possessions in Lombardy. In addition, the Senate agreed to invest him, "by the hands of the most illustrious lord doge," with the title Count of Chiari. The county earned Carmagnola an annual income of 6000 ducats.[123] In spite of all this, Visconti continued to court the military captain. These overtures prompted the Senate in July to warn Carmagnola "to stand always with his shield in hand," in other words to be on guard against the duke's blandishments.[124] The situation grew more dangerous when in December Florence declared war on Lucca, and Visconti began funneling aid to the Lucchesi while at the same time harassing the Marquess of Monferrato, a Venetian and Florentine ally.[125]

In January 1430 Visconti wrote to Carmagnola, requesting a meeting, which the mercenary captain rebuffed. In March Carmagnola arrived in Venice, where the Senate warned him yet again to be on guard against the duke's machinations and to refuse further communications with him. Venetian suspicions of Visconti's intentions and doubts about Carmagnola's own loyalty grew in April, when it was discovered that there were differences between the versions of a compromise over various disputed territories that Visconti had forwarded to Carmagnola and the League and the version presented by Visconti's ambassador to Venice.[126] And as the war between Florence and Lucca continued, it seemed clear that sooner or later it would expand to engulf Milan and Venice.[127]

When Carmagnola returned to Venice in September to discuss preparations for war, the question of further territorial rewards for the mercenary captain arose. In July Carmagnola had purchased a house in Brescia which he intended to refurbish in such a way as to make it, according to the records of the Senate, a "magnificent and beautiful" ornament to the Lombard city. In return, Carmagnola asked to be made a citizen of Brescia and that he and his descendants be granted an exemption from all taxes on the property. The Senate complied with his request with 17 negative votes and 4 abstentions. But with the prospect of war clearly on the horizon, Carmagnola also asked that, should the Duchy of Milan be destroyed, he be rewarded with at least one Milanese-controlled city. On 1 September the Senate voted to offer him any city on the western shore of the Adda except Milan; two other proposals, including one to offer him Pavia and Piacenza, were defeated. A few days later the Senate agreed to restore to him his territories around Vercelli, lands originally granted to him by Visconti and seized when he joined Venice, should Milan not be completely destroyed. When Carmagnola returned to Venice in December for further consultations concerning the impending war, he secured a letter from Foscari clarifying and guaranteeing the territorial promises made in September.[128]

Carmagnola's quest for territory was relentless but, as already noted, it was not unusual. Instead it reveals the dilemma that governments across the Italian peninsula faced when dealing with the mercenary captains. In a very real sense the condottieri were competing with their employers for territory. It is more than possible that had the Duchy of Milan been destroyed, Venice would have found itself facing a new rival in the west, namely Carmagnola, who might have used the opportunity to knit together his foothold in Brescia and his disparate holdings around Vercelli, Chiari, and the as yet unnamed city he was to get as a reward for victory into a new territorial state. In fact, this potential threat never came to fruition (at least not in the case of Carmagnola), but war with Milan seemed inevitable. In November the Senate voted to move toward war, especially as Visconti's support for Lucca in its war with Florence had forced him to leave Lombardy undermanned. As the Senate noted, "It is a proverb most true that he who has time on his side, ought not to wait for time."[129]

Troublesome relations with condottieri were not the only unforeseen consequence of Venice's expansion onto the mainland. The acquisition of new lands, the need to administer subject cities, and the increased level of contact between Venetians and nearby regimes allowed members of the patriciate to establish friendship and patronage networks with foreigners, networks which further complicated Venetian policy. For example, Ambrogio Badoer, son of the late Albano, was a confidant of the Marquess of Mantua, Gianfrancesco Gonzaga; nobleman Tommaso Malipiero that of Carmagnola.[130] In certain circumstances, such relationships could compromise Venice's security. One such case came to the surface in 1429 and involved nobleman Pietro Marcello. It even touched men close to the doge.

It seems that Marcello, who had previously been banished from Venice and its territories for commercial fraud, had gone to Pisa and was attempting to organize a group of Pisan ships so that they could proceed to the east and disrupt Venetian trade in Syria and Alexandria.[131] When word of Marcello's machinations reached the Ten in April 1429, the council decided to detain and investigate his son Giovanni, his relative Bartolomeo, and Giovanni Trevisan with whom Marcello had commercial interests in grain. The gravity of the case led the Ten in May to include a *zonta* or "addition" of supernumerary members to deliberate further in order to give their final decision due weight and sanction. This was necessary because the Ten wished to question Marcello's father-in-law Bartolomeo Donato and his son Andrea about the case. Bartolomeo Donato, one of the two procurators of San Marco *de supra*, was not only one of the most powerful men in the Venetian regime, but – as revealed shortly – a close ally of the doge. On 3 May the Ten authorized the questioning of Donato and his son Andrea. However in June both Bartolomeo Marcello and Trevisan were released from jail, and a proposal put forward by Foscari and the *avogador di comun* Marino Lando to question Andrea Donato again failed to pass. In July the Ten ordered the confiscation and sale of all Marcello's goods; and in September they had his son Giovanni banished to Crete for two years.[132] In the fall the Ten were attempting to track both Marcello's and his son's travels in Florentine and Milanese territory. Certainly by the following summer Marcello had established himself as a regular attendant at the Visconti court where, according to both Morosini and Sanudo, he was revealing Venetian state secrets. At this point, the Ten placed a bounty on his head, at the same time forbidding his Donato relatives from participating in deliberations concerning his case.[133] The Marcello case, although extreme, does reveal how Venice's mainland expansion opened up new fields of activities for Venetian patricians, including those who did not have the city's best interests at heart.

In 1429–30, while events in Italy continued at a low simmer, the situation in the eastern Mediterranean boiled over again. Ever since the Venetian annexation of Thessalonica in 1423, conditions in the city had deteriorated badly: the local inhabitants were discouraged by what they perceived as misguided Venetian rule while the Venetians for their part were distrustful of the Greeks and resentful of the expense of defending the city, which they estimated at 60,000 ducats per year.[134] Relations with the Ottomans took a dramatic turn for the worse as well when in spring 1429 Giacomo Dandolo, the Venetian captain of the city, undertook an embassy to Sultan Murad. According to the chronicles, the sultan asked Dandolo if he was authorized to surrender Thessalonica, and when he replied that he was not, the sultan had him arrested. The sultan's more aggressive stance toward Venice may have been prompted by the fact that the Turks were at that very moment finalizing a three-year truce with Emperor Sigismund, a truce mediated in part by the Milanese with the goal of damaging Venetian interests.[135] In response, Venice moved its warships to the region under the command of the captain of the Gulf, Andrea Mocenigo. In July Mocenigo led an assault against the Turks at Gallipoli, but suffered a serious defeat when his junior officers refused to follow his orders. These officers were later prosecuted but got off with relatively mild sentences; Foscari himself advocated harsh punishment, in the case of the vice-captain, nobleman Vittore Duodo, beheading.[136]

In March 1430 the long agony of Thessalonica finally came to an end when Sultan Murad himself laid siege to it. As the Turks entered the city, they sacked and looted it and forced an estimated 7000 inhabitants into slavery. News of the loss reached Venice in April. Dolfin's chronicle records that during their dominion, the Venetians had spent an estimated 700,000 ducats maintaining the city and its inhabitants.[137] The lesson in all this was, as one authority puts it, "that the survival of the Venetian commercial empire in Romania and the Black Sea now depended not on the goodwill of the Byzantine Emperors but on the favor of the Ottoman Sultan."[138] To that end, in late April the Senate ordered Silvestro Morosini, the captain-general of the sea, to undertake peace negotiations with the sultan, yet also instructing him to keep up the military pressure on the enemy. According to the treaty that was signed in September, Venice agreed to pay tribute and not attempt to retake Thessalonica, while the sultan agreed to respect Venice's control of the seas south and west of the island of Tenedos.[139] The Venetians had secured "a freedom of the sea which the Turks would never have allowed them while they held Thessalonica."[140] In May 1430 the Venetians renewed their treaty with the Byzantine emperor John and spent much of the summer negotiating with the Mamluk sultan of Egypt over the particulars of the lucrative spice trade. Henceforth Venetian policy with regard to the east was geared toward the protection of trade rather than the expansion of political dominion.[141]

The on-going threat from Milan and the Thessalonica debacle served only to exacerbate the preexisting rifts and dissensions within Venice's ruling class. Legislative activity from the year 1430 allows one to delineate the three critical fault lines in the façade of noble unanimity. The first, as discussed, was institutional and concerned the continuing rivalry between the Great Council and the smaller and more prestigious councils, especially the Senate. In a law passed in June 1430 the Great Council reiterated its position as the foundation of the state and complained that other councils, including the Senate, were interfering with those offices traditionally under the Great Council's jurisdiction. In a sharply divided vote (461 in favor, 170 opposed with 32 abstentions), the Great Council prohibited those bodies from abolishing, revoking, or lowering the salaries of offices which came under its purview.[142] The bill was proposed by the heads of the Forty, who like the tribunes of ancient Rome served as the defenders of the less powerful.

The second fault line was economic and social, pitting those lesser nobles who depended on government jobs for their livelihoods against the richest nobles who controlled the highest offices of the state. As noted earlier, this division found institutional expression in the rivalry between the Great Council and the Senate. In March 1430 the Great Council considered a proposal by the heads of the Forty, a proposal that prohibited women from wearing the extremely high shoes or clogs for which Venetian fashion was famous. The prologue to the bill offered two justifications for this state-sponsored interference with women's apparel. The first was moral – the bill claimed that the shoes were causing preg-

1   School of Tintoretto, portraits of Doges Mocenigo and Foscari, Great Council
Hall frieze, Ducal Palace.

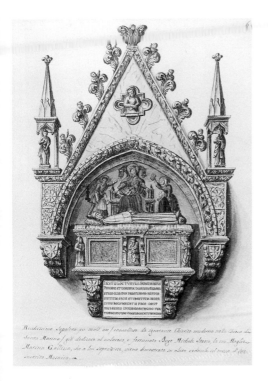

2   Tomb of Doge Michele Steno, from Jan
Grevembroch, "Monumenta veneta ex antiquis
ruderibus." Museo Civico Correr, MS.
Gradenigo–Dolfin 228/II, fig. 69.

3   Tomb of Doge Tommaso Mocenigo, from
Jan Grevembroch, "Monumenta veneta ex
antiquis ruderibus." Museo Civico Correr, MS.
Gradenigo–Dolfin 228/II, fig. 72.

4   Gold Ducat of Doge Foscari (obverse and reverse).

5   Portrait of Doge Foscari, from Porcellio Pandoni, "Commentariorum secundi anni de gestis Scipionis Picinini." Biblioteca Nazionale, Florence, Nuovi acquisti 445.

6 Portrait of Doge Foscari, from Mariegola 124, Museo Civico Correr.

7   Antonio Gambello or Antonello Griffo, copper alloy medal of Doge Foscari (obverse) and *Venetia* (reverse). Samuel H. Kress Collection, National Gallery of Art, Washington.

8   Guariento, *The Coronation of the Virgin*, fresco, formerly in the Great Council Hall, Ducal Palace.

9 Statue of *Veneçia*, façade of Ducal Palace.

10　Defaced portrait of Doge Marino Falier, alongside portrait of Doge Andrea Dandalo, Great Council Hall frieze, Ducal Palace.

11　Piazzetta wing of Ducal Palace, showing the Foscari extension.

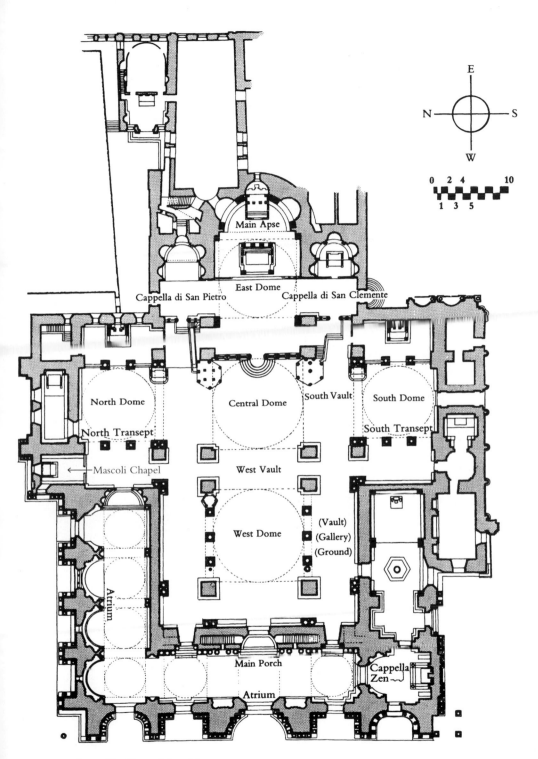

E
N — S
W

0 2 4 10
1 3 5

Main Apse

East Dome

Cappella di San Pietro   Cappella di San Clemente

North Dome   Central Dome   South Vault   South Dome

North Transept   South Transept

←Mascoli Chapel   West Vault

(Vault)
(Gallery)
(Ground)

West Dome

Atrium

Main Porch   Cappella Zen

Atrium

12   Plan of basilica of San Marco.

13   *The Birth of the Virgin*, mosaic, Chapel of the Madonna (Mascoli Chapel), San Marco.

14   *The Presentation of the Virgin*, mosaic, Chapel of the Madonna (Mascoli Chapel), San Marco.

15 *The Visitation*, mosaic, Chapel of the Madonna (Mascoli Chapel), San Marco.

16 *The Dormition of the Virgin*, mosaic, Chapel of the Madonna (Mascoli Chapel), San Marco.

17   Altar and altarpiece, Chapel of the Madonna (Mascoli Chapel), San Marco.

18   *(facing page top)* Inscription in the Sala dello Scrutinio, Ducal Palace.

19   *(facing page bottom)* San Tarasio Chapel, San Zaccaria.

QVI PATRIAE PERICVLA SVO PERICVLO EXPETVNT, HI SAPIENTES PV-
TANDI SVNT, CVM ET EVM, QVEM DEBENT, HONOREM REIP. REDDVNT,
ET PRO MVLTIS PERIRE MALVT. QVAM CVM MVLTIS. ETENIM, VEHEMETER
EST INIQVVM VITAM, QVAM A NATVRA ACCEPTAM PROPTER PATRIAM
CONSERVAVERIMVS, NATVRAE, CVM COGAT REDDERE PATRIAE, CVM
ROGET NON DARE. SAPIENTES IGITVR EXISTIMADI SVNT, QVI NVLLVM
PRO SALVTE PATRIAE PERICVLVM VITÃT. HOC VINCVLVM EST HVIVS
DIGNITATIS, QVA PRVIMVR, IN REP. HOC FVNDAMETVM LIBERTATIS, HIC
FONS AEQVITATIS, MENS, ET ANIMVS, ET CÕSILIVM ET SÈTÈTIA CIVITATIS.
POSITA EST I LEGIBVS, VT CORPORA NRA SINE MÈTE, SIC CIVITAS SINE
LEGE SVIS PARTIBVS, VT NERVIS, AC SÃGVINE, ET MBRIS, VTI NÕ POTEST.
LEGVM MINISTRI MAGISTRATVS, LEGVM ITERPRETES, IVDICES, LEGVM
DENIQVE ICCIRCO OVNES SERVI SVMVS, VT LIBERI ESSE POSSIMVS ☙

20 Tomb of Pietro and Jacopo Loredan, formerly in the church of Sant'Elena, Jan Grevembroch, "Monumenta veneta ex antiquis ruderibus." Museo Civico Correr, MS. Gradenigo-Dolfin 228/II, fig. 57.

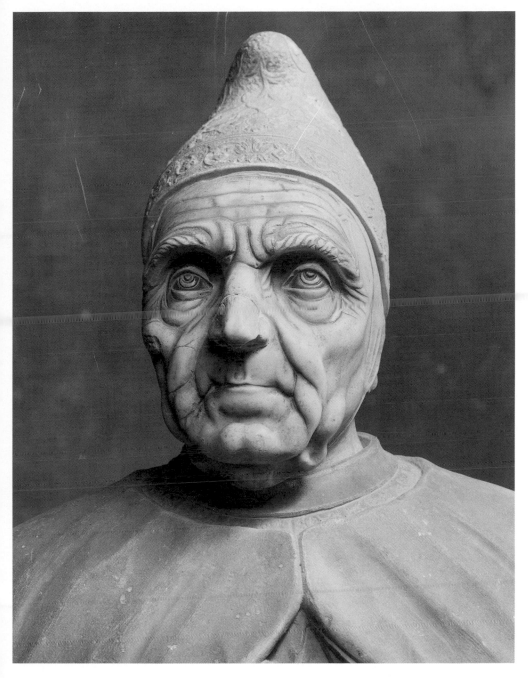

21 Original portrait head of Doge Foscari from the Porta della Carta. Museo
dell'Opera del Palazzo Ducale.

22 Porticato Foscari or Portico della Carta, Ducal Palace.

23 The covered staircase known as the Scala Foscara in the Ducal Palace courtyard, from Cesare Vecellio, *Degli habiti antichi et moderni,* 1590.

24 Donatello, statue of Gattamelata, Campo del Santo, Padua.

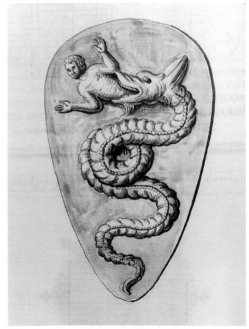

25 Visconti viper, from Jan Grevembroch, "Varie venete curiosità sacre e profane." Museo Civico Correr, MS. Gradenigo–Dolfin 65/III, fig. 27.

26 *(above)* Fondaco dei Turchi.

27 *(left)* Palazzo Medici, Florence.

28 Cà Foscari, at the turn of the Grand Canal.

29 Cà Foscari, third-floor frieze.

nant women to fall and abort their fetuses. The second (and likely the crucial concern) was economic. The higher the shoes, the longer the dresses had to be to reach them; the extra cloth added greatly to the expense. Clearly Venetian women (and their male relatives) were engaged in sartorial competition with high shoes and long dresses serving as markers of economic power and social prestige. In another sharply divided vote (527 in favor versus 197 opposed with 37 abstentions), the Great Council prohibited women from wearing such shoes and cobblers from manufacturing them.[143]

The third division within the patriciate ran along kinship and patronage lines and was also manifest in the competition for offices. In November 1430 the Great Council approved several changes regarding the conduct of elections. The first prohibited the announcement of vote totals for individual candidates until all the balloting for a particular election was completed. The second forbade relatives of candidates who were required to vacate the Council Hall during balloting from standing in the doorways. Evidently, they were following the letter rather than the spirit of the law and trying to influence elections by their visibility just beyond the confines of the room. The third and most significant rule change forbade the solicitation of votes by "friends and relatives" of candidates. According to the law, these partisans were wandering among the benches seeking votes and thereby undermining the free play of conscience in casting ballots. Unlike the bills discussed above, this electoral reform measure passed with little opposition on a vote of 302 yeas, 34 nays, and 20 abstentions.[144]

It is against this increasingly partisan backdrop that one of the most dramatic moments in Foscari's reign must be considered, one that had a profound impact on the doge. It occurred on Saturday 11 March 1430 as Foscari was, according to some accounts, going to Mass or, according to others, going to fulfill the responsibility imposed by his *promissione* to exhort the various palace magistrates to render justice equitably. He was being escorted by a contingent of nobles, including ambassadors from Siena as well as members of the Signoria. As Foscari neared the stone stairway close to the door of the old Great Council Hall, he was approached by nobleman Andrea Contarini, son of the late knight Niccolò Contarini of the parish of Santi Apostoli, in a way suggesting that the nobleman wished to speak with the doge. He was carrying a large pointed stick or cane, with which he proceeded to strike Foscari, hitting him between the mouth and nose, but aiming, at least according to Sanudo, for his neck. As blood gushed from Foscari's wound, guards cornered and seized Contarini. The doge was taken away to be cared for by physicians; the force of the blow turned out to be not very great.[145]

As word of the attempted assassination spread, the Council of Ten, the body with jurisdiction in such matters, convened and immediately began to consider its response. That same day, it voted unanimously to proceed against Contarini "for the insults and wounds aimed at the person of the most Serene lord doge of Venice."[146] Contarini was then taken to the torture chamber in the palace where, according to Morosini, he claimed that he was avenging his father's death; Morosini also explains, however, that Contarini's father had died before Foscari became doge. Both Morosini and Dolfin state that Contarini was mentally deranged, having shown symptoms of mental illness for some time. Sanudo offers this same version but then adds an elaboration drawn from other accounts, which relate that Contarini's ire had been aroused by his humiliation in a recent election held to fill the post of the captain of the Marches coastal patrol. According to this version, Contarini garnered just a few votes in the balloting; and when his relatives asked him if he knew why he had not been elected, they answered their own question by replying, "Because the doge orchestrated it." And so Contarini decided to seek revenge.[147]

The cryptic records of the Ten offer no explanation for Contarini's action. However, on the same day, the Ten ordered the failed assassin removed from the torture chamber and proposed that he be led to the stone staircase where his right arm (presumably the arm with which he had dealt the blow) be amputated and hung around his neck. He was then to be taken to the gallows between the two columns in the Piazzetta, where he was to be hanged and his body left until the following Monday. This proposal passed the Ten with a single dissenting vote. A note records that "it was carried out as contained in the law." Four days later the Ten granted all those who had taken part in the proceedings the right to three armed bodyguards.[148]

As was the case with Foscari's election, it is difficult at the distance of almost six hundred years to know exactly what happened, what prompted Contarini's attack on the doge. Clearly the writer most con-

temporary with the events, the chronicler Antonio Morosini, saw this as
the act of a madman. He notes that the "entire city felt compassion and
sorrow for that young man." Perhaps the single dissenting vote in the
Ten was prompted by similar feelings. Both Dolfin and Sanudo offer
largely similar versions, recording that even though Contarini was mentally disturbed, the Ten decided to hang him, as Morosini states, as a
"good example for the entire Republic of Venice."[149] Nevertheless,
certain doubts remain because of that troubling second version of events
recorded by Sanudo, according to which Contarini was out to avenge
an electoral defeat. If there is any truth to that version, it demonstrates
how serious the competition for offices had become. Furthermore, even
the accounts that present Contarini as mentally ill say that he committed the deed to avenge his dead father. Perhaps before he became doge
Foscari had slighted the Contarini in a way that lodged in the family's
collective memory and festered in the young man's mind.[150] The decision to offer bodyguards to the members of the Ten, although not
unusual in such cases, suggests that the Ten themselves were wary that
some larger conspiracy might be afoot.

A third possibility is that Contarini committed the act either to
avenge his father or repay his own electoral slight, but that the Ten then
went to some pains to present this publicly as the act of a mad and, significantly, a *young* man. Whatever its motives, the assassination attempt
can only have heightened the tensions gripping the patriciate at this
time and made everyone conscious of individual safety.

The sources offer no direct indication of how the assassination attempt
affected Foscari, but its impact was surely profound, for although several
early doges of Venice had died at the hands of assassins, no doge in centuries had suffered such a fate. It is easy of course to imagine possible
emotional responses: anger, fear, resignation, resolution, but the written
sources are mute on this point. Nevertheless, as described in an essay
published in 1961, the art historian Michelangelo Muraro believed that
he discerned one of Foscari's responses, namely the momentous decision to build a new chapel in the basilica of San Marco.

Muraro put forward the intriguing idea that Foscari constructed the
Mascoli Chapel (plate 5), originally known as the New Chapel or the
Chapel of the Madonna, as an ex voto "in pious acknowledgement to
the Madonna" that he had survived the assassination attempt.[151] Muraro

based his theory on the inscription placed on the wall directly above the altarpiece which reads:

MCCCCXXX DUCANTE INCLITO DOMINO
FRANCISCO FOSCARI PROCURATORIBUS VERO
S MARCI DOMINIS LEONARDO MOCENIGO ET
BARTHOLOMEO DONATO HEC CAPELA CONDITA FUIT

(1430 During the reign of the illustrious lord Francesco Foscari this chapel was founded by the procurators of San Marco lords Leonardo Mocenigo and Bartolomeo Donato)

For Muraro, the coincidence in the timing of the chapel's foundation and the assassination attempt suggested to him that it was built as a "votive chapel." His theory has found wide acceptance and sometimes is even cited as established fact.[152] However, there is little basis for accepting this explanation for the chapel's construction for the simple reason that none of the chronicles mentions the founding of the chapel and certainly none links it in any way to the attempt on Foscari's life. Yet if Foscari had begun the chapel as an ex voto, this is precisely the kind of information that fifteenth-century chroniclers, particularly a religiously inclined one like Morosini, would have mentioned. One therefore needs to look elsewhere for an explanation of why Foscari constructed the chapel. Before doing so, however, an examination of the chapel is in order.

The Chapel of the Madonna (now known as the Mascoli Chapel) is situated in the left-hand corner of the north transept of the basilica, directly opposite the treasury in the church's south transept and adjacent to the chapel of San Isidoro (fig. 12). Its renaming as the Mascoli Chapel occurred when it was taken over by the confraternity of the Mascoli in 1618, an appellation which obscures the chapel's significance. The structure measures 7.11 meters in depth, 4.21 meters in breadth, and reaches a maximum height of 7.95 meters.[153] It consists of a simple barrel-vaulted space, raised one step above the floor of the rest of the basilica. A waist-high balustrade with tracery also serves to separate the chapel from the rest of the church. The only source of light other than that emanating from the interior of the church itself is a small oculus on the rear wall.

What most distinguishes the chapel is the richness of its decoration, extravagant even by the standards of the ducal basilica. The floor, con-

sisting of Istrian white marble and Veronese red, is the only plain
element. By contrast, the walls are clad in rich and precious marbles,
including the luxurious *cipollino rosso* which covers the rear wall and
serves as a dramatic backdrop for the altar. A carved leafy entablature or
cornice separates the walls from the vault, which is completely covered
with mosaics. The mosaic on the rear wall, the one most visible to
observers, depicts the Annunciation. Mary is shown sitting at a desk
reading a book, while the patient archangel Gabriel assumes a posture
of humility and reverence. From above the window God the Father
directs the Holy Spirit in the form of a dove on the divine mission to
impregnate the Virgin. Presumably, once this act is complete, Gabriel will
spring into action with his angelic announcement.

Mosaics depicting scenes from the life of the Virgin cover the sides
of the barrel vault. On the left-hand wall are *The Birth of the Virgin* and
The Presentation of the Virgin (figs 13 and 14). The birth takes place on
the porch or loggia of an extravagant palace while the presentation
occurs naturally enough at a temple; both palace and temple display distinguishing Gothic elements. The buildings on the opposite side of the
vault are very different in style. *The Visitation* is set in what appears to
be the atrium of a Roman palace complete with a classicizing frieze,
while in *The Dormition* Mary's bier is placed before a Roman-style triumphal arch which caps the entry to a city street (figs. 15 and 16).[154]
Christ hovers in a mandorla in front of the arch, where he receives the
soul of the Virgin into his bosom. The top of the vault is covered with
a decorative band and three tondi with the Madonna, the prophet Isaiah,
and David.

The lower left corner of *The Presentation* is inscribed *Michael Çambono
venetus fecit* (Michele Giambono Venetian made this). However, the style
of the mosaic decorations betrays the influence of a number of artists,
including the Florentine master Andrea del Castagno. Florentine intervention in the design of the mosaics has led to other extravagant interpretations, most notably on the part of Muraro and Ettore Merkel who
attempt to chart in the shifting style of the mosaics on the left- and
right-hand sides of the vault and especially in what was clearly an altera-
tion in the grouping of the apostles surrounding Mary's bier, the changing diplomatic and military relations between Venice and Florence over
the course of Foscari's reign. Specifically, they see Michele Giambono's
reworking of Castagno's design for the *Dormition* mosaic as symptomatic

of Venice's rejection of Florentine artistic influence after Florence broke with Venice and allied with Milan in 1451.[155] But, as explored in chapter 4, such claims are problematic. In addition, they lead one away from understanding what the chapel meant at the time of its foundation. In fact, it took as many as thirty years for the mosaicists to complete the decoration; so it is more than possible that the chapel's significance to Foscari and others shifted over time.[156]

Before addressing those concerns, however, the other decorative element of the chapel, namely the altar and altarpiece, deserves attention (fig. 17). The altar table consists of a large block of *pietra d'Istria* raised one step above the floor of the chapel. Two carved angels censing a cross adorn its front. The table is surmounted by a sculpted marble altarpiece depicting the Virgin and Child with two saints, usually identified as Mark on the left and John the Evangelist on the right. This work has been attributed to various sculptors, including Michele Giambono and an unnamed Florentine follower of Lorenzo Ghiberti, although many ascribe it to Bartolomeo or Giovanni Bon.[157] Above the altarpiece is the dedicatory inscription.

So what exactly can one make of the Chapel of the Madonna and its possible place in Foscari's reign? Two events are noteworthy since they may have provided the opportunity and justification for this major intervention in the church. The first was the fire in San Marco in March 1419, the event that prompted procurator Foscari to divert funds to the church. On the 6th of that month cinders from a chimney in the Ducal Palace landed on the roof of the basilica and caught fire. Aided by strong winds, the flames destroyed the roof, melting the lead and burning the wooden rafters.[158] As discussed in the previous chapter, as a procurator *de citra*, Foscari helped transfer funds to repair the roof of San Marco. The on-going repairs to the basilica may have afforded the chance to convert this space into a chapel. The chapel's proximity to that of San Isidoro is also intriguing. Despite having been elected on the vigil of the feast of Saint Isidore, the doge may not have wished to intervene in that space since it was already associated with his deposed predecessor Marino Falier, beheaded in 1355.

The second event did not involve Foscari directly but rather the procurators named in the dedicatory inscription. According to Morosini, it occurred on 9 September 1428 when the senior procurator of San Marco *de supra*, Leonardo Mocenigo, brother of the late doge Tommaso, was consigning some of the reliquaries and other jewels in the treasury to his new colleague Bartolomeo Donato. While this was taking place, the procurators "discovered" four crosses which, again according to Morosini, had not been seen for hundreds of years. They had been covered in dust and dirt and lay neglected. One silver-plated cross with an etched figure of Christ was unusually large. In the center was a carved and enameled head of Christ with a diadem and Greek lettering. All the crosses were bejeweled and of great value. Morosini notes that the crosses had been acquired by the Venetians during the conquest of Constantinople in 1204 or even earlier. Upon their rediscovery, they were displayed, "honorably throughout the city."[159] It is possible that with the city of Thessalonica under increasing stress from the Turks, the recovery of these crosses of Byzantine origin served in some measure to reaffirm Venice's ties to that region.

Perhaps the procurators decided to commemorate their miraculous rediscovery (an event reminiscent of the rediscovery of the relics of Mark himself in 1094 after they had been "lost" during a rebuilding of the church) and planned an altar or perhaps even a chapel to do so.[160] After all, the altar table in the chapel shows two angels censing and adoring a large cross. But it is also possible that the plan was changed so that the veneration of the cross became a minor element in a chapel dedicated to the Virgin. In order to understand how this may have occurred, one needs to consider more fully the status of the church of San Marco, patronage rights over the church, and the relationship between Foscari and these particular procurators.

Today San Marco is the seat of the Patriarch of Venice, but this was not always the case. Until 1807 San Pietro di Castello in the far eastern reaches of the city beyond the Arsenal served as the city's cathedral. San Marco, by contrast, was the proprietary church of the doges. Indeed some have characterized San Marco as Venice's palatine chapel. But just as the dogeship evolved from a semi-monarchical position into a legally circumscribed one, so San Marco changed from the private chapel of the doge into what was in essence Venice's state church, although ducal associations remained strong. In the mid-thirteenth century Pope Innocent IV conferred on the *primicerio* or chief priest of the church the symbols of episcopal authority, namely the ring, mitre, and crozier.[161] But in 1367 the *primicerio* and the Bishop of Venice clashed when the bishop (ironically one of Foscari's ancestors) ordered the *primicerio* and the chaplains to appear before him in a controversy over the death tax. The *primicerio* protested, claiming that San Marco was not subject to the pope but only to the doge.[162] Also in the fourteenth century, the doges sought to increase their presence in San Marco through the placement of ducal tombs in the church.

As possessors of *iuspatronatus* or patronage rights over the church, the doges enjoyed both a number of privileges over and obligations to San Marco. Among the most important privileges was the right to appoint the *primicerio* and the canons. While a number of doges selected non-nobles for the office of *primicerio*, Foscari chose in 1425 his cousin Polidoro, son of his uncle Franzi.[163] This served to secure further Foscari's hold over the church. Among the ducal obligations to San Marco was the requirement that each incumbent present the church with a cloth for the high altar. These altar cloths were embroidered with the ducal coats of arms. Among the items listed in an inventory of the treasury dated 1463 was the altar cloth that Foscari presented with his family arms. Ducal arms were also displayed along the transept of the church.[164]

But the doges did not enjoy sole responsibility for the church of San Marco; rather they shared it with the procurators *de supra*, who, as observed earlier, controlled the church's income and finances and had primary responsibility for the building's fabric and maintenance.[165] Moreover, there was a countervailing tendency, perhaps encouraged by the procurators themselves, which sought to limit the appropriation of San Marco for individual ducal uses. According to the *Cronaca Magno*, for example, following the death of Doge Andrea Dandolo in 1354, a clause prohibiting any further ducal burials in San Marco was added to the ducal *promissione*. No such prohibition has been found by historians in the extant legislation, but the tradition may reflect a growing belief on the part of contemporaries that the ducal presence in San Marco had become too grand and was inappropriate in a republic.[166]

And so, although the doges enjoyed jurisdiction and patronage rights over San Marco, administration of the church's finances meant that they had to work in tandem with the procurators. This is reflected in the inscription on a project undertaken by one of Foscari's predecessors. The magnificent rood screen of the church commissioned from the brothers Pierpaolo and Jacobello dalle Masegne bears the following inscription:

MCCCXCIIII Hoc opus rectum fuit tempore Excelsi Domini Antonij Venerio, Dei gratia Ducis Venetiarum, ac Nobilium Virorum Dominorum, Petri Cornerio, et Michaelis Steno, Honorabilium Procuratorum praefatae Ecclesiae Benedictae Beatissimi Marci Evangelistae

(1394 In the time of the excellent lord Antonio Venier, by the grace of God, Doge of Venice, and of the noblemen the lords Pietro Corner and Michele Steno, honorable procurators of the blessed and most holy church of the Evangelist Saint Mark).[167]

The inscription records that the work was erected during the reign of Doge Antonio Venier and during the procuratorships of Pietro Corner and Michele Steno, suggesting a kind of joint patronage. The inscription in the Chapel of the Madonna assigns a more prominent role to the procurators than the read screen one does, saying that it was built by them during the reign of Foscari. Foscari's reticence in advertising his part in the chapel's construction may also have been motivated by a desire not to appear too proud. In 1443, for example, the members of the Scuola Grande di San Giovanni Evangelista decided that individual patrons ought not to put their epitaphs or personal insignia on projects built by the *scuola* since such displays were pompous and vainglorious.[168] Despite the absence of a more self-assertive inscription, it is impossible to imagine that an intervention as important as the building of a new chapel in San Marco could have been undertaken without impetus from Foscari, especially when his own cousin was *primicerio*.[169]

The assumption that the doge and procurators worked in tandem is further strengthened by knowledge of the personal ties between Foscari and at least one of the two procurators, Bartolomeo Donato, the procurator caught up in the Pietro Marcello scandal. Just two years after the chapel was begun, Donato's son Andrea married Foscari's daughter Camilla. Andrea was one of the two rectors in charge of Thessalonica, when the city fell to the Turks. Along with his colleague Paolo Contarini he fled the city and was tried for this by the *avogadori di comun*. But Donato managed to rehabilitate his reputation. The marriage was his second and the third for Camilla and ultimately produced many children.[170]

Given all this, one still needs to try and discern what lay behind the decision by Foscari to build the chapel with the procurators' help. The key almost certainly lies in the chapel's dedication for it significantly increased the Marian presence in the church. Mary, especially as the Orant Virgin, had been represented in the church of San Marco before. Images of the Virgin appeared in several mosaics including those in the central apse and the chapel of San Clemente. And one of the most venerated images in the church was the Nicopeian Madonna, which the Venetians attributed to Saint Luke the evangelist. Furthermore, according to a *catasto* or survey of 1308, an altar in the church was dedicated to "Santae Mariae de Columpna." This altar was apparently situated in the church's crypt where a confraternity dedicated to Mary met. But the Chapel of the Madonna was different; it was far grander.[171]

So by building the chapel, Foscari and the procurators further strengthened the associations between Venice and the Virgin, especially the notion that the city's destiny was determined by its founding on the feast of the Annunciation in the year 421. But the building of the chapel did more than this, for it also helped centralize Marian devotion in the city and located it securely within the confines of Venice's state church. This was the culmination of a process that had begun in 1379 with the abolition of the festival of the *Marie* or Marys, a festival that had its origins in the twelfth century if not earlier. Marked by the ritual parading of twelve wooden figures or Marys about the city, it was staged by the city's parish communities every spring around Candlemas and celebrated women and marriage. The factors that led to the abolition of the festival included conflicts within and between parishes for control of the event, bacchanalian excesses associated with it, and a waning sense of parish solidarity as well as the financial crisis brought on by the War of Chioggia. A ducal procession to the parish church of Santa Maria Formosa on 1 February and ducal attendance at Mass on the feast of the Purification of the Virgin, 2 February, Candlemas proper, replaced it. The exact date of the beginning of this practice is unknown, but certainly by the late fifteenth century doges were attending the Candlemas service *in* the Chapel of the Madonna. At that service, the doge distributed candles to members of the *scuole grandi*, clergy, and priors of the city's hospitals.[172]

It seems clear then that the building of the Chapel of the Madonna was part of an effort by the government (that is Foscari and the procurators) to tie Marian devotion ever more strongly to the state. However, it would be a mistake to discount entirely Foscari's personal motivations.

Foscari evidently had a strong personal devotion to the Virgin: perhaps this had been cultivated in his youth at the family's Marian chapel in San Simeon Apostolo; it certainly culminated in his burial at the Frari, a church dedicated to the Assumption of the Virgin; it is even possible that Foscari intended that the Chapel of the Madonna in San Marco serve as his eventual burial site. The motif of the censing angels on the altar table front was a funerary image, first used in tombs of French ecclesiastical officials but then adopted in northern Italy for use on the tombs of secular rulers including those of doges Jacopo and Lorenzo Tiepolo, who reigned in 1229–49 and 1268–75 respectively.[173] Apparently, despite what the Magno chronicle relates, there was no legal prohibition on ducal burials in San Marco. Certainly if Foscari had been buried there, it would have broken a one-hundred-year tradition and thus represented a major increase in ducal visibility, one made even greater by the rich nature of the materials used in the chapel.

But even if this was not the intent (and of course it never came to pass), the many trials and tribulations that Foscari faced during the first years of his reign, including the devastating recurrences of the plague, the loss of his uncle and two of his sons (Donato in 1425 and Giovanni in 1429), and yes, perhaps even the assassination attempt, provided ample motivations for Foscari to demonstrate his piety by building the chapel.[174] Foscari may well have found solace in a role with which he was already familiar from his stint as procurator of San Marco and at which he excelled, namely overseer and administrator of pious establishments. Furthermore, if the Candlemas tradition of the doge distributing candles to the *scuole* and hospitals in the chapel began during his reign, as seems likely, then it provides further evidence of a man who found comfort and gained strength from his role as the benefactor and impresario of charity.

In late 1430 Foscari had at least two other occasions on which to do his duty and demonstrate his personal devotion and concern for the community. In November Foscari attended along with hundreds of others, including the ambassadors from Florence and Milan and the Marquess of Ferrara, events celebrating the consecration of the great Dominican church of Santi Giovanni e Paolo, commonly known as San Zanipolo.[175] More pertinently, in December Foscari took the lead when plague again threatened the city. Apparently word had reached Venice that ships returning from the Romania line might be infected. Accordingly, on 2 December Foscari proposed in the Senate that, as prescribed in the law of August 1423, the admiral of the port inspect the returning ships and send anyone found to be infected immediately to the Lazzaretto. When later in the month news arrived that the *Delfina*, a ship returning from Tana on the Black Sea, was infected, Foscari proposed in the Senate that it be diverted to Istria and that those on board be prevented from coming to Venice for two months.[176] And so, just as at the very beginning of his reign, Foscari took the initiative in a time of plague. Although such chroniclers as Marino Sanudo do not emphasize this aspect of his character, Foscari seems to have been a man with a pronounced sense of his responsibility to the community and a deeply felt personal piety. It is precisely in this light that one should view the Chapel of the Madonna, certainly the most enigmatic of the building projects undertaken during Foscari's reign.

With the prospect of renewed war with Milan looming, the Venetian government sought divine favor as it had done many times before. On 22 January 1431 the Senate voted to donate 5 ducats to each of twenty monasteries scattered about the city and the lagoon. This was done so that the monks and nuns might offer up prayers and supplications to God in order to win his grace for the "conservation [. . .] augmentation and prosperity" of the Venetian state. In May, the Great Council decided to reduce the number of votes required for the passage of *grazie* or pardons. The council hoped that by so doing God might be induced to show clemency in turn to the state. And when in July the Senate voted to make a further donation to monasteries, it did so with the hope that the almighty would favor both Venice's naval and land forces.[177] Divine aid was certainly needed: in this war as in the previous ones, Carmagnola revealed himself to be a particularly problematic commander.

The Third Venetian-Visconti War began in late December 1430 or early January 1431 when a certain Soccino di Viscarino offered to betray to Carmagnola the town of Lodi on the western side of the Adda. Carmagnola attacked on 22 January but was unable to take the city.[178] With that opening salvo, both sides began in earnest to make military preparations and secure the allegiance of allies. In Venice the Senate elected nobleman Stefano Contarini captain of the Po fleet, but he refused the post; Niccolò, son of the procurator Giacomo Trevisan, was elected in his stead.[179] The city sought the neutrality of the Duke of Savoy, and the direct assistance of Rinaldo Palavicino for an assault on Parma and Piacenza, the Marquess of Monferrato for an attack on Alessandria, and the Fieschi for one against Genoa. For his part, Visconti could count on the experience of his two great mercenary captains, the distinguished Niccolò Piccinino and the up-and-coming Francesco Sforza, as well as the aid of various cities, including Siena and Lucca, which were currently at war with Florence.[180] Also at this time, another event occurred that would have far-reaching repercussions. On 20 February Pope Martin V died, and in early March a Venetian, Angelo Condulmer, ascended to the throne of Saint Peter and took the name Eugenius IV. The long-term effect of Condulmer's election was to bring Venetian and papal policy closer and to reconcile Venice with the emperor.[181]

After his initial assault on Lodi, Carmagnola reverted to his usual hesitation and delays. Frustrated, his Venetian employers sent him instructions to build a bridge across the Adda and take the war to Milan.[182] In May the Senate prepared to open a second front by electing Pietro Loredan captain-general of the sea and dispatching him to make trouble for Visconti in the waters around Genoa. In an effort to counter the charge that it was pursuing war only in order to further its own ambitions, the government presented Loredan with a flag emblazoned with a red cross against a white background and labeled with the words *Libertas Janue* (Freedom of Genoa) in gold letters which he was to display on his ship.[183] In that same month in Brescia, Carmagnola received the flags of both San Marco and the League. The Senate was careful to note that the flag of San Marco was the same one that Carmagnola had carried in the last war and whose disposition in the church of San Marco was the cause of so much dispute. And as in the previous war, the Senate gave him full authority to negotiate for the surrender of lands belonging to the duke.[184]

In June the Venetian Po fleet consisting of thirty-eight galleons and forty-eight other ships came up against the Milanese fleet of twenty-eight galleons and other ships under the command of Pasino Eustacchio and the Genoese Giovanni Grimaldi near Cremona. The Venetian forces under Niccolò Trevisan suffered a crushing defeat, losing most of their ships and suffering heavy casualties. Trevisan fled. In response the Senate authorized his arrest as well as that of the other noble commanders of the galleys. Among them was Andrea Donato. If Trevisan was caught, he was to be beheaded, as were Francesco Cocco and Antonio Rizzo, the admiral of the fleet.[185] But suspicion also fell on Carmagnola who had been unable or unwilling to provide assistance to the doomed naval forces, even though he was in communication with Trevisan and had overall responsibility for Venetian forces on the terraferma. He wrote to the Senate justifying his actions.[186] Following the defeat, the Senate again urged Carmagnola to take the offensive. In a letter that Foscari himself proposed, the Senate instructed the proveditor to the army, Paolo Correr, to encourage the captain-general to seize a bridge or fort which would allow the Venetian forces to cross the Adda. But further efforts to spur Carmagnola to action were in vain. He even proposed withdrawing from the field by the end of August.[187]

Fortunately for Venice, its fleet operating in the sea off the coast of Liguria was more successful. On 27 August Pietro Loredan scored a major victory against the Genoese admiral Francesco Spinola, a victory that he reported in letters to the Signoria. As thanksgiving to God and Saint Mark, the Senate decided to spend 1000 ducats to help the wounded and the families of the dead.[188] The victory also served to solidify even further Loredan's reputation for military prowess. Indeed the secretary who was recording the Senate's secret deliberations in this period was so caught up in the excitement and so taken with Loredan's exploits that he interrupted his usual cursive script to write Loredan's name in capital letters. He did something similar again the following December when he wrote not Loredan's name but that of the Saviour.[189] Once more it appeared that the sturdy and methodical doge had been upstaged by the mercurial and rash sailor.

Foscari was clearly annoyed with Loredan. On 18 September he placed a bill before the Senate forbidding participants in the battle from reporting via letters what had transpired during the engagement to relatives in Venice. Apparently, various officers had been sending letters home praising the actions of some and condemning those of others. Although the warning was directed at Loredan's junior officers, it was sent to Loredan as well and reveals ducal frustration with the kind of self-promotion at which the captain-general of the sea excelled.[190]

Carmagnola, by contrast, remained inactive, refusing to move against Soncino as advised by the Senate and allowing an opportunity to take Cremona slip through his fingers by arriving late on the scene.[191] Carmagnola had begun the Lombard campaign of 1431 at the head of a large and well-equipped army and ended it, as his biographer observes, "without having risked a battle, without having taken a fort, without having added a handful of land to the conquests of the years 1426–1428."[192] The Senate's displeasure with its commander was readily understandable.

Although the captain-general was unwilling to take action against the Duke of Milan's forces, he was persuaded to counter an autumn incursion into Friuli by the Hungarians.[193] After they were repelled, Carmagnola came to Venice for consultations and then returned to Brescia. In late December an extraordinary proposal was put forward in the Senate. The preamble minced no words but baldly stated the obvious, namely that, "by many indications and conjectures it is rather clearly understood that the magnificent Count Carmagnola our captain-general aspires to the dominion of Milan." Therefore in order to shorten the costly war by spurring him to bold action, the bill proposed that Carmagnola be offered for himself and his heirs dominion over Milan and all its territories on the far side of the Adda. In return, however, Carmagnola would have to renounce the earlier promises he had received regarding the city of Pavia as well as all claims to territory in the Bresciano. The bill contained a number of other provisions, including that for the first three months of the agreement he would serve at his own expense, and that if Milan were taken in that period he would pay an annual tribute of 30,000 ducats to Venice for ten years. But the proposal received only 52 votes in favor, and the Senate decided to table the matter until a number of other issues had been resolved, including some peace overtures then being floated through the mediation of Niccolò d'Este.[194]

This bill is significant for it reveals much about the intentions of Venice and Carmagnola and relations between the two at this moment. Clearly, Carmagnola aspired to a state of his own, but he was not going to be content with Chiari and his Brescian territories, or even with Pavia; he wanted Milan, the biggest prize of all. The Venetians, perhaps out of financial exhaustion, were at least willing to entertain this possibility because they believed that he would pose less of a threat than the treacherous Visconti. Indeed, the Venetians were so anxious to be rid of the duke that in October the Council of Ten authorized investigation of a proposal by a certain Micheletto Mudazio to poison him, but abandoned the idea in December when it became public.[195] The fact that

Carmagnola had no male heirs may also have encouraged them to offer him Milan, for they knew that upon his death possession of the duchy would again be in play and they would likely be in a better financial position to take it for themselves. Nonetheless, the Senate reasserted in the bill of 28 December that it had been drawn into war unwillingly and not out of "ambition for dominion," but for the "health and conservation of honor and of our state and the liberty of Italy."[196]

But soon – and perhaps inevitably – the ambitions of Carmagnola and his Venetian masters again collided. The government remained anxious for Carmagnola to cross the Adda. In late January 1432 the Senate again considered offering him dominion over Milan. And again the bill failed, but this time the vote was 95 opposed, 35 in favor, and 20 abstentions.[197] Indications that Carmagnola finally planned to take action again came to nothing, while efforts of Visconti's emissary Cristoforo Ghilino to meet with Carmagnola earned him stern warnings from the Senate to repel Milanese overtures. It is still an open question whether or not Carmagnola disobeyed these orders and met with representatives of Milan. It is also unclear whether or not he was relaying all messages he received from Milan on to his Venetian masters. What is certain is that while Milanese troops went on the offensive in several areas, Carmagnola let an opportunity to take Soncino slip through his fingers yet another time.[198]

At this point, and almost certainly on the basis of new and damning information, members of the Council of Ten decided to act. First, however, they concluded that they needed to proceed with more authority and so authorized the addition of a twenty-member *zonta* to their deliberations. On that same day, 28 March, they considered but rejected a proposal to have the rectors of Brescia arrest the captain-general directly.[199] Instead, they decided to set a trap. On the 29th the Ten approved a plan whereby the citizen-secretary Giovanni de Imperiis would go to Brescia and tell Carmagnola that he was needed in Venice for urgent consultations regarding the future course of the war. Imperiis was to inform him that the Marquess of Mantua had also been invited to these discussions. If Carmagnola refused to come, then the secretary was to meet with the rectors of Brescia and the proveditor Francesco de Garzoni and arrange for Carmagnola's arrest and detention in Brescia. They were authorized to take custody of his papers and monies and to seize his wife as well. If, on the other hand, during the trip to Venice Carmagnola became suspicious or got wind of the plan and fled, then all the rectors of the Venetian dominions were to do their utmost to capture and detain him. On the recommendation of Foscari, the council voted unanimously to keep its decision top secret.[200] On the 30th letters in Foscari's name were written to Venice's most important mercenary captains, informing them of the necessity of taking action against Carmagnola for the "honor and conservation of our dominion;" they were also instructed to obey orders from the rectors of Brescia and proveditor Garzoni as if they came from the mouth of the doge himself.[201]

Suspecting nothing, Carmagnola – accompanied by the council's secretary Imperiis – arrived in Venice on 7 April. Once at the Ducal Palace Carmagnola was met by what he presumed to be an honor guard comprising eight nobles. The doors of the palace were locked. Carmagnola and the nobles then proceeded to the Sala delle Do Mappe where they awaited the arrival of Foscari. After cooling his heels for a while, the captain-general was informed that Foscari had been taken ill so that the meeting between them would take place the following morning. In the meantime, Carmagnola's personal escorts had been told the opposite, namely that their master would be dining with Foscari; they were dismissed from the palace. At this point, Carmagnola planned to return to his Venetian palace to dine and await the next day's colloquy with the doge. As he made his way downstairs, he was told, according to Sanudo, "Signor Count, come this way along the corridor of the prisons." But when his escorts showed him toward the prison door, he said: "This is not the way;" and they replied, "This is indeed the right way." Carmagnola exclaimed, "I see all too well that I am dead," and let out a great sigh.[202]

On 6 and 7 April the Ten sent letters to the rectors of Brescia and the proveditors of the army, urging them to be on guard for the security of the region, to pay Carmagnola's troops, and to arrest the Countess Carmagnola. The rectors of other terraferma cities and Venice's ambassadors at peace negotiations in Ferrara were also informed of the Ten's actions, which were necessitated by "the bad intentions and depraved deeds of the count."[203] On the 9th the Ten began the proceedings against the captain-general by setting up a special college to investigate the case, authorizing not only the examination of Carmagnola and his chancellor Giovanni de Moris, but also the use of torture. In addition, they ordered the transfer of the countess to Venice, as well as another woman known as La Bella, presumably Carmagnola's mistress.[204]

Records of the trial of Carmagnola are missing; however, Dolfin and Sanudo state that he was tortured on the 11th. Because Carmagnola had an injured arm, the Ten were not able to use their preferred torture method, hoisting on a cord with the arms tied behind the back; instead they burned the soles of his feet until he confessed everything. Also witnesses were questioned, and various papers examined. The trial was suspended for Holy Week but resumed on 23 April. On 5 May the Ten heard the charges and evidence and decided by a vote of 26 in favor versus 1 against and 9 abstentions to convict the count for being a "public traitor." They then proceeded to the sentencing phase of the trial. Three of the ducal councilors as well as the three heads of the Ten and the *avogadori di comun* recommended that Carmagnola be led, gagged with his hands tied behind his back, to the place of justice between the two columns in the Piazzetta where he would be beheaded. This proposal got 19 votes. An alternative put forward by Foscari and the other three ducal councilors recommended that he spend the rest of his life in prison. That proposal got only 8 votes in favor and 9 abstentions and thus failed.[205] Given his position as head of state, the fact that Foscari was inclined to show relative leniency toward Carmagnola is surprising, especially as he often demonstrated harshness in other sentences. What led Foscari to make the judgement he did must remain a mystery. As a seasoned politician, one accustomed to the high-stakes game of power politics, perhaps he understood that Carmagnola had gambled and lost but did not deserve to die for his actions. Or he may have been inclined to clemency when he considered the feelings of the countess and her daughters.

Certainly Foscari was not alone in considering Carmagnola's family. Indeed, the death sentence contained a whole series of clauses making provision for Carmagnola's heirs. His wife was to live in Treviso and receive a stipend based on the interest from a fund of 10,000 ducats invested in the Monte; however, if she left Venetian dominions, she was to lose everything. As for his two unmarried daughters, they were each to get 5000 ducats invested in the Monte for their dowries, the interest of which was to be used to maintain them until they married. However, they could not marry without the consent of the Ten. If either girl died before marrying, she could dispose of up to 1000 ducats in her will; once married, she could bequeath all 5000 ducats. A third daughter, who was already betrothed to Sigismondo Malatesta, was to receive the same as her sisters should Malatesta decide, in the circumstances, not to go forward with the marriage, as indeed he did. The rest of Carmagnola's riches were to devolve to Venice.[206]

At the hour of Vespers on 5 May, Carmagnola was led into the Piazzetta. Dressed in scarlet and wearing a hat "alla Carmignolla," he was accompanied by members of the congregation of Santa Maria Formosa bearing a cross. With three strokes of the blade, he was beheaded as prescribed in his sentence. The religiously inclined chronicler Antonio Morosini judged that he died "rather devoutly." His body (and, as Sanudo is careful to point out, his head) were placed in a boat and, accompanied by priests, taken to the observant Franciscan monastery San Francesco della Vigna for burial; but as it turned out, Carmagnola had asked to be buried at the Frari the city's conventual Franciscan church. Accordingly, his body was transferred to the latter and buried in the cloister.[207]

On 14 May the Ten, meeting without the *zonta*, decided that an altar cloth commissioned by Carmagnola should be donated to the Frari, as should the clothing he had been wearing at the time of his execution, as he himself had requested.[208] Three years later, in March 1435, the Ten decided to donate the captain-general's silk pennant to San Francesco della Vigna, but only after it was altered so as not to be identifiable as Carmagnola's. A similar proposal made in May 1433 had been tabled. A few years after that, the condottiere's body was moved to the church of San Francesco in Milan, where he had had a marble tomb constructed. The church was destroyed in the early nineteenth century, so there is no record of the tomb's appearance.[209]

For its part, the Venetian government confiscated the balance of Carmagnola's property, including the palace which it had awarded to him, and took special care to pay his creditors.[210] In July the countess, who probably had been under house arrest in her husband's palace since her arrival in April, agreed to lodge at the convent of Santa Maria delle Vergini. But the nuns exacted a price for their hospitality. Among Carmagnola's goods that the government planned to sell was a brocaded cloth of gold silk which the captain-general had been in the custom of lending to various Brescian churches on feast days. The nuns, with the countess's concurrence, now asked the government to give it to them so that they could use it to adorn their high altar. The Ten approved the request as a way of augmenting the faith and of showing reverence to the "creator and his glorious mother the Virgin Mary." In August 1433 the Ten permitted Carmagnola's widow to take up residence on the mainland. By April 1434, however, she and her daughters had escaped to Milan.[211]

The story of Carmagnola, like that of Foscari himself, became the stuff of legend with a special appeal for nineteenth-century painters and writers, among them Alessandro Manzoni, who wrote a play entitled *Il conte di Carmagnola* (1820). However, these romanticizing works tend to obscure the real significance of Carmagnola's life and death. For his life is a lesson in the problems and pitfalls that the Venetian state faced in attempting to organize the military defense of its recently acquired mainland state. Venice had decided, like the other Italian states, to entrust that defense to mercenaries rather than to citizen armies, but then had to find a method of controlling the captains-general it placed at their helm. Their system relied on long-distance supervision by the Senate, including control of the purse strings, and direct oversight by the proveditors. But the captains and proveditors often clashed over issues of strategy, negotiations with the enemy, and mobilization of the troops. The problems eased somewhat after the 1430s as more Venetian nobles gained experience working with their mercenary employees.[212]

Further complicating the mix were the egos and ambitions of the condottieri themselves. In an age of territorial consolidation, they had to find their place in the rapidly diminishing interstices of regional power. This was less a problem for mercenary captains like the Gonzagas of Mantua and the Estes of Ferrara, who already ruled independent states, and more so for upstarts like Piccinino, Sforza, and Carmagnola who aspired to dominion. Unfortunately for Carmagnola, he was not content with his territories around Brescia, and Chiari, or even with the promise of Pavia. He was, in Sanudo's estimation, too proud and ambitious.[213] He aspired to Milan, and for this he paid with his life. Carmagnola's execution by the Ten sent a powerful message that reverberated for the rest of the century, namely that Venice's mercenary captains were expected to subordinate their own interests to those of their employer or pay the ultimate price. Although the Ten did not actively seek Carmagnola's betrayal, it certainly served their purposes well by sending, as one historian observes, "a salutary shock to his fellow captains and eventual successors."[214]

Unfortunately, the specific crime that brought about Carmagnola's demise can never be ascertained. But given the extraordinary patience his Venetian masters had shown him over the years, offering him ever greater rewards even when he avoided action, they must have had incontrovertible proof that he had betrayed his masters and was now colluding with Milan.[215] Apparently, Visconti's relentless overtures to Carmagnola had paid off; one hypothesis can be discounted, however, namely that Visconti set Carmagnola up in order to avenge the captain's desertion to the Venetian side eight years earlier, as too intricate even by the standards of Renaissance politics.[216] For the truth is that Carmagnola's heart lay in Milan: he was after all married to one of Visconti's relatives and all his properties lay in Lombard territory. He had even had his tomb constructed there. Living or dead, as lord or yet again as captain-general, Carmagnola always hoped to return to the Lombard capital.[217] This is not to say that his years of Venetian service were simply a ruse; only that his aspirations lay on the other side of the Adda, the river he had refused to cross so many times.

Even with Carmagnola's death, the war dragged on. Gianfrancesco Gonzaga, the Marquess of Mantua, was placed in command of the Venetian forces, but with the lesser title of governor-general. In a solemn ceremony conducted in San Marco and attended by Foscari, "the imperial gilded banner of Saint Mark the Evangelist," as Morosini describes it, was blessed and sent to Gonzaga who was in the field.[218] During the summer the Venetian land forces took several towns including Bordolano, Romanengo, Fontanella, and in late August the long-sought-after Soncino. The Venetian forces then moved into the Valtellina where in November they suffered a humiliating defeat. Visconti's army under the command of Niccolò Piccinino managed to capture several Venetian condottieri as well as the proveditor Giorgio Corner who was taken prisoner to Milan.[219]

For much of the spring and summer, little action occurred on the Ligurian front of the war. Pietro Loredan kept shifting his fleet between Portovenere and Pisa rather than moving toward the liberation of Genoa from Milanese control. His tactics provoked a particularly bitter dispute when on 14 July the Senate debated the wording of a letter to Loredan and the proveditors. Foscari as well as several *savi* proposed a strongly worded letter, complaining that Loredan's delaying tactics were giving the enemy time to gets its fleet in order, leading to "infinite evils and inconveniences," and contributing to a diminution of the League's "honor and reputation." Even today the letter seems heavy-handed and intended more than anything else to give offense.[220]

And offend it did. Loredan's relative, senator Francesco Loredan son of the late Giorgio, became furious and started making *ad hominem* attacks on Foscari. This prompted in turn a sharp rebuke from Lazzaro Mocenigo, Antonio Michiel, and Alvise Donato, the heads of the Ten. They warned Loredan that if he continued to attack the doge, they would fine him the massive amount of 1000 ducats, saying that "if he wished to speak or to say anything, let him speak simply about the bill and not against the person of the most Serene lord doge."[221] This episode, about which too little is known, is significant for two reasons. First, it provides the best proof yet that a bitter and on-going enmity existed between Foscari and members of the Loredan family. Yes, Foscari and Loredan were able to work together at times; but clearly there was no love lost between these two giants of Venetian politics.[222] Second, it reveals the frustration and tension that the war provoked within the ruling class in general. Some of the tensions and fissures that the Lombard wars created are considered above, and this third Venetian–Visconti conflict did nothing to ease those tensions; in fact it exacerbated them.

One of the primary causes of tension was the fiscal burden imposed by the war. According to Sanudo, military expenses were costing the government 70,000 ducats per month.[223] This in turn threatened confidence in the Monte as interest payments fell into arrears. In January 1432 Foscari and Leonardo Mocenigo offered a bill that worried holders of Monte shares even more. They proposed that the delayed interest payments due the past September be cut in half. The bill passed but only over a good deal of opposition: the vote was 68 yeas, 35 nays, and 12 abstentions.[224] It was now clear that the expense of the war would be felt by everyone – the rich and not just the poor, Jews, and residents of the terraferma. Certainly this contributed to greater rancor within the ruling elite. In spite of the burden, other special outlays had to be undertaken; and so the government embarked in September 1431 upon a major renovation of the dilapidated Rialto Bridge at a cost of a little more than 2300 ducats.[225]

The third war with Milan also rekindled various constitutional issues, including the advisability of creating a special council along the lines of the former Council of One Hundred. In July 1431 Foscari and five of the ducal councilors proposed that a special council of ninety sages (Morosini calls them "elders") be established to deal with major issues such as the war and forced loans. Foscari and his advisors couched this innovation in traditional terms, claiming that they were following Venice's progenitors in changing governmental structures as the times dictated. The ninety members were to be elected by the Great Council, but only men already holding high office or members of the Senate or Forty would be eligible. Up to three members of a family could be elected. Once elected, the ninety would then select by scrutiny an additional thirty members to sit with them. Only one member of any particular family could be among the thirty. The council would handle major issues such as those involving forced loans and the war and would be elected every six months until the reestablishment of peace with Milan. This extraordinary proposal clearly represented a bold-faced attempt to concentrate power in the hands of the wealthiest and most powerful nobles and by means of the *zonta* of thirty to eat away at the Great Council's electoral privileges. A very heated debate or, as Sanudo calls it, a *desputacion grande* ensued. The proposal received only 264 votes, while a countermeasure put forward by the defenders of the lesser nobles, the heads of the Forty, to leave the matter in the hands of the Senate passed on a vote of 519 in favor, with 21 against and 19 abstentions.[226] In their zeal to control the war, Foscari and the men around him had overplayed their hand and in the process offended the lesser nobles.

The frustration felt by these lesser and younger nobles continued to build. Desperate for salaried jobs and some influence over decisions, various nobles resorted to influence peddling and other forms of electoral chicanery. In July 1431, for example, the Senate complained that when votes were held for the posts of bowmen of the quarterdeck (*balestrieri alle pope*), the candidates' relations were engaging in dishonest tactics. The position of bowman, a job on the state owned galleys, was much coveted by poorer nobles because it offered a modest salary as well as a number of privileges including the right to carry a specific amount of merchandise on board. At least one merchant, Andrea Barbarigo, used the post to begin rebuilding his family's fortune.[227] Yet nothing that had occurred heretofore to win elections compared with the conspiracy uncovered in January 1433.

On the 22nd of that month, the Ten decided to establish a committee of four men to question – and if need be to torture – noblemen Giovanni, son of Azone Trevisan, and Zaccaria, son of the late Hector Contarini, concerning a "sect or company" that had been formed to undermine "justice and equity" through the manipulation of elections for office in the Great Council. The rhetoric of the Ten's decision conveyed their alarm. They feared that the conspirators had shown disdain not only for God but also for the honor of the state. The following day the Ten authorized the questioning of four more noblemen: Marco Magno, Marco Cicogna, Andrea Pisani, and Benedetto Barbarigo. Furthermore, as the extent of the plot began to come into focus, the Ten decided on the recommendation of Foscari and the heads of the Forty, to add a ten-member *zonta* to the case. Under questioning Contarini named names, and on the 24th the Ten authorized the round-up and interrogation of those suspects, as well as of Giovanni Soranzo who had come forward on his own.[228]

By the 28th the Ten had completed its investigation and was ready to proceed with the condemnation and sentencing of the conspirators. As usual their records are frustratingly cryptic, but the chronicler Giorgio Dolfin gives a cogent summary of the plot. Like the Ten, he describes the conspiracy as the action of a "company or sect," one that was in the habit of dining together. Whenever a member of the group decided that he wished to be elected to a particular office or post, the others swore that they would support his candidacy and only his candidacy. In this way, according to Dolfin, "they worked to help one another and to distribute all the offices and posts which they wanted."[229]

As it turned out, the ringleader of the plot was nobleman Marco Cicogna; and on the 28th the Ten sentenced him. Although various punishments were proposed, that of Foscari and Benedetto Emo passed. The Ten sentenced the fugitive Cicogna to perpetual banishment from Venice and its district: should he be captured, he would spend a year in jail and then suffer rebanishment. Furthermore, his crime would be read out annually for ten years during meetings of the Great Council, "as an example to others." The other four chief conspirators, noblemen Marco Magno, Zaccaria Contarini, Benedetto Barbarigo, and Andrea Pisani, were prohibited from ever holding office again; they were to suffer banishment for five years, and, like Cicogna, to have their names publicly read in the Great Council for ten years. On the same day, twenty other members of the conspiracy got lighter sentences, including one year's banishment, exclusion from office for ten years, and the humiliation of having their names published for five years. Their number included representatives from some of Venice's most famous families, such as the Venier, Dandolo, and da Mosto; as well as such smaller and less distinguished ones as the Orso, Guoro, Cocco, and de Renier.[230] But as it turned out, the case was not finished for new revelations were still to come. In early February, the Ten sentenced nine more nobles for participation in the plot, including nobleman Paolo dalle Boccole at whose home some members had dined together. And on 25 February three more men were condemned as well: Marco Boldu, Luca Mudazzo, and Pietro de Rugerio.[231]

The condemnation of so many noblemen from so many different families exposed the members of the Ten and their zonta to the danger of retribution, both physical and legal. Consequently, on the 28th, the Ten acted to protect those involved in the investigation and prosecution of the case. First, they granted themselves the right to go about with up to five armed men; second, they ruled that in the future the condemned could not serve as judges or witnesses in cases involving themselves or their sons; finally, they imposed a strict gag order on their own proceedings, making it illegal for any of their members to discuss what had been said or who had put forth various proposals. These bills passed unanimously with 21 affirmative votes. On that same day, the Ten approved a rule imposing permanent banishment from all Venetian lands on members of the Great Council who ever again dared to form any sort of "sect, confederation, league, or company" designed to corrupt elections and in so doing to undermine "the tranquility and *ben comune*" of the Republic.[232]

The conspiracy struck a particularly sensitive nerve. Morosini called it an "iniquitous and most wicked novelty" and an "abomination," while Dolfin believed that it was designed "to destroy the government of Venice." It threatened for two reasons. First, it served, in the words of the Ten, to undermine the "justice and equity of offices in our regime."[233] Indeed these were the principles upon which the entire Venetian political system had been based ever since the *Serrata* of the Great Council of 1297, for at that time the members of the ruling elite had decided that the foundation of the regime would be equal access (what they referred to as equity) to the offices of state for members of the Great Council by means of election. And although that theoretical equity was compromised by such factors as personal wealth and family connections, they clung tenaciously to the principle that nobles should have an equal chance in elections based solely on the principle of merit. Certainly, what made the *Serrata* a stroke of political genius and what so distinguished Venice from the other Italian states was the possibility of high office that it offered to a large number of men. In this way, it reduced the danger of factionalism and the exclusionary tactics that factions entailed. In fact, later in this very year the Medici family and their supporters would be expelled from Florence by their rivals the Albizzi and their followers.[234] The electoral conspiracy of 1433 threatened to undermine the equity and unanimity of the ruling class through the formation of secret pacts. It opened the door, in other words, to factionalism.

The second reason the conspiracy proved so threatening was that it exposed the hypocrisy of the notion of equity by laying bare for all to see the inequalities of wealth and power within the Venetian nobility. The chroniclers described the conspiracy as one of young men aimed at the regime, and certainly some of the conspirators were young. However seventeen of the thirty-eight condemned men are listed as having fathers who were deceased. This suggests that they were not all young. What they almost certainly were was poor; and many came from small, even obscure, families; while those with well-known last names came from poorer cadet branches. Indeed the term "young" may have been at least in part a codeword for poor and powerless. If this was the case, then it also casts the assassination attempt by Andrea Contarini, who was described as young, in a different light. And so this was a conspiracy "among poorer nobles to gain for themselves more than their fair share of the largesse that the state offered to the nobility in the form of offices."[235] It revealed just how divided and vulnerable to factionalism the Venetian ruling class, which constantly publicized its unanimity, really was.

During the summer of 1433 the government took remedial action to alleviate the economic plight of poorer nobles. Noting the need to assist them, the Senate voted in June to authorize two *balestrieri* on each of the six ships traveling to Syria. In August that same body passed overwhelmingly a bill designed to provide relief to poor nobles who had been banned from meetings of the Great Council and thus made ineligible for offices because of their inability to pay their forced loans and other tax impositions. And in November the Senate, declaring that justice ought to be equally rendered to all, decided to extend relief to non-nobles as well.[236]

It was during these very years that the Sala dello Scrutinio was erected adjacent to the Great Council Hall in the new wing of the Ducal Palace. As its name indicates, it was the room used by the electoral nominating committees which made their recommendations to the council members. Like the Great Council Hall itself, the Sala dello Scrutinio was destroyed by fire in 1577 and redecorated. But "a presumably original inscription with his [Foscari's] coat of arms was restored after the fire and left *in situ* [. . .] on the tribune wall" (fig. 18).[237] The lengthy text reads as follows:

QVI PATRIAE PERICVLA SVO PERICVLO EXPETVNT ... CAPIDILITES I V /HANDI SVNT. CVM ET EVM / . QVEM DEBENT. HONOREM REIP. REDDVNT./ ET PRO MVLTIS PERIRE MALVNT . QVAM CVM MVLTIS ET ENIM. VEHEMENTER / EST INIQVVM . VITAM . QVAM A NATURA ACCEPTAM PROPTER PATRIAM / CON- SERVAVERIMVS. NATVRAE . CVM COGAT REDDERE PATRIAE . CVM /ROGET NON DARE . SAPIENTES IGITVR EXISTIMANDI SVNT. QVI NVLLVM / PRO SALVTE PATRIAE PERICVLVM VITANT. HOC VINCVLVM EST HVIVS / DIGNI- TATIS. QVA FRVIMUR IN REP. HOC FUNDAMENTVM LIBERATIS. HIC /FONS AEQVITATIS. MENS. ET ANIMVS ET CONSILIVM ET SENTENTIA CIVITATIS. / POSITA EST IN LEGIVS. VT CORPORA NOSTRA SINE MENTE. SIC CIVITAS SINE / LEGE SVIS PARTIBVS. VT NERVIS. AC SANGVINE. ET MEMBRIS. VTI NON POTEST. / LEGVM MINISTRI. MAGISTRATVS LEGVM INTERPRETES. IVDICES. LEGVM / DENIQVE ICCIRCO OMNES SERVI SVMVS. VT LIBERI ESSE POSSVMUS.[238]

(Those who at risk to themselves court danger for their country must be thought wise when they render to the Republic the honor they owe, and would rather perish for the many than with the many. Indeed it is very unjust not to give the life, which we have received from nature and have preserved for our country's sake, to nature, when she compels, when she requests that it be surrendered for the country. Therefore they must be considered wise who avoid no danger for their fatherland's well-being. This is the bond of that dignity which we enjoy in the Republic, this is the foundation of freedom, this is the font of equity. The mind and spirit, the counsel and will of the city are situated in the laws. Just as our bodies without mind so a city without law cannot use its parts, like muscle and blood and limbs. We are ministers of the laws, magistrates, interpreters of the laws, judges, indeed we are all therefore servants of the laws so that we may be free.)[239]

Perhaps this exhortation to political sacrifice and reverence for the law was placed on the tribune wall following the scandal of 1433. Certainly if its precepts had been followed, the scandal would not have occurred in the first place.

Following the defeat of Venetian forces in the Valtellina in November 1432, the Senate decided to confer the captain-generalship on Gian-francesco Gonzaga, the Marquess of Mantua, promising him in the event of victory several territories including Crema and Caravaggio.[240] In March 1433 he received the symbols of command from Foscari in an elaborate ceremony in San Marco; in 1430 he had already been awarded, as noted earlier, the house on the Grand Canal known as the Palace of the Two Towers.[241] But by spring, the peace negotiations being con-ducted in Ferrara were nearing completion. Apparently, both Visconti and Venice were ready for peace; it was the Florentines who presented a stumbling block for they were demanding the restoration of the town of Pontremoli. According to Morosini, Foscari was able to smooth the rift between the two allies when in April he addressed two ambassadors from the Florentine Republic with a particularly eloquent speech.[242] News of the conclusion of the peace treaty, known as the Second Peace of Ferrara, reached Venice on 26 April and was met with joyous cele-brations. The treaty essentially reaffirmed the status quo ante bellum. Most importantly for Venice, Visconti agreed to restore lands that he had taken in the Bergamasco. But for all the expense and trouble it had caused, very little had been achieved.[243]

Certainly one of the factors pushing Milan toward peace was the growing rapprochement between Venice and the emperor-elect Sigis-mund, a warming of relations facilitated by the Venetian pope Eugenius IV. Sigismund was able to achieve an important goal when, on 31 May, he was finally crowned Holy Roman Emperor by Eugenius in Rome. Shortly thereafter, the emperor and Venice renewed for another five years the truce between them. As a reward, the emperor honored Andrea

Donato, Venice's representative to him, with a knighthood. Donato was by this point Foscari's son-in-law, having married Foscari's daughter Camilla a year earlier.[244]

Foscari chose this moment when peace had been achieved to do something entirely unexpected. On 26 June he announced to his six ducal councilors that he intended to renounce the dogeship. Morosini gives a fairly full account of the reasons Foscari gave for his decision. Looking back over the ten years of his reign, Foscari saw little of which to be proud. The city was suffering from dearth and penury; and the many years of war had produced little profit and heavy taxes. As Dolfin recounts, "all the time in which he had been doge, never was there anything but war and tribulation and death." Faced with this bleak record, Foscari's one desire now was to leave these responsibilities behind, quiet his soul, and "live in peace." According to Morosini, at the time Foscari made his announcement, he was in full maturity [he gives his age as sixty-two] and a very rich man." He also states that the doge had only three children living with him in the Ducal Palace: a son about five years of age, another son between ten and twelve years old, and a young daughter, whose age he does not specify.[245]

The picture that emerges from Morosini's description is of a man who had been worn down by the burdens of the office and discouraged by political and diplomatic setbacks and the poor state of the economy. Yet these were events and factors beyond any man's control. What is more likely is that Foscari was driven to resign by personal attacks on him and by the increasingly bitter struggles within the innermost circles of power. After all, during the previous three years, Foscari had not only been the object of an assassination attempt but also of *ad hominem* attacks and an increasingly bitter rivalry with Pietro Loredan. Even an effort in 1431 to elect Foscari's brother Marco to the vacancy in the procuratorship *de supra* created by the death of Foscari's friend Bartolomeo Donato had failed.[246] The terrible personal losses that Foscari experienced during these years also surely counted heavily in his decision. Foscari's sons were carried away with frightening regularity during the first decade of his reign. As noted above, his son Donato died in 1425 and Giovanni followed in 1429. But perhaps the greatest loss of all was of his son Lorenzo, who died in 1431.[247] Lorenzo appears to have been an impetuous, high-spirited youth, the kind of son of whom Renaissance fathers were proud. Just a year before his death he had been prosecuted along with four other nobles and a non-noble for causing a commotion by illegally entering the convent of Santa Maria delle Vergini on the day of the consecration of the new abbess. This was just the sort of youthful prank which, although officially condemned, actually earned the perpetrators a reputation for male prowess and carried no long-term career disabilities.[248] Now, as Morosini says, Foscari had only two young sons left – a meagre legacy for a man originally blessed with so many male heirs and a disturbing familial prospect in a city where patrilineage counted for everything.

And so Foscari's desire, as chronicled by Morosini and Dolfin, was to leave earthly cares behind and live instead in peace and quiet. According to Renaissance treatises on the ages of man, it was appropriate for older men to retire from active engagement in the world and turn their thoughts to God and the afterlife. Foscari's wish to renounce the dogeship serves as further proof of his piety, a piety most clearly represented in the construction of the Chapel of the Madonna. But the ducal councilors thwarted his plan. According to the ducal *promissione*, Foscari could resign only if all six councilors were in agreement; yet they were not, and so the resignation was not accepted.[249] Clearly Foscari saw the reestablishment of peace as a propitious moment to renounce politics and seek a different life. Instead he remained burdened with the dogeship. The succeeding few years would see Venice engaged yet again in war with Milan and Foscari fully developing the power and prestige of the ducal office. Quite unexpectedly, the pious administrator laboring under the special protection of the Virgin would make way for the full-fledged imperial leader.

3

The Royal Way
1433–1442

Franciscus Foscari dux [. . .] sub quo magni motus in tota Italia fuerunt ipsique populus venetus plurima bella gessit.

(Francesco Foscari doge [. . .] under whom there were many great changes in all Italy itself and the Venetians waged many wars.)

Aeneas Silvius Piccolomini[1]

In October 1440 the Venetian Senate decided that henceforth it would record its non-secret deliberations in two separate and distinct sets of registers labeled *terra* and *mar*, land and sea.[2] This seemingly minor change in the Senate's record-keeping procedures was in fact a very tangible and concrete acknowledgement that Venetian foreign policy had undergone a major transformation in the preceding decades, that the terraferma had taken its place alongside the eastern Mediterranean in the Venetian imagination, and that foreign affairs had grown so complex that the Senate needed a better method for keeping track of policy decisions. Most of all, this change reflected the fact that now land and sea together would determine Venice's fate. The pressure brought about by managing that transformation and the problems that issued from it led Foscari to attempt to resign the doge-ship in June 1433.

But Foscari's abdication attempt little prepares one for the next stage in his reign for although the underlying problems and stresses that led him to his decision remained largely unchanged, his approach to the dogeship shifted considerably. During the next few years he was reinvigorated as he responded to both political and economic crises with a revived activism and engagement in affairs. Just as significantly, Foscari assumed new visibility both at home and on the international scene as he and his wife Marina hosted visits from foreign dignitaries and staged elaborate wedding celebrations for their son Jacopo. In so doing, Foscari chose a new approach to the dogeship, emphasizing its princely rather than its ministerial aspects while at the same time infusing the position with additional layers of symbolic meaning drawn from the twin founts of northern chivalric and Roman imperial culture.

This redefinition of the ducal office was in large part Foscari's attempt to ameliorate the two great issues generated by the new mainland state, namely the problem of executive authority and the need to integrate the terraferma cities and their inhabitants into the Venetian realm. For now as a mainland power, Venice found itself in constant and direct contact with princely regimes across the breadth and length of Italy. The absorption of the smaller states by the larger ones meant that the great powers now virtually abutted one another with the result that simple border disputes or other disagreements could easily spiral out of control and into more general conflagrations due to the interlocking alliances that crisscrossed the peninsula. Additionally the timeframe for decision-making had shrunk dramatically: whereas it typically took more than a month for news to reach Venice from Constantinople and almost two months from Alexandria, thereby allowing the government time to weigh its decisions, news arrived from Milan in three days and could in special circumstances take as little as one.[3] Such conditions tended to favor princely states where governmental decisions could be made relatively quickly and resources mobilized without the burden of reaching consensus as required in republican regimes. Indeed, at this very moment, Venice's republican ally Florence was about to undergo just such a transformation as the Medici began to create a kind of shadow government operating from within their household and through the auspices of their international bank. In Venice, Foscari's elevation of the ducal role was both in keeping with and a response to these new pressures. At the same time the Council of Ten offered an alternative model for concentrating power, one that was capable of bringing doge and council into conflict.

Foscari's heightened visibility also represented an effort to bind the subject cities and their inhabitants to the *dominante* through the personage of the doge and by means of a common symbolic and ritual language. When the Venetians conquered the cities of the terraferma, they made the fateful decision not to create a standard legal code or to extend membership in the Great Council and with it Venetian citizenship to the elites of those subject cities. They opted instead to allow a degree of local self-governance.[4] This was a failure of imagination common to all the Italian cities but especially acute among the Venetians, conditioned as they were by a perception of themselves as distinct and set apart from the rest of Italy and by the subject cities' own glorification of their Roman past: while Padua, Verona, and the other mainland cities could all proudly trace their origins to ancient Rome, the Venetians could make no such claim.[5] Furthermore, whereas the terraferma cities partook of a chivalric inheritance as subjects of the Holy Roman Emperor, the Venetians found themselves lacking an indigenous knightly culture. Foscari, a count by virtue of the family holdings at Zellarino, attempted to bridge this cultural divide in a number of ways, not least of which was architecturally in the grand design for the new entry system into the Ducal Palace, the Porta della Carta. Ominously, however, for Venetian republicanism, the lynchpin in the entryway's decorative program was the figure of the doge himself. For Venice's new imperial age, Foscari created an imperial dogeship.[6]

Immediately following the Second Peace of Ferrara a major reshuffling of alliances and personnel across Italy occurred, as if a great bottleneck had been removed or dam burst. In Florence the failure of the war with Lucca led in September 1433 to the expulsion of the Medici and their supporters by the Albizzi and their allies. The head of the family, Cosimo de' Medici, was sentenced to exile in Padua, while his brother Lorenzo was sent to Venice.[7] When Cosimo himself visited Venice, he was met by an escort of boats and warmly received at the Ducal Palace by Foscari. According to a letter written by Cosimo's cousin Francesco di Giuliano:

He [Foscari] embraced him [Cosimo] warmly, greatly lamenting his misfortune, and then he sat down between Cosimo and Lorenzo, as if they had been ambassadors . . . and I can hardly describe the brotherly affection which all these citizens have extended to them, and to all our house, and above all my Lord the Doge, who really has shown and continues to show his friendship in every possible way, so that one may call him a true friend.[8]

Venetian attempts to reconcile Cosimo and the Florentine regime came to naught but did result in the Florentine government granting permission to Cosimo to take up residence in Venice, where he was able to carry on his banking business, undertake patronage projects perhaps including the construction of a library at San Giorgio Maggiore, and plot his return to Florence. A number of Florentine artists, among them Michelozzo, accompanied Cosimo to Venice.[9]

For their part, the Venetians persisted in their efforts to forge an alliance with Sigismund and Eugenius IV. The stumbling block, despite Sigismund's recent coronation in Rome, was the Council of Basel, which the pope was threatening to dissolve. Eugenius and Venice both feared that the council, whose current agenda included dealing with John Huss, would limit papal authority and diminish the position of the papacy beyond the Alps.[10] The Venetians, who in June 1433 renewed for five years their truce with the emperor, worked furiously to bring the pope and emperor into accord regarding the council. In July the Senate voted a levy based on the *estimo* in order to raise the 10,000 ducats that Venice had promised to the emperor in return for his support of the pope at Basel, and Foscari's son-in-law Andrea Donato was elected as Venice's emissary to the church meeting. In August the Senate selected twelve distinguished gentlemen to escort Sigismund through Venetian lands on his way from Rome to Basel; among these were Giovanni Contarini, Antonio Venier, and Francesco Barbaro, all three of whom Sigismund knighted.[11] In yet another favor to the emperor, the Ten decided in November to lift the bounty that the Republic had placed on the head of Brunoro della Scala, pretender to the Scaligeri lordship of Verona and Sigismund's courtier. All Venice's efforts paid off when in December Eugenius revoked his dissolution of the council.[12]

The Venetian strategy with regard to Basel was also designed to drive a deeper wedge between Sigismund and Visconti. They were assisted in this by Visconti's refusal to meet Sigismund during the emperor-elect's progress through Italy on his way to Rome for his coronation. Visconti was also making threatening gestures toward the pope. When the lands of Saint Peter, most notably Ancona, rose in revolt against Eugenius, Visconti dispatched his condottieri Francesco Sforza and Niccolò Fortebraccio to stir up trouble, but Eugenius was able to lure Sforza to his side by playing to his territorial ambitions and awarding him the March of Ancona. However, when the Eternal City itself rebelled in the spring of 1434, Eugenius was forced to flee to Florence.[13]

In April 1434 the reshuffling of personnel across Italy continued as the condottiere Erasmo da Narni, better known as Gattamelata, entered into a contract with Venice, along with his comrade Count Brandolino Brandolini. About the same age as Foscari, Gattamelata had trained for the military under the mercenary captain Braccio da Montone, eventually receiving his own *condotte* (contracts) from Martin V and Eugenius IV and serving them in the Romagna.[14] The Romagna was becoming a new theater of struggle between Milan and the League, and Venice responded by dividing its army, sending one branch under Gattamelata to guard the Romagna while Gianfrancesco Gonzaga continued to serve in Lombardy.[15] In August the allied Venetian and Florentine forces under Gattamelata and the Florentine commander Niccolò da Tolentino suffered a crushing defeat at the hands of Niccolò Piccinino at Castel Bolognese. Many of the League's commanders, including Tolentino and Cesare Martinengo, were taken prisoner. In the wake of the defeat, Francesco Loredan and Andrea Donato were sent as proveditors to help reorganize the forces; and Cosimo de' Medici offered a loan of 15,000 ducats in aid.[16] In that same month a pro-Medici priorate was selected to take office in Florence in September, and Cosimo began preparations for the return to his native city. The realignments were complete when in the fall Francesco Sforza reached an accord to serve the League.[17]

These dramatic transformations on the international scene were accompanied by a period of retrenchment and belt-tightening at home. On 9 May 1433, just a few days after the publication of the peace treaty, the Senate authorized the Collegio to examine and reduce any superfluous mainland expenses, though it forbade the cashiering of mercenary troops. But less than a month later the Senate, on the recommendation of Foscari and many others, itself decided to reduce the size of the army to 5000 cavalry and 2000 infantry, a decision that led some of the senior captains to abandon Venetian service. By December, however, Venice was again taking on troops in order to meet new threats in the Romagna.[18]

In the effort to raise revenue, the government showed more consistency. In June 1433, for example, the Senate decided to delay payments that were due to the Jews; and in July the Ten authorized the sale at auction of Carmagnola's palace at San Stae as well as his estates on the mainland. The money was to be used to buy back shares in the Monte. Matteo Vitturi, son of Foscari's deceased ally Bulgaro Vitturi, purchased the palace at a cost of 6360 ducats, slightly less than the 6500 ducats which the Ten had set as a minimum price.[19] Similarly, in the spring of 1434 the government decided to sell some property at Rialto on the Ruga dei Milanesi (the Street of the Milanese) as well as lands it had acquired in Bergamo, the Val Camonica, and Brescia.[20]

But the most significant fiscal measures involved the Monte itself. First, in accordance with the law, the Senate authorized a revision of the *estimo* and appointed a fifteen-member panel to review and if necessary to revise the assessments.[21] On 11 February 1434 Foscari himself proposed that Monte shares be repurchased at 40 percent of their face value; his proposal failed with only 35 votes in favor, while a measure to repurchase shares at 45 percent of face value passed.[22] Then in a more extreme and sweeping move, the Senate voted that same day on a number of measures to put the Monte, which it called the "principal foundation of our state," on a more secure footing. In addition to the usual methods of selling lands, raising the fiscal obligations of the Jews, and adjusting the duties on inhabitants of Treviso, Belluno, Bassano, Ceneda, and Feltre to match those of Vicenza, the Senate decided that it would require all governmental officials and office-holders making up to 400 ducats per year in salary and fees to contribute 10 percent of that income and those making more than 400 ducats annually 15 percent in order to raise money to repurchase shares in the Monte. The original bill exempted the Grand Chancellor from this obligation; however Foscari and Giovanni Navagero proposed that no exemptions be allowed and their version passed.[23] On 14 March the Great Council affirmed the Senate's decisions by a vote of 639 yeas, versus 131 nays, and 25 abstentions. The nays likely came from the poorer nobles who saw a 10 percent impost on their salary (effectively a 10 percent reduction in pay) as a threat to their already shaky financial situation.[24] Still, some members tried to find a way around this new fiscal burden, prompting the Great Council to pass a law in April forbidding salary increases in order to compensate for the reduced pay except as approved by the Great Council. That measure passed overwhelmingly by a vote of 780 in favor versus 20 opposed and 19 abstentions.[25]

Refinement of this new policy continued to occupy the councils for the rest of the year. In April the Senate voted on procedures for making these salary payments and decided that nobles who failed to pay would be ineligible for election to other posts until they cleared their debt.[26] On 7 November the Senate took the drastic step of dramatically increasing the levies: it raised the imposts on nobles serving outside the city by increasing the contribution on those with salaries below 400 ducats to 30 percent and those above 400 ducats to 40 percent. And on the 9th it ruled that noble officials and non-noble office staff in Venice would now be required to contribute a third of their salary. Foscari's brother Marco objected that the latter bill was particularly unfair to minor staff; but on the 11th the Great Council approved the imposts as set forth in the two Senate bills. And on 2 December Foscari alone made a proposal regarding how late payments should be handled.[27] What is evident here is not only the gripping pressure to find money in order to protect the solvency of the Monte, but also Foscari's own dynamic involvement in decision-making, just months after his attempt to resign the dogeship. At this point he was again fully in control of the power of the ducal office.

While all this was going on, Venice was further strengthening its new links to the Holy Roman Emperor and thereby making significant advances in legitimizing its legal claims to its terraferma possessions. As observed above, in June 1433, a few days after Sigismund's coronation in Rome, Venice renewed for another five years its truce with him. Venice's representative at the negotiations was Andrea Donato. According to the truce, the Venetians got the right to trade freely in the empire, while Sigismund secured guarantees to travel through Venetian territories and be received in its cities. Both parties agreed not to interfere in each other's territories or wars, although Venice reserved the right to come to the aid of its allies, the Estes of Ferrara, the Gonzagas of Mantua, as well as Monferrato and Ravenna. These provisions were an acknowledgement that Venice would not assist Milan should Sigismund attack the duchy.[28]

For his part Visconti responded to the new accord between Venice and the emperor by encouraging the legal challenges made by Ludovico di Teck, Patriarch of Aquileia, to Venetian control of Friuli. At the Council of Basel, di Teck leveled the charge that Venice had usurped church lands. Partly in an effort to strengthen its international claims to its subject territories, Venice had decided to send to Basel a large contingent of clergy, including not only representatives from each of the nine congregations of clergy within the city but also from the terraferma territories, not least Aquileia. Friuli remained, along with Dalmatia, a serious bone of contention between Venice and the emperor in his guise as King of Hungary. But di Teck remained intransigent, rebuffing Venetian attempts at a compromise.[29]

Despite the patriarch's machinations, relations between Venice and the emperor grew stronger. In January 1434 the Senate sent instructions to its ambassadors at Basel, including Donato, to work toward a more lasting agreement with the emperor aimed against Milan. At a minimum, the Venetians wanted the emperor to recognize their right to all lands east of the Adda, while lands to the west would remain at the emperor's disposition. Even so, Venice instructed its ambassadors to push for beachheads on the far side of the river, namely the town of Lodi and the castle at Trezzo. Negotiations for an anti-Milanese league between Venice, the emperor, and the pope proceeded over the next many months.[30]

In August 1435 Venice and the emperor were eventually able to reach an agreement for a league against Visconti designed to last for ten years. Among the provisions were the following: neither party could negotiate with Visconti without the consent of the other nor make a peace that was prejudicial to the other party. Should they agree to wage war on Visconti in Lombardy, the emperor would supply at least 4000 cavalry and come to Lombardy in person, while the Venetians would contribute 10,000 cavalry and 4000 infantry, give free passage to the emperor and his troops, and furnish them with supplies. The captured territories were to be divided as discussed in the earlier negotiations, that is Venice would receive lands on the eastern shore of the Adda; the emperor those on the western shore. Sigismund further agreed to seek support for the league from his vassals and dependents, especially the Duke of Savoy, while provision was also made for both the pope and Florence to join the alliance. But, perhaps most importantly, the emperor promised to invest Venice in the person of Foscari with all the lands that it currently held, except Vicenza and Verona.[31]

This last condition, Sigismund's designation of Foscari as imperial vicar, constituted a fundamental transformation in Venice's relations both with the emperor and its own terraferma subjects as well as in the doge-ship itself: according to the terms of the pact, Foscari agreed, in return for his investiture, to swear an oath of fealty to the emperor and present him annually with a golden cloth worth 1000 ducats. In so doing, the doge acknowledged that on the terraferma at least, he was subject to the emperor. This was highly significant since for centuries Venice had zealously maintained that in many respects the doge was coequal with the pope and emperor; this was achieved by publicizing Doge Sebas-tiano Ziani's role as mediator between the two powers in the Peace of Venice of 1177, not only in chronicles but also in paintings in the Ducal Palace. While this position was tenable so long as Venice remained pri-marily a maritime power, it no longer carried the same weight once Venice occupied mainland cities that were indisputably part of the empire.[32] On the terraferma at least, Venice was recognizing its subor-dination to the emperor.

With regard to the subject territories, the vicariate legitimized Vene-tian claims to sovereignty and inserted Venice into a still viable system of feudal obligations and privileges, allowing it to concede liberties and immunities like other feudal overlords. Internally the vicariate completed the process whereby Venice evolved from a commune into a Signoria or *dominium*, a transformation not only of nomenclature but also of power, first signaled in the revision of the *promissione* which Foscari swore on entering office and in the abolition of the Arengo.[33] It empha-sized a greater and greater concentration of power and authority in the innermost circles of government, especially the dogeship, as well as a growing sense of social stratification and hierarchy.

But just as important as the political and legal implications of the vic-ariate were its cultural ones, for what the vicariate also did was open the way for Venice in general and Foscari in particular to make fuller use of both Roman imperial and feudal/chivalric imagery. Heretofore, when Venice had made use of imperial imagery in architecture, rituals, and the like, it had most often done so by making reference not to Rome but to Constantinople, its erstwhile eastern overlord. So, for example, the medieval design of Piazza San Marco was intended to recall the imperial fora of the Byzantine capital. But now the doge was to be a vicar of the Holy Roman Emperor; and over the next century ancient Rome would provide one of the primary inspirations and reference points by which the Venetians understood themselves and their relations to the rest of the world.[34] Just as significantly, the vicariate gave Venice and the doge access to a feudal/chivalric system of which Foscari was already a part by virtue of his estates on the terraferma.[35] Both of these symbolic systems helped solidify Venice's control over the Roman-founded mainland cities which had been ruled for the most part by signorial regimes with vibrant feudal/chivalric traditions.

The actual investiture, which did not take place until 16 August 1437, naturally emphasized the feudal aspects of the vicariate. It took place at Prague. Foscari did not attend in person but was represented instead by the ambassador Marco Dandolo. Doges very seldom traveled outside the constricted limits of the *dogado* and only then with the permission of their councilors. In this particular instance, there were added incentives for the doge not to go in person but to be represented instead by proxies since the sight of Foscari himself doing fealty to the emperor would have emphasized far too strongly for Venetian taste the Republic's subordination to the emperor. The Venetians wanted it both ways: they were eager to gain the legitimacy the vicariate offered but wary of compromising their venerable claim to parity. Additionally, had Foscari attended in person, it might also have created the impression that he was being invested with the vicariate in his own right rather than as the representative of the Venetian state.[36]

According to Dolfin's account of the investiture, the emperor had a magnificent platform constructed in front of Prague's main church. One hundred knights were sent to fetch Dandolo; he was then brought to the platform, where he was awaited by the emperor along with many distinguished lords and barons. On mounting the stage, Dandolo dropped to his knees. The sovereign then raised him up and asked to see his commission and what he sought. Dandolo then explained to the emperor the terms of his commission, which included his right to speak on behalf of the government of Venice. After Mass, Sigismund read a decree (Dolfin calls it a "privilege") by which he conferred on the doge and his successors as well as on the Signoria of Venice all of its imperial lands. Dandolo swore an oath to the emperor on behalf of Foscari, pledging his fidelity and obedience. The emperor then granted a special honor to the ambassador by knighting him. According to Dolfin, the emperor presented Dandolo with a cloak of gold cloth worth 500 ducats and a special hat. Following this, Sigismund gave a speech praising Venice and had letters of similar ilk dispatched "to all parts of the world." He then issued a proclamation that Visconti should appear before him within two months in order to answer charges that he had acted against the emperor; should he fail to do so, Sigismund would proceed against him, "as God and justice demand."[37]

With this public ceremony, Venice received imperial sanction for its policy of territorial conquest; and the realignment of Venice and the empire was complete. Sigimund invested Foscari with Treviso, Feltre, Belluno, Ceneda, Padua, Brescia, Bergamo, Casalmaggiore, Soncino, Piadena, S. Giovanni in Croce, and all castles and burgs in the Cremonese as well as all territory east of the Adda.[38] Two omissions, however marred Venice's triumph for no mention was made of Vicenza and Verona out of imperial regard for Brunoro della Scala; nor was there any reference to disputed Friuli. Nonetheless it was a coup for Venice and a personal, if vicarious, triumph for Foscari as well. At the same time, it may have appeared to some that the doge had gone too far in subordinating Venice to the empire and in exalting himself, for the annual tribute of golden cloth was allowed to lapse and none of Foscari's successors ever again pledged their loyalty to the emperor in this way.[39]

The Prague ceremony was certainly the most conspicuous example of Venetian participation in ceremonies associated with feudal and chivalric rights and customs, but it was not the only one. And Dandolo was not the only representative of Venice to be knighted. Andrea Donato had received this honor on a previous mission to Sigismund, as had (as noted earlier) Giovanni Contarini, Antonio Venier, and Francesco Barbaro, three of the twelve gentlemen whom the Republic dispatched in August 1433 to escort the emperor through Venetian lands on his way to Basel.[40] Antonio Morosini's description of the sumptuary privileges that were accorded these men offers some sense of the prestige of knighthood, also of the powerful hold that chivalric culture had on the imagination of the merchant/administrators of republican Venice. According to the same chronicler, the four were made Knights of the Golden Spur and given collars of red and gold silk. In addition, each received a small gold cross (*croxieta*) with a carved griffin and the imperial device, which they could carry or wear, as Morosini was careful to note, "as often as they please."[41]

Andrea Donato's elevation to a knighthood was an honor not only for himself but also for his father-in-law the doge. About this same time, Foscari's brother Marco also gained in rank and prestige when in November 1434 he defeated Silvestro Morosini in the election to replace the recently deceased Fantin Michiel as procurator of San Marco *de citra*, having failed in an earlier effort to replace Bartolomeo Donato as procurator *de supra* (see chapter 2 above). And so he succeeded to his brother's former procuratorial post, the one that Albano Badoer held after Foscari and to which Foscari and his allies had attempted to elect the doge's brother-in-law Santo Venier in 1428. Now this pool of charitable funds was back securely in the hands of the Foscari and their allies. Together the two Foscari brothers stood at the summit of power.[42]

Sigismund's agreement in August 1435 to confer on Foscari the imperial vicariate could not have come at a better time for just a few months earlier, in the spring of that year, the Ten uncovered a serious plot to betray the city of Padua, the most important of Venice's mainland possessions, and restore it to Carrara family rule. Foscari's response to the conspiracy shows him at his most forceful, but it also indicates just how precarious Venice's hold on the terraferma remained.

Throughout these years Venice was constantly on the lookout for any signs of a resurgence of Carrarese sympathy in Padua. In October 1434, for example, the Ten arrested Carolo da Collalto when it learned that the Carrara arms, consisting of a wheel (*carro*) and the Collalto family device together adorned the façade of his house in Treviso. The Collalto were an important Trevisan family with strong connections to the Carraresi. In the end, the Ten determined that the paintings were old and hence not intended as a provocation, and released Carolo from jail. They also ordered that his pennant, which they had had confiscated and brought to Venice, be returned to him.[43] The Carraresi were not the only concern; the Venetians also worried that the remnants of the house of Scaligieri might become the focal point for rebellion in Verona. This explains their preoccupation with Brunoro della Scala's presence at Sigismund's court.

The first indication that something serious was afoot in Padua appears in the Ten's deliberations of 17 March, when on the basis of a denunciation they ordered the rectors of the town immediately to arrest and interrogate two men they identified as Bartolomeo and Melchiore Sartore (or Sartorelli) and to take any additional steps needed to secure the town. They also ordered the troops stationed in the Vicentino, Padovano, and Veronese to stand ready to respond to the rectors' demands and authorized the immediate dispatch of extra soldiers under Paolo Parenzano to Padua to assist the rectors if need be in securing the city's castle.[44]

The Ten's deliberations for that day convey a sense of the seriousness of the threat and how Foscari and the other members of the Ten responded. Their next decision was to add more men to their consultations: they authorized both the *savi della terraferma* and the *savi del consiglio* to attend their meeting. They then decided to augment even further the troops defending Padua by ordering the podestas of Chioggia, Torcello, and Murano as well as the captain of the Marches coastal patrols to send reliable troops. Foscari also proposed that two members of the Ten go to Padua to assist the rectors as special proveditors; they selected Silvestro Morosini and Andrea Mocenigo for this task. But when the heads of the Ten wanted to authorize the rectors and proveditors to deliver justice to the conspirators, Foscari and Benedetto Dandolo recommended that that decision be deferred until more information became available. In their final resolution during that very busy day, the Ten decided on the recommendation of the heads of the Ten, that six men – namely two heads, two other members of the Ten, as well as two ducal councilors – should pass the night in the Ducal Palace with the doge to handle any emergencies. They must have feared that the conspiracy would spread to Venice itself, especially as the travel time between the two cities was only six hours.[45] This resolution conveys, more clearly than any other, how the timeframe for decision-making had dramatically changed with the acquisition of the terraferma dominion.

On 18 March the Ten wrote to the rectors and to the two newly appointed special proveditors encouraging them to be diligent in their investigations, especially as the names of several notable persons had surfaced in connection with the conspiracy. The following day they wrote ordering them to inquire whether or not Marsiglio da Carrara was in the Trentino or elsewhere. By the next day, Carrara had been captured; and the Ten ordered his transfer under exceptionally heavy guard to Venice. They also voted rewards for the men who had revealed the conspiracy and the peasants who had helped capture some of the participants.[46]

The conspiracy itself focused on Marsiglio da Carrara, last legitimate descendant of the late ruler of Padua, Francesco Novello da Carrara. Marsiglio had made it his life's goal to retake the city, allying himself at various times with Sigismund and Visconti. The current plan, which had the tacit support of Visconti, was for Marsiglio's supporters inside the city to occupy the castle, open the city to him, and arrest the rectors and Venetian sympathizers. In addition, a squadron of troops under the command of Cristoforo da Tolentino and loyal to Visconti was to make its way to Padua to help the rebels. But snow delayed Marsiglio's descent on Padua from the Trentino and allowed time for informants to reveal the conspiracy to the Venetians. Marsiglio's attempt to escape north failed.[47]

On the 22nd the Ten authorized a special commission of four men to interrogate Marsiglio and torture him if need be. The day before, in thanksgiving for the successful thwarting of the plot, Foscari proposed and the Ten unanimously approved the distribution of 6 ducats each to twenty monasteries, churches, and hospitals in Venice and the lagoon, including the hospital of the Pietà dedicated to the care of orphans. Here again is evidence of Foscari's deeply felt personal piety.[48] But another aspect of his personality is revealed in another proposal he put forward on the 22nd. Apparently the preceding evening he had ordered a large group of noblemen who were lingering around the Ducal Palace to disperse. Given the air of suspicion and tension in the city and the approach of nightfall, this order made good sense; but the nobles ignored it. In response, Foscari proposed that the three heads of the Ten send for two or three of the recalcitrant nobles and interrogate them, and that the heads be authorized to deal with the other nobles as they saw fit. But Foscari's proposal received only 8 votes in favor. An alternative one, that the matter be dropped but that any nobles who lingered the current night get a sentence of one month in jail, similarly failed. Instead, the council approved a measure authorizing a committee to levy such penalties as it thought appropriate should nobles not exit the palace that evening or in the future.[49] Foscari's proposal indicates just how much the conspiracy had put him on edge.

As for Marsiglio, he confessed everything during a four-and-a-half-hour interview in the torture chamber. After hearing the evidence, the

Ten voted to condemn him as a traitor "who wished to take the dominion of our city of Padua from our hands." For some unknown reason,
six men abstained while eighteen voted in favor of the resolution.
However, when Foscari and many others proposed that Marsiglio be
beheaded between the columns of justice in Piazza San Marco, only two
members abstained. A number of Marsiglio's fellow conspirators were
also executed, including Giovanni da Milano, a familiar of Visconti. As
a warning their bodies were put on display at Fusina, the embarkation
point for boats heading to Padua. The Ten also condemned Ludovico
Buzzacarini to death and exiled his son Francesco to Crete. The Buzzacarini were one of Padua's most distinguished families and long-time
allies of the Carraresi.[50]

In the succeeding months Foscari continued to show concern for
affairs in Padua. On 6 April he proposed that the condottiere Taddeo
d'Este, who had arrived with his troops to help protect the city during
the conspiracy, be given the confiscated house of Ludovico Buzzacarini;
in so doing, Venice rewarded one of its most loyal captains and assured
that he would now have a personal stake in Padua's security. On the
27th of that same month the doge put forward procedures for the disposal of the rebels' goods. And when in May Marco Dandolo, podesta
of Padua, sought permission to return to Venice in order to attend a
court case filed against him, Foscari proposed that the case be delayed
since he did not want Padua left untended, "considering events that
recently occurred in our city of Padua."[51]

Noteworthy in all this is the degree of Foscari's personal involvement
in management of the Paduan conspiracy. He was fully engaged, making
decisions, ordering the distribution of alms, even trying to maintain order
and safety both in Padua and in Venice at the Ducal Palace. In his funeral
oration for Foscari, delivered more than twenty years later, Bernardo
Giustinian paid special tribute to the doge's action during those dangerous days, exclaiming of Foscari's actions in putting down the conspiracy, "Oh what singular presence of mind! Oh what admirable
swiftness!"[52] Certainly Foscari's concern was prompted by his recognition of Padua's strategic importance, but it also may have been motivated
by his own very personal attachments to the town. After all, his father
and uncle had been central in the original decision to conquer Padua.

In spite of Venetian efforts to pacify the city, many of Padua's citizens remained dissatisfied with Venetian rule.[53] In 1439 yet another con-

spiracy came to the surface. This one occurred during a time of renewed war with Milan, when much of the Veneto was overrun by Milanese troops. It involved an effort by Jacopo Scrovegni, a member of one of Padua's most distinguished families, to betray the city to Milan. Again Foscari took the lead, putting forward proposals in the Ten to secure the city and capture the conspirators. The Venetians placed a bounty on the escaped Scrovegni's head while it exiled others and confiscated their goods.[54] And in May 1456, just a year and a half before Foscari's death, the Ten became alarmed when they discovered that certain Paduan citizens were visiting in the city's cathedral a sculptured effigy reputed to be that of the late lord Francesco da Carrara. The Ten worried that this strange form of pilgrimage might incite discontent and so ordered the effigy removed from Padua as inconspicuously as possible and placed in their own armory for safekeeping. They also ordered inquiries to discover who had placed the image there and who went to see it.[55] More than half a century after its conquest by Venice, some in Padua remained nostalgic for the Carraresi and for Paduan independence. And those feelings lingered. During the war of the League of Cambrai in the early sixteenth century the Paduans were quick to throw off the Venetian yoke. Clearly, although the Venetians had conquered the mainland, they had not yet welded it solidly to the capital.

The death of Giovanna II, Queen of Naples, on 2 February 1435 further complicated the international situation: she had first named Alfonso V of Aragon who already possessed Sicily as her heir but then revoked the designation in favor of René, Duke of Anjou and Count of Provence. Visconti sided with René and sent the Genoese fleet to aid him. However, following a major naval victory at Ponza in August in which Alfonso was captured, Visconti infuriated the Genoese by releasing the prisoners. The Genoese rose in revolt against Milan, and the Venetians came to their assistance. Venice's new ally Sigismund also placed pressure on Visconti to restore Genoa's freedom and lands. Feeling the stress of the forces aligned against him, Visconti reached a peace accord with the pope and restored Imola to him.[56]

The goal of Venice and its allies at this point was the encirclement of Milan. And that goal seemed within reach when in May 1436 Genoa joined the League. Genoa's adherence also increased the strategic importance of Lombardy, particularly Brescia and Bergamo, whose possession by Venice isolated Visconti's troops in the north and impeded their movement south into Tuscany and the Romagna. This meant that Lombardy would be the primary field of military operations against Visconti and that the burden of the conflict would fall to Venice not Florence.[57]

Venice's concern with Brescia and Bergamo was manifest in a number of ways, especially as it sought to find the right men to serve as the rectors of those cities and their territories. When Benedetto Emo the captain of Bergamo died in June 1436, an interim proveditor was elected since the city was, as the Senate described it, "on the frontier and of the greatest importance and it is not good for there to be only one rector."[58] When in November the government needed to elect a new podesta of Bergamo, Foscari proposed that it be done by two nominating committees of the Great Council and a scrutiny of the Senate rather than through the normal procedure of four Great Council nominating committees. He also recommended the extraordinarily large salary of 1300 ducats in order to help ensure that an especially good candidate be found, since "the preservation of the said city is the preservation of our other Lombard lands."[59] In July the Ten investigated a plot to betray the castle at Brescia to Visconti, and in August the Senate forbade all castellans in Brescia and the Bresciano to leave their posts for any reason.[60]

But it was not until 1437 that the war really began to heat up. In mid-March Gianfrancesco Gonzaga, the commander of the Venetian forces, tried to take the fight to Visconti by crossing the Adda at Medolago west of Bergamo but was rebuffed. At this point, the goals of Venice and its ally Florence began to diverge. The Venetians and Genoese wanted to make an all-out assault on Milan. In fact in May the Senate sent instructions to Pietro Loredan, proveditor of the army, to encourage Gonzaga to pursue "the ruin and destruction of the Duke of Milan and his state." The Florentines, by contrast, were concerned with Piccinino's threats to Tuscany and wanted Sforza to concentrate his efforts there.[61]

In September Visconti launched a counteroffensive in Lombardy when his commander Piccinino moved his troops into the Bergamasco and took several castles. Finally Sforza responded to the threat by entering the Parmigiano.[62] But little came of these efforts, and on 28 October Gianfrancesco Gonzaga informed Venice that he wished to withdraw from Venetian service. The Republic sent Pietro Loredan as a special emissary to meet with him. Loredan had spent much of the year serving as a proveditor to the army, although he had had to withdraw in August on account of illness. Before going, he asked permission to take his son Jacopo with him on the mission; and the Senate granted him the favor in recognition of Loredan's "laudable mores and habits."[63] Noblemen were eager to include their sons on missions like this so that they could not only learn diplomatic protocol but also make valuable personal contacts. In this particular instance, however, Jacopo saw his father's mission fail. Gonzaga's relations with the Venetian proveditors had grown strained; and he may have feared that he was being lured back into Venetian service, only to be delivered the same fate as Carmagnola.[64] Fortunately for the Venetians, with the approach of winter Piccinino pulled his forces back from the Bergamasco. In late December they placed Gattamelata in command of their armies but refused him the title captain-general, designating him instead simply as "governor."[65]

The international situation was again thrown into chaos with the death on 9 December 1437 of Venice's former enemy and current ally Sigismund. For his part, Sforza returned with his forces to Tuscany, as Cosimo de' Medici made his way to Venice for consultation.[66] Cosimo's visit revealed just how much relations between the allies had deteriorated as their interests diverged. The Venetians were disturbed by the accord that the Florentines had reached with Visconti regarding Lucca and by Sforza's refusal to come to their aid in Lombardy. At this point, Sforza was already negotiating a possible return to the Milanese side; he did so in the hope that he might arrange an eventual marriage between himself and Visconti's daughter Bianca and thereby further his own territorial ambitions.[67] On 31 December the Senate debated how to respond to Sforza's failure to cross the Po and to Cosimo's demand that the Venetians pay their share of Sforza's stipend. Foscari and Antonio Contarini proposed a very immoderate response: they wanted Sforza to be informed via his emissary that he "is paid and obligated not only to the Florentines, but to the League, to which League and not to the Florentine he owes obedience; and that the Florentines are not and ought not to be considered the whole League." And they wanted Cosimo to know that in the opinion of the Venetians, Piccinino was using a ruse to draw Sforza back into Tuscany (and away from Lombardy) and that if Piccinino returned to Lombardy, then Sforza should return, without first getting the consent of the Florentines. But their proposal failed to pass in favor of one stating that, so long as Sforza refused to cross the Po, Venice would not pay any part of his stipend.[68] Foscari's proposal reveals that his personal relationship with Cosimo had worsened considerably since the days of Cosimo's exile in Venice when they were on the friendliest of terms. Vespasiano da Bisticci, the Florentine bookseller who composed a biography of Cosimo, reports that during his mission, Cosimo "grew to hate them [the Venetians] on account of their bad faith."[69] The clash of personalities between Cosimo and Foscari surely exacerbated the tension between the two allied republics. By contrast, Cosimo's personal relations with Sforza were cordial and strong.[70]

All the while, the Venetians were preparing for a visit by the Byzantine emperor John VIII and the Patriarch of Constantinople Joseph II, who were making their way to Ferrara on Venetian ships hired by the pope for a council designed to bring about a union of the Greek and Latin churches. Eugenius had transferred the council from Basel to Ferrara, over the objections and resistance of the majority of the delegates to Basel.[71] In December 1437 the Senate decided that it would house the patriarch at San Giorgio Maggiore and the emperor at the Marquess of Ferrara's palace at San Stae, also approving a proposal from Foscari and Luca Tron that the city spend 1000 ducats on hospitality.[72] The visitors arrived at San Niccolò on the Lido on 8 February. An advance party proceeded to the Ducal Palace to make arrangements for the formal entry and to inspect the accommodations the Venetians had provided. During the meeting with the advance party, Foscari informed the delegation that he planned to make a courtesy call on the emperor.[73]

Later that day Foscari and a group of nobles proceeded to the ships anchored near the Lido to greet the emperor and then the patriarch.[74] Various prelates and representatives of the pope also went to greet them both. Even though it was drizzling, the Byzantines' formal entry into Venice took place on Sunday 9 February. Foscari mounted the *bucintoro* for the trip to the Lido, accompanied by what Dolfin describes as "all the nobility of Venice" and a flotilla of other ships and boats. The *bucintoro* had been specially decorated for the occasion with imperial flags and other symbols, and the crew outfitted with costumes sporting both the lion of Saint Mark and the imperial eagle. On the top deck, the Venetians arranged various allegorical tableaux. Once at the Lido, Foscari and the Signoria transferred to the emperor's ship to greet him again.

The doge sat at the emperor's left while John's brother Demetrius sat on his right.[75] Silvester Syropoulos, a Greek prelate who kept a record of his trip to the Council of Ferrara, noted that Foscari used this occasion to present his younger son Domenico to the emperor. It is unclear why his older son Jacopo was not also introduced; perhaps he was away studying in Padua. The emperor then declined a request to transfer to the *bucintoro*, preferring instead to remain aboard his own galley. As he was hampered by physical infirmities perhaps he chose to do so in order to assert his dignity and retain his independence from Venetian control.[76] And so his ship, with the *bucintoro* in tow, made its way past San Marco and up the Grand Canal to the emperor's lodgings at the palace of the Marquess of Ferrara at San Giacomo dall'Orio, originally the palace of the Pesaro family and later presented to the Este family by the Venetian government. It is known today as the Fondaco dei Turchi (fig. 26).[77] Other palaces and monasteries were also commandeered into use as Venice had to supply accommodations for the more than nine hundred persons in the Byzantine delegation.

Over the next several days emissaries from the pope arrived in Venice to extend their greetings to the emperor, as did Niccolò d'Este, all of whom were formally received by Foscari as well. During the stay Foscari offered advice to the emperor regarding the conflict between the proponents of Basel and the pope and accompanied the patriarch on a tour of the treasures in San Marco.[78] The emperor remained in the city until 27 February while the patriarch lingered a few days longer; both then made their separate ways to Ferrara. The church council met in Ferrara from January 1438 until January 1439 before transferring to Florence in February 1439 and finally to Rome in 1443.

The imperial visit provided an important opportunity for the Venetians to show off their riches and power. The city's military might was put conspicuously on display as the imperial entourage passed the Arsenal on the way to Rialto and its spiritual wealth in the visit to San Marco. John's visit also offered Foscari the chance to assert the princely dignity of the ducal office by appearing on the civic stage in the company of an emperor. He also used the occasion to promote his son Domenico, much as Pietro Loredan had promoted his son Jacopo during his mission to Gonzaga. But Syropoulos reports that just days after Domenico's presentation to the emperor, the boy died, apparently of the plague. His death prompted Francesco Barbaro to compose a consolatory letter to the boy's brother Jacopo, expressing concern for the doge upon whose life and health the republic depended.[79] Fate had delivered Foscari yet another terrible blow: he was now left with only Jacopo, a startling fact for a man who had entered office so rich in sons. As often happened during his reign, personal losses accompanied Foscari's public triumphs.

Perhaps the doge took solace in the advancement of another of his relatives: the previous May Foscari's sister Elena had been installed as abbess of the venerable Benedictine convent of San Zaccaria. Situated not far from the Ducal Palace, San Zaccaria was arguably the city's most prestigious convent; and the nuns who called it home came from the most distinguished families. San Zaccaria also held special significance for the dogeship for it was the destination of one of the annual ducal *andate*. This one took place at Vespers on Easter Sunday and commemorated the legendary refuge which the ninth-century abbess Agostina Morosini offered Pope Benedict III. In recompense for the hospitality, the pope rewarded the nuns with a number of favors and gifts, including a jeweled crown, which Morosini subsequently presented to Doge Pietro Tradonico, whence originated (or so the story had it) the ducal *corno*. The Venetians used this story to invest the ducal office with yet another layer of sacrality since they could claim that the doge derived the *corno* ultimately from the pope. The *andata* itself consisted of a procession to San Zaccaria, followed by the hearing of Vespers and a visit to the tombs of the early doges buried at the church.[80]

Perhaps to commemorate her election as abbess, Elena donated 80 ducats of her own money in order to purchase a new organ for the monastery during her first year in office. She followed this up in subsequent years with a complete renovation of the chancel of the church, now known as the San Tarasio Chapel (fig. 19). The newly renovated apse, in the most current Gothic style, was decorated with frescos by Andrea del Castagno and Francesco da Faenza and furnished with three magnificent altarpieces at a total cost of 1874 ducats. The central altarpiece, which cost 180 ducats, was a gift of Elena and the prioress of the convent, Marina Donato, sister of Bartolomeo, while the other two were donated by the chamberlains Margarita Donato and Agnesina Giustinian. Although some of the images on the altarpieces commemorated the patrons (for example, the small statue of Saint Helen holding a cross on the right of the central altar), most were connected to relics housed in the church. Indeed, except for San Marco, no other Venetian church possessed relics of as many full bodies (as opposed to bits of bodies) as San Zaccaria. And so the altarpieces added lustre to the convent's reputation by emphasizing the nuns' special role "as custodians of civic as well as religious treasures."[81]

The rebuilding of San Zaccaria during the administration of Abbess Foscari was not the only building project undertaken in these years. Just north of the Rialto Bridge, nobleman Marino Contarini had recently completed construction of his fine Gothic palace, the Cà d'Oro on the bank of the Grand Canal; and in July 1437 the Scuola Grande di San Marco petitioned to build its new *albergo* (meeting hall) next to the recently consecrated Santi Giovanni e Paolo.[82] But Elena's additions to San Zaccaria added new distinction to what was already one of Venice's most important religious sites and gave it a Foscari overlay. Moreover, with Elena as abbess, Foscari's first cousin Polidoro as *primicerio* of San Marco and then (in 1437) as Bishop of Bergamo, and Marco as procurator *de citra*, the Foscari family had succeeded, perhaps as part of a political calculus, perhaps out of heartfelt piety, in placing themselves at the helm of some of the city's most important religious institutions. In November 1438 Marco and his colleague in the procuratorship *de citra* added to their already considerable portfolio of responsibilities when the Senate transferred to them jurisdiction over the Lazzaretto.[83] Regardless of their motives, these Foscari relatives lent further prestige to their kinsman the doge. This would have been particularly apparent during the annual *andata* to San Zaccaria, when Foscari was greeted by his own sister the abbess.

While chroniclers always took special note of such ceremonial occasions as the emperor's visit to Venice or the consecration of San Zanipolo, they did not bother to record the many daily, weekly, and annual responsibilities and rituals that absorbed much of Foscari's time as doge. In addition to attending all the most important councils, the doge had many other obligations. All these events made the dogeship a physically, intellectually, and at times emotionally taxing position. A few examples convey some sense of the burdens that Foscari (and other doges) dutifully bore. As outlined in the *promissione*, one of these was the supervision of the various administrative offices that made up the government. For instance, when it was discovered that thefts had occurred from the *ufficio alla messetteria*, an office that imposed taxes on various kinds of sales, Foscari proposed to the Senate that it be moved to a safer location.[84] The doge was also responsible for periodically visiting and overseeing Venice's main military establishment, the Arsenal. Thus in June 1437 he recommended to the Senate that a *proto* (master shipwright) named Niccolò Greco be placed in charge of the construction of all galleys, since his were determined to be of the best design.[85] Another ducal obligation was the supervision of the hospitals and other religious establishments that came under the doge's direct patronage. Therefore in November 1436 Foscari decided to award the small island of San Cristoforo, near Murano, to Fra Simone da Camerino, a member of the Augustinian order of Monte Ortone, so that he could establish a monastery there.[86] More generally, the doge was responsible for the overall welfare of the city. For this reason, in June 1437 Foscari made recommendations to help stabilize the city's declining population and boost the potters' guild.[87] Still another ducal responsibility, one which accorded well with the doge's princely position, was to hold a weekly audience and hear petitions for favors. One gains a sense of this from some of the bills that Foscari recommended – these clearly grew directly out of supplications to the doge. In April 1436, for example, Foscari made a proposal to the Senate that the Ospedale di San Marco be allowed to sell a number of properties that it owned at Muggia in Istria as their distance from Venice made them inconvenient for the hospital to administer. The money derived from the sale was to be invested instead in shares of the Monte.[88] In acts of February and April 1436, Foscari recommended that the community of San Giovanni in Croce, near Casalmaggiore, be remitted the tax that was usually collected on taverns there for two years: this would help cover expenses, including repair to the town's walls.[89] As all the above-mentioned examples illustrate, the doge's time was filled not only with decisions of international significance, but also with a dizzying variety of administrative tasks, many involving mundane matters affecting the lives of ordinary people.

The fact that the Venetians were loath to see any of these obligations lapse, despite the burden on the doge, was made clear when in May 1437 bad weather forced the cancellation of the annual marriage of the sea ceremony held on Ascension Day. In this ritual the doge traveled on the *bucintoro* to the Lido, where he tossed a ring into the waters while reciting the words, "We espouse thee, O sea, as a sign of true and perpetual dominion." This ritual served to substantiate Venice's claim to control of the Adriatic and its commercially valuable sea lanes. Because of the weather, the Senate decided to reschedule the ceremony for the following Sunday as they determined that it would not be "good for the honor and fame of our city and republic to abandon such an honorable custom." The Senate further ordered the ducal councilors to attend the rescheduled ceremony under penalty of a fine, but made an exception for Paolo Correr who was in mourning.[90]

The year 1438 began with Milan again on the offensive. In the spring Visconti's commander Piccinino attacked various cities of the Romagna, including Imola, Forlì, and Bologna; but most seriously for Venice, its protectorate Ravenna was betrayed to him. For his part, Sforza had reached an accord with Visconti by which the duke agreed to give his illegitimate daughter Bianca to Sforza in marriage and to name him his heir. With Sforza (and thus by extension Florence) neutralized for the moment, Visconti unleashed Piccinino on Venice and its territory. By late June he had captured several strongholds in the Cremonese, taken Casalmaggiore, and crossed the River Oglio.[91] His entry into the Mantovano was facilitated by Venice's former commander Gianfrancesco Gonzaga, who announced in July that he intended to join the Milanese side, despite offers of territory and the best efforts of Ambrogio Badoer. According to his pact with Visconti, Gonzaga would receive Verona and Vicenza once they were taken from Venice.[92] The Venetians responded to what they perceived as Gonzaga's betrayal, by placing all Mantuan merchants in their territory under arrest and confiscating their goods.[93]

Gonzaga's defection revealed the flaws in a military policy that relied on the loyalty of the smaller princely satellite states of Mantua and Ferrara.[94] The rupture with Mantua also exposed the Venetian state's flank, for now both Brescia and Verona were vulnerable to attack. Gonzaga moved his forces toward the Veronese, quickly taking Nogarola and positions near Legnago. Meanwhile Piccinino advanced into the Bresciano, taking Sirmione and Rivoltella on Lake Garda, other towns including Chiari and Soncino, and then establishing a siege of Brescia itself, a siege that would not be broken until 1440. Brescia was heroically defended by Taddeo d'Este and its rector Francesco Barbaro, the latter best remembered as an accomplished humanist and the author of *De re uxoria* (On wifely duties), dedicated in 1416 to Cosimo de' Medici's brother Lorenzo on the occasion of his marriage to Ginevra Cavalcanti.[95]

The Venetians reacted to the Milanese offensive in a variety of ways. On 6 July the Senate ordered the Collegio to meet daily in order to supervise affairs.[96] That same month Venice began to organize a huge Po fleet, which it placed under the veteran commander Pietro Loredan. Putting aside his differences with Loredan for the moment, Foscari proposed that the Senate accept Loredan's choices for ship captains.[97] And in August the Venetians were able to bind Niccolò d'Este to their side and secure his continuing military service and their safe transit of the Po by promising to restore to him the Polesine, a region long coveted by both states, which the Venetians held as surety for a loan they had made to Niccolò.[98] That same month they pursued negotiations to have Francesco Sforza rejoin their side; Sforza was increasingly frustrated with Visconti's delays in bringing about the marriage to Bianca; according to Sanudo, the impetus behind the overtures to Sforza came from Foscari himself.[99]

With the Milanese siege of Brescia deepening, in September Gattamelata executed a daring maneuver designed to secure Verona. He marched his troops out of Brescia and led them on a trek that took them through the rugged mountains around Lake Garda to the north, descending back onto the plains near Verona. Along the route, the Bishop of Trent's forces, allies of Visconti, harassed Gattamelata's army, which also had to contend with treacherous mountain trails and swift-flowing alpine streams. The humanist Giovanni Pontano compared Gattamelata's march with Hannibal's crossing of the Alps.[100] It certainly appeared a deed worthy of the ancients. The Venetians were so relieved that Gattamelata had managed his escape that they rewarded him generously. On 1 October the Senate finally agreed to designate him captain-general and arranged to have Marco Foscari and Paolo Tron convey to him the symbols of command. The Senate also voted to reward him with the palace in San Polo that had formerly been given to the commander Alvise dal Verme. They followed this up in July 1439 by granting him and his heirs admission to the Great Council.[101]

As for the Po fleet under Pietro Loredan, it finally sailed in late August. Two of Loredan's sons also contributed to this naval effort: Lorenzo was captain of the reconnaissance ships for the Po armada, while Jacopo was in charge of the ships patrolling the Adige.[102] In stark contrast, Foscari's son Jacopo appears to have had little or no career in arms and held no offices, instead performing certain ceremonial duties; in August, for example, he went with his uncle Marco as far as the parish of San Zulian in order to greet on their return the ambassadors whom Venice had sent to the newly elected Holy Roman Emperor.[103]

During the fall the Po armada saw little action, although Loredan's quick thinking saved the ships from being stranded when Gonzaga had the levies breached in order to lower the level of the river.[104] Then in October Loredan wrote asking to be relieved of his command on account of ill-health. Foscari and two others proposed in the Senate that Loredan be granted permission to repatriate and that a new captain be chosen in his place. The Senate accepted this proposal and elected Stefano Contarini as the new commander. Francesco Loredan and several others put forward an alternative, which among other things would have allowed one of Loredan's sons to command his flagship until the new admiral arrived, but this failed to pass.[105] The Loredans apparently were trying to position the next generation for positions of authority. On 26 October a gravely ill Pietro Loredan returned to Venice.[106]

On 11 November, at age sixty-six, Loredan died.[107] Venice's most distinguished homegrown military hero was gone. In his will he left explicit instructions regarding his funeral and burial. He asked to be buried at the Olivetan monastery of Sant'Elena, located on the eponymous island at the far eastern end of the city beyond the Arsenal. As for the funeral, he requested a simple affair: he wanted only the friars of Sant'Elena and the Jesuati of Sant'Agnese to attend and threatened malediction on his sons should they permit otherwise. He asked that his body be stripped of the accoutrements of power, that he be buried barefoot and with a stone for his pillow. He left 10 ducats for immediate payment to the monastery and another 60 to its building fund; his other charitable bequests included 30 ducats to be distributed to help dower the daughters of sailors. The previous June he had donated to the monastery a book containing the sermons of Pope Leo, bound in leather and embossed with the Loredan arms.[108]

But while humility characterized these particular legacies and wishes, Loredan's last will and testament also revealed his profound sense of personal pride and family honor. At the time of his death, Loredan had four sons: Jacopo, Paolo, Francesco, and Lorenzo. He left to them equally not only the balance of his estate, minus the various bequests he made, but also a gold reliquary which the Byzantine emperor had awarded him after his victory against the Turks at Gallipoli in 1416. It contained a trove of precious relics, including a piece of the true cross, a fragment of the Virgin's clothing, and bones of Saints Stephen and John Chrysostom. He commanded that the reliquary pass from male heir to male heir, "such that it always remain in our house." He similarly disposed of two flags or ensigns: the first, the flag of Saint Mark, he had received when he was elected captain-general in 1432; the second, the Genoese standard of Saint George, he had captured in 1431. The flags were among Loredan's most prized possessions and most likely were displayed in the main salon (*portego*) of his palace in San Canciano. In both instances, Loredan gave brief synopses of the victories in his will, including the number of ships engaged in the battles. Loredan wanted these symbols of his military prowess and imperial favor to remind future generations of the family of their illustrious ancestor and spur them on to similar deeds.[109] Pietro's son Jacopo, in his will dated 1471, passed these items on to his own son Antonio.[110]

Although Loredan left explicit instructions regarding his funeral, he made no mention of his tomb or how he wished it to be decorated. In all likelihood it was marked by a simple inscription in keeping with his injunction that his funeral be humble. But when Jacopo died in 1471, his sons Antonio and Pietro had an elaborate floor tomb constructed. It no longer exists; it was removed in the nineteenth century and subsequently lost. But its appearance is known from a drawing made by Jan Grevembroch in the 1750s (fig. 20). It consisted of an elaborately carved rectangular marble floor slab, with a leafy border. Sculpted in the center of the slab were the recumbent figures of Pietro and his son Jacopo, set within a simple arch supported by slender columns with Corinthian capitals. In the spandrels were the Loredan arms. Both men were depicted in armor from head to toe; and both wore breastplates decorated with the winged lion of Saint Mark. The only notable variation between the figures was in the decorative border around the lions. The men's heads rested on cushions under which were halberds, while a pole with two small flags of Saint Mark separated their figures. An inscription above the effigies recounted and commemorated their victories.

The Loredan family chose to remember these two illustrious kinsmen primarily as warriors. Although the epitaph briefly mentioned that both held the post of procurator of San Marco, the martial element predominated. Stylistically, the tomb seems retardataire, despite the rectangular form and Roman-style arch. The effigies, decked out as they are in full armor, appear to take inspiration from soldier tombs of an earlier age. This is particularly striking given that the tomb is unlikely to date from earlier than 1471, the year of Jacopo's death. Venice was engaged in the 1470s in war with the Turks, a period of national emergency. This tomb suggests that the Loredans wished to locate their ancestors within a long-standing familial and civic tradition of naval sacrifice for the good of the state.

Sanudo reports that the city was deeply saddened by Loredan's death.[111] One can only speculate how Foscari reacted to the demise of his long-time rival, the man whose career path and personality differed so markedly from his own. But certainly the disputes and rivalries that characterized their earlier years continued right up to the end and eventually prompted unfounded rumors of foul play. What is true is that over the years Foscari and members of the Loredan family had come into conflict over issues great and small that festered and apparently soured relations between them. In November 1433, for example, the syndics of the Levant prosecuted Daniele Loredan, former *bailo* (governor) and captain of Negroponte, for corruption. It was Foscari who proposed the harshest penalty for Loredan, namely that he spend a year in jail, pay 800 ducats in fines and restitution, and be deprived of offices for five years. The Senate accepted his recommendation; this cannot have gone down well with the Loredans.[112] In another incident during February 1435, the commune of Brescia sent appeals to the government in Venice over certain rulings made by the rectors Ludovico Storlado and Francesco Loredan, nephew of Pietro. Foscari proposed that one of Brescia's appeals be granted. Loredan may have interpreted this as undercutting his action.[113] Foscari and Francesco Loredan locked horns again in May that year when Loredan was serving as one of the three heads of the Council of Ten. A dispute arose between the doge and the heads over access to records of sodomy cases which were held for safekeeping in the offices of the procurators of San Marco. Perhaps the heads of the Ten wished to reopen a case that might prove embarrassing to Foscari or his allies. In 1433, for example, Alvise Foscari, son of Filippo, was involved as the victim in what appears to have been a sodomy case.[114]

Conflict between the two families could splash over in surprising ways into other disputes between nobles. On 17 November 1438, for example, a meeting of the Senate got out of hand when, according to the Ten, several nobles said "ugly and dishonest" things about other members. The Ten were so disturbed by the incident that they convened a *zonta* to help investigate the case. What had occurred was this: during this critical war year, there was a shortage of grain in the city; a rumor apparently began circulating that Niccolò d'Este had granted noblemen Orsato Giustinian and Daniele Vitturi special privileges that allowed them to ship and hoard grain. This is what got mentioned in the Senate. On the 26th the Ten issued an order forbidding disruptive words or deeds in council meetings that might endanger the state. They also sent a letter to the newly appointed captain-general of the Po fleet, Stefano Contarini, to investigate the charges. But perhaps most disturbing of all was the accusation that the recently deceased Loredan had known about the contract but done nothing to stop it.[115]

On 9 December the Ten ruled that the charges were false, that Giustinian and Vitturi had been publicly defamed, and that the result was scandalous not only for them but for their "relatives and friends." Now in order that their good names (*fama*) might be restored, and "so that ensuing hatreds and rancor might be completely removed and stopped," Leonardo Contarini and Ermolao Donato, two of the heads of the Ten, proposed that Foscari speak to the Senate; using "such good and pertinent words as his wisdom dictates," he should declare the truth, namely that Giustinian and Vitturi were innocent and without guilt. Yet in what is most likely a symptom of how bad relations had become, Foscari did not want to make such a public statement; he proposed instead that one of the heads of the Ten give it. But neither proposal got the necessary votes. When the Ten took up the matter again on 11 December, however, Contarini and Donato's proposal did pass by a vote of 17 to 4 with 2 abstentions. On that same day the *zonta* was dissolved.[116]

This incident is significant for a number of reasons. First, it indicates that the strains of the war effort were eroding the façade of civility within the councils and opening or reopening long-standing tensions and rivalries within the patriciate. Indeed, just a few months before, the same Orsato Giustinian had had words with nobleman Paolo Tron (the topic is not known).[117] The decorum of meetings was being badly breached. Second, it suggests that these personal insults were taking an ominous turn as they came to be perceived as injurious not only to the individuals involved, but also, as the Ten noted, to their networks of relatives and friends. At this moment, Venice seemed to be on a very dangerous path, one taken by many Italian cities before, namely the road to factionalism.

The Loredans, with their tradition of military service, may have had a keener sense of family solidarity and honor than other Venetian elite families, making them especially prone to allow insults or slights to escalate into something serious. Sanudo is reported to have observed that the Loredans "never forgot or forgave a wrong."[118] This seems likely for two years after the grain-hoarding incident, the Great Council debated whether or not to reduce the number of votes needed to grant a pardon to Giovanni della Colona, who had in some way injured Domenico Loredan. The proposal was that the number of votes for a pardon should be lowered, provided that Domenico and his relatives forgive and make peace with della Colona. However, the proposal was roundly defeated by a vote of 107 in favor versus 439 against and 52 abstentions – this despite the preamble having declared that a recent victory in the war with Visconti made this a propitious time to show mercy.[119]

Exacerbating the problem of division even further was Foscari's own behavior. Rather than assuming a neutral position, Foscari seems to have plunged into these conflicts, often taking sides. Sanudo reports, for example, that when Giustinian and Tron had words in August, Foscari drew advantage from the spectacle.[120] He could have enveloped himself in the sacral aura of the ducal office, served as a kind of disinterested arbiter, and thus eased tensions. But he resisted that role; as noted above, he did not even want to be the one to exonerate publicly Giustinian and Vitturi, perhaps because he had lingering doubts about their innocence or perhaps because the rumors also involved his old rival Loredan. On one level, of course, Foscari's behavior is understandable. He was deeply, even passionately, engaged in the issues and wished to make his opinions known. Furthermore, the doge was not expected to be neutral, a mere figurehead above the fray. Yet during these stressful times, Foscari contributed to rather than ameliorated the problems. In July he himself insulted Tommaso Duodo during Senate deliberations.[121] Yet there is no evidence to support the fantastical rumor put forward in later centuries that Foscari had Pietro Loredan poisoned. As discussed in chapter 6 below, this is a later interpolation by historians and chroniclers intent on explaining subsequent events in Foscari's reign but in fact illuminating the values of their own times.[122]

At this very moment of wartime crises and internal divisions Foscari, drawing on imperial and chivalric traditions, determined to assert himself by offering a new and more complex vision of the dogeship. It was on 10 November, just one day before Loredan's death, that the *provveditori al sal e sopra Rialto* (the Salt Officers), administrators officially in charge of major public works involving the Ducal Palace, signed a contract with the stonemasons Giovanni and Bartolomeo Bon to construct the new entryway into the palace, the Porta della Carta. The decision to begin work on the gateway almost certainly indicates that the extension of the palace along the length of the Piazzetta was nearing completion and that the entry system into the palace could now be reorganized and systematized.

The fact that the contract was signed by the Salt Officers raises the complex issue of how to understand Foscari's agency in this (and similar) commissions. In this regard it is important to recall that he was prohibited by the terms of his *promissione* from spending more than 100 *lire di piccoli* a year for work on the Ducal Palace. As a result, any major project he wanted carried out on the palace had (according to the *promissione*) to be approved by at least five of the ducal councilors, the three heads of the Forty, at least thirty votes within the Council of Forty, and two-thirds of the members of the Great Council. Prior approval was intended as a safeguard against extravagant spending and over-reaching attempts by doges to advance their image.[123] However, a politician as skillful as Foscari was more than capable of securing governmental approval for projects he advocated, especially when they promised to advance the reputation of Venice itself. In Florence, Cosimo de' Medici and his grandson Lorenzo the Magnificent both frequently worked their will through building commissions with a decidedly republican tint.[124]

During the preceding years there had been, in addition to construction of the Foscari wing, work on a number of lesser projects on the complex around the Ducal Palace and San Marco. In June 1436, for instance, a fire forced the reconstruction of the shops around the campanile of the church.[125] It was precisely the need to obviate the danger of fire that led the Senate in December 1437 to authorize the Salt Officers to reconstruct the vaults in the prisons housed within the Ducal Palace. The palace housed a whole complex of prisons, including one for women. Previously the vaults had been made of wood, but now the Senate wanted them rebuilt in more fire-resistant stone.[126] The Senate's concern with the palace prisons serves as a salutary reminder that the Ducal Palace of the fifteenth century was not the staid and rather sterile place it is today but a bustling governmental complex: it housed not only the apartments of the doge and his family, but also governmental offices and council halls, as well as a large staff of stewards, ushers, house-keepers, and personal retainers, such as the ducal barber.[127] In having, for example, a bakery and an adjoining room in which the doge's bakers slept, the palace was not very different from princely residences in other states, such as the palaces at Urbino or Mantua; the exception was that it housed no stables.

In Venice the Ducal Palace also had considerable defensive capability, an aspect of the complex that historians seldom take into account. Indeed, historians and art historians often draw attention to the fortress-like architecture of such governmental centers as the Castello Sforzesco in Milan or even the Palazzo Vecchio in Florence, contrasting their for-bidding features with the seemingly open and welcoming exterior of the Ducal Palace, characterized by its graceful arcade and elegant tracery. But to do so is to misapprehend a central feature of the palace, for once the gateways were secured, it was easily defendable; furthermore, its wells and stores of food and wine made it possible for the inhabitants to with-stand a siege. Disgruntled sailors learned just how secure the palace was when, in November 1436, they tried unsuccessfully to force their way inside.[128] Moreover, the Ten maintained a substantial armory, so that the palace was well equipped with weapons. During military shortages, whenever the Ten dispatched cuirasses and other items from the palace's cache to troops in need, they would ensure that the stocks were replen-ished.[129] The Ducal Palace was in every sense the nerve center of the Venetian government.

The contract that the Salt Officers Tommaso Malipiero, Antonio Marcello, Paolo Valaresso, and Marco Moro drew up with Giovanni Bon and his son Bartolomeo for the Porta della Carta is the only one that has survived for a Foscari project. According to the terms of the agree-ment, the officers agreed to pay the Bons 1700 ducats. They would also supply much of the stone needed for the construction, including that for the piers and lintel and some of the marble for the sculpted figures, while for their part the Bons agreed to follow the design which they had presented to the Salt Officers and supply the balance of the stone needed for the project. In addition, the contract spelled out in writing several of the elements that were to be included in the project, namely that the father and son team would create a figure of Saint Mark in the "form of a lion" and an arched window with tracery, and that they would surmount the portal with a figure of Justice. On this last point, the Bons agreed that they would make the figure of Justice single- or double-sided, depending on the wishes of the officers. They likewise agreed to give all the work a polished finish, supervise the transport of the materials to the site, and complete the project within eighteen months.[130] At the time the contract was executed the Bons were among Venice's most distinguished stone carvers, having worked on Marino Contarini's Cà d'Oro and for the Scuola Grande di San Marco.[131]

In the Porta della Carta, which derives its name either from the fact that paper was sold in the vicinity or in acknowledgement of the governmental offices located nearby, the Bons created an elaborate architectural and sculptural ensemble (plate 6).[132] The entry is framed by two composite piers of white *pietra d'Istria* and red *pietra di Verona* with inlays of *verde antico* that are joined at the top by a mixtilineal arch – the same form used in the altarpiece in the Chapel of the Madonna. The upper portion is filled by a three-light window with elaborate quatrefoil tracery; the lower section by a large rectangular doorway. The decoration, which strikes "both a festive and a triumphal note," combines major as well as minor sculptural elements.[133] The niches of the piers contain figures of the active or cardinal virtues Temperance (in the lower left), Prudence (in the upper right), and Fortitude (in the lower right) as well as the chief contemplative or theological virtue Charity (in the upper left niche). Just below the elaborate finials are two sets of putti presenting the ducal coat of arms, the Foscari family arms surmounted by the ducal *corno*. A tondo of Saint Mark carved in white Carrara marble and supported by three angels carved of the same material is set into the arch. The outside of the arch is embellished with putti who frolic among gracefully swaying acanthus foliage. The interior Gothic arch is decorated with alternating lion heads and an inlaid lozenge pattern. A figure of Justice (the fourth cardinal virtue) seated on a lion throne caps the entire structure. She holds a sword in one hand and scales in the other. The wall behind the figure of Justice is a later addition; originally the statue stood clear against the sky. Finally, in the rectangular frame is a figure of Foscari kneeling before the winged lion. It is a nineteenth-century copy, the original having been destroyed in the aftermath of the

French Revolution (see chapter 6 below), although the portrait head was preserved (fig. 21). Initially some parts of the structure were painted and others gilded.

The date for the completion of the Porta della Carta remains uncertain as the sources provide bits of contradictory evidence. In his chronicle Dolfin states that "the portal of the Ducal Palace of the city of Venice, adorned as you can see was completed in 1439," while Sanudo says that the work began at this time but that it was completed under Doge Cristoforo Moro.[134] These statements are always cited as referring to the Porta della Carta; however, judging from Sanudo's mention of Doge Moro, it may be that he somehow conflated the Porta della Carta and another project, the Arco Foscari, whose superstructure was completed under Moro. Moreover, both Dolfin and Sanudo refer to the portal as the "porta del palazzo ducal," whereas the contract and a subsequent addendum describe it as the "porta granda del palazzo." Uncertainty persists, but what is securely known is that the Bons failed to meet the sixteen-month deadline: in April 1442 they promised the Salt Officers that they would finish the remaining work on the structure, namely the tops of the piers, the angels surrounding the tondo of Saint Mark, the tracery of the window and "the other figures." Should they fail to do so within a year, the officers would fine them 100 ducats.[135] It is likely that they missed this deadline as well, given that Giovanni died during the summer of 1443 and only Bartolomeo incised his name on the lintel.[136]

In the Porta della Carta, the Bons' skill, the Salt Officers' financing, and Foscari's impetus combined to create a majestic entryway into the Ducal Palace, what the poet Jacopo d'Albizzotto Guidi referred to as "a royal gate" (una porta rial).[137] Architecturally, the portal needed to fulfill three functions: it had to present a visually satisfying transition between the basilica of San Marco and the Ducal Palace; to provide a functionally well-defined threshold between the expansive piazza and the more circumscribed interior courtyard of the palace; and to make a suitably grand impression on those entering the palace, both nobles coming to attend council meetings and foreign dignitaries. It accomplished the first by incorporating architectural and decorative elements from both the church and palace. For example, the putti cavorting among the acanthus foliage echo the Gothic accretions to the façade of the church, while the quatrefoil tracery repeats in more elaborate form the central motif of the palace's second-floor loggia. The second was achieved by making the portal a liminal or transitional space by means of its slightly recessed position and well-defined rectangular doorway. And the grandeur was realized through the creation of an entryway that evoked both the sacral and temporal bases of Venetian power. The Porta combined the sacred form of a tabernacle with the rudiments of the twin-tower gateway, an antique architectural type undergoing a revival at the time in Italy, especially in the Kingdom of Naples.[138] The double representation of Saint Mark in both human and lion form reminded those entering the palace that the city was under the special protection of the evangelist, while the figure of Justice reiterated the theme of the Judgement of Solomon found on the corner of the palace.

But certainly the most innovative and striking element of the design was the glorification of Foscari himself. The four virtues in the niches celebrate his personal virtues, not those of the government. That is certainly how Francesco Sansovino understood them when he wrote in 1581 that the statues represented "le virtù nobili del Principe Foscari;" and in fact these same virtues would eventually reappear on Foscari's tomb.[139] They are arranged on the Porta della Carta so that Charity, the chief theological virtue, and Prudence, which according to some schemes was the chief cardinal virtue, enjoy pride of place in the top niches while Temperance and Fortitude (the latter was believed to encompass magnanimity) are placed below them.[140] The singling out of Charity among the three theological virtues is in keeping with Foscari's piety and charitable concerns. The double set of putti presenting the Foscari ducal arms serve as unmistakable identifiers. Most remarkable of all is the statue of Foscari kneeling before the winged lion, which forcefully evokes Foscari's persona. Although the lines may have been recut by a restorer, the face is startlingly realistic.[141] It shows an aging Foscari with heavily furrowed brow, baggy eyes, sagging jowls, and neck muscles that overhang the string of the *camauro*, the skullcap worn under the *corno* (fig. 21). The portrayal is of Foscari the man, not an idealized figure of a doge.

It is not known when or even if the original plan for the Porta della Carta was modified to incorporate the statue of Foscari. As noted above, the contract made no mention of such a statue; it specified merely that the Bons would create a Saint Mark "in forma di liom [*sic*]." The doge and lion group, as such ensembles have come to be known, evokes several different themes in Venetian political ideology. The inscription on the book held in the lion's paw (*Pax tibi Marce evangelista meus*) records the first words that an angel spoke to Mark in the dream in which he learned that Venice would be his final resting place. That angelic visitation announced Venice's predestination to greatness under Mark's protection, a theme that was redolent with meaning at this time of terraferma expansion. The figure of the doge kneeling with the *vexillum* serves as a visual reminder of the coronation ceremony in which he was invested with the symbols of power. The message of such groupings is unmistakable: the doge is specially chosen by and derives his power from Mark. If as one authority claims, "gates most of all displayed sovereignty," then Foscari was clearly sovereign.[142] Art historians continue to debate whether or not the first occasion on which a doge and lion group was assembled was for the Porta della Carta; if not, its antecedents did not match it in size or visual impact.[143] From its installation on, all those entering the Ducal Palace were reminded not simply of the place of the dogeship in the Venetian governmental system, but also of the power and greatness of Foscari himself. Into the delicate balance of Venetian politics Foscari added new weight on the side of ducal power. Perhaps in recognition of this fact, the humanist Filippo Morandi da Rimini described Foscari in his *Carmen* of 1440–41 as "dux augustus."[144]

But the full impact of Foscari's innovation in the Porta della Carta can be understood only by recognizing that it was simply one component of an entirely reconceived entry-system for the Ducal Palace. For it caps a passageway known both as the Porticato Foscari and the Portico della Carta, which now leads to the space directly in front of the late fifteenth-century Scala dei Giganti (fig. 22). The portico consists of six groin-vaulted bays, with medallions of the four evangelists capping the middle vaults; a door at one of those middle vaults served as an important ceremonial entry into San Marco for the doge and dogaressa. This covered portico predated the Porta della Carta and apparently was reworked so as to incorporate it into the new entry-system.[145] Another change was the addition of a covered staircase (now destroyed but visible in a print of 1590 by Cesare Vecellio), known as the Scala Foscara, which abutted the portico and led to the upper floors of the Ducal Palace (fig. 23).[146] The construction of this stairway concealed any loggia-like functions originally performed by the portico and transformed it more clearly into a passageway. The building of the Scala Foscara thus shifted the north–south orientation of the palace complex (running from San Marco to the Great Council Hall) to an east–west axis (linking Piazza San Marco to the ducal quarters of the palace) and thereby creating a "ducal thoroughfare" or "via triumphalis."[147]

Yet another monument, the Arco Foscari, punctuated the other end of this royal way (plate 7). The Arco as it now stands is the product of at least three different building campaigns. The Foscari stage of the project consists of the solid but graceful ground-floor rounded arch with alternating bands of white *pietra d'Istria* and red *pietra di Verona*. The Foscari arms adorn the spandrels (plate 8). During the Foscari phase, the monument terminated at this level and was in all likelihood surmounted by a balustraded balcony. The arch represented in the mosaic of *The Dormition of the Virgin* in the Chapel of the Madonna offers some idea of how the original structure might have appeared (fig. 16). The monument achieved "a Roman arch effect while remaining within the native Gothic tradition."[148]

In all this, Foscari created an entry system for the governmental center which offered a new vision of the Venetian state and its princely ruler. Henceforth visitors to the Ducal Palace entered by means of a triumphal way, with all its associations of imperial might. The incorporation of antique design elements, including the use of the twin tower gateway in the Porta della Carta and the triumphal arch in the Arco Foscari reinforced this idea of a Roman imperial revival. In this way, Venice was able to lay claim to a Roman inheritance and in so doing, to match or even trump the Roman pedigree of its subject cities on the terraferma. At the same time, Gothic elements persisted, especially in the flamboyant tracery of the Porta window, the rib-vaults of the Porticato, and the *pietra d'Istria* and *di Verona* colonettes of the Arco. In so doing, Venice succeeded in quoting an architectural language that was popular in the former signorial regimes, as evidenced, for example, by the flamboyant tombs of the Scaligeri in Verona. The result of all this was a curious amalgam – a Roman inheritance projected through the lens of chivalric traditions, what has felicitously been dubbed in reference to intellectual developments in the city of Ferrara, "gothic humanism."[149]

Although Foscari had no official role as patron as the Salt Officers technically paid for the project, the stamp of his personality is unmistakable here. And what the new entryway did was to elevate the place of the dogeship and emphasize its princely aspects. After all, the layout of the system now emphasized the ducal apartments rather than the council halls, and triumphal entries were the prerogative of generals and emperors. One wonders whether Carmagnola's desire to build a vaulted tower to commemorate his victory at Maclodio inspired Foscari to build this gateway connected to a vaulted passageway. Whatever the answer, Venice's newly appointed imperial vicar was drawing on an imperial architectural vocabulary. Just as significantly, the decoration of the Porta and Arco celebrated not just the abstract qualities of the ducal office, but Foscari himself. This was made clear in the conspicuous use of the Foscari coat of arms and especially in his sculpted portrayal. With only slight exaggeration, Garry Wills observes that "with Foscari's image [on the Porta della Carta], Renaissance humanism has arrived in Venice, and with it the lone heroic leader."[150] The logical terminus for the entryway was the Scala dei Giganti, commissioned and built by the Barbarigo doges Marco (1485–86) and Agostino (1486–1501), since it is the fullest architectural statement of Venice's Roman imperial inheritance and of ducal aggrandizement. It is certainly no coincidence that the obverse of Foscari's portrait medal reproduces the figure of Justice incorporated into the façade of the Ducal Palace or that it is inscribed with the words "VENETIA MAGNA" (fig. 9): under Foscari, both Venice and the doge had achieved new levels of greatness.

Despite a number of setbacks during the next phase of the war, Venetian forces continued to perform extraordinary feats aspiring to confirm that new magnitude. The most spectacular took place during the winter of 1438–39 in what was an effort to relieve the still-besieged city of Brescia, valiantly defended by Francesco Barbaro. The only safe way to get supplies to the city was by way of Lake Garda, but direct access to the lake via the River Mincio was blocked by Milanese forces. And so the Venetians adopted an audacious plan by the Cretan engineer/shipwright Niccolò Sorbolo to transport ships over the mountains from the Adige to the lake. The fleet, including a large number of small craft and between two and five galleys, traveled up the Adige as far as Mori a few kilometers south of Rovereto. The ships were then hauled by oxen overland: they went up Monte Baldo, along a specially built causeway, and were then lowered in "a perfect prodigy of mechanical skill" by means of pulleys, ropes, and cables, and conveyed to Torbole on

Lake Garda, whence they were launched. All this took place in the depths of winter. The spectacle of ships traversing snow-covered mountains symbolized Venetian determination to retain Brescia while seeming to defy nature itself. It remained fixed in the Venetian imagination; in the late sixteenth century a painting by Tintoretto and his workshop celebrating Stefano Contarini's eventual victory over the Milanese on Lake Garda was affixed to the walls of the Great Council Hall.[151]

In the spring of 1439 Piccinino again took the offensive. His forces overran the Veronese, capturing such towns as Legnago and Lonigo. Part of the blame for this fell on Andrea Donato, at the time proveditor to the army, who counseled against meeting Visconti's troops head on, despite the fact that Gattamelata had a major force at his disposal. As recounted shortly, the state attorneys eventually prosecuted Donato for his role in this defeat, despite Foscari's efforts to gloss over the matter as a way of shielding his son-in-law.[152] More positively for Venice, it renewed its alliance with Florence, the pope, Ferrara, and Sforza, and after much negotiation secured an agreement with Sforza to return to its service and aid Gattamelata in the task of clearing the Vicentino and Veronese of enemy forces. In June the Senate voted to accept Foscari's proposal that Sforza be sent the flags of Venice, Florence, and Genoa, while turning down an alternative proposal by the *savi del consiglio* to send only one with the insignia of Florence and Genoa emblazoned on it.[153]

The arrival of Sforza restored the initiative in the war to the Venetians. But just as suddenly, as if in a replay of relations with Carmagnola, the Venetians found themselves again with a condottiere in the driver's seat; indeed in a very real sense Sforza had become the arbiter of the war.[154] His monthly stipend of 1700 florins virtually equaled the entire sum that the Salt Officers agreed to pay the Bons for their work on the Porta della Carta, a comparison that puts into sobering perspective both the cost of military operations and outlays on architecture.[155] Furthermore, the Senate constantly sought to flatter Sforza, as when in May it described his wisdom as "our sole and only refuge and remedy for the conservation and reintegration of our state." They curried his favor, writing, for example, to Tommaso Malipiero, who had been with Sforza inquiring whether Sforza's "woman" (*femena*) – presumably his mistress since he was not yet married to Bianca – would prefer receiving the gift of a jewel or some gold cloth. The answer was cloth, which was then sent to Sforza via Giovanni Pisani.[156] Just as in the case of Carmagnola, the Venetians sought to meet Sforza's various demands and to spur him to further action with promises of territory. They acceded, for example, to his request that Pisani stay on as proveditor to the army. And when on 30 July the Senate voted to congratulate him for his campaign in the Veronese, they promised him Mantua or Cremona, or, if he should cross the Adda, the biggest prize of all, Milan.[157]

The conspiracy mentioned above, involving Jacopo Scrovegni's attempt to hand over Padua to the Milanese, occurred during this stressful summer, in August 1439. Had it succeeded, it would have dealt a crushing blow to Venetian efforts to regain control of its Veneto dominions. In September the Venetians suffered a very real strategic and psychological loss, what Dolfin called "a great defeat," when the Milanese bested Venice's Garda fleet, the one they had so heroically transported over the mountains the previous winter. A number of Venetian noblemen, including the commander Pietro Zeno, were taken prisoner.[158] But the government quickly resolved to rebuild the force, although this time it wisely decided not to challenge nature twice, but instead to transport the building materials to the lakeshore and assemble the ships there. The preamble to the Senate's decision invoked the aid of Jesus, the Virgin, and Saint Mark in undertaking this rebuilding project in order to restore Venice's lost "honor and reputation" and to aid Brescia.[159] Apparently this supernatural help was forthcoming: on 9 November the Milanese suffered a major defeat of their own at the castle of Tenno when they tried to intercept a Venetian force attempting to relieve Brescia. A number of important Milanese commanders were captured, including Carlo Gonzaga, Cesare Martinengo, and Sagrimoro Visconti. Piccinino himself managed to escape. Gattamelata and Sforza immediately dispatched a letter announcing the good news to Foscari; it arrived on the 10th. On the morning of the 11th the doge attended a special thanksgiving Mass in San Marco and a victory procession followed. A more elaborate victory celebration attended by the clergy and flagellant confraternities was held on the 15th.[160]

But the tide turned just as quickly again on the 17th, when the citadel of Verona was betrayed to Piccinino and Gianfrancesco Gonzaga. Mantuan sympathizers rushed about crying "Gonzaga," but Sforza and Gattamelata hurried to the city and managed to retake it within two days. According to Dolfin, the Veronese assisted the Venetian forces, crying "Marco, Marco," since they did not wish to pass under the tutelage of Gonzaga, as the agreement with Visconti for the division of captured territory stipulated. In thanksgiving, the Veronese voted to pay Sforza 10,000 ducats and Gattamelata 3000, although they apparently did so at the insistence of Andrea Donato.[161] For its part, Venice rewarded Sforza by presenting to him the Palace of the Two Towers on the Grand Canal in the parish of San Pantalon. This was fitting because it was the palace that the government had purchased in 1430 and donated to the turncoat Gonzaga but then confiscated after his defection. Venice also honored Sforza with membership in the Great Council.[162] In December 1439 the Ten authorized its heads to enter into negotiations regarding a plan to poison Gonzaga, Piccinino, and Alvise dal Verme, justifying the decision by claiming that it would contribute to the "quiet and peace" of "all Italy."[163]

As this brief account of military operations in 1439 indicates, the momentum in the war swung back and forth like a pendulum, the objectives of the parties, including allies, too varied and their forces too evenly matched for either side to win a definitive victory. It would still be a number of years more before the parties would reach the conclusion that continuing warfare was bankrupting their states and ultimately futile. The military campaign of 1439 was also Gattamelata's last. In late December he suffered a stroke while at Torbole overseeing the preparation of the new Garda fleet. It left him paralyzed and unable to speak. He was transported first to Verona and then to Padua and eventually to the baths at Siena. But in November 1440 he suffered another debilitating stroke. The Republic nevertheless continued to honor him with the title of captain-general and a yearly stipend of 1000 ducats. He lingered until January 1443 and was buried as he requested in Padua at the church of Sant'Antonio, known as the Santo. The humanist Lauro Querini gave the funeral oration, and Giovanni Pontano gave a second one a few days later.[164]

Compared with condottieri of unbounded ambition and pride – such as Piccinino, Sforza, and Carmagnola – Gattamelata was a reliably hardworking and resourceful mercenary captain and a trustworthy and relatively modest man. The modesty is most apparent in the way he handled his relations with Sforza. Once it became clear in early 1439 that the Venetians were anxious to reemploy the younger man, questions arose concerning the titles they should hold. When Sforza was granted the title of captain-general of the League, Gattamelata acceded to the lesser denomination of governor of the Venetian forces, although he eventually received the title captain-general of the Venetian forces.[165] This is not to say that Gattamelata was not concerned with his own emoluments and reputation, merely that he was a realist who did not let overweening pride sour relations with his employers. But in the end he got unwitting revenge on Sforza by means of the equestrian statue by Donatello that his son Giovanantonio had erected in front of the Santo at a cost of 1650 ducats – that statue continues to stand in his memory (fig. 24).[166] It shows him in the pose of a Roman emperor, majestically wielding the baton of command. Of course, even in this respect Sforza nearly trumped Gattamelata for his son Ludovico, known as il Moro, commissioned an even larger equestrian statue of his father by no less an artist than Leonardo da Vinci. But it was never actually cast since the bronze was confiscated, appropriately enough, to make cannons, thereby securing the place of Gattamelata's statue as the most famous equestrian monument of the Italian Renaissance.

During the first part of 1440 the theater of war shifted back to Tuscany and the Romagna as Visconti dispatched Piccinino to those regions.[167] As Florence's situation grew more and more precarious, it sent ambassadors to Venice urging Sforza's assistance. According to Sanudo, in April Foscari again gave a very undiplomatic response to the Florentine demands, saying that he did not believe that the Tuscan city was in as dire straits as its ambassadors portrayed. He based his view on the fact that Pope Eugenius, who was by nature a fearful man, was still in Florence and had not written to Venice about the urgent need for Sforza's aid. Nor for that matter had Venice's ambassador in Florence. In addition, Foscari noted that the Bishop of Padua, Pietro Donato, another timid man, continued to reside in Florence as did many other prelates. They were there attending the church council, which had transferred from Ferrara to Florence in early 1439. Lastly, Foscari threatened that Venice would stop paying its share of the League's expenses should Sforza transfer his operations to Tuscany, claiming that Sforza's departure would hurt not only Venice, but ultimately Florence and Sforza as well. Sforza had recently been for consultations in Venice, where he was assiduously courted and honored by the doge.[168]

    At the time these negotiations were proceeding, events were again turning in Venice's favor. After a major victory on Lake Garda led by the Venetian commander Stefano Contarini, the harrowing three-year-long siege of Brescia was finally broken.[169] The mid-fifteenth-century chronicler Cristoforo da Soldo offers a wrenching account of the situation within the besieged city: by the beginning of April the inhabitants had been reduced to eating grasses, snails, and horses; and every day hundreds of children crowded the city's main piazza, crying "Hunger, hunger! God have mercy!"[170] On 20 April ambassadors arrived from newly liberated Brescia in order to renew the city's adherence to Venice. On the appointed day they proceeded to the Ducal Palace, where they were greeted by Foscari. Then they made a turn around the piazza, going as far as the church of San Geminiano before entering the basilica for Mass. After the service, the ambassadors pledged Brescia's devotion to Venice and presented Foscari with the city's flag emblazoned with the motto *Brixia manipotens fidei sue ceteris urbibus testimonium tulit* (Powerful Brescia bears witness to its loyalty over other cities). According to Dolfin, Foscari gave as "a most notable speech," in which he praised the Brescians for their loyalty to Venice. The flag was then hung in the church "for future memory." Sanudo recorded that it was still there in his day.[171]

In May and June Venetian forces continued to retake castles and towns on the shores of Lake Garda, the Bresciano and Veronese, winning a stunning victory at Orzinuovi. In thanksgiving for that victory and the return of lands that had been lost, the Great Council voted unanimously to free all those imprisoned for debts of 20 ducats or less. Then on 29 June the Florentine forces scored a major victory of their own over Piccinino at Anghiari. This was celebrated in Venice with a thanksgiving procession described by Sanudo as "the most beautiful ever." The campanile was festooned with flags and tapestries, and bonfires were lit throughout the city.[172]

Venice made one other significant territorial gain in this period: in early 1441 it asserted its direct control over Ravenna, exiling Ostasio III, the last da Polenta ruler of the city, to Crete where he remained until his death. Venice's acquisition of Ravenna (for some time it had indirectly controlled the city through the da Polenta family) represented a significant turning point as the Republic now penetrated south of the Po and into the Papal State. This takeover threatened Venice's relations with both the pope and Ferrara and lent new credence to fears of the Republic's "imperialist intentions." Venetians such as Dolfin by contrast painted the episode in a different light, claiming that the people of

Ravenna freely placed themselves under Venetian rule with "benevolence and love."[173]

Recognizing that events in the war were not going his way, Visconti began to make peace overtures via the Marquess of Ferrara. He dangled before both him and Sforza the prospect of marriage with his only heir, his illegitimate daughter Bianca, or as Dolfin more accurately but indelicately put it, "he marketed his daughter Madonna Bianca (*feva de sua fia madona biancha una gran merchantia*), offering [her] first to one lord then to another."[174] Visconti also put out peace feelers to Sforza. This initiative, coupled with Sforza's own negotiations for Bianca's hand, worried his Venetian employers, who clearly were concerned that he would switch sides yet again, taking the momentum in the war with him. In late July the Senate sent a letter to Pasquale Malipiero, proveditor to the army, advising him to reassure the general that just as they had placed all their power in his hands, so they had full faith in his ability to treat for peace and do everything for "the good and welfare of our state."[175] But as the negotiations dragged on into the fall, the Venetians remained worried, cautioning Sforza "to keep an eye out" for Visconti's tricks.[176] Just what kind of game Visconti was playing is unclear. In Francesco Cognasso's view, it may have been cunningly designed to undermine Venetian confidence in Sforza's loyalty, prompting his deliverance to the same fate as befell Carmagnola.[177] Whether or not this was Visconti's intention, the reality is that the Venetians found themselves in a strikingly familiar situation, again at the mercy of their captain-general. But this time history did not repeat itself; when Sforza arrived in Venice in early 1441, it was not to be jailed and executed, but rather to celebrate the marriage of Foscari's son Jacopo. His entry was greeted with "all the triumphs possible."[178]

The marriage of Jacopo afforded Foscari another opportunity to celebrate his family, to emphasize again the princely aspects of the ducal office, and in so doing to increase its prestige. But it was not his only chance to do so. The many diplomatic comings and goings of these years provided numerous occasions for him to appear on the civic stage in the company of princes. The reception the Venetians gave to the Byzantine emperor John in 1438 is considered above. Other visitors were less distinguished than the emperor but nonetheless warranted conspicuous welcomes. In 1440 alone, Foscari hosted the Marquess of Ferrara, the papal cardinal legate, the Archbishop of Taranto, and Sforza, meeting them with the *bucintoro* and staging grand entries.[179] But the most distinguished visitor of 1440 was Medea, the daughter of the Marquess of Saluzzo and future Queen of Cyprus, who was making her progress east for her forthcoming marriage. She was met with the *bucintoro* not only by Foscari and the Signoria, but also by Dogaressa Marina and an escort of one hundred and twenty-four women dressed in extravagant finery. The queen's retinue numbered three hundred. A few days after her entry, Foscari paid a call on the queen at her lodgings in the home of Giovanni Corner. During her stay, she visited various religious establishments in the city, including San Zaccaria, in order to view their relics. She also toured the treasury of San Marco, the Great Council Hall, and the Arsenal. After about two weeks she continued on her journey to Cyprus, but not before receiving a jewel valued at several hundred ducats which the Great Council had voted to present her. Her visit, like the others, offered the Venetians an opportunity to educate foreigners about Venice's spiritual and material wealth and, as the visit to the Great Council Hall suggests, its form of government.[180]

The symbol of that government was the doge; he was after all the very likeness of Venice. And so it was perhaps inevitable that as the scope and reach of government increased, so too did the pomp and ceremony associated with the ducal office. In November 1440 the Senate approved a measure proposed by Vito da Canal, which was designed to better honor God and Saint Mark and to thank them for recent military victories. It decreed that henceforth the city would hold a procession on the feast of Corpus Christi, just as it did on the feast of Saint Mark. It also ruled that on the vigil of the feast of Mark, all the guilds with affiliated religious brotherhoods should come to San Marco, "for the purpose of honoring the church of Saint Mark and the most Serene lord doge." This strengthened even further the association of the doge and Mark and placed the *popolo* of Venice, as represented by the guilds, in a much more subordinate position than before. A faint marginal note next to the Senate law seems to indicate that the provision for the ceremony on the vigil was revoked, although some later commentators interpreted parts of the rituals on the feast of Mark itself as signs of the guilds' "vassalage." In all likelihood the law was repealed because it offended republican sensibilities by going too far in elevating the ducal office and person of the doge.[181]

Official ceremonies and rites like these were subject to strict rules and procedures; as a result it was difficult for Foscari or any other doge for that matter to rework them in such a way as to increase significantly his power. But this was less obviously the case with more purely family occasions such as weddings. In most monarchical and princely states the weddings of the rulers' children were grand occasions, used to solidify domestic and especially international political alliances. And with the prospect of consummation, they also held out the promise of dynastic continuity. It was just such concerns that prompted the Venetians in the thirteenth century to begin including in the ducal *promissione* clauses forbidding doges to contract weddings for themselves or their offspring with foreign powers without permission from the government.[182] Nevertheless, Foscari used his only surviving son's marriage to a Venetian noblewoman to elevate his family on both the civic and international fronts. And he spent lavishly on it. In December 1440 he got permission from the Senate to sell 5000 ducats' worth of his shares in the Monte, money he no doubt intended to use for the wedding celebrations.[183]

The marriage, which took place in early 1441, united Foscari's son Jacopo to Lucrezia, daughter of Leonardo Contarini of San Barnaba. As the date of Jacopo's birth is uncertain, so is his age at the time of the marriage. Most patrician males waited to marry until their mid- to late twenties or even early thirties; while the median age at marriage for noblemen in the decade of the 1440s was thirty, indirect evidence suggests that Jacopo was only around twenty.[184] As discussed above, the doge himself had also entered into his first marriage in his early twenties, and so it appears that the Foscari family was especially anxious to launch its sons into full adulthood as signified by marriage. But the meaning of adulthood in Jacopo's case is obscure, especially given that the Venetian regime was wary of any concentration of power in the hands of doges' sons and forbade them from holding most offices.[185] Perhaps with only one surviving son, Foscari was concerned to have grandsons in order to ensure the continuation of his branch of the family into the next generation.

In contrast to many patrician youths who got a practical education in trade, Foscari's son Jacopo devoted his early years, as remarked in chapter 1, to learning, to acquiring a thoroughly up-to-date humanistic education, perhaps under the tutelage of Antonio Baratella and Francesco Barbaro. In 1436 he was at the University of Padua, attending

degree ceremonies as a witness. In that same year he received a letter
from the Veronese humanist Isotta Nogarola in which she celebrated his
love of books and commented that he had to look no further than to
his father for a model of virtue and honor. She concluded that if he
followed that example, as well as that of other illustrious men such as
Barbaro, his good name would endure. Leonardo Bruni was another who
corresponded with Jacopo. In one letter he invited Jacopo's comments
on a work he was sending him; in another he exhorted him, as had
Nogarola, to emulate his father's virtues. It is clear that Jacopo moved
in the most distinguished humanist circles, and it was his encouragement that prompted Ludovico Foscarini to write the *Gesta Victoris et
Coronae* (the Passion of Saints Victor and Corona), which the author
dedicated to Jacopo. Jacopo also was in all likelihood himself a patron
of Ciriaco d'Ancona, the traveler and antiquarian. All this indicates that
Jacopo and by extension his father were conversant with the latest ideas
circulating among the humanists about ideal forms of government and
the nature of true nobility, ideas ripe with nostalgia for ancient Greece
and Rome and ones that could be put to use in raising the dignity of
Venice and the ducal office.[186]

It is fortunate that not only Dolfin's description of Jacopo and Lucrezia's wedding celebrations has survived, but also a letter dated 16 February from Lucrezia's brothers Ramberto and Giacomo to another
brother Andrea in Constantinople.[187] The letter provides a particularly
valuable private or familial view of the marriage. The Contarini family,
a *casa vecchia*, was perhaps the largest and certainly one of the most distinguished Venetian noble families; and the marriage of one of their
daughters to the son of a sitting doge can only have added to their prestige. Almost nothing is known about Lucrezia herself; but Venetian noble
brides in this period were usually in their teens and hence much
younger than their husbands.[188] Given Jacopo's youth, it is likely that
Lucrezia was in her early teens. In the letter her brothers refer to her
as a "girl" (*garzona*) and comment that she comported herself during the
festivities better than expected, the kind of remark brothers would make
upon realizing that their little sister has grown up.

The letter begins with a thorough account of the dowry and trousseau
as well as the groom's counter-gifts. Lucrezia brought to the marriage a
dowry of 1600 ducats, an additional 2000 ducats in Monte shares, and
a trousseau valued by her brothers at 600 ducats. These figures are rather

modest, given that she married the son of the doge, but the Contarini surely did not want to exceed the legal limit of 1600 ducats established for dowries by the Senate in 1420.[189] The 1600 ducats were to be paid in cash. Where the dowry surpassed the legal limit was in the Monte shares. However, given the shaky status of the funded debt, they were certainly worth far less than their face value. The sum of 600 ducats for the trousseau was a bit higher than normal, but the brothers noted that they could not spend less, as Lucrezia was marrying "into the dogeship." They also observed that it more or less equaled the sum for their other sister Paola, except that in place of a simple housedress, they had spent 125 ducats on a gold brocade outfit. They wrote that a cash installment of 1000 ducats was due in a few days, but that the doge, dogaressa, and Jacopo were so pleased with Lucrezia, having found in her "everything that they were looking for," that they seemed unconcerned with the cash and were themselves spending with abandon.

The brothers' account of the gifts the Foscari gave Lucrezia confirms their assessment of Foscari extravagance. First, they had four outfits made for her at the extraordinary cost of 2000 ducats. The brothers described in detail each dress, the most extravagant of which was made of crimson cloth costing 18 ducats a *braccio* (about 64 centimeters), with open sleeves lined in fur. Then there were the jewels. These included a clasp adorned with a large pearl, a ruby, emerald, and diamond; a brooch with a diamond, pearl, and balas (a colored crystal) valued at 3500 ducats, numerous rings including four large balases worth 2000 ducats, and most significant of all, a necklace worth 8000 ducats, which the future Queen of Cyprus had worn during her recent visit. Indeed, the brothers noted that these things would be enough for "any great queen," and that Lucrezia had not had to ask for anything as the doge gave all of these things willingly.

"Gave" is not perhaps the right word, for if this wedding followed the practice of marriages elsewhere in Renaissance Italy, then these were not actually gifts to the bride but loans. It was common in this period for the groom or the father of the groom to make a show of outfitting the bride, but then to take back the goods, for what mattered on these occasions "was the ability to provide the proper set of accoutrements necessary for an honorable social occasion, an honorable ceremony, an honorable transition." In fact, it is likely that Foscari simply borrowed or rented many of the items, especially the jewels, and that he was especially fortunate in procuring the same necklace worn by the future queen; she herself had in all likelihood borrowed or rented the necklace in order to appear properly regal. In patriarchal and paternalistic Renaissance Italy, the outfitting of women was usually too important a task to be left to the women themselves. Instead it was the responsibility of male kin who were interested in making a show and promoting family honor.[190]

After giving their brother an account of the dowry and counter-gifts, Ramberto and Giacomo then described the marriage itself. Again, like marriages in Venice and elsewhere in Italy, it was a multi-stage affair. The first step was the sealing of the alliance between the two parties: unlike similar rites in Florence, this included the bride and groom themselves.[191] According to the brothers, Lucrezia and a company of sixty women traveled in two boats to the Ducal Palace. Usually this was an occasion when the bride was on display. In order to prevent such a "spectacle," however, and to protect symbolically the virginity of the bride, a number of other boats of noblemen and youths shielded those carrying the women.[192] Presumably after some sort of ceremony, the doge hosted a party with music and a dinner for both his and Lucrezia's kin.

A few days later – the brothers are not precise – the *sposalizio* (what today would be considered the wedding proper) took place.[193] This ceremony, occurred in the house of the bride and was a private affair. The doge and dogaressa were in attendance, as were "a few relatives." Presumably on this day the couple exchanged vows, and Jacopo gave Lucrezia a ring. Mass was said, although this was not a requirement in the fifteenth century.

The third stage in the marriage process occurred on 29 January, a Sunday.[194] The third and final step in a typical wedding consisted of the "publicizing" ceremony, during which the young bride was transported to the house of her husband, whose kin and friends welcomed her with feasts and festivities sometimes lasting several days."[195] This is precisely what happened. On the morning of the 29th, members of the *compagnie della calza* (stocking companies) began to assemble in the piazza. These organizations of noble youths wore distinctive uniforms with multi-color stockings (hence their name) and put on fetes of various sorts. The Contarini brothers were dressed in the outfit of their company, as was Jacopo (it is unclear whether they were all members of the same company).[196] The entire ensemble, including more than two hundred and fifty horses, various nobles, and their servants, formed a cortege led by trumpets and fifes. Eustachio Balbi, who had been designated Lord of the Festivities by the companies, supervised the event.

The procession took a turn around the courtyard of the Ducal Palace and then the piazza before setting off for the parish of San Samuele. There it crossed the Grand Canal by means of a bridge of boats which had been specially constructed for the occasion, bringing the entire group to Lucrezia's home parish of San Barnaba. Lucrezia, accompanied by fifty women and two procurators, went to Mass in the church; it was followed by an open-air sermon which was attended by the doge, Sforza, various ambassadors, and such a throng of people that no one could move. The cortege of men then returned to the Ducal Palace, albeit boisterously along a circuitous route via San Polo and Santa Maria Formosa. After a meal at the palace, a group of one hundred and fifty women boarded the *bucintoro*. Accompanied by a multitude of smaller boats, they made their way to San Barnaba, where Lucrezia embarked with another hundred women. Having proceeded to the Palace of the Two Towers to collect Sforza, the *bucintoro* then returned to San Marco with Lucrezia seated between Sforza and the Florentine ambassador. When the assembly arrived at the Ducal Palace, Foscari paid it the special honor of coming down and greeting it in the piazza. He placed Lucrezia between himself and Sforza and together they went to the staircase, where they were met by the dogaressa and fifty women. Curiously there is no mention of Jacopo in all this. Dancing and mummeries ensued, followed by dinner. The festivities lasted until three o'clock in the morning.

The next day, Monday the 30th, the brothers record that they again mounted their steeds; after making a round of the city they returned to the Ducal Palace, where Sforza hosted a joust in the piazza. The prize, awarded by Lucrezia herself, was a piece of silk cloth valued at 150 ducats. According to Dolfin, half went to one of Taddeo d'Este's men, the other half to one of Sforza's. The party held afterwards continued well into the night.

On Tuesday the various stocking companies made a tour of the city by boat and returned to the Ducal Palace for another dinner. And there were some additional military displays. The festivities continued on Thursday morning, when the companies again made a tour of the city. In the afternoon the Florentines staged a revel, which was followed by a tournament hosted either by the doge (as Dolfin claims) or the gold-smiths (as the brothers recount). This time the prize was divided among followers of Sforza, Gattamelata, and Taddeo d'Este. According to the brothers, "our festivities ended" with another party in the Ducal Palace. However, before concluding their letter, they gave their brother Andrea further details about the celebrations. They observed that the Great Council Hall, the site for many of the parties, had been lit with one hundred and twenty torches rather than the usual sixty; that the food at the meals, including oysters, capons, squabs, and peacocks, was so abundant that much of it had to be thrown away, and that a large number of foreigners attended. They noted that the government had ordered that women in mourning put aside their widows' weeds during the festivities and informed Andrea that they were themselves planning to host a party on the forthcoming Giovedi Grasso (Fat Thursday).[197] Dogaressa Marina, however, was not planning to attend as the party fell on the anniversary of the death of her son Domenico. And so Lucrezia was, in her brothers' words, going "to fill the dogaressa's shoes" (sarà [. . .] in pè della Dogaressa). They ended the letter with a brief round-up of the various marriages held that year, by which they presumably meant that Carnival season. They rather uncharitably judged many of the brides to be ugly.

The marriage of Jacopo Foscari to Lucrezia Contarini marked yet another significant step in Foscari's elevation of the ducal office. The lavishness of the ducal counter-gifts and meals, the jousts and parties, the attendance and participation of foreign ambassadors and condottieri, and the various parades by boat and on horseback about the city were all designed to impress both Venetians and foreigners alike with Foscari's munificence and magnificence. And impress they did. The Contarini brothers themselves observed that the city had never before witnessed such a "notable celebration." These celebrations left a distinctly regal or princely sensation; there was nothing republican about them. That point was made most markedly by Lucrezia's wearing the very necklace that had adorned the future Queen of Cyprus.[198]

In addition to the regal aspect, two other elements particularly stand out. The first is the international component of the events, for although the bride and groom were native Venetians, the festivities were designed to have a transnational impact – to send a message about Foscari's stature across the peninsula. To accomplish this end, the ambassadors from Florence and Sforza especially were given particularly prominent roles in the celebrations. In addition, the tournament judges were careful to ensure that the prizes were evenly divided among representatives of each of the city's most important mercenary commanders, including followers of Taddeo d'Este, a member of a cadet branch of the Ferrarese ruling house. In other words, this was not the typical Venetian patrician wedding designed to seal intra-city alliances; it was an international event, with diplomatic implications, and decidedly chivalric themes. The second notable element is its dynastic quality. To a very real degree the Contarini brothers and presumably others perceived Lucrezia as marrying into the dogeship itself – in fact they said just that. What is more, the doge rather than Jacopo figures most prominently in their description of the various festivities; and they observed how Lucrezia planned to stand in for the dogaressa during the Fat Thursday celebrations. The marriage appeared on one level at least to introduce the possibility of a Foscari dynasty – as if a new generation were being prepared for the dogal and dogaressal roles.[199]

Like the decoration of the Porta della Carta, the Foscari–Contarini marriage raised the visibility of the dogeship and in a curious way transformed the doge into the groom himself. The celebrations served to elide Venice and Foscari as they became increasingly intertwined, for what should have been essentially a private family matter, a marriage, now became a matter of state with international implications. Into the delicate balance between the magisterial and princely aspects of the ducal office, Foscari had yet again tipped the scales to the princely side.

The afterglow of the wedding quickly subsided, however, with the news that Piccinino had again gone on the offensive and taken Soncino. Sforza immediately took his leave and headed toward the Bresciano. Then in April, when the standards of Venice were being consigned to Sforza in Verona at the church of Sant'Anastasia, a miracle occurred. A white cross appeared in the sky and lingered there until the Mass was finished and the standards had been transported to Sforza's residence, after which it was not seen any more. Dolfin reports that many people witnessed the apparition. This sign, reminiscent of Emperor Constantine's vision of a cross before the Battle of the Milvian Bridge in the fourth century, seemed to augur well for Venice and especially for Sforza. Cristoforo da Soldo records that as a consequence of the vision, processions were held in Venice, Verona, and Brescia.[200]

Fighting during the summer of 1441 was concentrated in the Bresciano. In August Piccinino sent a message requesting a safe-conduct for himself and an agent of Visconti to visit Sforza's camp. An eight-day truce was declared, and so began the first discussions regarding an eventual peace. Visconti's emissary arrived with a very generous offer: the duke would give Sforza the hand of his daughter Bianca in marriage and the city of Cremona as her dowry. In addition, Sforza could retain the other cities, including Crema, which had been promised to him earlier. Soon thereafter Sforza traveled to Venice to discuss the terms with Foscari and the Signoria and with other members of the League. Eventually the peace talks moved to Sforza's camp at Cavriana in the Mantovano, south of Lake Garda. On 29 October Sforza married Bianca Maria near Cremona and took possession of the city. The peace, known as the Peace of Cavriana, was signed on 20 November and officially proclaimed on 18 December.[201]

According to the terms of the treaty, territories were returned to their status in the Second Peace of Ferrara (1433), and the River Adda was again designated the border between Venetian and Milanese possessions. The big losers were the Marquess of Mantua and Alvise dal Verme, who were forced to restore to the Venetians various towns they had taken, including Porto, Legnago, and Nogarola; subjects of Mantua living in Venetian territory, however, had their rights reinstated. The treaty acknowledged Genoa's independence from Milan, restored Imola and Bologna to the pope, established the rivers Magra and Panaro as the borders between Milanese possessions and Tuscany and the Romagna, and called for the restitution of prisoners.[202]

Apparently the cross that had appeared in the sky over Verona in April had been a very good omen indeed, for the biggest winner in the treaty was Sforza: he not only received Bianca as his wife and Cremona as her dowry, but now found himself well positioned to claim Milan upon Visconti's death. Moreover, it was he who had to all intents and purposes orchestrated the peace. In the words of the historian Michael Mallett: "It was at Sforza's camp at Cavriana, and very much as a result of Sforza's initiative, that a peace was finally agreed."[203] Venice's fortunes once again seemed to be in the hands of one of its mercenary captains. It is also significant that this was the second peace treaty with Visconti in which Venice did not make any important territorial gains. This fact impressed on the Venetians the point that their problems henceforth would be more political than military in nature.[204] But in the meantime, they greeted the treaty with their customary acts of charity by releasing prisoners from jail, dowering poor girls, and reducing the number of votes required for pardons (*grazie*). They staged processions and had Masses said to thank God and Saint Mark for the successful conclusion of the peace. In war-weary Brescia, thousands crowded the main piazza crying, "Peace! Peace!"[205]

In February 1442 Sforza made his triumphant return to Venice. He was received with great pomp. Foscari and the entire Signoria, as well as a great many other nobles, met him with the *bucintoro* and conveyed him to his palace at San Pantalon.[206] Sforza returned to Venice in May, this time in the company of Bianca Maria, affording the Venetians an opportunity to celebrate the couple's recent marriage. Traveling in different boats, Sforza arrived on 3 May at the island of San Giorgio in Alga, where he was met by Foscari, while Bianca Maria arrived at Santa Croce and was met by the dogaressa, her daughter-in-law Lucrezia, and a group of more than two hundred women dressed in finery and covered in jewels. A week before, on 26 April, the Senate had voted that for the occasion women ought to wear their "best clothes" as a way of honoring Sforza and Bianca and for the glory of Venice. Bianca was taken in the *bucintoro* to the palace of Gattamelata at San Polo, which had been requisitioned for her use; Sforza lodged at his Palace of the Two Towers at San Pantalon.[207]

On 4 May the dogaressa met Bianca at San Polo and together they made the trip to San Marco on foot, again escorted by a large group of women. This journey carried them through the Rialto market to the loggia at the foot of the bridge; they rested there for a while before crossing the Grand Canal and proceeding down the street of shops known as the Merceria. All the shops were decked out to display their merchandise, as was customary when important visitors were in town. Once at San Marco, they visited the high altar and toured the treasury of the church before dining in the Ducal Palace. On 1 May the Senate had expressed concern that unauthorized persons might board the *bucintoro* or enter the church during Bianca's visit. Sanudo reports that to prevent the latter possibility, all the doors of San Marco except the main entrance were locked and that officers with batons were stationed at the door to prevent any men from entering.[208] During her visit Bianca also got a tour of the Arsenal and received from the doge a jewel which

Dolfin valued at 1000 ducats – a figure double the amount the Senate had authorized for the purchase.[209] The couple left the city by sea. They were escorted as far as Malamocco on the Lido, where they boarded ships to take them to Ravenna and then into the Marches. Sforza wished to travel there as his hold on the region was increasingly under threat.

The restoration of peace allowed the Venetians to turn to other problems gripping the city, the most immediate of which (not surprisingly) was financial. Like the previous wars with Visconti, the third one placed a tremendous strain on the city's resources, and during its course the government adopted various measures to raise money, approving twelve imposts of the *estimo* in 1438 and eleven more in 1439, imposing new loans on the terraferma and Crete, and borrowing funds from private banks such as that owned by the Soranzo brothers.[210] In January 1439 the Senate passed a number of measures to raise money for the war effort, including new customs fees, a tax on rents, and a withholding or deduction of part of the interest payments on Monte shares. Most significant of all was the institution of a new tax known as the *boccatico*; despite its name, this was not a tax on individuals or "mouths" (*bocche*), but on houses or hearths. It was designed to replace the system of forced loans and was aimed at everyone, even foreigners, living in the city and the dogado. But unlike forced loans, there was no expectation that the funds collected would be repaid or interest paid on them. The *boccatico* represented something approaching a direct personal levy; as such it demonstrates the ways in which the demands of war were creating a stronger, more centralized state, one that intervened more and more in people's lives and gave greater power to those at the center.[211]

In March 1439 the Senate approved a measure whereby two men would be appointed to survey each parish and to impose on those who had not been previously assessed for the *estimo* an impost of up to 1 ducat per month. Only the truly destitute were exempt. The new tax was badly received and caused so much discontent – as the Senate put it, such "great grumbling" in the city – that on 31 March it revoked imposts of less than 6 *grossi* per month.[212] In April the Senate exempted all Florentines in the city, including the Medici, as they were already contributing to the war effort through taxes at home.[213] Overall, however, this effort to put the government's finances on a different tax footing was a failure. In August 1439 the Senate voted, on the recommendation of Foscari, Domenico Zorzi (one of the heads of the Forty), and the *savio del consiglio* Andrea Morosini, to return to the system of forced loans based on the *estimo* for those with the qualifying income, but to retain the *boccatico* for everyone else. In the end, the *boccatico* produced meager returns of a little more than 1000 ducats per year, not enough to make any significant difference in the government's overall financial situation.[214]

Still the search for funds went on unabated. In October 1439 the Senate gave permission to the officials in charge of auditing war expenses to take their investigation as far back as 1426, the beginning of the wars with Milan.[215] But as the war continued, so did the crushing burden of taxes. The government levied eleven more imposts of the *estimo* in 1440 and twelve more in 1441, together equaling a total tax of 30 percent of assessed wealth. Additionally, it suspended interest payments in 1439 and 1441, as Monte shares fell to 20 percent of their face value. From a financial point of view, 1441 was "the most disastrous year of all the period of the Lombard wars."[216]

Even the cessation of hostilities could not bring a quick amelioration. In January 1442 the Senate noted that every day men from the crew of one of the galleys that had served on Lake Garda were coming to the Ducal Palace demanding their pay, but it soundly rejected Foscari's proposal to pay them their due.[217] And in one curious cost-cutting measure in May 1442 the Senate decided that whenever a new city came under Venetian dominion, Venice should donate to that city an insignia of Saint Mark. However, from then on subject cities would be responsible for purchasing replacement flags. The Senate estimated that replacements were costing the government 400 ducats per year.[218] In spite of all these efforts, the financial situation remained so grave that it would soon provoke, as described in the next chapter, a tax revolt.

Not surprisingly, the stress of the war also continued to sharpen the various long-standing divisions and rivalries within the government and the broader society and to open up new ones as well. Among the latter was a growing rivalry between the Ten and the other councils. One salvo was fired on 27 September when, on the recommendation of their heads, the Ten passed by a vote of 9 to 5 a measure that essentially tried to limit speech in the Senate and other councils. The Ten complained, probably with good reason, that it often happened that speakers made accusations regarding the welfare of the state on the Senate floor, but when the Ten sought to investigate the allegations, they found either that the speakers had lied or else that they refused to cooperate with the investigation. The Ten therefore passed a measure that future speakers who made false allegations or who refused to cooperate in uncovering the truth should be deprived of offices and excluded from secret meetings of councils for a year; they would also be fined 500 ducats.[219] The Ten almost certainly had good intentions here. They did not want to waste their time pursuing patently false claims; at the same time they may have been trying to cool the tone of political rhetoric. But the other councils perceived this as an infringement of their right to free speech. The Great Council joined the fray when on 15 October it sought in turn to limit the power of the Ten. It observed that the Ten had overstepped its bounds by alienating goods belonging to the commune, a prerogative traditionally reserved for the Senate when approved by two-thirds of its members. In retaliation, the Great Council ruled that henceforth the Ten could not alienate property formerly belonging to rebels and traitors and raised the required number of favorable votes in the Senate to three-quarters. It also placed new restrictions on the Collegio.[220] On 8 November the Ten backed down, ensuring the dignity of the councils by restoring to members of the governmental councils the right "to say, counsel, and speak according to his conscience and opinion."[221] Although the Ten lost this particular fight, the issue demonstrates yet again the effort by those in the most powerful council to limit the rights of those in the other councils.

As far as the rivalry between the Foscari and Loredans is concerned, the death of Pietro Loredan appears to have lowered the heat by removing one of the key players. However, the nearly simultaneous prosecutions in August 1440 of Foscari's son-in-law Andrea Donato and Francesco, son of the late Giorgio Loredan, seem more than coincidental. On 5 August the Senate voted to punish Loredan for borrowing 500 ducats from the Salt Officers in order to build a small ship for transporting stones to Venice (the stones were probably intended for public works such as sea walls along the Lido) and using the money instead to build a cog, which the Senate judged to be "not fit for transporting stone." In other words, he did not use the loaned funds as he had promised. Foscari was deeply engaged in the case, even proposing a possible punishment.[222]

The prosecution of Donato stemmed from the episode in the spring of 1438 when as podesta of Padua and temporary proveditor to the army, he supposedly ordered, against the counsel of Gattamelata, the troops to retreat to Padua, Vicenza, and other towns rather than confront Piccinino at the Adige. But the entire affair has the odor of partisan politics. Sanudo claims that the doge tried to squelch the outcry in order to protect his son-in-law, while a modern analyst of the military campaign argues that it is unlikely that Gattamelata could have been so easily cowed by the proveditors, especially as he had received orders from the Senate on 17 April to prefer his own judgement to that of the proveditors, no matter who they were.[223] Furthermore, an examination of the Great Council vote to proceed against Donato indicates just how deeply divided the council was regarding the facts of the case. The first vote was inconclusive with 366 votes in favor of prosecuting Donato, 319 opposed, and 165 abstentions. It passed on a second vote with 411 in favor, 228 opposed, and 119 abstentions. Donato was fined 500 lire and prohibited from serving as proveditor to the army for five years. The state attorneys advocated a much harsher punishment, including that he spend two years in jail and be perpetually banned from serving not only in the post of proveditor but also that of ambassador.[224] Although there is no direct evidence of a connection between the Loredan and Donato prosecutions, their occurrence within a week of one another certainly created the opportunity for rivals to make mischief. Memories of slights and other embarrassments are always slow to fade.

Then in late June 1442 Foscari again did the unexpected. For a second time, he attempted to abdicate the dogeship. According to Dolfin, Foscari informed his councilors "with many notable words" that he "by no means" wished to remain in office. As with his first attempt in 1433, however, the members of the Ducal Council refused to accept his resignation. Foscari was steadfast, remaining in his apartments and neglecting to attend council meetings. Beseeched by the councilors and his relatives, he eventually changed his mind and resumed his duties, "just as he was previously accustomed to doing."[225] According to Sanudo, Foscari offered his age and health as the reasons for his desire to resign. He claimed that his "impotence," the term commonly used at the time to describe the frailties of old age, made him unable to perform his duties. Sanudo also copied into his version of events the editorial comment inserted by someone who was clearly writing as the events unfolded. Sanudo's anonymous source wrote: "I pray God that in the future he give to him [Foscari] and to us better luck than he has up until now."[226] These were sentiments Foscari obviously shared.

Foscari's perplexing second abdication attempt calls for explanation. The doge was now sixty-nine and beginning his twentieth year on the ducal throne. It is certainly possible that the ravages of time had left him physically broken and anxious to leave the burdens of office behind. On the other hand, there was nothing particularly remarkable about his age at this point. Indeed, as noted above, the average age at *election* for doges in the fifteenth and sixteenth centuries was seventy-two.[227] As a result, physical disability seems an unlikely explanation for his action. Another possibility, one bolstered by the fact that this was his second attempt at resignation, is that Foscari was prone to bouts of depression or at least to acute malaise. Yet there is no other evidence to point in that direction. Indeed, the sources record that Foscari gave eloquent speeches justifying his decision on both occasions. That hardly seems the behavior of a man caught in the grip of a profound mental crisis. The fact that he immediately resumed his responsibilities also militates against this argument. A more likely explanation for Foscari's action is that in this as in the previous episode he was simply tired of the constant intrigues and partisan struggles and disappointed that his effort to lead Venice to greatness had not met with greater success. The unknown author of the editorial insertion recorded by Sanudo certainly believed that neither Foscari nor Venice had had much good fortune in recent years, and that may have spurred him to retire.

The real key to unlocking the secret of Foscari's abdication attempts, however, is in their timing: in both instances, the doge waited until Venice was at peace before acting. In 1433 he tried to resign just two months after the Second Peace of Ferrara had been signed; in 1442 his decision followed the Peace of Cavriana by six months. What this indicates is that both efforts were thoughtfully considered rather than spontaneous decisions. They were not made in moments of national crisis; in fact the crises had passed. In both instances Foscari felt that he could step down knowing that even if he did not leave the city exactly triumphant, neither did he leave it in jeopardy. He was not shirking his responsibility; precisely the opposite was the case. He would be leaving when Venice was secure. Throughout the Renaissance moments of peace-making were commonly occasions for thanking God and the saints for their blessings and for making new beginnings of various sorts. It seems likely that Foscari's sense of piety, combined with his profound awareness of political realities, made him believe that now was the perfect time to resign and devote the rest of his life to his family and to God. He might even have had an earlier ducal precedent in mind, for in 1178 Doge Sebastiano Ziani retired to a monastery just months after helping orchestrate peace between the emperor and the pope.[228] But others had different plans for Foscari. His change of mind was surely caused not only by his councilors, but by the entreaties of his kinsmen, his brother Marco, his son Jacopo, and his wife Marina. They were, after all, the ones with the most to lose, not only in terms of actual power but also by being associated with a doge who had not seen his God-given responsibility through to the end.

What ultimately makes Foscari's attempt to leave the dogeship particu-larly difficult to understand is how it relates to his other actions during his second decade in that position. While during his first decade he was aiming to perfect the role of republican chief magistrate, exercising his administrative finesse and demonstrating his piety, in the second decade he was veering in the direction of princely power as he made a con-certed effort to raise the visibility and dignity of the ducal office and, especially in the Porta della Carta, to glorify himself, and in the case of Jacopo's wedding, his family. How that effort at personal and familial aggrandizement can then be reconciled with his attempt to resign requires further explanation.

The inquiry requires one to engage that most basic issue in biogra-phical studies, namely the role of the individual in shaping events, per-sonal agency, best summarized by the classic question: do the times shape the man or the man the times? Thus one must ask whether Foscari was leading Venice in a more princely direction in an effort to accumulate greater and greater power for himself and his family or whether he was simply following the flow of events as dictated by broader economic and political realities. The equivocal answer is: both. The bestowal of the imperial vicariate, the many entry ceremonies for foreign dignitaries – including those for the Byzantine emperor and the future Queen of Cyprus – the condoning of the erection of his statue on the Porta della Carta, and the extravagance of his son Jacopo's wedding were all acts designed to glorify Foscari and, in the last instance at least, to pave the way for his son's future success. And so to that extent one can argue that Foscari was indeed taking the Venetian state in a new direction, toward greater power for the prince. But that is not to say that he had any intention of undermining the city's republican foundations and establishing his personal rule.[229] For the doge was, as the Ten would soon claim, the *imago* of Venice: that elision of doge and state meant that Foscari's efforts to increase the visibility of the dogeship were simultaneously and inseparably efforts to increase the power and prestige of Venice.

The drive to augment the power of the state was itself a response to the new political realities of the Italian peninsula. The consolidation of the numerous city-states into a much smaller number of regional states, accomplished through warfare conducted by mercenary armies, necessitated the raising of vast sums of cash and, as observed above, the streamlining of decision-making processes.[230] In most states that meant awarding greater power to the prince, while in Venice it involved the concentration of power not only in the dogeship but also in the Senate and especially in the Ten. To that extent then, Foscari's quest for power was a quest for power for the central government, not for himself. His cultural program should be read in this way too. The evocations of imperial Rome in the Ducal Palace entry-system and the chivalric overtones of Jacopo's wedding celebrations were efforts to blend the culture of Venice and its newly acquired terraferma domains, to create what the art historian Colin Eisler terms the "Foscari style," which he defines as "allied with Florence and extravagant, celebratory, and militant."[231]

It is only with hindsight, with knowledge of later fifteenth-century doges, especially the brothers Marco and Agostino Barbarigo, and their efforts to incorporate even more princely elements into the dogeship, that one recognizes in Foscari's reign the beginnings of a disturbing trend toward personal rule.[232] According to Quentin Skinner, one characteristic of princely government was the transformation of values traditionally associated with the community "into a preoccupation with a series of purely personal qualities" associated with the ruler.[233] The presentation on the Porta della Carta of Charity along with the cardinal virtues as the personal attributes of Foscari rather than Venice as a whole is certainly in keeping with that change. But it is important to remember that Foscari could at best only dimly perceive where his actions might lead in the future. What is more, had he been allowed to resign the dogeship in 1442, he would have joined the vast majority of his ducal colleagues, just one more in a series of forgotten names and faces staring down at us from the walls of the Great Council Hall, the very epitome of republican magisterial anonymity. He would have been spared as well the personal heartbreak which even today guarantees his fame both in Venice and beyond.

4

The House of Foscari
1443–1453

*li Veneti progenitori non volevanno consentire che li Principi Veneti,
quando facevanno la ellectione de quelli, havessenno fiolli, perchè
cognoscevanno che li padri, inclinati ali fiolli, non potevanno tenire la
bilanza drecta.*

(Venice's ancestors did not wish when they held ducal
elections for the candidates to have sons, because they knew
that fathers, who are naturally inclined toward their sons,
could not maintain proper judgement toward them.)

Girolamo Priuli[1]

On 20 February 1445 the Council of Ten, supplemented by a *zonta*,
issued the following sentence:

> That, on account of his demerits, the plaintiff Jacopo Foscari, son of
> the lord doge, is perpetually banished from the city of Venice and its
> district and from all lands and places belonging to the commune of
> the Venetians, whether on the terraferma or overseas, except for
> Nauplion in Romania and its district, to which he is perpetually con-
> fined [. . .] and if he should disobey or if he should violate the terms

of his confinement, then he is to be captured wherever he might be and brought under heavy guard to Venice where between the twin columns of justice he is to be beheaded.[2]

The judgement passed with 22 favorable votes and just 4 abstentions.

One must ask how, only four years after his triumphal wedding to Lucrezia Contarini, things had reached the point that Foscari's only surviving son could suffer such a fate? The answer to this query leads deep into the international intrigues and domestic politics of the third decade of Foscari's dogeship as well as into the vexed position of a ducal son. And what one discovers along the way is that "the Jacopo affair," as it can legitimately be termed, was just part of a major breakdown in Venetian politics, one whose origins can be traced to the conquest of the terraferma. For now all the problems unleashed by the mainland adventure – control of the condottieri, the financial crisis, the quest for administrative jobs, the extension and transformation of patronage ties, and the fate of Milan, would bring in their wake corruption, dissension, and increasing factionalism within the Venetian patrician class. Jacopo Foscari was among the first victims of this crisis, but he was not to be its last.

The doge himself would react to Jacopo's predicament and to the swirl of events in a variety of ways, at times plunging into periods of despair and inaction, at other times firmly taking control of events. And then, just when it seemed that Jacopo's situation could get no worse, Foscari would take the extraordinary decision to begin building a family palace overlooking the Grand Canal. While in the first decade of his rule Foscari most often appeared in the guises of a republican chief magistrate and pious servant of God, and in the second decade as a princely figure drenched in chivalric and imperial associations, the persona that comes through most forcefully in this third period is that of *paterfamilias*. And, for the first time, the private man also begins to reveal himself.

The events that would engulf Jacopo, however, still lay some years ahead. In the aftermath of his second resignation attempt in June 1442, a very different set of problems confronted the doge and his government. The first of these not surprisingly was the ongoing fiscal crisis precipitated by the mainland wars. Apparently every day sailors from the Lake Garda fleet were coming to the Ducal Palace demanding their salary. The failure to pay the very men upon whom Venice's security and fortune depended was a particular embarrassment to the government. Foscari was especially troubled by this breach of faith and put forward proposals that the situation be rectified.[3]

But much more serious than the protestations of some disgruntled sailors was the growing sense among the populace, both in the city and on the terraferma, that the tax burden had grown intolerable; many stopped paying. In December the Senate passed a bill imposing penalties on those who refused to pay their own taxes and who encouraged others to do the same by crying out, "Don't pay! Don't buy pawns!" This constituted, according to one modern authority, a "more or less organized revolt against the fisc" that was brought under control not by the threat of legal penalties, but rather by the easing of levies for the next several years, a reduction made possible by the cessation of war.[4] Certainly the desire to avoid heavy taxes was universal. In May Foscari himself claimed that an error had been made in the assessment imposed on the Cà di Dio, the hospital for elderly women under the *iuspatronatus* of the doge.[5]

What sustained Venice even during this period of fiscal crisis was trade, which the Great Council justly referred to as "the foundation of our Republic."[6] It remained strong and grew even more secure when in 1442 the Venetians were able to reach a new accord with the Mamluk sultan of Egypt after years of conflict. In 1436 Venetian commerce had been thrown into turmoil when the sultan expelled Venetian merchants from his lands, including Damascus, Beirut, Tripoli, and Alexandria, so that he could take control of the pepper trade. According to Sanudo, Venetian merchants were forced to abandon 160,000 ducats' worth of goods in their warehouses in Beirut and another 75,000 in Alexandria.[7] It was partly to compensate for the closing of the Beirut and Alexandria lines that the Senate decided to launch the Barbary line and reopen the Tana line to the Black Sea. However, when fire destroyed the Venetians' warehouses in Tana in 1442 and claimed more than four hundred souls, they redoubled efforts to reach a new accord with the Mamluks, a change made easier by some conciliatory gestures from the new sultan.[8]

The man selected to head this delicate mission was Foscari's son-in-law Andrea Donato, who carried with him gifts for the sultan valued at more than 3000 ducats.[9] He departed in August in the company of Niccolò Soranzo, the newly appointed consul in Damascus, and fourteen ships, eight of which were headed to Alexandria and six to Syria. According to Dolfin, they were loaded with bullion and goods worth

400,000 ducats. In October Donato successfully completed his mission by securing a new accord with the Arabs.[10]

The situation in the eastern Mediterranean did not remain stable for long: just when relations with the Arabs began to improve, those with the Turks deteriorated as they placed new pressure on Constantinople. Emperor John's pleas for assistance drew a mixed response from the Venetians, who offered to mediate between him and the Turkish sultan and agreed to station some ships in Constantinople. But the main purpose of the ships, as Venice made clear, was to protect its own mercantile interests rather than provide for the emperor's security.[11]

John, who believed that the reward for the union of the Eastern and Latin churches achieved in 1439 at the Council of Florence ought to be a crusade against the Turks, got a more sympathetic hearing from the pope and Phillip III, the Duke of Burgundy, as well as from Ladislaus III, the King of Hungary and Poland, whose lands were threatened by the Ottoman thrust into the Balkans. The Venetians for their part remained non-committal since they did not want to jeopardize their trade with the Turks. Nevertheless, the pope moved forward with plans for the crusade and on 1 January 1443 levied a tithe on the church in order to raise money for the effort. The plan was for land forces to make their way from Hungary and for naval forces to sail from Venice in order to prevent the movement of Ottoman troops across the Hellespont from Asia into Europe. In May Pope Eugenius named his nephew and vice-chancellor Francesco Condulmer his special legate in charge of the fleet and dispatched him to Venice to oversee the preparation of the ten ships for which he had contracted. The Duke of Burgundy had promised to pay for an additional four.[12]

The fact that both the pope and his nephew were Venetians created special problems for the regime. For one thing, the Condulmers had personal ties to various members of the patriciate, ties that had the potential to divide loyalties and to undermine the integrity of the Venetian polity. In an effort to arrest such developments, Foscari put forward a bill on 17 May 1443 prohibiting nobles from soliciting either the pope or his nephew for appointments to captaincies and vice-captaincies in the papal fleet and another in May 1444 authorizing the state attorneys to investigate the methods by which nobles had secured positions on the ships outfitted by the Duke of Burgundy.[13] When it came time to appoint an admiral for the ships he was sponsoring, Eugenius made it clear that he wanted the procurator of San Marco Alvise Loredan in that post; and the Senate acceded by a vote of 118 to 6. Two other members of the Loredan family also held important positions in the crusader force: Paolo Loredan, son of the late Pietro, was captain of one of the papal galleys; and Antonio Loredan, captain of a Burgundian-sponsored ship.[14] With their family tradition of maritime service and expertise in the east, the Loredans brought an added layer of prestige to the venture.

But while the differing goals of the pope and the Venetians managed at least to dovetail in the east, the Republic and the papacy had very different political aims in mainland Italy, especially regarding Sforza. And so in August Foscari proposed to the Council of Ten that measures be taken to prevent Francesco Condulmer from funneling funds from Venice and its possessions to Piccinino who, with papal support, was seeking to drive Sforza from the Marches.[15] All in all, control of the papacy by a oo national was potentially ripe with pitfalls.

For their part, the Venetians used the struggle with the Turks as a pretext to secure additional territory along the coast of the southern Adriatic. In spring 1443 they took for themselves the city of Antivari, thereby securing "the whole Zetan coast," that is the coast of modern Montenegro.[16] The crusade itself, known as the Crusade of Varna, got under way in the summer. At its helm were Ladislaus and his general John Hunyadi; the papal representative was Cardinal Giuliano Cesarini. The former Serbian despot George Brankovic also joined in hopes of reclaiming the lands he had lost to the Turks. Since the Ottoman sultan Murad was engaged with problems in Anatolia, the crusaders had a fairly easy time of it as they marched down the Danube. They took the strategic town of Nis as well as Sofia. The Venetians took advantage of the crusaders' success to try to secure, with Turkish consent, the towns of Valona, Janina, and Argyrocastro along the Albanian coast.[17]

Faced with difficulties on two fronts, Murad opted to negotiate with the crusaders. He bought off both Brankovic and Ladislaus, the former by restoring the Serbian state, the latter by ceding to him the lands the crusaders had already conquered. The truce, worked out during June 1444, was set to last ten years and freed Murad to deal with the rebellion in Anatolia. But Cardinal Cesarini lobbied against the pact and convinced Ladislaus to disavow it so that soon the crusaders were again on the march and the papal fleet under way with Condulmer as the overall commander and Alvise Loredan as the captain of the Venetian ships. The plan was for one contingent of ships to guard the Dardanelles while another sailed up the Danube to help transport the land forces. But when the Senate learned that Ladislaus was again negotiating with the Turks, it hurriedly sent instructions to Loredan to make excuses to the sultan and explain to him that despite the Venetian makeup of the crew, the fleet was actually a papal one. This dispatch exposes the Venetians' opportunism; they joined the crusade in the hope that it would weaken the Turks and strengthen their own trade position. Indeed, they had already made known their desire to claim Gallipoli and Thessalonica as their share of the spoils. But in fact there was no truce, and when Murad's army finally engaged the crusaders at Varna in November 1444, it delivered them a crushing defeat. Both Ladislaus and Cardinal Cesarini were killed.[18]

The Crusade of Varna represented "the last attempt by western Christendom to drive the Turks out of Europe."[19] Eugenius hurled recriminations at his fellow Venetians for not providing sufficient tactical and material support for the effort and refused to meet his financial obligations for the fleet, while the Venetians hastened to repair relations with the sultan in order to protect their trade interests. In February 1446 they finally managed to secure a new treaty not only with Murad, who had retired following the victory at Varna, but also with his son and successor Mehmed II. In addition, they adopted a policy of non-engagement in the conflict between the Mamluk sultan and the King of Cyprus, especially with regard to the island of Rhodes. And in 1448 they renewed for what was to be the last time their treaty with the Byzantines. The Varna debacle simply ensured that everyone would maintain previously held opinions: the other western Christian powers saw the Venetians as shameless opportunists, while the Venetians held with some reason that they alone provided the only reliable bulwark against the Turks. For their part, the Byzantines saw both as unreliable allies and regretted their agreement for religious union.[20] While opinions varied, the fact remained that following Varna both the city of Constantinople and Venetian trade interests in the Aegean were more vulnerable than ever to the will of the Ottoman sultan.

Fortunately for the Venetians, these same years were relatively quiet on the terraferma front; at least they managed to avoid outright war. Attention continued to focus on the condottieri Sforza and Piccinino and on the eventual disposition of the Duchy of Milan. When last considered, Sforza was scurrying off to the Marches following Jacopo's wedding in order to protect his position there. He had good reason to be concerned since his father-in-law Visconti had been conspiring to turn Eugenius against him. In August 1442 Eugenius dismissed Sforza as Standard Bearer of the Church (*gonfaloniere della chiesa*) and replaced him with Niccolò Piccinino. Two months later Visconti, the pope, and Alfonso, the King of Naples, formed a league to attack him and retake the Marches. During the summer Sforza made desperate pleas for money, which only seemed to annoy his Venetian masters since, as noted above, they were facing their own financial crisis.[21]

But by the following summer Visconti had come to fear the growing influence of Alfonso and Piccinino and in yet another volte-face, reached an alliance with both Florence and Venice designed to protect Sforza. Aided by the league and by Alfonso's return to Naples, Sforza defeated Piccinino in November 1443. In retribution Eugenius excommunicated him and his son-in-law Sigismondo Malatesta the following April. But the military tide was with Sforza, who continued to win victories over Piccinino: at Montolmo in August 1444, for example, Piccinino's son Francesco was taken captive. The weight of this defeat rested heavily on the father's shoulders, and in October he succumbed at the age of fifty-eight to illness. He was preceded in death a month earlier by another famous condottiere, Gianfrancesco Gonzaga, the Marquess of Mantua, whom an unforgiving Dolfin described as a "rebel and traitor," a reference to his desertion to the Milanese side in 1438.[22]

Faced with this new reality, Eugenius reached a reconciliation with Sforza, who also reconfirmed for another three years his *condotta* with Florence and Venice.[23] In August Florence, Venice, and Bologna had agreed to a five-year alliance designed to prevent Visconti from interfering in the Romagna; then in November Florence and Venice reaffirmed their own alliance for another ten years.[24] But events were not settled for long since Leonello d'Este, the Marquess of Ferrara and son-in-law of Alfonso, was soon encouraging the Aragonese to take a more active role in northern affairs and to conquer Lombardy for themselves. At the same time Visconti and the pope renewed their machinations against Sforza. They were joined in this by Sigismondo Malatesta, who had fallen out with Sforza over the town of Pesaro – Sforza had purchased Pesaro from Galeazzo Malatesta in order to award it to his brother

Alessandro. Before long the combined forces of the pope, Naples, Milan, and Sigismondo Malatesta had Sforza on the defensive, wresting from him all of the Marches except the town of Jesi. At this point Sforza's main supporter, Cosimo de' Medici, urged him to carry the war to Rome itself, while the town of Ancona, coveted both by Venice and the Aragonese placed itself under Venetian protection in December 1445. Four years after the Peace of Cavriana, the stage was once again set for a more generalized war.[25] Venice did achieve one significant victory in June 1445 when, after years of conflict, it finally reached a settlement with the Patriarch of Aquileia over Friuli. The agreement gave the patriarch "absolute dominion" over the towns of Aquileia, San Vito, and San Daniele, while Venice gained undisputed claim to the rest of Friuli and Cadore. Venice agreed to pay an annual fee of 5000 ducats to the patriarch, but he was required in turn to purchase salt from Venice and rein in rebels and runners of contraband. This agreement marked Venice's assumption of the responsibility to protect the eastern Italian frontier from incursions by the Turks, a responsibility that neither the emperor nor the King of Hungary was able to bear alone any longer.[26]

During the interval of peace on the terraferma, the Venetian regime turned its attention to domestic matters and undertook a number of initiatives designed to assist the poor, both noble and common. Among the most significant of these was the Great Council's decision on 29 June 1443 to appoint a nobleman to handle the legal affairs of poor prisoners. According to the bill, such counsel was needed since the number of prisoners had grown dramatically on account of the enlargement of the state and the "most bitter war."[27] But it was the need particularly to assist poor nobles that preoccupied the government. Indeed on the same day that the council decided to appoint the advocate for the poor, it also passed (on a vote of 515 to 192 with 48 abstentions) a bill put forward by the heads of the Forty declaring office-holders ineligible for election to other posts for a period of time equal to their term of office. The intention, as the Great Council made clear, was to ensure that all nobles would have an equal opportunity to participate in office-holding and to enjoy the benefits thereof. Also on the same day the council expressed its concern that age qualifications for offices be observed and enforced.[28] A year later the council tackled the problem of poor nobles again by creating a number of minor administrative posts for which they were eligible. Most were in towns located on the eastern shore of the Adriatic Sea.[29]

Plague also remained a worry, prompting Foscari in December 1443 to put forward a bill modifying an earlier law regarding ships returning to Venice from plague-infested regions. Previously the Senate had given the Collegio the authority to grant entry to ships; Foscari's bill restored to the Senate alone the right to grant such licenses.[30] However a much more sweeping and comprehensive response to public health concerns failed on a legal technicality. In December 1444 the Great Council recognized the need for Venice to build a large hospital on the model of those then in existence in Florence, Siena, and elsewhere. It voted overwhelmingly to use the interest on 50,000 ducats of state loans left for pious purposes in the will of Giacomo Bernabovis to construct a hospital dedicated to Saint Mark on the site of the largely uninhabited Camaldoll monastery San Giovanni on the Giudecca. The doge and his councilors were to enjoy *iuspatronatus* over the new hospital, including the right to choose the prior and prioress; it was decided, however, that the first prioress would be Bernabovis's wife, whom the council described as a "most notable and apt" woman. But the plan fell apart a year later when the state attorneys ruled that Bernabovis's bequest could not be used in this way. In the end it took another thirty-two years for the Venetians to try to establish a hospital on the model of those found in other cities.[31]

And in March 1443 Marco Foscari put forward a measure designed at least in part to maintain what was considered the proper ordering of society. On the 20th of that month he proposed a bill in the Senate forbidding women from wearing dresses made with gold or silver thread and other sorts of luxurious brocades and silks; like other such sumptuary laws, however, it provided an exemption for the doge's daughter-in-law and daughters for as long as they resided in the palace. The preamble stated that men were spending up to 600 ducats on such outfits and expressed concern that this was causing the ruin of the city and provoking the anger of God. The measure failed on a first vote but passed on a second ballot with 65 yeas, 49 nays, and 9 abstentions.[32] However after the vote, five of the six ducal councilors argued on the basis of a Senate law of 29 March 1425 that the bill needed a favorable vote by three-quarters of the Senate in order to pass.[33] The state attorneys appear to have decided otherwise; nevertheless, four of the councilors, Maffeo Donato, Ludovico Storlado, Tommaso Duodo, and Zaccaria Bembo, refused to withdraw their decision. As a result, on 9 April the state attorney Andrea Morosini brought the case before the Great Council, which voted that the four should withdraw their decision or be penalized (340 to 244 with 60 abstentions). The following day, on order of the doge, the councilors' effort to void the vote was itself annulled.[34]

It is difficult to determine exactly what was at stake in this fight between Marco Foscari and the ducal councilors. Judging by the number of negative votes on both the original bill and on the ruling against the councilors, it appears that a large number of nobles resisted further efforts by the state to limit men's ability to outfit their wives and daughters in such a way as to establish clear-cut social distinctions between those nobles who could afford such extravagant expense (and in so doing accrue honor and reputation for themselves) and the larger number of nobles who could not afford such outlays. In fact, just a year before, in March 1442 the Great Council had defeated in another sharply divided vote a sumptuary law proposed by the heads of the Forty, whose preamble lamented practices that were causing "confusion and scandal among our nobles, who ought to enjoy one honor and dignity." Contraveners were, as in the bill of March 1443, subject to increments of their *estimo* assessments.[35] But it is also possible that the doge's enemies saw Marco's proposal as yet another effort by the Foscari brothers to shore up their support among poorer members of the ruling class (and ironically to increase the stature of Foscari women given the ducal exemption). As a result the debate over women's apparel took on added political significance.

One thing is clear, however, namely that the increasingly fractured ruling elite preferred to use legal maneuvering and bureaucratic infighting to inflict injury on their enemies, as can be observed in the councilors' efforts to derail Marco Foscari's sumptuary law. In the autumn of 1444 another such contest pitted the Loredans against a Foscari ally. It began on 23 September 1444, when the heads of the Council of Ten, Francesco Loredan (son of the late Giorgio), Tommaso Querini, and Lorenzo Minio, put forward a bill in the Ten: this was designed to put an end to the practice whereby nobles were lobbying members of various councils for offices and other kinds of benefices as well as pleading with them for special consideration in legal cases. Among the penalties they proposed for those who engaged in such special pleading was expulsion from the island of San Marco for six months. Since San Marco was the center of political life in Venice, this amounted to a kind of internal exile. The bill passed on a vote of 8 to 4 with 3 abstentions. In order that no one could claim ignorance of the law, its contents were to be read twice a year in the Great Council and four times a year in the Senate.[36]

On the surface, the bill's effort to root out electoral corruption seems reasonable and laudable. However, it quickly became a tool for punishing one's enemies. On 29 September Loredan and Querini decided to prosecute Matteo Vitturi, one of the state attorneys, who immediately before entering the Council of Forty's chambers had listened to an appeal by the Florentine ambassador to Venice. But Loredan's and Querini's colleague Lorenzo Minio disagreed with their decision. Minio's dissension suggests that the prosecution rested on shaky legal footing.[37] In fact, on that same day he, along with the doge and four others, argued that Vitturi should not be prosecuted since there was no specific prohibition in the original bill on pleas from the ambassador from Florence. Their bill received 10 votes. An alternative proposal that the law did apply to the ambassador got only 4 votes, while two members of the Ten abstained.[38]

The matter might have ended there, with bad feelings on both sides, except that a few days later, Vitturi and the other state attorneys, Andrea Mocenigo and Andrea Donato, decided to prosecute Loredan on the charge that he had publicly disclosed the names of those who had proposed the original bill in the Ten regarding pleas and bribes. At that point the new heads of the Ten, citing various legal precedents, challenged the authority of the state attorneys to prosecute a case before the Ten. But a constitutional crisis was averted when the three state attorneys decided not to pursue the case further. Mocenigo and Donato chose not to follow it up precisely in order to avoid a showdown with the Ten, while Vitturi admitted that he had pursued the case out of a sense of vendetta (the Latin term *vindicta* is used).[39] As part of the compromise, the heads of the Ten apparently agreed to pursue the case against Loredan themselves: on 7 October they asked for a vote in the Ten on the charges against him. But the Ten failed to convict him.[40] On that same day the doge proposed a strict gag order on all these proceedings. His proposal that contraveners be deprived of all offices for ten years was defeated by Giovanni da Pesaro's less stringent bill, which promised to exclude them only from sitting on the Ten for ten years.[41] A week later, on 14 October the Ten made changes to the original law regarding bribes and lobbying, including the requirement that all three heads be in agreement to prosecute; otherwise the decision had to be brought to the entire council for consideration.[42]

This convoluted case is significant for several reasons. It suggests that lobbying had taken on a new and more threatening character. Bribes and other efforts to influence policy or subvert elections were nothing new in Venice. The records of various councils are filled with legislation, most of which proved futile, designed to curb various forms of corruption. Yet as the pleas by the Florentine ambassador illustrate, Venice's direct involvement on the terraferma opened up a vast new arena for the exercise of influence and the cultivation of friendship and patronage ties. Indeed, in the immediate aftermath of the fall of Padua to Venice at the beginning of the century, it came to light that Venice's great naval hero, Carlo Zeno, had received bribes from the Carraresi.[43] As that early example illustrates, Venice's relations with its terraferma domains and with the neighboring Italian states were of a different order from those with its overseas dominions. For one thing, the terraferma's geographic proximity to Venice, coupled with its common linguistic and cultural ties, made it easy for terraferma inhabitants and residents of other Italian states to operate within Venice. Additionally, administrative stints on the mainland, ambassadorships to other Italian states, and appointments as proveditors of the army provided ample opportunities for members of the patriciate to develop bonds to the elites of provincial cities, foreign princes, and condottieri – bonds that could influence policy. Complicating the situation even further were the economic ties that many patricians had with the terraferma, the result either of their investment in land or accumulation of church benefices. Following the conquest of the terraferma, the vast majority of the bishoprics came under the control of native Venetians. The same was true of the cathedral canonries of Treviso and Padua.[44] As the example of the Condulmer family indicates, involvement with the church created a fertile environment for divided loyalties.

But the case of Vitturi is even more significant for what it reveals about the continuing deterioration of relations within the patriciate and the emergence of factionalism. To the growing rancor and the decline of decorum in council debates noted in the previous chapter was now added a new and even more dangerous element: as Vitturi openly admitted, he pursued the case against Loredan out of a desire for revenge. The fear that members of the patriciate would use the law in an effort to advance or avenge their kinsmen's interests was certainly not new. Since the mid-thirteenth century various laws had been designed to curb the influence of families by excluding them from deliberations in which their interests were at stake.[45] And it was increasingly common following decisions in particularly sensitive or high-profile cases for the relatives of those convicted to be prohibited from ever sitting in judgement on those who had prosecuted and decided the case. Such a prohibition was enacted in 1433, for example, following the conspiracy by young nobles to subvert elections.[46] What was novel in the Vitturi case was the use of the term "vendetta" (*vindicta*). For perhaps the first time in Venice, it was used to describe this type of legislative maneuvering. The articulation of this impulse marked a dangerous new step in the coalescence or reemergence of factionalism within the patriciate. Generally speaking, factions do not exist in a steady state; rather they ebb and flow. Like a virus in the body, they can lie dormant for years, only to emerge following even a trivial incident or slight. The Vitturi case marks one of those eruptions, for it pitted two of the doge's close associates (Vitturi and Donato) against the Loredans. In so doing, it rekindled the old rivalry between the two families, a rivalry that had gone into partial remission following the death of Pietro Loredan.

All of these elements – the influence of terraferma contacts, the use of the law to wage vendetta, and the growth of factionalism – converged in the case brought against the doge's son in February 1445. The proceedings against Jacopo began on the 17th of that month when the three heads of the Council of Ten, Francesco Loredan, Giovanni Memmo, and Ermolao Donato, proposed that Jacopo's manservant Gasparo, as well as any others the council deemed necessary, be detained, interrogated, and if need be tortured. As was usual in these matters, the scribes did not record why they were investigating Jacopo since that information was well known to the council members. On the same day the Ten took two other actions with regard to the case. First, given the importance of the matter before them, they authorized the addition of a ten-man *zonta* to their deliberations. Among those selected to serve were five procurators of San Marco: Federico Contarini, Alvise Venier, Paolo Tron, Leonardo Giustinian, and Marco da Molin. Clearly, the Ten wanted to give their proceedings an added air of legitimacy by selecting these distinguished office-holders. Second, they imposed the strictest secrecy on their dealings and threatened anyone who contravened the order with a 1000-ducat fine and exclusion from all councils and offices.[47]

The Ten's first order of business on 18 February was to strengthen the previous day's gag order. They then turned to more pressing matters. They authorized Jacopo's arrest, interrogation, and possible torture, observing that the actions of which he was accused were not only serious but also "clearly disgraceful and dishonorable to the government of our state." Furthermore, they decided that if Jacopo could not be found, then the doge was to make him appear by Nones on Saturday; otherwise they would continue to proceed against him *in absentia*. Rethinking their deadline, they moved it up to the next day by Terce. An annotation in the margin of the register records that the doge's response was noted in an accompanying folder (now lost). But Jacopo could not be found for he had fled to Trieste. According to Aeneas Silvius Piccolomini's brief biographical sketch of the doge, Jacopo fled aboard a forty-oared ship and took with him "much gold." And so, the following day the Ten ordered officials throughout Venetian lands to be on the lookout for Jacopo and to arrest and return him to Venice.[48]

The Ten certainly understood that they were treading into dangerous territory by demanding the arrest of the doge's son. What neither they nor anyone else knew was how Foscari, his allies within the patriciate, or even the *popolo* might react to the news. However, based on Foscari's response to their action of the day before, they must have concluded that the doge would not undertake drastic measures to save his son. Rather the Ten feared more subtle forms of retribution. Accordingly, they approved a measure put forward by Loredan and Memmo (but not by Donato). It prohibited Foscari as well as his and Jacopo's relatives – whom the Ten defined as those who had to excuse themselves from voting in the Great Council when a relative was up for election – from ever sitting in judgement in any judicial case involving any members of the Ten and their *zonta* or their sons. They did this, as they noted, so that all members could speak their conscience "for the honor and good of the state of the Venetians," and in order that each "might not fear at any time vendetta (*vindictam*) from anyone for administering justice." The secretaries then recorded in their register the names of all those involved in the case, including their own.[49]

What the Ten managed quite unwittingly to do by passing this law was to give shape and definition to what heretofore had been only vaguely defined interest groups. In essence they defined the core of the Foscari party – namely the Foscari kinsmen. In the process what they also did was to create a list (formally compiled by the secretaries) of those who, as a result of this bill, were now defined as an oppositional group to the Foscari – a group that was subject to possible vendetta by means of the law. It is unlikely that many members of the Ten and *zonta*, with the exception of Francesco Loredan, felt any particular animus toward the doge; but by their own action they had set themselves up as his opponents. Moreover, the extension of the legal protection to sons guaranteed that these groupings would survive at least into the next generation. The seeds had been sown for even greater discord within the heart of the government.

Those consequences would play out over time. The Ten's immediate concern was to continue their proceedings against Jacopo. On 20 February Loredan, Memmo, and Donato proposed a bill that provides some clues to the accusations against Jacopo. The three heads of the Ten noted that, based on their interrogations, they had learned that there was in the ducal apartments or in the doge's house (by which they presumably meant his family palace) or elsewhere a coffer containing various items that Jacopo had received, including "writings, jewels, and many other things." The Ten wanted this coffer confiscated. But the Ten and *zonta* failed to pass the measure by a vote of 12 to 12 with 2 abstentions.[50] Evidently they felt some qualms about this intrusion into the doge's private quarters.

It is unclear whether or not the Ten eventually got access to the coffer, but Dolfin's chronicle reveals why they wanted to examine its contents. For the accusation against Jacopo was that he had used his servants, especially Gasparo, as intermediaries to acquire "presents and gifts of money, jewels, and similar things" from various "lords, communities, and citizens" in clear violation of the laws of Venice, even including the ducal *promissione*. Among those attempting to influence Jacopo, as shown by Gasparo's later condemnation, were the Bishop of Concordia and, most shocking of all, Visconti. Both Dolfin, a relation of the doge and his son, and Sanudo, no admirer of the doge, were harsh in their condemnation of Jacopo's action. According to Dolfin, he was inspired by a malignant spirit to commit these acts, "not thinking of God or the honor of his fatherland." Sanudo, who clearly relied on Dolfin's chronicle for much of his account of the affair, notes that Jacopo brought "infamy" on the government. But it is impossible to confirm Dolfin's claim that Jacopo was examined for four days or Sanudo's that he was tortured with the *corda*. All this would have taken place in Trieste, but there is no indication in the Ten's extant records that such an examination was authorized there.[51]

With several centuries of hindsight, it appears that Jacopo was foolish rather than malevolent; that he was driven by greed and perhaps by the desire to appear important rather than by any intention to hurt the Venetian state. The awkward position of ducal sons has already been noted: they enjoyed special rank and distinction but were often excluded from most real positions of power.[52] This enforced leisure must have chafed Jacopo who occupied his time with humanist studies, an avocation that put him into contact with scholars and statesmen across Italy. But it might well have been those very contacts, coupled with his position as the doge's son, which made Jacopo a special target of those who wished to parlay gifts and bribes into favors and influence. None of this excuses Jacopo; he had to know that his actions were illegal and potentially damaging to the state. It merely recognizes that he was susceptible to the influence of foreign contacts; such influence had increased considerably for all patricians since the conquest of the terraferma.

Before proceeding to the sentencing of Jacopo, the Ten extended the same protection against retribution by the doge and Jacopo's relatives to all those who had testified in the case. But when it came to the sentencing phase, a disagreement developed among the heads of the Ten. Memmo and Donato wanted to move forward with the condemnation. Their proposal to do so received 20 votes. Francesco Loredan, by contrast, proposed that the *zonta* be reauthorized and various witnesses reexamined and re-tortured in order better to get at the truth. His proposal received a mere 6 votes, and so they proceeded to the sentencing.[53]

As noted at the beginning of this chapter, the Ten with its *zonta* sentenced Jacopo on 20 February 1445 to perpetual exile in the city of Nauplion in Romania, the term the Venetians used for the Byzantine or Greek east. Jacopo was to be transported to Nauplion – located in the Morea near the ancient city of Argos – on a ship known as the *Tre-*

visana. The Ten further ruled that once in Nauplion, Jacopo could retain no more than three male servants and that he had to report to the Venetian governors of the city every day and sleep within the city confines every night. The rectors of the city were to be instructed to treat him as a "private citizen." And if he escaped, he was to be returned to Venice and decapitated. The condemnation further authorized the heads of the Ten and the state attorneys to investigate from whom Jacopo had received the gifts and bribes and where they might be hidden. The plan was to restitute them to their donors, "for the honor of our dominion." The bill concluded with a number of clauses forbidding any efforts to revoke it.[54]

The Ten then spent the next several days clearing up a number of ancillary matters and punishing Jacopo's accomplices. First, they authorized bodyguards for themselves and for the *signori di notte* who had assisted them. They also extended this protection to noblemen Priamo Contarini and Andrea Dandolo, son of the late Giacomo, whom they described as the "principal witnesses" in the case against the doge's son. They condemned Jacopo's servants Gasparo and Pietro Varotari for assisting him with the bribes and gifts. Gasparo, who had fled the city, was to be banished for two years and permanently excluded from all offices and benefices in the city. Pietro was declared permanently ineligible for offices and was forbidden to serve the ducal family or to live in the Ducal Palace. A third servant by the name of Gianpietro was found to know about only one instance in which Jacopo had received a gift from an unnamed Greek. According to the Ten's records, Jacopo got the gift on account of his knowledge of the Greek language. Like Pietro, Gianpietro was forbidden to live in the palace or to serve the ducal family. And the Ten condemned Oliverio Albanese, the captain of Rialto, who had assisted in Jacopo's flight. Presumably he helped Jacopo secure the forty-oared ship that Piccolomini mentions. For his action, he was banned from all offices. The Ten also decided that henceforth the office of captain of Rialto should be awarded only to *cittadini originarii*, an elite core of citizens, a group in whom they placed special trust.[55]

On 25 February the Ten approved the commission of Marco Trevisan, the captain of the ship designated to transport Jacopo to the east. As many have noted in the past, the commission was drawn up in the doge's name, that is, in a strictly literal sense it was Foscari himself who ordered his son to be exiled to Greece. But, of course, this was merely a legal formality. Trevisan received orders to proceed to Trieste and, if Jacopo were there, to show him the order that he be transported to Modon. What this suggests is that, contrary to the reports of both Dolfin and Sanudo, Jacopo had not been captured; instead it appears that an agreement had been worked out, presumably with his father as mediator, that Jacopo would surrender himself within eight days in Trieste. During the voyage to Modon, Trevisan was to treat Jacopo as an "ordinary citizen" and was not, in any circumstances, to allow him to disembark. Once in Modon, Trevisan was to entrust him to the castellan who would arrange for his transfer to Nauplion within a month. In addition, Trevisan was told to find out if possible where Jacopo had stashed his money and other belongings, in order that the bribes could be restituted to those who gave them. Finally, if Jacopo's chancellor Bartolo da Cremona was with him, he was to be arrested and returned to Venice for interrogation.[56]

There is no explicit record of how Foscari reacted to his son's condemnation. However, the events of the next two months suggest that he was torn between his own paternal feelings and the dogaressa's entreaties to be merciful on the one hand, and his obligations as head of state on the other. The pressure mounted as Jacopo's departure from Trieste got delayed on account of sickness. He was apparently so ill that the dogaressa wanted to travel to Trieste to visit him. On 3 March Foscari made her desire known to his councilors, but by a vote of 11 to 3 with 1 abstention the Ten forbade her to do so, although they noted that their decision should be conveyed to the doge as diplomatically as possible.[57] The doge and Ten were again at loggerheads a week later, when according to the Ten's records, the doge insistently demanded that he be given a list of the items that Jacopo had supposedly acquired as gifts and bribes. For two days the Ten debated various responses to the doge's entreaty. One proposal, put forward by Francesco Balbi and Pietro Michiel, two of the three new heads of the Ten, was that Foscari order his son to go into exile since they were sure that Jacopo would obey his father's command. This same proposal also hints that some among the Ten were threatening to have Jacopo declared in violation of the exile order and hence subject to re-arrest and transfer to Venice for beheading. In the end, the only thing the Ten could agree upon was the need to appoint a new *zonta* of ten men.[58] On 7 April the Ten expressed their clear concern that their orders were still not being obeyed: Jacopo had still not gone into exile, and the bribes had still not been recouped. Furthermore, they ruled that a *zonta* had to be elected whenever Jacopo's case was under consideration and that at least seven members of the *zonta* had to be in attendance at meetings. Finally they declared that negotiations between the heads of the Ten and the state attorneys had in no way breached Jacopo's original condemnation.[59]

Clearly, Jacopo's failure to obey the order to go into exile represented a significant constitutional crisis – one that called into question the authority of the Council of Ten, Venice's most powerful body. And the one who appears chiefly responsible for this crisis was not Jacopo but the doge. As Balbi and Michiel observed, had Foscari brought his full weight as *paterfamilias* and doge to bear, he probably could have compelled Jacopo to obey. But the doge did not do that; instead, like Jacopo, he temporized, allowing what may at first have been a valid excuse, namely Jacopo's illness, to drag on while he apparently sought a more favorable outcome. In this Foscari clearly breached his ducal responsibility to uphold justice and execute it equitably. Just why he chose to do this remains unclear. Perhaps he knew Jacopo was guilty but allowed his feelings for him to interfere with his responsibility or maybe he believed that Jacopo had been framed and that the entire affair was nothing more than an effort to destroy him by means of his son. Regardless, Jacopo remained in Trieste, in direct violation of the Ten's orders. The crisis continued unresolved.

The affair remained at the center of domestic politics for much of the next year and a half as Jacopo lingered in Trieste in defiance of the Ten's orders. In October 1445 the Ten discussed some particulars of the case, at the same time imposing a gag order on their proceedings. A week later they appointed another *zonta* as required by the law of 7 April. But no further action was taken at that time.[60] Jacopo's condemnation evidently plunged the doge into a long period of official inactivity. The record shows, for example, that in January and February 1445, that is in the weeks immediately preceding the scandal, Foscari proposed six laws in the Senate but that he proposed none whatsoever during the rest of the year. He spent his energy instead working to secure a pardon for Jacopo. The Ten became concerned, for example, in January 1446 when they learned that the ducal councilors had recently given permission to Foscari to have a private discussion with Francesco Condulmer, whom they described as the Venetian cardinal, perhaps regarding Jacopo. The *promissione* forbade the doge to meet with ambassadors and nuncios except in the presence of his councilors, but a proposal in the Ten to reinforce the prohibition failed on a technicality.[61] In March and June 1446 the Ten again discussed particulars of the case but took no action. But they did pass laws forbidding anyone from informing the doge of what had transpired in their meetings and granting each participant the right of having up to five bodyguards.[62]

On 25 November the action moved to the Great Council, where the six ducal councilors proposed a bill authorizing the Ten to reconsider the sentence against Jacopo, based on the extraordinary circumstances that had conjoined to prevent his removal to Nauplion. According to the councilors, when it came time for Trevisan to transport Jacopo to the east, Jacopo was so ill that he was bedridden and in danger of dying. Furthermore, on his arrival in Trieste, Trevisan had himself taken ill and died on an unknown date. According to the councilors, it went against "all laws, all equity, and all justice and humanity" to proceed with something that clearly contravened the "divine will and disposition." They proposed that the Ten be allowed to review the case without incurring the penalties imposed in the original condemnation against those who might propose a pardon.[63] According to Dolfin, the Ten had given their approval for this measure to be put forward in the Great Council: the extant records of the Ten contain no such authorization, although they do note that on 23 November they examined the contents of a letter which they vowed to keep secret. It may well have concerned this case.[64]

What also seems likely is that the doge had worked to prepare the way for a change in the terms of Jacopo's exile by solidifying his support within the Great Council. Dolfin reports that after the bill was put forward Foscari addressed the council. In his speech he recounted for the assembled nobles all his efforts on behalf of the state, reminding them that he had never spared anything in this regard. He now asked them to concede to him in his old age the favor of having his last surviving son at his side. At this point in his speech, he became so distraught, crying and sobbing, that he was unable to finish and had to leave the Council Hall and return to his apartments. When debate continued, Pietro Querini and Michele Morosini spoke against the measure, while Niccolò Bernardo, Candiano Bollani, Andrea Barbo, and Antonio

1   Lazzaro Bastiani, portrait of Doge Francesco Foscari. Museo Civico Correr.

2   *(facing page top)* *Promissione* portrait of Doge Foscari, prologue page, fol. 4v. Private collection, Milan.

3   *(facing page bottom left)* *Promissione* portrait of Doge Foscari, prologue page, fol. 4v. Detail showing Foscari being presented to Saint Mark by Saints Francis and Nicholas.

4   *(facing page bottom right)* Leonardo Bellini (attrib.), portrait of Doge Foscari. Biblioteca Nazionale Marciana, Lat. Cl. X, 190 (3555), fol. 6r.

5   *(above)* Chapel of the Madonna (Mascoli Chapel), basilica of San Marco.

6 Giovanni and Bartolomeo Bon, the Porta della Carta, Ducal Palace.

7 *(facing page top)* Arco Foscari, Ducal Palace.

8 *(facing page bottom)* Arco Foscari, Ducal Palace, showing the first-floor Foscari phase of the project.

9 Cà Foscari.

10 Tomb of Doge Francesco Foscari, Santa Maria Gloriosa dei Frari.

11   Eugène Delacroix, *I due Foscari*. Musée Condé, Chantilly.

Venier (nicknamed Braxuola) spoke in its favor. The bill passed by a vote of 597 in favor, with 231 opposed and 80 abstentions.[65]

With the Great Council's authorization to do so, the Ten then took up the matter on 28 November, when the three heads of the Ten, Lorenzo Minio, Giovanni da Pesaro and Andrea Bernardo, using words taken almost verbatim from the preamble of the Great Council law, namely that divine will had impeded Jacopo's transfer to Nauplion, now proposed that "in the name of Jesus Christ" the Ten accept as "legitimate and honest" the reasons why the Ten's original order had not been carried out. Their measure passed with 15 votes. An alternative proposal by Marino Soranzo, that the matter be handled as a pardon rather than an actual bill, failed when it received 9 favorable votes and 1 abstention.[66]

With this action complete, the Ten then moved to change the terms of Jacopo's exile. Observing that Jacopo ought not remain in "foreign lands to the burden and interest of the most serene lord doge" but that he "should live in lands subject to the dominion of the Venetians and of this city, as was always the intention of this Council," the three heads of the Ten, now with the support of the ducal councilors Andrea Zulian, Marino Zane, and Niccolò Bernardo, proposed that Jacopo should be confined to Treviso and the Trevigiano as had been the case many times in the past for both nobles and *popolani*. The bill further provided that with a special license Jacopo could be allowed to go "in villegiatura," that is he could seek permission to visit the Foscari villa at Zellarino. But the bill also provided that if he broke the terms of his confinement, he would be imprisoned for a year in Treviso and fined 1000 ducats. It further detailed that all the gifts received by Jacopo had to be repaid from his personal accounts, and that if they were not sufficient, then from the doge's funds. Any unclaimed monies and gifts were to go into the communal coffers. Like the previous bill to accept Jacopo's excuses, this one passed with 15 votes. Again, an alternative bill by Soranzo failed when it got 10 votes. It placed slightly more restrictions on Jacopo, confining him to a more circumscribed area within Treviso and to the Cenedese, that is the region furthest from Venice. Furthermore, it specified that he was to receive no gifts or presents and that before taking up his exile in Treviso, he should hand over all the gifts he had received, which amounted to more than 1400 ducats' worth of goods, so that they could be returned to those who had given them.[67] Throughout the entire affair, the Ten demonstrated an almost obsessive desire to make sure that the gifts were returned. In this way they wished to purify the state and annul the obligations Jacopo had incurred by accepting them.

Dolfin reports that Jacopo reached Treviso on Sunday 4 December and that he himself was present when Jacopo arrived. The two men were second cousins, and upon seeing one another, they embraced. The occasion seems to have been a festive one for Dolfin also recounts that the podesta, Francesco da Lezze, turned out to greet Jacopo, as did "the entire community of Treviso."[68] In early January the Venetian humanist Lauro Querini sent fawning letters to both Jacopo and his father congratulating them on the return. In an effort to paint Jacopo's exile in a flattering light, he compared it with the exile of illustrious ancients, proclaiming that the disgrace of the exile in no way compared with the glory of the return.[69] In his account of the return Dolfin failed to note the irony of Jacopo's arrival on 4 December, the feast of Saint Barbara. That was the day on which the Great Council held its annual lottery, known as the *Barbarella*, to determine which noble youths would have the honor of entering the Great Council at eighteen rather than waiting until the customary age of twenty-five.[70] The occasion was surrounded by much excitement, and patrician families celebrated when their sons won this much-coveted privilege of beginning their political careers early. On this same day and in his own very peculiar way, Jacopo too had made a new entry into the sphere of Venetian politics.

Several months after his arrival in Treviso, Foscari and his son set about fulfilling one of the terms of Jacopo's return, namely the restoration of the gifts he had received. The Ten reported that the doge had a coffer in his possession and that it contained 2040 ducats or thereabouts as well as silverware and other items which, as both Foscari and Francesco Sforza's secretary certified, had been given to Jacopo by Sforza. On 5 April 1447 the Ten voted that a three-man delegation should go to the doge and retrieve the items and that the money should be used to help pay for the armament of a galley which the Ten had authorized on that very same day to conduct a special mission. Andrea Querini, Giovanni Malipiero, and Giovanni Giustinian were selected to get the contents of the coffer from the doge.[71]

Several questions remain unanswered here. Readers will recall that in February 1445 the Ten became aware of the existence of the coffer, but in a sharply divided vote (12 to 12 with 2 abstentions) failed to pass a measure to seize it.[72] At the time, the Ten believed that the coffer was in the Ducal Palace or "in the house of the lord doge," while their law of 1447 noted that the coffer was in Foscari's possession. Perhaps Jacopo had absconded with the box and its contents and then entrusted it to his father; but it seems more likely that it remained in one of the doge's residences. If it remained in the doge's possession the entire time, then it provides evidence that Foscari was actively hindering the investigation of his son, in clear violation of his duty, and that Venice's progenitors were right, as Girolamo Priuli observed at the beginning of the sixteenth century, to fear that ducal sons would cloud their fathers' judgement (as quoted in the epigraph to this chapter). With Jacopo now safely in Treviso, it must have appeared to Foscari that fortune's wheel had finally turned in his favor. But the galley which the Ten funded with the money from Jacopo's coffer had the mission of proceeding to the island of Crete to arrest yet another of Foscari's close kinsmen: his son-in-law Andrea Donato was now also snagged in the net of international intrigues.

By the time the Council of Ten ordered Donato's arrest, he had already enjoyed a long and distinguished career in politics, although not without its own share of controversy. He entered the Great Council in 1413 and held his first post, as captain of the Istrian guard, in 1417. After the death of his first wife, Maria da Canal, he married Foscari's daughter Camilla in 1432. Throughout the 1430s and 1440s he served the Republic almost without interruption, holding numerous posts in the city and on the terraferma, and traveling, as noted above, on important diplomatic missions to the Mamluk sultan and to Emperor Sigismund. It was during one of the latter that Sigismund knighted him. To commemorate that event, Donato inserted a rose into his coat of arms; henceforth his branch of the family was known as the Donà dalle Rose. Also as noted above, Foscari maneuvered to exculpate Donato for allowing Piccinino to overrun the Veronese in 1439.[73] It was during his various missions on the terraferma that Donato struck up a friendship with Sforza.

When the Ten ordered Donato's arrest, Venice and Sforza were moving rapidly toward a formal break in relations. As early as February 1447 the condottiere had reached a secret agreement with Visconti to form a league against Venice.[74] In March Sforza's secretary Angelo Simonetta went to Venice for the purpose of selling shares of Venetian government bonds as well as various properties he owned in the Padovano and Veronese. Clearly he was liquidating Milanese assets before the outbreak of conflict. He may have been on a bribery mission as well. The Ten ordered him arrested and tortured, at the same time imposing a strict gag order on their proceedings. Based on Simonetta's revelations, Donato came under suspicion of having been corrupted by Sforza and his agents. Accordingly, on 5 April the Ten ordered Donato's arrest.[75] At the time he was serving as the governor, or as the Venetians styled it, the Duke of Crete. It was during these interrogations of Simonetta that the Ten learned of the coffer containing the money and silver given to Jacopo. However, the contents of the coffer were found to amount to 2400 ducats, 1000 more than the amount that Jacopo had originally been charged with taking. The difference raises the question of whether or not Foscari himself had received gifts from Sforza. Perhaps in this moment of international crisis, the Ten chose to ignore that disturbing possibility.

On 12 April the Ten drew up in Foscari's name orders for Benedetto da Lezze to sail to Candia in Crete and take Donato, as they had done with Carmagnola, by means of a ruse. The plan was this: once on the island, da Lezze was to send a messenger to Donato telling him that he needed his advice concerning a mission he was on to the Levant. The Ten were sure that Donato, who had served on missions to the sultan, would hurry to da Lezze's galley for consultation with him. But if for some reason he should not comply, then he was to be arrested. Once on board, da Lezze was to sail for Venice immediately, making sure that during the return voyage Donato was unable to flee or communicate with anyone.[76]

On the same day that they gave the order for Donato's capture, the Ten dealt with several other nobles whose names had also come to light during Simonetta's interrogation. By a vote of 22 to 1 with 1 abstention, they decided not to pursue the case against Andrea Venier for the time being. The vote concerning nobleman Andrea Morosini, who was accused of receiving money from Giovanni da Cremona, was inconclusive. And in a sharply divided vote (13 in favor with 11 abstentions) the Ten decided to proceed against the estate of the late Giovanni Pisani for 200 ducats received from Sforza. A previous vote on this matter had failed when 14 members of the Ten abstained. The Ten voted to fine his estate 200 ducats and to add the money to the council's coffers. In addition, they ruled that neither Pisani's sons nor his grandsons should ever sit as judges in any cases involving the current members of the Ten. In the end the cases against Venier, Morosini, and Pisani came to naught. That against Venier was allowed to drop, while Morosini and Giovanni da Cremona were both found innocent. And in September 1448 Pisani's sons managed to get a posthumous pardon for their father. They admitted that their father had received 200 ducats from Sforza, but claimed that he had used the money to purchase bread for the troops.[77] In the meantime, the Ten had authorized the use of the confiscated funds to pay for boats to patrol the city during the current outbreak of the plague.[78]

Throughout these proceedings, the Ten were clearly concerned with their own security and that of the state. They voted bodyguards for themselves and ordered that once da Lezze boarded his galley for Crete, he should not disembark even while the ship remained in Venice.[79] The plan to trick Donato proceeded without a hitch: having been returned to Venice along with his wife Camilla (Foscari's daughter) and their family, he was imprisoned and interrogated by the Ten. According to Dolfin, he confessed to having received money from Sforza, who hoped for Donato's aid in promoting his interests with the Venetian government.[80] On 5 June 1447, by a vote of 15 to 4 with 8 abstentions, the Ten found him guilty and proceeded to sentence him. They ordered him jailed for a year and permanently banned from all offices in the government. Furthermore, they demanded that he surrender to the communal treasury the 900 ducats he had received from Sforza and an additional 900 as a penalty. They forbade any future granting of a pardon to Donato and ruled that neither his sons nor his grandsons should ever sit as judges in any cases involving members of the Ten or its *zonta*. That same day they also imposed a gag order on their proceedings.[81] Later in the month, the Ten voted to exile Simonetta to Crete. With its business finished, the Ten dissolved the *zonta* on 22 June.[82]

The entanglement of both Foscari's son and son-in-law in Sforza's plots illustrates just how vulnerable the doge's relatives had become to foreign machinations. They were natural targets for those hoping to influence the regime, especially since men such as Sforza who were more used to dealing with princely regimes across the Italian peninsula than with republican ones might naturally assume that the way to influence the doge was through his kinsmen. It seems clear that neither Jacopo nor Donato intended to harm in any way the Venetian state itself. Even as the Ten hatched their plot to trick Donato, they remained confident of his loyalty; that is, they were convinced that when da Lezze notified him that he needed his counsel, Donato would hurry to his side. But what both men did was allow their judgement to be clouded by Sforza's flattery and money.[83] Yet Jacopo and Donato were not alone in allowing personal relations and bonds of friendship with the mercenary captains and foreign princes to obscure the already ill-marked boundaries between public and private interests, thus rendering the regime more vulnerable to various forms of corruption.

Churchmen, as mentioned above, posed special problems as their loyalties were divided; but even laymen were vulnerable, especially where church benefices were concerned. The government was well aware that patricians whose kinsmen held important ecclesiastical posts might find it impossible to draw impartial and independent conclusions when it came to Venice's relations with the pope. In order to obviate this problem, the Ten had passed in 1411 a law forbidding nobles whose families held church benefices from participating in any meetings of councils in which relations between the Republic and the papacy or concerning other ecclesiastical institutions were discussed. But in July 1447 the Ten were confronted with the issue as it applied to the doge: as will be recalled from the preface, during a recent meeting Foscari had left the proceedings since they touched upon one of his nephews – Pietro, son of Foscari's brother Marco – whom the doge had recently named *primicerio* of San Marco and whom the pope had awarded several benefices. Wishing to clarify the situation for the future, Benedetto Vitturi, Benedetto da Mula, and Andrea Foscolo proposed in the Ten that the law not apply to the doge.[84]

Their bill with its extraordinary description of the doge as the *imago* of Venice reminds one not to lose sight of the very special regard in which the doge was held – a regard best illustrated by the placement of his image on the ducat (fig. 4). Doges were more than mere office-holders, they were veritable icons of the state, the living embodiment or representation of the Venetian polity, and the recipients of special authority through their relationship with Saint Mark. Doges were not, as the wording of the bill makes clear, simply the first among equals: they enjoyed a primacy that set them apart from other members of the patriciate; this carried as one of its privileges exemption from many of the rules as they applied to others. All this must be kept in mind in tracing the story of Foscari and his efforts to rehabilitate Jacopo. As doge, Foscari was able to draw on sources of power unavailable to any of his opponents, and he might well have felt that he was justified in seeking special treatment for his son.

As the efforts of Sforza to influence various members of Foscari's inner circle indicate, the situation on the Italian peninsula remained very much in flux as events continued to rotate around the eventual disposition of the Milanese state. In the midst of all the turmoil involving Jacopo, Venice again found itself starting in the spring of 1446 at war with Visconti. Conflict erupted when Sforza, who had been excommunicated by the pope, attacked territory in the Marches. In turn, Visconti acted to reclaim for himself the cities of Cremona and Pontremoli, which he had given to Sforza as part of Bianca Maria's dowry. In late April Milanese forces under Francesco Picchino entered the Cremonese and in early May occupied Soncino and Romanengo. The Venetian military commander Michele Attendolo, Count of Cotignola, massed his troops in the area, while the government encouraged Sforza to return from the Marches to protect Cremona. Finally, after a series of failed negotiations with Visconti, Venice and Florence decided to make a stand at Cremona. In late September the two sides met in battle at the island of Mezzano, near Casalmaggiore. Piccinino and the Milanese suffered a major defeat as the Venetians captured many of their captains, supplies, and four thousand horses. In Venice the victory was celebrated with processions and almsgiving. In addition the Great Council approved Foscari's proposal that Cotignola be granted membership of that body; and in January 1447 he received the town of Castelfranco in the Veneto as a fief. The captain-general followed up the victory by taking many towns, including Romanengo, Treviglio, and Caravaggio, and on 7 November entered Milanese territory. The Venetians' rapid success and what appeared to be the impending destruction of the Milanese state now alarmed the other powers in Italy, who feared growing Venetian success. It also unsettled Sforza, who had his own ambitions to control Milan. But rather than proceeding on toward Milan, the Venetian forces took up winter quarters; and the year ended with failed negotiations between Visconti and Venice in which the duke offered the Venetians Ghiaradadda but little else.[85]

The next year, 1447, was momentous, marked as it was by a number of changes across the peninsula. Already in the fall of 1446 Visconti had begun negotiating a rapprochement with Sforza, who, while encouraging these talks, was hesitant to break definitively with Venice. For their part, the Venetians counseled Sforza to hold firm to their alliance. In February, however, Visconti and Sforza reached a secret accord to form a league against Venice – a league that would also include the pope and Alfonso of Naples. At the same time, Visconti began negotiating with the French about their aid in recovering Bergamo and Brescia, in return for which Visconti would give up Asti. But all these plans were temporarily thrown into chaos with the death of Eugenius IV on 23 February and the election of Nicholas V in his stead.[86]

Recognizing that a break with Sforza was inevitable, the Venetians decided to send Cotignola to secure Cremona, which belonged to Sforza. At the same time, Sforza sent his secretary Simonetta to Venice on the mission that brought about the downfall of Donato. On the very day that the Ten decided to imprison Simonetta, they also voted to confiscate the Palace of the Two Towers, which the government had presented to Sforza: the Ten now referred to him as "our enemy." Claiming that the palace had become a haven for rebels, the Ten ordered it closed, the door shut, and all the inhabitants expelled except for a custodian who was to remain in the building until the Ten could decide upon its final disposition.[87]

The confiscation of Sforza's palace on the Grand Canal served as a highly visible demonstration of Venice's displeasure with the mercenary captain since, as noted above, the gift of a palace was among the highest honors the Venetian government could bestow upon a foreigner. In Sforza's case, the prestige was intensified by the palace's prominent position at the point where the canal turns in the journey from San Marco to Rialto. All those passing by would have had their attention drawn to Sforza and his special relationship with the Venetians. But now honor turned to shame, as the Ten used the palace to publicize the Republic's displeasure with Sforza. The closed door was particularly significant since, as architectural historians and anthropologists have demonstrated, thresholds are spaces redolent with meaning. At the beginning of the fourteenth century the Council of Ten had punished the noble Balduino family for their participation in the Querini-Tiepolo conspiracy by ordering that the door of their palace at Rialto remain perpetually open.

In so doing, they signaled that the Balduino were powerless in face of the government, unable to control their family property. In Sforza's case, the closed door signified that he had been shut out; that he was no longer able to enter a space that had once been designated as his. The Ten's characterization of the palace as a receptacle for traitors also suggests the almost totemic significance of palaces in the Renaissance. Sforza's palace had in a sense taken on the character of its inhabitant and as such represented a nefarious presence in the very heart of the city.[88]

During the summer Cotignola continued to make raids into Milanese territory while peace negotiations proceeded in Ferrara. However, the entire situation took another dramatic turn when on 13 August Visconti died. The man who for more than thirty-five years had been the focus of Venetian policy was gone, but not the problem he embodied – the settlement of Milan. The issue remained confused since during his lifetime Visconti had written four different wills, naming variously Visconti kinsmen, Sforza, and Alfonso of Aragon as his heir. The French as well as the Holy Roman Emperor also had an interest in the Milanese succession. But the citizens of Milan had a different plan for after nearly one hundred and fifty years of Visconti family rule, they quickly constituted the Ambrosian Republic, named after Ambrose, the fourth-century Bishop of Milan and the city's patron saint. At the same time, some of the subject cities threw off the yoke of Milanese rule; two of them, Lodi and Piacenza, placed themselves under Venetian protection. Control of these cities gave Venice effective control of the rivers Adda and Po and thus the ability to suffocate the Lombard capital. Meanwhile, in Milan itself, some favored an alliance with Venice, pending some territorial concessions; but in the end the Milanese chose to rely instead on Sforza, whom they hired as the city's captain-general with the promise that he would be rewarded with either Brescia or Verona once those cities were wrested from the Venetians.[89]

Now that a major conflict with Sforza was inevitable, the Senate made ready by authorizing on 4 September the creation of a huge Po fleet, observing that "it is certain that when one makes war well, one makes peace well."[90] The government also prepared for the conflict by resolving what clearly had come to be perceived as a major impediment to Venetian success, namely Foscari's continuing preoccupation with the fate of Jacopo. In September the Ten received a supplication from the doge in which he made the case for why Jacopo should be allowed to return from exile in Treviso. Foscari began by noting that Jacopo's situation had taken a terrible toll on his own mind and body, making it difficult for him in his "extreme old age" (he was now seventy-four) to do "that which he is obliged and that which he wishes to do for this Republic." He then painted a pitiful picture of Jacopo's plight. For the past three years Jacopo had been at loose ends, living in the houses of others. Worse still, a "terrible fever" now plagued the region around Mestre, where, according to the doge, there were "neither doctors nor medicine and more still, no one but servants." The fever had already claimed several victims: Jacopo's wife was ill, as were three of their four girls; Jacopo's dear elder son was sick, as was the wetnurse of his newborn son. The nurse's illness seemed destined to doom the nursling: one "could almost say that the boy is lost." All this was so much to bear that death itself would be dearer than continuing to live. And so the doge asked, as a "remedy" to his troubles, that "his only and most unhappy son be absolved of the exile and be returned to his own fatherland."[91]

In response, the heads of the Ten, Marco Longo, Matteo Vitturi, and Vittore Capello, proposed that the doge's petition be granted on several grounds. First, the present situation required that the state be headed by a prince who "is free and not preoccupied, [but] with his undivided attention, directs the government and republic." In the current circumstances, as the preamble to the bill made clear, this was not the case as was patently obvious to all. The doge was sick in both mind and body. Second, it was an act of piety to show the doge the same humanity and favor that had been shown to other nobles in the past, especially as God had shown such favor to the city. And finally, the doge's actions on behalf of the Republic merited this reward, especially since it concerned his sole surviving son. The Ten passed the bill with 19 votes in favor, 1 against, and 3 abstentions.[92]

As the bill makes clear, two arguments seem to have carried weight with the Ten and convinced them to repatriate Jacopo. The first regarded the welfare of the state. At this critical juncture in the Republic's history, with the fate of Milan in the balance, it was essential that the doge be a strong leader. Otherwise the future of Venice itself might be in jeopardy. But just as important was the appeal to the heartstrings. Four times in Foscari's petition and bill, Jacopo is referred to as the doge's "only son." During the summer of 1447 Venice was struck by a particularly devastating outbreak of the plague. Sanudo reports that processions were held, masses sung at specially constructed outdoor altars, and fires lit to purge the air.[93] Certainly members of the Ten watched as friends and kinsmen, including perhaps some of their own sons, succumbed to the disease. This no doubt led them to empathize with a man who had seen all of his sons save one snatched away by death. Of course politics played an essential role as well. One of the men proposing the bill was Foscari's ally Matteo Vitturi, son of the late Bulgaro. Foscari's supporters wished to set right what they saw as a wrong against the doge. And the petition itself was designed to elicit maximum sympathy for the doge with its carefully crafted description of his unrelenting service to the state and its pitiful depiction of his fever-ridden grandchildren. The characterization of Jacopo as homeless doubtless played well to an audience of nobles who placed great significance on palaces as repositories of family identity and believed that kinsmen ought to be gathered together between their sheltering walls. Inexplicably, however, neither Dolfin nor Sanudo takes note of Jacopo's repatriation.

With Visconti's death, a critical change occurred as Venice replaced the now-deceased ruler of Milan as the perceived aggressor in Italian affairs. Since the reign of Giangaleazzo Visconti, who died in 1402, Milan had earned the reputation as the greatest threat to its neighbors and hence to the stability of the entire peninsula. But with the future of Milan uncertain and with Venetian troops on the western shore of the Adda, the other powers began to fear what would happen should the Venetian Republic conquer the Lombard capital. Even Venice's putative ally, Florence, grew increasingly wary, with Cosimo de' Medici warning that it was crucial that "the Venetians not become the lords of Italy."[94] For their part, the Venetians waged an unsuccessful public-relations campaign designed to mute the growing chorus of criticism. When, for example, in July 1447 they were considering a second assault on Milan, the Senate authorized the fabrication of a flag with a red cross on a white field and below it a figure of Saint Ambrose with a banderol in his hand emblazoned with the words *Libertas populi Mediolani et liga* (Liberty for the *popolo* of Milan and the League). The banner was supposed to help convince the Milanese "that we are not making war on the duke out of ambition to rule but only in order to be and live in secure peace."[95] Similarly, when in September the Ambrosian Republic protested Venice's takeover of Lodi, the Senate responded that that city had "spontaneously

and of its own will" pledged itself to Venice and that otherwise it would
have fallen to Sforza, damaging both Milan and Venice. It is unlikely,
however, that such arguments, much less colorful flags, persuaded the
Milanese that they were safe, especially when thousands of Venetian
troops were already lodged in Lombardy.[96]

The Republic's new more vigorous stance also prompted an internal
debate within the patriciate over the rectitude of Venetian actions. Some
within the patriciate called into question the Republic's motives. Among
them was the humanist Francesco Barbaro. As his record of service to
the state, including his heroic action during the siege of Brescia indicates, Barbaro was not opposed to Venice's original expansion into
eastern Lombardy. But now he and others, including perhaps Pasquale
Malipiero and Jacopo Antonio Marcello, began to share the same
concern as that expressed by Cosimo de' Medici, namely that Venice was
too enamored of conquest and should instead be treating the Milanese
with "responsibility and equity."[97] What is also significant here is that
this major dispute over policy seems over time to have begun to follow
the rapidly developing factional lines: while Foscari and his allies were
forming a hawkish party, his opponents – many of whom were a generation younger than the doge – were forming a dovish one.[98] Herein
may lie the effort by Sanudo and others to read back into Foscari's election the origin of the debate over terraferma expansion.

As for the war itself, when Sforza's army finally encountered the
Venetian one at Piacenza in November 1447, he handed them a major
defeat.[99] In July 1448 he scored yet another victory at Casalmaggiore.
In that instance, Andrea Querini, the commander of the Po fleet, was
forced to set fire to the Venetian armada in order to prevent it from
falling into enemy hands. The state attorneys tried him for his actions
and condemned him to three years in prison, a fine, and permanent
exclusion from offices. As Dolfin and Sanudo note, it was Foscari
who proposed this punishment. The state attorneys recommended that
Querini be beheaded.[100] As Sforza's star rose, other condottieri decided
to seek their fortunes with the increasingly besieged Venetians. In February the Senate considered Francesco Piccinino's conditions for entering Venetian service, including his demand that he receive all lands west
of the Adda; but the talks failed. More successful were the negotiations
with the rising commander Bartolomeo Colleoni, who joined the
Venetian side in May.[101]

Following his victory at Casalmaggiore, Sforza moved on and laid siege to Caravaggio, one of Venice's last major territorial outposts on the eastern shore of the Adda. There, in September, he delivered the Venetians still another crushing defeat, capturing the proveditors Gherardo Dandolo and Ermolao Donato: rather than fleeing, they preferred, in Dolfin's words, to risk dying to protect "the flags rather than save themselves with a shameful and ignominious flight." But protect the flags they could not; and the Milanese placed the captured Venetian and Florentine standards in the church of Sant'Ambrogio. Word of the disaster reached Venice on Sunday the 15th. Sanudo reports that Foscari, rather than despairing of the news, "came into the Collegio with more vigor than ever."[102] Clearly, the decision to release Jacopo from exile so that the doge could devote himself to public affairs was paying off in renewed ducal engagement with affairs. But it appears that Foscari alone was energized by the defeat: according to Dolfin, as Sforza took advantage of the victory and raced across the Bergamasco and Bresciano capturing town after town, there was in Venice "great melancholy and worry;" he adds, however, that the Venetians had not lost the heart to regroup.[103] One of their first actions was to cashier their commander Michele Attendolo and eventually confiscate his fief at Castelfranco. Sigismondo Malatesta assumed the role of governor-general of the Venetian forces in February 1449.[104]

Venice was spared further military humiliation by the jealousies and suspicions that Sforza's success aroused in the Ambrosian Republic. As a result, Sforza began to negotiate with the Venetians, trusting that Venetian power could help make him Duke of Milan. On 18 October the two parties reached an agreement, known as the Treaty of Rivoltella, by which, again in Dolfin's words, Venice and Sforza became "common enemies of the Milanese."[105] The treaty stipulated that the Venetians agree to assist Sforza in his effort to become ruler of Milan by furnishing him with a force of 4000 cavalry and 2000 infantry and agreeing to pay him a stipend of 13,000 ducats per month. In return, Sforza promised to relinquish Crema and Ghiaradadda and restore all lands he had captured in the Bresciano and Bergamasco. Both sides agreed that the River Adda would serve as the boundary between their lands, but that Sforza would hold jurisdiction over the river itself. Sforza would release the prisoners he held, including Ermolao Donato. In addition, the Venetians agreed to restore to Sforza the Palace of the Two Towers. In January 1449 the

Council of Ten cynically decided not to entertain a plot to kill Sforza on the grounds that Venice was currently allied with him.[106]

The Treaty of Rivoltella marked yet another stage in the rearrangement of alliances among the peninsular powers. When ambassadors from the Ambrosian Republic went to Venice in November, the Senate informed them that they would not be received. The situation was particularly difficult for Cosimo de' Medici, torn as he was between sympathy for the Ambrosian Republic and personal ties to Sforza. In all this it was Sforza who was the winner, since the Venetians had now officially recognized and thereby legitimated his claim to the lordship of Milan.[107] But a quick survey of the situation in September 1449 reveals the opportunism of all the actors and a complete lack of guiding principles other than self-interest for their actions. For by that point Venice had reached a new accord with the Ambrosian Republic, essentially abandoning its alliance with Sforza. Accordingly, in November the Ten authorized a plot to try to assassinate the condottiere.[108]

What drove the Venetians back into the arms of the Milanese republic was their growing concern over Sforza's success, compounded by a new war with the Aragonese of Naples – a war that began in July 1449 and at whose heart lay a conflict over control of the strategically important islands of Cephalonia, Zante, and Santa Maura off the western coast of Greece.[109] The Venetians actually invited Sforza to join with them and the Ambrosian Republic in an agreement that would have divided up the old Duchy of Milan and guaranteed Sforza substantial holdings, including Cremona, Pavia, Piacenza, and Parma; but they never came to terms. The Senate tried to justify its actions to Sforza by informing him that it was unable to prosecute war on two fronts, that is, on the terraferma against Milan and on the sea against Naples.[110] But this was merely an excuse since in all likelihood Venice's goal was to neutralize Lombard power by creating two satellite states, neither of which alone would have been powerful enough to threaten Venetian interests. But such a triple alliance never came about, and Sforza continued his siege of Milan.[111]

The Milanese situation came to a head in early 1450. Famine gripped the city as efforts by Colleoni and Malatesta to get supplies to the beleaguered inhabitants failed. On the night of 25 February riots erupted in the city, during which the Venetian envoy Leonardo Venier was murdered. Proposals were made to invite in various overlords, including the

Duke of Savoy or even the French. But in the end, the Guelf party triumphed and offered the city to Sforza. Terms were reached with the condottiere on 11 March; he entered the city on the 25th, and the Milanese proclaimed him lord of the city on the 26th. Almost immediately the Venetians dispatched Jacopo Antonio Marcello to treat with the new ruler of Milan.[112] For their part, both the Florentines and the pope were pleased by Sforza's success since he seemed to offer the best hope of blocking further Venetian aggression. This sentiment, combined with Venice's rapprochement with Naples (they reached a peace accord in July 1450), served to widen the gap between Venice and its former ally Florence. In October the peace between Venice and Naples blossomed into a full-blown alliance aimed at carving up Milan, and the stage was very nearly set for the final phase of an apparently unending cycle of conflict and war.[113]

The Venetian army that took the field at the battle of Caravaggio in 1448 numbered 20,000 men. The mobilization and support of such a force was a vast undertaking, requiring huge financial outlays. One predictable result was a worsening of the financial crisis facing the government and further efforts to squeeze every possible source of revenue. During 1448, for example, there were thirteen levies of the *estimo*, which together amounted to an impost of nearly 15 percent of taxable wealth. Only in 1440 was there a higher tax burden.[114] In December 1450 the Senate lamented the meager revenues generated by the *boccatico* and ordered that foreigners be more assiduously surveyed and assessed, although an exemption was granted for subjects of Venice's newfound ally the King of Naples. Additionally, the funds entrusted to the procurators of San Marco were raided for loans. This prompted Alvise Loredan, one of the procurators *de supra*, to write in October 1448 that his office had no money left on deposit (*in depositum*). A month earlier the Senate had ordered the requisitioning of horses from terraferma subjects and that reimbursement be delayed as long as possible. The city's privately owned banks were also importuned for loans, although with such vast sums at stake (in April 1449 the Soranzo bank loaned 33,000 ducats to pay Sforza), the terms for repayment were clearly spelled out.[115] Venice's financial situation was further exacerbated by the Mamluk sultan's refusal to allow Venetian merchants to trade in Syria, although an agreement with John, King of Cyprus, opened that market to

Venetian commerce.[116] Foscari, for his part, was deeply engaged in the effort to keep the financial ship afloat, proposing various measures to help generate revenue.[117]

Where Foscari was less successful was in curbing the corruption among his relatives and disputes within the patriciate. One case involved his cousin Polidoro, former *primicerio* of San Marco. In 1437 Polidoro had assumed the strategically important and politically sensitive position of Bishop of Bergamo. He proved lacking in both discretion and finesse and managed to alienate his flock: among the acts that offended the leading citizens of the city was his removal from the cathedral of a marble block that was used in various civic ceremonies; he appropriated it for use in a fountain in the episcopal palace. Relations deteriorated even further when in 1448 the Bergamaschi accused Polidoro of appropriating for his own ends various objects pertaining to the cathedral, including books and silver. The Senate, by a vote of 101 to 5 with 8 abstentions, ordered him to return the property within twenty days; if he failed to do so, the revenue from his benefices would be sequestered until restitution was made. In response Polidoro quit Bergamo and spent the remaining two years of his life in the papal court. He had failed his native city by alienating the residents of Bergamo. But it is impossible to determine whether the Senate's condemnation of Polidoro was a result of its desire to placate the residents of an important subject city or the growing animosity toward members of the Foscari family.[118]

Another troubling case involved Cristoforo Cocco, who in 1429 had married Marco Foscari's daughter Maria; they had a son, Niccolò. Following Maria's death, Cocco joined the priesthood and became an apostolic notary. But like so many others in Foscari's circle, he got caught up in international intrigues. In 1446 the Ten accused him of collusion with Visconti and placed a bounty on his head, but Cocco fled to Rome. There, over the next several years, he continued to cause trouble for his native city, feeding information, some of it false, to both the pope and Alfonso of Naples, and forging letters from various Venetian nobles. Finally, under increasing pressure from Venice, the pope stopped protecting Cocco, who fled papal lands but was captured and returned to Venice for trial. The Ten found him guilty of "lese maiestatis" and decided to ask the pope to defrock him so that he could be punished. But illness killed Cocco before the government could; he died in the late fall of 1449.[119]

One of the men who appears to have helped inform the Ten of Cocco's actions was yet another of Foscari's relations by marriage, Francesco Venier, son of the late Santo Venier. On 1 October, Venier, who earned his living as a merchant, asked permission to return to Rome or Naples; but the Ten ruled that he could not leave Venetian territory without their authorization. A week later Venier tried to file a denunciation against Ermolao Donato, but the Ten ruled this invalid since, according to the law passed in February 1445, it was illegal for any of Jacopo Foscari's relatives to use the law against members of the Ten and *zonta* who had condemned Jacopo. Donato was one of those men. Here one sees the deleterious effect of the Ten's decision to guard against using the courts to wage vendetta for now, five years after that original case, the law was still being used to draw lines within the patriciate, to create factions. At the end of the month, the Ten again denied permission for Venier to leave Venetian domains.[120]

It was during this period of shifting alliances and suspicions within the ranks of the patriciate that an incident involving Foscari and nobleman Tommaso Duodo occurred. During a meeting of the Senate on 7 September Duodo uttered words that the Ten, in their subsequent investigation of the case, judged injurious to the doge. Unfortunately the Ten's records provide no indication either of what prompted this outburst or its nature: that is, whether it involved a dispute over policy or was more personal, touching perhaps in some way on one of the recent cases involving Foscari's relations. But it represented a breach of senatorial decorum, serious enough to require a response on the part of the Ten. Duodo was fined 500 lire and found ineligible to attend secret deliberations (as provided in the Ten's law of November 1438 against such outbursts); further, a gag order was placed on the proceedings.[121]

This incident, vague as it is, reveals that Foscari himself had become a lightning rod in Senate debates. It is difficult to determine precisely why this was the case. Certainly some of it was due to the difficult international situation and the fiscal crisis that it brought in its wake, problems increasingly identified with Foscari and his policies. But some of it may be attributable as well to the fact that Foscari had now been on the ducal throne for twenty-five years; some members of the ruling elite may have felt that the doge had simply lingered too long in office. Additionally, as recent scandals involving his kinsmen suggest, some members of his family (and the doge himself during Jacopo's exile) displayed contempt for the rule of law. The doge's long reign might well have been a factor in this by contributing to the perception among members of his family that they could do as they pleased. The decision to prosecute Duodo suggests that Foscari was deeply concerned with his own dignity and that of the ducal office. His effort to protect the prerogatives of the ducal office became apparent when, in April 1450, he complained to the Ten that the syndics of the Council of Forty were interfering with the work of the ducal *gastaldi*, officers who executed sentences and who were considered part of the ducal household. Foscari argued that it was his responsibility to handle problems within the ducal "family" and that any complaints against them should be brought to his attention when he held public audiences.[122]

But all the previous scandals swirling around the doge's kinsmen paled in relation to the "horrible case," as the Council of Ten put it, that broke in November 1450. On the night of 5 November nobleman Ermolao Donato, at the time a member of the Council of Ten and formerly a member of Jacopo's first trial committee, was attacked while returning home. According to Dolfin, he had stopped in an alley near the church of Santa Maria Formosa to urinate and was stabbed by an unknown assailant. Others report that he had reached the door of his home when the attack occurred. Severely wounded, he died two days later and was buried at the church of San Michele di Murano where two of his sons were monks.[123]

The Ten met the morning after the attack and immediately voted to add a ten-man *zonta* to their proceedings. Their sense of urgency was real enough since they had no way of knowing whether this was an attack aimed at Donato personally or part of a larger conspiracy, perhaps by Venice's enemies, to destabilize the government. Once constituted, the Ten and its *zonta* voted a generous reward to anyone who could offer information regarding the assault. According to Dolfin, nobleman Triadano Gritti consulted the Bishop of Jesolo, a well-known astrologer, regarding the case. The bishop predicted that the truth of the case would never be known. But this is almost surely an apocryphal story added by Dolfin, a Foscari partisan, as a way of discrediting the Ten's ultimate findings.[124]

Despite the reward, the Ten got few solid leads in the days and weeks following the assassination. During November they detained and interrogated various suspects, although it is not clear whether all of them were under suspicion in the Donato case. Certainly they suspected Luchino Zeno but cleared him of responsibility on 9 December. With their investigation going nowhere, the Ten voted on that day to increase the reward for information and threatened with death anyone who knew the truth but refused to reveal it.[125] They also took further steps to ensure the city's security. On 16 December they debated measures to make sure that police were regularly paid so that the city could be properly patrolled, and ruled that no one could go about after the third hour of the night without a torch since "the darkness of night" made it easy for evildoers to carry out their misdeeds.[126]

On 2 January 1451 the Ten finally got a break in the case when Antonio Venier, nicknamed Braxuola, came forward with the explosive accusation that Jacopo Foscari had commissioned his servant Oliverio to murder Donato. According to Venier, early on the morning after the attack, Benedetto Gritti was in Mestre, where he saw Oliverio. Having arrived in Mestre with a boat in order to get a load of firewood, Oliverio spoke to Gritti and asked him if he had heard of the attack on Donato. When Gritti replied that he had not, Oliverio reported the story to him. Returning to Venice, Gritti reported what he had heard to his kinsmen Triadano Gritti. Suspicions were aroused since the night before, just an hour or two before Donato was attacked, Oliverio had been seen passing through the Piazza San Marco and entering the Ducal Palace. Why was he in Mestre so early the next morning and on so trivial a task as picking up firewood, unless he had fled Venice after committing the crime? This is the story as reported by Dolfin, who adds that Oliverio was immediately detained and tortured but confessed nothing.[127]

The records of the Ten do not include this narrative, although they do confirm that an accusation was made by Venier. They also indicate that on the morning of 2 January they voted to add six members to their body by scrutiny since several members were absent or ill. The heads of the Ten put forward a measure to detain Jacopo, but this was immediately voted down in favor of a proposal by Melchiore Grimani, first to hear the name of his accuser and then to consider the arrest of Jacopo. After Vespers they debated but failed to pass three further measures: one to send for those named in the accusation; the second to have one of their chiefs visit the procurator Andrea Donato, brother of the deceased Ermolao (not to be confused with Foscari's son-in-law Andrea

Donato from a different branch of the family), to learn whether or not Ermolao had ever mentioned to him that he feared anyone in particular; the third to arrest Jacopo. Instead they passed unanimously a bill to keep their proceedings secret, and, as the notary's annotation indicates, took an oath on the Scriptures, to do so.[128]

The following day, 3 January, the Ten continued their deliberations. They passed a bill proposed by the heads (Francesco Zorzi, Giovanni Memmo, and Paolo Barbo), which authorized the detention of Jacopo and the immediate examination of those named in the accusation as well as Andrea Donato, Ermolao's brother, and any others they saw fit to interview. Given the gravity of the situation, they also decided that while the special subcommittee carried out its investigation, the full Council of Ten should remain in session. A countermeasure to examine the accusers before arresting Jacopo, proposed by Niccolò Bon and Gerardo Dandolo, failed to pass. The Ten took two other actions that day. First, they voted to detain nobleman Niccolò Mudazzo, described in the bill as the son-in-law of Francesco Zane, for unspecified suspicions in the case. Second, they voted to reconstitute the subcommittee charged with the investigation. In the end the subcommittee was made up of seven members: Luca da Lezze, Paolo Barbo (one of the heads of the Ten), Delfino Venier, Paolo Tron, Andrea Morosini, Cristoforo Moro, and Marino Soranzo.[129]

On the 8th the subcommittee reported to the Ten that they were divided on how to proceed next. Some favored conducting an examination of nobleman Matteo Vitturi, currently serving as the ambassador to the King of Aragon. According to some accounts, which Jacopo was denying under torture, he and Vitturi had celebrated following Vitturi's election to the post of *avogador di comun*. Therefore they wanted to write to Vitturi and have him report under oath the nature of his conversation with Jacopo and to give the names of those present. But the measure failed to pass, with 7 favoring the bill, 14 opposing, and 4 abstentions. By contrast, the council voted unanimously to free Niccolò Mudazzo.[130]

On 27 January the Ten voted to offer compensation in the form of jobs to the two men, Niccolò Zio and Jacobo de Dardani, who were serving as guards for Jacopo; and on the 28th voted to provide extra protection in the form of up to seven armed retainers to each member of the Ten and *zonta*.[131] That same day the Ten voted themselves legal protection as well when they approved a measure put forward by the heads (Zorzi, Memmo, and Barbo): this forbade the doge and his and Jacopo's kinsmen, whom they defined as all those who normally had to exit the Great Council on account of kinship when elections were held, from ever sitting in judgement on any members of the Ten, their sons, brothers, or grandsons. If this were done, everyone could speak his conscience and act according to what God and the "honor of the Venetians" required, and no one would fear "at any time vendetta from any person." The proposal further provided that the doge could not be present when there were discussions of cases involving his or their relatives. The measure passed by a vote of 23 to 4 with 2 abstentions. The bill then listed the thirty-five men, including the three scribes, covered by the law. Like the law passed during Jacopo's previous trial, this one tended to fix or institutionalize factions or parties within the patriciate by defining those who had reason to fear vendetta on the part of the doge and his relatives. Also like the previous bill, it circumscribed Foscari's right to be present when certain discussions took place. As such, it represented a limitation by the Ten on Foscari's power and prerogatives. Justly or unjustly, the father was paying a heavy price for his son's presumed actions.[132]

On 3 February the Ten decided to keep their chamber locked so that no one could enter; they also decided to assume another notary since the workload of the council had grown so great.[133] Three days later they tried to move forward with the case against Jacopo. The three new heads of the Ten, Francesco Zorzi, Andrea Marcello, and Stefano Trevisan, proposed that the subcommittee bring its findings regarding Jacopo to the full council the following day. But Mechiore Grimani put forward a different proposal: that the council should await the imminent return of Matteo Vitturi and question him (presumably about the conversation he had had with Jacopo after Vitturi's election as state attorney); they would also continue to follow up leads supplied by Antonio Biata, and try to locate a certain Giorgio mentioned in Biata's testimony. Most interesting of all was the motion put forward by nobleman Luca da Lezze, that Jacopo be freed because the accusation made by Antonio Venier (who reported the story of Oliverio's trip to Mestre) was not the "truth" (veritas) but merely "a juicy tidbit of gossip" (una gulositas) and that the torture of Jacopo had yielded nothing. Da Lezze's bill demonstrates that a small group within the Ten and its zonta believed the evidence against

Jacopo to be specious and almost certainly motivated by some sort of personal vendetta against him, in other words that he was being rail-roaded into a conviction. On a first vote the heads' proposal got 13 votes, Grimani's 6, and da Lezze's 5, while on a second vote those in favor of da Lezze's measure opted instead for Grimani's delaying tactic. Both the heads' measure and Grimani's were reintroduced on the 7th, and the council voted 16 to 9 with 4 abstentions to bring Jacopo's trial to a conclusion.[134]

On 10 February the Ten expressed frustration that the case against Jacopo had suffered a delay due to the illness of Delfino Venier and ordered the special subcommittee to move forward with the proceed-ings. But nothing happened for more than a month because of a decline in Jacopo's health, likely due to the rigors of the torture he had endured. On 13 March, with his health restored, the Ten again took up the case against him and ordered the interrogation of Oliverio in order to "extract" the truth. On the 26th, with the subcommittee itself divided on the issue, the Ten failed to pass a proposal by the state attorney Niccolò Bernardo to torture Oliverio again; and so on that same day the Ten moved to conclude the case.[135]

The three heads of the Ten, Francesco Zorzi, Carolo Marino, and Paolo Barbo, recommended that Jacopo be found guilty of the murder of Ermolao Donato despite their admission that they had been unable to extract a confession from him, even under torture; such a confession would have confirmed certain writings and testimonies that, in the opinion of the heads "clearly" demonstrated Jacopo's guilt. Instead, all that they had extracted from Jacopo, whom they described as "obsti-nate," were some words mumbled through clenched teeth. Nevertheless, they decided to move forward for the "good of our state," which had been paralyzed by the proceedings. They proposed that Jacopo be per-manently exiled to the city of Canea on the Venetian-controlled island of Crete, and that he be transported on the ship of Luca Mantello which was leaving shortly for the island. Once in Canea, he was to report to the authorities daily. Should Jacopo escape his exile and fall into the hands of the authorities, he was to be brought to Venice for beheading between the twin columns in Piazza San Marco and have all his goods and those of his sons confiscated by the government. Anyone who cap-tured the fugitive would get 1500 ducats for him dead, 3000 for him alive. The bill also included a number of long provisions designed to prohibit Jacopo from ever receiving any kind of pardon. The measure passed with 17 yeas, 7 nays, and 4 abstentions.[136]

The Ten then approved another measure put forward by the heads of the council forbidding Jacopo from being treated "honorifically" in his exile and prohibiting the rectors of Canea from using him as an advisor; rather he was to be considered nothing more than a "private citizen." Another provision forbade anyone from escorting him from Canea specifically or from Crete generally. The third required that Jacopo's condemnation be announced in the next meeting of the Great Council "for the information of everyone." Having made the fateful decision to condemn Jacopo seems to have freed up more members of the council to vote for this measure since it passed with only 1 negative vote and 2 abstentions. And they lifted the gag order on the proceedings, except that the names of interested third parties and those who made accusations were not to be revealed.[137] This bill was rather unusual since normally the Ten liked to keep their deliberations secret. However, given the political volatility of the case, the Ten thought it wise to make the charges and evidence against Jacopo as public as possible.

The Ten also acted to tie up a number of loose ends. They voted to exile Oliverio Sguri, Jacopo's servant, permanently from Venice and its territories, sent word to the ship's captain Luca Mantello not to depart from Venice, and promised rewards to the three men who had guarded Jacopo while in jail and to the extra notary, Pietro Encio, whom they had taken on to help with the increased workload. The Ten included special provisions designed to prevent the "lord doge" and his relatives from retaliating against these men.[138] Regarding Foscari, the council passed by a vote of 26 to 6 with 1 abstention a measure ordering the heads of the council, namely Zorzi, Marino and Barbo, to go "immediately" to see the doge and inform him of Jacopo's fate and "exhort his Serenity to good patience." The Ten were clearly concerned about Foscari's reaction and voted that the council should not adjourn until the heads returned from their delicate mission.[139]

On 29 March the Ten prepared for Jacopo's passage to Crete. They passed a measure requiring three of the *signori di notte* along with their patrolmen to stand ready to transfer the prisoner to Luca Mantello's ship during the night and prepared their mandate. They also composed the commission for Mantello, which – again in accordance with legal requirements – was written in the doge's name: the fictive Foscari was to inform Mantello of his responsibility, namely to remove Jacopo to Crete and to get under way as quickly as possible.[140] On this same day the Ten passed three other measures wrapping up the case. In the first they unanimously granted to the *signori di notte* who had stayed in the Ducal Palace throughout the proceedings the right to armed retainers. The second measure, however, was much more controversial. The heads proposed that Andrea Venier, the original informant, be granted a yearly stipend of 200 ducats from the Salt Office and that on his death the subsidy be granted to his legitimate sons for life. The measure passed only on a second vote; and even then the council was deeply divided with 14 in favor, 11 against, and 2 abstentions. Evidently, the councilors felt some unease about this reward, either because they viewed Venier's action as a patriotic responsibility not requiring recompense or more likely because they remained suspicious of Venier's character and motives. The councilors were more secure in their decision to extend to Venier the right to armed protection and immunity from retaliation by the doge and his and Jacopo's relatives.[141]

How are Jacopo's second trial and condemnation to be understood? Historians have differed markedly in their assessments. After carefully compiling and analyzing the evidence from the Ten's registers, Francesco Berlan, the last to undertake a step by step examination of the case, drew up a balance sheet of the arguments supporting both Jacopo's innocence (4 points) or guilt (7 points) and concluded in a *tour de force* of obfuscating language "to doubt highly in his [Jacopo's] innocence." Among the arguments pointing to Jacopo's guilt were, in Berlan's view, the fact that public opinion judged Jacopo guilty and that it was well known that there was bad blood between Jacopo and Donato. However, in both of these cases and also in another, Berlan based his analysis not on material in the Ten's records but on evidence from much later writers, including Giovanni Battista Egnazio and Flaminio Corner.[142] Samuele Romanin, an astute reader of the Ten's evidence, arrived at a very different and much more subtle interpretation. The decision to punish Jacopo with exile for as serious an allegation as murder was, in Romanin's opinion, a political "expedient" made necessary, as the Ten themselves observed, by the need to bring an end to a case that had stalled the government's ability to act on other matters. He adds that the punishment itself, a rather pleasant exile on the island of Crete, further points to the Ten's inability to bring the case to a definitive conclusion.[143]

My own view is that Jacopo was most likely innocent of the crime. There is nothing in his life to suggest that Jacopo was the type to authorize the murder of an enemy. His actions during his first exile indicate that he had the capacity to act foolishly, but not maliciously. More telling still is the fact that a small but significant minority of the members of the Ten and its *zonta* had serious doubts about the case: five of them voted in favor of Luca da Lezze's bill terming Venier's accusation nothing more than hearsay; and eleven members expressed their uncertainty either by rejecting or abstaining on the measure to condemn Jacopo. These numbers are all the more meaningful when one remembers that those with close kinship ties to Foscari were excluded from the deliberations. Furthermore, as explored below, over the course of the next several years rumors kept cropping up regarding Donato's murder requiring investigation. This suggests that there was a rush to judgement, possibly for the reasons Romanin suggested, namely, in order for the government to move forward.[144]

Given all this, Jacopo's condemnation must be attributed in large measure to the venomous atmosphere within the inner circles of power, an environment poisoned at least in part by the doge's own response to Jacopo's first exile but also by the corruption of so many of his kinsmen and associates. Their actions and the perception that some in Foscari's circle of intimates saw themselves as somehow above the law made it easier to believe Venier's accusation against Jacopo, despite the lack of corroborating evidence. To this must be added the desire on the part of at least some members of the Ten, men who had come to see themselves as opponents of the doge, to bring Foscari and his son low. Of the thirty-two nobles involved in Jacopo's second case and given immunity from retaliation by the doge and his relatives, eleven had served as judges in Jacopo's earlier trial and been granted similar immunity. The murder of one of their fellow judges surely made them suspicious of Jacopo. Of the four heads of the Ten during these months, two (Francesco Zorzi and Giovanni Memmo) had served on the earlier panel. The legalistic reification of a Foscari party and an anti-Foscari party began to show its dangerous potential. To what extent on-going resentment by the Loredans and their associates fueled the prosecution of Jacopo remains an open question. The procurator Alvise Loredan was a member of the 1451 *zonta*; and certainly some members of the panel had close ties to the Loredan family. Ermolao Donato himself had married Marina, Pietro Loredan's daughter.[145] Whatever the motives for their actions, members of the Council of Ten had taken an important decision which many perceived to be based on politics rather than on incontrovertible evidence.

During the next several months the Ten sought to expand their influence even further. In August 1451 they became aware of some sort of plot in the city of Crema, involving a certain Zanone da Crema. Proveditor Jacopo Antonio Marcello was ordered to secure the city's castle and gates. Although there is no evidence that the case involved Jacopo in any way whatsoever, the Ten decided to augment their numbers by calling in the *zonta* that had investigated the Donato murder case as well as the *savi del consiglio* and the *savi della terraferma* to deal with the Crema conspiracy. What this suggests is that Jacopo's trial had fostered the coalescence of a group of patricians who now saw themselves as helmsmen of the state.[146] And in November 1451 the Ten rejected, by a vote of 6 to 12 with 5 abstentions, a measure to move debate concerning the possible annexation of Cremona to Venetian control to the Senate, which the Ten conceded had jurisdiction over matters of "war and peace." Instead the council interpreted the matter to fall within its purview to deal with matters regarding security and the augmentation of the state.[147] During the final years of Foscari's reign, an increasingly activist Council of Ten asserted its authority to guide the Republic as the doge once again became preoccupied with the fate of his only son.

There was no respite in the international sphere. During the early months of 1451 storm clouds gathered both in Italy and abroad. In February the Turkish sultan Murad II died and was succeeded by his son Mehmed II. Underestimated by both the Greeks and the Latins, Mehmed had his eyes set on the reconquest of Constantinople. Unaware of (or unconcerned with) his ultimate goal, Venice dispatched an ambassador to reconfirm the treaty between the two powers.[148] The Byzantine emperor Constantine also sent an embassy to the new sultan but managed to insult him by hinting that he was prepared to support a pretender to Mehmed's throne. This prompted the emperor's vizier to upbraid the ambassadors with the warning: "If Constantinople eludes his [Mehmed's] bold and impetuous grasp, it will only be because God continues to overlook your [the Greeks'] devious and wicked schemes."[149] Late in the year Constantine sent a mission to Venice alerting them to the sultan's mobilization of forces to besiege the city and requesting assistance. But Venice responded in February 1452, as it had many times before, that it could provide aid only as part of a unified western effort. Among the excuses it offered was the renewal of war in Italy.[150]

During much of 1451 the Venetians made preparations for war against Sforza and their former allies the Florentines. First, however, they needed to get their military command structure in order. In February a vote was held to decide which of three candidates, Gentile da Leonessa, Bartolomeo Colleoni, or Jacopo Piccinino, should receive the nod. Suspicious of both Colleoni and Piccinino, the Senate awarded the post to Leonessa who received the title governor-general. Niccolò da Canal and Andrea Dandolo then traveled to his camp and presented him with the baton of command.[151] As a result of the decision Colleoni deserted the Venetian side, prompting the Ten to undertake a number of retaliatory measures, including holding his wife and children as hostages and freezing his assets. Nevertheless, he himself managed to escape to Milan, but only after many of his forces and supplies had been seized in a surprise attack led by Leonessa. Had that effort not succeeded, Colleoni could have, in Dolfin's estimation, inflicted "great damage" on the Venetian side.[152]

Just two days after requesting Borso d'Este's assistance in their efforts to capture Colleoni, the Ten issued a special order to all state officials forbidding them to have contact or undertake talks with any foreigners, including condottieri. If such a person presented himself at the private residence of a Venetian official, he was to be told that he would be received only in the public palace. The Ten aimed at controlling what had become the Achilles' heel of Venice's terraferma expansion policy, namely the development of potentially harmful personal ties between individual Venetians and foreigners – the very kind of tie that had led to Jacopo's first exile. Although such ties could, in the right circumstances, facilitate communication between states, their dangers were even more obviously apparent. Colleoni's recent desertion, coupled with the memory of Carmagnola's double-cross, brought the issue abruptly to the fore again, especially as it applied to condottieri.[153]

With the command issue settled and the effort to limit personal contacts in place, the Venetians next undertook to secure allies for the forthcoming conflict. As early as October 1450 Venice and Alfonso of Naples had formed a pact, negotiated on the Venetian side by Foscari's close ally Matteo Vitturi, designed to last ten years. According to the terms of the alliance, the two powers planned to restore Milan to liberty, dividing other territories in Lombardy among themselves and their allies. Venice, for its part, wanted Cremona, Pizzighettone, and "all other places on this side of the Adda." In May 1451 the league between Venice and Naples was officially proclaimed; it also included Savoy, Siena, and Monferrato. The opposing side consisted of Milan, Florence, Genoa, and Mantua.[154]

The Venetians made their third preparatory action on 1 June 1451, when the Senate ordered the expulsion of all Florentines from Venetian territory.[155] Venice's allies ordered similar expulsions. According to Dolfin, it was Alfonso who pushed for this action as retribution for the "great subvention of money" that the Florentines had been supplying to Sforza. It is well known that Cosimo de' Medici was Sforza's main financial backer. The expulsion of the Florentines from Venice must have been a particularly heavy blow since many Florentine merchants were active in the Venetian markets, but it also hurt Venetians who had commercial links with their Florentine colleagues. As a result, the Senate ruled on 7 June that no Venetians were to trade with or act as agents for Florentine merchants. Among the exemptions from expulsion that the Senate granted was one for Palla Strozzi and his sons who were not engaged in trade. Strozzi, who lived in Padua, had been exiled from Florence by Cosimo. But Palla's merchant son was ordered to leave.[156] On 5 June the Senate modified its order by declaring that the expulsion did not apply to Florentine artisans. This was not motivated by any particular regard for those from the working classes, but rather by the fear that artisans would return home, taking with them their business acumen, manufacturing expertise, and trade secrets. Indeed the Senate stated that their repatriation would result "in benefit to the lands of the Florentines and not a little detriment to our city."[157]

Among the projects in which the Florentines had been engaged was the design of the mosaic decoration in the Chapel of the Madonna in San Marco. Although the main structure of the chapel appears to have been completed rather quickly in the 1430s, work on the mosaics continued at a much slower pace. It was still under way in 1449 when Stamati, a thief of Cretan origin, bored through the walls of the basilica's treasury and stole a number of precious objects, including the ducal coronation beret. According to Dolfin, the robber hid the rubble from his nightly excavations under a ladder that the mosaicists used to climb to their work in the Chapel of the Madonna.[158] As noted in chapter 2, one of the most problematic aspects of the mosaic program is the odd arrangement and discordant styles of the figures in *The Dormition of the Virgin* (fig. 16). In their analyses of the chapel decorations, both Michelangelo Muraro and Ettore Merkel attribute the highly imbalanced placement of the figures at the head and feet of the Virgin and the abrupt change in style between the figures at her head (generally considered to be based on a cartoon by the Florentine Andrea del Castagno) and the more traditionally Venetian figures at her feet (some attributed by Merkel to designs by Michele Giambono and others by Jacopo Bellini) to the 1451 rupture in the Venetian-Florentine alliance and the expulsion of Florentines from Venetian-controlled lands.[159] Merkel interprets Giambono's reworking of Castagno's "revolutionary" program into a more traditional Venetian idiom as evidence of the Venetian state's and in particular Foscari's "coercion and instrumentalization" of artists. However such an interpretation is unlikely. It is far more reasonable to suggest that the design was changed so that all the apostles could be depicted (minus Judas, of course); it seems to have been the case that Castagno's cartoon was to include only four. Just a few years later Imperatrice Ovetari, one of Andrea Mantegna's patrons, sued him for depicting only eight apostles in his *Assumption of the Virgin*, a painting in the Ovetari chapel in the church of the Ermemitani in Padua.[160]

The continuation of work on the Chapel of the Madonna was not the only effort in these years to embellish San Marco. In March the Senate debated how to dispose of two gold brocade outfits and a piece of crimson velvet that the Byzantine emperor had presented to ambassador Niccolò da Canal. It concluded that it would be disrespectful to sell them at public auction and decided to donate them instead to the procurators of San Marco *de supra* for use as vestments or hangings for the church.[161] And in June the Senate, recognizing that the city's principal responsibility was to honor Saint Mark and "hold his church in the highest and greatest veneration" – and also that expenses were outrunning income – ruled that in the future every galley returning to Venice should present 200 pounds of white wax to the church, "for the honor and reverence of the divine cult and of our protector."[162] Certainly with the approach of war, the Senate felt the need to propitiate its saintly guardian. War itself was finally declared against Milan, Florence, Genoa, and their allies in December, following, according to Sanudo, "much dispute" in the Senate.[163]

An additional factor that would come into play during the war, especially as the pope sought to mediate a peace treaty among the belligerents, was the papal decision in October 1451 to raise the Venetian bishopric, that is the Bishopric of Castello, to the dignity of a patriarchate. For centuries the Bishop of Castello had been subordinate to the Patriarch of Grado. At the time of the bishopric's elevation, the incumbent was the Venetian patrician Lorenzo Giustinian, who – despite his misgivings about accepting the post – had been selected by his fellow countryman Eugenius IV to serve as Bishop of Castello in 1433. Eugenius decided to transfer the patriarchate from Grado to Castello precisely in order to increase papal influence in Venice and provide a counterweight to what the pope perceived as a too independent Venetian church, an independence symbolized geographically and ceremonially by the centrality of the church of San Marco to Venetian spiritual and political life and by the inaccessibility and obscurity of the bishop's seat at San Pietro di Castello. Eugenius failed in his efforts to transfer the patriarchate, but his successor Nicholas V managed to bring about the shift on 8 October 1451. The Venetian government greeted the elevation with little enthusiasm since they recognized it for what it was – a papal grab for power within its domain. For his part, Dolfin chose to pass over the transfer in silence; Sanudo merely noted its occurrence.[164] The transformation was complete when in December 1456 the pope authorized the patriarch's celebration of services according to the Roman rite rather than the older patriarchal rite, which accorded a role for the doge. That rite continued, however, to be performed in San Marco, the ducal chapel.[165]

War resumed on the terraferma in 1452 but with little prospect that the position of the major states would be transformed in any significant way. Alfonso centered his efforts in southern Tuscany while the Venetians undertook a new thrust across the Adda. In an effort to thwart Naples, the Florentines and Sforza called on the support of René of Anjou, the Angevin claimant to the Neapolitan throne, but his efforts proved halfhearted.[166] The Venetians tried various tactics to swing victory in their direction, including efforts to reinvigorate the Ambrosian Republic. The Senate encouraged Leonessa to fly the standard of the Republic that

Jacopo Piccinino had received when he was in its employ: this would be a way of signaling "to all that we desire to see the freedom and good standing of Milan."[167] In November the two great armies met at Montechiaro but failed to engage since the mercenary captains were afraid to risk everything on a single battle.[168]

Throughout the year, as throughout the entire history of the conflict, the condottieri continued to place their personal interests ahead of other concerns. Although he was not in Venice's employ at the time, having been dismissed after the defeat at Caravaggio (1448), Michele Attendolo went over to the Florentine side. But rather than immediately depriving him of his fief at Castelfranco, the Senate voted instead to sequester the revenues deriving from those estates. The government's leniency was certainly due to the fact that Attendolo had close ties to members of the patriciate. He was married to the daughter of nobleman Bartolomeo Pisani. It did eventually confiscate the fief.[169] But condottieri such as Attendolo do not deserve all the blame for their apparent lack of loyalty, for Venice was constantly encouraging commanders to switch sides (as were its enemies). Just months after Colleoni's desertion to the Florentines, the Ten were abetting his efforts to carve out a state for himself from the lands belonging to Sforza. They also decided to make overtures to Giovanni da Tolentino; he was to be offered possible rulership of Cremona in return for defecting from the enemy.[170]

As was the case so many times before, the resumption of war reignited the Republic's financial crisis and renewed what was becoming an increasingly desperate search for revenue. All the old expedients were tried, including new loans from the Jews and the terraferma cities as well as from private banks, renewed impositions of the *estimo* (after no assessments in 1451, there were five in 1452), and the reduction and delay of interest payments on previous forced loans.[171] In June the ducal chapel was feeling the effects of this last provision. Ruling that it was "neither dignified nor convenient that our protector Saint Mark and his church should be treated like other individual citizens and persons, but rather better and more honorably," the Great Council voted that the church should receive the full interest payments to which it was entitled.[172] Months earlier, in January, the Senate had ordered the Collegio to make sure that all those holding clerical benefices as well as observant friars and nuns were paying their proper taxes.[173] Perhaps feeling the moral weight of their decision, the Senate ordered on the same day as their ruling regarding the observants that 500 ducats derived from the recently passed measures should be given to the patriarch to distribute "for the love of God" (*amore dei*). Foscari was among those who put forward this bill. In this time of crisis he assumed a familiar role, that of pious servant of God.[174] In June, however, the Senate hedged its bets at least partly when it ordered that 4 ducats be given to each observant monastery in the city in order that the monks and nuns might pray "for the good of our state" and so that God might look favorably on the city's affairs.[175]

The government also undertook two other measures to raise more revenue, both of which had been tried in the past. In January the Great Council decided that all office-holders should contribute a portion of their salary to support the war, either by remaining in office for an additional period of time without receiving any pay, or by contributing a portion of their salary, depending on the position they held. It also appointed a special committee of five *savi* to oversee its implementation. The money was to be used only for the war.[176] A month earlier the Senate had voted to create another commission of *savi* to investigate those who were not paying forced loans. They were authorized to choose two men per parish who would gather information: they could then determine who should pay and how much.[177] But in June 1452 it became known that the *savi* still had not met and that two of them were no longer available for service. At this point Foscari put forward a proposal that two new *savi* be elected to bring the commission up to the requisite number and that they meet by the following Monday under pain of a 500-ducat fine per member should they fail to do so. The bill passed 82 to 19 with 5 abstentions.[178] Further changes were made to the commission in August; among other things, the *savi* were now authorized to appoint as many assessors per parish as they deemed necessary, depending on the "condition of the parishes."[179] However, none of these revenue-enhancing measures proved sufficient; and in December the Senate voted to create yet another special committee of three *savi* "to find money."[180]

In the midst of the renewed war and the fiscal crisis Foscari hosted what was to be the last imperial visit of his reign, that of Holy Roman Emperor Frederick III. The event was important in its own right since it offered another opportunity for Venice and the doge to present themselves on the international stage; details of the visit also provide important insights into Foscari's state of mind following Jacopo's exile to Crete, as well as into the domestic political climate. The emperor was passing through northern Italy on his way home to Germany following not only his marriage in Naples to Leonora, daughter of the King of Portugal and niece of Alfonso of Naples, but also his coronation in Rome by the pope. In early May 1452 the government began making preparations to host the emperor, empress, and their retinue, which according to Dolfin numbered fifteen hundred and consisted among others of bishops, barons, and various female attendants. On the 3rd of that month the Senate voted, since the Signoria and Collegio were so occupied with other affairs, to create a special committee of five proveditors to coordinate the imperial visit. Three days later the Senate changed course slightly and determined that the Collegio and special proveditors together should make decisions regarding the visit.[181] The most pressing matter was to find accommodation for the imperial visitors and their retainers. The government decided to lodge the emperor in the palace of the Marquess of Ferrara and the empress in the home of Matteo Vitturi at San Stae and to use the houses lining the Campo San Polo for other guests. Monasteries and hostels were also requisitioned to house the visitors.[182]

The property owners in San Polo used the occasion to try and wrest concessions from the government. The *campo*, the largest square in the city after Piazza San Marco, was the site of one of several government-sponsored archery ranges as well as a market. Dating back centuries, these practice fields were supposed to be used by citizens in order to keep their military skills well honed. But some of the residents of San Polo now felt that the range detracted from the square's beauty. On 8 May they approached the Ten about removing the archery field, citing the fact that they had offered their houses to accommodate the imperial retinue. The Ten agreed to demolish the range, but only if in return the property owners would undertake the paving of the *campo* with stones from the derelict monastery of Sant'Andrea. Acting on behalf of the parishioners, noblemen Giacomo Morosini and Pietro Querini refused the offer, citing the huge expense that paving the entire square would entail. As often happens, economics won out over beautification.[183]

In addition to finding housing for the visitors, the government wanted the city itself to be properly outfitted. On 13 May the Collegio expressed concern that there was not enough silk to honor the emperor. The silk was to be used as bunting for windows and to adorn ships. Accordingly, nobles and others were ordered to hand over their silks "for the ornament and honor" of the emperor. After his visit the fabrics would be returned and their owners compensated for any damage done to their goods. The bill did not apply to the silk guild, but the special proveditors were to meet with officials of that guild, no doubt to solicit their assistance and requisition their wares.[184] In addition, the Senate authorized the purchase of crimson velvet to outfit the beds to be used by the emperor, empress, and the emperor's nephew Ladislaus, King of Hungary. Afterwards, the velvets were to be sold "with the least [financial] damage to our government." All these preparations were serious business; the Senate expressed concern that Venice should surpass its subject cities in honoring the emperor.[185] Sanudo reports that stones used in on-going construction at the Ducal Palace were to be cleared from the piazza and that all those in mourning were required to put away their mourning clothes and dress instead in their colorful best.[186] But even while it concerned itself with what to modern eyes (but not to fifteenth-century ones) seem like fairly trivial matters, the Senate did not lose sight of the serious problems facing the government. Concerned that Foscari and other nobles would be kept very busy with the visitors, it ordered the Collegio to meet daily at the palace to oversee governmental business and the ducal councilors to meet for two hours to handle diplomatic correspondence and other pressing matters of state.[187]

Frederick arrived in Venice on 21 May accompanied by a legation of Venetian nobles who had gone to meet him at Chioggia and by a flotilla of Venetian ships and boats which Dolfin numbered at two thousand. Various guilds and the *compagnie delle calze* were put in charge of outfitting many of the ships. Foscari met the emperor at San Niccolò del Lido with the *bucintoro*, which had been festooned for the occasion with cloth of gold. The day before his arrival the Senate had debated the all-important issue of seating on the *bucintoro*. As it was, the emperor was seated with the King of Hungary and Duke of Austria on his right, while Foscari and the ambassadors from Naples, Savoy, and Siena were on his left. The division appears to have been based on geography; that is, the representatives of German lands were on one side of the emperor, those from the Italian lands on the other. It is also worth noting that the Italian side consisted of Venice's allies in the current war.[188]

The fifteen-year-old empress arrived on 25 May and spent a couple of days at San Niccolò before entering the city. Sanudo offers two different accounts of her formal entry. According to the first account, likely based on Dolfin's chronicle, he reports that the dogaressa, accompanied by two hundred women adorned with jewels and gold cloth, went to meet her with the *bucintoro*. He also reports that for this occasion the usual sumptuary laws were suspended. In the other it was Foscari, accompanied by sixty women, who went to meet the empress at San Niccolò. The government selected three women, described as "worthy and wise," to address the empress on behalf of the government. They were: Suor d'Amor, wife of Giorgio Corner; Creusa, wife of Alvise Diedo; and Cristina, wife of Girolamo Barbarigo.[189]

On 29 May the imperial couple attended Mass in San Marco, whose altars had been adorned for the occasion with the church's finest jewels. On the 30th they were guests at a party held in the Great Council Hall. The Venetians used the opportunity to present the pregnant empress with a jeweled crown valued at 2000 ducats and gifts of cloth. The emperor departed Venice on 1 June. Foscari accompanied him as far as Marghera, where Frederick knighted Marco Corner and Foscari's nephew Andrea Venier. The empress left a few days later; she traveled by boat to Treviso. Among her honor guard was nobleman Carlo Morosini, whose infant daughter the empress had taken as her goddaughter. Hospitality for the imperial guests and their retinue reportedly cost the government 1000 ducats per day.[190]

The imperial visit was not only an occasion for festivity but also for serious political negotiations on both international and domestic matters. First and foremost, the emperor offered, as Foscari reported to the Senate, to mediate among the warring Italian states. The Senate decided, in a particularly lopsided vote, respectfully to decline the emperor's offer and used the occasion to place the blame for the war squarely on Sforza's and the Florentines' shoulders. Clearly, they did not relish the possibility of imperial interference in these affairs.[191] The emperor let it be known that Sforza was seeking an alliance with him aimed at Venice. Almost certainly the emperor leaked this information as a negotiating tactic since he wanted Venetian assistance of various sorts. Not to be intimidated, the Senate voted to temporize, all the while asserting Venice's goodwill toward him.[192] Frederick sought to intervene in Venice's internal affairs as well by making appeals on behalf of two individuals. First, he asked the government to elevate one of its citizens to membership in the Great Council. That is, he wanted them to ennoble this unnamed citizen.[193] Second, he sought clemency for Foscari's son-in-law Andrea Donato, who had taken refuge at the papal court following his condemnation for taking a bribe from Sforza. The Senate decided by a vote of 143 to 10 with 10 abstentions to reject the emperor's requests, reminding him, as diplomatically as possible, that the decision regarding Donato had not been taken lightly but had been made instead by many councils and by "long and difficult paths." The Senate's refusal to bow to imperial pressure again suggests a hardening of lines against the doge and his allies.[194]

There is strong evidence that Jacopo's case continued to reverberate throughout the government and the city, affecting his father in profound ways and even throwing into jeopardy aspects of the imperial visit. As noted above, Jacopo's tribulations seem to have precipitated periods of inactivity and perhaps even depression on his father's part. In January 1452 the Council of Ten expressed concern that one of the foundations of the Venetian people's faith in the government, namely their conviction that their concerns were being heard and addressed, was being undermined because "for some time" and on account of "various events which have occurred" Foscari was not holding his daily audience as required in the ducal *promissione*. For that reason the Ten decided that the ducal councilors should hold audiences to clear the backlog of cases and restore the people's faith in the functioning of the government.[195] There is no explicit evidence that Foscari's preoccupation with his son's fate led the doge to neglect this duty and the Ten to take action; his ever-advancing age and the crush of international events may also explain his dereliction. But it seems likely that Jacopo's exile was a contributing factor.

Certainly it was impossible for Foscari or anyone else to put aside the events that had befallen Jacopo. There were many who felt that he had been unjustly condemned, while his prosecutors were equally convinced of the rectitude of their actions. Those who believed in his innocence had their convictions strengthened by persistent rumors that others were responsible for the crime. In February the Ten ordered the trial of the recently captured Bartolomeo Scarpaza, who in November 1450 had accused someone else of Ermolao Donato's murder. Most telling of all, the sitting members of the Ten decided that they would try Scarpaza

for making a false accusation; in other words, they ruled that they themselves had full legal authority and that there was no need to reconvene
the Ten and *zonta* who had heard the original case. Indeed they feared
that calling the original tribunal would lead to "great murmuring in the
city." In March the Ten found Scarpaza guilty and sentenced him, among
other things, to be put on public display and have his crime publicly
proclaimed. In so doing, the Ten hoped to squash the rumor and prevent
popular opinion from turning even more sharply against them.[196]

Jacopo's fate arose as an issue even during Frederick III's visit: according to Sanudo, the Ten forbade Jacopo's wife Lucrezia, "on account of
her husband," from boarding the *bucintoro* for its trip to meet the empress
at the Lido. In response to this insult to his daughter-in-law, Foscari
himself apparently balked at participating in the empress's entry, but the
Ten ordered him to do so. If Sanudo's information is accurate (and it
appears to be so, as he lists the ruling as just one of a number of provisions made for the visit – many of which can be confirmed inde-
pendently in the records of the Senate and Ten), then it indicates how
Jacopo's trial continued to create fissures within the ruling class. Clearly
some within the Ten were intent on shaming Foscari further by excluding Jacopo's wife from any role during this important occasion. Doubtless they justified their action on legal and diplomatic grounds, arguing
that it would be disrespectful to the empress for the wife of an exile to
participate in this ceremony. In response Foscari at least considered the
possibility of abrogating his responsibility at this most serious of times.
His reaction suggests that his negligence in holding audiences was in part
willful. Certainly Foscari continued to feel deeply the impact of his son's
exile. The incident regarding the *bucintoro* also confirms that Lucrezia and
her sons did not accompany Jacopo on his exile to Crete.[197] These factors
– Foscari's preoccupation with Jacopo's fate and the presence of his
grandsons in Venice – would soon come together to influence the doge's
next building project, the building of a family palace. But before considering that project, it is necessary to analyze the events of 1453, one
of the most momentous, if not the most momentous year, of Foscari's
long and increasingly troubled reign, for the doge's decision to erect the
palace was also influenced by the course of international events.

In the war against Sforza and Florence, 1453 began with Venice again
on the offensive in the borderlands between the Venetian and Milanese

states. Venetian forces recaptured much of the land in the Bresciano, Bergamasco, and Cremonese that Sforza had taken. But they suffered a setback when in March, during the siege of Manerbio, south of Brescia, Gentile da Leonessa was wounded. He died on 1 April. In response, Foscari himself proposed that two proveditors be dispatched to Brescia to take charge of the situation. The Senate selected the procurator Pasquale Malipiero and Jacopo Antonio Marcello for this task. Several days later the Venetians selected Jacopo Piccinino to succeed Leonessa as governor of the Venetian forces.[198] Events were further complicated for Venice and its ally Naples by a new expedition into Italy by René of Anjou, an expedition funded in large part by the Florentines. René's departure from France was delayed by several factors, not least the death of his wife; and once he landed in Italy, he met resistance from Savoy. Nevertheless, he soldiered on, arriving in Pavia in September and joining up with Sforza's army at Cremona in October. Backed by these French reinforcements, Sforza retook the offensive and managed to capture much of the Bresciano and Bergamasco. Sforza's success prompted new fears in Venice for the security of Padua.[199] Fortunately for the Venetians, the approach of winter forced both Sforza and René into winter quarters. Throughout the year Pope Nicholas V sought to bring about a general pacification of the peninsula. In October Venice commissioned Orsato Giustinian and Cristoforo Moro as its delegates to papal-sponsored peace talks; they were to demand that Venice keep everything on the eastern side of the Po and Adda as well as all territory beyond the Adda then held by Venice. Among the belligerents, the republics Venice and Florence were the most anxious to see the restoration of peace since they were feeling the weight of the war both in terms of its direct financial costs and its impact on trade. By contrast, Sforza and Alfonso were less eager to see a peace concluded before their territorial and dynastic ambitions could be fulfilled. Nevertheless, Venice and Sforza did begin a series of separate negotiations through the intermediary Fra Simone da Camerino, who had developed a strong personal relationship with both Sforza and Foscari.[200]

Certainly one of the major factors driving the various powers to the peace table, however slowly, was the precipitous transformation of events in the eastern Mediterranean, caused by the fall of Constantinople to the Turks in May 1453. As noted above, Constantine XI's warnings about

Mehmed II's ambitions and his own requests for western reinforcements met with the usual excuses and dilatory responses. But when Mehmed completed his new fortress of Rumeli Hisar on the European side of the Bosphorus in August 1452 (a complement to the fortress of Anadolu Hisar on the Asian shore), he proclaimed that all ships wishing to proceed through the straits had to get permission to proceed as well as pay a toll. Venice took notice, especially since Mehmed now effectively controlled access not only to the port of Constantinople but also to the Black Sea and its ports. In that same month the Senate ordered special preparations for the ships about to set sail on the Romania line and authorized Gabriele Trevisan, the vice-captain of the Gulf, to assess the situation in Constantinople and, if necessary, assist in the defense of the city. A counter proposal, to abandon the Byzantines to their fate, received only 7 votes. The Senate also voted to apprise Alfonso of the worsening situation. And it responded in November to the Byzantine envoy's urgent request for assistance by informing the pope and cardinals of the rapidly deteriorating situation in Constantinople.[201]

Mehmed's intention to control the sea routes in the area became dramatically clear to the Venetians in late November when his forces sank a Venetian merchant vessel, captained by Antonio Rizzo, traveling to Constantinople from the Black Sea with a load of barley, which refused to stop and get permission to proceed. Rizzo and his crew managed to get to shore but were captured. Despite appeals from the Venetian ambassador Fabrizio Corner to the sultan, they were all executed. The members of the crew were decapitated and Rizzo impaled. His body was left on the side of the road. The two sides were hurtling toward war.[202]

At a meeting held in December the substantial colony of Venetian merchants resident in Constantinople decided to cast its fate with that of the Byzantines. On 14 December the Great Council of the colony approved with only one negative vote the previous day's decision by Girolamo Minotto, the colony's *bailo* (governor), forbidding Venetian ships in port to depart without his permission, under threat of a 3000-ducat fine. Minotto's order overruled Gabriele Trevisan's instructions from the Senate to return to Venice with his two galleys and the three merchant vessels he was escorting from Trebizond, under the command of Alvise Diedo, which were in the harbor. Several other ships from Venice as well as three from Crete were also in port. The colonists did dispatch word of the increasingly desperate situation to Venice.[203]

The senators reacted to the alarm which reached them in February 1453 by voting to build two more ships. They also authorized the Great Council to elect a captain to command the fifteen galleys then in preparation; the man the Great Council elected for this task was Jacopo Loredan, son of the late Pietro. He was named captain-general of the sea. In order to fund this fleet, the Senate decided that merchants with commercial interests in the Romania line and at Tana would have to raise 16,000 ducats; it also ordered the preparation of ration shipments for the crews. On the diplomatic front, it voted to sound out Mehmed on his precise intentions and to inform Pope Nicholas, Emperor Frederick III, Alfonso of Aragon, and Ladislaus of Hungary, of their need to assist in the effort to save Constantinople.[204]

Dolfin places the blame for Venice's failure to act sooner on the procurator Paolo Tron and "some others" who on the basis of news they were getting from Tron's nephew Santo and from Giovanni and Niccolò Giustinian, merchants in Constantinople, had underestimated the threat to the Byzantine capital and continued instead to direct money toward the terraferma war effort.[205] By contrast, the Greek advisor to Constantine, George Sphrantzes, blamed Foscari, attributing Venice's lack of speed to the failed attempts to negotiate a marriage between one of the doge's daughters and Constantine when he was still despot of the Morea. According to Sphrantzes, Constantine agreed to the betrothal "not so much because of the dowry, but because his territories would be joined to those of Venice." But he adds that:

> once Constantine had become emperor and come to the City [Constantinople], this marriage was out of the question. What nobleman or noblewomen would ever receive the daughter of a Venetian – even though he might be the glorious doge – as queen and lady for more than a short time?

On account of this rejection, Foscari "became our enemy" and prevailed upon the Senate not to send the necessary aid.[206]

It is difficult to know what to make of Sphrantzes's story. On the one hand, there are reasons to credit it. Sphrantzes was a particularly close advisor to Constantine, having participated in other marriage negotiations for the future emperor, including his marriage in 1441 to a daughter of Dorino Gattilusi, Prince of Lesbos, from a Genoese family. Constantine's new wife died just a year later, and it was apparently at that time that the possibility of a marriage to one of Foscari's daughters was contemplated. If this chronology is correct, then these negotiations would have taken place just a year after Foscari staged the extravagant wedding of his son Jacopo. A marriage into the Byzantine imperial house would have capped in a spectacular way this most princely phase of Foscari's reign.[207] On the other hand, there are also reasons to be skeptical of Sphrantzes's claim. First and foremost, there is no mention of the negotiations in any other source; it seems unlikely that chroniclers such as Dolfin would have ignored matters of this importance.[208] Moreover, there is nothing in the Venetian sources to suggest that Foscari was actively opposed to helping the Byzantines. Most importantly, the ducal *promissione* would have required that Foscari get approval for the marriage from his councilors and the heads of the Forty, as well as the overwhelming majority of the members of the Forty and Great Council, an approval he was unlikely to receive. It may be that some preliminary discussions took place but that they were never formalized into an actual betrothal. What Sphrantzes's account does reveal (as was the case with the apocryphal speeches of Tommaso Mocenigo against terraferma expansion) is a tendency among many fifteenth-century commentators and chroniclers to attribute major policy decisions to the whims of individual rulers: on this occasion Foscari and his wounded pride became, for some Greeks at least, a convenient scapegoat.

Despite the increasing sense of urgency, preparations proceeded much too slowly for the recriminating and unfortunate Byzantines. Word arrived in Venice in early April that the pope was prepared to pay for five galleys; in its response the Senate could not resist the temptation to take a swipe at him, using the occasion to remind the pontiff of his predecessor Eugenius IV's unfulfilled promise to pay for the papal vessels during the Crusade of Varna. It also let him know that the armada had to reach Constantinople by the end of May; otherwise the prevailing winds would make it impossible for the ships to enter the straits.[209] On 13 April it ordered Alvise Longo to sail with just one ship to Tenedos and assess the situation, especially the location of the Turkish fleet. If the way was safe, he was to proceed on to Constantinople and assist in its defense.[210] On 7 May Jacopo Loredan was finally given his commission as captain-general of the sea. He was to sail to Corfu and take command of that island's galley and then proceed toward Tenedos, where he would be joined by the galleys from Crete. The Senate ordered him not to attack the Turks unless provoked; if upon reaching Constantinople he found that the emperor and sultan had already reached an accord, he was advised to withdraw to Corfu. In the event that peace had not been reached, he should look to the defense of Negroponte as well. Sailing with Loredan was Bartolomeo Marcello, Venice's ambassador to the sultan. His job was to mediate a peace between Constantine and Mehmed, while at the same time emphasizing to the sultan that Venice's actions were intended only to protect its interests. These included Constantinople itself, which the Senate described as being "ours on account of the laws and jurisdictions which we always have held and which we enjoy presently in that city." They based these assertions on the fact that they had a *bailo* and rector resident in the city who had the power to levy customs fees and that their flag flew "publicly" in the city.[211]

What the Senate did not know when it made this bold claim was that Mehmed's siege of the city was already in progress, for the sultan had assembled his massive army of 160,000 before the city on 5 April.[212] Many of the Venetians who were present in the now-doomed city took major roles in its defense. Among these were the *bailo* Girolamo Minotto, whom the emperor placed in charge of the defenses of the Blachernai Palace; Catarino, Filippo, and Jacopo Contarini and others were in command of various gates and sections of the city's massive walls; and the ships of Gabriele Trevisan and Alvise Diedo patrolled the port and Golden Horn, itself protected by a chain which stretched across the harbor to Galata.[213] Among the more dramatic episodes in the siege was the Turks' portage overland, around the chain protecting the harbor, of seventy-two vessels. (One of the witnesses to the siege, Leonardo di Chio, the Archbishop of Mytilene, compared this seemingly superhuman feat with the Venetians' own action in 1438, when they hauled their ships over the mountains to Lake Garda.) Another was the attempt to destroy the Turkish fleet by sending in a fireship; in this battle Giacomo Cocco, captain of one of the Trebizond galleys (whom Leonardo described as "avid for honor and glory"), broke formation, sailing his vessel directly at the Turkish ships. His ship was sunk, and his entire crew lost. Unfortunately, his impetuous act cost the Christian forces the battle.[214]

The final assault on the city began on the morning of 29 May. For several preceding days both the Turkish invaders and Christian defenders invoked God for assistance, while the leaders rallied their troops. Constantine made a speech to the assembled defenders. In Dolfin's version, he warned that the Turks intended to profane the city, which he described as "the city of Constantine the Great, your fatherland, the refuge of Christians, the asylum of all Greece." He rallied the Genoese, who had always defended "this, your mother city [. . .] against the insults of the Turks." And he addressed the "most potent" Venetians who many times had spilled Turkish blood, and who "in our days, by [the efforts of] Pietro Loredan captain-general have sent so many Turkish galleys and souls to infernal Cerberus." If the speech is authentic, then it indicates just how large Loredan's reputation loomed in both the Venetian and Byzantine imaginations almost forty years after his famous victory over the Turks at Gallipoli.[215] Although the defenders fought valiantly, in the end they were unable to repel the Turkish soldiers who, showing their own unrelenting valor, threw themselves in wave after wave against the city walls. Eventually, they managed to breach the fortifications and take the town. Constantine XI died fighting for the pathetic remains of a once great empire. Girolamo Minotto, his son, and several others were taken prisoner and beheaded. Other Venetian nobles and commoners, including Giovanni Loredan, Fabrizio Corner, and Gabriele Trevisan, were seized and eventually offered for ransom. Once it became clear that the city had been taken, the Turkish sailors patrolling the coast around the city deserted to participate in the looting; this allowed a number of Venetian, Genoese, and Cretan galleys to escape, although not the Venetians' merchant vessels.[216] Dolfin placed Venice's financial losses at at least 200,000 ducats; those of its Cretan feudatories and citizens at another 100,000 ducats. Modern estimates suggest half a million ducats as a likely figure.[217]

Refugees from the fallen city reached Negroponte in four days. There they conveyed the news to Jacopo Loredan, who was in a holding pattern, waiting to sail on to Constantinople. Letters announcing the news arrived in Venice on Friday 29 June, the feast of Saint Peter, when the Great Council was in session. According to Dolfin's account, when a ship arriving from Corfu was sighted coming into the *bacino* of San Marco, all the patricians rushed to the windows and balconies, seeking word of the fate of Constantinople, the Romania galleys, and their kinsmen. The letters were immediately taken to the Signoria who then made an announcement to the assembled councilors. Balloting for offices was suspended; and all the patricians began to wail, beating their hands and breasts and tearing their hair. Some "mourned for their fathers," as Dolfin observes, "others for their sons, others for their brothers, and others for their goods." The Signoria called for silence as one of the secretaries of the Council of Ten read the full text of the letter to the assembly. This recitation set off a new round of wailing. But mourning quickly turned to recriminations as those in the hall began to accuse the Signoria and Collegio of negligence and those in Constantinople itself of underestimating the Turkish threat. When the following Wednesday, 4 July, the Romania galleys arrived in harbor, their entry was subdued: no fifes or trumpets announced their return, and the crews decided not to hoist the banner of Saint Mark from the highest masts.[218]

Despite the many claims about the perfidy of the Turks, Venice, in typical manner, acted quickly in order to repair relations with the sultan and ensure the resumption of regular trade relations. The Senate sent instructions to Bartolomeo Marcello to continue on his mission to Mehmed and to Loredan to look to the defense of Negroponte, which had now become the frontline in the struggle. On 17 July it revised its orders to Marcello. He was to inform the sultan that Venice had every intention of honoring the peace accord signed with his father; but if Mehmed demanded modifications to that agreement, then Marcello should inform him that he would need to consult the government. He was to demand the restitution of all merchant ships and negotiate the ransom of hostages. If the sultan was amenable to the return of Venetian merchants to Constantinople, then he was to offer as a model for the new commercial accord a copy of the treaties that the Venetians had reached with the Byzantines. To smooth the way in these negotiations, the Senate decided on 12 July to increase the value of the gifts to be given to the sultan and his advisors from 500 to 1200 ducats. They judged the old amount to be inadequate, "given recent events."[219]

Anticipating all eventualities, the Venetians also opened negotiations in September with the Grand Karaman, the ruler of an emirate in Anatolia hostile to the Ottomans, to see if it would be possible to conduct trade for the Romania galleys through his lands.[220] At the same time it continued to encourage the pope and other Christian leaders to take action against the Turks, warning them that if the Turkish threat was not halted, the Greek lands and islands would be the next to fall and Apulia after that.[221] For the rest of the year Venice looked to the defense of the Morea and the fortification of Negroponte. At the end of August the Senate congratulated Jacopo Loredan on his capture of seventeen Turkish ships.[222] At home, relatives of those taken hostage pushed for their release. The Loredans pressed hard for the ransoming of prisoners, including Giovanni Loredan, son of the late Paolo, while one of Girolamo Minotto's sons got permission to travel as a *balestriere alla pope* to Constantinople to seek the liberation of his relatives, including his father the *bailo*. But when it became clear that the father had been killed, the government awarded annuities to his sons and dowries to his daughters.[223]

The fall of Constantinople and the extinction of the Byzantine empire sent shock waves throughout Europe; it was, in Sanudo's opinion, "the worst news for all of Christendom."[224] In its wake numbers of refugees made their way west, including scholars such as Cardinal Bessarion, who contributed to the advancement of Greek studies in Italy. Yet the conquest did not fundamentally alter the balance of power in the eastern Mediterranean since by the time it fell, the Byzantine empire was little more than a shadow of its former self. But what it did do was draw attention to the stark reality of Turkish expansion. The implications of the conflict were felt most strongly in Venice, which was on the frontline and which saw its interests most directly threatened.

Oddly enough, the impact of the fall was felt most keenly in the sphere of Venetian domestic politics for it suddenly called into question the wisdom of the policy of terraferma expansion and the seemingly endless wars with Milan. As already noted, news of Constantinople's collapse led to recriminations and finger-pointing; critics felt that if the Signoria and Collegio had not been so focused on events to the west, they would have better understood the reality of the threat to the east. Moreover, the demands of the Lombard wars made it virtually impossible for Venice to take decisive action in the east, action that might have halted at least temporarily the Turkish advance. As Dolfin observes, the decision to act as quickly as possible to repair relations with the sultan following the conquest was necessitated by "the insupportable weight [of affairs] concerning Duke Francesco [Sforza] of Milan."[225] Venice simply did not have the resources to fight wars on both fronts. While Sphrantzes blamed Foscari personally for Venice's failure to help Byzantium in time, his fellow Greek Cardinal Bessarion did not share that view; instead he wrote to Foscari in July 1453, encouraging the Venetians to carry on in their effort against the Turks.[226] But many of Foscari's fellow Venetians did blame him and the policies with which he was associated for the collapse and the losses to Venice's commercial interests. That anger, coupled with further intrigues involving Jacopo, would soon transpire to make Foscari yet another notable victim of the fall of Constantinople.

Contributing to the internal discontent was the ever-worsening state of the Republic's finances, a crisis that culminated in December with the collapse of the Monte, the last exaction of which was made in February 1454. The situation was further exacerbated by a serious grain shortage in the city, as well as by a shortage of bullion.[227] Throughout 1453 the government sought to find money from a variety of sources, including the sale of shops at Rialto and in Padua. It was so desperate for funds that in January the Senate approved a measure that if anyone could devise a way of generating income that would not impose new burdens, the inventor would be rewarded with five percent of the take. As another Senate law stated, "if ever there was a time to find and exact money, it is now."[228] The situation grew even worse in September with the collapse of the Soranzo family bank. The precipitating event was the flight of the bank manager and cashier, non-nobleman Alvise Venier; but the underlying causes of the bank's failure were the heavy exactions it was forced to pay to the state, the bullion crisis, as well as the collapsing chains of credit caused by the fall of Constantinople.[229]

As for the Monte, each new levy generated less and less income, while the costs of the wars continued to increase. In November the Senate appointed a special board of sages "to find money." Among the members was Foscari's nephew Filippo.[230] In December it became clear that the old system of raising money through forced loans based on *estimo* assessments was no longer working. Noting that if money were not quickly found the state would be "in the greatest danger," the Ten decided on 6 December to follow a recommendation made by Doge Foscari and Bernardo Michiel, Marco Longo, and Pietro Bembo, to forbid judicial or legislative retribution against anyone proposing emergency financial measures.[231] Observing that they were no longer concerned "with the glory and dignity [of the state] but with its very health and freedom," the Senators approved a series of emergency measures designed to generate between 700,000 and 1,000,000 ducats in income. They decided first that from 1 January fees and other duties would be devoted to the war effort and that most other outlays would be delayed. Second, they ordered that the revenues which normally accrued to various office-holders as part of their compensation should be directed instead into the state's coffers. Third, taxes were imposed on properties and rents both in the city and on the terraferma, and new customs duties assessed. The Jews, always a favorite target of governmental taxation, were given an additional burden: those residing on the terraferma were to contribute an additional 8000 ducats, as would those living in Venice's overseas possessions.[232]

The significance of these measures cannot be exaggerated for they represented a fundamental change in the way the Republic of Venice generated revenue. The old system of relying on forced loans and the concomitant interest payments on those loans – a system that had been in operation since the thirteenth century – was suspended in favor of a new, more direct system of taxation. These laws and the suspension of interest payments constituted "a decisive step" toward the imposition of a system of direct taxes "on the entire body of taxpayers." The cost of war had opened the way for a new intrusion of the state into the financial lives of its citizens. Viewed from another angle, it placed in jeopardy the system of interest payments on forced loans upon which many charitable institutions and individuals had come to rely. In acts dated 18 and 31 December the government passed legislation to ensure enforcement of these new measures.[233] And on the 21st, the doge's brother Marco, who had largely dropped out of sight in recent years, renewed his push for sumptuary laws designed to limit spending on women's clothing, in this case jewelry. The goal, as the law made clear, was to honor God and to ensure that money remain in circulation and not go into consumables. But Foscari's proposal failed in a lopsided vote.[234]

In February 1453, several months before the collapse of the Monte, the Council of Ten had decided to generate additional revenue for the war effort by putting up for public auction the Palace of the Two Towers (as explained above, this palace had been awarded to Sforza but then confiscated from him and locked tight). The Ten established a minimum sale price of 7000 ducats. However, when the financial situation continued to worsen and no buyers came forward, the Ten amended its decision and ruled that the house should be sold for the highest price that the government could get for it. It appears that by May an offer had been tendered: the Senate ruled that the house could not be sold for less than 5500 ducats and that the buyer would have to pay cash for the house within one day of its sale. Among those recommending the sale on these terms were both the doge's brother Marco and his nephew Filippo. Although no record of the sale has come to light, it is known that the ultimate buyer of the property was the doge himself. Thus began one of Foscari's most important and revealing building projects.[235]

The House of the Two Towers stood on the shore of the Grand Canal, at the spot where it makes its turn toward San Marco, although one authority suggests that it was set back from the water, that it was located where the courtyard of Cà Foscari stands today.[236] The property was also bordered on another side by a smaller canal which today takes its name from Cà Foscari. While little is known about the shape or appearance of the Palace of the Two Towers, it certainly consisted of a main house (*caxa grande*) and courtyard as well as a smaller one-story property or outbuilding (*caxeta pizola*) which jutted beyond the main articulated boundaries of the palace complex. Some architectural historians have speculated on the basis of the palace's name that it resembled the now heavily restored Fondaco dei Turchi, whose Grand Canal façade, with two vestigial towers on each end, was built in the mid to late thirteenth century by the Pesaro family in a self-consciously Byzantinizing style. As noted above, the building had subsequently been awarded by the government to the Marquesses of Ferrara (fig. 26).[237] Apparently, the government found this building type especially appropriate for distinguished allies and military commanders.[238]

By the time the Palace of the Two Towers was sold to Foscari in 1453, it is likely that it was in a poor state of repair, especially since it stood at such a vulnerable location with canals on two sides and had sat unused for the past six years. Certainly the palace must have seemed old-fashioned and architecturally out of date, particularly when compared with some of the palaces that had been built in the previous few years, especially Marino Contarini's recently completed Cà d'Oro. There was a good deal of construction taking place in the immediate vicinity of the palace. The brothers Niccolò and Giovanni Giustinian were in the process of building their new palace on land directly contiguous. In

1451 they had petitioned for and been granted permission from the government to purchase the small outbuilding belonging to the Palace of the Two Towers which jutted toward their property and which they wished to tear down since it was interfering with their own construction project. Among the reasons they offered for their desire to acquire the *caxeta* was that their new palace would bring both great "ornament" and "honor" to the city.[239]

Almost immediately upon purchasing the Palace of the Two Towers, Foscari had it razed and began construction of the grand palace that still bears the family name (plate 9). His decision to purchase the property was determined by a whole complex of reasons, some personal and familial, others redolent with domestic political and international diplomatic implications. Naturally, given Jacopo's exile, the three were intertwined. But there can be no doubt that Foscari's goal first and foremost in building Cà Foscari was to establish an impressive new home for his direct line of male heirs at one of the most conspicuous locations on the entire Grand Canal, the turn (*volta*) the canal makes on the journey from Rialto to San Marco. Probably Foscari did not intend to live in the palace itself (unless he still hoped to resign the ducal office) since doges traditionally died in office and hence as residents of the Ducal Palace. In choosing this location, Foscari forsook the family's traditional home parish, San Simeon Apostolo, at the far reaches of the city; that property devolved to his brother Marco and his heirs.[240] Instead he chose a site in the very center of the city. In this way, he made a powerful statement about what he perceived to be his and his heirs' place in Venice. In a poem in praise of the palace, written some time between 1457 and 1460, that is after Jacopo's death, the poet Giovanantonio Romano wrote that Foscari built the palace for his grandsons.[241] However, it seems plausible that Foscari erected the palace with the hope that it might someday be occupied by Jacopo himself. One of the themes that the doge emphasized in his petition of 1447 for Jacopo's return from exile in Treviso was that his son was forced to live in "the houses of others," that he was not under the paternal roof.[242] The doge's goal of repatriating Jacopo was not an entirely unrealistic one for, despite the terms of Jacopo's banishment – specifically that it could not in any circumstances be revoked – experience taught the old man that anything was possible, that circumstances might change enough to allow even for a revocation of his son's punishment. This was particularly true if, as he believed, his son was innocent of Ermolao Donato's murder and that information might soon come to light that would exonerate him; there were after all constant rumors about the case. Barring that possibility, Foscari could also hope that political circumstances might again strengthen his hand enough to make it possible for him to petition again for his son's return, as he had done before. In this way, the palace delivered a powerful message to the doge's opponents within the city about his own and his family's resilience.[243]

Foscari used the palace to send equally powerful messages to Venice's international enemies, specifically to the architects of the current alliance against Venice: Francesco Sforza and Cosimo de' Medici. Foscari's warning to Sforza was clear and unequivocal. No one who saw Cà Foscari rising on the very land where Sforza's palace had once stood could misinterpret its meaning: as Foscari did to Sforza's Palace of the Two Towers, so he intended to do to Sforza and Milan, namely to destroy them. Romano wove this interpretation too into his poem: addressing the palace itself, he wrote, "you occupy the site that the bearded viper once held."[244] The reference is to the Visconti family and their symbol the viper, the family whose female heiress Sforza had taken as his bride and upon whose legacy Sforza consciously built. Images of the Visconti viper could still be seen in Venice; there was one in the parish of San Pantalon, for example, perhaps on a property that had formerly belonged to the Visconti family (fig. 25).[245] Certainly, the restoration of peace between Venice and Milan in 1454 led Romano to soften his criticism of Sforza by evoking the Milan of Filippo Maria Visconti rather than the new Milanese ruler. Given Sforza's own appropriation of a Visconti family legacy through his wife Bianca Maria, however, including incorporation of the Visconti viper into his own device, the original meaning of Foscari's building project as a rebuke to Sforza endured as a subtext of the poem.[246]

While Foscari's challenge to Sforza was explicit, that to Cosimo de' Medici was implicit and hence more subtle. As discussed in chapter 2, within two years of taking office as doge, Foscari broke with Venice's traditional ally Milan and opted instead for an alliance with republican Florence. Foscari warmly received Cosimo and his brother Lorenzo when they were exiled from Florence in 1433. But relations between Foscari and Cosimo rapidly deteriorated, mirroring those between their two republics. The stumbling blocks to good relations were commercial competition between Florentine and Venetian merchants and Cosimo's unmitigated support for Sforza. At the same time the fiscal and diplomatic pressures leading to a diminution of power in the Great Council and toward a concentration of power in the dogeship and the Council of Ten were also operative in Florence. In the Tuscan case, however, the momentum was away from a republican tradition built on support of the city's guilds and institutionalized in the city's executive committee, the priorate, which resided in the Palazzo Vecchio and toward an informal clique of great merchant and manufacturing families allied in one way or another to the Medici. Especially when compared with Foscari, Cosimo was handicapped by having no formal hold on power; furthermore any efforts on his part to remedy that situation were sure to ignite opposition from proponents of Florence's republican traditions. Unlike Foscari, who after all was a prince, Cosimo had to exercise caution when promoting explicitly princely traditions.[247]

Yet Cosimo's most forthrightly self-assertive act in this regard was his decision to build a new family palace (fig. 27). Begun in 1445, it was not completed until 1459. Designed by Michelozzo or perhaps by Filippo Brunelleschi, Cosimo's new home impressed first with its location on a "sharp curve" on the Via Larga, second with its massive size, and third with its architecture, a combination of native Tuscan and ancient Roman elements. Among its many distinctive architectural features were the heavy rustication of the ground floor, likely adapted from the Augustan wall of Trajan's forum in Rome, the biforate arched windows similar to those used on the Palazzo Vecchio, and the great height of the garden wall, a defensive element common in earlier Florentine palaces. Opinion differs widely on what meaning to attach to Palazzo Medici. Some have seen it as an expression of Cosimo's princely aspirations; one authority even argues that the palace resembled a "princely *camera*." Others, notably Dale Kent in her study of Cosimo's patronage activities, contend that the palace was "representative of the highest ideal of the Roman, Ciceronian, and Florentine republican citizen's obligation to his family, neighbors, friends, and ultimately to his city." But Kent also concedes that "the structure of the palace accommodates an interpretation [. . .] of princely luxury and power." In the end she concludes that Palazzo Medici "perfectly exemplifies the family's relation to the city, located complexly between honoring the city and themselves." Certainly, it had the ability to envelop all those meanings.[248]

Foscari never saw the Palazzo Medici. But there can be no doubt that he heard about its construction from Venetian envoys reporting on activities in Florence or from Venetian merchants who had business in the Tuscan city. It is also possible that he got some sense of its appearance, perhaps from one of the Florentine artists who sojourned for various periods of time in Venice and Padua. The leaders of the various peninsular states regularly kept themselves well informed about cultural projects in other cities and competed in obtaining the services of the most popular artists. In May 1452, for instance, Alfonso of Naples wrote to his ally Foscari, whom he addressed as "our dearest friend," requesting his help in securing the services of Donatello. Alfonso wanted the sculptor to replicate his equestrian statue of Gattamelata, although likely with himself as the mounted warrior, in order to adorn the triumphal arch he was then constructing in Naples.[249] Word of Cosimo's building project may have inspired Foscari to undertake his own palace and offer it as a challenge to Sforza's main financial backer. Certainly Cosimo would have greeted the news that Foscari had undertaken the project during the height of the war with some consternation, especially since he himself had had to postpone the building of his palace until 1445, when a temporary peace had been achieved and the financial situation stabilized.[250] Foscari, by contrast, undertook his palace in a time of war and in the midst of a severe financial crisis.

Although Foscari might have been inspired by rivalry with Cosimo, stylistically Cà Foscari bears no resemblance whatsoever to Cosimo's edifice; rather it operates within the traditions of Venetian Gothic domestic architecture – albeit with some features that point in the direction of the new "Renaissance" style, the origins of which were then emanating from Tuscany. The two ways in which it is similar to Palazzo Medici are, first, in its situation as the focus of a particularly impressive urban vista, the kind of location much favored by writers of Renaissance treatises on architecture and urbanism; and also in its massive proportions, especially when juxtaposed with other palaces on the canal (fig. 28).[251] Clearly both patrons wanted to leave their imprint on the urban fabric. The visual impact of Cà Foscari at the time of its construction is difficult to grasp, given that larger and even more magnificent palaces were built in subsequent centuries and now tend to attract greater attention. But it is worth noting that when he wrote his guidebook to Venice some fifty years after the doge's death, Sanudo singled out only two palaces on the Grand Canal for particular remark: Giorgio Corner's palace at San Samuele and Cà Foscari.[252]

By any measure the palace creates a grand impression. A foundation of white *pietra d'Istria* supports the red-brick four-story façade, whose very nearly square shape is now obscured somewhat by subsidence and a rise in the water level.[253] The sides of the façade are defined by alternating quoins also in *pietra d'Istria*; the top by a substantial cornice made of the same material, while string courses mark the various floors. The ground floor is interrupted by six simple windows with ogee arches and by the broad-arched water-entrance. The second floor (the first of two *piani nobili*) is not as high as the third story and is set apart by an eight-light window graced with ogee arches set within a rectangular frame with marble revetment. The third floor (the second and taller of the two *piani nobili*) is also defined by an eight-light window with arches which support seven quatrefoil and two bi-foil openings, a direct quotation of the loggia of the Ducal Palace. Surmounting the window is a frieze in low relief, "an architectural element completely extraneous to Venetian tradition" (fig. 29).[254] In the center of the frieze is a helmet with flowing drapery surmounted by a nearly illegible winged lion of Saint Mark, which was defaced following the fall of the Republic in 1797. It is flanked on both sides by two sets of winged putti who present the Foscari family coat of arms. These were also destroyed in the same rush of revolutionary fervor but were replaced in 1924.[255] The top floor is distinguished by a four-light window with crossed inflected arches with elaborate tracery. Two single-light windows on either side of that central aperture align with the outer openings of the eight-light windows on the two floors below and define the central portion of the façade. The outer sections of the façade are marked on each story by two sets of two single-light windows which match the other windows of that particular floor. The broad expanses of brick between those windows subtly create the impression of two towers flanking the central portion of the structure.[256] The interior of the palace has undergone numerous alterations over the centuries, but it can be discerned from the façade that, as in most Venetian palaces, there was a large central space known as the *portego* on each floor (marked by the massed windows) with smaller rooms on both sides leading off from this central room. The center space on the ground floor was known as the *androne* and allowed for entry to the house by water from the front or by land from the rear.[257] In later centuries a massive addition was built onto the back of the palace. What seems to be original is the large rear courtyard with its crenellated wall and huge portal surmounted by an arch into which has been set a frieze, again showing two putti displaying the Foscari arms. The only difference between this coat of arms and those on the façade frieze is that a third putto hovers above it and prepares to crown his companions (fig. 30).

As noted above, Cà Foscari is a transitional work. Some have judged it to be the apogee of Venetian Gothic architecture. In *The Stones of Venice* (first published in 1851–53), for example, John Ruskin described it as "the noblest example in Venice of the fifteenth-century Gothic."[258] Certainly it operates both structurally and decoratively within native traditions. But others have called attention to its Renaissance elements, a claim that may seem strange to those more familiar with the characteristics of Tuscan architecture. The present-day scholar and architect Antonio Foscari, a descendant of the doge, identifies four elements of the façade as "Renaissance-like" (*rinascimentale*). These are the palace's massive size, which broke with the tradition of emphasizing "parity" among the members of the nobility; its axial symmetry; the development from bottom to top of ever more delicate architectural elements, which "seem to evoke the Vitruvian theory of the superimposition of the architectural orders then being diffused by Leon Battista Alberti;" and, fourth, the façade's square shape.[259] To these can be added the alternating quoins of antique inspiration, an element rare in Gothic palaces.[260]

Like the Porta della Carta, when read both architecturally and contextually, Cà Foscari offers a variety of different meanings and interpretations, but most fundamentally it represents a powerful statement by the doge of his own and his family's place in Venice and an assertion of their ducal heritage. That point is made most clearly in the architectural quotations from the Ducal Palace itself.[261] But how observers were to understand those associations, as republican or princely, is less clear. While the symbol of the Republic, the lion of Saint Mark, enjoys primacy of place on the third-story frieze, its repetition as an element in the Foscari family's coat of arms suggests an identification between the state and the family, the glorification of one contributing to the glorification of the other. Moreover, the impression created by the frieze is not Venetian, but Roman and imperial, although with Early Christian overtones.[262] And the helmet adds a martial element, possibly alluding to the family's heritage as counts of Zellarino. Certainly it evokes the chivalric traditions characteristic of the mainland states.[263]

Whatever other meanings the doge wished to be attached to it, he meant first and foremost for people to see Cà Foscari as the architectural embodiment of his role as *paterfamilias*.[264] As the poet Romano put it, "At tu perpetuum fato mansura per aevum/Foscareae aeternum gentis celebrabere factis": the palace would last to eternity and stand as a monument to the deeds of the Foscari family.[265] By building the palace, Foscari was celebrating his family's past and laying the groundwork for its future; certainly he envisioned that future as holding out great prospects for his two grandsons, the sons of Jacopo. He may even have hoped that the future would yet hold a place for Jacopo as well. In this sense, the house of Foscari perfectly epitomizes the uneasy (and not entirely successful) balancing act that Foscari was trying to perform between his duties and responsibilities to the state as doge and his loyalties and solicitude for his family. From the point of view of many others in the government, however, the choice was obvious: the doge's first obligation, as his *promissione* made clear, was to subordinate his family's interests to those of the Republic. That was a choice that Doge Foscari was hesitant to make. And it would bring him to ruin.

5

Last Judgements
1454–1457

nec est secundum deum, nec mores nostri dominii, quod pater penam patiatur pro filio iniquo.

(it is neither godly nor customary in our state that a father should suffer a penalty on account of an evil son.)

The Council of Ten,
in a case involving a certain Amadeo Montagna[1]

Vir fuit enim semper fortunatus. Nunc autem in filio infelix est.

(Indeed the man [Foscari] was always favored by fortune. Now, however, he is unhappy in his son.)

Aeneas Silvius Piccolomini[2]

By the time he began in 1453 to build his new family palace on the Grand Canal, Francesco Foscari had either reached or was approaching eighty years of age and had been on the ducal throne for thirty years. This was an extraordinary length of time by any standard and particularly so in republican Venice, where doges usually reigned, on account of their advanced age at election, a decade or less. These indisputable biological and chronological facts were to shape the remaining years of

Foscari's dogate and, in a very real sense, to determine its final outcome. The doge's age meant that he found it increasingly difficult to shoulder the heavy demands of the ducal office; and although there is plenty of evidence that Foscari remained engaged much of the time with his official duties, he also lapsed into periods of inactivity, brought on either by illness or by his constant preoccupation with the fate of Jacopo. Equally importantly, Foscari's long tenure in office meant that an entire generation had grown up knowing no other doge. The youngest members of the Great Council, those who qualified in the *Barbarella* lottery at eighteen and even those who entered at the normal age of twenty-five, had not even been born when Foscari entered office. More significantly, two generations of the Republic's leaders had passed or were passing from the scene. Among the deaths during the first two decades of Foscari's reign were those of men who were his elders, men who remembered well the War of Chioggia and the initial conquest of the terraferma: this group included some of Foscari's closest allies, for example Albano Badoer and Santo Venier, though there were also some contemporaries, such as Pietro Loredan. But now those who had taken leadership positions in the subsequent period, the years of the extended Lombard wars, had themselves reached old age and were beginning to die: Andrea Zulian in 1452; Francesco Barbaro in 1454; and the city's first patriarch Lorenzo Giustinian in 1456.[3] Furthermore, Foscari's sister Elena, the Abbess of San Zaccaria, died in 1455. For Foscari, the passing of his relatives and contemporaries, both allies and opponents, must have evoked a combination of nostalgia and melancholy, tinged with regret and a sense of opportunities lost. And yet he reigned on. Foscari's longevity led to a general fatigue with his dogeship and growing resentment toward him, combined with a longing for a new beginning, and an unspoken desire on the part of Pasquale Malipiero, Cristoforo Moro, and others to assume the dogeship themselves, to fulfill their own ambitions, to steer the Republic in different directions.[4]

One of the factors contributing to the desire for change was frustration with the wars in Lombardy. Ever since the initial successes in Brescia and Bergamo in the 1420s, these wars had absorbed huge amounts of manpower, diplomacy, and treasure, but resulted in few tangible benefits. Fortunately, for the Venetians the growing desire to bring the conflict to an end was shared by Florence and increasingly by Sforza, although less so by Venice's ally Alfonso of Naples. Spurred by the futility of military efforts as well as by the conquest of Constantinople, some began to search for a way out of the impasse. In July 1453 Pope Nicholas V let it be known that he was interested in mediating a peace between the Italian powers. Secret negotiations had already begun between the Venetian patriarch Lorenzo Giustinian, the Archbishop of Florence Antoninus Pierozzi, and a third unnamed religious.[5] In October Nicholas convened formal peace talks in Rome; the knight Orsato Giustinian and the procurator of San Marco Cristoforo Moro represented the Republic. As its initial bargaining position Venice demanded, "for its security," everything on "this" side of the Po and Adda, as well as all territory it currently held beyond the Adda. Assisting informally in the effort to bring about a peace was Andrea Donato, who had taken up residence in Rome. But the negotiations dragged on for months with little progress.[6] While the envoys from the various states haggled and debated in Rome, an effort to bring about a separate peace between Venice and Sforza was progressing under the auspices of the Augustinian friar, Simone da Camerino, who was possibly the unnamed religious involved in the earlier mediation efforts between Patriarch Giustinian and Archbishop Antoninus.

Fra Simone had a close personal bond with Foscari stretching back decades, so close that one historian of the order of Augustinian Observant friars has characterized him as "the doge's man."[7] Described by one chronicler as "a man of little learning but full of faith and of charity," Simone was, in other words, a man in whom one could have complete confidence.[8] The relationship between the two was bound up with their mutual interest in the monastery of San Cristoforo, located on an island of the same name between Venice and Murano. The island no longer exists for it was later absorbed into the cemetery island of San Michele. Foscari's engagement with the site dated at least as far back as his days as procurator of San Marco and to his concern with hospital reform, for the island was for a time home to the Ospedale di Santi Cristoforo e Onofrio which was under ducal patronage but which had fallen into ruin. Soon after becoming doge, Foscari awarded the island to the members of the Order of Saint Brigit, but they abandoned the site after Eugenius IV ordered a reform of their order. Then in November 1436 Foscari conveyed the monastery to Fra Simone and the members of his congregation of Augustinian friars of Monte Ortone, itself founded at about the same time as the island's transfer.[9]

The congregation took its name from one of the peaks in the Euganean Hills near Padua. In 1428 a certain Pietro Falco, suffering from the plague, had ascended that mountain, received a vision of the Virgin Mary, and been cured. The Paduan jurist Ludovico Buzzacarini quickly took charge of the cult that developed around the site; by 1433 the monks tending the pilgrimage destination had been incorporated into the order of Augustinian friars. In essence Simone's association with Monte Ortone might have been a political act orchestrated by Foscari. It had to do with the doge's preoccupation with the security of Padua as Buzzacarini, the original orchestrator of the cult, was a ringleader in Marsiglio da Carrara's abortive attempt to reclaim Padua for his family in 1435; as noted above, Buzzacarini was executed for his part in the conspiracy. Thirteen months later, in April 1436, the prior general of the order of Augustinians named Simone as vicar over three houses: Santa Maria di Monte Ortone; Santa Maria in Campo Santo, near the town of Cittadella in the Paduan *contado*; and the island monastery of San Cristoforo. At the same time and on the order of Foscari, the hospital of San Marco located in the Prato della Valle in Padua was also conveyed to Simone; and in July 1436 Eugenius IV formally licensed the congregation.[10] As for the island of San Cristoforo, Foscari transferred it to Simone on 25 November 1436; and construction of the church began in December 1437. The monastic complex eventually included the main church with several side chapels, a dormitory, as well as a chapel dedicated to Saint Humphrey (Onofrio), which was located in the orchard (fig. 31).[11]

The link between Foscari and Simone paid off when, as noted above, the friar undertook separate peace negotiations between Venice and Sforza. His counterparts on the Milanese side were also Augustinian Observant friars: Giovanni Rocco Porzi da Pavia and Agostino Cazzuli da Crema. For months during the winter of 1453–54 Simone shuttled back and forth between Venice and Milan carrying proposals.[12] The previous chapter considers at some length the factors driving Venice to the peace table, including the increasing threat from the Turks, a threat felt more acutely by Venice than by the other Italian powers, given the city's dependency on trade. Financial exhaustion also played a significant role. According to Dolfin, the land war was costing the Republic 550,000 ducats a year.[13] Similar concerns also influenced Sforza, especially given that the Florentines and Genoese were slow to funnel money to him.

But paramount in his mind was his need to consolidate his hold over his newly acquired duchy. Venice's efforts to lure Colleoni from his service also figured in his calculations.[14]

The courting of Colleoni depended to some measure on the personal trust that had developed between the mercenary captain and nobleman Andrea Morosini, who served as the intermediary between Colleoni and the Republic. The condottiere let it be known that he was interested in returning to the Venetian side, although his demands were high: he wanted 100,000 ducats per year and appointment as captain-general. What made these negotiations even more unusual was that they were overseen by the Council of Ten rather than the Senate. This represented "a significant extension of its authority," one brought about by the need for security. Certainly some contemporaries disapproved of the Ten's aggrandizement of its own power: Dolfin comments that the Ten's involvement was "against the law of that council." Both Dolfin and Sanudo also report that another facet of the negotiations to rehire Colleoni involved a proposal for him to marry one of his daughters to Morosini's son Paolo, who was to receive in turn a *condotta* with Colleoni's forces. Paolo died before this took place. Nevertheless, by the end of February an agreement for Colleoni to reenter Venetian service had been sealed. At the same time the Republic attempted to lure the Marquess of Mantua as well as Sigismondo Malatesta, the captain of the Florentine forces, back to its side.[15]

As regards the peace talks, both those conducted by Simone and those held under papal auspices, the major sticking points were control of Bergamo and the Bergamasco as well as the final disposition of the town of Crema. Sforza wrote a letter to Cosimo de' Medici, saying that Simone kept urging him to "give up Crema, give up Crema."[16] But there were other issues as well, especially as they involved the allies. The Florentines, for example, wanted the restoration of castles that had been taken from them by Alfonso and by the Sienese.[17] Venice and Sforza eventually reached an agreement; and on 18 March the Senate voted 147 to 8 with 3 abstentions to accept the terms as outlined by Fra Simone. The senators agreed to send representatives to finalize the terms; ten days later they commissioned on a unanimous vote Paolo Barbo to accompany Simone to conclude the accord. According to some accounts, Barbo traveled in disguise as a friar so as not to allow word of the talks to leak out.[18] On 1 April Sforza went to the town of Lodi to meet Barbo and Simone, and on the 9th the two sides signed what has come to be known as the Peace of Lodi. The peace was officially promulgated in Venice on the 14th, Palm Sunday.[19]

According to the terms of the treaty, Sforza agreed to relinquish to Venice all the territory he had conquered in the Bresciano and Bergamasco, as well as Crema, while retaining for himself the Ghiaradadda, including such towns as Caravaggio and Triviglio, as well as the parts of the Cremonese he had captured. He also retained rights over the Adda. Both sides agreed to return prisoners and restore property that had been sequestered or occupied during the war. The pact even included a special arrangement to return to Sforza's chancellor Angelo Simonetta his property in Verona and compensate him for his other losses. For their part, the Venetians were to persuade the Duke of Savoy, the Marquess of Monferrato, and the lords of Correggio to restore to Sforza lands which they had occupied; if they failed to do so, Sforza could move against them. Should that in turn provoke Alfonso to make war on Sforza, Venice would inform the king of the terms and deny him aid in the effort. Generally speaking, the treaty was designed to remove, as far as possible, any future pretexts for war between Milan and Venice. Over the next several months Fra Simone continued to travel between the two cities, ironing out outstanding concerns. In May, for example, Foscari commissioned him to work out the disposition of Brescello, which had been promised to the lords of Correggio; and in August, fearing that otherwise he would be taken for a liar, Simone worked to make sure that the provisions in the treaty forbidding retribution against those in Bergamo and Brescia who had cooperated with the other side were observed.[20]

The treaty also included provisions for allies on both sides to sign on to the agreement within predetermined time limits. But Venice's main partner, Alfonso of Naples, was unhappy with the settlement, not because he objected to its provisions but because the Venetians, his reputed allies, had not deigned to inform him in advance. According to one report to Sforza, the king complained bitterly that Venice "had shown so little regard for him." The pope also took offense and "made his adherence conditional upon that of the king."[21] But Venice, Florence, and Milan again went their own way and agreed in August 1454 to form a twenty-five-year league, sometimes referred to anachronistically as the Concert of Italy, which amounted in essence to a mutual non-aggression pact. The terms of the pact, which was shepherded along by Venice, dictated that each member state would maintain a prescribed number of soldiers in its army and come to the others' aid should they suffer attack. In case of war they agreed neither to enter into a separate peace nor to form any other league which might compromise the present one. The signatories promised within two months to name their allies who would ratify the agreement within an additional two months. They also decided to invite both the pope and Alfonso to join the alliance. Bologna soon joined the League, and the major powers named their allies and adherents.[22] Again Alfonso was offended, as was the pope, but the king finally gave his assent to both the Peace of Lodi and the League in January 1455. He did manage to get some concessions: Genoa, for example, on which he had designs, was not included.[23] On 25 March Foscari proclaimed the entry of the pope, Naples, and the Duke of Modena into the League, concluding with the words "Long live San Marco!"[24]

The Peace of Lodi and the subsequent Italian League, which are often conflated, have assumed a prominent place in many accounts of the history of western Europe: the League in particular has often been characterized as a prototype or model for the kind of balance-of-power configurations that dominated Europe right through the Cold War of the twentieth century. Additionally, historians have viewed the effort to maintain the delicate equilibrium required by the League as the impetus for the development of modern diplomatic practices, including most especially the dispatch of resident ambassadors.[25] Taking a shorter view, it is clear that the League demonstrated "the sterility of conflict between the major Italian powers."[26] That is, after nearly thirty years of war and a tremendous sacrifice of men and money, it was apparent to everyone that none of the major powers was in a position to dominate the entire peninsula; a *de facto* balance of power had been achieved, the agreement simply gave *de iure* recognition to that reality by discarding "the traditional practice of opposing leagues in favor of a grand alliance of all the Italian powers."[27] The League had another important function as well; it was also designed to "isolate Italian politics from European ones," that is, to neutralize the threat of foreign intervention in Italian affairs, especially by the French – who claimed both the Duchy of Milan and the Kingdom of Naples as theirs – and by the Holy Roman Emperor.[28] Finally, it had an additional purpose of maintaining the social and political equilibrium within each of the member states.[29] In this way it was an essentially conservative agreement.

The Venetians greeted the Peace of Lodi with elaborate processions and celebrations, including the pealing of bells and lighting of bonfires. For its part, the Senate agreed to free all debtors both in Venice and the subject territories who owed 50 ducats or less and to give the patriarch Lorenzo Giustinian 500 ducats to distribute *pro amore dei* as he saw fit. The Senate also issued an order recalling all those who had been sent into exile, but excluded those who had broken their exile and those who had been exiled from Crema. Nor did it apply to those banished by the Council of Ten. The latter group included, of course, Jacopo Foscari.[30]

Following the success of the peace talks, Fra Simone was not reticent about presenting his own demands, fulfillment of which he believed he deserved as recompense for his efforts. In May he put before the government a petition requesting that the monastery of San Cristoforo be renamed San Cristoforo della Pace in honor of the agreement, and that properties owned by Santa Maria di Monte Ortone and Santa Maria in Campo Santo in Cittadella be exempt from governmental imposts. On 17 May 1454 the Senate approved Simone's request to rename the monastery. It further agreed to give Simone 100 ducats a month for two years to support construction at San Cristoforo and thereafter to provide 30 ducats annually to the monastery and to exempt Santa Maria di Monte Ortone and Santa Maria in Campo Santo from taxation.[31] The renaming of the monastery meant that the Peace of Lodi was now commemorated in the nomenclature of the lagoon.

The peace also found forms of architectural expression. Most importantly, apparently even before the treaty was signed, Simone was trying to get Sforza's Palace of the Two Towers on the Grand Canal returned to him.[32] But on 12 June the friar reported to Sforza that when he addressed the issue, the senators replied that had the palace not been razed, they would have done so. Sforza's concern with acquiring a new Venetian residence indicates just how deeply the confiscation of the Palace of the Two Towers had offended him and how strongly he felt that his honor be restored by means of another palace. Simone made those feelings known to the Venetians. On 18 June he wrote to Sforza, describing how he had told the Signoria that such a donation would be a sign of "the love that you have for the said lord [Sforza]" and that no other action "would please him more." On that same day, first the Collegio and then the Senate agreed to find him a new residence. In his letter Simone reported how he thanked the Venetian government for its response, saying: "Oh what honor, oh what fame this gift will bring to your most illustrious Signoria! This is a sign of great affection and love!"[33] He also told Sforza that the vote was unanimous when in fact there were 19 votes against (123 voted in favor). Either the Venetians deliberately misinformed Simone of the vote, creating the impression that it was unanimous, or Simone, fearing that Sforza would take umbrage at the negative votes, chose to veil the facts to Sforza. In any case, Sforza was to get the palace that he so "vehemently" (as the Senate put it) desired.[34]

However, finding another property for Sforza proved difficult. Only after a wait of two more years did the government finally award him one. The palace they chose was situated in Campo San Polo and had formerly been the property of Gattamelata and his heirs. When Gattamelata's son Giovanantonio died without issue in April 1456, the government donated the house to Sforza in June that year.[35] But Sforza was not particularly pleased with the new property since it was in a state of disrepair and still bore the Gattamelata arms.[36] Worse still, it was not on the Grand Canal and hence not, in his view, a sufficiently distinguished and honorable site. He also judged it unequal to his station since the surrounding canals were not navigable by the *bucintoro*; this presented a sticking point since Sforza was used to being received in Venice by the ducal barge; and a palace that the *bucintoro* could not approach directly threatened to create all sorts of protocol concerns.[37] Accordingly, Sforza's agents began to search for a more suitable residence. After a series of negotiations involving various locations, they settled on a property situated across the Grand Canal but within view of Cà Foscari; it belonged to Marco Corner, father of Caterina Corner, future Queen of Cyprus. Sforza purchased the partially constructed palace in 1461, although many more controversies regarding the sale followed. The palace, which was designed on a grand scale but never completed, is known even today as the Cà del Duca (fig. 32).[38] In spite of all these tribulations, the fact that Sforza was once again a property owner in Venice signaled the rapprochement between the two powers. Cà Foscari itself was also reinterpreted to accord with the changed international situation. In his laudatory ode Giovanantonio Romano addressed the palace itself: "After Italy which had given itself to cruel warfare was pacified by divine decree, then you [Cà Foscari] suddenly were built, in a time of eternal peace."[39] Even reimagined, this new interpretation could not completely obliterate the palace's original message as an affront to Sforza.

Another decisive step in the growing détente between Venice and Milan occurred in November 1455, when Sforza sent his eldest son Galeazzo Maria, then eleven years old, on a mission to Venice. The boy made his entry into the city aboard the *bucintoro*, which met him at Chioggia. Accompanied by a retinue of almost three hundred barons, knights, and gentlemen, he lodged at the palace of the Marquess of Ferrara since his visit occurred before his father was awarded Gattamelata's former palace. The Venetian government authorized the expenditure of up to 2000 ducats on the visit. During his eleven-day stay he toured the city, visited the glassworks on Murano, cast a ballot in a meeting of the Great Council, and participated in the religious festivals being celebrated at the time.[40] Commissioned by his father, as Dolfin put it, to "bow" to Foscari, to whom he considered himself obligated, as well as to the entire Senate, he gave an oration in Latin: after excusing himself for his lack of eloquence, he celebrated the restitution of "the peace and ancient friendship" between the two states, a peace he characterized as not having been so much destroyed during the years of conflict as merely "interrupted." He pledged to lend to Venice his every faculty of mind, spirit, and body, just "as sons do to their fathers;" he went on to say that Milan and Venice were not, "two empires, two jurisdictions, or two republics, but rather one principality with two different names, one in spirit, mind and will, and also conjoined." Speaking on behalf of his parents, brothers, and himself, he concluded with an expression of love and benevolence toward the Venetians.[41] Although, as Dolfin notes, Galeazzo did not compose the oration himself, he did deliver it most successfully; Sforza's agent in Venice proudly reported that he read it not like a boy, but like a grown man.[42]

Soon after the youth's departure, Foscari sent a letter to Sforza on behalf of Venice, congratulating the duke on the visit of his "most dear and most splendid" son, whom he described as an "ornament" to his principality. He even referred to the boy as "our son in common." Galeazzo's mother Bianca Maria was so pleased with the letter that she preserved it among her "arcane treasures," as Dolfin put it, so that she could read it from time to time.[43] Sforza responded in turn with a letter to Foscari thanking him for showing Galeazzo "that intimacy that a father shows his son" and reiterating that he and his heirs were at Venice's disposal. The duke added that he took special pleasure in Foscari's designation of Galeazzo as their "son in common," and concluded by recording that should Galeazzo or any of his other sons fail to demonstrate goodwill toward Venice, he would curse and deprive them of their "paternal inheritance."[44] Like so many diplomatic exchanges of the period, these letters are redolent with what now might seem overly lavish familial language, but which was an essential element of Renaissance diplomacy.

During his stay Galeazzo toured several islands in the lagoon. Among the places he visited was the monastery of San Cristoforo, now renamed with the modifier "della Pace."[45] Various descriptions of the island state that a plaque commemorating the peace was attached to the walls of the monastery near the cloister. It is possible that this tribute to peace was commissioned at the time of Galeazzo's visit or some time thereafter in commemoration of the visit. Like nearly everything else on the island, the plaque has been lost or destroyed. But a drawing of it by Jan Grevembroch survives (fig. 33), showing that the plaque was rectangular in shape and framed with billet molding. It displayed the arms of Venice, the winged lion of Saint Mark, and the arms of Francesco Sforza, namely a quartered shield decorated with eagles and with Visconti vipers. An iron chain threaded through a ring at the top of each shield conjoined them, with the words "PAX QUIS SEPARABIT NOS" (Peace, who will divide us) inscribed between. Several previous scholars who were unaware of the drawing wrongly concluded that the plaque linked the Foscari and Sforza coats of arms.[46] Nevertheless, the incorporation of the lion of Saint Mark into the Foscari arms would have allowed for some confluence of the two; and certainly the reputations of the doge, Fra Simone, and the monastery itself were tied to the peace. Indeed the friars of the Congregation of Monte Ortone continued to cultivate the association: the epitaph on Fra Simone's tomb at Monte Ortone alludes to the peace; and the friar's role in mediating the treaty was also commemorated in a seventeenth-century painting by Giambattista Bissoni once in the sacristy of the church of Monte Ortone and in another painting by an unknown artist in San Cristoforo.[47]

Despite the expressions of goodwill that Foscari made to Galeazzo (Sanudo says that the doge "cherished him greatly"), the visit by the son of one of his chief rivals must have pained the doge, especially when he compared the reception accorded the boy and the esteem in which he was held with the infamy that had befallen his own son and heir. Indeed Foscari seems to have envied Sforza: twice in 1456 Sforza's agent in Venice wrote to his master informing him that Foscari had described Sforza, his wife, and children as enjoying a "paradise here on earth."[48] From time to time during these years, issues involving Jacopo continued to surface, reminding the doge of his son's fate. But every time the Ten revisited Jacopo's case, they remained intransigent. In July 1454, for example, a question arose concerning the disposition of a stone image (*imago lapidea*) which had belonged to Jacopo; having been found in the Customs House, it was now in the possession of Giovanni Capello. Unfortunately, nothing else is known about this sculpture, whether it was religious or secular in subject matter. Perhaps, given Jacopo's humanist interests, it was an antique fragment. In any case, the Ten wanted it disposed of properly; two of the heads of the council, Lorenzo Soranzo and Giacomo Dandolo, proposed that master stonecutters estimate its value and if Capello was willing to pay what they judged its worth to be, he could have it as he had been promised. Otherwise the piece was to be given to the procurators of San Marco so that they could use it to "ornament" a spot they considered appropriate. In no circumstances was it to be sold, given as a gift, or otherwise alienated. Their proposal received 5 votes. A counter-proposal, by Leo da Molin, the third head of the council, denying Capello's claim and ordering that the piece be given to the procurators as above, passed with 10 votes in favor and 1 against. The prohibition on offering the sculpture for sale or as a gift suggests that the Ten were worried that it might in some way become a kind of talisman of Jacopo or a rallying point for his followers, much like the Carrara image that would cause such concern in Padua in 1456. Incidents like this recalling Jacopo's fate surely increased the doge's bitterness, not only when he compared what had befallen his son with the obvious successes of Sforza's son Galeazzo but also with those of Cosimo de' Medici's son Piero.[49] Certainly Foscari felt deeply the familial disability that set him apart from his princely peers.

The Peace of Lodi was not the only treaty concluded in the spring of 1454. On 18 April, just four days after the publication of the agreement, the Venetian envoy to the Turks Bartolomeo Marcello reached an accord with Sultan Mehmed II amplifying the pact that the two sides had signed the previous September. The treaty essentially confirmed Venetian privileges as they had stood under the Byzantine emperors, including the right to trade throughout the sultan's lands and maintain a resident *bailo* in Constantinople, but with the important difference that now Venetian merchants were required to pay a 2 percent duty on goods they sold in or shipped through the sultan's realm. This tax represented "an affirmation [by the sultan] of sovereignty, attuned to the new power relationships that the fall of the Byzantine Empire had provoked in the eastern Mediterranean." Among the other privileges that the sultan guaranteed the Venetians was the right to ship slaves from the Black Sea region so long as they were not Muslims; merchants were required to pay the same 2 percent duty on them as they paid on other merchandise. The treaty essentially recognized the economic benefit that both sides derived from trade between their states.[50] But it also represented little more than a pause in the larger battle between the two for control of Greece and the Greek islands and for the rest of the Balkan peninsula. Indeed, the Peace of Lodi allowed Venice to direct more of its resources toward the east.[51]

It did this by giving the Republic the opportunity to scale back its standing army to numbers close to those outlined in the creation of the League; namely 6000 cavalry and 2000 infantry. One of the men unhappy with this reduction was the captain-general Jacopo Piccinino, who decided to seek his fortune elsewhere. His Venetian employers saw little reason to retain him, especially since they had already secretly agreed to reemploy Colleoni and award him the title captain-general. The task of informing Piccinino that the Republic no longer required his services fell to the doge. Apparently Foscari carried out this delicate operation with great finesse for the Senate learned that Piccinino was gratified by the great "humanity" with which Foscari delivered the news. Again the doge's renowned eloquence served him well.[52] Certainly past experience taught the Venetians that there was no reason to burn their bridges as far as Piccinino was concerned, especially given how quickly events could change. With Piccinino's departure the title of captain-general and the baton of command passed to Colleoni, whom the Venetians established in a fief at Malpaga near Bergamo, while another commander, Braccio da Montone, was stationed at Brescia. These postings helped safeguard the still vulnerable western frontier.[53] Also, the death in February 1455 of Belpetro Manelmi da Vicenza, the nobleman who had served for decades as collateral-general or chief army administrator, offered the government the opportunity to reorganize that office, save yet more money, and provide jobs for Venetian nobles as collaterals.[54]

The pressure to save money was acutely felt since the viability of the Monte had still not been determined. Despite the many financial problems, the Republic was not yet prepared to abandon entirely the old system of forced loans and continued to search for a way to save the Monte. In September 1454 the Senate elected five special *savi* to investigate the loan office; the five elected were Niccolò Bernardo, Guglielmo Querini, the procurator Paolo Tron, as well as two future doges, procurators Pasquale Malipiero and Cristoforo Moro.[55] Within days they recommended measures to save money, including the cashiering of the condottiere Guido Rangoni and a reduction of Carlo Gonzaga's stipend. The size of the infantry was also reduced at this time.[56] But money-saving measures such as these were not enough to solve the fiscal crisis, and the following June the Senate authorized yet another committee of five *savi* who in turn presented a series of recommendations designed to raise 46,000 ducats. In September the Great Council approved still other measures to revive the Monte. Unfortunately, the council could not come up with any genuinely new ideas; instead it again called for officials to give back a portion of their salaries and officers to prorogue their terms. The plan was to use the savings generated from these and other expedients to buy up shares of the debt.[57] Yet more than a year later, on 29 November 1456, the Senate had to reiterate the need for officials who were supposed to surrender a share of their salaries to do so immediately in order to sustain the Monte which it continued to describe as the "root of our state and the axis which sustains it and around which revolve all our interests."[58] In the end, none of these solutions proved sufficient to revive the Monte or solve the underlying problem of how to raise revenue. The government would continue to rely on stop-gap measures such as these until 1463, when it instituted a new form of taxation known as the *decima* which was based on real estate holdings.[59]

The drive to find salaried positions for poorer nobles provided one of many countervailing forces to the cost-cutting measures designed to save the Monte. Lodi allowed the government to address these and other domestic and constitutional issues which had arisen in the preceding years but which had had to be put on hold for the duration of the war. The Senate recognized as much in December 1454, when it acknowledged that "after the peace was made, many things were put in order and regularized."[60] Reading through the legislation for the period 1454–57, one gets a sense of the discontent, rivalries, and resentments that had festered during the war years and now cried out for attention.

For one thing, the restoration of peace allowed divisions to resurface within the ranks of the nobility, especially between the poorer nobles and the wealthier ones. In September 1454, for example, the Great Council, the bulwark of the poorer patricians, passed a law restricting all terms of office to one year, except for the lords of the Arsenal and the supervisors of the state-owned rope factory, the hemp officials, in order to maintain "equality" among members of the patriciate. The exceptions were designed to guarantee managerial continuity in Venice's naval defense industry. The preamble to the law observed that several offices currently carried a two-year term. The goal of the legislation was to allow more nobles to participate in office-holding by rotating posts more frequently; and it passed with 591 votes in favor, 182 against, and 76 abstentions. In the same spirit, the Great Council decided in October to modify the rules regarding the terms of offices for castellanies and other posts such as rectorships on the terraferma so that "many more nobles will be able to participate in these benefices." It voted (693 to 36 with 19 abstentions) that such offices currently held for between three and five years should henceforth be held only for two and that those held for two years should be reduced to one year. It also ruled that castellanies awarded in the Great Council by special favor (*per gratiam*) could no longer be held for four years, but only for two.[61]

The Great Council's effort to assign castellanies to patricians placed the leaders of the government in an awkward position for they were caught between the demands of two groups: fellow nobles who wanted these low-level but salaried positions; and loyal subjects of the regime, both Venetian *popolani* and residents of the subject territories, who also coveted them. The issue was of such importance that the Ten decided on 9 April 1455 to add a *zonta* of twenty members to investigate why offices that had been promised to non-nobles and men from the subject realms were being assigned instead to members of the nobility through *grazie*. The Ten were worried because the practice was causing "much

grumbling" among those who felt they were being disenfranchised as
well as contributing to "a diminution of the honor of our nobility."
They ordered an immediate halt to further grants of offices until they
and the *zonta* could investigate the matter thoroughly.[62] Noting two
days later that many offices had been awarded "out of friendship and
not through equity" and that this was causing quarrels and discontent
within the noble class, the Ten debated several different measures and
finally voted to nullify the law of the previous October allowing the
awarding of castellanies by *grazie*. The following day they also debated
increasing the number of bowmen of the quarterdeck as a way to help
poor nobles, but that measure failed to pass. Recognizing just how
explosive the issues they were debating were as well as the fact that they
were treading into arenas usually reserved for the Great Council, they
imposed a gag order on their proceedings and then prosecuted one of
their secretaries for breaking it. In order further to protect themselves
against retribution, they passed another law. This stated, first, that anyone
who spoke or acted against the members of the Ten and its *zonta* would
be deprived of all offices for five years; and second, that any noble who
had received an office by *grazia* and then had it revoked by the Ten
would be forbidden from sitting in judgement in any case involving any
of the members of the Ten or the *zonta* which approved the change.[63]
Perhaps as a response to the Ten's promise to find other remedies for
poor nobles, the Senate approved on 23 April a proposal that all galleys
add to their crews two more bowmen. In approving the measure, the
senators observed that the number of poor nobles had grown so great
that there were now "in truth" more than four hundred who wished
to be assumed as *balestrieri*. It also noted that the benefit from these
positions accrued not only to the recipients themselves but also to their
fathers, brothers, sisters, and children, in other words, to a "very, very
big number" of patricians. The measure passed on a vote of 74 to 61
with 11 abstentions.[64]

Three observations are worth making in regard to the critical issue
of office-holding. First, it is clear that the awarding of positions by *grazie*
posed a serious threat to the regime: it not only undermined the principle of equality which sustained that regime and the vetting of candidates which elections assured, but it also fostered a system whereby the
richest and most powerful nobles were able to reward their followers
and build clienteles by distributing governmental jobs. Second, the

Council of Ten's intervention in this arena represented, as it was well aware, yet another extension of its authority into areas traditionally the prerogative of other councils. The Ten justified their intervention on the grounds that both the Great Council and the Senate had failed to take action to avoid these "scandals."[65] Third, the Senate's sharply divided vote on the measure to increase the number of bowmen indicates just how deep the division between wealthy and poor nobles had grown. In the Senate, one of the bastions of the elite, almost as many men voted against the bill as voted for it. Obviously there were many senators who in this time of financial belt-tightening were unsympathetic if not downright hostile to the needs of their fellow patricians.

The tension between the competing demands to maintain equality among patricians and the desire on the part of the wealthy and more powerful ones to set themselves apart became abundantly clear when in June 1454 the Ten, again stepping into the arena of electoral procedures, established rules regarding how candidates should be identified when the election lists were announced. Observing that in recent elections it had become customary to offer a summary of offices that candidates had held as well as notice of candidates who had not held office, the Ten ruled, again in an effort to preserve "equality," that candidates should be identified only by their name, by that of their father and family, and by the parish in which they resided. But then the Ten decided that in addition it could be announced whether a candidate was the eldest member of a family bearing that particular name (*el grando*), and whether or not he held a special dignity, that is, if he was a ducal councilor or head of the Ten, a procurator of San Marco or state attorney, and "if his father had been doge or a procurator of San Marco." If the candidate was described in any other way, his name was to be removed from the electoral slate.[66] In approving these exceptions, the Ten undercut its own effort to preserve equality by allowing those who had held the highest and most prestigious offices of state to be so identified. Of particular note was their exemption of ducal sons as well as sons of the procurators of San Marco. Clearly, the dogeship and procuratorships were so exalted that the prestige associated with them transcended generations. And so yet again one is reminded just how badly Jacopo squandered the legacy of his father and jeopardized the future aspirations of his lineage. By allowing these exceptions, the members of the Ten revealed their own sense of status hierarchies and in so doing further undermined the very equity they were ostensibly striving to preserve. But in September the Ten had to backtrack when they concluded that their effort to ensure equity had had unintended consequences: without some summary of candidates' experience, it had become impossible to make an assessment of their qualifications, especially since not all members of the patriciate knew one another. The Ten modified their earlier ruling, deciding that from now on each candidate could be identified by only one previously held office or position.[67]

The increasing bifurcation of the ruling class into rich and poor, the demand for jobs by the poorer nobles, and the desire of richer nobles to reward clients seem to have combined in various ways in these final years of Foscari's reign and contributed to two trends which can be judged deleterious to the good of the Republic: first the further development of factions or interest groups within the patriciate and second a new rash of serious electoral corruption cases. With regard to the first, the evidence suggests that during these years there was a renewed emphasis on the cultivation of patron/client relationships within the patriciate. One factor contributing toward their recrudescence was the effort by poorer nobles to find powerful patrons who could reward them with jobs and favors of various sorts and by rich nobles to create clients who could support them with votes. In December 1454, for example, the Great Council revised the rules for electing the heads of the Council of Forty since recent changes had led to lobbying by "relatives and friends."[68] Such relationships were relatively harmless as long as they remained informal and did not coalesce into better defined associations aimed at promoting particular policies or controlling elections in a systematic way. But it was just such a concern that apparently prompted the Council of Ten in March 1454 to approve a measure, albeit by a narrow margin, forbidding nobles from entertaining in their homes more than three or four nobles who were not related to them. If a noble did host such a meal, then all those who attended it would, for a year from the day of the gathering, be required to exit the Great Council, Senate or Forty, just as kinsmen had to do, whenever a fellow attendee was up for a vote. The goal of the measure, as the Ten stated specifically, was to prevent "conventicles and dangers" which could result from such gatherings. The Ten were especially concerned that such meetings would lead to a mixing of "old, young and middle-aged" noblemen. Normally members of the patriciate divided along kinship and generational lines.

Clearly, the Ten were worried about what would happen should a group develop that was able to bridge that generational divide; it would have the ability to bring together a significant voting bloc. But the very next day and without explanation the Signoria ordered the suspension of the law until another vote could be taken on it.[69] Nevertheless, the very fact that the issue was debated indicates that it had become a worry.

Two much-publicized cases of electoral corruption in 1457 validated the Ten's concern. The first involved nobleman Donato Corner, who tried to rig an election for the post of podesta of Ravenna in favor of his father Giacomo. He did so by convincing several fellow nobles to cast more than one ballot. When the fraud was discovered, the Ten assembled a *zonta* to investigate the matter. Their inquiry uncovered the complicity of noblemen Paolo Giustinian, Ettore Soranzo, Andrea Civran, Girolamo Zane, and Adorno Contarini in the scheme. Soranzo and Civran were permanently excluded from all offices and had their right hands, the ones with which they cast the illegal votes, amputated; a similar fate would greet the fugitive Contarini, should he be caught. No further action was taken against Zane. As for Corner and Giustinian, judged to be the ringleaders, they were both exiled to Crete. But should they break the terms of their exile and return to Venice, they were to be beheaded.[70] The severity of the punishments indicates just how seriously the Ten took this threat to electoral integrity.

The other case broke at almost the same time and was so blatant that Dolfin devoted an unusual amount of space to it in his chronicle. The mastermind of the "conspiracy or sect," as Sanudo referred to it, was nobleman Bartolomeo Pisani, son of the late Pietro Pisani and son-in-law of the condottiere Michele Attendolo. He was in his early thirties, tall and handsome, and his plan was to make others beholden to him by engineering their election to various posts.[71] One of Pisani's associates was nobleman Andrea Corner, son of the late Giorgio, who wished to be elected to the Senate. In order to ensure Corner's election, Pisani had to be certain that his own men, that is men who were in on the plot, would win the forthcoming election for the new heads of the Council of Forty since it was the heads of the Forty who counted the ballot balls in elections held in the Great Council, as well as in their own council. As the sole head of the Forty at the time, Pisani was able to count the ballots for the new heads in secret, with the result that Alvise Lombardo, Francesco Bon, and Lorenzo Baffo won the election.

But when the election results were announced, various members of the Forty began to complain that they had not voted for the winning candidates. Word of the grumblings among the members of the Forty reached the Council of Ten by means of Antonio Venier, nicknamed Braxuola, the same man who had implicated Jacopo Foscari in the murder of Ermolao Donato. According to Dolfin, Venier was a gossip, who knew "every little thing that was happening in the city."[72] When Niccolò Miani, one of the heads of the Ten, happened to run into the busybody, Venier, hoping to receive a reward for the information, asked if Miani knew about the rumors regarding the recent election of the heads of the Forty. Alerted to the case, the Ten launched an investigation by polling the members of the Forty as to whether or not they had voted for Lombardo and Bon. The results showed that they could not have won the election fairly. As word of the investigation leaked out, Pisani fled the city. And soon it came to light that many other elections in the Great Council, including Andrea Corner's election to the Senate, had been rigged. In addition to those named above, nobleman Francesco da Canal and the secretaries Andrea della Costa and Polonio Donati were also found to be involved in the conspiracy.

The punishments meted out were severe and geared to fit, as the Ten described them, these "most wicked and detestable excesses," which touch "the viscera of our heart."[73] The harshest penalties were reserved for Pisani, Baffo, and Bon. They had all fled the city. They were banned from all Venetian lands, and bounties were placed on their heads. If they were ever caught, they were to be brought to Venice to be hanged at the two red columns on the loggia of the Ducal Palace; their bodies would be left there for three days.[74] Corner was given the choice of permanent exile to Crete or Cyprus, while Francesco da Canal and Alvise Lombardo were banished for five years and excluded for five additional years from the Great Council. The notary Andrea della Costa was also exiled.[75] Although the two cases of electoral fraud were unrelated, the Ten were meting out punishment to those involved simultaneously; this prompted Dolfin to comment on the amputations ordered for those involved in the Donato Corner case. He noted that this punishment prompted a good deal of talk throughout the city since never before had noblemen's blood been spilled for a similar crime.[76]

Another victim of the Pisani conspiracy was Marco Corner, the distinguished older brother of Andrea. Marco, who was a knight, was punished for not revealing the plot to get his brother elected to the Senate. He was sentenced to two years' exile from Venice and banned an additional two years from holding any offices in the city.[77] Corner's secondary involvement had one other consequence as well. The legal difficulties that befell him and his brother seem to have been the motivating factors in Marco's decision to sell for Francesco Sforza's use the house that his brother had been building on the Grand Canal. The Cà del Duca thus enters this story once again.[78]

So does another palace, that of the brothers Niccolò and Giovanni Giustinian, who were building next to Cà Foscari. The Ten became concerned in July 1455 when they learned that the brothers had mounted on the walls of their palace their coat of arms along with some eagles. This contravened a law that prohibited nobles from sporting either eagles or lilies, the symbols of the Holy Roman Emperor and the King of France respectively. The vote was sharply divided, but in the end the Ten apparently decided that the eagles should be removed. The brothers' decision to adorn their house with these imperial symbols is significant for it suggests that members of the patriciate were increasingly willing to advertise their loyalties and that the atmosphere in the city had become more markedly partisan than before.[79]

It is difficult to determine the degree to which divisions between rich and poor nobles were a factor in the Pisani plot. Certainly Pisani himself and Andrea Corner came from distinguished families, but Pisani was very young at the time, just at the beginning of his career. His effort to use the heads of the Forty, the body known to represent the interests of the lesser nobles, does suggest that he intended to build his career with the support of those nobles, much as Foscari had done decades earlier. Again, Dolfin states that he expected a "great prize" from those whom he had helped; and several of his accomplices, including Baffo, Bon, Lombardo, and da Canal, came from families that were not particularly distinguished at the time.[80] This might have concerned the Ten when they approved a measure designed to prevent similar cases in the future. Observing that a statute of 1344 requiring members of the Ducal Council to count the ballots in the Great Council was still valid, the Ten ruled that henceforth ballots were to be counted by the ducal councilors and not by the heads of the Forty.[81] In order to prevent the more simple kind of electoral fraud perpetrated in the Donato Corner/Paolo Giustinian case, namely the stuffing of the ballot urns, the Ten arranged for them to be more carefully safeguarded during elections. It also passed measures designed to prevent lobbying and other forms of corruption in senatorial elections.[82] But proposals aimed at ensuring fair elections were ineffective against those bent on circumventing them, and electoral fraud would remain a problem until the very end of the Republic. Measures were also passed to protect those who had investigated these corruption cases from retribution by the relatives of the condemned.[83] But the number of men declared ineligible by reason of consanguinity was so great that the Ten realized that there might be problems in reaching the necessary quorums to conduct elections for offices, and so they were forced to modify the prohibition. They decided that if a quorum could not be reached on account of the exclusions, the deficiencies should be made up by selecting additional members by lottery, first from the ranks of the three state attorneys, then from the heads of the Ten, and finally, if need be, from the three *auditori vecchi*, officials charged with the appeal of civil cases.[84] Herein was revealed one of the problems of a closed and highly inbred ruling elite.

In the years immediately following the Peace of Lodi there is strong evidence of popular disaffection as well, fueled in part by a serious grain shortage. In August 1454 the Ten became concerned that the escalating price of grain might "induce the *popolo* to fury" and ordered the state attorneys to inspect the supplies in the communal grain depots and investigate whether a law of March 1453 prohibiting the export of grain was being obeyed. In early September the state attorneys reported that there was more grain in the warehouses than they had expected but also that many had broken the law and so the Ten imposed new penalties, basically declaring that anyone who had exported grain now had to import double the amount that he had exported from the city.[85] But by the winter of 1456, the danger of famine had grown even greater, prompting the Ten to pass an entire series of measures designed to ensure that the city was adequately supplied with grain.[86] It was still a concern in October 1456 when Foscari himself was a sponsor of bills aimed at alleviating the grain shortage.[87]

Another source of popular discontent was the government's delay in paying its sailors. In October 1454 they were marching to the Piazza San Marco every day, voicing their demands, and making threats. According to a bill proposed by Foscari as well as five of his councilors, these demonstrations were the source of "tumult, scandal, and dishonor to the

Signoria, which sees those [sailors] and hears them." Consequently, the Ten voted to find money to pay the sailors what they were owed.[88] As mentioned above, this same issue had arisen back in 1442, when Foscari had taken the lead in getting the problem resolved. Indeed, this is one of the few instances in these final years of his reign when he was one of the co-sponsors of a bill, a responsibility he had undertaken quite often earlier in his career as doge. It seems that his old sense of obligation to the poor, coupled with the very real threat of violence, motivated him to act. However, the doge was not involved in February 1456, when the galley sailors were again complaining that they were not being paid; the Ten voted, on the recommendation of five of the ducal councilors, to take 3000 ducats from the Salt Office to satisfy their demands. In this instance, the three heads of the Ten opposed the measure, saying that this was a matter for the Senate to decide. Nor was Foscari involved in July 1456, when the sailors were still complaining about being owed 600 ducats.[89] Foscari's sporadic engagement was likely due to his advanced age and his renewed concerns for Jacopo. Dolfin reports that in 1455 the doge had begun to use a walking stick, although, as a Foscari partisan, he was quick to add that he continued to "govern the city as he had always done before."[90]

Yet another "tumult," but one that seems to have brought together nobles and commoners alike, was the result in early 1456 of nobleman Francesco dalle Boccole's inquiries into overdue interest payments on Monte shares. Apparently, in return for informing investors of the balances due them, dalle Boccole demanded a fee. But when he called the investors together for a meeting at Rialto, the Ten became alarmed since "easily hundreds, maybe thousands of persons crowded together" in order to devise a way to recover what was owed them. Alarmed at this prospect, the Ten had dalle Boccole arrested for organizing an illegal gathering and interfering with normal legislative procedures; they banished him to Zara for three years. Some among the population may have viewed dalle Boccole, who came from one of the lesser noble families, as a champion of the small investor in the government's funded debt.[91]

A terrible recurrence of the plague in 1456 further exacerbated the tensions within the city. The first notice of its return appeared in April, when the Senate ordered that the procurators of San Marco *de citra* immediately fill the vacant post of prior of the Lazzaretto. In June the Senate ordered a stop to the traffic in Slavs and Albanians (often employed as domestic servants and in the naval industries) as a way to halt further spread of the disease. Then in July it elected three special officials to find a place to send people who had been cured at the Lazzaretto but who were not yet ready to be readmitted to the city. They selected San Pietro in Volta on a barrier island in the southern lagoon near Pellestrina, but in August work was suspended on account of finances and as the number of cases started to decline.[92] Throughout the summer it became increasingly difficult for the government to carry out its work because so many nobles and other officials had fled the city; in September the situation was so bad that even the *savi del consiglio* were absent from work. And so the Senate voted to add a special *zonta* of three *savi*; the three they selected were Marco Foscari, Orsato Giustinian, and Triadano Gritti.[93] As in earlier outbreaks, special police patrols were added to protect the nearly deserted city (deserted of elites that is); and six special barbers were selected to minister to poor victims. The Senate also voted more alms in the form of grain for monasteries and the poor.[94] After its winter respite, the disease returned to further afflict the city during the spring and early summer of 1457. When in early August 1457 it appeared that the plague had finally passed, the Senate ordered the patriarch to hold processions in thanksgiving and voted to award 200 ducats in alms.[95] Unlike in previous outbreaks, there is no evidence to suggest that Foscari took any role in organizing efforts to combat the disease; again this is likely the result of his own increasing infirmity.

It is against this backdrop of increasing divisions and partisanship within the patriciate, popular discontent, and plague that one needs to view the major events of Foscari's last two years as doge, namely the final investigation and condemnation of Jacopo and Foscari's own forced removal from the dogeship. As was the case with the earlier charges against Jacopo, these events, in addition to revealing much about the state of Venetian politics and governance at this time, provide dramatic insights into the personality, thoughts, and feelings of the doge himself.

The first official notice of renewed problems regarding Jacopo appears in the Council of Ten's records of 7 June 1456. On that day the three heads of the Ten, Luca da Pesaro, Leo Duodo, and Jacopo Loredan, son of the late Pietro, recommended that a twenty-man *zonta* be convened to assist the council in its deliberations regarding new allegations leveled against him. The Ten learned of the allegations through letters sent from Venice's administrators in Crete as well as from Alvise Bocheta, who had been the *ballotino* during Foscari's election and so was known by the nickname Ballotino. Recognizing the "moment and importance" of the case, the Ten voted 15 to 1 to approve the *zonta* and immediately elected its members. They were: Cristoforo Moro, Pasquale Malipiero, Paolo Tron, Andrea Contarini, Triadano Gritti, Bernardo Michiel, Marino Zane, Andrea Foscolo, Niccolò Marcello, Niccolò Miani, Stefano Trevisan, Benedetto Morosini, Luca da Lezze, Gherardo Dandolo, Guglielmo Querini, Francesco Balbi, Ettore Pasqualigo, Niccolò Soranzo, Angelo Gradenigo, and Marco Zeno. But Trevisan, Dandolo and Gradenigo were declared ineligible for various reasons; so Luca da Pesaro, Andrea Dandolo, and Donato Barbaro were elected in their stead. On the same day the Ten and the *zonta*, on the recommendation of the heads, imposed a gag order on their proceedings, making it illegal even for members to speak with each other about the case. The councilors Zaccaria Valaresso and Vittore Capello pushed for the right for members to discuss the case among themselves, but failed in their effort.[96]

Dolfin recounts the allegations made against Jacopo. According to his version, Alvise Bocheta (the *ballotino*) who had accompanied Jacopo in his exile to Crete, arrived in Venice on 1 June with news that Jacopo had written a letter to Francesco Sforza, reminding him of the many favors he had received from his father when he was in Venetian service and seeking Sforza's intercession in securing from the Signoria a revocation of Jacopo's exile. As Dolfin tells the story, the letter to Sforza was a ruse by Jacopo designed to ensure that he would be remanded to Venice for investigation since he wanted to see his "father, mother, and wife and children before he should die." The scheme was as follows: Jacopo "pretended" to write to Sforza and then left the letter in plain view on his desk, knowing full well that when Bocheta saw it, he would report it to the Ten, believing it to be "full of treason." And just as Jacopo planned, Bocheta spied the missive and reported it to the Ten, hoping thereby to get a reward for his denunciation. To back up this version of events, Dolfin reports another story involving his "acquaintance" Damiano di Chiavari, a Genoese who while traveling from Chios to Genoa, put in to the port of Canea where he had a colloquy with Jacopo. Jacopo explained his plan to Damiano, who when he arrived in Venice told his "acquaintance" Luca Gritti, whom he happened to meet in the Piazza San Marco, how Jacopo "fabricated" the letter so that he could see his family once again. Gritti then reported this information to his father Triadano. Triadano in turn relayed the story to the Ten for it seemed to him, in Dolfin's words, "a great thing to have learned indeed the truth of the matter."[97]

This is the "truth" of the matter as Dolfin understood it. An analysis of his understanding of the case follows shortly, but first it is important to continue the narration of the Ten's handling of the investigation. On 8 June the Ten and the *zonta* approved overwhelmingly (34 to 2) a measure put forward by the heads Pesaro, Duodo, and Loredan, to provide legal protection against possible "vendetta" by the doge's and Jacopo's relations, who were forbidden from ever sitting in judgement or voting on cases involving members of the investigatory committee or their brothers, sons, and even grandsons. "Relations" were defined as those who normally had to excuse themselves from elections on account of consanguinity. In addition, the bill reaffirmed the gag order imposed the day before and ordered that anyone who broke the prohibition would be permanently banned from all councils and offices and have his goods confiscated. This even applied to nobleman Niccolò Memmo, who had been mistakenly called to take part in the council and then dismissed when the error was discovered. There follows a list of all those accorded the protection against vendetta and sworn to secrecy. In addition to the members of the *zonta* listed above, it included the six ducal councilors (Benedetto Barozzi, Zaccaria Valaresso, Lorenzo Loredan, Girolamo Donato, Vittore Capello, and Paolo Barbo), the three state attorneys (Niccolò Tron, Ludovico Foscarini, and Zaccaria Trevisan), the eleven members of the Ten (Luca da Pesaro, Jacopo Loredan, Leo Duodo, Antonio Venier, Orsato Giustinian, Giovanni Dolfin, Niccolò Bernardo, Francesco Zorzi, Ermolao Pisani, Marco Corner, and Giovanni Trevisan) as well as the three members of the ducal chancery who served as notaries.[98]

The next matter revealed the deep divisions within the Ten and *zonta* itself. The ducal councilors Valaresso and Capello, the same men who the day before had objected to the prohibition on members talking with each other about the case, put forward a proposal to deal leniently with Jacopo. They based their argument on several factors. First, although they conceded that the letters which had been shown to the council did mention Sforza, they argued that further investigation of the case would lead only to "new scandals and disturbances," which might disrupt the newly secured peace with the ruler of Milan. Second, they called attention to the fact that Jacopo was in reality a lightweight, somebody who was not in a position to do any real harm. Their exact phrase was, "attentive to the triviality (*levitate*) of the same ser Jacopo Foscari, which is understood by everyone." Therefore they recommended that the Ten write to the rectors in Canea and have them admonish and reprimand Jacopo, "with the most acerbic words," that henceforth he should conduct himself properly; otherwise he would face a punishment that he would always regret. In addition, they proposed that the officials in Canea select two trustworthy men to serve as chaperons for Jacopo both day and night and that he never be left unattended. They proposed a salary of 3 ducats a month for each of the attendants, as well as living expenses, all of which were to be paid for by the doge. It appears that Valaresso and Capello accepted the same explanation of events as Dolfin, namely that Jacopo concocted his ridiculous plan in order to return to Venice.

The counter-proposal, by the three heads of the Ten, took the threat more seriously either because its sponsors believed that Jacopo really intended to write to Sforza or because they were themselves waging a vendetta against Jacopo and his father. Calling attention to the evidence which they had been shown and judging it to touch "our honor and the heart of our state," they proposed that a galley be dispatched to Crete to fetch Jacopo and return him to Venice for further investigation. The votes on the two proposals indicate that the council was sharply divided. On the first ballot, the proposal by Valaresso and Capello got 12 votes in favor, 2 against, and 5 abstentions. On the second ballot, it got 11 yeas, no nays, and 5 abstentions. Since it had not achieved a majority, it failed. The counter-proposal by the heads, including Jacopo Loredan (son of the late Pietro), got 17 positive votes on the first ballot and 20 on the second, giving it a majority of the 36 possible votes; hence it passed. The Ten and its *zonta* then elected Lorenzo Loredan (another son of the late Pietro) as captain of the galley to be sent to Crete and ordered the overseers of the Arsenal to have the ship ready within three days, that is by the coming Friday.[99]

On 12 June the Ten and *zonta* approved Loredan's commission. Following the required legal formula, it was issued in the name of "Francesco Foscari by the grace of God doge of the Venetians." It charged Loredan to sail immediately and directly to Canea and to make no stops unless constrained to do so by necessity. The captain was ordered to confiscate all letters that members of the crew were carrying and to hand them over to the Ten on his return. Clearly the Ten were worried that there might be informants among the ship's staff. Once in Crete, the ship was not to dock but remain offshore so that no unauthorized persons could disembark. Loredan himself was to make his way to the rectors of Canea, take possession of Jacopo and his servants, including his cook, and any of Jacopo's papers confiscated by the rectors, and then return immediately to Venice, making sure all the while that Jacopo talked with no one and had no opportunity to escape. Once in Venice, Loredan was to send the ship's scribe to inform the Ten of their arrival and await their orders. In no circumstances were members of the crew to leave the ship nor were other ships to be allowed to approach Loredan's vessel.

The same bill also included the text of the letter to be delivered to the rectors of Canea. It contained a bombshell, one that went unmentioned in Dolfin's chronicle. The Ten began the letter by acknowledging receipt of certain materials that the rectors had forwarded to them, including "authentic letters" in Jacopo's hand as well as some pages in cipher. And it praised the rectors for their work. The Ten took special note of some material contained in the dossier, specifically that following a shipwreck several Genoese had taken refuge in the home of Jacopo Giustinian, a Genoese living in Canea. Among these was a certain Battista with whom Jacopo struck up a friendship, "speaking with him daily and telling him much about himself." Eventually, Jacopo asked if Battista would do him a favor: he asked whether Battista would dispatch for him letters to the "emperor of the Turks," namely to Sultan Mehmed II. According to the Ten, Jacopo asked the sultan in the letters to send a ship to Canea to rescue him, "hoping in this way to escape the penalties and strictures contained in his trial and sentence." The Ten ordered the rectors to take depositions from both Jacopo Giustinian and Battista and to forward the material to them. They were especially interested in learning whether or not Jacopo had received a response from the sultan. They also commanded the rectors to turn over Jacopo's servant Giorgio and his cook to Loredan, as well as any other servants who had served him since January. They ordered a further search of Jacopo's belongings and wanted any materials found to be sent on with the galley. The bill concluded with a warning to future heads of the Ten that should Jacopo not be dealt the death penalty, they should expedite his return to Crete. Regarding this last provision, the current heads apparently feared that at some future point, perhaps when the heads were better disposed toward Foscari, the doge and his allies might use Jacopo's return to try to secure a pardon for him. The measure passed with 31 votes and only 2 abstentions.[100] Also on 12 June the council voted to offer protection from his creditors to Bocheta for four months from the time of his arrival in Venice, also arranging for Lorenzo Loredan to transport Giovanni Mussi, the man who had carried the Canean rectors' denunciation to Venice, back to Crete.[101]

According to Dolfin, Loredan made the trip to Crete and back in thirty-four days, arriving in Venice on 19 July. Jacopo was immediately placed in the prison known as the Torricella within the Ducal Palace walls.[102] On 23 June the Ten elected their heads for July: Marco Corner, Orsato Giustinian, and Ermolao Pisani replaced the outgoing chiefs Pesaro, Duodo, and Loredan.[103] However, on 14 July Pisani was selected to investigate some unrelated matters in Crema. On that same day the Ten created its special subcommittee to handle the case. The seven members were: the ducal councilor Zaccaria Valaresso, the head Marco Corner, the state attorney Zaccaria Trevisan as well as Niccolò Bernardo, Pasquale Malipiero, Paolo Tron, and Jacopo Loredan.[104] On the 21st the Ten expressed worry that with Pisani on mission to Crema, the council could not function properly without three heads, especially given the amount of business it currently had on its agenda. Consequently, when on the 24th they selected the heads for August, they decided that one of the three should be chosen by lot not only to serve during that month but also to fulfill the final week of Pisani's July term. The three men elected to serve in August were Jacopo Loredan, Niccolò Bernardo, and Francesco Zorzi; and it was Loredan who won the right to assume office early as a replacement for Pisani.[105]

Assuming that Dolfin's date for Jacopo's arrival in Venice is correct, the investigating committee acted with great speed: on 23 July the three heads of the Ten (Giustinian, Corner, and Loredan) and the three state attorneys (Niccolò Tron, Ludovico Foscarini, and Zaccaria Trevisan) proposed that having heard and read the evidence against Jacopo, they proceed to the sentencing phase. That motion passed on a sharply divided vote: there were 19 in favor, 11 opposed, and 4 abstentions.[106]

According to Dolfin, Jacopo was tortured but stuck to his story that he had "fabricated" the letter (to Sforza) so that he would be recalled to Venice and thereby have the opportunity to see his family.[107] On the 24th the Ten debated Jacopo's punishment. Four different proposals were put forward. The first was made by five of the six ducal councilors (Benedetto Barozzi, Lorenzo Loredan, Girolamo Donato, Vittore Capello, and Paolo Barbo), Orsato Giustinian, one of the three heads of the Ten, and the three state attorneys (Niccolò Tron, Ludovico Foscarini, and Zaccaria Trevisan). It called for Jacopo to be rebanished to Crete and that he sail with the galley *Leona* which was about to depart. In addition, four guards were to be permanently assigned to watch him; their salaries were to be paid by the doge. Jacopo was to be admonished never again to write to "any lord, dominion, or commune." And should word ever reach the Ten that Jacopo had again written to foreign powers, he would spend the rest of his life in jail in Canea. The second proposal, put forward by Zaccaria Valaresso, included all of these provisions, but it also stiffened the sentence by requiring that upon his return to Canea, Jacopo spend a year in jail. Another, by the head Marco Corner, was the most lenient of the proposals; it recommended that Jacopo resume his exile on the previous terms. The fourth, put forward by Jacopo Loredan, citing the "letters, writings and other depositions against ser Jacopo Foscari read in this Council," called for the defendant to be beheaded between the columns of Saints Mark and Theodore in the Piazza the following Monday. The severity of Loredan's recommendation shocks even today. When it was time to vote on the various proposals the thirty-four voting members of the Ten and its *zonta* cast their votes as follows: on the first ballot 8 voted for the proposal to return Jacopo to Crete and to warn him not to write further letters; 14 voted for Valaresso's proposal for the same sentence but with a year in jail; 2 voted for Marco Corner's relatively lenient sentence, 3 abstained altogether, and 7 voted in favor of Loredan's proposal to behead Jacopo. On the second ballot, the voters moved to the middle, abandoning entirely Corner's lenient sentence and Loredan's harsh one; neither got any votes on the second ballot; instead 12 voted to return Jacopo to Crete; 22 voted for the additional year in jail; no one abstained.[108] The Ten had ruled, but then in one small act of kindness they decided (by 21 to 2 with 10 abstentions) that before his departure for Canea, the doge and other relatives could visit Jacopo in the Torricella.[109]

That permission opened the way for one of the most famous episodes in the life of Doge Foscari, an event that did much to inspire the nineteenth-century Romantic writers, composers, and painters who were to take up the Foscari story. The original report comes from Dolfin. According to him, following the sentencing, the dogaressa, Jacopo's wife Lucrezia, and Jacopo and Lucrezia's children went to visit the prisoner in the Torricella, where he was found suffering the effects of his torture – he had been subjected to thirty hoistings by rope. Some time afterward he was transferred to the room known as the *camera dale oselle del cavalier*, where his father went to see him. Again according to Dolfin, even though Foscari found his son "disfigured, macerated, and tormented with his beard disheveled and unkempt," the doge maintained a detached and stoic attitude toward him, so much so that "it seemed that he wasn't his son." Then when Jacopo asked his father to find a way for him to stay in Venice, Foscari, in what has come to be his most famous utterance, responded, "Jacopo, go and obey the wishes of the city and don't seek anything more." If Dolfin is to be believed, Jacopo was then led away and transported to the ship which carried him back to Crete. But once Jacopo had departed, Foscari's stalwart façade crumbled. He threw himself on a chair crying and wailing, "Oh, great pity." Certainly, Dolfin paints a heart-wrenching scene of the aged and now decrepit doge bidding what he must have known would be his final farewell to his son.[110]

Following their judgement of Jacopo, the Ten acted to tie up the loose ends of the case. On the same day as the sentencing, the council approved a measure put forward by Loredan and Marco Corner to reward the informer Alvise Bocheta with the priorate of the Cà di Dio. Since it enjoyed ducal *iuspatronatus*, the doge normally appointed the prior; in fact it was an important bit of ducal patronage. The ducal councilors objected to Loredan and Corner's proposal, arguing that it was not proper to expel someone from a benefice, namely the current prior – a Foscari appointee – in order to benefit someone else and furthermore that "for the honor of God and the good of the paupers," the priors ought to be good men of integrity. They put forward a counterproposal that Bocheta be rewarded at the next appropriate job vacancy. But the proposal to appoint Bocheta prior of the Cà di Dio carried the day.[111] Next, the Ten voted unanimously to release Jacopo's two servants from jail and to see that they were paid what was due them from

Jacopo's funds; they also approved a payment of 10 ducats each to the men who had guarded him while he was in prison. They then imposed a gag order on their proceedings and voted themselves the right to go about with two bodyguards each. On the 28th, they approved Bocheta's petition to have two bodyguards as well.[112]

On the 29th the Ten drew up the commission for the galley captain Maffeo Leon. Again, as the law required, the commission was drafted in the doge's name; it charged Leon to transport "Jacopo, our son" back to Crete. Leon was to take special precautions against anything going wrong; for this reason he was to make his way directly to his destination, stopping only if forced by necessity. He was to make sure that Jacopo was guarded "with diligence" and once in Canea was to consign Jacopo to the rectors of the city. Finally, the Ten ordered Leon to depart on Saturday 31 July and to rejoin the captain of the Gulf in the waters off Modon once his mission was complete. And on that Saturday the Ten ordered the *signori di notte* to transport "ser Jacopo Foscari, son of the lord doge," from the Ducal Palace to Leon's galley which was anchored at San Niccolò on the Lido. As the ship got under way and headed out into the waters of the Adriatic Sea, Jacopo bid a final farewell to his native city.[113]

What is one to make of Jacopo's final trial and investigation? Had he indeed communicated with foreign princes, including the Turks, as his critics claimed? Or was he, as his supporters contended, a victim of his own foolish plot, a plan that gave his and the doge's opponents the opportunity to persecute them further? As in the earlier cases involving Jacopo, it is difficult to reach a definitive conclusion since much of the evidence, most notably the papers confiscated by the rectors in Canea, has been lost to history. Yet what clues do survive – included in the records of the Ten, Dolfin's account, and reports to foreign governments – can be sifted for the insights they provide.

It seems certain that Jacopo did write or intended to write to Sforza (and perhaps others) seeking their help in procuring a pardon and that it was not, as Jacopo contended, merely a ruse to see his family a final time. Even Jacopo's defenders conceded as much, acknowledging that the confiscated materials "make mention of the Duke of Milan."[114] Also there appears to be a pattern to Jacopo's behavior: the accusation against him – communicating with foreign powers – is the same one for which he was condemned during his first trial in 1445. But Jacopo's plan was not entirely fanciful since it was common in Renaissance Italy for well-connected men and even those who were not well-connected to seek the assistance of the rich and powerful. The letters to the Medici of Florence are the best-known example of this; they are replete with requests for direct assistance or for the Medici to serve as intermediaries in securing favors. Jacopo himself had been approached in such ways. In 1437, for example, he received a letter from Francesco Barbaro commending a candidate for the Bishopric of Bergamo.[115] And in 1455 Paolo Barbo, one of Jacopo's judges, courted the favor of Sforza by presenting him with two dogs, one black and one red.[116] Jacopo may have calculated that with the restoration of peace between Venice and Milan and the recent triumphant visit of Sforza's son Galeazzo to Venice, now was the perfect time to importune Sforza to press for a favor for Foscari's son. What Jacopo did not understand – and what he seems never to have understood – was the delicate position he was in: while the overt manipulation of informal contacts and the bestowal of conspicuous favors was perfectly permissible for the sons of princes in signorial regimes and even for Medici sons, this was simply not acceptable by the more rigorous standards of republican Venice where suspicion of ducal sons was encoded in the ducal *promissione* and other laws of the state. But Jacopo was either too arrogant, too stupid, or both successfully to act the princely son without offending Venice's republican sensibilities.

Jacopo's lack of subtlety and understanding was not, however, entirely his fault. Many of the doge's own actions, sent mixed messages to Jacopo about his father's willingness to enforce strictly the customs and practices of the republican regime. After all, the doge himself had asserted the princely aspects of his office, not least including the placement of his statue on the Porta della Carta, the staging of Jacopo's magnificent wedding celebrations, and the construction of a remarkable family palace; furthermore, he had accepted (and promoted) the delays in enforcing Jacopo's first exile, and his efforts to get that exile revoked were ultimately successful. The very longevity of Foscari's reign also bolstered the princely trajectory; this was a ducal reign different from any that Venice had experienced before. Jacopo was not the only one to misread the signals or assume that things had changed: as noted above, several of the doge's other relations also cultivated foreign connections in the manner of foreign princes. But mistake the signals he did.

Once caught, Jacopo seems to have concocted the excuse that the letters were really just a stratagem to return to Venice one last time, but that reasoning rings hollow. If Jacopo wished the letters to be spied, why were there also materials written in cipher? Similarly, Jacopo's desire to have one final visit with his family reads like an explanation arrived at after the fact. In any case, Jacopo and the doge's supporters, including Dolfin, took up this defense, portraying Jacopo's actions as motivated by the perfectly understandable wish to see his loved ones once again. Furthermore, any of these explanations might have been invented as a means of countering those who wanted to punish Jacopo severely. It is telling that Dolfin, a relative and friend of Jacopo, makes no mention of the letters to the Turks. If Jacopo did indeed write those letters – and Berlan for one thinks he did and that they were actually sent – then he was even more stupid than before, displaying no understanding whatsoever of what was acceptable to his countrymen and what was not.[117] It was one thing to write to the Italian prince and one-time Venetian commander Sforza, it was quite another to write to the infidel Turk. The notion that the sultan would send a vessel to rescue him from Crete, an island that was clearly in the Venetian sphere of influence, was preposterous. It may be that Jacopo's years in exile had caused him to lose touch with native Venetian sensibilities. As a way of minimizing the dangers of what he had done, his supporters among the Ten and its *zonta* drew attention to the fact that he was a man of little consequence. For reasons explored below, they also chose to emphasize the doge's scrupulous adherence to the law, as recorded in his final words to Jacopo.

The evidence suggests that of the thirty-four members of the Ten and its *zonta*, approximately a third were supporters of Jacopo and his father. This is based on the fact that twelve men voted in favor of the motion put forward by Valaresso and Capello on 8 June, that Jacopo simply be reprimanded on Crete for his actions, and that eleven voted against finding Jacopo guilty in the ballot of 23 July. Unfortunately, besides Valaresso and Capello, the records of the Ten do not reveal the identities of the voters. According to Dolfin, Capello joined Paolo Barbo and Orsato Giustinian, both members of the Ten and its *zonta* at the time of Jacopo's condemnation, as well as other "good men" in trying to secure a pardon for Jacopo after his return to Crete.[118] So one is inclined to count Giustinian among his partisans. But Giustinian was one of the heads who proposed that Jacopo be found guilty in the first place. His colleague as head of the Ten, Marco Corner, is another who seems to have vacillated: he joined Giustinian and Loredan in proposing that Jacopo be found guilty; on the other hand, he put forward the most lenient punishment for Jacopo. Their actions suggest that both Giustinian and Corner were sympathetic to Jacopo and his father but nonetheless believed that Jacopo had to pay in some measure for his deeds. But their desire to punish Jacopo may have been counterbalanced by an almost equally strong feeling that some members of the Ten were out to get him. The original effort by Valaresso and Capello to allow members of the Ten and *zonta* to discuss the case among themselves – a proposal that was defeated – implies that Jacopo's partisans were worried about his being railroaded into a conviction while his detractors were fearful that any discussion among the Ten might derail that effort.

While Jacopo's supporters minimized the significance of his actions, excusing them as the machinations of someone who was not to be taken very seriously, then his opponents – or at least some of them – believed just the opposite, that Jacopo's behavior threatened the honor and integrity of the Venetian state. These men looked at exactly the same evidence and saw not the harmless maneuverings of a political nobody, but rather the intrigues of a ducal son who was willing to flout the laws of the Republic. They saw themselves in turn as upholders of the law and defenders of Venice's republican regime; since corresponding with foreign princes was expressly prohibited in the ducal *promissione*, Jacopo's recidivism in this regard called for stern action.[119] Such an interpretation puts their actions in the best possible light: it seems undeniable that there was a small subgroup among Jacopo's detractors who harbored particularly intense feelings of animosity toward him. These were the seven men who voted in favor of Jacopo's beheading. The leader of this group was Jacopo Loredan and must have included his brother Lorenzo as well. Jacopo's efforts to correspond with the sultan would have been particularly distasteful to them since the family had a long record of military service against the Turks. Of course it is possible that Loredan had only the best of intentions, that is, to uphold the law. But that is not the way Foscari's supporters saw it, nor is it what Sforza's agent Antonio Guidobono reported to his master concerning the case.

To my knowledge, Guidobono's reports to Sforza have not been examined previously for information regarding Jacopo. They provide extremely valuable new insights into the case, especially regarding the opponents' motivations. On 9 June he wrote to Sforza telling him of Bocheta's arrival in Venice. According to Guidobono, Bocheta had served in the Foscari household for thirty-three years, a date which seems correct given that he was selected as *ballotino* in 1423. Presumably on account of his long service and associations with the doge, Bocheta was chosen to accompany Jacopo in his exile to Crete and to look after him. But word got back to the doge that Bocheta was abusing his relationship by maltreating Jacopo, even to the point of hitting him and drawing blood. He was therefore released from service and returned to Venice.

In retaliation for his dismissal Bocheta went directly to the Ten, to whom he reported Jacopo's letters. According to Guidobono, the Ten and its *zonta* were filled with Foscari's enemies and none of his partisans. He also informed Sforza that although the Ten's proceedings were top secret, a ship had been dispatched to Crete to retrieve Jacopo. But then Guidobono offered an explosive interpretation of what was happening – he told Sforza that the presumed objective of the Ten was to proceed against Jacopo and sentence him to death and that in this way they would be able to offer a legitimate reason to force Foscari from office and hold a ducal election. To quote Guidobono: "And they would come to a new ducal election because by laying hands on the son, that is by causing him to die, they will be able in all honesty to arrive at this privation [of the ducal office] and a new election." The ambassador attributed the Ten's motives at least in part to their belief that Foscari had simply ruled for too long; the Republic was no longer being well served since he neglected all his duties except for the morning audience in the Collegio. He ended the letter by remarking that Foscari was enduring these tribulations with remarkable constancy and fortitude.[120] Five days later, on 14 June, Guidobono reported to Sforza that the ship had sailed. It is also clear that in the intervening days popular opinion had turned in Foscari's favor and that many were expressing the view that he should be allowed "to die as doge in peace." Guidobono again commented on Foscari's fortitude in face of this situation and noted that during the two months it would take for the ship to return to Venice with Jacopo, Foscari would have sufficient time to rally his forces.[121]

In his next letter to Sforza on this subject, written on 23 July, Guidobono reported that Jacopo was being held in the Torricella and tortured, but not too severely since his body was already broken from his previous trials. One of the main points of the interrogation concerned the letters that Jacopo had sent to Sforza. He also relayed Jacopo's reason for writing the letters, namely that he had done so in order to return to Venice to see his family. According to Guidobono, the Ten included "the greatest enemies that the doge has in the city," although he noted that the doge still had his supporters and that public opinion as well as "innocence and justice" were on his side. In the ambassador's estimation, Foscari was going to great lengths to make it appear that he was unaffected by these events, while his "relatives and friends" were doing everything in their power "to put out this fire."[122] And in his last letter on the subject, dated 28 July, Guidobono said that Jacopo was expected to be returned to Crete the following Saturday even though he was extremely ill. In fact, most expected him to die before his departure since "he values life so little [at this point]."[123]

Antonio Guidobono's letters to Sforza offer the best contemporary evidence that there was more both to this case and to the subsequent deposition of Foscari than simply the misdeeds of a ducal son, that in fact the desire to punish the doge figured as well. While Guidobono makes clear that Foscari's enemies were extremely concerned about his neglect of ducal duty – and he seems to confirm that Jacopo did in fact write to Sforza – he also characterizes the Ten as a kind of kangaroo court, one that was out to destroy the doge and force a new election. Although he does not name names, one can assume that the ringleader was Jacopo Loredan since it was he who proposed that Jacopo be beheaded. The draconian nature of Loredan's preferred punishment suggests that he and his followers allowed the long-standing rivalry between the Foscari and the Loredans to shape their actions, although it was, after all, Jacopo who gave them the opportunity to act in the first place. Further proof that Jacopo Loredan took pleasure in thwarting the doge comes from the proposal that he made (surprisingly, along with Marco Corner) to remove Foscari's appointee to the priorate of the Cà di Dio and to replace him with Bocheta. It is also worth noting that when it came to other cases tried while he was a chief of the Ten, Loredan was not always, as he was in Jacopo's case, an advocate of the most severe punishments.[124]

As in Jacopo's earlier trials, much of the evidence against him was based on information supplied by informants, men who stood to profit from their revelations. This calls for an assessment of the credibility of men about whom little is known. It seems telling that rumors continued to circulate about the killing of Ermolao Donato, including a report that nobleman Niccolò Erizzo had confessed to it on his deathbed. So too is the fact that in 1458 the Ten were forced to remove Bocheta from the priorate of the Cà di Dio for maladministration and misappropriating the hospital's income in order to pay off his own debts. The Ten decided instead to reward Bocheta with a stipend of 30 ducats every three months for the rest of his life. It may be that the administration of this important charitable institution was simply beyond Bocheta's limited competence, but it seems more likely that he was a rather unsavory character since the Ten demanded that he hand over to them the hospital's inventories and certain goods which he had apparently taken for himself.[125] Overall, Bocheta comes across as a man who was willing to inform on the doge's son for personal gain. If that was the case, then the Ten sacrificed Jacopo to the testimony of men of limited credibility in order to fulfill their own ambitions.

In the end, as is so often the case when examining the fragmentary evidence of past legal proceedings – one thinks here of the mid-sixteenth-century case of the impostor Martin Guerre as well as present-day allegations of wrongdoing – it is difficult if not impossible to establish the truth beyond a reasonable doubt. That Jacopo composed some letters seems certain – indeed, as noted above, Guidobono mentions the letters to Sforza rather matter-of-factly, neither making any effort to deny their existence nor expressing any outrage that his master was implicated in these events. This suggests that they were authentic, but whether they were the harmless fantasies of a prodigal son or a genuine threat to the regime remains open to debate. What is known – and this is the salient point – is that Jacopo's final trial revealed deep rifts within the ranks of Venice's ruling class, rifts based in part on notions of right governance and in part on personal animosities. What has come down through time as evidence – evidence that historians of the past have often taken as solid and unequivocal – is the detritus of those partisan debates, with all sides trying to present their case in the best possible light and to attribute to themselves the best of motives. Dolfin's chronicle, which is very detailed for these years, has been characterized as almost diary-like, but it was composed *post-factum* and therefore presents what occurred in light of subsequent events.[126] It may well be, for example, that Dolfin's most famous scene, Foscari's farewell to his son, was intended to establish beyond a shadow of a doubt that Foscari adhered strictly to the laws of the Republic: in that scene, playing the part of defender of the law, the doge advises his son to obey the wishes of the city; such adherence to the law would later be a cornerstone of the doge's own defense against those who wished to remove him from office. Even Guidobono's seemingly neutral third-party letters to Sforza need to be used with caution since he may simply have been reporting events as the doge's supporters saw them. Nevertheless, his letters are crucial for they show that many contemporaries understood the prosecution of Jacopo as an effort to destroy the doge; that they believed that a desire for vendetta was involved. What they demonstrate without question is that the patriciate was now deeply divided into pro- and anti-Foscari camps, with the opponents out to get Foscari and the doge rallying his supporters.

A marginal note added to the Ten's deliberations by the council's scribes provides a pathetic coda to the case. It records that Jacopo died on Crete on 12 January 1457, presumably while serving his year in jail. That is what the rectors of Canea informed the Ten. But they neglected to give a cause of death; and Sforza's new agent in Venice, Antonio di Clivio Marchese, called Marchese da Varese, wrote to his master that no more than a cryptic announcement of the death had been made.[127] On 17 March the Ten wrote to the rectors ordering them to forward to the council "by secure passage" all of Jacopo's writings.[128] And so on a winter day in early 1457 Jacopo Foscari ended what can only be judged a wasted life in a Cretan jail. The great Florentine humanist Leonardo Bruni had once written to Jacopo, "Know that a great burden has been laid upon you," a reference to his father's many achievements.[129] But, trapped in part by the legal restrictions on his actions as a ducal son, Jacopo failed to live up to that paternal example. He left behind instead a tarnished reputation as well as a wife, children, and a father, now bereft of all his sons. Varese for one thought the old man deserving of compassion.[130]

Jacopo's condemnation had a profound impact on the doge. As Dolfin indicates, Foscari's immediate reaction was despair. The doge's acceptance of his son's fate contrasts sharply with the action he took following Jacopo's first exile, when he worked to get his son's punishment overturned. But that earlier determination now gave way to a resignation from which the aged Foscari only occasionally roused himself. The numbing aftermath of Jacopo's departure must have contributed to the doge's lethargy during the plague which raged during that summer. Foscari did rally somewhat in the autumn of 1456; for example, in October he was engaged with bills designed to help alleviate the grain shortage then gripping the city.[131] But word of Jacopo's death seems to have sent him into a new tailspin of despair which in turn exacerbated his increasing health problems. According to Dolfin, after the news of his son's death, Foscari engaged himself little "in the governance of this Republic;" and Ottone del Carretto, Sforza's agent in Rome, wrote in the fall of 1457 that he had heard that for more than a year Foscari had not been presiding at meetings or attending council sessions. Foscari was not, however, entirely disengaged: in April 1457 Varese wrote that Foscari had discussed with him letters received from Naples. At best, it appears that Foscari's engagement was sporadic and that the government, although still functioning, lacked a clear sense of direction. In the doge's absence there was no one, according to the ducal councilors, willing to reject unjust petitions and no one "appropriate" to respond to "legates and foreigners and subjects who appeared [before the government]."[132] Without him the government felt rudderless, even though the councils continued to function quite successfully. It was after all during the summer of 1457 that the Ten dealt with the electoral conspiracies of Donato Corner and Bartolomeo Pisani. Certainly, one important element in the Ten's accretion of power, as considered above, was the vacuum at the very top of the government created by Foscari's inactivity.

The prospect of a headless state proved very unsettling for members of the Ten. The first sure indication that the Ten as a body had become concerned with the situation appears in their deliberations of 18 June 1457, right in the midst of the electoral corruption scandals. On that occasion they discussed some important matters concerning the doge as well as nobleman Jacopo Polani and "other nobles" and then voted to keep these discussions "most secret" under pain of beheading.[133] The details of their discussion are not known, but the severity of the punishment suggests that it was a matter of the greatest importance and almost certainly had to do with finding a way out of the dilemma posed by Foscari's condition. It is unclear whether or not the issue of Polani was in any way related.

The Ten took no further action on the problem until mid-October, when for the first time since the previous summer and Jacopo's final trial,

Jacopo Loredan was again one of the heads of the council. His colleagues were Girolamo Donato and Girolamo Barbarigo. The other members of the Ten were: Orsato Giustinian, Antonio Venier, Paolo Barbo, Ottaviano Valier, Luca da Lezze, Leonardo Contarini, and Domenico Diedo. The ducal councilors were Orio Pasqualigo, Giovanni Loredan, Davide Contarini, Matteo Barbaro, Leo Diedo, and Giacomo Memmo, a head of the Forty who was substituting for the ducal councilor from the *sestiere* of San Marco. The other two heads of the Forty were Marco Barbo and Benedetto Loredan. The state attorneys were Niccolò Bernardo, Triadano Gritti, and Carolo Marino. On 19 October, preparing to consider matters concerning the doge, the Ten voted, on the recommendation of the heads, to exclude Leonardo Contarini from the discussion since he was related to Jacopo's father-in-law. His relative, the ducal councilor Davide Contarini, was also excluded.[134]

Having expelled these obvious Foscari partisans, the three heads then proposed that a twenty-five man *zonta* be added to their deliberations to deal with the matter of "our most Serene lord doge [who] for a long time now has vacated the governance of our State, and is now reduced to such advanced old age that he is not able to engage himself in the matters of our State, nor is there any hope that in the future he will be able to come to the tribune or to our councils." The Ten approved the measure 13 to 1 with 1 abstention and elected the twenty-five members of the *zonta*. According to Dolfin, the heads did not inform the members of the Ten, the ducal councilors, or the state attorneys before the vote what they intended to propose.[135] The twenty-five members of the *zonta* were: Paolo Tron, Pasquale Malipiero, Cristoforo Moro, Matteo Vitturi, Niccolò Bon, Giorgio Valaresso, Andrea Bernardo, Luca da Pesaro, Ludovico Storlado, Andrea Foscolo, Leo da Molin, Niccolò Miani, Luca Vendramin, Ermolao Pisani, Benedetto Morosini, Leo Viaro, Francesco Trevisan, Bernardo Balbi, Alessandro Marcello, Lorenzo Soranzo, Giorgio Bembo, Lorenzo Honoradi, Benedetto Barozzi, Pietro Balastro, and Pietro Grimani. When Honoradi was released from the committee on account of his propinquity to Malipiero, the Ten decided that they would proceed with just twenty-four members.[136] The Ten voted to impose a gag order on their proceedings. Anyone who contravened the order would be fined 1000 ducats and permanently excluded from all offices and benefices. In order not to arouse suspicion, Leonardo Contarini was ordered to make his way to the Ten whenever it was called, although he could not participate. He was also warned not to tell anyone of what had happened to him.[137]

Then on 21 October the three heads of the Ten put forward their proposal. Calling attention to Foscari's long vacancy from the governance of the state, brought on by personal matters and by his "old age and decrepitude," which was causing "great inconvenience and detriment" to the state, they proposed that the ducal councilors and the heads of the Ten consult with Foscari and point out to "his Sublimity" the dangers that the present situation created. Furthermore, they should urge him as a "good Prince and true *Pater Patriae*" to renounce "freely and spontaneously" the dogeship which "for many reasons he ought to do." To sweeten what they knew to be a very bitter pill, the heads further proposed that Foscari be offered an annual stipend of 1500 ducats as well as any part of his remaining salary. The heads wanted the council and *zonta* to remain in session until they got the doge's response; if Foscari asked for time to consider the issue, they would give him only until the next evening. The measure passed by a wide margin on a vote of 29 to 3 with 6 abstentions.[138]

Dolfin's account, obviously written after the events, states that once a new doge had been elected to serve in Foscari's place, the plan was for Foscari to continue to enjoy the "usual salary, regalia, and honors" as long as he lived. As noted above, this was not precisely what the Ten approved; their proposal made clear that Foscari was to renounce the dogeship and receive only a stipend. Dolfin also errs when he states that the Ten and its *zonta* debated the proposal for days, sometimes meeting throughout the night and arousing amazement in the city as people wondered what issue was of such import that the Ten could be so occupied. He also claims that the Ten placed the doge's brother Marco under what amounted to house arrest in the Ducal Palace so that no one would suspect what they were debating. But once the issue had been "well considered and ventilated," the Ten voted "by a few ballots" that the heads and councilors should visit the doge and encourage him "to renounce the dogeship and allow that another man, a vice-doge, govern at the tribune and councils in his place, retaining for as long as he [Foscari] lived all the usual provisions, salaries, regalia, and benefits as before."

There are some obvious problems with Dolfin's account, including his statements that the issue was debated for days, that there were several ballots, and that Marco Foscari was arrested. None of these assertions can be found in the official records of the Ten. On the other hand, he does get many things right; and one does wonder how the Ten kept Marco Foscari, who was after all a procurator of San Marco and hence used to being consulted on important issues, from becoming suspicious of what was afoot. What is especially interesting is the notion of a vice-dogeship. One can well imagine that some members of the delegation presented the situation to the ailing Foscari in this manner as a way of softening the blow. After all, as noted in chapter 1, Foscari's *promissione* made provision for the ducal councilors to select a vice-doge if he became incapacitated.[139] Dolfin's account seems to reflect the story as it was told by members of the committee after the fact and also as it was remembered by Foscari partisans, people who wanted to believe that the members of the Ten deliberated for days, were divided in their votes, and called for something less than total renunciation of the dogeship.

Where Dolfin got things absolutely right was in beginning his account of Foscari's deposition: "at this time in the Venetian state, [there was] a great and unheard of novelty." Removing a doge from office on account of old age and decrepitude was virtually unprecedented in Venice, a city known for its reliance on rule by the aged. Indeed respect for the wisdom of the elderly and confidence in their ability to govern had been deeply embedded for generations. One of the extremely rare examples of removing men from any office on account of old age occurred in 1428, when the ducal councilors proposed that a certain Giorgio Belcovich be relieved of his office as a captain in Sebenico since "on account of old age he is not able to exercise his office."[140] In most of such instances, the government tried, as it did with Foscari, to ensure that those removed from office did not suffer financial difficulties. Such was the case with Zaccaria Rizzo, a book-keeper in Padua, and with nobleman Tommaso Soranzo, an employee of the gold estimators' office at the Mint who "on account of his antiquity is not able to attend to his duty except with great inconvenience to his person." The Great Council decided to elect another in the latter's place but agreed that he, Soranzo, should continue to enjoy half his salary for as long as he lived and even that he could exercise his office along with his replacement whenever he felt up to it.[141] But perhaps the most striking example, ironically enough, was that of the procurator of San Marco *de citra* Giovanni Barbo, who in 1416 was judged no longer able to carry out his duties on account of his "infirmity and illness" and so was "replaced" by a third procurator, namely the young Francesco Foscari, while Barbo continued to enjoy the perquisites of the office. The hesitancy that the government displayed in relieving the elderly from their responsibilities indeed makes Foscari's case all the more remarkable and inevitably raises further questions about the Ten's motives.

On 22 October, the day after their decision to send a delegation to Foscari urging him to resign, the Ten took up the matter of the doge's response. As required by the previous day's decision, the ducal councilors and the heads of the Ten had met with Foscari on the evening of the 21st and tried to persuade him to renounce the dogeship. Foscari's reply, according to the records of the Ten, was that he did not want to give a definitive answer at that time but wished instead to keep his options open (*libertatem suam conservare volebat*). Fearing even graver problems, presumably that Foscari would rally supporters to his cause (as Guidobono said he had done during Jacopo's final investigation), the Ten and its *zonta* now voted to send its delegation back to the doge to learn "his definitive intention." They also agreed to remain in session so that once they learned the doge's decision, they could act accordingly. The vote on this measure was nearly identical to that of the day before, except that two more men now decided to abstain, bringing the number of abstentions to eight.[142]

Following that decision, the delegation made its way back to see the doge. Having had the night to consider his options, the wily old man threw a completely unexpected wrench into the Ten's plans. Dolfin's account of Foscari's answer is worth recording in full:

> He responded that he had sworn at his installation to observe his *promissione*, which oath he did not wish and was not able to disobey but rather obey; and if they wished to make other provisions, they were at liberty to have four of the ducal councilors go and propose a bill in the Great Council; and if the bill passed in the Great Council he was ready to comply. But since it had pleased the Republic to elect him as its doge and prince for life, he wished, as long as God granted him life, to remain, live, and die in the dogeship, alleging that it was not the business of the Council of Ten to provide for this matter, but rather the Great Council.[143]

Although his body may have been failing him, it is clear that Foscari remained in complete control of his mental faculties and could still play political hardball. By responding in this way, the doge placed two major obstacles in front of the Ten. First and most significantly, he challenged the Ten's legal authority to depose him. He argued, in essence, that since the Great Council had elected him, only that body had the power to remove him from office. If the Ten wished to proceed, he declared, they should do so legally, as outlined in his *promissione*, by having the ducal councilors make a proposal in the Great Council.[144] If the bill passed, he would abide by the decision. By putting this challenge to the Ten, the doge hoped that his appeal to the laws of Venice would force the Ten to reconsider their precedent-setting action. But Foscari had another trick up his sleeve as well: he reckoned that if the Ten capitulated and brought the issue before the Great Council, he could rely on support from the poorer members of the nobility – a group he had cultivated throughout his career – to defeat the measure. He figured as well that resentment at the Ten's grab for power would drive many who were not particularly well disposed toward him to vote in his favor as a way of signaling their displeasure with the Ten. Foscari's decades of experience with governmental procedures and a lifetime of effort in championing the poor paid their rewards as he threw the Ten off balance.

Disconcerted, the Ten and its *zonta* debated for some time the issue posed by the doge, namely whether the entire matter was properly theirs to consider or fell under the jurisdiction of the Great Council. There were, by their own admission, within the Ten, "diverse opinions and judgements" and good arguments to be made on both sides. Proponents of Foscari's position could argue, as he did, that only the Great Council, the embodiment of the will of the entire community, had the authority to elect or depose a doge. After all, the Venetians believed that the doge as earthly representative of Saint Mark was chosen through the elaborate system of nomination, lottery, and voting and that only the Great Council could reverse the vote. But those arguing for the Ten could make solid legal arguments to support their position. The Council of Ten had been formed to handle matters of state security; an ineffective or inactive doge certainly threatened the welfare of the state. More specifically, they could point to Foscari's own *promissione*, which contained provisions for selecting a vice-doge by the ducal councilors. Since the ducal councilors were meeting with the Ten, it was not going too far to suggest that the Ten as a whole should decide this matter.

After debating the legal issues involved, the Ten and its *zonta* decided to vote on two declarations: the first, proposed by Donato and Barbarigo, was that "this material ought to be defined in the Great Council;" the second, put forward by Loredan, stated "that the above-said matter of our Prince ought to be defined and settled by this council with the *zonta*." The council voted four times: on the first three ballots, the motion to refer the issue to the Great Council got 16 votes, while the motion in favor of the Ten got 19 votes; there were 3 abstentions. Thus neither motion had a simple majority. But on the fourth ballot, two proponents of the Great Council switched sides, giving Loredan's motion in favor of the Ten a slight majority and so the measure carried.[145]

Having narrowly ruled that the matter was properly theirs to decide, the Ten again closed ranks and voted as "true citizens of the fatherland" on a resolution put forward by the six ducal councilors and the three heads that the following morning the delegation would return once again to the doge and inform him that, since he had twice refused to renounce the dogeship "spontaneously and freely," he was now deposed and had to vacate the Ducal Palace within eight days. They were to reconfirm the previously discussed financial settlement, namely that he would get a yearly stipend of 1500 ducats as well as his salary pro-rated to that day. The bill also stated that if Foscari did not comply within the allotted time, then all his goods would be confiscated and would devolve to the state; the matter of electing a new doge would proceed in the Great Council, "according to the usual methods and procedures." This passed 28 to 5 with 5 abstentions.[146]

With their fateful decision made, the Ten then unanimously passed three additional measures designed to protect both their persons and reputations. First, they voted to forbid any members of the council from lobbying to be elected the next doge. They wanted to guarantee instead that all voting would be done "by conscience and according to God['s wishes] and not by importuning." This law was clearly designed to quash any potential rumors (such as those reported to Sforza by Guidobono) that some among them had voted to depose Foscari in order to promote themselves to the dogeship. The concern was not unfounded since Pasquale Malipiero and Cristoforo Moro, the next two doges of Venice, were both members of the committee. Next, they imposed a strict gag order on their proceedings. Finally, they voted to protect themselves, their sons, brothers, and grandsons from any sort of legal reprisals by the doge or his relatives, whom they defined as all those who had to excuse themselves from elections on account of propinquity.[147]

According to Dolfin, when Foscari was informed by the delegation of ducal councilors and the heads of the Ten that there had been a vote to depose him, he responded that since this was "the firm disposition and will of the Signoria and of the Council of Ten," he would obey; and so he renounced the dogeship on 23 October 1457. The ducal ring was removed from his finger and smashed and the horn and gold brocade band were cut from the ducal *corno*. He promised the delegates that he would vacate the Ducal Palace within two days and go to Cà Foscari. As the members of the delegation turned to leave his apartment, Foscari fixed his sight on Giacomo Memmo, the chief of the Forty who was substituting as the ducal councilor for the *sestiere* of San Marco. Foscari called him over and taking his hand asked him, "Whose son are you?" Memmo responded, "I am the son of ser Marino Memmo." To which Foscari replied: "He is my dear friend. Tell him on my behalf that it would mean much to me if he would come and visit so that we can go together by boat and enjoy ourselves in visiting the monasteries." Cognizant of the fact that Foscari had detained Memmo, the other members of the Ducal Council stopped him afterwards and questioned him about their conversation as they were worried that he might have revealed what had been said during their meetings.[148]

If Dolfin's report can be trusted, then it indicates that Foscari, having played the constitutional card by demanding that the matter be taken up by the Great Council, had no other tricks up his sleeve; instead, just as he had encouraged Jacopo to do, he decided to obey the will of the government. Of course, Foscari's partisans had every reason to portray the doge as compliant since this cast him in a favorable light and made him appear a martyr. By contrast, the description of the delegation's paranoia about the nature of the conversation between Foscari and Memmo placed them in an unfavorable light. The most heart-wrenching aspect of the meeting was the exchange between Memmo and the doge. If accurate, it suggests that Foscari now planned to turn his attention to matters of the next world, as he had intended more than twenty years earlier on his first attempt at resigning from the dogeship; his old friend and later enemy Cosimo de' Medici would do the same in the final year of his life. As Cosimo's biographer Vespasiano da Bisticci put it:

in his latter days Cosimo fell into irresolute mood, and would often sit for hours without speaking, sunk in thought. In reply to his wife who remarked on his taciturnity he said, "When you propose to go into the country, you trouble yourself for fifteen days in settling what you will do when you get there. Now that the time has come for me to quit this world and pass into another, does it not occur to you that I ought to think about it?"[149]

The most awkward moment in Foscari's deposition, however, must have been when he was forced to remove the ducal ring from his hand and watch it be destroyed and then to have the ducal *corno* taken from him and stripped of its ornaments. These were rituals usually performed on the death of a doge.[150]

The next day, again according to Dolfin, Foscari departed the Ducal Palace accompanied by his brother Marco, other relatives, and familiars. He descended what Dolfin describes as "the stone stairway," using a walking stick but otherwise without assistance. When Marco, addressing his brother as "Most Serene Prince," suggested they exit the palace by the "other stairway below that is covered," Foscari responded that he intended to leave by the same stairway that he had ascended on his entry into the dogeship.[151] Again, it is not possible to judge the accuracy of this scene. If true, it indicates not only that Foscari remained proud, but also that he intended to arouse sympathy for himself by making a very public departure from the precincts of government. If apocryphal, it was designed to garner yet more sympathy for the doge and to solidify his image as a martyr to the Ten. Furthermore, Dolfin's description does not reveal anything definite about the architecture of the palace. The stone stairway cannot have been the covered one built to abut the Porticato Foscari since it did not exist at the time of Foscari's election. Presumably it refers to a stairway on the side of the palace facing the *bacino*. Marco wanted them to use a less conspicuous, private stairway that must have been located in the part of the palace housing the ducal apartments, one that led directly to the canal bordering that wing.

Dolfin next states that when word of the deposition got out, it upset the *popolo* and *cittadini*, who complained that nothing since the foundation of the city had displeased them more. Their grumblings reached "to the stones of the foundations of Venice" as they protested that Foscari had been created doge for life; especially given his advanced age and his "poor convalescence," he had little time left and should therefore have been allowed to end his life as doge. Then in what is clearly Dolfin's own commentary he adds:

> Nor is one to marvel that Venice was displeased with the deposition, especially [with Foscari] having exalted and amplified the Venetian state and name, with such prudence and wisdom as is manifest to all. It appeared that there was no one else in Venice who was as worthy as him of such excellence as the governance of the dogado. This Republic also advanced with him with love and sincere will. And this should not have been the reward for so many efforts and troubles that he suffered on behalf of the Republic.

Dolfin concludes: "These then were the sentiments that motivated the grumblings among the citizens."[152]

The Ten's records indicate that displeasure with their decision extended beyond the *popolo* and *cittadini*. On 26 October they became concerned that "some of our nobles, having heard the provisions made by this most excellent council with its *zonta*, concerning the election of a new doge, began to object." The Ten found this intolerable and so passed a law authorizing the heads of the council and its inquisitors to investigate who was speaking up and what they were saying and to report back so that the Ten could take whatever action the "honor and reputation of this council" requires.[153] It seems likely that the resentment was fueled not only by the Ten's action but also by their attempts to portray Foscari's removal from the ducal throne as in some measure voluntary. For example, the notice on the 24th that the Great Council had been called into session to begin preparations for the election of the next doge characterized Foscari's removal as an "absolution" from the dogeship, prompted by his not being able "to exercise it on account of old age."[154] The rewriting of the past, even when it was merely a day old, had already begun. This must have proved particularly irksome to Foscari's supporters when they recalled how twice during his reign he had not been allowed to resign; but now that he was being forced from office, the Ten described it as a resignation.

How should one understand the deposition, this "great and unheard of novelty" in Venetian politics, this unprecedented assertion by the Council of Ten of its power even over the dogeship? Was the Ten's action justified, given Foscari's declining health and failure to fulfill his duties, or was it spurred by a desire on the part of Loredan and his allies to take vengeance on Foscari and his kinsmen? Is it mere coincidence that it was only when Loredan was again a head of the Ten that the council decided to act? Over the centuries, as discussed in the next chapter, political commentators, historians, and others have come down on one side or the other of these questions, based on shifting social and political concerns. Yet what previous analysts fail to recognize is that there is no need to choose, since both arguments are true in the sense that various people at the time believed in those truths and then acted accordingly. This conclusion does not represent a renunciation of the historian's responsibility to interpret the past or a capitulation to the impossibility of ever knowing what really happened; rather it is a simple recognition of the fact that the truth is what people make of it. This *is* what happened in the past: some believed that the Ten had acted properly; others saw Foscari as the victim of a vendetta. Most foreign chroniclers repeated the Ten's official line that Foscari left office on account of old age; but at least one, the anonymous compiler of events in Forlì, wrote that Foscari, whom he described as "a most wise man," was deprived of the dogeship out of "passion and hatred, rather than with reason."[155] Archbishop Antoninus of Florence offered both explanations, writing, "Some say the reason for his deposition was old age; others say rather [that it was] the envy and ambition of others."[156] These twin "truths" or beliefs about Foscari's deposition would help shape Venetian politics for at least the next half-century.

It is worth examining the two positions in a bit more detail. The idea that Foscari was the victim of a vendetta waged by his enemies, especially the Loredans, long held sway as the most widely accepted view of the deposition. This viewpoint is already discernible in Dolfin's account and in Guidobono's letters. There was, after all, a great deal of "truth" in this interpretation for it was Loredan who took unusually harsh positions regarding both the doge and his son. It was he who proposed that Jacopo be beheaded, and it was he alone who proposed that jurisdiction over the deposition remain in the hands of the Ten and not be referred to the Great Council. No historian has heretofore recognized this latter point, largely because Berlan's 1852 transcription of the law creates the misleading impression that the three heads of the Ten jointly put both propositions forward for a vote. However, an examination of the original page of the Ten's deliberations clearly shows that this was not the case (fig. 34). Loredan's colleagues proposed that the matter be referred to the Great Council. Loredan, by contrast, wanted to be sure that it remained in the more exclusive precincts of the Ten and its *zonta*. There seems little doubt that the Loredan family harbored a dislike for Foscari; nevertheless, Loredan would not have been able to act had not Foscari and his son handed him the opportunity to do so.

Dolfin also makes clear that there was a group of men within the Ten whom he considered Foscari's enemies or rivals. Describing Foscari's death, Dolfin observes how the doge left behind

> a great reputation for justice and good works with the great praise of his family, who ought right away to be known as a saint than by any other name, given his patience in all the many labors and troubles he had, and for his son and his son-in-law and relatives, persecuted by fortune and by many of his rivals and enemies; he was another Job on earth, given his constancy in face of so much adversity.[157]

According to Dolfin, Foscari's troubles were caused by his enemies, not by anything he or his relatives had done. And when he records the Ten's debate on how to handle Foscari's funeral arrangements, he says that they agreed on a state funeral only "after much opposition from his enemies who, persecuting him in life, so did not cease to do so in death."[158] For Dolfin and other Foscari partisans, both the doge and his son were victims of vindictive enemies.

Most of those in the Ten at the time, including Loredan, maintained the opposite view: that the reason for Foscari's deposition was his inability to perform the duties of his office any longer; this has generally speaking become the prevailing view among historians. This position started to gain ground when, in the mid-nineteenth century, scholars began to rely not only on chronicles but also on documentary evidence from the councils themselves to reconstruct the past. Not surprisingly, anyone who reads the Ten's records will be swayed to believe, as the Ten repeatedly proclaimed, that their sole concern was the welfare of the state.

Taking up the Ten's defense, there is some truth in the claim that Foscari was increasingly incapacitated and unable to function fully as doge; Dolfin did nothing to counter that view. The evidence shows that Foscari neither sponsored nor co-sponsored any bills at all during 1457; he had indeed become increasingly inactive; and Sforza's agent noted in

January that year that Foscari was enduring the suffering that was common among the aged.[159] The Ten faced the dilemma of what to do when a leader is incapacitated. Further support for the Ten's contention that they acted for the good of the state seems to emerge from the tentativeness of some of their actions: they did, after all, debate whether or not they had the authority to decide the doge's fate; and some of them seem to have entertained the idea of a vice-dogeship. Casting Loredan in the best possible light, the distinguished nineteenth-century historian Samuele Romanin – not coincidentally the leading Venetian proponent of the then new document-based history – described him as "a rigorous upholder of the laws in the manner of Cato, rather than a personal enemy of Foscari."[160]

So, there were two versions of what occurred, each valid for those who believed it and who were ready to act on that belief. Recognizing this debate for what it is, one can step back to ask not which is correct, but what can be learned from Foscari's deposition, what light does it shed on Venetian politics and society in the sixth decade of the fifteenth century. What it reveals, first and foremost, is the growing power of the Council of Ten. In tracing this growth, this book, has shown that it was a response in large part to the new exigencies of war and international diplomacy, factors demanding a strong executive and tight secrecy. The alternative, which Foscari at times pursued, especially in the decade of the 1440s, was driven by many of the same imperatives: to exalt the position of the doge, to raise its dignity to that of foreign princes. The deposition thus throws into high relief the institutional conflict the Venetian Republic faced as it struggled to redefine its executive structure in a changing world.

The deposition also illustrates another development that this book has tracked in some detail, namely the growing bifurcation of the Venetian ruling elite into two corps, one consisting of the rich and powerful centered in the Senate and Ten, the other composed of poorer nobles with loci of power in the Forty and the Great Council. Foscari's effort to have the matter of his deposition taken up by the Great Council makes this divide clear. At issue were two visions of Venetian patrician society, one communitarian and egalitarian; the other hierarchical and stratified. This is not to claim that Foscari was himself a member of that lesser nobility; he clearly was not, but he and his brother Marco aimed to portray themselves as advocates of the lesser nobles.

The legally defined Venetian nobility was at the same time nothing more than an agglomeration of family or kinship groups. And so the deposition should be read in familial terms as well. Here is where the rivalry between the Foscari and the Loredans becomes an issue: just as the struggle for power had institutional and socio-economic foci, so, too, it had kinship components. The difficult – indeed, nearly impossible – question to answer is the extent to which the family rivalries mirrored socio-economic ones. It would take a team of historians working many years to identify all the members of the ruling elite at the time and to try to discern their economic investments and interests, a process that would be made even more difficult by the loss of such materials as account books. Simple identifiers such as family name are no guarantee of political alliance: as noted above, for example, Jacopo was accused of murdering Ermolao Donato at the same time that Andrea Donato was one of his father's closest allies. Similarly, while Niccolò Bernardo was an enemy of Foscari, his kinsman Pietro had been married to Foscari's daughter Camilla.[161] What this study has shown is that the Foscari had important economic investments on the terraferma, while the Loredans were heavily engaged in eastern trade. But no clear-cut distinction can be made for the Foscari too had vital trade links to the east. Career choices and administrative experience might have been more significant determinants. Early on the Foscari developed a reputation for terraferma expertise and cultivated ties to citizens of other Italian states; the Loredans, by contrast, came to be known for their heroism in military service and knowledge of naval and eastern Mediterranean affairs. The expanding geographic sphere of Venetian influence and the burgeoning bureaucracy fueled this career diversification and helped create new criteria for distinguishing one patrician family from another.

Related to these career choices were contrasting notions of Venetian masculinity. Few of the Foscari distinguished themselves on the battlefield; instead they became known for their work as civil servants and dedication to the church and – at least in the case of Jacopo and to some extent his father – for their humanistic learning. Flavio Biondo praised the doge's knowledge of letters. Others, as noted earlier, commented on his eloquence. The Loredans, by contrast, cultivated an image as brave and intrepid naval commanders, men who were ready to risk their very lives for the Republic. Biondo included Pietro Loredan in his list of distinguished Venetian writers even though, as he admitted, Loredan was illiterate in Latin. But Loredan did write "copiously" in Italian, including, according to Biondo, on the art of sailing.[162] Of course, it was vital for Venice to have men with expertise in all these areas. But when voting on candidates for doge, members of the nobility had to decide which kind of leader could best advance the state's interests at any particular moment in time: the learned administrator or the natural commander.

In the end Foscari's deposition was conditioned by many variables. But one fact is indisputable: it constituted a major crisis for Venice, the likes of which the Republic had not faced since the conspiracy of Doge Marino Falier in 1355 and would not witness again until the defeat at Agnadello in 1509 during the War of the League of Cambrai. Like Foscari's deposition, those crises raised issues about respectively the nature of ducal power and the consequences of terraferma expansion. What the deposition reveals first and foremost is the dilemma that the Venetians confronted as they tried to redefine a polity which was no longer a city-state with a communal form of government, distant colonial possessions, and a relatively homogeneous ruling class, but had become a regional state with a complex bureaucracy requiring career specialization, maritime and terraferma interests under threat from both other Italian states and overseas powers, and a socially and economically stratified ruling elite. At the very center of this struggle was a debate over the nature and character of the dogeship itself.

Two Venetian humanist writers who were active at the time, Lauro Querini and Giovanni Caldiera, provide insights into this debate and into the institutional and intellectual tangle into which the Venetians had knotted themselves. Querini, scion of a noble family, was born around 1420. An intimate of the Foscari family (as noted above, he wrote to both Jacopo and his father on the occasion of the latter's transfer to Treviso), he devoted much of his time to humanist studies. In 1452 he left Venice for Crete where he remained until his death.[163] The works for which he is best known date from the 1440s. In a letter to Pietro Tommasi and in two treatises on the subject of nobility, Querini challenged the Florentine humanist Poggio Bracciolini in his contention that true nobility depends on virtue rather than birth.[164] According to Querini, Poggio was correct that virtue is the very essence of nobility, but the Florentine did not understand that virtue is transmitted through blood. Furthermore, the truly noble, those blessed with this innate superiority, are called to rule other men.[165] Querini thus presented a forthright defense of Venice's hereditarily defined ruling elite, of which he himself was a member. In *De republica* (*c.* 1449–50) Querini extended his defense of the Venetian patriciate's claims to innate superiority into an apology for their aristocratic republic. Drawing on Aristotle's *Politics*, Querini argued that a city can follow one of three forms of government: monarchy, aristocracy, or democracy, but of the three, he judged aristocracy the best.[166]

Querini's tracts on nobility and on the republic also lauded Venice's special role as a kind of new Rome. He observed that "most happy Venice preserves therefore Roman liberty, without sect, without faction, without any division." But Venice superseded the ancient capital for, he continued:

> No other republic ever, no empire, no kind of city, so long endured as a harmony of minds of one accord, if I may so speak, without domestic discord, as long as has excellent Venice. For now for more than one thousand years, the gods willing, she has ruled in just empire (*iusto imperio*) with virtue and dignity the greater part of Italy and nearly the whole of the Mediterranean Sea.[167]

Querini thus tried to meld in his treatise two contrasting views of Venice, one as a beacon of liberty to the rest of Italy, the other as an empire commanding a large part of Italy and much of the sea. Venice was heir to two Roman legacies, the freedom-loving inheritance of the Roman Republic and the imperial inheritance of the Roman Empire.

The destabilizing potential of this dual inheritance was clear in the dedication of the *De republica*, which reads, "Francisco Fuscaro principi optimo Laurus Quirinus felicitatem." Querini took up this trope of the doge as *princeps* when he observed that just as ancient times had produced their Caesars and Augustuses, so his own age was no less worthy of being glorified for having produced Foscari, a man in no way inferior to those rulers.[168] Thus in a treatise specifically devoted to illustrating the superiority of aristocratic republican rule, Querini found himself comparing Foscari favorably with Rome's imperial rulers. It would be easy to dismiss these words as nothing more than the fulsome rhetoric typical of such dedications. But like the sculptural and architectural program of the new entry system into the Ducal Palace, Querini's treatise shows the Venetians struggling to define the appropriate role for the doge in their polity which was both a republic and an imperial power.

This same uneasy alignment would reappear in Bernardo Giustinian's funeral oration for Foscari.

The writings of Giovanni Caldiera, a member of the Venice's *cittadino* class and also an intimate of Foscari, reveal a similar quest to situate or position the dogeship, although Caldiera's solution was quite different from Querini's. As noted in chapter 1, during his student days Caldiera had been a beneficiary of Foscari's patronage: while he was a procurator of San Marco, Foscari had directed some of the procuratorial funds to help pay for Caldiera's university expenses.[169] In his treatise entitled *De concordantia poetarum, philosophorum et theologorum* (On the concordance of the poets, philosophers, and theologians), a work in which Caldiera travels through several mythical realms, he repaid the favor by assigning Foscari a place of honor under the special protection of the goddess Respublica. The encounter occurs on an island city where the liberal and mechanical arts are practiced. Foscari sits at the foot of the throne of Respublica and around him are arrayed the other members of the government arranged according to rank. Foscari greets the visitor with an oration praising Venice's wealth and achievements in civic arts as well as its aristocracy, "which resembles supercelestial government and imitates the form of divine institutions."[170] And so, although Foscari is presented in a republican setting and indeed as under the special protection of Respublica herself, the context is clearly hierarchical.

These emphases are even more clear in Caldiera's other work, actually a trilogy, the *De virtutibus*, *De oeconomia*, and *De Politia*, the first of which he dedicated to one of Foscari's successors, Doge Cristoforo Moro. Composed in 1463, *De Politia* portrays the doge as a veritable monarch, "superior to the law on account of his virtues, and assisted by a series of councils functioning as consultative bodies subordinate to the dogal will." A kind of philosopher-king, the doge seeks advice from these other organs of government, but it is his innate sense of what is right that guides the polity. One significant exception exists to this ducally controlled government, namely the Council of Ten, which tolerates "nothing threatening to the republic." Caldiera's solution to Venice's problem of executive authority is to entrust it to a realm of moral responsibility where, as Margaret King observes, "the same hierarchical pattern of rule exists in Venice as in the order of nature [. . .] and is concordant with the will of God."[171] There is, then, in the works of both Caldiera and Querini, an effort on the part of intellectuals close to

Foscari to reconcile the princely and republican aspects of the office. It was ultimately this dilemma, played out through the events surrounding Jacopo, that brought Foscari down.

Little is known of how Foscari passed his days after the deposition. Perhaps he sought solace and aid from the saints, as the humanist Ludovico Foscarini had once exhorted Jacopo to do.[172] But certainly his rapidly declining health would have prevented him from visiting monasteries in the lagoon as he wished. The one thing known for certain is that on 29 October 1457 he drew up his last will and testament. It seems unlikely that this is the only will Foscari made during his lifetime, although there is no mention that it supersedes previous ones. In any event, it is the only one that has survived. It is quite short, especially for a man as wealthy and powerful as Foscari; its only surprise is its brevity. Otherwise, it conforms entirely to testamentary practices of the time. First, Foscari names his wife Marina, his brother Marco, and his grandsons Francesco and Niccolò, the sons of Jacopo, as his executors, although the boys are not to undertake this responsibility until they reach age twenty. Like most wills of the period, it includes both charitable bequests and legacies to family members. The charitable bequests include 100 ducats for the Patriarch of Venice and "his church," another 100 to be distributed in amounts of 5 ducats to help twenty girls marry, yet another 100 ducats to be allotted to the poor according to the discretion of his executors, and finally a request that 50 ducats be dispersed in installments of 2 ducats each to twenty-five monasteries in the city. In return the religious are to recite masses of Saint Gregory for his soul. Foscari leaves the choice of monasteries up to his executors, "according to their conscience."

The bequests to kin are similarly simple and straightforward. There are no elaborate provisions either for what should happen to his estate far into the future or should his grandsons die before reaching maturity. He does not seek to entail his properties; in fact he does not even enumerate them. Instead, he sets out to assist his immediate kin. First, he bequeaths his daughter Maria an annual stipend of 100 ducats to pay for her maintenance, and he asks that she live with her mother, Foscari's wife Marina. Described in the will as a "domicella," Maria must have been destined for spinsterhood since he neither makes any provisions for a dowry nor for her to enter a convent. He leaves it to the discre-

30 *(top)* Cà Foscari, sculpture over rear courtyard gate, from Jan Grevembroch, "Saggi di familiari, magnificenze." Museo Civico Correr, MS. Gradenigo–Dolfin 229, fig. 45.

31 *(middle)* Island monastery of San Cristoforo della Pace, from Vincenzo Coronelli, *Le singolarità di Venezia*, 1697.

32 *(bottom)* Cà del Duca.

p Jacobuſ Lauredano
p Jeronimuſ Donato
p Jeronimuſ Barbadico
Capita

uemadmodum huic Ex̃ conſilio notũ eſt: heri dñi Conſiliarij et Capita ſe contuleziũt ad
Illu. Principem noſtrũ. Et in executione partiſ ⁊ deliberationiſ capte in iſto conſilio explica
uerūt ſue Ex̃ quantũ fieri debeat ut pſuderet ad renũtiandũ rc̃. Ipſe aut̃ Princeps noſter
inter ceteza respondit q̃ nollebat dicere de ſic. nec de non: q̃q̃ libertate ſuaz ſibi c̃ſuaie uolebat
Et examinatiſ condicionibs et neceſſitatibus Regiminis ⁊ ſtatus nri que oĩa ad cutãda maioza
et grauioza incõuenietĩa requirit prouiſione: fiebat pro ſtatu ſuo intelligere diffinitiua ſue
tione eiuſdem Illu. Principis. vz. ſi intendat renũtiare cũ condicionibs capti ⁊ declaratis ſue cel.
nec ne propterea ___ Vadit par⁹

Q̃ dñi Conſiliazij et Capita huĩ Ex̃ conſilij ſe conferre debeat ad Ipm. ſ. principe dicendo ſibi per
tinentibus et accomodatis uerbis. Q̃ quia Ex̃ ſua heri ſero inter ceteza dixit de ſic. nec de no̅ Conſiliũ Ipm cũ Additione
deliberauit mittere Ipoſ dñoſ Conſiliaz⁹ ⁊ Capita ad Ex̃ ſuaz pro intelligendo diffinitiua eiuſ
intentione: ut ea intellecta prouidere ⁊ deliberare poſſit ſicut ſibi uidebitur.
Conſiliũ aut iſtud no recedat ſed ſic unitũ ſtare debeat: ut intellecto reſponſo preſati Principiſ
conſultare ⁊ deliberare poſſit utilitate et comoda nri ſtatus.

De parte _____ 27
De non _____ 3
Nonſinc _____ 8   Die XXII. Octobr̃ cũ Addic̃

Quoniam in hac materia Illuſtri̅ Principiſ que diu diſputata eſt in hoc c̃ſilio ſicut omẽ intel
ligere potuerūt ſūt diuerſe opiniones ⁊ huĩ vz. ſi reſ iſta in iſto conſilio aut in maioz c̃ſilio
diffiniri debeat. Vadit par⁹ ⁊ ſuaz declaratioz

p Jezonimuſ Donato
p Jeronimuſ Barbadico
Capita

Q̃ materia Ipi diffiniri debeat in maiozi conſilio
De parte _____ 16 _____ 16 _____ 16 _____ 14

p Jacobuſ Lauredano
Caput

Q̃ materia iſta principis nri diffiniri ⁊ expediri debeat per iſtud conſiliũ cũ Addic̃
De parte _____ 19 _____ 19 _____ 19 _____ 21
De non _____ 0
Nonſinc _____ 3 _____ 3 _____ 3 _____ 3
Die XXII. octobr̃ cũ Addic̃

p ornuſ Paſqualigo
p Matheuſ Barbaro
p Johãet Lauredano
p Dauid Contareno
p Leo Duodo
Conſiliazij
p Jacobuſ Memo cap
⁊ xl. loco conſiliazij
p Jacobuſ Lauredano
p Jezonim⁹ Donato
p Jeronimuſ Barbadico
Capita

 Htellexit hoc Ex̃ conſiliũ quid reſpondezit Illu̅ Princeps nr̃ ad ea que heri ⁊ hodie cũ deliberatione
ipſius conſilij p dñoſ Conſiliaz⁹ et Capita ſibi explicata fuerūt: tam in exportando ⁊ rogando eũ
ut pro neceſſio. et euidentiſſimo comodo ſtatus et Regiminis nri renũtiaze uellet q̃ ⁊ ut diffinitue
dicere uellet intentione ſua rc̃. Et ſicut clare et aperte agnoſcitur ſua Sub. que nihil diffinitiue
uoluit reſpondere: querit ducere rem iſtas in tpuſ. ⁊ perſiſtere in ducatu cũ tanto detrimeto
et preiudicio ſtatus nri: quanto omẽ intelligit. q̃a ex abſentia et inhabilitate pſone ſue: negocia
ſtatus et Regiminis nri: quotidie de malo in peiuſ nudent procedere. Niſiq̃ prouideat certiſſimũ
tenezi poteſt q̃ in ſucceſſu tpuſ: multo maioza ⁊ grauioza incõuenietĩa ⁊ picula expectaturi ſum⁹
Que ſi uezi cuiuſ patrie ſimuſ: totis nriſ ſenſibus totis uiribus cuitare debemuſ. propterea

Vadit par⁹ Q̃ auctoritate iſtus conſilij cũ Additioe capti ſit. Q̃ dñi Conſiliazij ⁊ Capita huĩ cõſilij
in craſtinũ de mane ſe conferre debeat ad Illuſtri̅ Principe: dicendo ſibi q̃am p duaſ uiceſ cõ
ſiliũ iſtud miſit eos ad eius pñtea: perſuadendo ⁊ rogando eũ ut pro neceſſio bono ⁊ euidentiſſimo
comodo ſtatus nri ſponte ⁊ libere renũtiare uellet. Cũaz rem ſua Sub. facere recuſaret pretez id
quod conſiliũ Ipm ſibi firmiter p̃ſuadebat: qua ſicut ſua Ex̃ optime intelligit: penitus neceſſiũ
eſt pro euitandiſ caſibus ⁊ piculis q̃ contingere poſſent: ut prouideatur. Ideoq̃ declarat̃ ſibi
deliberatiũ ⁊ capti eſſe p preſati̅ conſiliũ iſtud cũ Addic̃. Q̃ deponat a Ducatu ⁊ teneat̃ recedere ex
palatio infra dieſ octo p̃x. Declaret̃ tñ ſibi: q̃ habebit ſingulo año ⁊ ab officio nro ſalui due
millequingetoſ auĩ in uita ſua: de pecuniſ ſpectantibus nro dñio: q̃ ſibi dent̃ ſingulo mẽ p ratas.
Et ultra hoc ſiquid hc̃ reſtat de ſalario ſuo uſq̃ in pñtez diem: p ipm officiũ ſibi ſoluet̃ in mẽ
ſex p ratas: ſicuti et ſue cel. oblata fiũt.

Volue.

33 *(facing page top)* Memorial plaque commemorating the Peace of Lodi at San Cristoforo della Pace, from Jan Grevembroch, "Varie venete curiosità sacre e profane." Museo Civico Correr, MS. Gradenigo–Dolfin 65/I, fig. 100.

34 *(facing page bottom)* The Council of Ten's deliberation for 22 October 1457. Archivio di Stato di Venezia, Consiglio dei Dieci, Deliberazioni misti, reg. 15, fol. 140r.

35 *(above)* Scala dei Giganti, Ducal Palace.

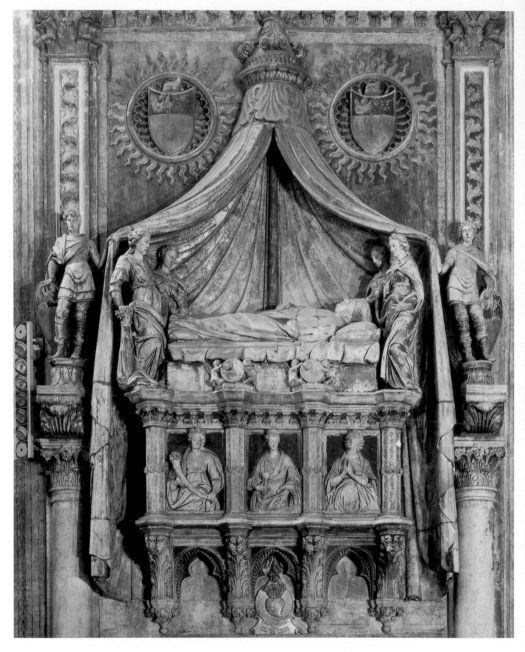

36   Tomb of Doge Foscari, Santa Maria Gloriosa dei Frari. Detail of sarcophagus.

37   *(facing page top)* Tomb of Doge Foscari, Santa Maria Gloriosa dei Frari. Detail of effigy.

38   *(facing page bottom)* Tomb of Doge Foscari, etching by Marco Sebastiano Giampiccoli, 1777. Museo Civico Correr, Stampe Gherro 290.

ALOISII FOSCARI
HIC COR
HIC IPSO IVBENTES
ANNO DEI MDCCX

ACCIPIE CIVES FRANCISCI FOSCARI VESTRI DVCIS IMAGINEM
INGENIO MEMORIÆ ELOQVENTIA AD HAEC IVSTICIA
FORTITVDINE ANIMI CONSILIO SI NIHIL AMPLIVS CERTE
SVMMORVM PRINCIPVM GLORIAM AEMVLARI CONTENDI
PIETATER GA PATRIAM MEAE SATISFECI NVNQVAM MAXIMA
BELLA PROVESTRA SALVTE ET DIGNITATE TERRA MARIQVE PER
ANNOS PLVS QVAM XXX GESSI SVM MA FELICITATE CONFECI
LABANTEM IAM DV MISI ITALIAE LIBERTATEM INBATORES QVE
ARMIS COMPESCVI BRIXIAM BERGOMVM RAVENAM CREMAM
IMPERIO ADIVNXI VESTRO OMNIBVS ORNAMENTIS PATRIAM
AVXI PACE VOBIS PARTA ITALIA INTRANQVILLVM FOEDERE
REDACTA POST TOT LABORES EXHAVSTOS AETATIS ANNO LXXXIII
DVCATVS III SVPRA XXX SALVTIS QVE MCCCCLVII KLENDIS
NOVEMBRIBVS AD AETERNAM REQVIEM COMMIGRAVI VOS
IVSTICIAM ET CONCORDIAM QVO SEMPITERNVM HOC SIT
IMPERIVM CONSERVATE

39   Tomb of Doge Foscari, epitaph.

FRANCISCO
AVO
DIVO DVCI
FRANCISCO
GERMANO
PIENTISSIMO

NICOLAVS
IACOBE
MONVMENTVM
HOC
MAGNIFICE
POSVIT

40   Tomb of Doge Foscari, inscription on
base of left column.

41   Tomb of Doge Foscari, inscription on
base of right column.

42 (left) Porta della Carta, Ducal Palace, without doge and lion group.

43 (below) Francesco Hayez, *The Last Farewell of the Son of Doge Foscari to his Family*, oil on canvas, Galleria d'Arte Moderna, Florence.

44   Francesco Hayez, *Doge Francesco Foscari Deposed*, oil on canvas, Museo Brera, Milan.

45   Poster for *Il due Foscari*, film directed by Enrico Fulchignoni
with Rossano Brazzi as Jacopo.

tion of Marina to free the family slaves, but with the proviso that she should "reserve" one or more female slaves to serve Maria.

Foscari bequeaths Jacopo's widow Lucrezia 25 ducats annually, to do with as she pleases. But his major legacy to her is his injunction that she continue to live with his wife and grandsons and treat the boys well, in return for her upkeep. At the same time he enjoins his grandsons to be obedient to her, "as they ought to." Through these bequests, Foscari tries, as did many testators of this period when leaving legacies to widowed mothers, to prevent Lucrezia from becoming what was sometimes described as a "cruel mother," that is, a widow who remarried, abandoning her children for another household and just as importantly removing her dowry from the patriline. Indeed, Foscari's major preoccupation, as his will makes clear, is the welfare and future of his grandchildren, Jacopo's offspring. He leaves 2500 ducats each for the dowries of his granddaughters, although he does not bother to mention how many there are or even to record their names. They are referred to simply as the sisters of his grandsons Francesco and Niccolò. The bulk of his estate, what was known as the "residuum," he bequeaths to the two boys with the proviso that they live "quietly and obediently" with their mother and grandmother. Only at age twenty will they come into full possession of the estate; and even then they are forbidden to sell any of its possessions until they reach thirty. If they should decide to sell some of the estate's property and their uncle Marco wishes to buy it, he is to receive a 15 percent discount off the lowest price. As a token of his esteem for his brother, Foscari bequeaths him 100 ducats "out of love." The will contains no specific bequests to Marina, nor does it include any provisions for Foscari's burial. He also makes no specific mention of his new palace.[173]

If one did not know whose will it is, one would never guess that it was written by a (former) doge. It does not include, as some doges' wills do, bequests to ducal servants or others who were employed in the Ducal Palace.[174] Even the charitable bequests are modest, especially given Foscari's wealth and status and his past history of helping the poor. He neglected, for example, hospitals such as the Lazzaretto and the Cà di Dio, one of his abiding lifetime concerns. Certainly the effort to help poor girls with their dowries harked back to his days as a procurator when he used such monies to help build a clientele; but this was one of the most common types of testamentary bequests in Renaissance

Venice. There is nothing unusual here. His major preoccupation, almost his only one, was that his grandsons be brought up well by his wife and daughter-in-law. One cannot help but read into this a desire on his part to perpetuate the memory of his son Jacopo and preserve the glory of his lineage.[175]

While Foscari passed his days after leaving office quietly preparing for death, the government moved rapidly to begin the elaborate process of electing his successor. On Tuesday 25 October the alternating rounds of nomination and lottery got under way so that by the 27th the final committee of forty-one electors had begun meeting in conclave. They met until Sunday the 30th, when they elected Pasquale Malipiero the new Doge of Venice. He was immediately presented to the city in San Marco and installed in office.[176]

One of Malipiero's first actions was to write to various foreign governments informing them of his election (there are copies of his announcement in the archives of Milan, Florence, and Siena). In the letter, Malipiero again presented the official, that is the Ten's, version of events, stating that Foscari had "vacated" the ducal throne "on account of his decrepit age and long-standing ill-health and disability." Malipiero also used the letter to quash any rumors that the Venetian government was seriously divided or that there had been a *coup d'état*, for he added that his election had been conducted according to the usual rites and solemnities and greeted with great joy, applause, and "unanimous" assent. He was putting foreign powers on notice that they should not try to take advantage of Venice's change of regime in order to better their own positions.[177] Sforza for one was clearly annoyed that news of the deposition had taken him by surprise. He chastised his agent in Venice for not keeping him better informed and continued to press him for details of what had happened. Marchese da Varese reported that he knew little except that he could perhaps forward to Sforza the names of the men who had taken part in the Ten and the *zonta*.[178] But the Milanese prince was also quick to send a letter congratulating Malipiero on his elevation to the ducal throne, observing that in removing Foscari from the "weight" of the office, the "Senate" (as he called it) had acted sagely.[179]

On All Saints' Day, Tuesday 1 November 1457, just two days after Malipiero's election, Francesco Foscari died at his home in the parish of San Pantalon at age eighty-four. Dolfin explains the suddenness of his death through his belief that neither God nor Saint Mark wished for

Venice to have two heads, "since just as it is not right for a body to have two heads, so it was not right that there ought to be two doges of Venice."[180] Rumors about the circumstances of Foscari's death raced through the city. According to one of them recorded by Dolfin, just "as a ripe piece of fruit falls from a tree with the slightest bit of wind," so when Foscari heard the bells of San Marco announcing the election of his successor, a vein in his stomach burst, and he died from the hemorrhage. Another version had it that he had a tumor on his tongue which metastasized and cut off his windpipe so that he suffocated on the phlegm. Yet another was that he died of melancholy, "seeing himself," as Sanudo puts it, "tossed out of the Ducal Palace and his ducal chambers."[181] The first version in particular provided combustible fuel for the imagination of such Romantics as Byron and Verdi.

It fell to Foscari's son-in-law, the recently repatriated knight Andrea Donato, to inform the members of the Signoria of the doge's death. Donato found them in San Marco, where they were attending High Mass for All Saints' Day. He informed Doge Malipiero and the Signoria that Foscari had expired that morning. Dolfin, who was present at the Mass, captures the scene perfectly:

> Hearing this news, everyone looked around from one to another; saying that if they had only waited 10 days more to act, they would not have branded the city with inconstancy in this way. It seemed to everyone a marvel, and they were stupefied by such a thing, that he had expired so soon and it displeased many concerning the privation [of office] of such a prince, like whom there never was and never will be a similar one in this city.[182]

As soon as the Mass ended, the Pien Collegio met with the Ten to consider how to respond to this unexpected and shocking development. They eventually decided – but only over objections from his enemies, including especially Niccolò Bernardo, whom Dolfin described as a "depraved and vindictive man of evil nature" – that Foscari should be accorded all the pomp and honors of a full ducal funeral. Accordingly, the bells of San Marco immediately began to toll, announcing to the city that Foscari had died.[183]

Foscari's body was transferred at dawn on 3 November from Cà Foscari to the Ducal Palace, where it lay in state either in the chamber of the *signori di notte*, as Dolfin reports, or in the hall of the *giudici del piovego*, as Sanudo relates. His corpse was adorned with all the trappings of the ducal office. Robed in his gold brocade *manto*, Foscari had the ducal *corno* on his head, spurs on his feet, and a golden sword at his side. His coat of arms was placed by his head. In the afternoon, Doge Malipiero and the Signoria, along with representatives of all the secular and regular clergy of the city and the *scuole grandi*, heard offices sung in his honor. Twenty noblemen, dressed in scarlet and representing the city, flanked the body, ten on each side. The room was decorated with the banners of the *scuole piccole*. The body was hoisted by members of the Scuola di San Marco and carried "under a golden umbrella with solemn pomp and great illumination" by sailors from the Arsenal, the doge's customary honor guard, along the Merceria, across the Rialto Bridge and to the Frari. The cortege included both patricians and *popolani* dressed in mourning garb. Following the most solemn obsequies, the humanist Bernardo Giustinian delivered a funeral oration which reportedly lasted four hours. Awaiting more permanent burial arrangements, Foscari's body was placed in a temporary grave either at the Frari or, as another source has it, in the parish church of San Pantalon.[184]

Bernardo Giustinian faced an extremely awkward situation when he was asked by Foscari's brother Marco to deliver the eulogy. Never before had a living doge been present at the funeral of his predecessor. Moreover, the events of the last tragic year of Foscari's reign presented a variety of difficulties for Giustinian: the conventions of classically inspired rhetoric required him to present a summary of the deceased's life, including a praiseworthy treatment of his family, personal qualities, and deeds.[185] The orator also had to tiptoe through a minefield of issues, pleasing the family and assuaging their interests while not offending the members of the Signoria who had recently deposed the deceased.[186]

Giustinian used the occasion to present an *apologia* for Venice's actions during the Italian wars and terraferma expansion. Indeed, most of the lengthy oration is taken up with an account of foreign affairs during Foscari's reign both in Italy and overseas. Giustinian countered the charge leveled by Venice's enemies (and by some of the doge's enemies as well) that the conquest of the terraferma was driven by cupidity and a desire for domination by arguing instead that Venice had been drawn reluctantly into mainland affairs, but that under Foscari's leadership it had accepted its destiny, its *fortuna*, to protect the *libertas Italiae*. Going on to define that liberty in a particular way – not as some later scholars would have it as an allegiance to republican values, but rather as a commitment to maintaining a system of independent states – Giustinian then argued that "in protecting her own freedom, [Venice] had also protected the liberty of her neighbors."[187] Yet, like Lauro Querini, the eulogist did not shy away from describing Venice as an empire, observing that under Foscari Venice had taken possession of a number of cities, including Brescia, Bergamo, Crema, and Ravenna; he described the last of these as a "most ancient and celebrated city, the seat of kings and emperors." Addressing the deceased doge directly, Giustinian proclaimed, "These [cities], Francesco, are your monuments; the fruits of your labors by which the splendor of your name is rendered immortal."[188]

Attentive to the circumstances in which he was speaking, Giustinian presented Venice's actions during Foscari's reign as directed by the doge but with the support of the other members of the ruling elite. Several times, in his account of military exploits, he mentioned Pietro and Alvise Loredan by name.[189] Giustinian chose to ignore entirely the deposition, noting only metaphorically that Foscari had survived many tempests and arrived at a tranquil harbor.[190] He also sought to dampen the flames of internal conflict by claiming that Foscari whom heaven had chosen to take from them had been reincarnated in the figure of Malipiero ("Non enim ablatus a nobis Franciscus est, sed in hoc Paschasio restitutus").[191] He did, however, include one passage which could be read as a criticism of the Loredans: after summarizing the achievements of Foscari's reign, he observed that – contrary to the view that he might deserve less glory for having prevailed not by force of arms but by counsel and wisdom – Giustinian himself stood with better minds who valued "wise rule" over "military discipline."[192] Nevertheless, Giustinian's funeral oration for Foscari stands as one of the great monuments of Venetian myth-making, in which tensions among the ruling elite are glossed over and the contradictions between a republican commitment to liberty and the acquisition of an empire subtly resolved into a vision of a unified community with an immortal leader.

In terms of his task to please the family and celebrate the deceased, Giustinian delivered a rhetorical *tour de force*. He made fatherhood and lineage two of his central themes, subtly weaving their personal and political meanings throughout the eulogy. In the speech's exordium, he evoked the paternal connotations of the ducal office, relating how

Foscari had devoted almost all his life to public affairs and that for more than thirty-four years he had ruled his subjects more as a parent than as a prince.[193] As already noted, representations of the doge as father were rare in Venetian political discourse because they carried princely overtones which threatened the delicate balance between the ducal office and the various councils. Yet in these circumstances, Giustinian did not shy away from the term "pater," although he was careful to apply it to the other leaders of the state as well.[194]

He further evoked the paternal theme, although this time in its classical guise, by twice honoring Foscari with variants of the appellation *Pater Patriae*. In the first instance, Giustinian deployed its conjugal possibilities noting that Venice, cast here as the wife, had been widowed by the loss of her husband ("certe viduata tali principe civitas, orbata parente patria").[195] The second use occurred in the context of Giustinian's discussion of Foscari's charitable activities during his time as procurator of San Marco. Noting the doge's efforts on behalf of the poor, the orator contrasted the Caesars who received the title *Pater Patriae* before they merited it, with Foscari who had taken on the responsibilities of the title before being honored with the title itself.[196] Through these phrases, Giustinian carefully constructed an image of Foscari as political husband and father. Members of the Ten could not object to this usage since they themselves had encouraged Foscari to assume the role of the "true *Pater Patriae*" and renounce the dogeship.

At the same time the eulogist used the oration to situate Foscari within a more private, familial context. It was customary in Renaissance eulogies to establish the deceased's pedigree, to illustrate the glories of his lineage.[197] Giustinian used this convention to laud the Foscari patriline, to describe an unbroken chain of males extending from Foscari's grandfather all the way to the doge's grandsons Francesco and Niccolò, while never mentioning the disgraced Jacopo by name. Foscari's grandfather Giovanni was recalled for his great deeds on land and sea, while the doge's father Niccolò was remembered not only for his administration of cities on the terraferma (again, a way of invoking the imperial theme) and the many offices he held within Venice itself, but for having produced so distinguished a son who in attaining the office of doge fulfilled the family's destiny.[198] The special relationship of father and son was further emphasized when Giustinian recalled how, most extraordinarily, at the age of only thirty-one Francesco succeeded his father as state attorney. Such precocity was almost unheard of in Venice; and, according to the orator, a father could only rejoice when his son surpassed him in virtue.[199]

Having at the beginning of the speech recalled the family's past, Giustinian ended by looking to its future. He called on Foscari's brother Marco, to whom the doge had entrusted the care of his grandsons, to hold their grandfather up to them as a model so that these "common grandsons" (*nepotes communes*) might be inspired by his "most glorious image" (*gloriosissimam imaginem*). At the close of the eulogy, Giustinian again addressed Foscari as "Father" (*Francisce pater*) and asked God and the saints to protect the city and preserve the peace.[200]

Another device Giustinian used to evoke the familial theme was to make several references to his own patriline. He remarked that when Marco Foscari asked him to undertake the speech he was pleased to do so since Foscari was beloved by his father Leonardo and by the entire Giustinian family. He recalled a time when together the doge and his father counseled military action in Friuli as well as a naval victory led by his cousin Orsato, whom in the circumstances Giustinian called "pater." And he noted the honor that accrued to Venice during Foscari's reign when Pope Nicholas V raised its bishopric to the dignity of a patriarchate with his uncle Lorenzo as the first incumbent.[201] By paying homage to his own family, Giustinian reinforced one of the central images of his oration.

By focusing on the themes of fatherhood and lineage, Giustinian was able to celebrate the Foscari family. Moreover, by carefully constructing an image of the patriline as a continuum of distinguished men, he subtly paid homage to Jacopo without mentioning him by name. Given the difficulty of the task before him, Giustinian accomplished his seemingly impossible goal of celebrating the doge and his family without offending the Signoria. At the same time he began the delicate process of repairing the family's tarnished image, a process that would take place on many fronts, not least of all in the doge's tomb.

While Giustinian proved himself to be a consummate diplomat in his attempts to heal the wounds inflicted by Foscari's deposition, others offered more partisan assessments. In contrast to Giustinian's measured oration, which reveals little about Foscari himself but much about Venetian political mythologizing, Dolfin's account is entirely laudatory. As noted above, it includes not only a Foscari sympathizer's explanation for the deposition, namely that he had been "persecuted" by his enemies, but also his recollection of the reign as an age of prudence, wisdom, justice, and "good works", when Venice had extended its realm and glorified its name with "love and true purpose." For Dolfin, Foscari was the agent of Venice's success, not simply the representative of a perfect polity; it was he who had "exalted and amplified the state and the name of Venice."[202]

Foscari's deposition helped to draw together a group that can be labeled the Foscari party. At its center were the doge's closest kinsmen. One can identify this inner circle from a note recorded at the end of the Ten's register of deliberations for this period. It lists the men whom the Ten considered Foscari's closest kinsmen, the men who were excluded from ever involving themselves in cases regarding Jacopo's prosecutors, for fear that they would use the courts to wage vendetta. Unfortunately, it is impossible to determine precisely when this list was compiled and to which of the several prosecutions of Jacopo it applied. But clearly it had to do with one of Jacopo's cases since Andrea Donato and Marco Ruzzini are described as "brothers-in-law," which was their relationship to Jacopo. Nevertheless, the list is also valid for the period following the doge's death since the kinsmen did not change; furthermore, the prohibition applied to future generations as well. Not surprisingly, of the fifteen men listed, the greatest number were Foscari themselves: these included the doge, Jacopo, and Marco as well as their cousins, descendants of Franzi – Filippo, Urbano, Ludovico, and Giovanni Foscari. The other men listed were all related by marriage either to the doge and/or Jacopo. These included, as noted above, Jacopo's brothers-in-law Donato and Ruzzini as well as his cousins Andrea Venier, and Francesco Venier, son of the late Santo; Jacopo's nephews Niccolò Mudazzo, Pietro Bernardo, and Girolamo Michiel, son of the late Niccolò; and Jacopo's father-in-law Leonardo Contarini and his sons and sons-in-law.[203]

These were the Foscari associates, men who could be expected to seek to avenge the wrong done to the doge and his son. The civic atmosphere was highly charged. As the Ten's deliberations of 26 November indicate, members of that council feared retribution: the question had arisen whether or not the prohibition on Foscari's relatives using the courts to seek vengeance excluded them from collecting debts they were owed by members of the Ten and its *zonta*; it also needed to be established whether or not they could fulfill their responsibility as executors of estates if those estates had some claim against members of the Ten and the *zonta*. In both instances the Ten answered in the affirmative, voting that the Foscari relatives could seek payment of what was owed them and fulfill their fiduciary responsibilities. In the end, however, the Signoria determined that both measures had failed to pass since neither had received the unanimous vote required by the original legislation of 22 October which forbade Foscari's relatives from using the legal system to avenge the doge.[204]

The man around whom Foscari's sympathizers rallied was his brother Marco, who as early as 30 December 1457, a little less than two months after his brother's death, was again making proposals in the Senate in his capacity as a *savio del consiglio*.[205] Retribution came, at least in one form the following fall by means of a series of reforms within the Council of Ten itself. On 23 October 1458, a year to the day after Foscari's deposition, the heads of the Ten – Benedetto Vitturi, Giovanni Loredan, and Lorenzo Soranzo – proposed that a *zonta* of twenty noblemen be convened to consider a whole range of questions concerning the power of the heads of the Ten. These included the growing jurisdiction of the Ten in matters not traditionally part of its purview, especially matters that were customarily the competence of the Great Council, as well as regarding the penalties that the Ten meted out. It took three rounds of voting for this measure to pass by a vote of 9 to 2 with 5 abstentions. Once passed, the Ten elected the twenty-man *zonta*: among those elected were Marco Foscari, Andrea Donato, and Orsato Giustinian. Pressure from the doge's circle of allies as well as discontent among both the poorer nobles and the *popolo* seem to have forced the Ten's hand; this probably explains Loredan's co-sponsorship of the measure.[206]

On the 25th the Ten and its *zonta* passed three measures addressing these concerns. All three bills were put forward by the ducal councilors Antonio Contarini and Jacopo Barbarigo and by the heads Vitturi and Soranzo; Loredan was not a co-sponsor. The first bill began with a prologue observing that recently the Council of Ten had concerned itself with matters regarding the ducal *promissione* and that it might do so again in the future, "with great scandal and danger to our State." Given that the council had been created to prevent scandals rather than be the source of them and to provide "for the peacefulness and evident good of our State," the Ten decided that henceforth they should not concern themselves with the ducal *promissione* or its contents. The only exception involved conspiracies, like that of Doge Falier, the traditional responsibility of the council. This new rule was henceforth to be read to members twice a year, "for the information of everyone." It passed 31 to 1 with 4 abstentions. But then a question arose whether or not they should announce their decision to the Great Council. The heads and ducal councilors, with the exception of Domenico Diedo, wanted it published but without the self-accusatory prologue; Diedo did not want any part of the bill published in the Great Council. His proposal carried the day with 23 votes; 13 voted for the other measure.[207] At this point apparently many of the legislators did not want to add fuel to the fire of discontent in the Great Council by having the Ten publicly acknowledge that it had overstepped its authority.

The second measure observed that over the past twelve or thirteen years the heads of the Ten had enlarged their jurisdiction by issuing decisions, commissions, and letters without authorization from the entire council. Noting that not even the ducal councilors could issue such rulings unless three of them were in agreement on the matter, that the heads of the Ten had even less authority to do so than they did, and that the dignity of the Signoria was being diminished as petitioners clamored to have audiences with the heads of the Ten, the Ten and *zonta* ruled by a vote of 32 to 4 that henceforth the heads could not issue such papers and rulings without authorization from the council and then only in matters that were within the province of the Ten. The only exception was for some "important case," namely a state emergency, but even then the heads were required first to consult with the Signoria and to bring the matter to the full Council of Ten as soon as possible thereafter.[208] Both this measure and the previous one carried heavy penalties for their violation.

What is clear from these decisions is that noble sentiment backed by popular opinion blamed the Council of Ten and most especially its heads for what had happened to Jacopo and his father. It is likely that they blamed Jacopo Loredan in particular. One can discern as the background to these measures the Foscari party's explanation of the doge's deposition, namely that he was a victim of persecution by his enemies; and one can understand action being taken on the basis of that explanation. But the third measure is in many ways the most interesting of the three for it was clearly designed to tamp those same flames of factional conflict within the patriciate. Observing that it was essential "by all possible means" to maintain "our united and peaceful State in its united and peaceful regimen" and to obviate even the smallest "division or scandal" which could bring about "ruin and desolation," the Ten noted that in the past ten years the council had begun to issue certain penalties which deprived kinsmen of their right to sit as judges in cases; in its previous ninety-five years this eventuality had not arisen, even for crimes deserving death. The Ten voted 34 to 2 that henceforth they could not issue sentences depriving "offspring or relatives" of the condemned either of offices or their judicial rights. In approving this measure the Ten noted that it was not proper to deny members of the nobility the privileges that their "noble origins and liberty and the laws of the city of Venice" conferred upon them, nor was it right for anyone to bear the blame for something that was not his own fault. But two exceptions were allowed. One involved treason, in which case the Ten could act as they saw fit. The other concerned cases in which the Ten judged the character of the condemned and "of their sons" to be of sufficient danger that they could be deprived of these rights. But even then the penalty was to extend only to the fathers and sons and not beyond them. The Ten had ruled in 1453, as the first of the two epigrams at the beginning of this chapter indicates, that a father should not suffer for the wrongs of his son. They made that ruling in the case of a man whose son had aided the enemy. Now they retreated partially from that principle at least when father and son shared a similar character. No member of the Ten can possibly have considered these exceptions without thinking of the recent cases of Jacopo and his father. And so even here when the issue was the unity of the ruling class, members of the Ten and its *zonta* vacillated in their assessment of the Foscari.[209]

Even with these efforts at self-reform, the issues raised by Foscari's deposition about the role and place of the Ten in Venetian governance would not go away. Ten years later, in September 1468, the Great Council intervened by reiterating the traditional competencies of the Council of Ten, namely treason and conspiracies against the state, sodomy, and supervision of the *scuole*, but otherwise prohibiting the Ten from expanding its jurisdiction, especially warning the heads to observe those limits. The bill passed by a vote of 450 to 166 with 110 abstentions. This vote shows evidence yet again of the deep division between the smaller and more powerful group of nobles and the bulk of poorer nobles who hoped to maintain the authority of the Great Council and other bodies.[210]

Although the laws of 1458 and 1468 constituted major reforms, they by no means resolved the issue of executive authority in the Venetian Republic. It would persist as the demands of international politics continued to push in the direction of concentrating power in an ever narrower circle of men. In response to that pressure, several of Foscari's successors in the dogeship would continue to pursue the alternative route that Foscari himself had pioneered in the 1440s, a route toward an ever more princely dogeship, one heavily imbued with Roman imperial associations. This trend would reach its apogee in the brothers Marco and Agostino Barbarigo who, as noted above, served consecutive terms as doge in 1485–86 and 1486–1501. Their program found architectural expression in a triumphal stairway, later dubbed the Scala dei Giganti, which completed the reworking of the Ducal Palace entry system inaugurated by Foscari with the Porta della Carta (fig. 35).[211]

In the aftermath of Foscari's deposition and death, the government sought to find a new equilibrium among the various councils and a balance between them and the doge. Foscari's heirs had a different project to pursue: they wanted to memorialize the doge and in so doing to restore the family's tarnished reputation, thus preparing the way for future generations, especially the doge's grandsons, to assume leadership positions in the Republic. These tasks fell to two persons in particular, the doge's brother Marco and widow Marina, both of whom Foscari had named as his executors. But since Marco was involved in the more overtly political side of affairs and had his own sons' futures to consider, a good deal of this effort devolved to the former dogaressa.

By far the most important element in this program of commemoration involved the design and construction of Foscari's tomb. During the course of the fourteenth and fifteenth centuries, ducal tombs had become increasingly elaborate ensembles of sculpture, mosaic, and painting which presented not only the attributes of the deceased but also their visions of the polity and the place of Venice in God's scheme for the world. The selection of a burial site was particularly significant, especially as Venice's great Dominican church, Santi Giovanni e Paolo, was rapidly becoming the preferred choice of doges – so much so that it has often been described as a ducal mausoleum and compared with other royal burial sites such as Saint-Denis and Westminster Abbey.

In his will, Foscari did not designate a burial site. As discussed in chapter 2, he might originally have hoped to be buried in the Chapel of the Madonna in San Marco. If so, he would have broken the strong tradition against ducal burials in the basilica. A San Marco burial certainly would have been in keeping with his efforts to exalt the dogeship. But if that was Foscari's intention, it came to naught; and he apparently shifted his focus instead to the church of the Frari. The Frari had many things to recommend it. First and foremost it was dedicated to the Virgin, specifically to the Virgin's assumption into heaven. By choosing the Frari, Foscari could continue his Marian devotion.[212] In addition, it was a church of the Franciscan order – the order known for its commitment to the poor *and* his patron saint was Saint Francis. Finally, the Frari was located not far from Foscari's native parish and close to Cà Foscari; and at least one of his sons, Domenico, was buried there.[213] If, as seems less likely, the choice of location was not Foscari's but a task that fell to Marco and Marina, then their selection of the Frari rather than San Zanipolo needs to be read in light of the deposition and as an effort on their part to distance the doge from the government which had deposed him.

The tomb itself occupies the right-hand wall of the church's chancel (plate 10); that of Doge Niccolò Tron, who died in 1473, fills the opposite wall. Titian's great *Assumption of the Virgin*, completed in 1518, hangs between them. Foscari's monument is an example of a wall-hung tomb that has been augmented with a canopy or tent of honor and by a rich architectural setting, itself surrounded by a poorly preserved fresco painted to imitate a leather wall-hanging. Engaged Corinthian columns, resting on pedestals, rise from the floor. They are topped with warrior figures who lean on shields adorned with the Foscari coat of arms and who simultaneously pull back the curtains of the canopy to reveal the sarcophagus and effigy of the doge. Above the canopy are roundels with the Foscari arms, crowned by the ducal *corno*, against a shell background, with sunburst rays framing the roundels. Behind the warriors rise pilasters capped with Corinthian capitals which terminate in an elaborate cornice with paterae and putti. This is surmounted in turn by a curved Gothic gable adorned with leafy foliage and a finial. Flanking the gable are the figures of the Annunciation while a figure of Christ in a radiant mandorla accompanied by a small figure fills its center.

The sarcophagus below is adorned with five figures: on the left side Saint Francis; on the right Saint Mark; and on the front the theological virtues (from left to right), Charity, Faith, and Hope (fig. 36). Topping the sarcophagus is a sculpted bier on which rests the effigy of Foscari. He is shown in full regalia including the ermine cape, the skullcap, the ducal *corno*, the *manto*, slippers, and gloves. By his side is a sheathed sword (fig. 37). The recumbent doge is attended by the cardinal virtues: Fortitude and Temperance at his feet; Prudence and Justice at his head. In front of the bier are four putti holding roundels with the Foscari arms. Below the tomb is the epitaph in Roman capitals and on the base of the columns is a dedicatory inscription.[214]

The contract for the tomb is lost. Therefore many questions about its construction remain unanswered. Various dates have been set forth by art historians: some date it to the 1460s while others put it as late as the 1480s. The earlier date seems more likely. Also in dispute is the tomb's sculptor: Antonio and Paolo Bregno, Antonio Rizzo, and Niccolò di Giovanni Fiorentino have all been put forward as possibilities.[215] But while its attribution and dating remain points of contention, the meaning of the tomb is more readily discernible. The bottom half of the structure celebrates the character of Foscari as man and doge. Here the virtues that accompanied him on the Porta della Carta (now joined by Faith and Hope) return to keep vigil over his body. The cardinal virtues engage in a kind of *sacra conversazione* recalling his worldly achievements, as do the *all'antica* warriors, holding shields, an innovation of the Foscari tomb.[216] His personal patron, Saint Francis, and the city's patron, Saint Mark, likewise pay him honor and guard his corpse. The cornice marks the transition from the earthly to the heavenly realms in "an upward moving narrative program."[217] The Annunciation group recalls the good news of the Incarnation that finds its fulfillment in the Christ figure. But it also alludes to Venice itself and its legendary founding on the feast of the Annunciation. The sculptural group presents an admixture of personal, religious, and civic meanings. If, as Anne Markham Schulz argues, the Christ is meant to depict the ascending Christ, then it is unique in Italian funerary monuments. Tombs normally depict the resurrected Christ. Schulz has argued that, as the ascending Christ, the figure must be read in light of Foscari's deposition. According to her, "the *Ascending Christ* implies that, as doge, Foscari was directly responsible to Christ and not to the Venetian *Signoria*."[218]

Certainly, the tomb should be viewed in the context of Foscari's deposition, but Schulz's interpretation of the ascending Christ seems unlikely for it would go against the family's goal which was reintegration rather than further alienation from the inner circles of power. While it may be true that Christ was originally to be accompanied by two small angels, as Schulz argues, the fact is that only one is there now – and, as can be seen from Marco Sebastiano Giampiccoli's drawing of 1777 (fig. 38), has been for centuries. Even at close range the wings are difficult to discern, and from the ground they are nearly impossible to make out. It is more likely that the program was modified so that the figure is meant to represent, as most have interpreted it, the soul of the deceased and that viewers are to understand it to mean that Foscari, as a virtuous ruler, has been received in glory. Indeed, near the end of his eulogy to Foscari, Giustinian proclaimed "He is not here, he is shining in heaven."[219] The words are reminiscent of those spoken to the three Maries on Easter morning. The tomb presents then a kind of Christianized resurrection of Foscari, the doge's personal virtues leading to his salvation and the city's glory. And certainly Giustinian's words find sculptural expression in the Foscari arms in roundels with a sunburst surround; he *is* shining in heaven.

On a plaque below the sarcophagus is the epitaph (fig. 39):

ACCIPITE CIVES FRANCISCI FOSCARI VESTRI DUCIS IMAGINEM / INGENIO MEMORIA ELOQUENTIA AD HAEC IUSTICIA / FORTITUDINE ANIMI CONSILIO SI NIHIL AMPLIUS CERTE / SUMMORUM PRINCIPUM GLORIAM AEMULARI CONTENDI / PIETATI ERGA PATRIAM MEAE SATISFECI NUNQUAM MAXIMA / BELLA PRO VESTRA SALUTE ET DIGNITATE TERRA MARIQUE PER / ANNOS PLUSQUAM XXX GESSI SUMMA FOELICITATE CONFECI / LABANTEM SUFFULSI ITALIAE LIBERTATEM TURBATORES QUIETIS / ARMIS COMPESCUI BRIXIAM BERGOMUM RAVENAM CREMAM / IMPERIO ADIUNXI VESTRO OMNIBUS ORNAMENTIS PATRIAM / AUXI PACE VOBIS PARTA ITALIA IN TRANQUILLUM FOEDERE / REDACTA POST TOT LABORES EXHAUSTOS AETATIS ANNO LXXXIIII / DUCATUS IIII SUPRA XXX SALUTISQUE MCCCCLVII KLENDIS [*sic*] / NOVEMBRIBUS AD AETERNAM REQUIEM COMMIGRAVI VOS / IUSTICIAM ET CONCORDIAM QUO SEMPITERNUM HOC SIT / IMPERIUM CONSERVATE.

(Accept, citizens, the likeness of Francesco Foscari your doge; if nothing more, I strove to rival in our day with skill, eloquence, justice, strength of spirit, and sure purpose, the glory of the greatest princes; I never exhausted my piety toward the fatherland; for thirty years I conducted great wars on land and sea for your well-being and dignity and brought them to a happy conclusion; I supported the wavering freedom of Italy; I fought with arms the agitators of quiet; I added to your empire Brescia, Bergamo, Ravenna, and Crema; I enriched the fatherland with all ornaments; with Italy restored to peace in a tranquil league; after such exhausting labors, at the age of eighty-four, having reigned thirty and four years I passed on to eternal rest; You [citizens] conserve the peace and concord that they may be eternal in this empire.)

The epitaph reiterates the principal themes of Giustinian's funeral oration. Indeed it is generally attributed to him. It is as if Foscari were addressing his subjects a final time, proclaiming how he added Brescia, Bergamo, Ravenna, and Crema to Venice's "empire," while at the same time preserving the *libertas Italiae*. With his work complete, his soul has migrated (just as can be observed at the pinnacle of the monument) to its eternal rest. The epitaph contains only one oblique reference to the deposition, namely Foscari's injunction that those who read it work to preserve the city in justice and concord, qualities little on display during his final days in office. When compared with the epitaphs on Steno's and Mocenigo's tombs, it indicates that under Foscari Venice had fully accepted its imperial destiny while simultaneously presenting itself as the defender of Italian liberty.

The entire monument rests on columns, on the bases of which is the dedicatory inscription, which reads: (left base) "FRANCISCO / AVO / DIVO DVCI / FRANCISCO / GERMANO / PIENTISSIMO (right base) NICOLAVS / IACOBI / MONVMENTVM / HOC / MAGNIFICE / POSVIT" (For saintly grand-father doge Francesco, Niccolò son of Jacopo with his most pious brother Francesco erected this magnificent monument) (figs. 40 and 41). The inscription commemorates the grandsons' joint financial patronage of the tomb in their capacity as Foscari's universal heirs.[220] Despite the inscription, several pieces of evidence suggest that the real force behind the tomb was either the former dogaressa, the boys' grandmother Marina, or their uncle Marco. First, at the time of Foscari's death,

Francesco and Niccolò were much too young to make such important decisions as the location and the design of their grandfather's final resting place. The dates of their registration for the noble lottery, the Balla d'Oro, reveal that Francesco was fifteen and Niccolò ten when Foscari died.[221] Second, other evidence indicates that Marina and Marco took the lead in administering the estate as they were required to do since the boys were under twenty. In February 1458, for example, they returned to the procurators of San Marco a jeweled brooch or clasp that Foscari had apparently borrowed from their office after leaving 800 ducats as a guarantee of its return. A note recording the transaction indicates that the grandson Francesco returned the brooch accompanied by his uncle Marco.[222] Third, it is known from still other evidence that Marina was extremely interested in protecting these boys, who represented the living legacy of both her husband and their son. In June 1461 she petitioned the Collegio asking that the chancery notary Cristoforo di Pozzo be granted permission to accompany Niccolò, described as an adolescent (Francesco must have been deceased by this time), out of the city on account of plague.[223] All of this points to the two primary executors, especially perhaps Marina, as the force behind the tomb.

Armed with this knowledge, it is useful to take another look at the monument. And what that informed look reveals is that the tomb, like the funeral oration, is a subtle memorial not only to the doge, but to the house of Foscari and particularly to Francesco's direct male descendants. One of the most striking features of the tomb is the deployment of the Foscari arms as a decorative device. It appears no fewer than six times on the sculptural program. According to Debra Pincus, the foremost expert on ducal tombs, this was "the first Renaissance tomb to make the coat of arms a monumental component of the tomb program."[224] The dedicatory inscription, which commemorates the boys' financial contribution as residual heirs of the estate, becomes a subtle way to invoke in Venice the name of their father Jacopo who was buried in Crete. Three generations of the Foscari family are thus memorialized by the tomb, and Jacopo is returned in spirit if not in body to Venice to await the only tribunal that matters, that before the creator at the Last Judgement.

It is likely that Giustinian's funeral oration was so successful in pleasing both the family and the state that it served as the inspiration for the tomb. Like the oration, the tomb erases time by looking not only back to the glories of Foscari's reign recalled in the inscription, but also forward, to the heavenly reward awaiting the doge, as well as to the future of the lineage. The tomb was designed to rehabilitate the reputation of the doge and to open the way for future generations of the family to assume distinguished positions. Foscari's grandson Niccolò indeed went on to have a successful career, including several important ambassadorial missions and even a stint on the Council of Ten.[225] His sons, one of whom he named Jacopo, had even more distinguished lives, although no Foscari ever again attained the dogeship.[226] In addition, Cà Foscari became one of the most celebrated palaces in the Renaissance city. In 1574 the Senate selected it as the most appropriate setting to lodge Henry III, King of Poland, when he stopped in Venice during his journey to be crowned King of France.[227]

Unfortunately little is known about Marina in the years following the deposition beyond the details mentioned above. On 28 July 1458 she filed official notice with the *giudici del proprio*, the judges with jurisdiction over dowries, that she intended to reclaim her dowry, but there is no record of when the repayment was made.[228] Marina wrote her last will and testament in March 1473 and died some time before November that year. Only a portion of her last will and testament has come to light through the records of the *giudici del esaminador* who had jurisdiction over contracts involving real estate. She named as her executors her aunt Cristina Barbarigo, her nephew Bartolomeo Barbarigo, her daughters Paola, wife of Girolamo Michiel, and the unmarried Maria, as well as her grandson Niccolò. She bequeathed some properties to Cristina Barbarigo and to Cristina's son and divided the balance of her estate between Cristina Barbarigo and her own daughters Paola and Maria. The extant part of the will provides no clues to charitable bequests that she may have made, nor does it indicate where she wished to be buried.[229]

But Foscari's tomb became, as she and Marco had intended it, a focus of Foscari family pride and observance. Niccolò created an endowment in order that Mass could be said daily at the high altar in the doge's honor.[230] In addition, several members of the family chose to be buried close to the tomb. In her will dated 1511, for example, Niccolò's widow Caterina asked to be interred at the Frari "in our tomb of the house of Foscari."[231] Most likely this common tomb, a crypt, was located in the pavement immediately in front of Foscari's monument, as was the case with the Tron tomb immediately opposite.[232] Perhaps Marina's bones lie anonymously there as well. In any case, the tomb achieved its double function of memorializing the doge and rehabilitating the Foscari name.

Francesco Foscari was certainly one of the most complicated and complex figures of fifteenth-century Italy, a place and time overflowing with extraordinary personalities. As doge, he had the fortune (or perhaps the misfortune) to rule at a time when major changes were taking place not only in Venice, but throughout Italy and the wider Mediterranean world. In attempting to assess his dogeship, it is useful to look at the corrections made to the ducal *promissione* following his deposition for they provide valuable clues to what his contemporaries saw as his short-comings as well as evidence of what they wanted in his successors. Several of the changes seem to reflect the disquiet that Foscari's physical infirmity provoked. According to the revised oath of office, the new doge had to promise to attend all meetings of the Great Council and of the Senate, as well as of the Forty whenever the state attorneys were presenting an important case to them, and to hold weekly audiences to hear the petitions of foreigners. In addition, once a month he was to admonish the various judges to administer justice fairly and without prejudice. One revision reflects concern with Foscari's aggrandizement of ducal power, specifically with his ability to communicate with foreign princes as equals. The Great Council approved the correctors' recom-mendation that the clause forbidding the doge from opening letters from popes or emperors without his councilors present be extended to include letters from all foreign "princes, lords, and communes." And another correction appears to have grown out of Jacopo's case. It forbade the dogaressa, as well as ducal sons, grandsons, and daughters-in-law, from accepting any gifts except food when traveling outside Venice and even then for no more than one day. The correctors revoked the doge's immunity from taxes and other imposts, while at the same time affirm-ing Foscari's elevation of the ceremonial dignity of the ducal office by requiring the new doge to wear silk garments whenever he appeared in public, "for the dignity and honor of the dogeship." From now on as well the dogaressa was to dress in a *manto* whenever she appeared outside the palace. These changes to the ducal *promissione* reflect the ambiva-lence that many Venetians felt toward Foscari and the direction in which he took the dogeship.[233]

Foscari's policy successes are recorded in his epitaph and in his contemporaries' assessments of his reign. These included a significant expansion of the Venetian domain, especially on the terraferma, and a heroic defense of Venetian interests in the eastern Mediterranean.[234] These actions, together with Foscari's steady elaboration of Venice's image as the new Rome, helped the Republic to maintain, unlike many of the smaller states of the Italian peninsula, its place as a major player in European power politics until the middle of the sixteenth century; thereafter it could no longer compete with the nascent nation-states France, England, and Spain. Of course, these successes carried with them huge costs in manpower and money, the brunt of which was borne by the towns of the terraferma and by Venice's subjects both on the terraferma and overseas. They came at a huge personal price to Foscari as well.

Foscari the man is much more difficult to know and hence to assess. Dolfin, Giustinian, and others of the time used the traditional vocabulary of the virtues to describe him. To them he displayed the cardinal virtues, including prudence, justice, fortitude, and temperance, and the theological ones (faith, hope, and charity) as well as other qualities such as constancy and patience.[235] But such descriptions were commonplaces of Renaissance rhetoric and were used to describe all rulers, even those in whom these qualities were conspicuously lacking. Many, including Aeneas Silvius Piccolomini, noted Foscari's gift for eloquence. Archbishop Antoninus of Florence observed that he ruled with "great prudence" and "affability" (*affabilitate*). The latter term is perhaps best understood to mean his "courtesy." Bernardo Giustinian described Foscari as having a "strong" (*vehemens*) nature, while Pierantonio Paltroni, chancery official and advisor to Federigo da Montefeltro, the Duke of Urbino, characterized him as the "most dignified (*dignissimo*) prince that there ever was in that place [Venice] and a man of great genius (*ingegno*) and of the greatest prudence and eloquence."[236] If the historian Robert Finlay is right that the normally slow-moving Venetian *cursus honorum* tended to weed out men who were brash, favoring instead those who were given to compromise and deliberation, then it may well be that Foscari's precocity in politics set him apart from his contemporaries; there was no opportunity for years of service in minor offices and lesser councils to work their solvent effect and smooth out the rough edges of his personality.[237] No doubt this made him a target of those who were envious of his power.

From the evidence of his actions it is clear that Foscari had extraordinary strengths, including a daunting intelligence, a prodigious knowledge of the government and the intricacies of its procedures, an amazing skill with language in an age that valued eloquence, a sincere and deeply felt sense of piety, and a genuine empathy for the less fortunate which fit uneasily with a strong sense of class distinction. His great weakness was his inability (or refusal) to rein in his relatives and the perception, justified or not, that he was reluctant to make them pay for their misdeeds. In the end Foscari was caught between his public responsibilities as *Pater Patriae* and his personal loyalties as *paterfamilias*. That dilemma guaranteed that Foscari would live on as one of the most contested and controversial figures in the history of the Republic, enjoying an after life accorded few other figures from the Venetian past.

6

Remembering Foscari
1457–2007

> " 'Tis perhaps as true as most Inscriptions upon tombs, and
> yet no less A fable."
>
> Lord Byron, *The Two Foscari*[1]

Even in death, Foscari has remained a controversial and contested
subject. While the Venetian Republic persisted, he continued to figure
in debates over ducal authority and the direction of foreign policy, as
well as in formulations of the mythic and anti-mythic visions of the
polity. The events of his reign also played a role in the later evolution
of Venetian society, particularly in the consolidation of an aristocratic
identity and ethos emphasizing family honor and solidarity. With the fall
of the Republic to Napoleon in 1797 and the subsequent periods of
Austrian domination and Italian independence, Foscari assumed new significance as a tragic hero and as the perceived victim of an oppressive
government. And although in the late twentieth century and into the
twenty-first his image has begun to fade, he remains always lurking in
the background, ready to enter into new controversies such as those
regarding the centralization of power and the "failed" nature of the
modern Italian state. Since his death, not only his descendants, but poets,

playwrights, composers, historians, and painters have all laid claim to him, molding and shaping his image, creating not one or even (playing on the title of Byron's drama) two Foscari, but many – each of whom speaks to the concerns and interests of a particular time and place.[2]

Foscari's deposition and subsequent efforts by the Great Council to bridle the power of the Council of Ten did not resolve the particular questions raised by his reign regarding the nature of ducal or executive authority in Venice's governmental system. Indeed during the late fifteenth century there was a pronounced trend toward even greater glorification of the ducal office, as mentioned above, a process that began with Foscari and culminated in the consecutive dogeships of Marco Barbarigo (1485–86) and his brother Agostino (1486–1501). Agostino in particular pushed the limits of republican tolerance for princely gestures by requiring that those he received in audience genuflect and kiss his hand. He also constructed the elaborate staircase now known as the Scala dei Giganti as a new entry into the Ducal Palace, replete with his portrait and arms and allusions to a new "Augustan" age. (fig. 35). This serves as a compelling terminus for the Via Triumphalis which begins with Foscari's Porta della Carta.[3]

In addition, by the last quarter of the fifteenth century the policy decisions initiated during Foscari's reign began to reap their often bitter rewards. Although Venice continued to claim, as Giustinian had done in his funeral oration for the doge, that the Republic's conquest of the terraferma represented nothing more than an effort to safeguard its own liberty and that of the rest of Italy, its actions seemed to belie those avowals. Increasingly, Venice came to be perceived as the aggressor intent on subjugating as much of Italy as possible. The War of Ferrara (1482–84), in which Venice tried unsuccessfully to seize its southern neighbor, helped to solidify this image, as did the Republic's diplomatic and strategic machinations following the French invasions of Italy in 1494 and 1498. The climax came when the powers of Europe allied against the Venetians in the League of Cambrai and delivered them a humiliating defeat at Agnadello in 1509. In the space of a few short days Venice's terraferma dominion disintegrated as city after city threw off the yoke of Venetian rule. Although in time Venice recovered virtually all it had lost, the Treaty of Bologna in 1530 marked the Republic's decline to second-rank power status.[4]

As Frederic Lane observed, "If Venice had had Italy only to think about, she might indeed have proved strong enough to upset completely the Italian balance of power."[5] But the Republic had important interests and assets in the eastern Mediterranean as well, and these proved especially vulnerable to on-going pressure from the Ottoman Turks. After a sixteen-year war Venice signed a treaty in 1479, surrendering Negroponte and other Aegean islands to the Turks and giving up the Albanian town of Scutari. A renewed Turkish offensive in 1499 led to raids into Friuli and to the eventual loss of Modon and Coron as well as other Venetian outposts in Greece and Albania. Venice's resources proved incapable of protecting both its terraferma and overseas interests.[6]

Not surprisingly commentators and theorists looked to Foscari's reign for the origins of these foreign and domestic policy controversies. The military debacles briefly outlined above led many to ask when and how Venice had gone wrong. They found the answers in Foscari's dogate and in the fateful decision to press ahead with territorial expansion into Lombardy, that is, in the supposed debate between Doge Mocenigo and Procurator Foscari. As observed in chapter 1, Mocenigo's speeches are largely fabrications, elaborations of a nascent debate which undoubtedly took place, but which did not center on the two main figures. Yet as time passed and the consequences of the decision to intervene more actively on the terraferma became apparent, those whose economic, family, or career interests in the eastern Mediterranean suffered setbacks embellished and repeated the speeches, copying them into chronicles and other tracts, thereby creating a genealogy and precedent for their position.[7]

The diarist and businessman Girolamo Priuli, who was an eyewitness to the calamitous years around 1500, provides a good example. Priuli was a firm believer in what Lane called the "seaward-looking" position, which might also be termed the Mocenigan position.[8] Reacting in 1502 both to recent losses to the Turks and to the Portuguese importation of Indian spices, he wrote: "The city of Venice found itself in great distress for fear of losing the maritime dominion, whence came the benefit and honor of the Venetian state, for the fame and glory of Venice proceeded and came from its voyages and the reputation of the sea."[9] In addition, Priuli feared that the pleasures and luxuries of the mainland had made the Venetians soft.[10] All this seemed to confirm what now appeared to be prophetic words on Mocenigo's part. And of course the culprit, if only implicitly, was Foscari and his policy of terraferma conquest. The solution, according to Priuli, was a return to Venice's founding values and a rigorous life. As he put it, "If the Venetian rulers wish to keep their Italian possessions they will have to learn the military art."[11]

Priuli was not alone in expressing such sentiments. Domenico Morosini, who is considered more fully below, similarly saw the roots of corruption in Foscari's policy of terraferma expansion. In his opinion, the only well-run republic was one of modest dimensions.[12] Sanudo too viewed with disfavor the choice of the land over the sea. As Franco Gaeta observes, "the presence of the famous speeches of Tommaso Mocenigo against the 'politics of the terraferma' should be enough to understand from what point of view Sanudo reconstructed the most recent Venetian history."[13] Not surprisingly, Andrea Mocenigo, a descendant of Doge Tommaso, who in 1525 published a detailed account of the War of the League of Cambrai, the *Bellum Cameracense*, expressed similar views. He described the Cambrai debacle as a direct consequence of policies that Foscari had initiated and that his ancestor had judged to be "ruinous."[14] By contrast, the defenders of Foscari, or at the very least those who felt it was their job to defend Venetian actions during these difficult years, argued, as Giustinian had done in the funeral oration, that Venice's (and hence Foscari's) actions were inspired by the desire to promote liberty not only for Venice but for all of Italy.[15]

Another aspect of the Venetian response to these years of crisis, at least on the part of those in the "seaward-looking" party, was to attribute the blame to Foscari personally, to tie it to his character. Increasingly Venice's numerous enemies labeled the Republic as displaying unbridled ambition, as aiming toward the *imperio d'Italia*.[16] One means of defusing this claim was to find its origins not in policy decisions but in Foscari's personality. In essence, if Venice was being labeled the aggressor by the other powers, it was not Venice's fault but Foscari's. This formulation comes across most clearly in Sanudo, not only in Mocenigo's speeches, but also in Sanudo's account of Foscari's term as procurator. According to Sanudo, Foscari had "his eye on the dogeship" – it was his great ambition and impatience that led him to orchestrate the procuratorial vacancy by having Giovanni Barbo declared incompetent. Sanudo also claims that once in office Foscari used the procuratorship's resources to smooth the way for his election to the dogeship. It was no wonder then that Venice was led astray – it was led by an ambitious and over-reaching politician. Even the emphasis on Foscari's youth contributed to this view. While works such as Giustinian's funeral oration take Foscari's prodigious progress up the *cursus honorum* to be a sign of great ability and perhaps even of divine approbation, it could be read by less favorable eyes as yet another symptom of the doge's ambition, especially at a time when theorists such as Domenico Morosini were accusing the young of recklessness and placing the state at risk.[17] Again, the antidote for many writers such as Priuli was to emphasize what they perceived to be traditional Venetian values.[18] Other legends casting Foscari in an unfavorable light, including the accusation that he had had Pietro Loredan poisoned and that he survived in his old age on human breast milk, began to accrue to him as well.[19]

An ambitious doge not only threatened to lead Venice into international crises but also jeopardized the internal equilibrium of the Republic. And in the on-going debate over the role and place of the doge, Foscari continued to play a substantial part. One of the most important theorists of Venetian governance during the final decades of the fifteenth century was Domenico Morosini, who in 1497 began composing a treatise entitled *De bene instituta re publica*, a distillation of his ideas on the ideal republic and the need for reform in Venice.[20] Morosini, who observed Agostino Barbarigo's reign at close range, feared what would happen if an ambitious doge allied himself with the youthful malcontents who tended to dominate the Great Council. As a counterweight to such a threat, he advocated adding new checks on ducal authority and placing power firmly in the hands of elders, that is, in a Senate whose members were elected for life.[21]

Gaetano Cozzi has argued that Morosini had not only Barbarigo but also Foscari firmly in mind when he fashioned his recommendations concerning the dogeship. Following Barbarigo's death in 1501, the government created a new board known as the *Tre inquisitori sopra il doge defunto* (the three inquisitors regarding the deceased doge) whose job it was to conduct a judicial inquiry into the deceased doge's conduct and if necessary to fine his estate for violations of the *promissione*. It was clearly an effort to put the brakes on further ducal aggrandizement. But Morosini advocated going even further. He suggested that a sitting doge's conduct be examined every five years and that he be forced to abdicate if found to be corrupt.[22] According to Cozzi, the recollection of Foscari's reign led Morosini to pen this proposed reform.[23]

But circumstances as much as anything reversed the trend toward greater ducal authority. Ducal power had grown in step with Venice's empire. From 1500 on, with Venice in retreat on both land and sea, it became increasingly difficult for doges to press claims for more power. Although they were not mere figureheads (a popular saying of the period described them as "little more than tavern signs"), the future for them, as for Venice itself, lay not so much in the wielding of real power, but in the careful manipulation of "images of power."[24] With Venice's decline to second-rank status came a corresponding rise in ducal imagery and pomp and in the mythologizing of the state itself, a trend that Foscari certainly had a hand in originating.

Although with time the opposing views of Foscari's deposition lost their immediate political import, especially with regard to ducal power, the two views persisted, taking on new significance. They became, in fact, fundamental components of the mythic and anti-mythic views of the Venetian government.[25]

Some apologists for the Venetian regime and formulators of the sixteenth-century version of the myth of Venice such as Marc'Antonio Coccio Sabellico argued that Venice's actions in Italy represented a defense of republican liberty. In his *Rerum venetarum libri*, Sabellico helped formulate two of the essential components of the myth: Venice's claim to autonomy as a sovereign state and celebration of its remarkable durability.[26] Yet for proponents of the myth, Foscari's deposition and subsequent death presented a number of difficulties, revealing either the Republic's essential fragility (if one believed that Foscari aspired to princely power) or its cruelty (if one accepted that it persecuted an aged man who had long served the Republic well). Accordingly, those who wished to portray Venice and its institutions in a sympathetic and idealized light either attributed Foscari's deposition to incapacity brought on by old age or ignored the event entirely. For instance, in his account Sabellico effectively glosses over the controversy surrounding Foscari's final year in office. There is no mention of the Jacopo affair, and the author simply states that because Foscari was no longer able to carry out his duties, Pasquale Malipiero succeeded him (*surrogatus est*).[27] Two later proponents of the myth present similar views. In his treatise *Delle cose notabeli della città di Venezia*, published under the name Girolamo Bardi, Francesco Sansovino states that Foscari was dismissed from the dogeship "on account of his impotence." And Fulgenzio Manfredi in his *Dodici tavole*, a broadsheet, says only that Foscari was deposed, "on account of his advanced age."[28] Many Venetians apologists were unwilling to air their dirty linen in public, to expose to scrutiny some of the Republic's less than savory episodes.

Another adherent of the mythic view of Venice, Giovanni Battista Egnazio, followed a different tack. His *De exemplis illustrium virorum venetae civitatis atque aliarum gentium*, published in 1554, uses personages from history to explore institutions and aspects of the Venetian character.[29] There are, for example, chapters on everything from miracles to poverty, happiness to perfidy. The work comprises nine books with a total of eighty-three chapters. Foscari serves as an exemplum in seventeen of the chapters, Jacopo in three. In the chapter entitled "De venetorum institutis" Egnazio explains that Foscari was removed from office on account of old age, although he acknowledges that envy and other motives played a role as well.[30] Among the virtues Foscari exhibited were, according to Egnazio, fortitude in the prosecution of war, and patience and constancy in the face of tribulations.[31] The author holds up Foscari and his brother Marco as models of fraternal piety and the dogaressa Marina as the epitome of wifely loyalty. Egnazio was perhaps the first to report that when the government decided to give Foscari a ducal funeral, Marina refused to relinquish the body but was compelled in the end to do so.[32] Unlike Sabellico, Egnazio does not shy away from the details of Jacopo's life but uses them to illuminate instead how the doge's sense of duty and responsibility to the law allowed him to stifle his paternal feelings.[33]

In one sense, it could be argued that Egnazio stripped Foscari's reign of its political immediacy and refashioned it into a moralizing tale. In essence, he transformed figures from the Venetian past such as Foscari into ancient Roman statesmen or Christian saints, into embodiments of particular virtues or, in the case of Marino Falier, vices. But in another sense Egnazio's *De exemplis illustrium virorum venetae civitatis* is a highly political work – a commentary on the character of the men (and women) who created this ideal republic, and a prescription for its continuation.

So too are the writings of Paolo Paruta, including his *Discorsi politici sopra diversi fatti illustri e memorabili di principi e di repubbliche antiche e moderne*, published in 1599.[34] In this work Paruta refutes Machiavelli's claims that ancient Rome surpassed Venice as the exemplary govern-ment.[35] Although he concedes that Rome enjoyed a greater dominion, he also notes that it did not endure and that Roman civic life was marked by internal strife. The Venetian state, by contrast, is "rather modest" in size, but tranquil in the "union and concord of its citizens."[36] As part of his effort to secure Venice's status in a much-changed world by portraying it as perfect and immobile, Paruta seeks to lay to rest, once and for all, the opposition between the land and sea policies. According to his formulation, maritime capability grows in direct rela-tion to land power. Thus Venice was able to put to sea a really sub-stantial fleet only after it had acquired its terraferma dominion. This success was thanks to Foscari, whom Paruta describes as a "prince of singular prudence," one who recognized that the path to maritime greatness lay on the mainland. Even so, the Venetians came late to this policy and thus encountered obstacles which prevented them from achieving even "greater empire."[37] But in recompense, they had created a perfect republic.

At the same time that Egnazio, Paruta, and others were casting Venice in a positive light, fashioning it into the exemplary Republic, another group of writers and commentators were beginning to look at it much more critically, seeing its government not as something to be admired and imitated, but rather feared and despised. They were creating what has come to be known as the anti-myth of Venice. The anti-myth, like the myth itself, had venerable origins, traceable some contend to Gio-vanni Conversino da Ravenna in the late fourteenth century. Certainly, Venetian policies in the years leading up to the War of the League of Cambrai added fuel to anti-Venetian fires. Luigi da Porto, a nobleman from Vicenza, questioned Venice's claim to be the defender of Italian liberty, arguing instead that, at least with regard to its subject cities, the *dominante* was tyrannical and corrupt. Machiavelli was a particularly harsh critic of the Serenissima, accusing it of ambition and insolence while grudgingly acknowledging its durability.[38]

But it was in the later sixteenth century and beyond and especially outside Italy that the anti-myth took firmest hold. Instead of praising Venice for its stability and longevity, writers criticized it for its lack of freedom, its oppression, and even terror. The anonymously published *Squitinio della libertà veneta* (1612) questioned Venetian claims to inde-pendence and viewed the *Serrata* as a coup against democracy.[39] One of the images that emerged most strongly in anti-mythic discourse was of a government entertaining secret denunciations, torturing the accused, and executing the condemned.[40] Even Egnazio's positive Venetian virtues could become incriminating evidence of the Venetians' inability to resist a corrupt system, as when, for example, the Frenchman Abraham Nicolas Amelot de la Houssaye said of the Venetians, they "know how to obey."[41]

Naturally Foscari's reign easily fit such formulations and those wishing to portray Venice in a negative light found plenty of material even in works that celebrated the Republic, especially in the seventeenth and eighteenth centuries, when the history of Foscari and the Loredans received a thorough elaboration. A good example is Alessandro Maria Vianoli's *Historia veneta*, published in 1680–84. According to this account, for years the Loredans secretly cultivated their hatred of Foscari; a spurned marriage offer and other vexations are supposed to have fueled the animosity between the families. Vianoli further recounts how Foscari claimed that he would not truly be doge as long as Loredan was alive. Jacopo Loredan then took advantage of the doge's incapacity in the wake of his son's troubles to seek his revenge for the injuries to his own father, which had been recorded not only in the family's account books but also in his heart.[42]

The elaboration of Foscari's deposition as the final working out of a long-standing vendetta on the part of the Loredans served more than just anti-mythic political purposes. In a curious way, like the actual waging of vendetta, the telling and retelling of the story of Pietro Loredan's grudge against Foscari and Jacopo Loredan's settling of the account served to strengthen noble family solidarity and reinforce aristocratic values at a time when admission to the Venetian nobility was up for sale and the ruling class had lost much of its cohesion.[43] In his brief lives of the doges, entitled *Fasti ducales* (1696), Giovanni Palazzi traced the origins of the rivalry between the two families to a spurned marriage offer. In this account Foscari sought to reconcile the two families by offering his daughter to the second-born son of Loredan, but the offer was rejected.[44] While several historians credit this version of events, it is strikingly similar to that which the Florentines used to explain the origins of factionalism in their city, namely Buondelmonte de' Buondelmonti's repudiation of his bethrothed. The purpose of such "narrative fantasies" (as Trevor Dean calls vendetta accounts) was not political but social, namely to instill in noblemen, especially members of distinguished houses, the obligation to defend and protect their family honor.[45] The anonymous author of one eighteenth-century compilation of acts regarding the Council of Ten stated that he had seen in the home of Andrea Querini of Santa Maria Formosa a Loredan descendant's claim to have set eyes on Jacopo Loredan's original account book, the one in which he cancelled the debt owed his father and uncle. The author observed that "powerful men hold it a terrible wrong to forget injuries and not to avenge them," although in his own view he added that the pursuit of private wrongs should not interfere with the public welfare.[46]

The revenge narrative proved especially problematic for Foscari family members. They could have chosen to emphasize it and to cast their ancestors as the victims of Loredan's intractability and the Ten's severity; it was after all this version of events which they accepted as accurate. But it would have been humiliating to do so, especially as it would have placed them in the awkward position of not having avenged in turn the wrong done to the doge and Jacopo. Consequently they adopted the same tactic that they had first used in relation to the tomb, namely they chose to celebrate Foscari's dogeship and to ignore the deposition completely. An eighteenth-century list of family portraits and their accompanying inscriptions that were on display at La Malcontenta, the family's Palladian villa on the River Brenta, indicates that the Foscari assembled a portrait gallery of distinguished ancestors, "a continuum of outstanding men."[47] In an effort to establish the family's ancient Venetian pedigree, they included the portrait of a certain Giorgio Foscari described as a tribune in the year 804. The next portrait was of the doge's great-grandfather Giovanni, the first count. The doge's portrait was accompanied by a lengthy inscription which described his accomplishments in international affairs and claimed that his departure from office was a "renunciation" (renuntiatio) of the dogeship.[48] This carefully chosen word obfuscated what had really occurred and created the impression that the doge's action was voluntary. The gallery also included a portrait of Jacopo. The inscription below his portrait stated merely that he was the son of the doge and a "knight" (eques). No mention was made of his crimes, exile, or fate. But it is significant that again, as in the inscription on the base of the doge's tomb, members of the family chose to include and commemorate Jacopo. The final portrait mentioned in the list is that of a Sebastiano Foscari who died in 1739.[49]

Another eighteenth-century member of the family, Alvise III, chose to associate himself with his illustrious ancestor in a most unusual way. In his will dated 1714 he asked that after his death, his heart be placed in the doge's sarcophagus.[50] A plaque with a relief of a flaming heart placed in the wall below the tomb chest commemorates his decision (fig. 36). Nothing better epitomizes the family's reverence and celebration of their famous forebear.

The democratic impulses unleashed by the French Revolution ultimately snuffed out the Republic. It was Napoleon Bonaparte's threat to take the city by force which finally brought the independent Venetian state to an end as the Great Council presided over by Doge Ludovico Manin voted itself out of existence on 12 May 1797. Among the tasks the new revolutionary government set for itself were not only the eradication of the old system of government and the creation of a new regime but also the reinvention of Venetian time and space. Accomplishing the latter goal required reappropriation of Venice's ritual space, the Piazza San Marco, and a return to the "democratic" times before the aristocratic usurpation of power accomplished in the *Serrata*.[51] But before the Piazza could be reclaimed, it had to be purified. And so, in a wave of iconoclastic fervor, statues of the lion of Saint Mark along with other symbols of the Venetian old regime were pulled from monuments and destroyed. One of the most conspicuous of these was the doge and lion group on the Porta della Carta. The statues of both Foscari and the lion were destroyed (fig. 42). But nobleman Ascanio da Molin did manage to salvage the doge's sculpted head (fig. 21).[52] As noted above, the frieze on Cà Foscari was also defaced. Francesco Foscari, who had in the past and would again in the future assume many subtle meanings, became in this revolutionary instant a symbol of the entire Venetian governmental enterprise.

Venice's cession to Austria in 1815 by the Congress of Vienna created a new political and social situation that is considered more fully below, but the repercussions of the French Revolution continued to be felt as the anti-myth gained even wider circulation, thanks in large part to a seminal work by Pierre Antoine Noël Daru, the *Histoire de la République de Venise*, first published in 1819.[53] Daru, a nobleman and functionary under Napoleon, paints a devastating picture of the defunct Republic and its institutions. This comes across most clearly in his exposition of

Foscari's reign. Daru relates Jacopo's three trials before what he calls the "terrible tribunal," namely the Council of Ten.[54] He also argues that the man who intercepted Jacopo's letter to Sforza was not a mere merchant but a spy sent by the Ten to watch over him.[55] When describing the doge's stoicism in his last colloquy with his son, he observes that tyranny can produce "cruel circumspection."[56] He then goes on to recount the history of the doge's deposition, including the story of the account book, framing it as a vendetta on the part of Jacopo Loredan.[57]

In attempting to explain why the doge's deposition provoked no reaction, Daru attributes it to the fear generated by a newly created institution, the three state inquisitors. Basing his evidence on a manuscript entitled the *Statuti, leggi et ordini delli signori inquisitori di stato*, Daru contends that this "monstrous tribunal" originated in 1454, not in the mid-sixteenth century as earlier thought, and that it became the predominant instititution, more powerful even than the Ten. Summarizing its authority, Daru writes, "its duration was permanent, its members temporary, their power absolute, their forms arbitrary, their executions secret, except when they judged it appropriate, and their acts, left no trace, not even that of widespread blood."[58] In other words, the perversion of the Venetian system began during Foscari's reign, and he and his son were ironically enough its first victims. Daru's much vaunted source, the capitulary of the state inquisitors, turned out to be a fake: the office of the state inquisitors was not formed until the sixteenth century, but Daru had created an indelible image of Venetian terror, a view shared by other historians such as J. C. L. Sismonde de Sismondi.[59] And soon this view was to acquire even wider dissemination, not through the ponderous tomes of historians but rather through the works of poets, playwrights, composers, and painters.

Foscari's image and reputation underwent its most profound and lasting transformation in the early nineteeth century. This was due in large measure to the publication in 1821 of Lord Byron's play *The Two Foscari*.[60] Byron arrived in Venice in 1816, remaining there for several years. During that time he became well acquainted with both the city and its history.[61] In his play Byron transposed the story of Foscari from civic history into historical drama, imbuing the events of Foscari's reign not only with atmospherics appealing to Romantic sensibilities, but also with a critique of oppressive government that exuded the air of early nineteenth-century liberalism. By emphasizing such universal themes as the conflict between the law and familial interests, and the powerlessness of the individual before the state, Byron endowed the story of Foscari and Jacopo, the two Foscari of his title, with a significance that made use of but went well beyond the particulars of Venetian historical and political discourse. Byron's own reputation ensured that the play earned a wide readership; and as a result, the Foscari story became grist for artists working in a variety of media.[62]

Byron's five-act play, subtitled *An Historical Tragedy*, includes six major characters, as well as various supernumeraries. The six named characters (two of them English variants) are: Francis Foscari, Jacopo Foscari, James Loredano, Marco Memmo, an unnamed Barbarigo described simply as "a Senator," and Marina, wife of Jacopo. (In reality, Jacopo's wife was named Lucrezia; his mother Marina.) Act One takes place in a hall in the Ducal Palace and opens with Loredano and Barbarigo discussing Jacopo's recent torture by the Ten. Both men are united in their "hate of the ambitious Foscari" (180), although Loredano is the more implacable of the two, for while Barbarigo feels some pity for Jacopo's physical suffering, he thinks that Loredano pursues his "hereditary hate too far" (180). Loredano believes that the doge poisoned his father and uncle and plans to pursue his vendetta until the debt which he has recorded in his "books of commerce" (183) is repaid. Soon Jacopo is led in by guards on his way to another round of torture; but he is first taken by his sympathetic escorts to a window where he gazes upon his beloved Venice. Jacopo recalls such youthful pleasures as competing in regattas and swimming in the billowing waters of the lagoon. For him a third exile from his native city would be worse than death itself.

Memmo and another senator enter as Jacopo is led off for further interrogation and torture. The two admit that even as nobles they know little of the Ten's secret ways. When the senator asks Memmo if he aspires to the dogeship, he replies that he would "rather be an unit / Of an united and imperial 'Ten' / Than shine a lonely, though a gilded cipher" (191). Marina appears and protests the injustice of the torture which takes place offstage. Her "Despair defies even despotism" as she accuses the Ten of trampling "on all human feelings, all / Ties which bind man to man" (196). At this point, Memmo and the senator provide crucial background information, noting that Jacopo confessed that he had written to the Duke of Milan, but did so only in order to return home, that the accusation of bribery against him remains unproven, and that Jacopo's culpability for the death of Ermolao Donà (Donato) has been vindicated by Erizzo's confession. The act concludes as Barbarigo and Loredano return from the torture chamber. The interrogation had ended when Marina rashly burst into the proceedings. Loredano remains unmoved despite Jacopo's suffering, telling Barbarigo that he will wage war, "With all their house, till theirs or mine are nothing" (201).

Act Two takes place in another hall in the Ducal Palace. The scene opens as the aged doge with the help of a senator puts his signature to what is clearly the Peace of Lodi, a treaty which brings an end to "Thirty-four years of nearly ceaseless warfare" (204). Foscari makes a brief speech in which he recounts the accomplishments of his reign, noting that he found Venice "queen of ocean, and I leave her / Lady of Lombardy" (204). When the senator asks the doge when he will be ready for the next meeting of the Ten, Foscari responds whenever they wish since he is "the state's servant" (206). The senator leaves and Marina enters, informing the doge that the Ten have revoked their permission for her to accompany Jacopo to his prison cell. In the ensuing dialogue Marina launches into a diatribe against the Ten, describing them as

> The old human fiends,
> With one foot in the grave, with dim eyes, strange
> To tears save drops of dotage, with long white
> And scanty hairs, and shaking hands, and heads
> As palsied as their hearts are hard, they council,
> Cabal, and put men's lives out, as if life
> Were no more than the feelings long extinguish'd
> In their accursed bosoms. (210)

In reply to her rebukes, Foscari answers, "I have other duties than a father's" (214) and recalls his earlier efforts to abdicate. Loredano arrives and tells Foscari that Jacopo is to be exiled yet again. Over Marina's protests, both Loredano and the doge reply that the state's commandments must be obeyed. This prompts Marina into another tirade:

> Keep
> Those maxims for your mass of scared mechanics,
> Your merchants, your Dalmatian and Greek slaves,
> Your tributaries, your dumb citizens,

And mask'd nobility, your sbirri, and
Your spies, your galley and your other slaves,
To whom your midnight carryings off and drownings,
Your dungeons next the palace roofs, or under
The water's level; your mysterious meetings,
And unknown dooms, and sudden executions,
Your "Bridge of Sighs," your strangling chamber, and
Your torturing instruments, have made ye seem
The beings of another and worse world! (221)

Marina curses a city whose "laws / Would stifle Nature's" and accuses Foscari of being "more a Doge than father," to which Foscari replies, "I am more citizen than either" (226–27). But in the end his fatherly instincts break through his dutiful façade as he agrees to visit Jacopo before he sails.

Act Three takes place in a dank and dark prison within the walls of the Ducal Palace. Marina arrives to tell Jacopo the news that he is to be exiled again to Crete. He greets the news with despair saying, "I could endure my dungeon, for 'twas Venice" (235). Marina answers, "This love of thine / For an ungrateful and tyrannic soil / Is passion, and not patriotism" (236). Loredano himself comes to the prison to announce the sentence or perhaps, as Marina surmises, to gloat; and then the doge makes his way to the prison cell. Jacopo learns that he must leave behind his children for they are, as Loredano says, "the state's" (250). The act ends as Marina and Jacopo prepare to bid farewell to their children and sail for Crete.

In Act Four Loredano reveals to Barbarigo his plan that "This day / Shall be the last of the old Doge's reign" (255). Memmo and the senator reappear as they have been selected to be among the *zonta* of twenty-five to assist in the ducal deposition. The doge, Jacopo, and Marina enter; and Foscari commands his son, in a paraphrase of the Dolfin chronicle to "Go and obey our country's will" (261). When an officer and guards come to escort Marina and Jacopo to the ship, Jacopo grows suddenly faint and dies. Marina does not want to relinquish the body, and finally Foscari breaks down, throwing himself weeping on his son's dead body. Marina asks him, "Where is now / The stoic of the state?" (268). Exiting from the meeting of the Ten, Loredano and Barbarigo come upon the pathetic scene. Implacable, Loredano tells Foscari that he is summoned

by the Ten in an hour's time. After Foscari and Marina leave, Barbarigo
chides Loredano again for his hard-heartedness. But Loredano replies:

> The feelings
> Of private passion may not interrupt
> The public benefit; and what the state
> Decides to-day must not give way before
> To-morrow for a natural accident. (272)

He further explains his motivation, saying that the ghosts of his dead
father and uncle haunt his bed and urge him to vengeance.

The doge's apartment is the setting for the fifth and final act of the
tragedy. It opens as the Signoria and head of the Ten solicit Foscari's
resignation; but he refuses, and they depart. Marina and Foscari also leave
to visit Jacopo's corpse, and when Loredano and Barbarigo return, Barbarigo again assails Loredano for his single-mindedness. When Barbarigo
speaks some incautious words against Loredano's *zonta*, Loredano warns
him to watch his tongue, to which Barbarigo replies: "Oh! they'll hear
as much one day / From louder tongues than mine; they have gone
beyond / Even their exorbitance of power: and when / This happens
in the most contemn'd and abject / States, stung humanity will rise to
check it" (287).

Foscari now returns, as does the deputation from the Ten. When the
head of the Ten reads the degree of deposition, Foscari relents with the
words "I obey" (289). Foscari removes the ducal *corno* and ring, noting,
in a reference to Ascension Day rituals, that "The Adriatic's free to wed
another" (290). As Foscari prepares to exit the palace, he is told that
Pasquale Malipiero has already been elected as his successor. To which
Foscari responds:

> Earth and Heaven!
> Ye will reverberate this peal; and I
> Live to hear this! – the first doge who e'er heard
> Such sound for his successor! Happier he,
> My attainted predecessor, stern Faliero –
> This insult at the least was spared him. (292)

Foscari refuses to depart the palace by a private staircase, choosing to
exit instead by "the Giants' Stairs" (293). When the head of the Ten
protests that this act will bestir the people, Foscari counters: "The people!

– There's no people, you well know it . . . / There is a *populace*, perhaps, whose looks / May shame you; but they dare not groan nor curse you, / Save with their hearts and eyes" (294). Suddenly the bells of San Marco toll, announcing the election of Malipiero; and at the sound, Foscari expires. All of the assembled, except Loredano, immediately agree to accord him a ducal funeral. But Marina protests the plan, saying: "I have heard of murderers, who have interr'd / Their victims; but ne'er heard, until this hour, / Of so much splendour in hypocrisy / O'er those they slew" (299–300). At the same time, Loredan is seen writing something in his account book. When Barbarigo asks him what he records, Loredano, pointing to the corpse, responds, "That *he* has paid me!" (300).

While most critics agree that Byron's *The Two Foscari* is not particularly successful as a piece of theater (in fact Byron may not have intended for it to be performed on stage),[63] the drama operates on several levels simultaneously, not only locating the tale of Foscari and Jacopo securely within the discourse concerning the nature of Venetian republicanism, but also creating a universal tale of political oppression and the sacrifice of individuals to the state. As mentioned, Byron subtitled the play *An Historical Tragedy*, even writing to a friend that it was "rigidly historical."[64] To emphasize that fact, the appendix to the first printed edition included excerpts from Daru's *Histoire de la République de Venise* and Sismondi's *Histoire des Républiques Italiens du Moyen Age*, explicating the events of Foscari's reign. The inclusion of the excerpts served in crucial ways to authenticate Byron's claim to historicity. It also signaled the author's acceptance of Daru's and Sismondi's strongly anti-mythic views of Venice.[65]

It is the terror of the regime that comes through most strongly in the drama. The Ten work in secret, trampling on human rights, and using torture to achieve their ends. Even Memmo and the unnamed senator fear its power, and at the same time aspire to join its ranks. The third act, set in the prison, is the most terrifying; for it is in this prison that Jacopo sees the wall scratchings of those who have come before him. Characters allude in the play to the fate of both Falier and Carmagnola. Yet everyone, with the exception of Marina, accepts the system as it is, even Foscari. Despite his brief breakdown at the end of Act Four, the doge remains, as Marina calls him, "the stoic of the state." The tragedy for Foscari is that his sense of duty forces him to sacrifice that which is most precious – his only surviving son – and in the end, to yield to the Ten's demand for his deposition.[66] The horror for the reader/audience is that Venice has created such automatons.

In spite of its anti-mythic tone and message, the play is also replete with references to the more positive and laudatory myth of Venice. Ironically, it is Jacopo who gives fullest voice to it. Despite all that has happened to him, Jacopo longs to remain in Venice, the city he loves – even if only as a prisoner. The recollections of his youth evoke a placid and serene city where noble oarsmen competed in regattas, "While the fair populace of crowding beauties, Plebeian as patrician, cheer'd us on" (186). Throughout the play, there are references to monuments (the Scala dei Giganti) and ceremonies (the marriage to the sea), which recollect a positive image of Venice's republican regime.

Despite its claims to historicity, the play is filled with inaccuracies, anachronisms, and tamperings with actual events, not all of which are attributable to Byron's sources. Byron was certainly aware of some of these; but he was determined that the play conform to the classical unities of time, place, and action. Therefore all of the events take place within the Ducal Palace and in the space of twenty-four hours, and both Foscari and Jacopo die in similar ways.[67] Why Byron substituted Marina for Lucrezia Contarini, Jacopo's real wife, is unclear. It may have been accidental; on the other hand, it afforded him a unitary voice of opposition and the opportunity to have Marina resist efforts by the government to claim both corpses. The many anachronisms indicate that Byron was more concerned with the universal aspects of the story than with historical accuracy. Perhaps it is for this reason that he includes allusions to the Bridge of Sighs and the Scala dei Giganti, neither of which existed in Foscari's time.

It was doubtless the universal themes and the romantic setting that appealed to nineteenth-century audiences. Despite its location in a specific place and time, *The Two Foscari* served as a vehicle to explore such ideas as freedom versus oppression, duty versus feeling, nature versus law, and youth versus age. While critics have suggested that Byron identified with Jacopo (Byron himself was effectively exiled from his native England), it is with the female character, Marina, that Byron's sympathies lie.[68] She is an Antigone-like figure, who resists the unfeeling legalism of the duty-bound old men who surround her. While her efforts are doomed to failure, the play foresees a future when, as Jacopo says, humanity will arise to check the power of tyrannical goverment. In his appendix to the play Byron responded to various charges against him: "Acts – acts on the part of government, and *not* writings against them, have caused the past convulsions [i.e. the French Revolution], and are tending to the future" (327). Byron, who was active in the Italian revolutionary movement known as the Carbonari, died at Missolonghi, fighting for Greek independence, just two and a half years after the publication of *The Two Foscari*.

Byron's *The Two Foscari* was widely read; and artists and composers in particular began to explore in a variety of media the subjects and themes first presented in the play.[69] Foscari's story became a favorite topic among those involved in the movement known as historical romanticism – one in which themes from Venetian history played a prominent part.[70] Byron also wrote a play entitled *Marino Faliero*, which cast that discredited doge as a freedom fighter.[71] That work inspired an opera of the same name by Gaetano Donizetti, first performed in Paris in 1835. However, it fell not to Donizetti, but the young Giuseppe Verdi to transform Foscari's story into an opera.

I Due Foscari was Verdi's sixth opera. In the winter and spring of 1844 he and his librettist Francesco Maria Piave were considering several new projects, including an opera entitled *Lorenzino de' Medici*. However, Verdi feared that that subject would run into difficulties with the Austrian censors and so encouraged Piave to work on the Foscari project as well in case they needed an alternative. Verdi wrote to Piave that he liked the topic and advised him to reduce Byron's five-act play to three acts, placing Jacopo's death at the end of Act Two.[72] By mid-May he had received a plot summary from Piave and wrote to him on the 14th, describing it as a "beautiful drama, very beautiful, most beautiful!" However, although he liked the characterization of Foscari and Marina, he found that of Jacopo too weak: he encouraged Piave to make Jacopo more "energetic" and to add "something robust in order to have a beautiful aria" in the scene following Jacopo's paean to Venice. He also asked Piave to revise the scenes between Marina and her servants. And although he found the second act "most touching" (*toccantissimo*), he now advised the librettist to move Jacopo's death to the beginning of Act Three. In addition he wanted that act to open with a chorus of men and women in the Piazzetta and to include a gondolier in the distant lagoon singing "a verse (*ottava*) of Tasso." He also urged Piave to keep the recitatives brief, especially those of Loredano and Bar-barigo.[73]

Verdi wrote again on 22 May after receiving Piave's revisions. He informed him that he had sent the plot summary to Rome for approval by the papal censors. He also suggested further changes to the libretto, encouraging Piave yet again to render Jacopo "more energetic." Among other things he wanted revisions to Jacopo's cavatina and a "gran Duetto" at the end of Act One between Foscari and Marina – one filled with "great feeling" and "beautiful poetry." He also asked if Piave could set the third act in the evening, "thus adding a sunset which is a beau-tiful thing."[74] In yet another missive, Verdi indicated that he was still worried about the opera's lack of drama, observing "that in the work of Byron there isn't that scenic grandiosity that is needed in works of music." He encouraged Piave to put his mind to it and to "come up with something that creates a little ruckus, especially in the first act."[75]

By the early summer Verdi was negotiating with the Venetian opera house La Fenice to premier *I due Foscari* during the 1844–45 Carnival season. The first performance of Verdi's *Ernani* had been given there on 9 March 1844 and the management of the opera house was anxious to have another Verdi opening. In July the composer wrote to Guglielmo Brenna, manager at La Fenice, informing him of the Foscari project as well as of another project based on the life of Catherine Howard. He wrote of *Foscari*, "It's a Venetian topic and should stir a lot of interest in Venice; besides it's full of passion and is very musical."[76] On 9 July Verdi wrote to Count Alvise Mocenigo, president of La Fenice's board, saying, "I lean toward *I due Foscari* because, even though it's a little less grandiose than *Caterina [Howard]*, the subject is more passionate, and it doesn't contain the odious characters of the other, and also because it's differ-ent in style from *Nabucadonasor* [*Nabucco*] and the *Lombardi* [*I Lombardi alla Prima Crociata*]."[77]

On 26 July Brenna sent a letter to Verdi, "On the express order of the President of Spectacles, Count Alvise Mocenigo." The letter informed Verdi that La Fenice was refusing both *Caterina Howard* and *I due Foscari*. The directors did not want to present the former because of its "excessive atrocity." The reasons given for the refusal of *Foscari* were even more extraordinary. Brenna wrote on behalf of Mocenigo, "as to the second, that is the two Foscari, [it is refused] because it takes a hard look at families still living in Venice, particularly the Loredans and Barbarigos, who would lament the odious image that it would present of their ancestors."[78] But not wanting to alienate Italy's most sought-after young composer, Brenna encouraged Verdi to present them with another project.

The Gran Teatro La Fenice was by far the most prestigious of the several theaters in Venice. The property of its boxholders, it was closely identified with the city's aristocracy, and the Mayor of Venice regularly attended the governing board's meetings *ex officio*.[79] What is clear is that nearly four hundred years later and even after the fall of the Republic, the events of Foscari's reign still threatened to disrupt the social world of the city's elite. While Mocenigo's stated reason for refusing the work was the offense the opera might cause the Loredans and Barbarigos, he was likely concerned with the reputation of his own family as well, for although no Mocenigo appears in the work, its presentation would call to mind for those who knew their history (as many nobles did) Doge Tommaso Mocenigo's deathbed speech. Thus the Mocenigos would be cast as early opponents of the heroic Foscari. In addition, there were Foscari descendants living in the city, so the play had the potential to create new social rifts. Mocenigo left unstated possible objections to the play on political grounds. Both Byron's play and Verdi's opera presented an unflattering view of aristocractic rule. Mocenigo might have feared such calls to freedom at a time when many Venetian aristocrats, himself included, were collaborating with their Austrian rulers. He was married to the daughter of Venice's Austrian governor.[80]

Rebuffed by La Fenice, Verdi offered *I due Foscari* to Antonio Lanari, the impresario of the Teatro Argentina in Rome. It passed without revision the pontifical censors; and during the summer Verdi and Piave worked sporadically on the opera. In October Verdi traveled to Rome to prepare for the opening. *I due Foscari* had its premiere in Rome on 3 November 1844. It was, in the words of Verdi, a "mezzo-fiasco," partly because the singers were out of tune and partly because expectations had been raised too high. Piave noted, however, that, "the music of *I due Foscari* is divine and I do not doubt that it will be appreciated more and more."[81]

Despite the problems on the opening night, the opera was performed throughout Italy in the succeeding months. The Roman premiere was followed by performances at Livorno and Trieste in December 1844, Florence in January 1845, Naples in February, and Parma on 24 March.

The opera had its Venetian opening on 30 March 1845, not at La Fenice, but at the less prestigious (and socially charged) Teatro San Benedetto, also known as Teatro Gallo. The Teatro Apollo restaged it in 1846, and *I due Foscari* was eventually put on at La Fenice in February 1847. It was restaged there during the Carnival season 1854–55.[82]

While the libretto for Verdi's opera is based on Byron's play, the two works are actually quite different, and not simply in the condensation from five acts to three. The opera opens with a chorus singing of the silence and mystery that enshroud Venice. As in Byron's play, Loredan's hatred and Jacopo's love of his native city are quickly established. The second scene takes place in the Foscari palace where (the correctly named) Lucrezia Contarini gets news from her friend Pisana that Jacopo is to be sent back into exile. The action moves again to the Ducal Palace where the chorus sings of Venice's impartial justice, and the doge privately struggles with Jacopo's fate while publicly remaining aloof. The act ends when Lucrezia convinces Foscari to visit Jacopo, and exclaims to the doge, "your tears Once more allow me to hope!" (9).

Act Two opens in the state prison where Jacopo, in a delirious state, sees spectres of earlier prisoners, including Carmagnola. Lucrezia arrives and tells Jacopo his fate. Foscari appears and reveals his deep love for his son, exclaiming "Here I am not the Doge" (13). But as he takes his leave, he informs them that when they see him again "it will be as Doge" (15). Loredan enters and announces that the Ten have forbidden Lucrezia to accompany Jacopo to Crete. The act ends in the Council Hall where Jacopo entrusts his weeping children to their grandfather.

The third and final act opens on a festive scene in the Piazzetta where at sunset (as Verdi requested of Piave), the people are making merry and singing of Venice, "Daughter, bride, mistress of the sea" (22). Loredan comments that to the people "it does not matter if a Foscari is Doge, or a Malipiero" (22). The festivities are interrupted as Jacopo is led to the ship that will take him into exile. In the next scene Barbarigo announces to the doge in his private apartment that Erizzo has confessed to Donato's murder. Foscari's elation is quickly dashed, however, when Lucrezia arrives with the news that Jacopo has died. The Ten then enter this unhappy scene and compel the doge to resign. As in Byron's play, the ringing of the bells of San Marco announces Malipiero's election. Foscari dies with the words "My son!" on his lips, while Loredan records the payment of his debt.

Like Byron, Piave was careful to establish the historicity of the events portrayed. To this end he included at the front of the libretto a two-page preface entitled "To the reader" in which he summarized the events of Foscari's reign, arguing that the conflict between Foscari and the Loredans dated to the time of the doge's election. He also cautioned his readers that he had had to take certain liberties with the story as befit this kind of work.[83] Freed of the need to observe the classical unities, he set the action both in the Ducal Palace and elsewhere and included more detailed descriptions of the sets than did Byron. He advised, for example, that Act One, Scene Seven be set in Cà Foscari in a room lined with portraits of various "Procurators, Senators, etc of the Foscari family" and that the Grand Canal and the old Rialto Bridge be visible through Gothic arches.[84]

Apart from these changes, however, what Piave and Verdi did was transform Byron's story into a personal or domestic tragedy. They chose to deemphasize the political elements of the story, both the rhetoric of mythic and anti-mythic Venice as well as the veiled calls to present-day revolutionary action. But in recompense, Piave rendered the doge a more interesting and complex figure. Whereas in Byron's play, one has very little sense of Foscari's inner torment, in Piave's libretto and Verdi's music it plays a major role, especially in the doge's third act aria, "Questa dunque è l'iniqua mercede," in which he rails, "This then is the iniquitous reward/You reserve for an aged warrior?/This then is the prize for the valor and faith/Which have protected and expanded the empire?"[85] Lucrezia too is shown as a fully three-dimensional figure. But Jacopo remains, as Verdi feared from the beginning, a weakly drawn character. And the cumulative critical judgement does not place the opera among Verdi's better works. Verdi himself summarized critical opinion when he wrote: "in subjects that are naturally sad, if one isn't careful, one ends up producing a funeral, as for example I Foscari, which have a tint, a color that is too uniform from beginning to end."[86] But at least in Verdi's hands, the doge had been transformed from a political symbol into a very particular kind of romantic hero.

In the nineteenth century a number of painters, inspired either by Byron's play, Verdi's opera, or both, set about to depict critical moments in the Foscari melodrama.[87] Many of the paintings seem to reproduce the stage sets, costumes, and actions that might have been used in various dramatic and lyric productions. They appear almost as tableaux, frozen at the moment when the curtain falls. The theatricality of these paintings is not surprising given the classicism that inspired both Byron's play and the history painters' craft. In addition, these painters moved in the same circles as costume and set designers, even on occasion undertaking those roles themselves.[88] In 1858 the painter Domenico Morelli produced *I due Foscari*, which depicted the doge, Lucrezia, and some servants carrying away the body of Jacopo. The painting became part of Verdi's personal collection.[89]

Certainly the best-known works of this kind were executed by the history painter Francesco Hayez. Born on the island of Murano in 1791 to a Venetian mother and a French father, the academically trained Hayez spent most of his career working in Milan. His major contribution to painting was the substitution of themes from Italian history for the classical and mythological subjects which previously had dominated the history painters' repertoire. His first great success came in 1820 with his painting *Pietro Rossi, Lord of Parma, Despoiled by the Scaligeri*, a scene derived from Sismondi's history. It was followed in 1821 by *Carmagnola Accompanied to his Death*, a painting inspired by Manzoni's play. Images such as these were fed by and in turn nurtured the nationalistic ferment at work in Italy at the time.[90]

Hayez painted various episodes of the Foscari story at many different points in his career, often reproducing the same subjects for different patrons. He painted several versions of *The Last Farewell of the Son of Doge Foscari to his Family*, a canvas he first exhibited in Milan in 1832. The version reproduced here, which dates from 1851–52 (fig. 43), was acquired by the poet Andrea Maffei.[91] It illustrates well Hayez's theatricality. The scene takes place on the sun-bathed loggia of the Ducal Palace. One glimpses in the distance through the mist of the lagoon the (anachronistically depicted) churches of San Giorgio Maggiore and the Zitelle. Also visible are the two columns of the Piazzetta. Doge Foscari and Dogaressa Marina occupy the central space, while between them one of their innocent granddaughters – her innocence highlighted by her white dress – appeals donor-like to her grandfather. To the left kneels a beseeching Jacopo, dressed in black and white, chained at the waist and attended by a sympathetic youth who clutches his hat to his breast. To the doge and dogaressa's immediate right stands a very subdued Lucrezia surrounded by three of her pathetic children. Her pose resembles that of a Madonna of Mercy. Finally to the far right stand three patricians. Loredan is the figure in red – the color of high office. But he is set apart. He occupies a different plane from the other principal figures. His position, gesture, and envelopment in shadow subtly call to mind depictions of Judas at the Last Supper. In the background, groups of patricians and noble adolescents seem oblivious to the scene taking place before them. The sunlight (which seems awkwardly to emanate from two different points) is critical for it catches the white clothing worn by the five central family members. What comes across is a domestic tragedy – one largely stripped of its political dimensions and only decipherable if one already knows the story.

Probably the best known of Hayez's works in the Foscari cycle is *Doge Francesco Foscari Deposed*, a scene he painted several times. A version of 1844 was commissioned by the Marchese Filippo Ala Ponzoni and is now housed at the Museo Brera, Milan (fig. 44).[92] The action is set inside the Ducal Palace in the private apartment of the doge. Visible through the loggia is one of the cupolas of San Marco and an elaborate Gothic gateway (which appears to stand on the site of the present-day Arco Foscari). The architrave over the doorway is inscribed "FRANCISCUS FOSCARI DUX VEN," while the rear wall is adorned with armour, a triptych with a kneeling donor doge, and a plaque with a lion of Saint Mark and three ducal coats of arms below it. To the left is a standard, a lantern, and a curtain, while the wall beyond seems to be covered with a fresco not dissimilar to the one surrounding the Foscari tomb. The aged doge sits just slightly off-center. His gesture indicates that he has just taken off the ducal *corno*, and his expression is desolate and disconsolate. To the far left sits the stunned dogaressa attended by a nurse. Her tense and contorted hands signal her inner turmoil and foretell the resistance that she will exhibit after her husband's death. In front of the table stands Lucrezia with her daughter. Foscari's two young grandsons hover by his throne, while to the right stand six nobles, including again the red-robed Loredan, who asserts himself with an imperious gesture. Two ladies-in-waiting, four men, and a single male with his head sharply turned to observe the doge (perhaps meant to indicate the repentant Barbarigo) occupy the background. But in spite of its subject matter, the painting seems, like Verdi's opera, to lack the requisite drama.

What Hayez displays in this work is an almost archaeological interest in his subject. He evidently made a concerted effort to furnish his painting with all the props necessary to secure the work within a Venetian ambience. Moreover, there are motives, figures, and techniques quoted from Venetian Renaissance masters. The young man in the background with his hand on his hip and dressed as a member of one of the *compagnie delle calze* is strongly reminiscent of Carpaccio's depictions of such young men, while the single man in the background near the balustrade evokes Titian's *Man with a Blue Sleeve* in the National Gallery, London. The drapery in the painting is Veronese-like in its luxury and rich green color. Fernando Mazzocca has even argued that in works such as these Hayez "resumed the 'narrative' tradition" of Cinquecento Venetian painting.[93] But in spite of their Byronic inspiration, the works have been stripped of their revolutionary political content. What they call to mind is an age of Venetian artistic rather than political florescence. The message is not threatening, so much so that Ferdinand I himself commissioned a cycle of Foscari paintings from Hayez. The painter Michelangelo Grigoletti placed himself in competition with Hayez when, in response to the Austrian emperor's request for the rendition of a historical subject, he produced his own version of the last farewell of Foscari and Jacopo.[94]

The engraver Giovanni Brizeghel in turn produced an engraving of Hayez's *Foscari Deposed* from which two hundred lithograph copies were made.[95] But this was not the only means by which Foscari's story achieved international fame. Foreign artists also took up the theme. The most famous example by far is Eugène Delacroix's *I due Foscari* of 1853, now housed at the Musée Condé, Chantilly (plate 11). Twenty-six years earlier Delacroix had drawn inspiration from Byron's *Marino Faliero* and painted his *Execution of Marino Faliero*, a canvas exhibited at the Paris Salon of 1827.[96]

Delacroix's *I due Foscari* contrasts sharply with the paintings by Hayez. Unlike the latter's works, which are presented frontally, Delacroix's composition is arranged diagonally: the steps and canopy of the ducal throne and the windows of the hall draw the viewer's eye from the figure of the doge, to Jacopo and finally into the dark recesses of the vast architectural space, thus emphasizing the narrative elements of the painting. To employ a modern metaphor, if Hayez's paintings resemble photographs, Delacroix's canvas calls to mind the cinema. In addition, whereas Hayez's paintings are highly polished, Delacroix's work exhibits much freer brushstrokes, reminiscent of Rubens and Titian. This too serves to highlight the emotional intensity of the scene.[97]

In Delacroix's *I due Foscari*, a tense and dejected Foscari sits with downcast eyes as a patrician functionary reads the sentence of banishment against the shirtless and Christ-like Jacopo who appears to swoon as the sentence is read. The figures surrounding Jacopo are arranged in such a way as to recall depictions of Christ's descent from the cross. The meaning is therefore clear; yet another innocent is being wrongly condemned; another individual is destroyed by the secular authorities whose power is symbolized by the "oppressive architecture."[98] Delacroix's painting stands somewhere between Byron's political commentary and Verdi's domestic tragedy. Except for the doge's robes and *corno*, there are few props or backdrops that allow the viewer to recognize this place as Venice or that make reference to Venetian political imagery, so that the painting lacks the distinctly Venetian elements of Hayez's canvases.

Yet decorative elements played an important role in many history paintings, serving as a kind of "antiquarian documentation."[99] Their authenticity was often the subject of lively and sometimes bitter debates. One of these involved the depiction of fourteenth- and fifteenth-century doges as bearded. Contemporary paintings such as the Bastiani portrait show that mid-fifteenth-century doges were clean shaven; beards came into fashion only at the end of the century. In 1874 a critic who compared Grigoletti's and Hayez's renderings of the last farewell of the doge and Jacopo found Grigoletti's work wanting, going so far as to suggest that he should not have competed with Hayez but chosen another subject instead. But he did praise Grigoletti for "rendering more exactly the costumes of the period" and for having "the courage to shave the beard of the doge."[100] And in 1840 a debate raged in the *Gazzetta privilegiata di Venezia* as to whether or not the singer playing Falier in a Venetian production of Donizetti's opera *Marino Faliero* should appear beardless.[101] This debate over historical accuracy was about to take a much more serious turn, however, as scholars began to exploit archival materials in an effort to uncover the past. Their efforts would result in the debunking of many of the romantic legends surrounding Foscari.

The quest for a new "scientific" history, with its accompanying mania for documentary or archival sources, began in the mid-nineteenth century. There was an eighteenth-century precursor, however, in the erudite nobleman Flaminio Corner, who published a life of Foscari in

1758, including a number of documentary sources.[102] The most famous advocate of this new approach was the German historian Leopold von Ranke. He himself made extensive use of Venetian sources, particularly ambassadorial *relazioni* (reports), and wrote three essays on Venetian history.[103] But the method found its most accomplished local practitioner in Samuele Romanin, who between 1853 and 1861 published his ten-volume *Storia documentata di Venezia*.[104] Drawing heavily on the records of the now defunct Republic, Romanin even appended transcriptions of relevant documents to each volume. The explosion of governmental record-keeping in the fifteenth century provided ample material for Romanin's corrective impulses. Indeed he wrote at the beginning of his fourth volume, "arriving now at the fifteenth century, the documents are in such abundance that the account [of the past] is drawn almost exclusively from them, and hence will present many things which are entirely new or in a new light and with views in fact different from those with which they were treated heretofore."[105]

On the basis of archival evidence, Romanin sought again and again to unmask the errors of previous historians. In his footnotes he repeatedly expresses exasperation with his predecessors. To cite only two examples: "one reads nothing in the historians regarding the particulars of this embassy"; and "Count Sagredo [. . .] without justification writes [. . .]."[106] He is unforgiving as well of fiction writers; he calls the "sorrowful farewell" between Carmagnola and his wife in Manzoni's play *Carmagnola* nothing but a "poetic invention."[107] But he reserves his harshest criticism for Sismondi and Daru, attacking Sismondi for his reflex criticism of Venice and Daru for his inventions.[108] Noting that the doge and other relations were indeed prohibited from participating in deliberations concerning Jacopo's fate, Romanin writes: "From this one sees how much faith one can place in the pathetic descriptions of Daru and even more so of Galibert, who arriving to complete the triad with Laugier and with Daru, pushes sentimentalism to the ultimate degree." He then adds, "I am sorry for the novelists (*romanzieri*), but the history of Venice has been turned too much into a novel and it is time to stop it."[109]

Romanin's criticism of Daru in turn reveals a great deal about his view of Foscari. In his opinion, the doge was not a bellicose leader intent on war, but instead a larger-than-life personality whom contemporaries, out of jealousy or envy, blamed for the troubles of the times.[110] Regarding the deposition, Romanin argues that it was not the product of a vendetta on the part of the Loredans. The historian concludes that Jacopo Loredan's action in consoling Foscari (apparently a later interpolation into the story of the deposition), "does not jibe at all with the idea of a vendetta for the death of his father and with that famous [phrase]: 'he has paid'."[111] As noted earlier, Romanin sees Loredan as another Cato, "rather than as a personal enemy of Foscari."[112] And his final assessment of Foscari's reign is positive; in his opinion it was "one of the most memorable in Venetian history," marked by "military glory, territorial acquisitions, fetes, and magnificence."[113] In hesitating to label Venice the aggressor and in discounting the idea of a vendetta, Romanin showed himself to be an apologist for the Venetian Republic, what might be termed a "neo-mythologizer." As a counter to Daru's depiction of Venice as rapacious and marked by vindictiveness, Romanin portrayed a city drawn reluctantly into war and ruled by law not emotions.[114]

Working at the same time as Romanin, another historian, Francesco Berlan, was pursuing a similar documentary course. Indeed at least twice in his footnotes, Romanin felt compelled to write that he had completed his own research before the publication of Berlan's studies, although he reluctantly conceded that Berlan had refuted "the inexactitudes of ancient and modern historians on this argument [i.e. the Jacopo case and the deposition]."[115] Like Romanin, Berlan set about correcting the errors of previous historians and others in his study *I due Foscari*, which he published in 1852.[116] As he noted, "on the faith of traditions and chronicles, prosators, poets, novelists and painters made paladins of innocence and virtue these two ancients [the doge and his son], crying out against the injustice of the Council of Ten, which deposed the first from the ducal throne in 1457 and condemned the second three times to exile." And although he acknowledged that Corner had consulted and even published some documents, he stated that "one or more documents cannot give but some information; only a series of ordered documents are conducive to drawing an informed judgement."[117]

With this approach in mind, Berlan undertook his study of the two Foscari, although he limited himself to an examination of Jacopo's trials and the doge's deposition. As noted above, after extensive research and a weighing of the evidence, he concluded that Jacopo was likely guilty of misconduct; and that if he was not "an infamous man," he certainly "was not a hero."[118] At the same time, Berlan argued that the doge was deposed as a result of incompetence brought on by old age, not of vendetta by the Loredans.[119] And because of its action, the Ten's power was quickly circumscribed. In order to substantiate his conclusions, Berlan included over ninety pages of documents taken from the records of the Ten, Senate, and Great Council.

Like Romanin, Berlan was an apologist for the Venetian regime and a strong Italian nationalist.[120] On the title page of the book, he identified himself as "Francesco Berlan Veneziano." Writing in the wake of the failed revolution of 1848, he saw it as his task to rescue Venice's past from the calumnies of its critics, especially members of what he termed the "French school."[121] In his view, the "envious and ignorant" were dragging through the mud "the venerable flag of San Marco, in order thus to affirm that even in its most splendid days it was all befouled." He believed that these corrected lessons of the past would serve a constructive purpose, namely to revive the memory of the medieval Italian communes, which were and remained "an Italian glory."[122] He was thus creating the genealogy for a new Italian state, one that would not deny its communal past.[123]

Of a piece with Berlan's and Romanin's intentions was the restoration of the Porta della Carta. A mid-century intervention included the renovation of several architectural elements, including parts of the pilasters. A much more thorough restoration was undertaken between 1879 and 1883. This culminated in 1885 with the placement on the monument of a new doge and lion group by the sculptor Luigi Ferrari. His commission required him to reproduce the original as closely as possible.[124]

During the nineteenth century members of the Foscari family continued to make efforts to link themselves to their illustrious past. For example, when Michelangelo Cappello and Giovanni Bernardi published information about Foscari's election from the records of the Great Council and from one of the chronicles in the Biblioteca Marciana, they dedicated the volume to Cesare Foscari on the occasion of his marriage to Elisabeta, daughter of Niccolò Barozzi.[125] Other documents relating to Foscari's reign were published to celebrate the marriage between Pietro Foscari and Elisabetta Widman-Rezzonico in 1897.[126] Also in the last years of the century Pietro Gradenigo, a Foscari relation, undertook a detailed although highly schematic history of the family. Gradenigo adopted a largely prosopographical or biographical approach and celebrated the family's accomplishments with, among other things, a tabu-lation of the offices held by family members.[127]

In spite of the new emphasis on documentary studies, some contin-ued to hold that Foscari was hounded out of office by members of the Loredan family intent on revenge. The leading proponent of this view at the end of the nineteenth century was Edoardo Vecchiato, whose short essay *I Foscari ed i Loredano* appeared in 1898. After giving a very abbre-viated account of Foscari's reign, including his territorial conquests, Vecchiato asks if there is any credible explanation for a successful doge's removal from office other than a personal vendetta on the part of his enemies, the Loredans. He answers his own question in the negative, even crediting the account book legend. But in Vecchiato's awkward hands, the anti-mythic version of the Foscari story is deprived of its venom. It is no longer a diatribe against a corrupt Venetian system, as it had been under Daru, but rather a gripping story of personal passions and family interests.[128] Furthermore, the weakness of Vecchiato's refuta-tion of Romanin seemed to augur the demise of the vendetta narrative. However, it still held sway with some historians working in a more popular vein, as, for example, in John Addington Symonds's *Renaissance in Italy: The Age of the Despots* (1888).[129]

At the beginning of the nineteenth century Lord Byron had brought Foscari's reign to the public by means of a theatrical melodrama. At the end of the century Alethea Wiel, the only female writer to concern herself with Foscari in an extended way, produced a book entitled *Two Doges of Venice*, which covers both Mocenigo's and Foscari's reigns.[130] It is based largely on the work of Romanin and Berlan, but incorporates Wiel's own reading of some of the primary sources, especially the Dolfin chronicle, which, as she points out, Berlan did not know.[131] The result is a judicious and highly readable assessment of Foscari's dogeship. Nothing better indicates the success of Romanin's efforts to de-romanticize the reign than a popular writer's decision that a balanced account would be as compelling for readers as a retelling of the old tales, although Wiel did concede that "we almost resent the colder though truer view of his life which must break through the veil our commiseration had woven around his fate and story."[132]

The conditions that had made the debate over Foscari's deposition such an important topic in the nineteenth century faded rapidly in the twentieth only to be replaced by new concerns. No longer were such issues as the stance of the individual before the state and notions of noble honor and family solidarity of such moment. They were superseded by twentieth-century concerns with the nature of executive authority and the perceived weakness of the Italian nation-state. And as was true of Venetian scholarship more generally, these topics occupied different segments of the scholarly community. The impact of Foscari's dogeship on Venetian republicanism interested primarily (though not exclusively) Anglophone historians while Italian scholars showed more interest in examining the nature of the regional state created during his reign. However in both categories the debates centered less on Foscari's fate (as had been the case in the nineteenth century) than on his and Venice's intentions.

For those interested in Venice's republican tradition, Foscari's reign represented a time of great vulnerability, when the city was in danger of succumbing to the power of one individual or family, as Florence did to the Medici. In this configuration of events Sanudo's portrayal of the doge took on new persuasive power. Thus Frederic Lane viewed Foscari as a "proud, imperious" politician who advocated an "adventuresome assertive policy" toward both east and west. Lane also characterized the doge as an "ambitious politician."[133] Hugh Trevor-Roper, who published a brief biographical essay on Foscari in 1965, also labeled him "ambitious," while in 1984 Michael Mallett described him as "formidable."[134] For many historians Foscari's dogeship represented a moment when Venice dangerously toyed with the lure of signorial rule. In 1970 David Chambers, for example, wrote of Foscari's "flamboyant princely style," a fashion which would continue until it reached its apogee in the reigns of the Barbarigo doges; Franz Babinger's publication of 1957 refers to him as the "last lofty personality" in a republic characterized by impersonal rule.[135] For some historians who lived through World War II and the Cold War, Foscari evoked if only faintly the spectre of republican regimes undermined by dictatorial rule.

Correspondingly, some of these same historians viewed the deposition as a necessarily corrective legal or constitutional measure designed to prevent possible ducal abuses of office. Giuseppe Maranini argued that Foscari was deposed "only on account of [his] old age" and inability to perform his duties and for reasons that were "objective and impersonal."[136] Trevor-Roper, who believed that the Loredans "mercilessly persecuted" Foscari, nevertheless interpreted the deposition as the final stage in the constitutional perfection of the Venetian Republic, since after him no doge aspired to be anything more than a figurehead.[137] And although not addressing Foscari specifically, the Franco-Italian historian Alberto Tenenti claimed that the actions of the Ten saved Venice from drastic changes of government and from "the transformation of its republican regime into a princely one."[138]

However this view of the deposition as a legal and hence commendable action did not prevent some of these same historians from also discerning less honorable personal motives behind it. Lane, for example, argued that when Milan checked Foscari's policy of territorial expansion and when the tax burden to support the war effort became unbearable, his rivals "took revenge."[139] The late twentieth-century movement known as the "new social history" actually strengthened this view: Robert Finlay, who examined the impact of kinship and patronage networks on Venetian politics, could thus argue that, although incompetence brought on by old age was the primary cause of Foscari's deposition, "the aims of a faction [the Loredans and their followers] coincided with those of the *Primi* as a whole."[140] And Elisabeth Crouzet-Pavan has characterized Foscari's removal from office as "an act reeking of a vendetta nourished by centuries of family hatreds."[141] Trevor-Roper was the only one, however, to revive the old revenge narrative wholesale and to argue that Foscari was the victim of the Loredans' "undying jealousy and hatred."[142] He did, however, as noted above, put forward the idea that the personal vendetta had a positive outcome, namely the restraint of ducal power. Finlay offered by contrast a much more subtle interpretation, suggesting that Foscari's removal from office, "far from signaling the end of ducal power [. . .] testifies to the continued authority resident in the dogeship and to the importance of maintaining an able and energetic individual in the key office of the government."[143] In his view, Foscari's reign was just one moment in an on-going debate about the nature of executive authority in the Venetian Republic, a view I share.

While Italian scholars of the twentieth century did not ignore these issues (in fact Trevor-Roper's opinion is suspiciously close to that of Roberto Cessi), many had a different set of research and political aims and looked to Foscari's reign as the crucial moment in the evolution of the territorial state, the precursor for good or ill of the Italian nation-state. Thus for Cessi the advance onto the terraferma was not a result of Foscari's personal ambition but the product of the "entire nation."[144] In Gaetano Cozzi's view, it makes no sense to debate the merits of the supposed Mocenigo and Foscari positions since "in reality, that which had the upper hand was an irresistible logic, the logic of the territorial state."[145] Consequently, while Andrea da Mosto could claim that Foscari was "a historical personage of the first order," and Giuseppe Gullino could argue that he was "the greatest doge" that Venice ever had, in the works of most late twentieth-century historians Foscari has been largely stripped of his agency, becoming merely the pointman for economic and geopolitical forces that were sweeping Venice and the rest of Italy along.[146] The contrast with the nineteenth century could not be greater: having been viewed first and foremost as an individual, Foscari has been transformed into a trend. One area of continuity between the centuries is the Foscari family's on-going effort to tie their identity to that of their ancestor. For example, since 1999 the family has supported the publication of three volumes of source materials concerning Foscari's reign in a series entitled "La Malcontenta."[147]

And in 2005 Giuseppe Gullino, one of the most distinguished historians of Venetian politics, presented his interpretation of the "saga of the Foscari." In his view, the fate of Jacopo and his father was the result of a fierce contest between two powerful family blocs: one made up of the Foscari and their allies and relations (the Donatos, Giustinians, Michiels, Veniers, and Vitturi), the other comprising the Loredans, Barbarigos, Duodos, Mocenigos, and another branch of the Donatos. According to his interpretation, Jacopo's foibles merely provided the pretext for the rival group to humble the Foscari party, which had profited greatly from Venice's terraferma expansion. While I share Gullino's view that the impact of terraferma expansion was central, I view the events of Foscari's reign less as a clash of particular families (excepting of course the rivalry with the Loredans) than as a contest that had an institutional and class basis, that is a contest between the Ten, Senate, and Great Council and the members of the patriciate they represented. However, I cannot credit Gullino's hypothesis that members of Foscari's own circle had Jacopo assassinated in Crete in order to silence him and to protect their mutual interests. It seems likely that historians of later periods will view this new conspiracy theory as the understandable product of an age which has become all too familiar with governmental cover-ups and lies.[148]

It is appropriate, in a study which understands images as occupying a central position in Foscari's politics, reign, and legacy, to include a few observations about the production of two films featuring the Foscari. In 1923 the director Mario Almirante made a silent film entitled *I due Foscari*; a second version was made in 1942 by the director Enrico Fulchignoni, assisted by Michelangelo Antonioni and starring Rossano Brazzi as Jacopo (fig. 45).[149]

Both films take considerable liberties with Foscari's reign, transforming events even more markedly than did Byron or Verdi. In the Almirante version, Jacopo's sworn enemy is a certain Ezio Contarini, who discovers that Jacopo has secretly returned from exile in order to see his wife Lucrezia. Contarini denounces Jacopo to the Council of Ten which, impervious to the pleas of both his wife and father, sentences him to death. And while Jacopo is escorted to the gallows, the Ten force his father to resign. In Fulchignoni's version, a vicious rivalry exists between the Foscari and the Faredanas [sic]. When Foscari is elected doge, his rival Faredana is so vexed that he dies of a heart attack, and his son vows revenge. He seeks that revenge by falsely accusing Jacopo of treason; Jacopo is imprisoned but escapes by jumping from his prison window and swimming under the Bridge of Sighs. Re-arrested, he is accused of murdering Donato Almarò [sic]. But during the trial, Jacopo succeeds in proving his innocence and revealing the actual perpetrators of the crime. A happy ending is thwarted, however, when the old doge dies before he is able to greet his exonerated son.

The writer Ugo Ojetti recorded his reactions to the Almirante filming, which took place in Piazza San Marco in October 1922. Noting that Byron had rendered the Foscari story in verse, Delacroix in paint, and Verdi in music, it was, according to Ojetti, inevitable that "the two unfortunates would end up with a slide onto film."[150] Ojetti described the scene in the piazza as the director of the film struggled to get the extras to stop smoking and watch the gallows, not him. But whenever he got the crowd quiet and in place, the horn of a vaporetto would sound or a flock of pigeons swoop in, upsetting the Quattrocento ambience. The set designer's efforts to hide the lamp-posts around the basilica led one native Venetian to exclaim, "Il ga mascarà anca San

Marco" (He's even masked San Marco). But the tourists were happy as they watched the actor playing Jacopo ascend the gallows. As Ojetti observed, "for foreigners Venice is all a theater, a marvelous and continuous stage set; and whether the Ducal Palace is stone or papier-maché matters little to them, so long as it is between the Riva and the Basilica, with those forms and those colors."[151] The point – and it is one with which Foscari himself might have agreed – is that images have power.

Over the centuries Foscari's image has been constantly reshaped and altered, rendering him at times a figure of unbridled ambition, at other times the victim of a relentless vendetta on the part of his enemies. These viewpoints have had the effect of obfuscating the institutional and political questions the Republic faced during his reign. By characterizing Foscari as ambitious, the Venetians (and subsequent historians) were in a sense able to lay the blame for Venice's aggressive foreign policy at his feet. Similarly, the vendetta narrative provided a convenient smokescreen capable of concealing the crisis of governance the Republic faced as it tried to meet the challenges of managing its terraferma dominion. This is not to say that Foscari did not have enemies out to destroy him. The Milanese ambassadorial reports show that he did. But despite the optimism expressed by Romanin and Berlan that documentary evidence would allow historians to discover what actually happened, it is now clear that even the official governmental records present highly partisan accounts. Yet those accounts were themselves fundamental components of the historical processes, shaping visions of the past and actions in the present.

The nineteenth-century Romantics who did so much to perpetuate Foscari's memory chose to depict his life as a tragedy. Tragic it certainly was, but not in the way in which they understood it. Instead it is possible to view Foscari as the sacrificial lamb offered up by the Venetian state to atone for its transformation from a city-state into a territorial state. That shift required institutional adjustments of all sorts and just as significantly cultural realignments as well. Unfortunately for Foscari, the most compelling cultural model for such a state was the Roman Empire, and this required a re-positioning of the doge as emperor. Yet this new imperial dogeship did not fit with Venice's republican traditions, and Foscari paid the price. Perhaps for this reason it is more accurate to characterize Foscari as the scapegoat for Venice's new imperial age.

At the same time, Foscari's tragedy was a personal one, brought on by the corruption of his kinsmen, particularly his son. Yet bound as he was by the imperatives of a strictly patrilineal society, Foscari allowed his regard for Jacopo at times to blind him to his duties as doge. It is easy to condemn Foscari for not having had the foresight to realize where their actions would lead them. But who does not fear judgement by the unforgiving standards of historical hindsight?

ABBREVIATIONS

b.	busta, buste	mv	*more veneto*
ch.	chapter		[Venetian calendar year]
ed., eds.	editor(s)	n., nn.	note(s)
fasc.	fascicle	pt.	part
fig., figs.	figure(s)	reg.	register(s)
fol., fols.	folio(s)	ser.	series

LIBRARIES AND ARCHIVES

Unless otherwise noted, all archival references are to the Archivio di Stato, Venice.

AAVa – Archivio Apostolico Vaticano
ASF – Archivio di Stato, Florence
ASM – Archivio di Stato, Milan
BAV – Biblioteca Apostolica Vaticana
BNM – Biblioteca Nazionale Marciana, Venice
BN Biblioteca Nazionale, Florence
MCC – Museo Civico Correr, Venice

ARCHIVAL SERIES, VENICE

AC – Avogaria di Comun
CI – Cancelleria Inferiore
DM – Consiglio dei Dieci, Deliberazioni Misti
MC – Maggior Consiglio, Deliberazioni
PSM – Procuratori di San Marco
SM – Senato, Deliberazioni Misti
SMar – Senato, Deliberazioni, Mar
SS – Senato, Deliberazioni Secreti
ST – Senato, Deliberazioni, Terra

FREQUENTLY CITED WORKS

DBI – Dizionario biografico degli italiani (Rome: Istituto della Enciclopedia Italiana, 1960–).
Dolfin – BNM, It. Cl.VII, 794 (8503): Zorzi (Giorgio) Dolfin, "Cronica."
Morosini – BNM, It. Cl. VII, 2048–49 (8332.1–2): Antonio Morosini, "Cronica" (continuous pagination).
Predelli – R. Predelli et al., *I libri commemoriali della Republica di Venezia: Regesti.* Monumenti storici pubblicati dalla R. deputazione veneta di storia patria. 1st ser., Documenti. 8 vols. Venice: Tipografia Visentini. 1876–1914. N.B. All references cited as Predelli are to the printed volumes by Predelli rather than to the volumes of the original books in the archives. Following the volume number is the page number as well as the number assigned to the act.
Romanin – Samuele Romanin, *Storia documentata di Venezia*, 3rd edition. 10 vols. Venice: Filippi Editore, 1972–75.
Thiriet – F. Thiriet, ed., *Régestes des délibérations du sénat de Venise concernant la Romanie.* 3 vols. Paris: Mouton, 1958–61. N.B. Following the volume number is the number of the act as assigned by Thiriet.

Since I have used microfilms of some of the Senate series photographed before the folios were renumbered, I have given in every case the date of the act as well as the folio number. Similarly for the series Archivio Sforzesco the numbering of the documents is in some instances illegible, contradictory, or non-existent. Therefore I have supplied the date of each letter.

NOTES

PREFACE

[1] Antoninus, 1913, 98.

[2] Byron, 1905, 129.

[3] Mathews, 1993, 11.

[4] Gleason, 1993, 110–28.

[5] The phrase comes from Bouwsma, 1974.

[6] This is also reflected in the fact that there are so few ducal biographies. For the doges listed here, see Madden, 2003; Lazzarini, 1963; Tafuri, ed., 1984; Seneca, 1959. See also Gaetano Cozzi's biography of doge Niccolò Contarini (Cozzi, 1958) and the collective biographies in Da Mosto, 1983.

[7] For this description of the doge, see Muir, 1981, ch. 7.

[8] Lane, 1973, ch. 8.

[9] DM, reg. 13, fol. 78v (5 July 1447). *Dominium* might also be translated here as the Signoria, the executive committee comprising the doge, his six councilors, and the three heads of the Council of Forty.

[10] Belting, 1994, esp. 10, 474; Trexler, 1980, 61–73.

[11] Chojnacki, 2000.

[12] Finlay, 1980, ch. 3.

[13] For the classic statement of the transformations taking place, see Mattingly, 1955, esp. pt. 2. See also Besta, 1899, 144; Fubini, 1982, 327. Alternatively, *ad hoc* committees known as *balie* were frequently used in republican regimes. Although such special committees were also employed in Venice, the Ten often took these responsibilities for themselves. See Cracco, 1979, 77; Caferro, 1998, 186–87.

[14] Giustiniano, 1798, 34.

[15] The literature on the Medici is vast. One can profitably begin with D. Kent, 2000, and F. W. Kent, 2004.

[16] Muraro, 1961a.

[17] Berlan, 1852; Romanin. For the full range of views regarding Foscari from his death to the present, see chapter 6 of this book.

[18] There are many editions and translations of Burckhardt's *Civilization of the Renaissance*

in Italy (German original, 1860; Eng. trans. S. G. C. Middlemore, 1890). For a recent effort to understand Cosimo de' Medici through his patronage, see D. Kent, 2000.

CHAPTER 1   BECOMING DOGE, 1373–1423

[1] Piccolomini, 1991, 29.

[2] The calculation of Foscari as the sixty-eighth doge is based on Marino Sanudo's list of doges (Sanudo, 1980, 65–68). By contrast, Francesco Sansovino, writing under the name Girolamo Bardi, lists him as the sixty-fifth doge (Sansovino, 1587, 103), while Giovanni Palazzi lists him as the sixty-fourth (Palazzi, 1696, 148).

[3] For these "succession portraits" and other information on the decoration of the Great Council Hall, see Sinding-Larsen, 1974, 30; Brown, 1988, 261–65, 272–79.

[4] Joachim Strupp suggested to me in conversation that the portrait is perhaps a copy of the Great Council portrait, intended for private use; given the extant fifteenth-century fragment showing the doges in three-quarter view, however, that does not seem at all certain. In the Polish city of Łódź there is a portrait of Doge Steno in profile (see Weber, 1993, 32, and fig. 10). The arched effect at the top of the work suggests that it might have been copied from a frieze that ran along the top of a wall. Steno is depicted facing right; if his successor Mocenigo was facing left, then, according to the order of succession, Foscari would also have been facing right, as he appears in the Bastiani portrait. However, another profile portrait of Foscari in the Baldo Collection in Milan shows him facing left (see Heinemann, 1962–91, 3:111, and fig. 190; Eisler, 1989, 21). Heinemann attributes the Baldo Collection portrait to Gentile Bellini and suggests that it was painted from life, perhaps

in celebration of the Peace of Lodi. The Bastiani portrait has also been attributed to other artists, including Gentile Bellini, Jacopo Bellini, and Bartolomeo Vivarini, although it is now usually attributed to Bastiani, who was active between 1449 and 1512. Edoardo Arslan remains skeptical of the Bastiani attribution. Whether it was painted from life or after death, it is likely a copy of an official portrait (if not of the Great Council portrait), perhaps intended for family use. See, among others, Heinemann, 1962–91, 3:111; Paoletti, 1929, 75–79; Arslan, 1965, 167. Rab Hatfield suggests that profile portraits often constituted "pictorial eulogies" (Hatfield, 1965, 329).

[5] On the Byzantine origins of the *corno*, see Pertusi, 1965, 83.

[6] Giuseppe Gullino states that Francesco was born on 19 June 1373 but offers no source for that information (Gullino, 2005b, 25). For much of the family information and the itinerary of Foscari's career before the dogeship, I follow the very complete information found in Girgensohn, 1996, 2:756–83; and the various biographies of Foscari family members in *DBI* 49:293–351, especially Gullino, 1997.

[7] Lazzarini, 1895, 5.

[8] Lane, 1971; Chojnacki, 1974.

[9] For an explanation of these terms, see Finlay, 1980, 92–96.

[10] For genealogical charts of the family, see Girgensohn, 1996, 783; Gullino, 2005b, 187.

[11] See Kohl, 1998, 192–93. For some of his properties, see Scuola di Santa Maria del Rosario, b. 28, Arm. Com. Girardi, Cassella II, Mazzo III, Proc. 7, fol. 28r–v.

[12] Lazzarini, 1895, 6–8; Zoccoletto, 1999, 15–17. The latter also publishes the original diploma granting the investiture (55–56).

[13] Lazzarini, 1895, 8–9. For copies of the will dated 8 January 1340mv, see Archivio

Gradenigo, Rio Marin, b. 340, pp. 153–54; Scuola di Santa Maria del Rosario, b. 28, Arm. Com. Girardi, Cassella II, Mazzo III, Proc. VI, fols. 3v–13r; and MCC, PD 274-C/III.

[14] For the careers of Giovanni and his son Paolo, see Ravegnani, 1997, 320–21, 336–38. Copies of Giovanni's will are in Scuola di Santa Maria del Rosario, b. 28, Arm. Com. Girardi, Cassella II, Mazzo III, Proc. VI, fols. 89r–92v; and in b. 29, fascicle marked "Arm. Com. Girardi, Cassella III, Mazzo IV, Proc. IV," parchment no. 54. Giovanni's wife Franceschina left 8 ducats in her will for the building fund for San Simeon Apostolo ibid., b. 29, Arm. Com. Girardi, Cassella III, Mazzo IV, Proc. V, parchment no. 26; will dated 22 February 1402mv.

[15] For the income from various properties in Venice and the terraferma, see Scuola di Santa Maria del Rosario, b. 28, Arm. Com. Girardi, Cassella II, Mazzo III, Proc. VI, fols. 73r–85r.

[16] Gullino, 1997, 333–35; Girgensohn, 1996, 2:775–83.

[17] Marco's birthdate is based on the registration of 1412 for the *balla d'oro* (usually done at the age of eighteen). See AC, reg. 162, "Balla d'Oro," fol. 72r.

[18] CI, Notai, b. 228, notary Angeleto di Andreuccio, protocol 1418–21, fol. 37v, act dated 1 August 1418. For a discussion of the *corredo*, see Chojnacki, 2000, 76–94.

[19] In his will Donato asked to be buried in the ground at San Simeon Apostolo, without any monument. For his will, see Scuola di S. Maria del Rosario, b. 29, Arm. Com. Girardi, Cassella III, Mazzo IV, Proc. XII, will dated 8 October 1421; see also Girgensohn, 1996, 2:781, n. 59. For an earlier will, see NT, b. 858, notary Marco Raffanelli, unbound testament 5, dated 30 August 1409.

[20] NT, b. 1255, notary Petrus Zane, protocol, fols. 191v–192r.

[21] Ibid., fols. 105v–106v.

[22] Gullino, 1997, 304; for the dowry figure in ducats, see Girgensohn, 1996, 2:756, n. 7; for the history of the castle of Dragameston, see Scuola di Santa Maria del Rosario, b. 29, Arm. Com. Girardi, Cassella III, Mazzo IV, Proc. X, fol. 2r–v.

[23] In 1420 Franzi emancipated his son Filippo, who immediately thereafter acknowledged receipt of a 1200-ducat dowry from his wife Ysabeta, daughter of Azone Trevisan. See CI, Notai, b. 228, notary Angeleto di Andreuccio, protocol 1418–21, fol. 204r, acts dated 4 March 1420.

[24] Scuola di Santa Maria del Rosario, b. 29, Arm. Com. Girardi, Cassella III, Mazzo IV, Proc. XI, parchment no. 12 (27 August 1432).

[25] Gullino, 1997, 304–06; Girgensohn, 1996, 2:756–65; Lazzarini, 1893, 11–12.

[26] Chojnacki, 1974.

[27] In his nineteenth-century history of the family, Pietro Gradenigo states that the doge's father Niccolò was a "padrone di nave" but cites no source for this information (Archivio Gradenigo, Rio Marin, b. 333, Pietro Gradenigo, "Lavoro storico cronologico biografico sulla veneta famiglia Foscari, con prospetti, documenti e note," entry 29). Doris Stöckly's detailed study of the control of state-owned galleys makes no mention of Foscari engagement in maritime matters (Stöckly, 1995).

[28] For the urban properties, see Scuola di Santa Maria del Rosario, b. 29, Arm. Com. Girardi, Cassella III, Proc. IV, fols. 14r, 16r, 18r–29tris verso.

[29] Piccolomini, 2001, 204–05, 234.

[30] Grendler, 1989.

[31] Morosini, 1107, 1513–14; Cumming, 1992, 355–56. I cannot imagine why Andrea Da Mosto judged Foscari "poco colto in materia letteraria," a point repeated by Colin Eisler (Da Mosto, 1983, 163; Eisler, 1989, 20).

I have relied on the version of Morosini's chronicle in the Biblioteca Nazionale Marciana, Venice, which is a copy of the original now held at the Nationalbibliothek in Vienna. However, as the recent editors of Morosini's chronicle observe, the Marciana copy is very reliable, except "for a few small errors [. . .] of a minor nature" (Ghezzo, Melville-Jones, and Rizzi, eds., 1999, ix).

[32] King, 1986, esp. 372–73.

[33] For the example of the merchant Andrea Barbarigo, see Lane, 1944, 17–22.

[34] Giudici di Petizion, Sentenze e Interdetti, reg. 8, fols. 32r–33r. When he left Damascus, he placed his brother-in-law Santo Venier in charge of trying to collect the debt. This suggests that these young men had been sent east in order to manage their families' business interests.

[35] For Priuli, see Mueller, 1997, 103–06, 182, 429.

[36] Quoted in Cracco, 1979, 1:80. For background information on Caresini, see Carile, 1977, 80–83.

[37] Lane, 1971.

[38] For a convenient summary, see Lane, 1973, 57–65.

[39] Ibid., 42–43.

[40] Ibid., 189–201.

[41] Lane, 1992, esp. 129–37; Lane, 1944, 45–52; Lane, 1966, 36–55, 193–226; Stöckly, 1995.

[42] Brown, 1988, 37–40.

[43] Lazzarini, 1895, 6, 9–10. According to Lazzarini, once Venice began to acquire terraferma domains, the prohibition no longer made sense.

[44] Lane, 1973, ch. 6, esp. 64–65.

[45] These events are conveniently summarized in Mallett, 1984, 7–16.

[46] For detailed accounts of these events, see Kohl, 1998, ch. 10; and Raulich, 1890. For shorter accounts, see Cozzi, 1986, 11–13; and Mallett, 1996a, 181–89.

[47] SS, reg. 2, fol. 109v (5 May 1405).

[48] Ibid., fol. 132r (31 July 1405); Kohl, 1998, 333; Raulich, 1890, 86.

[49] Kohl, 1998, 333–36.

[50] Mallett, 1996a, 189.

[51] Cozzi, 1986, 14–18.

[52] Indeed Franzi appears to have suffered from a physical disability that made him unfit for military service. This may have contributed at least in part to the dramatic contrast between the Foscari and the Loredans, Venice's premier military family. See SS, reg. 2, fol. 110r (12 May 1405); also Gullino, 1997, 304.

[53] Gullino, 1997, 304–05; Girgensohn, 1996, 2:759–60.

[54] Gullino, 1997, 334; Girgensohn, 1996, 2:777.

[55] DM, reg. 8, fol. 24v (20 October 1395).

[56] Girgensohn, 1996, 2:767. In this role, Foscari advocated greater preparedness for a possible war with Genoa. See SS, reg. 1, fols. 112r (3 November 1403), 133r (16 February 1403mv).

[57] Zannini, 1996, 424.

[58] Gullino, 1997, 306.

[59] SS, reg. 1, fol. 142r (4 April 1404). See also Gullino, 1997, 306; Girgensohn, 1996, 2:767.

[60] Including in Bernardo Giustinian's funeral oration for Foscari (Giustiniano, 1798, 25).

[61] As, for example, in Romanin, 4:53.

[62] For an account of the surrender of the symbols, see Gatari and Gatari, 1909–31, 577–79; a translation in Dean, 2000, 243–44. For the tomb, see Wolters, 1976, 1:233–34, but note the error in his transcription of the epitaph by consulting the photo in vol. 2, cat. no. 538.

[63] Mallett, 1996a, 189–90.

[64] Cozzi, 1986, 21.

[65] Ibid., 27; Gullino, 1996a, 26–32; Fine, 1987, 503–09.

66 Gullino, 1997, 307; SS, reg. 4, fols. 21v (1 June 1409); 22v–23r (4 June 1409).

67 SS, reg. 4, fol. 36v (1 July 1409).

68 SS, reg. 4, fol. 42v (29 July 1409); Gullino, 1997, 307; for Cabrino Fondulo, see Covini, 1997, 586–89; and for Pandolfo Malatesta, Zanetti, 1961, esp. 868–76.

69 SS, reg. 4, fols. 54v–55r (5 and 7 September 1409); Gullino, 1997, 307; Girgensohn, 1996, 2:767–68.

70 Gullino (1997, 307–08) suggests he refused the post so that there would be no impediment to his uncle Franzi sitting in the Collegio as a ducal councilor (the law would have prohibited two members of the same patriline from sitting together in the Collegio), but Girgensohn's data suggest that it was Francesco who was elected a ducal councilor in the second half of 1410, whereas Franzi completed a term on the Council of Ten in May 1410 and was elected an *auditore delle sentenze* in June (Girgensohn, 1996, 2:760, 768).

71 See SM, reg. 48, fols. 157r–158r (acts dated 28 June 1410 and 3 July 1410); ibid., reg. 49, fol. 54r (13 September 1411). See also Gullino, 1997, 307; Molà, 2000, 79.

72 Gullino, 1997, 307–08.

73 SS, reg. 5, fol. 9v (27 March 1412). His term lasted until 1 October.

74 Gullino, 1997, 308. For the troop inspection, see SS, reg. 5, fol. 17v (19 April 1412); the effort to combat fraud, SM, reg. 49, fol. 125r (18 June 1412); the creation of a special emergency committee, SS, reg. 5, fol. 39r (28 June 1412).

75 See, for example, DM, reg. 11, fol. 119r–v (17 March 1435).

76 Gullino, 1997, 308. See SS, reg. 5, fols. 49v (20 July 1412), 50r (21 July 1412), 54r (30 July 1412).

77 As especially noted by Giustinian in his funeral oration (Giustiniano, 1798, 25). See also Gullino, 1997, 334.

78 Cozzi, 1974.

79 Queller, 1986, 29–50; Zannini, 1996.

80 Giustiniano, 1798, 25–26.

81 AC, Raspe, reg. 3646, fols. 153v–154r.

82 For some examples, see ibid., fols. 150r–v (Ieronimo Secreto and Iohannes Zancarolo); 155v–157r (Nicoleto Querini, Marino Dandolo, Karolus Querini, Niccolò Corner); 159r (Angelo Simetecolo); 163v (Andrea Querini). I wish to thank Stanley Chojnacki for bringing this issue to my attention. See also O'Connell, 2004.

83 Gullino, 1997, 308; Girgensohn, 1996, 2:768. Foscari's commission as ambassador to Sigismund is found in SS, reg. 5, fols. 136r–137v (6 June 1413).

84 SM, reg. 50, fol. 36r (30 September 1413); DM, reg. 9, fol. 107r (17 August 1413); Girgensohn, 1996, 2:768–69; Gullino, 1997, 308. For the *savi grandi*, see Da Mosto, 1937–40, 1:22. It is also worth noting that at about this time Foscari's middle brother Donato began his climb up the *cursus honorum*. On 1 October 1414 and again on 1 April 1415 he was elected a *savio agli ordini*, but died a few years later, probably in 1421. SM, reg. 50, fol. 164v (1 October 1414); reg. 51, fol. 13v (1 April 1415).

85 Girgensohn, 1996, 2:769; Gullino, 1997, 309. For the commission, see SS, reg. 5, fols. 168r–170v (10 December 1413).

86 Gullino, 1997, 308–09; Girgensohn, 1996, 2:769. SM, reg. 50, fol. 165r (1 October 1414), reg. 51, fol. 78r (30 September 1415), reg. 51, fol. 119v (31 March 1416).

87 AC, reg. 106, "Liber nuptiarum," fol. 67v.

88 Giudici del Proprio, Vadimoni, reg. 4, fol. 16r. I wish to thank Stanley Chojnacki for this reference. It is unclear which of the first two stages of the traditional three part marriage ceremony took place on 12 February. Foscari recorded in his account book, "die 12 fevrir fui novizo in Marina fia de

ser Bartolamio Nani." He may have been referring to either the betrothal or to what would now be considered the marriage itself; the third stage, which took place on the 27th, was the public transfer of Marina to her new husband's home. For the steps in the marriage ceremony, see Klapisch-Zuber, 1987, 183–87. For the *corredo* and for dowries in this period, see Chojnacki, 2000, 76–94.

[89] Finlay, 1980, 134.

[90] Girgensohn, 1996, 2:771–72, 783; ibid., 772, n. 124, for the suggestion that Jacopo was born in 1418.

[91] CI, Notai, b. 228, notary Angeleto di Andreuccio, protocol 1418–21, fol. 21r, act dated 13 May 1418. I wish to thank Paula Clarke for this reference.

[92] What follows is taken largely from my essay on Foscari's career as procurator: D. Romano, 1998. While procurator, Foscari also continued to be elected to such posts as *savio del consiglio*. See, for example, SM, reg. 51, fol. 168v (30 September 1416).

[93] Sanudo, 1980, 104.

[94] For the office, see Mueller, 1971.

[95] MCC, MS. Cicogna 1645, "Cronica Dolfina," 3 (1405–22), 518–20. Until 1468 the procurators were nominated by two committees, thereafter by four. For background on Pietro Dolfin, see Aricò's introduction in Sanudo, 1989, xxxix–xli; and Zaccaria, 1991, 562–65.

[96] MC, reg. 22 (Ursa), fol. 15r–v. See also BNM, It. Cl.VII, 380 (7471), Marco Barbaro, "Procuratori di San Marco," 27–29; for the cases of 1355 and 1361, ibid., 21–23.

[97] See, for example, Klapisch-Zuber, 1985, 68–93; Kent and Kent, 1982, 2.

[98] D. Kent, 1978, 61–71.

[99] D. Romano, 1987b, 120–31.

[100] Mueller, 1971, 117, 187.

[101] BNM, It. Cl.VII, 125 (7460), "Cronica Sanuda," fol. 239r. Despite this title, the work is in fact a section of Sanudo's *Le vite dei*

dogi. For this manuscript and other copies of the text, see Angela Caracciolo Aricò's introduction in Sanudo, 1989, xxi–xxiii. For another but undated account, see Morosini and Morosini, eds., 1897, 16–17, n. 7.

[102] Sansovino, 1968, 491. However, it should also be noted that Antonio Morosini's contemporary account makes no reference to Foscari's use of the office in this way: Morosini, 380–90.

[103] Such a conclusion assumes that old accounts were not consolidated and their records systematically destroyed, a point the manuscript cited by Domenico Morosini may call into dispute (Morosini and Morosini, eds., 1897, 16–17, n. 7). See also Mueller, 1971, 118; D. Romano, 1998, 43, n. 26.

[104] Mueller, 1971, 117.

[105] D. Romano, 1998, 44, n. 30.

[106] PSM, Misti, b. 12, notebook 1 (1377–1484), pages with heading "Dabimus pro maritando pauperas domicellas," entries dated 15 February 1415mv to 3 February 1418mv; and ibid., b. 145a, Commissaria of Giovanni Gabriel, notebook entitled "Quaternus noviciarum de miser Ziorzi Morexini." See also D. Romano, 1998, 45.

[107] The notebook in the Gabriel estate indicates that Foscari distributed funds for Maria, a second daughter of the late Giacomo Priuli. Again, the payment was made to Andrea Priuli. However, this selection is not recorded in the records of Morosini's estate. See the "Quaternus noviciarum de miser Ziorzi Morexini" (cited in the previous note), act dated 24 March 1419. The identification of this Priuli as Foscari's former father-in-law is based solely on his name.

[108] PSM, de citra, b. 96, Commissaria of Pietro Corner, notebook 1, page entitled "Quo dabimus pauperibus domicellis," act dated 9 May 1421.

[109] Ibid., b. 87, Commissaria of Leonardo Vitturi, will dated 1305, and notebook 6 (1414–22) unpaginated, page with heading "Quo dabimus pauperibus propinquis [. . .] pro paga septembris 1415 et marci de 1416."

[110] CI, Notai, b. 191, notary Federico de Stefanis, leatherbound protocol with acts dated 27 May 1419, 27 September 1419, 14 January 1420mv, and 14 April 1423.

[111] See King, 1989, 42; and more generally, King, 1986, 98–117, 344–45.

[112] PSM, Misti, b. 145a, Commissaria of Giovanni Gabriel, "Quaternus noviciarum de miser Ziorzi Morexini."

[113] Sanuto, 1733, col. 925–96.

[114] SM, reg. 52, fol. 167v (8 May 1419). For della Scala's will and the transfer of funds, see PSM, Misti, b. 98a, notebook 1393–1480, unpaginated. See the last clause of her will and act of the procurators under the rubric "Dabimus ecclesiis," dated 10 May 1419.

[115] MC, reg. 22 (Ursa), fol. 36v. The law is also found in PSM, de citra, b. 332, Capitolare della Procuratia Eccelentissima de Citra, 210–11. One of the hospitals affected was that endowed by Zorzi Basegio in his will dated July 1385 and under the jurisdiction of the procurators de citra. The Great Council law was copied into one of the procurators' notebooks concerning the estate (see PSM, de citra, b. 53, Commissaria of Zorzi Basegio, fasc. 3, notebook II [1418–90], inside cover).

[116] DM, reg. 10, fol. 11v (31 May 1419). The property had once belonged to one of the participants in the 1310 conspiracy led by Baiamonte Tiepolo and Marco Querini to overthrow the government.

[117] Cicogna, 1969–70, 3:382–83; Gullino, 1996a, 30–31.

[118] Ibid.

[119] Sanuto, 1733, cols. 901–09. There is also a long excerpt in Romanin, 4:54–56.

[120] CI, Notai, b. 228, notary Angeleto di Andreuccio, protocol 1418–20, fol. 275v (16 January 1420mv), protocol 1421–23, acts dated 1 April 1422, 3 October 1422. I wish to thank Paula Clarke for these important references.

[121] Gullino, 1997, 309; Cozzi, 1986, 21; Romanin, 4:57–58.

[122] Romanin, 4:51–52; Gullino, 1997, 309. For the commission, see SS, reg. 7, fols. 2r–4r (6 March 1418).

[123] Cozzi, 1986, 22–23; Romanin, 4:58–59.

[124] Cozzi, 1986, 22–23; Romanin, 4:60–64; Cicogna, 1969–70, 3:383. In negotiations with the pope regarding the annexation of Friuli, Foscari insisted on Venice's rights and argued as well that the annexation was motivated not by "ambition" for a larger state, but only as a defense against Sigismund. See SS, reg. 7, fols. 177v–178v (acts dated 8 and 9 September 1420).

[125] Mallett, 1996a, 192; Cozzi, 1986, 23–24; Romanin, 4:65–69.

[126] Lane, 1973, 226; Cozzi, 1986, 129 (citing later reflections of the diarist Girolamo Priuli); Gullino, 1996b, 406–07; Gullino, 2005b, 153. However although Zannini (1996, 438) argues that there was an increasing demand for jobs, he also suggests that the number of jobs grew proportionally to the increase in the number of nobles. And Mallett (1996a, 239) contests the idea that it was poor nobles who benefited most from terraferma expansion. For a discussion of some of the other economic issues possibly motivating the expansion onto the terraferma, see Luzzatto, 1961, 155–64.

[127] Sanuto, 1733, cols. 946–66. For the manuscript version, see BNM, It. Cl. VII, 800 (7151), "Vite dei dogi," fols. 478r–488r.

[128] BNM, It. Cl. VII, 763 (7960), with the catalogue title "Tommaso Mocenigo, Discorsi." See also Stahl, 1995, 286.

[129] Sanuto, 1733, col. 952; BNM, It. Cl. VII, 800 (7151), "Vite dei dogi," fol. 482r.

[130] In this section I follow the slightly different version printed in Besta, 1912, 94–97, since the first sentence of this section in Muratori's transcription makes little sense. His version reads: "Ma que' che dicono di volere Ser Francesco Foscari, dicono bugie e cose senza fondamento, e sopra più che non fanno i falconi." The Marciana manuscript 800 (fol. 487v) reads: "Ma quelli che dicono di voler ser Francesco Foscari dice busie e cose senza algun fondamento e sora più che non fanno li falconi." Another transcription of the speech is found in Romanin, 4:70–72.

[131] Baron, 1955, 201.

[132] Ibid., 204.

[133] Ibid., 212.

[134] The same is true of another detailed chronicle for this period, that of Donato Contarini: BNM, It. Cl. VII, 95 (8610).

[135] Sanuto, 1733, col. 946: "Questa è una copia tratta dal Libro dell'Illustre Messer Tommaso Mocenigo Doge di Venezia per dar risposta agli Ambasciadori de' Fiorentini." In the Marciana manuscript: "Questa he una copia nel libro del Illustre miser Toma Mozenigo doxe de Venexia per dar resposta ali ambasadori de Fiorentini" (BNM, It. Cl. VIII, 763 [7960], unpaginated). Baron (1955, 186) suggests that they come from Mocenigo's copybook.

[136] This point is especially clear in the Marciana manuscript, where there is a list of wars fought between 1295 and 1418 and then several blank pages between what is essentially the end of Sanudo's life of Mocenigo, that is his transcription of Mocenigo's epitaph, and the "speeches" (BNM, It. Cl. VII, 800 [7151], fols. 475r–477v). In other words, there is no continuous narrative here. It should be noted, however, that Sanudo does briefly mention

near the end of his narrative of Mocenigo's life that ambassadors from Florence arrived in Venice seeking a league and that there were "varie dispute" in the Senate with Foscari advocating the league and Mocenigo opposing them in his speech (Sanuto, 1733, col. 945; Marciana manuscript 800, fol. 474r).

[137] In this regard it is also useful to note that in the second speech Mocenigo castigates the young procurator, telling him that he should not make speeches if he first does not have "buona intelligenza e buona pratica" (Sanuto, 1733, col. 952; Marciana manuscript 800, fol. 482v). Such a remark seems unlikely given the experience and intelligence that Foscari had demonstrated in his career so far, including having served with Mocenigo on an ambassadorial mission at the time Mocenigo was elected doge.

[138] Luzzatto, 1954, 271–84; Lane, 1992, 253; Stahl, 1995, 287–88.

[139] Poppi, 1972–73, 463–97.

[140] Stahl, 1995, 300.

[141] Lane, 1992, 253. According to Stahl (1995, 301), the speech represents "a retrospective vision of a golden age" that "would provide an example of how the unwise policies taken by Doge Foscari had fulfilled the worst fears of his predecessor." Cozzi (1986, 3) suggests that Sanudo himself may have been responsible for reworking the speeches. Stöckly (1995, 328–30, 345) argues that the rift between patricians with maritime interests and those with terraferma interests began to show only at mid-century.

[142] Lane, 1973, 359.

[143] In the second speech, Mocenigo considers Venice's acquisition of Padua, Vicenza, Verona, and Friuli to have been justified; the last of these was accomplished in his reign. Sanuto, 1733, 958.

[144] Romanin, 4:69.

[145] SS, reg. 8, fol. 99r–v (31 March 1423).

[146] Gullino, 1997, 305.

[147] For investments in the terraferma, see D. Gallo, 1994. Stöckly (1995, 338–39, 343) concludes that nearly all patrician families participated to some extent in international maritime commerce and that they invested in both commerce and the terraferma. For Loredan's push for benefices (which failed), see Del Torre, 1992–93, 1194.

[148] For the generational conflict, see Cessi, 1981, 365–67.

[149] As Romanin (4:76, n. 28) says: "anche sotto Foscari lungamente si esitò avanti di abbracciare il partito della guerra e si abbracciò soltanto dopo esauriti tutt'i mezzi di pace."

[150] As cited in Wolters, 1976, 1:239, but with several mistakes in the transcription. See also Cumming, 1992, 337–38. The translation is that of Cumming.

[151] Cessi, 1981, 365.

[152] Luzzatto, 1961, 168.

[153] Musatti, 1888. For the texts of the earliest promissioni, see Graziato, ed., 1986.

[154] MC, reg. 22 (Ursa), fols. 54r–55v.

[155] For the Arengo, see Lane, 1973, 91, 95–96. As early as 1417 the Ten had considered limiting the authority of the Arengo during ducal vacancies. See DM, reg. 9, fol. 161r–v (acts dated 27 January 1416mv).

[156] MC, reg. 22 (Ursa), fol. 56r. Cozzi, 1986, 25; Romanin, 4:73–74.

[157] MC, reg. 22 (Ursa), fols. 56r–57r.

[158] Foscari's promissione has been published by Dieter Girgensohn (see Girgensohn, ed. 2004). Before its publication, I relied on another transcription (not noted by Girgensohn) found in MCC, Prov. Div. 2362/II, "Promissione ducale di Francesco Foscari [ms. Pergamenaceo proprietà delle sorelle Félissent (Treviso)], presso il duca Eugenio Catemario di Quadri, Udine, Palazzo Torriani." The earlier transcription was done in 1949.

[159] See, for example, Girgensohn, ed. 2004, 57–58 (clause XLIII), 59 (clause XLV), 29 (clause XIIII). See also Muir, 1981, 254–56.

[160] Girgensohn, ed. 2004, 69 (clauses LIIII and LV), 125 (clause CXVI).

[161] MC, reg. 22 (Ursa), fols. 54v–55v; the rules for the election of Foscari's successor Pasquale Malipiero are chronicled in Dolfin, 450v–452r.

[162] Lane, 1973, 111.

[163] Quoted in Boholm, 1990, 122.

[164] Ibid., 123–24.

[165] Finlay, 1980, 142.

[166] MC, reg. 22 (Ursa), fol. 55r.

[167] MC, reg. 22 (Ursa), fols. 57v–58v; Sanudo, 1999, 5.

[168] A description of the ducal election procedures is included in the poem "El sommo della condizione di Vinegia" by Jacopo d'Albizzotto Guidi, dated 1442: Guidi, 1995, 117–19. A copy of the poem (with an expanded title) is in the Biblioteca del Seminario Patriarchale, Venice, MS. 950, "El sommo della condizione e stato e principio della citta di Vinegia," unpaginated. I wish to thank Don Gianni Bernardo for his kind assistance in consulting it.

[169] Sanudo, 1999, 8–12. But note that the editor is wrong in saying that Bartolomeo Storlado's name does not appear in the Great Council records. For Sanudo's hopes of eventually reworking the manuscript, see Angela Caracciolo Aricò's introduction in Sanudo, 1999, xxx–xxxi; for his use of archival sources, see her introduction in Sanudo, 1989, lxiv.

[170] For the addition above the text (in the same hand), that it was the feast of Saint Isidore, see the original manuscript in BNM, It. Cl. VII, 125 (7460), "Cronica Sanuda," fol. 2r (242r). The saint's feast day is in fact 16 April.

[171] Sanudo, 1999, 3–7.

[172] Finlay, 1980, 124–41.

[173] In his deathbed speech, Doge Mocenigo did not mention his brother. This too suggests that Sanudo's source was a pro-Mocenigo account intended to avoid drawing attention to the brother's failed candidacy.

[174] Syracuse University Library, Ranke MS. 41, "Historia venetiana di Agostino Agostini," fol. 141r.

[175] The Agostini chronicle gives the figure of 15,000 ducats (ibid., fol. 141v).

[176] The Agostini chronicle (ibid., fol. 141v) presents Pisani and Correr as Foscari's defenders, whereas Sanudo (1999, 6) seems to say that they attacked him.

[177] Sanudo, 1999, 6–7. The most problematic phrase is "Fo tolto poi per do et per 12," which I have translated here as "He gained two votes and got 12."

[178] Syracuse University Library, Ranke MS. 41, "Historia Venetiana di Agostino Agostini," fol. 142r–v. The number 17 is also reported in Cornelio, 1758, 107.

[179] For the *portonari*, see Sanudo, 1980, 87; and the poem of Jacopo d'Albizzotto Guidi (Guidi, 1995, 117), which states: "du altri soficienti [è] alla scrittura/più giovan', che ricolghino el partito/ben lïalmente, colla mente pura." See Cornelio, 1758, 106. See also Morosini and Morosini, eds. (1897, 12), with excerpts from a manuscript in the Morosini archive. According to that account, the doorkeepers also had the job "à conzar i letti massime quei di Vecchi, e servirli, nelle quali operationi si raccomandava, e pregavali darli la ballotta, dicendo che quella volta non toccava a lui, ma che havrebbe servito in altre Vacanze, li quali vedendo, che non poteva esser fatto, gliela davano, onde in ogni ballottation andava crescendo."

[180] Sanudo, 1999, 4; Romanin, 4:73, n. 16.

[181] Sanudo, 1999, 6.

[182] The notary Federico de Stefanis made the same mistake, noting that on 16 April

"facto Arengo fuit." See CI, Notai, b. 191, notary Federico de Stefanis, leatherbound protocol, act dated 16 April 1423.

[183] Dean and Lowe, 1998, 12–13. My own attempt to try to identify Foscari's eleven partisans in the forty-one proved unsuccessful since there were a vast number of ties linking various members to one another. In this regard it is instructive to keep in mind the remark by the Florentine Giovanni Rucellai that the Rucellai lineage's marriage ties involved "half the city." Cited in F. W. Kent, 1995, 178.

[184] Muir, 1981, 284. Other accounts suggest he ascended a porphyry throne rather than the *bigonzo*. See Boholm, 1990, 133. For the *bigonzo*, see Hopkins, 1988, 183–85.

[185] For the doge as a sacral figure and the instrument of divine illumination, see Pincus, 2000a, esp. chs. 6 and 8; Pincus, 2000b. See also her discussion of the ducat in Pincus, 2000a, 77–79.

[186] For accounts of the coronation, see Dolfin, 319v–320r; Sanudo, 1999, 12; Morosini, 390. For the illustration by Giacomo Franco of the coin-tossing ceremony, see Muir, 1981, 287. Of course, this image too requires careful interpretation since it was likely intended to depict "popular" disorder.

[187] Muir, 1981, 281–89.

[188] This was an idea already expressed clearly by Petrarch. See Sarnelli, 2004, 39.

[189] Lowe, 2001. Hatfield (1965, 333) notes that profile portraits were "symptomatic of a mentality which sees excellence in terms of social rather than personal values."

[190] Woods-Marsden, 2001, 69.

[191] Ibid., 75.

[192] Heinemann, 1962–91, 3:111, and fig. 190. Heinemman attributes it to Gentile Bellini. Eisler (1989, 21) suggests it may come from the workshop of Giambono. I

have been unable to locate this portrait. Eisler lists it as being housed in the Baldo Collection in Milan. However, in personal correspondence he is unable to recall where or how he found the portrait (e-mail, 11 November 2005). I have also contacted the authorities at the *sovrintendenza* in Milan who have no knowledge of this collection (e-mail, 30 January 2006).

[193] Girgensohn, ed. 2004, xx–xxi. Galli (1997, 238–43) incorrectly dates the manuscript to 1422; it is clearly later, as Girgensohn suggests.

[194] For Nicholas's veneration in Venice, see Muir, 1981, 97–101.

[195] MCC, Mariegola 124. On a sheet included with the image in Mariegola 124 is an indication (from the eighteenth century) of yet another manuscript showing Foscari in the act of receiving a book from its author. Barbaro says that he saw an ancient rendition of the Foscari arms without the lion painted on a wall. Unfortunately, there is no way to determine when and why the arms were added. Marco Barbaro, "Arbori de' patritii veneti," photocopy in Archivio di Stato, Venice, vol. 15, p. 503.

[196] BN, Nuovi acquisti 445, Porcellio Pandoni, "Commentariorum secundi anni de gestis Scipionis Picinini exercitus Venetorum imperatoris." On the tangled history of Pandoni's treatise and its various dedicatees, see Picotti, 1908.

[197] Pertusi, 1970, 290–91.

[198] Eisler, 1989, 509.

[199] BNM, Lat. X, 190 (3555), fol. 6r. The *promissione* appears to have a confused history. The first sentence identifies it as the *promissione* of Doge Antonio Venier, who was elected in 1382. However, in clause 53, the list of doges includes Foscari. It may be that this particular *promissione* was intended for use by a ducal councilor (it includes the capitulary of the ducal councilors) and that it was "recy-

cled" so that the portrait of Foscari was added later. I wish to thank Helena Szepe for her assistance in thinking about this image. For a discussion of it and of Bellini, see the catalogue entry by Susy Marcon in Zorzi, ed., 1988, 156; Marcon, 2004, 76–78.

[200] For a discussion of the medal and its attribution to Griffo, see Stahl, 2001, 306–07. It is sometimes attributed to Antonio Gambello.

[201] Paoletti (1929, 79) suggests that the medal might be a copy of the Bastiani portrait or vice versa.

[202] Some have mistakenly suggested that it quotes the figure of Venice at the summit of the Porta della Carta. However that figure holds a sword and a balance and lacks the small figures of the furies below.

[203] Wolters, 1976, 1:178–79. I wish to thank Rob Ulery for his help with the translation.

[204] Scher, 1994, 15–21, 43–44.

[205] Lazzarini, 1963, 202–03. Since the conclave of forty-one electors was meeting, the Council of Ten decided to defer the procession until some time after the election. According to the Ten, the *andata* traditionally took place on 16 April. See DM, reg. 10, fol. 57r (14 April 1423).

[206] Muir, 1981, 217–19. Sanudo's account was amended to note that it took place on Saint Isidore's feast day ("fo San Sidro"). See Sanudo, 1999, 12. However, both there and in his guide to Venice Sanudo (1980, 56) incorrectly gave the date of that saint's feast as 15 April.

[207] Lazzarini, 1963, 293.

CHAPTER 2   TRIBUTE TO THE VIRGIN, 1423–1433

[1] Quoted (with minor variations) and translated in Cumming, 1992, 336.

[2] Ibid., 333–41.

[3] Ibid., 341–46 for the text, translation, and commentary. Humanists, no doubt hoping to gain ducal patronage, composed various works in honor of Foscari's elevation to the ducal office. For the poem *Foscara*, written by the Paduan humanist Antonio Baratella to celebrate Foscari's election, see Marconato, 2002, 83–86; and for an oration by the Bergamasco humanist Antonio Carabello, see Segarizzi, 1904, 6.

[4] Sanudo, 1999, 7.

[5] MC, reg. 22 (Ursa), fol. 59v (20 May 1423); Sanudo, 1999, 7.

[6] Hurlburt, 2006, 69–74.

[7] Ibid., 38–43.

[8] DM, reg. 10, fol. 80r (20 June 1425). The following October the Ten authorized the gold-beaters to hold their celebrations: ibid., fol. 83v (24 October 1425). Perhaps di Monte's motet was composed for this Paduan celebration of Foscari's election. Cumming (1992, 357) suggests something similar but does not identify this specific event as a likely occasion for the work's composition. For further discussion of the guild receptions, see Hurlburt, 2006, 49–56.

[9] Morosini, 393–94.

[10] For the text and discussion, see Cumming, 1992, 346–53, quotes on 349 and 350.

[11] Ibid., 356, for the suggestion that both the *Christus vincit* and Romano's *Carminibus festos* may have been composed for that first meeting of the Great Council. Cumming fails, however, to consider the significance that the laudatory motet with its Marian associations would have had as a pendant to Guariento's fresco.

[12] As with the election, Sanudo gives two different versions of this first Great Council meeting. According to one account, the meeting took place on 23 April 1423 in the "salla nuova fabrichata." However, later he says that a meeting took place on 20 April in the "salla granda" (Sanudo, 1999, 7, 13). For a complete survey of the issues regarding the construction and decoration of the Great Council Hall, see Martindale, 1993.

[13] Francastel, 1965; Rosand, 1984; Rosand, 2001.

[14] Martindale, 1993, 92; see also Saxl, 1957, 1:147–49.

[15] Sanudo, 1999, 8, 23 (but with the incorrect date of 13 April); Morosini, 394. Da Polenta had been awarded membership in the Great Council as a reward for his assistance during the struggle with the Carrara. See Barbiani, 1927, 27. The letter from Pope Martin V congratulating Foscari on his election is in AAVa, Arm. XXXIX, vol. 6, "Breviarum," fols. 85v–86r.

[16] Morosini, 393–94. Because of a tear in the pages upon which the most recent version of Sanudo's life of Foscari is based (Sanudo, 1999, 7–8, 23), I rely here on the less reliable Muratori edition of 1733 which reads, "Venne al Consiglio il Marchese di Mantova, e fu fatto entrare in elezione, e a requisizione del Doge tolse Procuratore in luogo di sua Serenità Ser' Albano Badoero." Sanuto, 1733, col. 968.

[17] Dolfin, 320v; Sanudo, 1999, 14; Morosini, 397–98; see also Nicol, 1988, 358–60; Setton, 1978, 19–23.

[18] The phrase comes from Nicol, 1988, 353–54.

[19] Morosini, 403.

[20] Dolfin, 320v–321r; Sanudo, 1999, 14.

[21] SM, reg. 54, fol. 127r–v (2 and 7 July 1423); SS, reg. 8, fols. 111v–112r (7 July 1423); see also Thiriet, 2:1891–92.

[22] SM, reg. 54, fol. 131r (13 July 1423); SS, reg. 8, fols. 115v–119r (27 July 1423); Thiriet, 2:1894, 1898.

[23] Nicol, 1988, 361.

[24] SS, reg. 8, fol. 111v (7 July 1423).

[25] Morosini, 424–26.

[26] SM, reg. 54, fols. 152v–153r (20 October 1423); Thiriet, 2:1908; Nicol, 1988, 362–63.

[27] Sanudo, 1999, 20.

[28] SS, reg. 8, fols. 151r–152r; Thiriet, 2: 1931. See also Sanudo, 1999, 20.

[29] SM, reg. 55, fol. 25r (19 May 1424); Thiriet, 2:1934.

[30] For remarks about Florentine entrance ceremonies which are also in many ways applicable to Venice, see Trexler, 1978, 10–11, 25. And for Venice, see Brown, 1990.

[31] MC, reg. 22 (Ursa), fol. 63v (11 December 1423).

[32] Morosini, 439; Dolfin, 322r; Sanudo, 1999, 16.

[33] MC, reg. 22 (Ursa), fol. 60r (10 June 1423).

[34] The events of John's mission are nicely summarized in Nicol, 1988, 364–66.

[35] Dolfin, 323v; Sanudo, 1999, 25.

[36] Setton, 1978, 19, 30; Fine, 1987, 516–36.

[37] MC, reg. 22 (Ursa), fol. 61r (8 August 1423); Morosini, 422–23; Sanudo, 1999, 15. For the population estimate, see Mueller, 1979b, 95, graph 1. The chronicle of Donato Contarini, however, says that 6300 people died: BNM, It. Cl. VII, 95 (8610), fol. 218r.

[38] DM, reg. 10, fol. 60v (11 August 1423).

[39] SM, reg. 54, fol. 140v (29 August 1423). The law is printed in *Venezia e la peste:1348/1797*, 1979, 365.

[40] MC, reg. 22 (Ursa), fol. 62r (10 October 1423). See also Mueller, 1979a, 84–86.

[41] Crouzet-Pavan, 1992, 2:693, n. 70 (I was unable to locate the document in the archives as cited by Crouzet-Pavan).

[42] SM, reg. 54, fol. 140r (28 August 1423); for the doge/popolo "binary," see Cracco, 1979, 75–77.

[43] Crouzet-Pavan, 1995.

[44] SM, reg. 54, fols. 132r, 133v (acts dated 19, 25, and 27 July 1423).

[45] MC, reg. 22 (Ursa), fol. 50v (27 September 1422). The law is published in Lorenzi, 1868, 58–59.

[46] Morosini, 456–57; Sanudo, 1999, 19.

[47] Guidi, 1995, 15. Guidi moved to Venice from Florence in 1427.

[48] SM, reg. 55, fols. 4v, 8r (acts dated 11 and 23 March 1424). See also Cessi and Alberti, 1934, 61–64; Howard, 2000, 117–18.

[49] I wish to thank Gary Radke for bringing this commonality between the projects to my attention.

[50] Wirobisz (1965, 318) has characterized the fifteenth century as a period of "intense" building activity.

[51] For a full analysis, see Raulich, 1888, 441–68, 661–96.

[52] Dolfin, 324; Romanin, 4:75–76.

[53] SS, reg. 8, fol. 156r (13 May 1424); Romanin, 4:77.

[54] Dolfin, 324v–325r; SS, reg. 8, fol. 174v (6 October 1424); Raulich, 1888, 444.

[55] Sanudo, 1999, 27–28; Dolfin, 325v.

[56] Raulich, 1888, 448–51. These included a mission by Francesco della Siega to Milan. SS, reg. 8, fol. 188r–v (17 February 1424mv).

[57] Dolfin, 325v–326r; Sanudo, 1999, 28–29.

[58] SS, reg. 9, fol. 2r (acts dated 2 and 9 March 1425). The acts are published in Raulich, 1888, 464–65 and in Battistella, 1889, 476–77; and discussed briefly in Battistella, 1889, 100–01, and Mallett, 1984, 32. See also Morosini, 530; Dolfin, 326v; Sanudo, 1999, 33–34. For the lance, see Mallett, 1984, 69.

[59] Mallett, 1984, 11–33, quotes on 28.

[60] Bueno de Mesquita, 1972, 582–83, quote on 583. See also Battistella, 1889, 3–93.

[61] Dolfin, 326v; SS, reg. 9, fols. 2v–4v (acts dated 22 and 24 March 1425); printed in Raulich, 1888, 465–68. See also Battistella, 1889, 101–03.

[62] Dolfin, 327r–v, 330r–v; Sanudo, 1999, 45; SS, reg. 9, fol. 53r (23 November 1425); Romanin, 4:78–79.

[63] SS, reg. 9, fols. 55r–58v (3 December 1425); Raulich, 1888, 457–58; Predelli, 4:65–66, no. 197; Morosini, 606–09; Sanudo, 1999, 43.

[64] Cozzi, 1986, 25; Cessi, 1981, 373–74; for the official publication of the League, see SS, reg. 9, fol. 67r (21 January 1425mv). In a letter sent to Foscari from Crete in early 1426 by the secretary and chronicler Lorenzo de Monacis, the author emphasized that Foscari (and Venice) had undertaken the war with Milan not out of any desire for domination but only to protect the "welfare of Italy and of our fatherland." See Pertusi, 1970, 285, n. 2. For the new Venetian vision, see Mallett, 1996a, 194–96.

[65] SS, reg. 9, fols. 64r and 65r (acts dated 12 and 13 January 1425mv); Dolfin, 331r–v; Morosini, 617–18.

[66] MC, reg. 22 (Ursa), fol. 71v (21 December 1425); Dolfin, 330v; Sanudo, 1999, 43–44; Maranini, 1974, 2:140–43; Besta, 1899, 134.

[67] These events are summarized in Romanin, 4:85–88; Raulich, 1888, 661–96.

[68] SM, reg. 56, fol. 2v (23 March 1426); Dolfin, 331v–332r.

[69] Raulich, 1888, 672–76; Dolfin, 333v.

[70] SS, reg. 9, fols. 116r, 118r (acts dated 11 and 25 May 1426). The act of 11 May is published in Battistella, 1889, 484. See also Morosini, 649–50.

[71] SM, reg. 56, fol. 23v (29 June 1426); SS, reg. 9, fol. 140v (8 July 1426). The June act was proposed by Foscari and by the procurator Leonardo Mocenigo.

[72] Dolfin, 336v; Morosini, 727–28; Sanudo, 1999, 545.

[73] Raulich, 1888, 688–96; Predelli, 4:75–77, no. 232; Dolfin, 338r; Romanin, 4:87–88.

[74] Dolfin, 338r–v; Morosini, 762–63; Sanudo, 1999, 65. Each gives a different figure for the value of the gifts to Carmagnola's wife.

[75] Sanudo, 1999, 65–70; Dolfin, 338v–339r; Battistella, 1889, 151–55; Romanin, 4:89–91. For the pleas by the One Hundred for Carmagnola to act, see SS, reg. 10, fols. 47v and 48r–v (26 and 27 April 1427), passim.

[76] Battistella, 1889, 155; Mallett, 1984, 34–35.

[77] Battistella, 1889, 155–66, 175–77, 180–81; Romanin, 4, 91–93; SS, reg. 10, fols. 80v–82r; 85v–86r (1 and 7 September 1427).

[78] For the battle and the number of troops and prisoners, see Battistella, 1889, 183–91; see also Dolfin, 340v–41r; Sanudo, 1999, 550–51; Morosini, 832–35.

[79] Morosini, 835. In November the Great Council authorized the release of certain debt prisoners as well as the reduction of sentences for other prisoners by three months. MC, reg. 22 (Ursa), fol. 76v (9 November 1427).

[80] SS, reg. 10, fol. 96v (15 October 1427); Dolfin, 341r, 345v; Morosini, 943–44; Sanudo, 1999, 551, 558.

[81] Mallett, 1984, 190–91; Tassini, 1970, 622–23.

[82] Mallett, 1984, 187–90, quote on 187.

[83] See Guerrini, 1933, 338–50. It includes a flawed and incomplete transcription of the law (doc. 1). For the original, see SM, reg. 56, fol. 138v (7 December 1427). The victory was also celebrated in a polemic by Guarino Veronese. See Battistella, 1889, 511–19; and Sabbadini, 1896.

[84] Battistella, 1889, 202–05.

[85] SM, reg. 56, fol. 184v (10 May 1428); Romanin, 4:94–97.

[86] For the terms of the peace, see Dolfin, 342v–343v; Morosini, 871–75; Sanudo, 1999, 553–55; Predelli, 4:125–26, no. 15.

[87] SM, reg. 56, fols. 184r, 188r (9 and 24 May 1428); Dolfin, 344r; Morosini, 883–86; Sanudo, 1999, 556.

88 Dolfin, 344r–v; Morosini, 891–93.

89 Cessi, 1916, esp. 370–71; Battistella, 1889, 221–22; Mallett, 1984, 35 (for the phrase "permanent billets").

90 Morosini, 881–82.

91 BAV, Vat. Lat. 6085, "Cronica di Venetia," fol. 129r–v; Stöckly, 1995, 93–176; Lane, 1973, 337–42.

92 SM, reg. 56, fols. 130v, 131r (acts dated 29 October 1427). Knapton, 1986, 309, 315–17; Pezzolo, 1996, 707–08.

93 Information in this paragraph is taken from Mueller, 1997, 459–72, 488–92.

94 Ibid., 522–23, 465–69.

95 SM, reg. 56, fol. 48v (19 August 1426).

96 SM, reg. 56, fols. 9r–10r (30 April 1426); Dolfin, 333v.

97 DM, reg. 10, fol. 88v (9 October 1426).

98 For a provocative interpretation of these conflicts see Cracco, 1979, 80–90.

99 MC, reg. 22 (Ursa), fol. 73v (29 September 1426).

100 Ibid., fol. 77r–v (13 December 1427).

101 Ibid., fol. 78v (17 May 1428); SS, reg. 10, fol. 151v (following act dated 10 May 1428); Maranini, 1974, 2:143 (but with the incorrect year). It should be noted, however, that in September 1428 the Great Council approved a zonta (addition) of forty nobles to the Senate. MC, reg. 22 (Ursa), fol. 80v (28 September 1428).

102 SM, reg. 56, fol. 2v (18 March 1426). This act suggests again Foscari's reliance on the Great Council. For the process of Senate scrutiny as a substitute procedure for nominations, see Queller, 1986, 102.

103 MC, reg. 22 (Ursa), fol. 64v (13 April 1424).

104 Lane, 1973, 226, 323–24. The tradition appears to derive from the sixteenth-century diarist Girolamo Priuli. See Queller, 1986, 33; Mallett, 1996a, 239.

105 MC, reg. 22 (Ursa), fol. 70r (2 September 1425).

106 SM, reg. 55, fol. 156v (18 August 1425). For similar attitudes among the elites of Florence, see Molho, 1979, 9–11.

107 MC, reg. 22 (Ursa), fol. 70r (10 August 1425).

108 Ibid., fol. 82v (30 November 1428).

109 Rizzi, 2001, 2:111, entry 1077.

110 SM, reg. 55, fol. 102r (24 March 1425).

111 Ibid., reg. 56, fol. 120v (20 August 1427). The bill passed 48 to 20 with 1 abstention.

112 MC, reg. 22 (Ursa), fols. 74v–75r (acts dated 18 March 1427); Queller, 1986, 132–33.

113 Cicogna, 1969–70, 3:383.

114 Morosini, 759.

115 SS, reg. 10, fols. 39v, 42v–43r (26 and 31 March 1427); Morosini, 770.

116 Girgensohn, 1996, 763.

117 Ganudo, 1999, 7.

118 Dolfin, 345v.

119 SM, reg. 57, fols. 115v, 123r (acts dated 14 June and 1 July 1429).

120 BNM, It. Cl. VII, 380 (7471), Marco Barbaro, "Procuratori di San Marco," 29–30. It is Morosini (936–37) who reports that the avogadori di comun ruled the proposed contest between Venier and Donato invalid.

121 Battistella, 1889, 229–33; SS, reg. 10, fol. 224v (18 January 1428mv).

122 SS, reg. 10, fols. 239v–240v (15 February 1428mv); Morosini, 945–48; Predelli, 4:151–52, no. 101; Battistella, 1889, 234–36.

123 SS, reg. 10, fols. 224v, 241r (10 January and 22 February 1428mv); Battistella, 1889, 239.

124 SS, reg. 11, fol. 21r (9 July 1429); Battistella, 1889, 243–44.

125 Romanin, 4:100–02; Battistella, 1889, 245.

126 SS, reg. 11, fols. 92r–v, 99v–100v (21 and 23 April 1430). One part of the act of 23 April is transcribed in Battistella, 1889, 492. Romanin (4:102–03) thinks Venetian suspi-

cions of Carmagnola were growing; for a contrasting view, see Battistella, 1889, 245–51.

[127] Battistella, 1889, 254.

[128] SM, reg. 57, fol. 233r (6 July 1430). It is published in Battistella, 1889, 493. SS, reg. 11, fols. 132r, 133r, 134r, 154v (acts dated 1, 5, and 11 September 1430, and 15 December 1430). The December decision is also published in Battistella, 1889, 493–95.

[129] SS, reg. 57, fol. 149r (20 November 1430): "Et sit proverbium verissimum quod qui habet tempus non debet expectare tempus."

[130] Mallett, 1984, 204.

[131] Morosini, 958–59. For the commercial fraud, see Sanudo, 1999, 77–78.

[132] DM, reg. 10, fols. 108v–109r, 111v, 113v, 119v–121r (acts dated 28 April, 2 and 3 May, 8 June, 6 July, 22 and 28 September 1429). For Marcello's and Trevisan's grain interests, see ibid., fol. 110r (1 June 1429). In August and then in September the Ten authorized the release of some of the money in order to support Marcello's wife and children: ibid., fols. 117v, 119r (31 August and 15 September 1429).

[133] DM, reg. 10, fols. 122v–124v (acts dated 27 November through 29 December 1429); reg. 11, fols. 12r–14v (acts dated 2, 23, 30 August, 19 and 27 September 1430); Morosini, 1112–14; Sanudo, 1999, 81. Morosini was particularly incensed by Marcello's actions, saying (1113) that he had made himself, the "servant, slave, and man of the Duke of Milan."

[134] Nicol, 1988, 367–70.

[135] Sanudo, 1999, 560; Morosini, 951; G. Romano, 1890, 605–07; Gullino, 1996a, 36; Cozzi, 1986, 29.

[136] Sanudo, 1999, 561–62; Gullino, 1996a, 36; Nicol, 1988, 371. For the punishments, see SM, reg. 57, fols. 183v, 185r (acts dated 9, 12, and 27 January 1429mv); Dolfin, 348r; Morosini, 1053, 1055–56.

[137] Morosini, 1077, 1086–90, Dolfin, 348v–349r.

[138] Nicol, 1988, 372.

[139] SS, reg. 11, fols. 102r–103r (29 April 1430); Thiriet, 2:2192. For the treaty, see Dolfin, 350r; Morosini, 1124–27; a copy is published in Thomas, ed., 1969, 2:343–45.

[140] According to Nicol, 1988, 372.

[141] For the treaty with Byzantium, see SM, reg. 57, fol. 212v (8 May 1430); Thiriet, 2:2194; for the negotiations with Egypt, see SM, reg. 57, fols. 221r, 225v–230r (acts dated 17 June, 1 July 1430); Ashtor, 1983, 283–92; Nicol, 1988, 373.

[142] MC, reg. 22 (Ursa), fol. 89r (18 June 1430).

[143] Ibid., fol. 87v (2 March 1430). See also Bistort, 1969, 170; Frick, 2002, 157.

[144] MC, reg. 22 (Ursa), fol. 91v (11 November 1430).

[145] I have pieced together this account from Morosini, 1067–68; Dolfin, 348r–v; and Sanudo, 82–83, 564–65. As if the assassination attempt were not bad enough, Contarini's blow was directed at the face, which as the Great Council observed in 1443, constituted the "most noble" part of the human body. See MC, reg. 22 (Ursa), fol. 151v (29 June 1443).

[146] DM, reg. 11, fol. 7v (11 March 1430).

[147] Morosini, 1068; Sanudo, 1999, 82–83, 565.

[148] DM, reg. 11, fol. 7v (11 and 15 March 1430).

[149] Morosini, 1068.

[150] The reader will recall that a Contarini ran against Foscari for doge in 1423. Foscari's son Jacopo married a Contarini in 1441. Its many branches made the Contarini almost certainly the largest noble family in Venice.

[151] Muraro (1961b, 264–65) gives an error-filled account of the assassination attempt, arguing that it was carried out by

"a ruffian, undoubtedly hired by the patrician Andrea Contarini, the fierce leader of the party opposed to Foscari" (quote on 265). His transcription of the dedicatory inscription (265) is also unreliable.

[152] Ibid., 265. For examples of those following Muraro's theory, see Eisler, 1989, 20; Brown, 1996, 105; Merkel, 1973, 76–77, n. 2 (with the assassination attempt wrongly dated to 1431).

[153] Muraro, 1961b, 264, n. 2.

[154] On the different use of perspective on the left and right sides, see ibid., 273–74.

[155] Ibid.; Merkel, 1973, 65–80.

[156] Muraro, 1961b, 265, n. 10.

[157] For a full discussion of the altarpiece and the many theories regarding its authorship, see Wolters, 1976, 1:107–11 and cat. no. 235 (1:277–78).

[158] Dolfin, 308v–309r. Sanudo (1999, 77) mistakenly dates the fire ten years later, to March 1429.

[159] Morosini, 912–13. Sanudo (1999, 76–77) gives a much shorter version of these events.

[160] For the earlier rediscovery of Mark's relics, see Brown, 1996, 24–25.

[161] Pincus, 2000a, 36–38. There was also a private chapel within the Ducal Palace itself: ibid., 10.

[162] Cozzi, 1992–93, 10–11; Ravegnani, 1997, 336–37; Girgensohn, 2005, 280–83.

[163] For the *primicerio*, see Ongania, 1886, 258, citing the work of Nicolò Doglioni. For Polidoro, see Del Torre, 1997b, 347–50; for the date of his election, see Archivio Gradenigo, Rio Marin, b. 333, Pietro Gradenigo, "Lavoro storico", entry 41.

[164] PSM, de supra, Serie Chiesa, b. 79, fascicle 12, inventory of 30 September 1463. See also R. Gallo, 1967, 251; Ongania, 1886, 254.

[165] For the procurators as patrons, see Chambers, 1997.

[166] Pincus, 2000a, 146–47; Ongania, 1886, 14 (doc. 105).

[167] Quoted in Ongania, 1886, 252–53; for a different transcription with significant variants, see Wolters, 1976, 1:224. The translation is from Paoletti and Radke, 2002, 138.

[168] DM, reg. 12, fol. 131v (22 May 1443).

[169] Jacoff (1993, 111) holds a similar opinion regarding ducal involvement in San Marco. For the importance of *opera* or building committees as aspects of Medici patronage, see F. W. Kent, 2004, esp. 21–28.

[170] Gullino, 1991, 706.

[171] Demus, 1960, 43, 123–25; Gallo, 1967, 146. Muraro's claim (1961b, 265, n. 7) that the Chapel of the Madonna represented the first time that scenes from the life of the Virgin had appeared in Venetian art is incorrect. See Lafontaine-Dosogne, 1996.

[172] For the festival of the Marys, see Muir, 1981, 135–56; D. Romano, 1984, 74–76; Boholm, 1990, 153–78; Crouzet-Pavan, 1992, 527–56. For the feast of the Purification, see Muir, 1981, 155; Gallo, 1967, 146.

[173] Pincus, 2000a, 28–30.

[174] For the dates of his sons' deaths, see Sanudo, 1999, 7. Sanudo's date for the death of another son, Domenico, appears to be wrong. He died in 1437.

[175] Morosini, 1134–39; Sanudo (1999, 81) gives a brief description but misdates the event to 1429.

[176] SM, reg. 58, fol. 21r (28 December 1430).

[177] Ibid., fols. 30v, 69r (22 January 1430mv and 30 July 1431); MC, reg. 22 (Ursa), fol. 93r (28 May 1431).

[178] Romanin, 4:103–04; Battistella, 1889, 259–60.

[179] Dolfin, 351r. For Trevisan's election, see also SM, reg. 58, fol. 46v (27 March 1431).

[180] Romanin, 4:104–05.

[181] Dolfin, 352r; Morosini, 1180, 1183–84; Battistella, 1889, 311; Cozzi, 1986, 34–37.

[182] Battistella, 1889, 260–63.

[183] SS, reg. 11, fol. 199r (9 June 1431); Dolfin, 354r; Morosini, 1223.

[184] SS, reg. 11, fols. 191r, 195r (12 and 26 May 1431); Dolfin, 354; Morosini, 1218–19. The act of 26 May is printed in Battistella, 1889, 496–97.

[185] For the battle, see Dolfin, 354v–355r; Battistella, 1889, 272–77; for the Senate's action against the commanders, see SM, reg. 58, fols. 61r (30 June 1431), 67r–68v (14–24 July 1431).

[186] For the various opinions regarding Carmagnola's actions during this battle, see Battistella 1889, 277–89. See also Baldrighi, 1977.

[187] SS, reg. 12, fol. 7r (1 August 1431); Romanin, 4:107–08; Battistella 1889, 292–95.

[188] For the victory and Loredan's letter, see Dolfin, 355v–356r; Sanudo, 1999, 96–100. For the aid to the families, see SM, reg. 58, fol. 78r (4 September 1431).

[189] SS, reg. 12, fols. 18r (4 September 1431), 47v (4 December 1431).

[190] Ibid., fol. 26r (18 September 1431).

[191] For the Senate's effort to get him to move against Soncino, see ibid., fol. 20r–v (10 September 1431), also printed in Battistella, 1889, 497–99; for the failed move against Cremona, see Battistella, 1889, 305–10; Romanin, 4:108.

[192] Battistella, 1889, 310.

[193] Dolfin, 357r–v; Sanudo, 1999, 109; Battistella, 1889, 311–15. There is some uncertainty as to whether or not he ever made it to Friuli. See Mallett, 1984, 36.

[194] SS, reg. 12, fols. 52v–53r (28 December 1431); also printed in Battistella, 1889, 499–501.

[195] DM, reg. 11, fols. 28v, 29v–30v, 31r, 32r (acts dated 10 October, 7, 14, 21, 28 November, and 5 December 1431).

[196] SS, reg. 12, fols. 52v–53r (28 December 1431); Battistella, 1889, 499.

[197] SS, reg. 12, fol. 62r (28 January 1431mv); Battistella, 1889, 331–32.

[198] Battistella, 1889, 332–38.

[199] DM, reg. 11, fol. 37v (acts dated 28 March 1432); the proposal to have the rectors of Brescia detain him is also published in Battistella, 1889, 502, but incorrectly dated there as 27 March.

[200] DM, reg. 11, fols. 38r–39r (acts dated 29 March). Romanin (4:112–15) gives a translation of the orders to Imperiis.

[201] DM, reg. 11, fols. 39r–40r (letters dated 30 March). See also Romanin, 4:115–16.

[202] Sanudo, 1999, 590–91; Sanudo's account is very similar to the one found in Dolfin, 359r–v. Morosini (1349–63) also agrees in the essentials, with only some details differing.

[203] DM, reg. 11, fols. 41r–42v (acts dated 6 and 7 April 1432), quote on 42v. See also Battistella, 1889, 352–55.

[204] DM, reg. 11, fols. 43r–44r (acts dated 9–11 April 1432).

[205] Ibid., fol. 45r (acts dated 5 May 1432); Sanudo, 1999, 591; Dolfin, 360r. For a brief explanation of Venetian trial procedures and an Italian translation of the condemnation, see Romanin, 4:111–12, n. 33, 118–19.

[206] DM, reg. 11, fol. 45r (5 May 1432). Romanin identifies the unnamed Malatesta as Sigismondo.

[207] Morosini, 1362–63; Sanudo, 1999, 591–92; Dolfin, 360r. Their accounts differ in some details. For the burial at the Frari, see Battistella, 1889, 363.

[208] DM, reg. 11, fol. 47v (14 May 1432), also transcribed in Romanin, 4:120, n. 50.

[209] Ibid., fols. 77v, 117r (acts dated 27 May 1433 and 9 March 1435); Romanin (4:120, n. 50) gives the wrong date for the second act, as does Battistella, 1889, 363–64. For the move to Milan, see Battistella, 1889, 364.

[210] DM, reg. 11, fol. 47v (14 May 1432), *passim*.

[211] Ibid., fols. 51v, 53v, 85v, 95v (acts dated 23 July and 7 August 1432, 27 August 1433, and 14 April 1434).

[212] Mallett, 1974, 98–100; Mallett, 1984, 153–80.

[213] Sanudo, 1999, 591. See also Dolfin, 360r.

[214] Mallett, 1984, 37.

[215] Battistella, 1889, 387, and esp. 420 (where he cites near-contemporary non-Venetian sources); Romanin, 4:122–24.

[216] Cognasso, 1955, 286.

[217] Battistella (1889, 438) thinks Visconti may have promised him Brescia.

[218] Dolfin, 360r; Morosini, 1359; Sanudo, 1999, 594.

[219] For a brief summary of these events, see Sanudo, 1999, 599; Mallett, 1984, 27; Romanin, 4:121.

[220] SS, reg. 12, fols. 108v–109r (14 July 1432).

[221] DM, reg. 11, fol. 51v (14 July 1432). This was not put up for a vote.

[222] Perhaps the enmity dated from when Foscari became a procurator of San Marco, since his colleague was Alvise (Ludovico) Loredan, father of Pietro. It may well be that Alvise resented the upstart's meddling in an office in which he had served for years.

[223] Sanudo, 1999, 92.

[224] SM, reg. 58, fol. 95r (31 January 1431mv). For the general situation, see Mueller, 1997, 468–69.

[225] Sanudo, 1999, 109.

[226] MC, reg. 22 (Ursa), fols. 93v–94r (acts dated 2 July 1431); Sanudo, 1999, 94–95; Morosini, 1235–36; Besta, 1899, 134. Morosini writes that the proposal was "molto desputada."

[227] SM, reg. 58, fol. 68r (16 July 1431). For the position of bowman, see Queller, 1986, 34–39. For Barbarigo, see Lane, 1944, 17–18.

[228] DM, reg. 11, fol. 64r–v (acts dated 22–24 January 1432mv).

[229] Dolfin, 363v–364r. Sanudo's account (1999, 117–19) is very similar to Dolfin's.

[230] DM, reg. 11, fols. 65r–67v (acts dated 28 January 1432mv). Romanin (4:126) has some errors in his description of the penalties meted out.

[231] DM, reg. 11, fols. 69v–70r (acts dated 11 and 20 February 1432mv), 71r–72v (acts dated 20 and 25 February 1432mv).

[232] Ibid., fols. 68r–68v, 69r (acts dated 28 January 1432mv); see also fol. 70v (20 February 1432mv).

[233] Morosini, 1480; Dolfin, 363v; DM, reg. 11, fol. 64r (22 January 1432mv).

[234] Lane, 1971; D. Kent, 1978.

[235] Queller, 1986, 79–80. For my count of the conspirators with deceased fathers, I relied on the records of the Ten, rather than on the lists in the chronicles. For how notions of status were tied to notions of age, see D. Romano, 2005.

[236] SM, reg. 58, fols. 213v, 222v (24 June and 3 August 1433), reg. 59, fol. 12r (3 November 1433).

[237] Sinding-Larsen, 1974, 80; Lorenzetti, 1975, 282. I wish to remember Patricia Labalme, who first brought this inscription to my attention. Sanudo (1999, 663) offers an Italian translation.

[238] I have spelled out the abbreviations in the inscription.

[239] I wish to express my sincere gratitude to Robert Ulery for his great help with the translation of this inscription.

[240] Romanin, 4:121.

[241] Romanin, 4:121. For the ceremony, see Dolfin, 364v; for the palace, Mallett, 1984, 191.

[242] SS, reg. 12, fols. 174v–175r (20 March 1433); Romanin, 4:121; Morosini, 1513–15.

[243] For the terms of the peace, see Dolfin, 364v–365v; Predelli, 4:174–75, no. 183;

Romanin, 4:121–22; for the celebrations, Morosini, 1516–22.

[244] Dolfin, 365v; Sanudo, 1999, 600; Romanin, 4:127–28; Predelli, 4:177, no. 189. Cognasso (1955, 298) blames Visconti for the growing distance between the emperor and Milan.

[245] Morosini, 1531–33; Dolfin, 366r; Sanudo, 1999, 122, 600.

[246] According to Sanudo (1999, 94), Marco lost to Giacomo Trevisan, who got 285 votes to Foscari's 198.

[247] Sanudo, 1999, 7.

[248] AC, Raspe, reg. 3648, fols. 47r–48r (7 August 1430). Four of the participants got minor punishments; Lorenzo and the non-noble were absolved. For youthful indiscretions which had no long-term impact on a political career, see Chojnacki, 2002, 227–43.

[249] Girgensohn, ed. 2004, 69 (clause LV); Morosini, 1531–33; Dolfin, 366r; Sanudo, 1999, 600.

CHAPTER 3   THE ROYAL WAY, 1433–1442

[1] Piccolomini, 1991, 26.

[2] ST, reg. 1, fol. 2r (1 October 1440); SMar, reg. 1, fol. 3r (4 October 1440). Stöckly, 1995, 330.

[3] Sardella, 1948, 56–57.

[4] For useful summaries of Venice's relations with the terraferma, see Grubb, 1988; Knapton, 1998.

[5] This led the Venetians to claim a moral superiority over Rome. See Brown, 1996, 25, 99–100, passim.

[6] For Venice's imperial age, see the book of the same name, i.e. Chambers, 1970.

[7] D. Kent, 1978, 295.

[8] ASF, MAP, V, 703, 14 November 1433. The translation is from D. Kent, 1978, 305–06.

[9] For Cosimo's time in Venice, see Gutkind, 1938, 88–90; D. Kent, 1978, 306.

For Michelozzo, see Foscari, 1993; Muraro, 1961b, 270–73.

[10] Cozzi, 1986, 34–35.

[11] SM, reg. 58, fol. 216v (1 July 1433); SS, reg. 12, fols. 198v–199r (3 August 1433); Dolfin, 366r–v; Sanudo, 1999, 123, 601–02; Morosini, 1559–60, 1566. Morosini dates Donato's election as occurring in September.

[12] DM, reg. 11, fol. 88v (4 November 1433); Morosini, 1574–79; Cozzi, 1986, 36.

[13] Romanin, 4:128–29.

[14] Eroli, 1879, 7–62 (the condotta is published as doc. ix, 264–70); Dolfin, 368r.

[15] Mallett, 1984, 38.

[16] Dolfin, 369v–370r; Sanudo, 1999, 127–28, 605; Romanin, 4:131–32; Eroli, 1879, 72–73. D. Kent (1978, 330) quotes a letter from Jacopo Donato stating that Cosimo and Lorenzo loaned Venice 30,000 ducats. The original is ASF, MAP, IV, 331, letter dated 11 September 1434.

[17] D. Kent, 1978, 328; Dolfin, 371r; Sanudo, 1999, 611; SS, reg. 13, fols. 117r–118r (28 October 1434).

[18] SM, reg. 58, fol. 201v (9 May 1433); SS, reg. 12, fol. 188r (4 June 1433); Mallett, 1984, 38.

[19] SM, reg. 58, fol. 212r (20 June 1433); DM, reg. 11, fols. 80v–81r, 84r, 88v (acts dated 8 and 23 July, 12 August, 29 October 1433); Morosini, 1554; Dolfin, 366v.

[20] SM, reg. 59, fols. 37r–v, 49r (acts dated 9 March and 17 May 1434). The order to sell the Rialto property was revoked on 6 April (fol. 42r).

[21] Dolfin, 367v–368r; SM, reg. 59, fols. 21r–23r (8 January 1433mv).

[22] SM, reg. 59, fol. 26r (11 February 1433mv).

[23] Ibid., fol. 27r–v (acts dated 11 and 12 February 1433mv); the law is published in Besta, 1912, 103–06.

[24] MC, reg. 22 (Ursa), fol. 105r–v (14 March 1434); the law is discussed in Luz-

zatto, ed., 1929, ccxxxvii–ccxxxviii and published on 272–73.

[25] MC, reg. 22 (Ursa), fol. 105v (18 April 1434).

[26] SM, reg. 59, fol. 40v (1 April 1434).

[27] SM, reg. 59, fols. 77v–78r, 81v (7 and 9 November, 2 December 1434); MC, reg. 22 (Ursa), fol. 108r–v (acts dated 11 November 1434). The second of the Great Council laws is published in Luzzatto, ed., 1929, 274–75; see also the discussion by Dolfin (371r), who wrongly dates the laws to September.

[28] Predelli, 4:177, no. 189; Romanin, 4:127–28; Hazlitt, 1966, 1:908. Both Romanin and Hazlitt incorrectly give the date of the agreement as 1432.

[29] Romanin, 4:130–32; Cozzi, 1986, 36–37.

[30] SS, reg. 13, fols. 42r–v 94v–96v (22 January 1433mv, 2 and 4 August 1434).

[31] Predelli, 4:201–02, no. 1.

[32] Romanin, 4:136.

[33] Gullino, 1996c, 355; Zamperetti, 1991, 34–44. By contrast, Cozzi (1986, 37) viewed the vicariate as "piuttosto riduttiva," given the reality of Venetian control of the terraferma.

[34] J. Schulz, 1991, 438–40; Brown, 1996, 8–9, 11, 17–18, 108–15; Chambers, 1970, 12–30.

[35] Gullino, 1996c, 355.

[36] I wish to thank Gary Radke for calling my attention to this latter possibility.

[37] Dolfin, 375v–376r. Sanudo (1999, 154–62) gives Italian translations of the concession made by Sigismund and the oath of fealty by Foscari.

[38] For the list of cities I follow Predelli, 4:213, no. 25. However Romanin (4:137), following Sanudo (1999, 154, 156), lists in place of Piadena, Platina or Peschiera.

[39] As noted by Romanin, 4:138. For the exception of Verona, see Law, 2000, X:9–11.

[40] For Donato's knighting, see Morosini, 1558; Dolfin, 365v; for those of Contarini, Venier, and Barbaro, see Morosini, 1566.

[41] Morosini, 1566.

[42] For Marco's election, see BNM, It. Cl. VII, 380 (7471), Marco Barbaro, "Procuratori di San Marco", 30.

[43] DM, reg. 11, fols. 110v, 112r (acts dated 21 October and 10 November 1434); for the Collalto family connections to the Carraresi, see Kohl, 1998, 192, 292.

[44] DM, reg. 11, fol. 118v (acts dated 17 March 1435). I have been unable to determine whether or not the Ten were poorly informed at this point regarding the names of the two. As it turned out men named Antonio and Benedetto Sartorelli were among the principal conspirators: ibid., fol. 124r (act dated 23 March 1435). For the conspiracy see also Segarizzi, 1916.

[45] DM, reg. 11, fol. 119r–v (acts dated 17 March 1435). For the travel time, see MC, reg. 22 (Ursa), fol. 187r (13 February 1451mv).

[46] DM, reg. 11, fols. 119v–120v (acts dated 18, 19, 20 March 1435).

[47] For accounts of the conspiracy, see Dolfin, 371v–372r; Sanudo, 1999, 612–14; Segarizzi, 1916; and Montobbio, 1989, 198–200. In addition, the humanist Jacopo Zeno wrote an account of the conspiracy. See Bertalot, 1975, 103–29.

[48] DM, reg. 11, fol. 121r (acts dated 21 and 22 March 1435).

[49] Ibid., fol. 121v (acts dated 22 March 1435).

[50] Dolfin, 372r. For Marsiglio's condemnation, see DM, reg. 11, fol. 122r (23 March 1435); for various other condemnations and rewards, ibid., fols. 122r–129r (acts dated 23 March to 1 April 1435). For the Buzzacarini family's connections to the Carraresi, see Kohl, 1998, 97, 113, 167, 174.

[51] DM, reg. 11, fols. 130v–131r (6 and 27 April 1435); SM, reg. 59, fol. 107v (4 May

1435). For the reward to Este, see also Mallett, 1984, 189.

52 Giustiniano, 1798, 34.

53 For efforts by the Bishop of Padua Pietro Dolfin (uncle of Foscari's son-in-law Andrea) to celebrate Paduan cultural traditions while also allying the city more closely to Venice, see Holgate, 2002.

54 For accounts of the conspiracy, see Dolfin, 385v, Sanudo, 1999, 256–57, 259, Montobbio, 1989, 207–08. For the actions of the Ten, see, for example, DM, reg. 12, fols. 34v–38r (various acts dated August 1439), fol. 40v (15 October 1439), fols. 42r–46v (various acts dated November 1439).

55 DM, reg. 15, fols. 94v, 95v (acts dated 26 and 31 May 1456).

56 Dolfin, 372v–373r; Sanudo, 1999, 614–16; Romanin, 4:132–34.

57 Cessi, 1981, 381–82.

58 SM, reg. 59, fol. 161v (8 June 1436).

59 Ibid., fol. 183r (22 November 1436).

60 DM, reg. 11, fols. 149v–150r, 152r (acts dated 23 and 25 July and 22 August 1436); SM, reg. 59, fol. 168r (6 August 1436).

61 Mallett, 1984, 39; Cognasso, 1955, 322–23; for the instructions to Loredan, see SS, reg. 14, fol. 38r (28 May 1437).

62 Dolfin, 377r; Cognasso, 1955, 323–24.

63 SS, reg. 14, fols. 29v–30r, 51r, 74v (acts dated 9 April, 11 August, and 26 November 1437). At the same time the Senate agreed to reserve for Jacopo an office with the *rason vecchie* (an office with jurisdiction over various rectors) that he currently held.

64 Eroli, 1879, 96; Mallett, 1984, 39; Tarducci, 1899.

65 SS, reg. 14, fol. 84r (23 December 1437); Eroli, 1879, 97–98.

66 Dolfin, 378r; Cognasso, 1955, 324.

67 Romanin, 4:135; Cognasso, 1955, 324– 28.

68 SS, reg. 14, fol. 86r (31 December 1438).

69 Da Bisticci, 1997, 218.

70 Gutkind, 1938, 145–48.

71 For crucial background on the negotiations leading to the church council's move to Ferrara, see Gill, 1961a, 46–98.

72 SM, reg. 60, fol. 46r (3 December 1437). See also Thiriet, 3:2455.

73 I have relied for my account of the emperor's visit on: Syropoulos, 1971, 213–27; Dolfin, 379v–381r; Sanudo, 1999, 162–68, 627–29; Gill, 1961a, 98–104; and Romanin, 4:139–40.

74 Syropoulos (1971, 217) says that Foscari greeted them at San Giorgio Maggiore.

75 Sources differ as to whether Foscari sat on the emperor's right or left: ibid., 217, n. 6.

76 Ibid., 217, n. 5.

77 J. Schulz, 2004, 152–57.

78 Syropoulos, 1971, 221–25.

79 Ibid., 217; Sanudo (1999, 168) also reports the death. For the letter, see Barbaro, 1991–99, 2:228–29. Barbaro reports that Domenico died of the plague. See also Gothein, 1932, 177.

80 Muir, 1981, 221–23; and for a different legend, Radke, 2001, 446–47. For Elena's election, see Radke, 2001, 440.

81 Radke, 2001, 440–45, quote on 445. For an interpretation of the chapel as a celebration of the Venetian state under Doge Foscari, see Aikema, 2000, esp. 33. For the identification of Marina as sister of Bartolomeo and thus aunt to Andrea Donato *miles*, see Holgate, 2002, 8.

82 For the Cà d'Oro, see Goy, 1992; for the Scuola Grande di San Marco, see DM, reg. 12, fol. 2r (3 July 1437).

83 SM, reg. 60, fols. 110v–111r (14 November 1438).

84 Ibid., fol. 3v (23 March 1437).

85 Ibid., fol. 17r (4 June 1437). On the *proti* and the doge's responsibility as overseer of the Arsenal, see Lane, 1992, 54–55; R. C. Davis, 1991, 152.

86 Corner, 1990, 307–08.

87 SM, reg. 60, fol. 17r–v (acts dated 4 and 8 June 1437).

88 SM, reg. 59, fol. 155v (20 April 1436).

89 SM, reg. 59, fols. 141v, 155v (acts dated 3 February 1435mv and 20 April 1436). For another example, which preserves the wording of the petition of the Scuola di Santa Maria della Giustizia to the doge, see DM, reg. 13, fol. 5r (26 May 1445).

90 SM, reg. 60, fol. 10r (10 May 1437). For the ritual itself, see Muir, 1981, 119–34.

91 Dolfin, 381r–382v; Sanudo, 1999, 171, 633–34.

92 However, much to Gonzaga's dismay, Visconti kept changing the terms of their agreement. See Tarducci, 1899, 274–75, 294, 315, 325, 329.

93 Sanudo, 1999, 634–35; Dolfin, 382v–383r; SS, reg. 14, fol. 129r (9 July 1438).

94 Mallett, 1996a, 197.

95 Sanudo, 1999, 635; Romanin, 4:142; Eroli, 1879, 112–15.

96 SS, reg. 14, fols. 126v–127r, 129r (acts dated 6 and 9 July 1438); Sanudo, 1999, 181–82.

97 Ibid., fol. 133v (19 July 1438); Sanudo, 1999, 181.

98 Dolfin, 383r; Sanudo, 1999, 639; Tarducci, 1899, 304–05.

99 Sanudo, 1999, 185; Tarducci, 1899, 306–07.

100 Eroli, 1879, 115–21; Hazlitt, 1966, 1: 919; Sanudo, 1999, 639–40.

101 Soranzo, 1957, 85–88. For the designation captain-general, see SS, reg. 14, fol. 156r–v (acts dated 1 and 2 October 1438); for the palace, see Dolfin, 383v–384r; for election to the Great Council, see Eroli, 1879, 121, 333–34.

102 Sanudo, 1999, 181, 189; SS, reg. 14, fols. 129v–130r (11 July 1438).

103 Sanudo, 1999, 184.

104 Dolfin, 384r–v; Sanudo, 1999, 642–43.

105 SS, reg. 14, fol. 161r (21 October 1438).

106 Sanudo (1999, 196) incorrectly reports that Giacomo returned on that date. But Dolfin (384v) reports that it was Pietro.

107 Gullino (2005a, 778) states that Loredan died on 28 October, not 11 November as reported by Sanudo (1999, 199).

108 A copy of his will is found in PSM, Misti, b. 52, testament 41. Sanudo (1999, 199–200) reports that he was buried with the stone pillow and barefoot. Other information about his funeral and the bequest of the book to Sant'Elena is found in Sant'Elena in Isola, b. 1, parchment notebook titled "Liber importantissimo," fols. 13v–14r. For a transcribed extract, see Cicogna, 1969–70, 3:384, n. 1.

109 PSM, Misti, b. 52, testament 41. For the display of banners and arms in porteghi, see J. Schulz, 2004, 25; Brown, 2004, 19–20.

110 PSM, Misti, b. 52, testament 37. And Jacopo left some other flags to his grandsons, children of his son Luca.

111 Sanudo, 1999, 200.

112 SM, reg. 59, fol. 13r (6 November 1433). See also Thiriet, 3:2332.

113 SM, reg. 59, fol. 92r (7 February 1434mv).

114 DM, reg. 11, fol. 132v (5 May 1435). The capi for May were Loredan, Niccolò Capello, and Alessandro Zorzi (ibid., fol. 131v). For the possible sodomy case involving Alvise, son of Filippo Foscari, ibid., fol. 76v (13 May 1433). In July 1433 Foscari proposed a strict gag order on a recent sodomy case: ibid., fol. 83r (30 July 1433). Many Venetian noble families had cadet lines, traceable to an illegitimate ancestor. Some of these cadet lines enjoyed cittadino status (Grubb, 2000, 352). This was likely the case as well with the Foscari. A certain Andrea Foscari was a ducal gastaldo. His son was convicted of sodomy. See DM, reg. 12, fol. 16v (28 May 1438).

115 Ibid., reg. 12, fols. 23v–24v (acts dated 17–26 November 1438).

116 Ibid., fol. 25r–v (acts dated 3 and 11 December 1438).

117 Sanudo, 1999, 188.

118 Finlay, 1980, 81. The quotation is Finlay's, but note that I have been unable to track Sanudo's remarks based on the citation given by Finlay.

119 MC, reg. 22 (Ursa), fol. 130v (24 June 1440).

120 Sanudo, 1999, 188, 201. For the meaning of the verb which Sanudo used to describe Foscari's action ("galdeva"), see Boerio, 1973, 295 ("galdèr").

121 Sanudo, 1999, 634.

122 There were also rumors that Visconti had had Loredan poisoned.

123 Girgensohn, ed. 2004, 115 (clause CVII).

124 D. Kent, 2000, 29–31; F. W. Kent, 2004, 62–64, 70, 92, 103–04.

125 Dolfin, 374r.

126 SM, reg. 60, fol. 45v (14 December 1437). For the agreement with a master mason named Steffanim to carry out much of this work, see Lorenzi, 1868, 66–68.

127 AC, Raspe, reg. 3647, fol. 243v (17 July 1426).

128 DM, reg. 11, fol. 155v (21 November 1436).

129 In June 1428 the Ten passed an act to purchase cuirasses, helmets, bows, and other items for their armory, as printed in Lorenzi, 1868, 65.

130 Provveditori al Sal, b. 6, reg. 3, fol. 84r–v. A generally reliable copy of the contract is found in Lorenzi, 1868, 68–69; a translation of the original agreement (but not of the later amendments) is in Chambers, 1971, 66–69.

131 A. M. Schulz, 1978b, 7–25, 68–70.

132 Most of what follows derives from Pincus, 1976, 48–56. For the name, ibid., 42, n. 13; for the clever translation "Document Gate," see Wills, 2001, 100.

133 Pincus, 1976, 52.

134 Dolfin, 386v; Sanudo, 1999, 288.

135 Lorenzi, 1868, 70.

136 A. M. Schulz, 1978b, 71.

137 Guidi, 1995, 8. See also Rossi, 1893, esp. 414.

138 Pincus, 1976, 48, 56, 155–61.

139 Sansovino, 1968, 319. As Serena Romano notes, the Porta ties together "indissolubly three images and three concepts: his [Foscari's] person, the idea of justice, and Venice" (S. Romano, ed., 1979, 12).

140 For the schemes of the virtues, see Skinner, 2002, 61–64.

141 A. M. Schulz, 1978b, 47–48. Debra Pincus informs me that the recutting is not certain and that the *corno* is a restoration.

142 Rollo-Koster, 2003, 94. She is referring to gates in city walls, but the point seems as true in the case of the Porta della Carta since Venice did not have city walls.

143 For a discussion of the doge and lion group, see Pincus, 1976, 384–401. However, Pincus now believes that the first ensemble (on the Porta della Carta) may date to the 1440s.

144 Marx, 1978, 9.

145 Pincus, 1976, 64, 69–70.

146 Ibid., 64–69. Gentile Bellini's drawing of *The Judgement of Solomon* in his Louvre notebook also gives some sense of how the Portico and Scala were related. Eisler, 1989, 284, plates 153–54.

147 Pincus, 1976, 73–75; the phrase "via triumphalis" first appears in Hubala, 1965, 641. Giorgio Bellavitis (2005, 96) has suggested that the new entryway created the equivalent of a *portego* into a typical Venetian palace.

148 Pincus, 1976, 76–103, quote on 97.

149 Gundersheimer, 1973, 96, n. 10.

150 Wills, 2001, 101.

151 I have taken this account from: Sanudo, 1999, 291–92; Romanin, 4:144–45; Hazlitt,

1966, 1:921–22; Soranzo, 1957, 92–93; Mallett, 1984, 98–99; King, 1994, 247. The quote is from Hazlitt. For the painting in the Great Council Hall, see Lorenzetti, 1975, 276.

[152] SS, reg. 14, fol. 192r (23 March 1439); Romanin, 4:145; Soranzo, 1957, 97–98. For Donato, see also Sanudo, 1999, 229–30, 241, and MC, reg. 22, fol. 131v (12 August 1440).

[153] SS, reg. 14, fol. 210r (23 June 1439); Sanudo, 1999, 211, 214; Dolfin, 385r; Soranzo, 1957, 100–02.

[154] Mallett, 1996a, 197; Cessi, 1981, 383.

[155] Predelli, 4:218–19, no. 45; Soranzo, 1957, 102. King (1994, 247) gives the incorrect figure of 18,000 ducats.

[156] SS, reg. 14, fols. 202v–203r (6 May 1439); also quoted in Soranzo, 1957, 100. Malipiero was so offended that he did not get to deliver the cloth that he insulted Foscari by making an obscene gesture. Sanudo, 1999, 245.

[157] Sanudo, 1999, 246, 249; SS, reg. 14, fol. 214v (30 July 1439); Romanin, 4:145.

[158] Dolfin, 385v; Sanudo, 1999, 267; Soranzo, 1957, 93.

[159] SS, reg. 14, fols. 231v–232r (10 October 1439); Sanudo, 1999, 268–70; Mallett, 1984, 99.

[160] Dolfin, 385v–386r; Soranzo, 1957, 107–08; Romanin, 4:145–46. For the text of the letter to Foscari, see Sanudo, 1999, 271.

[161] Dolfin, 386r; Sanudo, 1999, 273–76; Soranzo, 1957, 108–09; Mallett, 1984, 192.

[162] Sanudo, 1999, 277; Soranzo, 1957, 109; Mallett, 1984, 191.

[163] DM, reg. 12, fol. 50r (30 December 1439).

[164] This information on Gattamelata's illness and death is taken from Soranzo, 1957, 110–14. For the texts of the orations, see Eroli, 1879, 348–61. For a brief biography, see Menniti Ippolito, 1993.

[165] Soranzo, 1957, 102; Eroli, 1879, 328–31; Mallet, 1984, 156–57.

[166] For the arbitration of the price, see Eroli, 1879, 208–15.

[167] Dolfin, 386v; Romanin, 4:146–47.

[168] Sanudo, 1999, 308, 310, 315–16; Dolfin, 386v. More measured language is used in Orsato Giustinian's commission as ambassador to Florence: SS, reg. 15, fols. 19v–20v (19 April 1440). See also Hazlitt, 1966, 1:928–30. For the transfer of the church council to Florence, see Gill, 1961a, 176–89.

[169] For the naval victory on Garda, see Sanudo, 1999, 312–13; Dolfin, 386v–387r. And for the victory celebrations and alms-giving, see SM, reg. 60, fols. 205r, 208v (acts dated 12 April 1440).

[170] Da Soldo, 1938–42, 1:45.

[171] This account of Brescia's rededication is taken from Dolfin, 387r; Sanudo, 1999, 312.

[172] Sanudo, 1999, 330–33, 339; Dolfin, 387v; MC, reg. 22 (Ursa), fol. 130v (29 June 1440).

[173] For the takeover of Ravenna, see Barbiani, 1927, 34–42; Berti, 2001, 305–16. For fears of Venetian imperialism, see Mallett, 1996a, 197–99. For Venetian views of the takeover, see Dolfin, 387v–388r; Sanudo, 1999, 326, 343–44.

[174] For the negotiations via Este, see SS, reg. 15, fol. 28r (25 June 1440); Sanudo, 1999, 335. For Bianca Maria, see Dolfin, 388r; Sanudo, 1999, 344.

[175] SS, reg. 15, fols. 31v–32r (30 July 1440). For Malipiero's election as proveditor, see SM, reg. 60, fol. 211r (3 May 1440); and for his commission, SS, reg. 15, fol. 23r (18 May 1440).

[176] SS, reg. 15, fols. 46v–47r (4 October 1440).

[177] Cognasso, 1955, 340.

[178] Sforza arrived in Venice in December for consultations; he appears to have departed and then returned for the wedding. For this and the quote, see Sanudo, 1999, 345.

[179] Sforza made numerous visits that year, each warranting a reception. For the visits of various dignitaries in 1440, see Sanudo, 1999, 289, 298, 307, 314, 345.

[180] For the future queen's visit, see Sanudo, 1999, 320–25; Dolfin, 387r–v; SM, reg. 60, fol. 211r (1 May 1440). For Dogaressa Marina's role in this and other visits, see Hurlburt, 2006, 96–105.

[181] ST, reg. 1, fol. 5v (26 November 1440); Muir, 1981, 84–85.

[182] For the prohibition in Foscari's *promissione*, see Girgensohn, ed. 2004, 95 (clause LXXXIIII); see also Lane, 1973, 94–95.

[183] ST, reg. 1, fol. 6v (4 December 1440). Members of the Collegio were also prohibited from selling Monte shares while in office.

[184] It will be recalled (see chapter 2 above) that at the time of his first abdication attempt in 1433, Morosini claimed that Foscari had two sons: one age five and another between ten and twelve. The five-year-old must have been Domenico who died in 1438. That would place Jacopo's birth between 1421 and 1423, and his age at marriage in 1441 between eighteen and twenty. For the average age of Venetian males at marriage, see Chojnacki, 2000, 185–205, esp. 195.

[185] Finlay, 1980, 134–35; for the prohibition, see Girgensohn, ed. 2004, 61 (clause XLVII).

[186] For Nogarola's letter, see Nogarola, 1886, 1:46–54 (as well as letters to him by her sister Ginevra [2:329–34] and by Guarino Veronese [1:55–60]); and now a translation of her letter to Jacopo in Nogarola, 2004, 45–48. For Bruni's letters, see Bruni, 1741, 2:96–97, 109. For the work by Foscarini, which he wrote while captain of Feltre (Victor and Corona were Feltre's patrons), see Frazier, 2004, 58–59, 387. For a fuller account and bibliography of Jacopo's humanist interests, see King, 1986, 372–73.

[187] The letter was first published by Flaminio Corner (Cornelio, 1758, 167–72). A version is also found in Sanudo, 1999 (349–55) but not in Sanuto, 1733; I have relied on the former.

[188] Chojnacki, 2000, 187.

[189] Ibid., 43. Corner's version of the letter gives the dowry amount as 16,000 ducats, but it is much more likely that it was within the legal limit of 1600.

[190] Frick, 2002, 128–32, quote on 129.

[191] In her description of marriage rituals in Florence, Klapisch-Zuber (1987, 183) describes the first stage as the sealing of the alliance ("fermare il parentado"). I believe that this is what occurred as the first stage in this wedding, as the brothers begin the description, "El zorno 'landò in parentà tra de una parte e de l'altra" (Sanudo, 1999, 350).

[192] In another measure designed to protect the bride, the Senate passed a law on 21 January regulating who was allowed on the *bucintoro* when it went to retrieve Lucrezia. ST, reg. 1, fol. 11v (21 January 1440mv).

[193] For the *sponsalia* or *sposalizio*, see Klapisch-Zuber, 1987, 185–86. Tellingly the brothers use the verb "fo sposada" to describe what occurred on this day (Sanudo, 1999, 350).

[194] Dolfin (388r) gives different dates for the various stages of the marriage process. He says that the transfer of the bride to the Ducal Palace occurred on 5 February.

[195] Klapisch-Zuber, 1987, 186–87.

[196] Among those who enjoyed membership in the same company as Jacopo was Federigo di Montefeltro. See Paltroni, 1966, 45.

[197] For the Fat Thursday celebrations in Venice, see Muir, 1981, 156–61.

[198] And for the ambiguity provoked by the use of the Great Council Hall, see Casini, 1996, 290–91.

[199] For a different interpretation of the wedding, especially its significance in terms of Venice's urban history, see Crouzet-Pavan, 1992, 606–11.

[200] Dolfin, 388v; Sanudo, 1999, 355; Da Soldo, 1938–42, 1:53. Dolfin and Sanudo report that it appeared on 24 April, which they call the feast of Saint George (recte 23 April). Da Soldo says it occurred on 25 April, the feast of Saint Mark.

[201] Sanudo, 1999, 356–58; Dolfin, 388v–390r; Romanin, 4:147–48.

[202] Predelli, 4:262–66, no. 183; Romanin, 4:148.

[203] Mallett, 1984, 40.

[204] Cessi, 1981, 384.

[205] Dolfin, 389v–390r; Sanudo, 1999, 358; MC, reg. 22 (Ursa), fols. 138v–139r (acts dated 26 November and 21 December 1441); DM, reg. 12, fol. 36r (14 December 1441); Da Soldo, 1938–42, 1:57.

[206] Sanudo, 1999, 358; Dolfin, 390r.

[207] I have compiled this description of their visit from the accounts by Sanudo and Dolfin, accounts that differ in many particulars. Sanudo, 1999, 359–63; Dolfin, 390r–v. For the Senate vote, see ST, reg. 1, fol. 66v (26 April 1442).

[208] SMar, reg. 1, fol. 95r (1 May 1442); Sanudo, 1999, 361.

[209] The Senate authorized spending between 500 and 600 ducats. Perhaps Dolfin overestimated its value. SS, reg. 15, fol. 119v (10 April 1442).

[210] For imposts of the estimo, see Mueller, 1997, 465, 528, and slightly different figures in Pezzolo, 1996, 709. For the taxes on the terraferma and Crete, see SM, reg. 60, fols. 125r–v, 126v (acts dated 21–23, 27 February 1438mv). See also Thiriet, 3:2488, 2489. For loans from the Soranzo bank, see ST, reg. 1, fol. 59r (5 February 1441mv).

[211] SM, reg. 60, fols. 121r–122r (acts dated 27 January 1438mv); extract transcribed in

Luzzatto, ed., 1929, 278–79; see also Sanudo, 1999, 210–11. For an evaluation of the significance of the boccatico, see Luzzatto, ed., 1929, ccxxxii; Pezzolo, 1996, 708–10.

[212] SM, reg. 60, fols. 132r, 134v (acts dated 9 and 31 March 1439); Sanudo, 1999, 223, 226.

[213] SM, reg. 60, fol. 137v (17 April 1439).

[214] SM, reg. 60, fol. 168r–v (22 August 1439); printed in Besta, 1912, 107–10; and extract in Luzzatto 1929, 279–81; Sanudo, 1999, 258; see also the discussion in Luzzatto, 1929, ccxxxiii; Pezzolo, 1996, 710.

[215] SM, reg. 60, fol. 173v (13 October 1439).

[216] Mueller, 1997, 465, 468, 528; Pezzolo, 1996, 708–12, quote in Luzzatto, ed., 1929, ccxliv.

[217] ST, reg. 1, fol. 52v (4 January 1441mv).

[218] Ibid., fol. 69r (24 May 1442).

[219] DM, reg. 12, fol. 91r (27 September 1441).

[220] MC, reg. 22 (Ursa), fol. 137v (15 October 1441).

[221] DM, reg. 12, fol. 93v (8 November 1441).

[222] SM, reg. 60, fol. 247v (5 August 1440). See also AC, Raspe, reg. 3648, fol. 206v (4 August 1440). It should be noted that in December Paolo Bernardo was tried for the same offence. ST, reg. 1, fol. 6r (8 December 1440). For the small cargo ship, called a maran, see Lane, 1992, 53, n. 57.

[223] Sanudo, 1999, 229–30, 241; Soranzo, 1957, 97–99.

[224] MC, reg. 22 (Ursa), fol. 131v (12 August 1440). See also AC, Raspe, reg. 3648, fol. 207r (12 August 1440).

[225] Dolfin, 391r–v.

[226] Sanudo, 1999, 364.

[227] Finlay, 1980, 125.

[228] Lane, 1973, 93.

[229] Tenenti (1996, 333), for example, while not discussing Foscari directly, argues that

during the late Trecento and especially the Quattrocento the Council of Ten saved Venice from becoming a princely regime.

230 For a Genoese response to the same imperatives, see Shaw, 2005, 71.

231 Eisler, 1989, 22.

232 Muraro, 1961a.

233 Skinner, 2002, 121–23.

CHAPTER 4   THE HOUSE OF FOSCARI, 1443–1453

1 Priuli, 1912–40, 4:40. My translation differs somewhat from that in Finlay, 1980, 134.

2 DM, reg. 12, fol. 174v (20 February 1444mv); also printed in Berlan, 1852, 72–74. By Romania, the Venetians at various times meant the Byzantine empire or their possessions in Greece.

3 ST, reg. 1, fols. 52v and 84v (acts dated 4 January 1441mv and 18 December 1442).

4 Ibid., fol. 84r (28 December 1442); also published in Luzzatto, ed., 1929, 293–94 (but with the wrong date). For the tax revolt, see especially Mueller, 1997, 505–06.

5 ST, reg. 1, fol. 68r (16 May 1442).

6 MC, reg. 22 (Ursa), fol. 113r (22 January 1435mv).

7 Sanudo, 1999, 132.

8 Ashtor, 1983, 297–305; Stöckly, 1995, 148–49; Gullino, 1996a, 46.

9 Sanudo, 1999, 364. Dolfin (391r) gives the figure as 4000 ducats and says he accepted for fear of the penalty for refusal. Leonardo Contarini, father of Jacopo's wife, was also elected but refused the post. For the election and Donato's commission, see SMar, reg. 1, fols. 107r–v, 109v, 114v–115v (acts dated 17 and 24 July, 4 August 1442).

10 Dolfin, 391v; Sanudo, 1999, 370, 374–76; Ashtor, 1983, 305.

11 Thiriet, 3:2590–92; Nicol, 1988, 382.

12 Nicol, 1988, 381–83; Thiriet, 3:2607–08.

13 SMar, reg. 1, fol. 174r (17 May 1443); reg. 2, fol. 2r (8 May 1444).

14 SS, reg. 16, fols. 65r, 105v (13 February 1443mv and 7 July 1444); SMar, reg. 1, fol. 228v (23 March 1444). See also Thiriet, 3:2638.

15 DM, reg. 12, fol. 137r (25 August 1443). See also ibid., fol. 138r (6 September 1443).

16 Fine, 1987, 533–34; Romanin, 4:175.

17 Sanudo, 1999, 391–92; Fine, 1987, 530–34; 548; Nicol, 1988, 383; Thiriet, 3: 2623, 2659.

18 Fine, 1987, 549–51; Nicol, 1988, 383–84; Thiriet, 3:2651, 2655–56, 2668.

19 Nicol, 1988, 384.

20 Thiriet, 3:2663, 2675, 2681; Predelli, 4:296, no. 289; Nicol, 1988, 385–88.

21 Sanudo, 1999, 365-67; SMar, reg. 1, fols. 111r and 130v (acts dated 27 July and 12 October 1442); SS, reg. 15, fols. 129v and 131r (acts dated 11 and 18 July 1442).

22 Dolfin, 398v, 401v; Sanudo, 1999, 386–87, 390, 398, 400–01; Cognasso, 1955, 351–55. Malatesta's second wife was Polissena, illegitimate daughter of Sforza.

23 SS, reg. 16, fols. 123v–125r (3 and 5 October 1444).

24 Cozzi, 1986, 41.

25 Cognasso, 1955, 358–63; Romanin, 4: 153–54; Gill, 1961b, 158.

26 Cozzi, 1986, 40.

27 MC, reg. 22 (Ursa), fols. 150v–151r (29 June 1443).

28 Ibid., fols. 151v–152r (acts dated 29 June 1443).

29 Ibid., fol. 157v (7 June 1444).

30 SMar, reg. 1, fol. 204r (19 December 1443).

31 MC, reg. 22 (Ursa), fols. 159r and 162r (acts dated 28 December 1444 and 4 January 1445mv). The Hospital of Gesù Cristo di Sant'Antonio, which the Venetians founded in 1476, took its inspiration from the general

hospital of Milan, but did not, in the end, become the all-encompassing centralized hospital originally intended. See Pullan, 1971, 197–215.

32 ST, reg. 1, fol. 91v (20 March 1443); Sanudo, 1999, 393.

33 Collegio, Notatorio, reg. 7, fol. 62r, act 194 (20 March 1443).

34 MC, reg. 22 (Ursa), fol. 150r (9 April 1443); Collegio, Notatorio, reg. 7, fol. 62r, cancellation of act 194 dated 10 April 1443.

35 MC, reg. 22 (Ursa), fol. 140r (4 March 1442). The laws of March 1442 and March 1443, as well as that of 1425, are briefly discussed in Bistort, 1969, 122–23.

36 DM, reg. 12, fol. 163r–v (23 September 1444).

37 Ibid., fol. 186r [*sic*] (29 September 1444).

38 Ibid., fol. 164r (29 September 1444).

39 Ibid., fol. 185v (5 October 1444).

40 Two votes were taken. The first resulted in 4 yeas, 4 nays, and 4 abstentions; the second in 4 yeas, 5 nays, and 3 abstentions. Ibid., fol. 164v (7 October 1444).

41 Ibid.

42 Ibid., fol. 165r (14 October 1444).

43 Lane, 1973, 227–28; Queller, 1986, 193.

44 Del Torre, 1992–93, esp. 1183–87, 1201.

45 Cessi, ed., 1970, 2:26 (clause xxix).

46 DM, reg. 11, fol. 68r (28 January 1432mv).

47 Ibid., reg. 12, fol. 172r–v (3 acts dated 17 February 1444mv); Berlan, 1852, 67–68. These acts as well as the others involving the cases against Jacopo were published by Francesco Berlan, although he gives the older pagination. In each case, I give the archival reference as well as the Berlan page references.

48 DM, reg. 12. fols. 172v–173r (acts dated 18 and 19 February 1444mv); Berlan, 1852, 68–70; Piccolomini, 1991, 28–29.

49 DM, reg. 12, fol. 173r–v (19 February 1444mv); Berlan, 1852, 70–71.

50 DM, reg. 12, fol. 174r (20 February 1444mv); Berlan, 1852, 71.

51 For the two accounts, see Dolfin, 402r–v; Sanudo, 1999, 405–07. For the condemnation of Gasparo, see DM, reg. 12, fol. 175v (25 February 1444mv); Berlan, 1852, 75–76.

52 Girgensohn, ed. 2004, 61 (clause XLVII). Jacopo was elected to serve in the Senate, either its regular membership or its *zonta*; in all but one case, however, his name was crossed out. See Segretario alle Voci, reg. 4, fols. 96v, 97r, 100v, 103r, 106r, 108v, 110r (Jacopo's name not cancelled), 113r. I wish to thank Ben Kohl and Monique O'Connell for checking their electronic databank of the *Segretario alle Voci* records.

53 DM, reg. 12, fol. 174r (acts dated 20 February 1444mv); Berlan, 1852, 71–72.

54 DM, reg. 12, fol. 174v (20 February 1444mv); Berlan, 1852, 72–74.

55 DM, reg. 12, fols. 175r–176v (acts dated 20 and 25 February 1444mv); Berlan, 1852, 74–77; Piccolomini, 1991, 28.

56 DM, reg. 12, fols. 176v–177r (25 February 1444mv); Berlan, 1852, 77–79.

57 DM, reg. 12, fol. 177v (3 March 1445); Berlan, 1852, 79.

58 DM, reg. 12, fol. 178r–v (acts dated 10 and 11 March 1445); Berlan, 1852, 79–81.

59 DM, reg. 12, fol. 180v (7 April 1445); Berlan, 1852, 81–82.

60 DM, reg. 13, fol. 18r–v (acts dated 20 and 27 October 1445); Berlan, 1852, 82–83.

61 DM, reg. 13, fol. 25r (26 January 1445mv); Berlan, 1852, 83–84. For background, see also Del Torre, 1997a, 134–36; and for the clause in the *promissione*, see Girgensohn, ed. 2004, 45 (clause XXXIII). Condulmer arrived in Venice in January but returned to Rome in February. See Olivieri, 1982, 763.

[62] DM, reg. 13, fols. 29r, 35v–36r (acts dated 30 March and 22 June 1446); Berlan, 1852, 84–85. Berlan apparently missed the law of 30 March.

[63] MC, reg. 22 (Ursa), fol. 165v (25 November 1446); Berlan, 1852, 85–86.

[64] Dolfin, 405v; DM, reg. 13, fol. 50r (23 November 1446). Berlan makes no note of this law.

[65] Dolfin, 406r. Dolfin's figures are confused, although his total of 908 votes accords with the vote recorded in the Great Council's records.

[66] DM, reg. 13, fol. 51r (acts dated 28 November 1446); Berlan, 1852, 87.

[67] DM, reg. 13, fol. 51v (acts dated 28 November 1446); Berlan, 1852, 88–89.

[68] Dolfin, 406r. For Dolfin's relation to Jacopo, see Zannoni, 1941–42, 9–10.

[69] BAV, Vat. Lat. 3194, fols. 11r–13r. See also Segarizzi, 1904, 12.

[70] Chojnacki, 2000, 227–43.

[71] DM, reg. 13, fol. 65r (5 April 1447); Berlan, 1852, 89.

[72] Ibid., reg. 12, fol. 174r (20 February 1444mv); Berlan, 1852, 71.

[73] This information is taken from Gullino, 1991, 708.

[74] Cognasso, 1955, 373.

[75] DM, reg. 13, fols. 57r, 61v–62r, 63r, 64v (acts 1, 29, 30 March and 5 April 1447).

[76] Ibid., fols. 65r–v (12 April 1447).

[77] Ibid., fols. 66r–v, 69v, 110r (12 and 28 April 1447, 12 September 1448).

[78] Ibid., fol. 80v (26 July 1447).

[79] Ibid., fol. 67r–v (acts dated 12 April 1447).

[80] Dolfin, 408v.

[81] DM, reg. 13, fols. 73v–74v (acts dated 5 June 1447). Sanudo (Sanudo, 1999, 427) briefly discusses the case, but incorrectly lists his fine as 1500 ducats. Donato's case is also mentioned in Queller, 1986, 194.

[82] DM, reg. 13, fols. 75r–77r (acts dated 14, 21, 22 June 1447).

[83] For a different opinion, that these men were "admirers" of Sforza, see Law, 2000, II:398.

[84] DM, reg. 13, fol. 78v (5 July 1447); Del Torre, 1997a, 136. For Pietro's career, see Fletcher, 1996.

[85] This summary of events is taken from Sanudo, 1999, 414–23; Dolfin, 404r–406v; Romanin, 4:153–55; Cognasso, 1955, 364–71. For the grants to Cotignola, see Sanudo, 1999, 417–19; Mallett, 1984, 187–88.

[86] Romanin, 4:155; Cognasso, 1955, 371–73.

[87] DM, reg. 13, fol. 62v (29 March 1447).

[88] For the Balduino case, see D. Romano, 1987a, esp. 151–52.

[89] Sanudo, 1999, 424–29; Dolfin, 407v–409r; Cognasso, 1955, 375–413; Romanin, 4:156–58; Cozzi, 1986, 42–43.

[90] ST, reg. 2, fol. 44r (4 September 1447); Dolfin, 408r.

[91] DM, reg. 13, fol. 83r (13 September 1447); Berlan, 1852, 90–91.

[92] DM, reg. 13, fol. 82v (13 September 1447); Berlan, 1852, 90.

[93] Sanudo, 1999, 427–28.

[94] Cited in Cognasso, 1955, 416. For Cosimo's distrust of Venice and for the commercial rivalry between the cities, see Gutkind, 1938, 145–46; Ilardi, 1959, 132; Mallett, 1967; Rubinstein, 1974; Rondinini, 1982, 253–54; Fubini, 1982, 291–97.

[95] ST, reg. 2, fol. 39r (5 July 1447).

[96] SS, reg. 17, fol. 167r–v (25 September 1447). Mallett (1984, 41) notes that in November Venice had at least 17,000 troops in Lombardy.

[97] Barbaro, 1991–99, 2:501–5; see also Pillinini, 1963; Rubinstein, 1974, 202–03; and Cozzi, 1986, 43–44.

[98] On Malipiero's and Marcello's later opposition to Foscari, see King, 1994, 115.

[99] Sanudo, 1999, 429–30.

[100] Dolfin, 410r–v; Sanudo, 1999, 431–32.

[101] For Piccinino, see SS, reg. 17, fol. 199v (7 February 1447mv). For Colleoni, ibid., fol. 225r (21 May 1448); also Predelli, 5:13, no. 23.

[102] Dolfin, 411r–v; Sanudo, 1999, 434–36.

[103] Dolfin, 412r.

[104] Mallett, 1984, 41, 182.

[105] Dolfin, 412v.

[106] For the terms of the treaty, see Predelli, 5:16–18, no. 32; Sanudo, 1999, 438; Dolfin, 412v–413r. Although Dolfin describes the palace as having been bought by Foscari, it is clear that he is referring to its later confiscation and sale for Dolfin's work is in fact a chronicle and not a diary. He is recording events in retrospect. For the decision not to pursue an attempt to kill Sforza, see DM, reg. 13, fol. 116v (8 January 1448mv).

[107] Romanin, 4: 160; Cognasso, 1955, 422–25.

[108] DM, reg. 13, fol. 163v (26 November 1449).

[109] For the war with Naples, see Gullino, 1996a, 47–51; Dolfin, 413v–415r; Sanudo, 1999, 446. For the strategic importance of the islands, see SS, reg. 18, fols. 96r–97r (8 July 1449).

[110] SS, reg. 18, fols. 122v–123r (25 September 1449).

[111] Sanudo, 1999, 444–45; Dolfin, 416r–v; Cognasso, 1955, 439–44; Romanin, 4:161–62.

[112] Dolfin, 417r–v.

[113] Ibid., 418v.

[114] For the troop size, see Mallett, 1984, 41; for the economic consequences, Mueller, 1997, 465, 529.

[115] ST, reg. 2, fols. 83v, 87r, 107r, 161v (acts dated 21 September and 21 October 1448, 26 April 1449, 7 December 1450). On bank loans to the state generally, see Mueller, 1997, 425–50.

[116] For Cyprus, see Thiriet, 3:2780; Stöckly, 1995, 202. For Syria, Thiriet, 3:2793; Ashtor, 1983, 306–08.

[117] For three examples from 1448 in which the doge alone proposed bills regarding finances, see ST, reg. 2, fols. 62v (19 March), 71v–72r (13 June), 83r (18 September).

[118] Del Torre, 1997, 348–49; for the Senate condemnation, see ST, reg. 2, fols. 68v–69r (20 May 1448).

[119] Gullino, 1982, 516–18. For the final stages of the Ten's trial of Cocco, see DM, reg. 13, fols. 156r–157v (acts dated 22 October 1449).

[120] Ibid., fols. 128v, 153r, 154v, 158v (acts dated 28 May and 1, 9, 29 October 1449).

[121] Ibid., fols. 149v–150v (acts dated 8 and 10 September 1449). For the law of 1438, see ibid., reg. 12, fol. 24r (26 November 1438).

[122] DM, reg. 13, fol. 177r (8 April 1450).

[123] Dolfin, 419r; AOM, Brollesco, carreggio 340, docs. 18–20 (letters dated 20 and 21 November 1450).

[124] DM, reg. 14, fols. 14v–15r (acts dated 6 November 1450); Berlan, 1852, 92–94; Dolfin, 419r.

[125] DM, reg. 14, fols. 16v, 17r, 19r (acts dated 27 November and 9 December 1450); Berlan, 1852, 94–95.

[126] DM, reg. 14, fols. 20r–21r (acts dated 16 December 1450). It is unclear whether or not the measure regarding police salaries passed.

[127] Dolfin, 419r–v.

[128] DM, reg. 14, fols. 23v–24r (acts dated 2 January 1450mv); Berlan, 1852, 95–97.

[129] DM, reg. 14, fols. 24v–25r (acts dated 3 January 1450mv); Berlan, 1852, 97–99.

[130] DM, reg. 14, fol. 26r (acts dated 8 January 1450mv); Berlan, 1852, 99–100.

[131] DM, reg. 14, fols. 27r–v, 29r (acts dated 21, 27, and 28 January 1450mv); Berlan, 1852, 100–02.

[132] DM, reg. 14, fol. 29v (28 January 1450mv); Berlan, 1852, 102–03.

133 DM, reg. 14, fol. 30r–v (acts dated 3 February 1450mv); Berlan, 1852, 103–04 (the latter reports only the law about keeping the chamber locked).

134 DM, reg. 14, fol. 31r–v (acts dated 6 and 7 February 1450mv); Berlan, 1852, 104–05.

135 DM, reg. 14, fols. 31v, 36r, 37v (10 February 1450mv, 13 and 26 March 1451); Berlan, 1852, 105–06.

136 DM, reg. 14, fols. 37v–38r (26 March 1451); Berlan, 1852, 106–08.

137 DM, reg. 14, fols. 38r–v, 39r (acts dated 26 March 1451); Berlan, 1852, 108–09.

138 DM, reg. 14, fols. 38v–39v (acts dated 26 March 1451); Berlan, 1852, 108–11.

139 DM, reg. 14, fol. 38v (26 March 1451); Berlan, 1852, 109.

140 DM, reg. 14, fols. 40v–41r (acts dated 29 March 1451); Berlan, 1852, 112–13.

141 DM, reg. 14, fol. 41r–v (acts dated 29 March 1451); Berlan, 1852, 113–14. On 9 May 1451 Foscari sent a letter to the Duke of Crete, Bernardo Balbi, among others, ordering them to give 30 ducats to Luca Mantello as a "gift" for his part in transporting Jacopo to the island. See BN, Fondo Tordi 1, "Copialettere del Doge di Venezia Francesco Foscari," fol. 24r.

142 Berlan, 1852, 35–37.

143 Romanin, 4:203–04.

144 Gullino (2005b, 51–61) also judges Jacopo innocent of the murder.

145 De Peppo, 1991, 723.

146 DM, reg. 14, fol. 69v (acts dated 28 August 1451).

147 Ibid., fol. 86v (acts dated 3 November 1451).

148 Thiriet, 3:2862. The treaty was reconfirmed in September. See Predelli, 5:65, no. 204. Nicol (1988, 393) argues that certainly by early 1452 Venice "had lost interest in the fate of Christian Constantinople," especially since trade with the Turks was flourishing.

149 Quoted in Nicol, 1988, 392–93.

150 Thiriet, 3:2881; Nicol, 1988, 393.

151 SS, reg. 19, fol. 44r–v (acts dated 24 February 1451mv); Sanudo, 1999, 459; Mallett, 1984, 42.

152 Dolfin, 420r; Sanudo, 1999, 460; DM, reg. 14, fols. 47v–57r (acts dated 5, 12, 22, 26, 29 May 1451). Colleoni's wife was housed at San Zaccaria: DM, reg. 14, fol. 136v (22 October 1452). The long reach of the Jacopo case appears to have made itself felt when the Ten were trying Francesco de Senis, Colleoni's chancellor. Leonardo Contarini, Jacopo's father-in-law, was forced to remove himself from judgement in the case: DM, reg. 14, fol. 62v (3 July 1451).

153 DM, reg. 14, fol. 53v (28 May 1451).

154 Dolfin, 419v–420r; Predelli, 5:55–56, 59, 60–61, nos. 171, 184, 186, 189; Rubieri, 1879, 2:247–48.

155 ST, reg. 2, fol. 192r–v (acts dated 1 June 1451); Dolfin, 420r; Sanudo, 1999, 461–63, including the text of Foscari's order expelling the Florentines.

156 ST, reg. 2, fols. 193v, 197r (7 and 22 June 1451). Strozzi's merchant son was ordered into exile. See also Sanudo, 1999, 461.

157 ST, reg. 2, fol. 193r (5 June 1451).

158 Dolfin, 415r–416r.

159 Muraro, 1961b, 274; Merkel, 1973, esp. 75–76.

160 Lightbown, 1986, 52. I wish to thank Gary Radke for helping me puzzle through this issue.

161 ST, reg. 2, fol. 177v (19 March 1451).

162 SMar, reg. 4, fol. 62v (10 June 1451).

163 Sanudo, 1999, 464; Dolfin, 420v.

164 Sanudo, 1999, 463. Dolfin does not mention the transfer where it should occur chronologically (420v). See also Cozzi, 1986, 243–44.

165 Cozzi, 1986, 245–46. For a brief summary of the papal bull, see Predelli, 5:65–66, no. 207.

[166] Mallett, 1996a, 200; Dolfin, 421v–423r; Sanudo, 1999, 468, 470–71, 476–77.

[167] SS, reg. 19, fol. 140v (25 May 1452). The issue of the Ambrosian flag arose again in September: DM, reg. 14, fol. 135r (17 September 1452).

[168] Romanin, 4:164.

[169] Mallett, 1984, 182.

[170] DM, reg. 14, fols. 105r, 114v–115r, 118r–v (acts dated 23 February 1451mv, 10 May and 12 June 1452). The final act is mistakenly dated 12 July in the register.

[171] For the Jews, see SMar, reg. 4, fol. 100r (7 January 1451mv), and Thiriet, 3:2880; for the terraferma cities, SS, reg. 19, fol. 120v (8 February 1451mv); for loans by the Ciera bank, ST, reg. 3, fols. 34r, 39v–40r (acts dated 3 July and 18 September 1452). For the forced loans and suspension of interest payments, see Luzzatto, ed., 1929, cclii–ccliv; Mueller, 1997, 469.

[172] MC, reg. 22 (Ursa), fol. 187v (24 June 1452); the act is also published in Luzzatto, ed., 1929, 306–07.

[173] ST, reg. 3, fols. 17r, 19r–v, 27r (acts dated 10 and 30 January 1451mv, 27 April 1452). See also Sanudo, 1999, 468 (with reference to the Collegio).

[174] ST, reg. 3, fol. 19v (30 January 1451mv).

[175] Ibid., fol. 33v (30 June 1452).

[176] MC, reg. 22 (Ursa), fol. 186r–v (23 January 1451mv). The vote was 827 to 114 with 105 abstentions. Both Sanudo (1999, 466–67) and Dolfin (420v) wrongly record the number of negative votes.

[177] ST, reg. 3, fol. 16v (31 December 1451).

[178] Ibid., fol. 31v (10 June 1452).

[179] Ibid., fol. 35v (16 August 1452).

[180] Ibid., fol. 49r (1 December 1452). See also Sanudo, 1999, 477–78.

[181] ST, reg. 3, fol. 28r–v (acts dated 3 and 6 May 1452); see also Dolfin, 421r; Sanudo, 1999, 464, 469.

[182] Dolfin, 421r; Sanudo, 1999, 469.

[183] DM, reg. 14, fol. 114v (8 May 1452).

[184] ST, reg. 3, fol. 29r (13 May 1452). The Senate notary recorded that this measure was passed by the Collegio and recorded in the Senate register by mistake.

[185] Ibid., fol. 29v (16 May 1452); Sanudo, 1999, 469. Clearly some senators were beginning to balk at the expense of the imperial visit; the vote on this measure was 79 to 68 with 2 abstentions.

[186] Sanudo, 1999, 474.

[187] ST, reg. 3, fol. 30r (20 May 1452).

[188] Dolfin, 421r; Sanudo, 1999, 472–75; SS, reg. 19, fol. 138v (20 May 1452).

[189] Sanudo, 1999, 472, 475; Dolfin, 421r–v.

[190] Dolfin, 421r–v; Sanudo, 1999, 472–73, 475. Dolfin (421r) offers the figure for the expense.

[191] SS, reg. 19, fol. 140v (23 May 1452).

[192] Ibid., fols. 140r, 141v (acts dated 23 and 25 May 1452).

[193] Giovanni Palazzi (1696, 154) identifies the unnamed citizen as Agostino Ciera, known as "dal Banco," a point repeated by Flaminio Corner in his life of Andrea Donato (Cornelio, 1758, 53).

[194] SS, reg. 19, fol. 139v (23 May 1452).

[195] DM, reg. 14, fols. 98v (5 January 1451mv), 100v (26 January 1451mv).

[196] Ibid., reg. 14, fols. 102v–103r, 108v (acts dated 16 February 1451mv and 15 March 1452).

[197] Sanudo, 1999, 474.

[198] For Leonessa's death and Piccinino's succession, see Dolfin, 423r; Sanudo, 1999, 479–80; Mallett, 1984, 42. For Foscari's proposals regarding the proveditors, see SS, reg. 19, fol. 191r (acts dated 3 April 1453).

[199] Sanudo, 1999, 480–81, 489–90; Dolfin, 422r, 423v, 435r–v. For René's progress, see Colombo, 1894; King, 1994, 285–90. For concerns about Padua, see ST, reg. 3, fol. 95v (26 December 1453), SS, reg. 19, fol. 232v (26 December 1453).

[200] For the papal peace negotiations, see Dolfin, 435r–v; Sanudo, 1999, 490; Catalano, 1956, 50, 55, 59. For the election of Giustinian and Moro, SS, reg. 19, fol. 212r (19 September 1453); Sanudo, 1999, 494; for their commission, SS, reg. 19, fol. 217r–v (12 October 1453). For Fra Simone, see Catalano, 1956, 59; Antonini, 1930, 252.

[201] Thiriet, 3:2896–97, 2905; Alexandrescu-Dersca Bulgaru, 1974, 249–53.

[202] Dolfin, 424v; Alexandrescu-Dersca Bulgaru, 1974, 253–54. Nicol (1988, 395) appears to be incorrect when stating that at this point Venice and the Turks were "technically at war." As late as May 1453 the Senate still insisted that the two parties were at peace. The Senate deliberation of 7 May 1453 is cited in Alexandrescu-Dersca Bulgaru, 1974, 258, n. 71.

[203] Barbaro, 1976, 11–12; Alexandrescu-Dersca Bulgaru, 1974, 254–55; Nicol, 1988, 396–97; Guilland, 1959, 170–71; Romanin, 4:182–83. For the Venetian community and the *bailo* in Constantinople after the conquest by the Turks, see Dursteler, 2006, esp. 23–40.

[204] Dolfin, 424r; for the Senate's actions, see SMar, reg. 4, fols. 171r–172r, 174r (acts dated 19 and 24 February 1452mv, 2 March 1453); SS, reg. 19, fol. 187r (24 February 1452mv); Thiriet, 3:2909–912; Guilland, 1959, 172–73; Alexandrescu-Dersca Bulgaru, 1974, 255–56; Nicol, 1988, 397.

[205] Dolfin, 424r.

[206] Sphrantzes, 1980, 71–72; also quoted in Romanin, 4:186, n. 66.

[207] For a chronology of marriage negotiations, see Sphrantzes, 1980, 17; Runciman, 1965, 51–55.

[208] Guilland, 1959, 154–55.

[209] SS, reg. 19, fol. 192r (10 April 1453); Thiriet, 3:2917.

[210] SMar, reg. 4, fol. 185r–v (13 April 1453); Thiriet, 3:2919.

[211] For Loredan's commission, see SS, reg. 19, fols. 193v–194r (7 May 1453); Thiriet, 3:2922. For Marcello's, SMar, reg. 4, fols. 188r–189r (8 May 1453); Thiriet, 3:2923; Alexandrescu-Dersca Bulgaru, 1974, 257–60; Nicol, 1988, 397–99.

[212] According to the account in Dolfin (425v), it began on 5 April.

[213] Dolfin, 428r–v; Nicol, 1988, 400.

[214] Di Chio, 1976, 136–39, 142–45; Dolfin, 427r; Sanudo, 1999, 483; Runciman, 1965, 104–11. Dolfin's major sources for the siege were a letter from Leonardo di Chio to Nicholas V and a description by Filippo Morandi, known as Filippo da Rimini: Dolfin, 424v.

[215] Dolfin, 430v–431v. The speech as recorded by Dolfin may be a composite of several different speeches, including one by Minotto. See Barbaro, 1976, 361, n. 116; Di Chio, 1976, 404, n. 54.

[216] Barbaro, 1976, 37; Dolfin, 433r–434r; Sanudo, 1999, 486–87; Runciman, 1965, 133–44. Nicol (1988, 406, n. 1, citing Thiriet, 3:2936) wrongly gives the number of Venetian dead as forty nobles and five hundred others, but that was the number of hostages, according to the Senate (see Romanin, 4:382–83); for a list of those who were taken prisoner or died, see Barbaro, 1856, 59–65.

[217] Dolfin, 434v; Mueller, 1997, 212–13.

[218] Dolfin, 434r–v; Sanudo, 1999, 487.

[219] SS, reg. 19, fols. 203v, 204v (acts dated 5 and 17 July 1453); Thiriet, 3:2932, 2935; Dolfin, 435r; Sanudo, 1999, 489. For the revised gifts, see SMar, reg. 4, fol. 201v (12 July 1453); Thiriet, 3:2934.

[220] ST, reg. 3, fol. 80r (14 September 1453); SMar, reg. 5, fol. 6v (15 September 1453).

[221] SS, reg. 19, fols. 205r, 216v (acts dated 18 July and 9 October 1453); the letter of 18 July is also transcribed in Romanin, 4:382–83.

[222] On Negroponte, see SS, reg. 19, fol. 216r (9 October 1453); Thiriet, 3:2946 (but misdated 8 October); SMar, reg. 5, fol. 15r (26 December 1453); Thiriet, 3:2951. On Loredan's taking of Turkish ships, see SS, reg. 19, fols. 210v–211r (31 August 1453); Thiriet, 3:2941.

[223] On the Loredans and Minottos, see SMar, reg. 4, fol. 202r–v (13 and 17 July 1453); Thiriet, 3:2935; Sanudo, 1999, 489.

[224] Sanudo, 1999, 487. The phrase reads, "fo pessima nuova a tutta la Christianittà." I follow the translation in Nicol, 1988, 405.

[225] Dolfin, 435r.

[226] For the text of Bessarion's letter, see Vast, 1977, 454–56. See also Setton, 1978, 149.

[227] For the grain shortage, see Dolfin, 435v; for the shortage of bullion and coins, Mueller, 1997, 215–19.

[228] ST, reg. 3, fols. 54v, 55r, 57r, 66v (acts dated 18 and 27 January 1452mv, 5 May 1453). For other measures taken in this period, see Dolfin, 423r.

[229] Dolfin, 436v; for full analyses, see Luzzatto, ed., 1929, ccliv; Mueller, 1997, 200–219.

[230] Luzzatto, ed., 1929, ccliii; ST, reg. 3, fol. 88v (10 and 14 November 1453).

[231] DM, reg. 14, fol. 185r (6 December 1453).

[232] ST, reg. 3, fols. 90v–92v (acts dated 6–8 December 1453); also printed in Besta, 1912, 116–27; and the summaries in Dolfin, 435v–436r; Sanudo, 1999, 492–94; Cozzi, 1986, 129; Pezzolo, 1996, 713–14.

[233] ST, reg. 3, fols. 94r, 96v (acts dated 18 and 31 December 1453); Pezzolo, 1996, 713–14; Mueller, 1997, 466, 570. The quotes are from Pezzolo.

[234] ST, reg. 3, fol. 95r (21 December 1453); see also Mueller, 1997, 217. For Marco's inactivity in these years, see Gullino, 1997, 327.

[235] These three acts, along with fifty-six other documents relating to the Palace of the Two Towers and Cà Foscari, are now published in Sartori, ed., 2001, docs. 10–12. It is important to note, however, that some documents relating to the property and palace have been omitted.

[236] Paoletti, 1893–97, 1:30, citing the genealogist Girolamo Priuli. This would have been in keeping with many of Venice's palaces built in the eleventh and twelfth centuries. See J. Schulz, 2004, 29. For an alternative view, see Foscari, 2005a, 55.

[237] For the brief description of the Palace of the Two Towers, courtyard, and outbuilding, see Sartori, ed., 2001, doc. 9; see also Foscari, 2005b. For speculation about the palace's appearance, see Howard, 1975, 123. For the presence of towers in Venetian palaces and the date of the Fondaco dei Turchi's façade, see J. Schulz, 2004, 12–13, 23, 163.

[238] I wish to thank Deborah Howard for bringing this point to my attention. One wonders whether other palaces awarded to condottieri, such as the one awarded to Gattamelata, also sported towers. I disagree with Antonio Foscari, however, who argues (Foscari, 2005b, 37) that in purchasing the Palace of the Two Towers the doge was assuming for himself "il ruolo del condottiero." Foscari's public persona never included military elements.

[239] Sartori, ed., 2001, doc. 9.

[240] In February 1443 Foscari and his cousin Filippo, son of the late Franzi, had agreed to the division of other properties. See Scuola di Santa Maria del Rosario, Commissaria Girardi, b. 29, proc. IV, parchment 56 and paper protocol, fols. 18r–29tris verso.

[241] It reads in part, "Insignis dux ipse sui monumenta futuris/Iam senior sedem voluit fundare nepotum." Antonio Foscari has pub-

lished a commentary on the poem and the palace (Foscari, 2001, ix–xxxiv). For Marco's property in San Simeon Apostolo, see Tassini, 1970, 605.

242 DM, reg. 13, fol. 83r (13 September 1447). The phrase reads, "andare ramengo per le case de altri." As Giuseppe Boerio notes, "andare ramengo" means to wander about the world, while "star ramengo" means to be outside one's homeland and paternal household (Boerio, 1973, 551).

243 I see little reason to believe, as Antonio Foscari hypothesizes, that Marco Foscari directed construction of the palace (Foscari, 2001, xxxii).

244 "Quemque locum dono serpens barbatus habebat" (Foscari, 2001, ix, xii).

245 For a photo of the sculpture as it currently appears as well as other indications in Venice of the Visconti viper and the Sforza arms (some of which postdate Foscari's reign), see Rizzi, 1987, 600, 622–23, 654–55.

246 Foscari, 2001, xix–xxi, but note the error in n. 6, where Foscari's sister is misidentified as Marta.

247 The literature on Florence and the Medici is vast. For an introduction to the family's bases of support, see D. Kent, 1978.

248 Information about the Palazzo Medici is taken from D. Kent, 2000, 217–38, quotes on 224, 226, 228, 230. For the "princely camera", see Trexler, 1980, 425. For Brunelleschi as the architect, rather than Michelozzo who is traditionally credited with the building, see Preyer, 1990, 65–73.

249 See Hersey, 1973, 54 and the text of the letter on 66; see also Ryder, 1990, 345–46.

250 D. Kent, 2000, 218.

251 Ibid., 228.

252 Sanudo, 1980, 20–21.

253 My description of the palace largely follows Foscari, 2001, xii–xvii, nn. 2–3; Bianchi, 1994, 178–80; and Arslan, 1971, 255–56.

254 Foscari, 2001, xvii.

255 Ibid., xviii, n. 5.

256 But this impression was characteristic of many Venetian palaces. See Howard, 2000, 140.

257 For a convenient and extremely clear account of palace interiors, ibid., 134–40.

258 Ruskin, 1860, 3:309.

259 Foscari, 2001, xvi; for some similar remarks, see Bianchi, 1994, 178–80, and Concina, 2006, 225–26.

260 I wish to thank Gary Radke for the observation about the quoins.

261 Antonio Foscari suggests that the palace played visually on both the Ducal Palace and the offices of the Procurators of San Marco, thus evoking "the two most prestigious moments of his [the doge's] political career" (Foscari, 2001, xvii).

262 In particular the winged putti holding the coats of arms recall Early Christian models. See Pincus, 2000a, 64–66.

263 Gullino, 1997, 313.

264 For some stimulating remarks on the builder as pater, see D. Kent, 2000, 219, 230–35.

265 Foscari, 2001, ix; Foscari also refers (xvii) to the palace as the doge's act of "auto-celebration."

CHAPTER 5   LAST JUDGEMENTS, 1454–1457

1 DM, reg. 14, fol. 143v (19 January 1452mv). The case involved Montagna's son who had defected to the enemy.

2 Piccolomini, 1991, 29.

3 For Zulian, see Troilo, 1932, esp. 7, 157.

4 In his diary Girolamo Priuli noted that the city grew tired of doges who lived for a long time and even came to hate them: Priuli 1912–40, 4:372. See also Finlay, 1980, 135.

[5] SS, reg. 19, fol. 204r (12 and 17 July 1453); Romanin, 4:164. For other efforts to bring about a peace, see Greppi, 1913, 332–33; Antonini, 1930, 236–38.

[6] SS, reg. 19, fols. 212r, 217r–v, 218r, 221v (acts dated 19 September, 12 October, and 10 November 1453); Cessi, 1981, 388.

[7] Walsh, 1989, 91: "un uomo del Doge."

[8] British Library, London, MS. Add. 15586, "Historia de l'origine di Venetia, e delle valorosissime imprese fatte sino l'anno 1460," fol. 99v.

[9] For the early history of the island and hospital, see Corner, 1990, 307–08; for Foscari's early interest, see AC, Raspe, reg. 3647, fol. 84r–v (10 January 1420mv), and Collegio, Notatorio, reg. 5, fol. 139r, act 479, 19 June 1420.

[10] Walsh, 1989, 88–92.

[11] Copies of many of the monastery's most important charters, including a copy of Foscari's conveyance of 1436, are in San Cristoforo della Pace: b. 3, large notebook with the words "S. Cristoforo Muran, Testamenti" on the spine; and b. 11, notebook with incipit "Origine della Congregatione." For the "chiesiola di S. Onofrio nell'Horto," see the note at the end of the will of Antonia Pino dated 1451, on one of the unnumbered pages in the back of the notebook in b. 11. A copy of Foscari's charter is also in Cornelio, 1749, 1:272–73. For the beginnings of constructions, see Dolfin, 376v; King (1994, 224) wrongly gives the date as 1439.

[12] Walsh, 1989, 95–96; Walsh, 1979, 182–83; SS, reg. 20, fol. 4r (14 January 1453mv).

[13] Dolfin, 439v; Sanudo, 1999, 499.

[14] Canetta, 1885, 524–25, 545; Antonini, 1930, 262–63, 275; Fossati, 1957, 15–19; Fubini, 1982, 306.

[15] DM, reg. 14, fols. 187v, 188r, 190r, 192v, 193r–v, 194v (acts dated 9, 10, 29 January and 20, 27 February 1453mv); Dolfin, 436r–v;

Sanudo, 1999, 495; Predelli, 5:90–91, no. 284. On the efforts to get the Marquess of Mantua, see DM, reg. 14, fols. 190v–191r (29 January 1453mv); on Malatesta, see Antonini, 1930, 259. For the quote regarding the expansion of the Ten's power, see Mallett, 1984, 164; for the negotiations regarding the possible marriage, ibid., 204.

[16] SS, reg. 20, fol. 8v (4 February 1453mv); Canetta, 1885, 550–52, quote on 551; Antonini, 1930, 256–57.

[17] Antonini, 1930, 244, 252–53.

[18] SS, reg. 20, fols. 13v–15v (acts dated 18–28 March 1454); Dolfin, 438r.

[19] The Florentines had been pushing for an accord and agreed to it shortly thereafter. Canetta, 1885, 555–56; Rubieri, 1879, 2:291–93; Soranzo, 1924, 13.

[20] Predelli, 5:87–90, nos. 282–83; Dolfin, 438v; Sanudo, 1999, 497; Romanin, 4:103, Antonini, 1930, 271–72; Greppi, 1913, 335; Canetta, 1885, 556–57. For Foscari's letter to Simone regarding Brescello, see San Cristoforo della Pace, b. 11, notebook with incipit "Origine della Congregatione," 18–19; for Simone's concern for his reputation, DM, reg. 15, fol. 16v (14 August 1454).

[21] Ryder, 1990, 261, 289.

[22] Predelli, 5:100–104, nos. 313–22; Dolfin, 439v; Sanudo, 1999, 501. For the characterization of the League as a mutual non-aggression pact, see Pillinini, 1970, 50.

[23] Ryder, 1990, 290.

[24] Sanudo (1999, 516–17) includes a copy of the proclamation.

[25] Soranzo, 1924, 123–67; Mattingly, 1955, 76–77. For an excellent summary of the historiography of the League, see Pillinini, 1970, 38–59.

[26] That is the view expressed in Ryder, 1990, 290.

[27] The quotation is from Ilardi, 1959, 143.

[28] That is the view of Cessi, 1981, 391. Pillinini (1970, 59) argues that forces far

larger than those of the League helped maintain the status quo.

29 Catalano, 1956, 80; Chittolini, 2005, 247–48.

30 Dolfin, 438v; ST, reg. 3, fols. 111r, 112v (acts dated 13 and 15 April 1454).

31 ST, reg. 3, fol. 116r (17 May 1454); Sanudo, 1999, 510, 622; Walsh, 1989, 96. The Senate act is also printed in Cornelio, 1749, 1:277.

32 Greppi, 1913, 336.

33 The two letters from Simone to Sforza have been published in slightly different versions in Greppi, 1913, 352–54, and Sartori, 2001, 36–38.

34 The Senate law is published in Greppi, 1913, 354. Greppi, like Simone, reports the vote as unanimous; the final line of his transcription reads, "De parte omnes." However the original Senate register clearly indicates a vote of 123 to 19 with no abstentions: SS, reg. 20, fol. 22v (18 June 1454).

35 The law awarding the property to Sforza is published in Greppi, 1913, 355.

36 ASM, Sforzesco, carteggio 344, letter from Marchese da Varese to Sforza dated 31 December 1457.

37 Greppi, 1913, 341–43.

38 For the sale contract, see Beltrami, 1906, 22–26. See also Greppi, 1913, 343–51.

39 Foscari, 2001, xxv.

40 Dolfin, 440bisv. Sanudo's account (1999, 515) differs in several specifics, for example in stating that Galeazzo Maria was met at San Clemente rather than Chioggia. Regarding the expenses, at first the Senate authorized 1000 ducats but later raised it to at least 2000: ST, reg. 3, fols. 177v, 183v (26 September and 7 November 1455). There are numerous reports back to his father on the progress of Galeazzo's visit. For the trip to Murano and balloting in the Great Council, see ASM, Sforzesco, carteggio 342, letter from Galeazzo to his father dated 24

November 1455 and from Antonio Guidobono to Sforza dated 25 November 1455.

41 The Latin text of Sforza's speech is found in Libri commemoriali, reg. 14, fol. 176v, no. 336. Predelli (5:111, no. 340) simply describes it as a "gratulatio". Dolfin (440bisv–441r) and Sanudo (1999, 660–62) offer Italian translations.

42 Dolfin, 440bisv; ASM, Sforzesco, carteggio 342, letter from Antonio Guidobono to Sforza dated 18 November 1455.

43 Foscari's letter is found in Libri commemoriali, reg. 14, fol. 177r, no. 337. See also Predelli, 5:111, no. 341. For Bianca Maria's preservation of the letter, see Dolfin, 441r.

44 Libri commemoriali, reg. 14, fols. 177r–v, no. 338. See also Predelli, 5:111, no. 342.

45 ASM, Sforzesco, carteggio 342, letter from Galeazzo's chaperones to Sforza dated 24 November 1455.

46 Greppi, 1913, 336; King, 1994, 226. Among those who have successfully identified the Grevembroch drawing are Rizzi, 1987, 662. Greppi (1913, 336, n. 1) cites letters of Fra Simone to Sforza dated 1464 interpreting the sculpture, but I have been unable to find them in the Archivio di Stato, Milan. I believe that the plaque may be visible in the engraving of the monastery by Coronelli (1697, vol. 3) as the small square on the exterior wall. According to Cornelio (1749, 1:259) it was on the western corner of the church. However, Sagredo (1839, 16) reports that the sculpture was placed as it appears perhaps in the engraving "sul muro versante ponente," that is on the western-facing wall. If it was placed on the exterior wall, it would have been visible to those traveling to Murano. However, it should be noted that Sagredo wrongly records that the sculpture linked the Foscari and Sforza arms.

47 For the works in Monte Ortone, see Tomasino, 1644, 43–44; Righetti, 1993, 27,

30; and Donzelli and Pilo, 1967, 93. It is unclear whether or not the Bissoni is extant. For the painting at San Cristoforo, see MCC, MS. Cicogna 3234/III/29, fasc. "S. Cristoforo della Pace," description of the church.

[48] ASM, Sforzesco, carteggio 343, letters from Marchese da Varese to Sforza dated 25 and 30 September 1456. See also Sanudo, 1999, 515.

[49] DM, reg. 15, fol. 10v (31 July 1454); also printed in Berlan, 1852, 115–16.

[50] The quotation is from Cozzi, 1986, 47. A copy of the treaty is published in Romanin, 4:383–87; and its provisions are epitomized in Predelli, 5:91–92, no. 288.

[51] Gullino, 1996a, 59–60; Fine, 1987, 564–68.

[52] On military changes in this period, see Mallett, 1984, 43–45; for the negotiations with Piccinino, see SS, reg. 20, fol. 40r–v (acts dated 12 and 16 October 1454).

[53] Mallett, 1984, 44; for Colleoni, see SS, reg. 20, fols. 42r–43r (19 and 22 October 1454); Dolfin, 441v.

[54] Mallett, 1984, 104–08.

[55] SS, reg. 20, fol. 34r (6 September 1454); and in Luzzatto, ed., 1929, 308–09, but wrongly dated 10 September (see also his comments on p. cclvii). On 3 September the Senate had voted to appoint 3 *savi* who were to find ways to save money by examining the contracts of the condottieri, but that task appears to have been subsumed by the five *savi* appointed to examine expenses: ibid., fol. 33v (3 September 1454).

[56] Ibid., fol. 35r–v (acts dated 12 and 13 September 1454); ST, reg. 3, fol. 131r (20 September 1454).

[57] SS, reg. 20, fol. 66v (28 June 1455); MC, Deliberazioni, reg. 23 (Regina), fols. 8r–9v (21 September 1455), and in Luzzatto, ed., 1929, 309–13; ST, reg. 3, fols. 174v–175v, 178r (acts dated 15 and 25 September 1455); the act of 25 September in Luzzatto, ed., 1929, 313–14; Dolfin, 442v.

[58] ST, reg. 4, fols. 29v–30r (29 November 1456).

[59] Mueller, 1997, 466.

[60] ST, reg. 3, fol. 141v (9 December 1454).

[61] MC, Deliberazioni, reg. 22 (Ursa), fol. 196r–v (acts dated 21 September and 27 October 1454).

[62] DM, reg. 15, fol. 40v (9 April 1455).

[63] Ibid., fols. 41v–43v (multiple acts dated 11 and 12 April 1455). The issue is also briefly mentioned in Mallett, 1984, 108.

[64] SM, reg. 5, fol. 85r–v (23 April 1455).

[65] DM, reg. 15, fol. 41v, preamble to motion by Zaccaria Valaresso and Lorenzo Loredan (11 April 1455). In April 1456 the Ten prohibited the awarding of tax farms, fishing rights, and other communal properties by *grazia* without their permission: ibid., fol. 91v (14 April 1456).

[66] Ibid., fol. 3v (19 June 1454).

[67] Ibid., fol. 20r (18 September 1454).

[68] MC, Deliberazioni, reg. 22 (Ursa), fol. 197v (1 December 1454).

[69] DM, reg. 14, fol. 197v (27 March 1454, with marginal note dated 28 March 1454).

[70] Dolfin, 445v; DM, reg. 15, fols. 117r–118r, 129v–132r (acts dated 9, 11, 16 February 1456mv and 14, 20, 21 June 1457); see also the discussion of the case in Queller, 1986, 98.

[71] Dolfin, 446r–447v; Sanudo, 1999, 527–30.

[72] Dolfin, 446v; Sanudo, 1999, 528.

[73] DM, reg. 15, fols. 125v, 126v (acts dated 27 and 30 May 1457).

[74] Ibid., fol. 127r–v (acts dated 3 June 1457). The condemned were usually executed between the two columns in the Piazzetta. Perhaps the columns of the loggia were chosen instead because of the condemneds' effort to subvert elections which took place in the Ducal Palace.

[75] Ibid., fols. 127v–128r, 131r (acts dated 3 and 20 June 1457).

[76] Dolfin, 447r. The two cases were quite distinct, as the Ten made clear: DM, reg. 15, fol. 128r (3 June 1457). However, Dolfin tended to conflate the two a bit.

[77] Ibid., fol. 133r (30 June 1457); Dolfin, 447r–v. Queller (1986, 99) wrongly reports his sentence.

[78] Greppi, 1913, 343–51.

[79] DM, reg. 15, fol. 65r (30 July 1455). The Ten's decision is unclear since the proposal that the eagles could remain got 17 votes, while that suggesting their removal got only 14. However, according to an amendment immediately below (with an accompanying cross indicating passage), the prohibitions of earlier laws were to be observed. Although from a different branch of the family, Bernardo Giustinian had given a speech three years before welcoming Frederick III as he made his way to Naples for his marriage. Perhaps this accounted for the decision to sport imperial eagles. See Labalme, 1969, 112, 135–40. Ironically, Bernardo was eventually knighted by the King of France: ibid., 165–66.

[80] Dolfin, 446v.

[81] DM, reg. 15, fol. 127r (1 June 1457); Dolfin, 447r; Sanudo, 1999, 529; Queller, 1986, 100.

[82] DM, reg. 15, fols. 118v, 129v–130r (23 February 1456mv and 18 June 1457); Queller, 1986, 98–99.

[83] Ibid., fols. 128r–v, 131v, 133r (acts dated 3, 20, and 30 June 1457).

[84] Ibid., fol. 132r (21 June 1457).

[85] Ibid., fols. 14v–15r, 17r (acts dated 22 August and 4 September 1454).

[86] Ibid., fols. 76r–v, 77v, 78r, 79v, 80r–v (acts dated 22 October, 5, 12, 26 November, and 17 December 1455).

[87] ST, reg. 4, fol. 21r (12 October 1456); SS, reg. 20, fol. 106r (12 October 1456).

[88] DM, reg. 15, fol. 23r (31 October 1454).

[89] Ibid., fols. 82v, 102r (4 February 1455mv and 21 July 1456).

[90] Dolfin, 443v.

[91] This summary is taken from Mueller, 1997, 481–83.

[92] ST, reg. 4, fols. 3v, 11v, 13v–14r, 16r–v, 18v (acts dated 1 April, 26 June, 17 and 27 July, 3, 12, 31 August 1456); Dolfin, 443r–v; Sanudo, 1999, 521. See also Mueller, 1979a, 85; Palmer, 1979, 104.

[93] For those not attending work, see MC, Deliberazioni, reg. 23 (Regina), fols. 14v, 15v (acts dated 8 August and 12 September 1456). For the Senate's action, see ST, reg. 4, fol. 19v (6 September 1456); Dolfin, 445v; Sanudo, 1999, 525.

[94] DM, reg. 15, fols. 104v, 112v (11 August and 24 November 1456); ST, reg. 4, fols. 16r, 19v (3 August and 9 September 1456); Dolfin, 445v.

[95] DM, reg. 15, fols. 121r, 132r (6 April and 22 June 1457); ST, reg. 4, fol. 49r (6 August 1457).

[96] DM, reg. 15, fol. 96r–v (acts dated 7 June and 7 July 1454); Berlan, 1852, 116–17.

[97] Dolfin, 443v–444r. Sanudo's account (1999, 521–24) appears to have been taken from Dolfin and offers no further insights.

[98] DM, reg. 15, fol. 96v (8 June 1456); Berlan, 1852, 117–19.

[99] DM, reg. 15, fol. 97r (acts dated 8 June 1456); Berlan, 1852, 119–21.

[100] DM, reg. 15, fols. 97v–98v (12 June 1456); Berlan, 1852, 121–25. For the fears of an effort to secure a pardon for Jacopo, see Berlan, 1852, 54.

[101] DM, reg. 15, fol. 98v (12 June 1456); Berlan, 1852, 125.

[102] Dolfin, 444r.

[103] DM, reg. 15, fol. 99v (23 June 1456).

[104] Ibid., fol. 101r–v (14 July 1456); Berlan, 1852, 125.

[105] Ibid., fol. 102r (acts dated 21 and 24 July 1456).

[106] Ibid., fol. 102r (23 July 1456); Berlan, 1852, 126.

[107] Dolfin, 444r.

[108] DM, reg. 15, fols. 102v (24 July 1456); Berlan, 1852, 126–27. In reporting the vote on Loredan's proposal, the usually very reliable Berlan makes a serious error: in his transcription of the second ballot, he records that Loredan's proposed punishment got 5 votes (in fact it got none). It also gives the mistaken impression that 3 men abstained on the second ballot when, in fact, they abstained on the first.

[109] DM, reg. 15, fol. 103r (24 July 1456); Berlan, 1852, 129.

[110] Dolfin, 444r–v.

[111] DM, reg. 15, fol. 102v (24 July 1456); Berlan, 1852, 127–28. Bocheta is not included in the list of priors of the Ca di Dio compiled by Flaminio Corner. See Cornelio, 1749, 8:330.

[112] DM, reg. 15, fols. 102v–103v (24 and 28 July 1456); Berlan, 1852, 128–30.

[113] DM, reg. 15, fol. 103v (29 and 31 July 1456); Berlan, 1852, 130–31.

[114] That was the wording in Valaresso's and Capello's original proposal that Jacopo not be brought back to Venice but merely admonished severely. See DM, reg. 15, fol. 97r (8 June 1456); Berlan, 1852, 119.

[115] Barbaro, 1991–99, 2:201.

[116] ASM, Sforzesco, carteggio 342, no. 182, letter from Antonio Guidobono to Sforza dated 20 August 1455 and Sforza's response to Guidobono (no. 187, 25 August 1455), telling him to thank Barbo for the present.

[117] Berlan, 1852, 53.

[118] Dolfin, 444v.

[119] For the prohibition on correspondence, see Girgensohn, ed. 2004, 61 (clause XLVII).

[120] ASM, Sforzesco, carteggio 343, no. 70, letter from Antonio Guidobono to Sforza dated 9 June 1456. For background on

Sforza diplomacy, including information about his various envoys, see Cerioni, 1970; Margaroli, 1992; and Senatore, 1998.

[121] ASM, Sforzesco, carteggio 343, no. 77, letter from Antonio Guidobono to Sforza dated 14 June 1456.

[122] Ibid., no. illegible, letter from Antonio Guidobono to Sforza dated 23 July 1456 (N.B. on the front of the letter a later hand has incorrectly written the date as 18 July).

[123] Ibid., no. 170, letter from Antonio Guidobono to Sforza dated 28 July 1456.

[124] I have looked at cases from the following months when Loredan was one of the heads: March 1456, June 1456, late July/August 1456, October 1457, February 1458, May 1458, and August 1458. Of the six cases during those years in which the Ten meted out punishment for various crimes, in three Loredan was an advocate of the harshest proposals; in three others he recommended less severe measures. Interestingly, in light of his effort to have Jacopo beheaded, in two of the instances in which he advocated a relatively lenient punishment, others wanted the defendants to be executed. For all of these cases, see DM, reg. 15, fols. 87v–88r, 100r, 153r, 159r (acts dated 3 March 1456 [3 cases], 30 June 1456, 25 May 1458, and 23 August 1458).

[125] DM, reg. 15, fols. 144v, 146v, 149v (acts dated 11 January 1457mv, 22 February 1457mv, and 23 March 1458); Berlan, 1852, 56, 194.

[126] Carile, 1991, 499.

[127] DM, reg. 15, fol. 102v, marginal annotation dated 12 January 1456mv; Berlan, 1852, 127; ASM, Sforzesco, carteggio 344, no. 65, letter from Marchese da Varese to Sforza dated 16 March 1457.

[128] DM, reg. 15, fol. 119v, 17 March 1457; Berlan, 1852, 131.

[129] Bruni, 1741, 2:96–97; I follow the translation in King, 1986, 31.

[130] ASM, Sforzesco, carteggio 344, no. 65, letter from Marchese da Varese to Sforza, dated 16 March 1457.

[131] ST, reg. 4, fol. 21r (12 October 1456); SS, reg. 20, fol. 106r (12 October 1456).

[132] Dolfin, 448r; ASM, Sforzesco, carteggio 46, no. 170, letter from Ottone del Carretto to Sforza dated 25 November 1457; carteggio 344, no. illegible, letter from Marchese da Varese to Sforza dated 27 April 1457. Within a few years rumors even began to circulate that Foscari survived only by drinking human milk: Soranzo, ed., 1915, 93.

[133] DM, reg. 15, fol. 130v (18 June 1457); Berlan, 1852, 182.

[134] DM, reg. 15, fol. 139r (19 October 1457); Berlan, 1852, 182–83. For the list of members, see Dolfin, 447v.

[135] Dolfin, 447v.

[136] DM, reg. 15, fol. 139r–v (acts dated 19 and 21 October 1457); Berlan, 1852, 183–84; Dolfin (447v) offers a slightly different list and so should be used with caution.

[137] DM, reg. 15, fol. 139r (19 October 1457); Berlan, 1852, 184.

[138] DM, reg. 15, fol. 139v (21 October 1457); Berlan, 1852, 185–86. The heads stated that Foscari would have until the "third hour," that is three hours after sunset to make his decision.

[139] Girgensohn, ed., 2004, 69 (clause LIIII).

[140] The ducal councilors agreed to award Belcovich 100 lire a year for as long as he lived: SM, reg. 28, fol. 15r (30 June 1428).

[141] Rizzo retained his salary but not the other benefits of the office of book-keeper: SM, reg. 58, fol. 156r (22 November 1432). For Soranzo, see MC, Deliberazioni, reg. 22 (Ursa), fol. 118v (29 June 1437). For the office of the gold estimators, see Stahl, 2000, 136–40, 147–52. There are a few other instances: in one, the Senate agreed to continue to employ "for as long as he will live" a constable from Padua who feared he

would be fired on account of his age; in another the Great Council agreed to designate Giovanni di Domenico, a *cittadino originario* and an elderly ship's carpenter who was no longer able to work, a *povero al pevere*, that is the beneficiary of a special charity. For the constable from Padua, see ST, reg. 1, fol. 198v (21 July 1446); for di Domenico, see MC, Deliberazioni, reg. 23 (Regina), fol. 10r (19 October 1455).

[142] DM, reg. 15, fol. 140r (22 October 1457); Berlan, 1852, 187.

[143] Dolfin, 448v.

[144] Although Dolfin reports that four of the councilors had to agree, Foscari's *promissione* required that all six make the motion before the Great Council. See Girgensohn, ed., 2004, 69 (clause LV).

[145] DM, reg. 15, fol. 140r (22 October 1457); Berlan, 1852, 188. To my knowledge no previous historian (certainly not Berlan or Romanin) has noted that the heads of the Ten divided here, with Donato and Barbarigo proposing that the matter be referred to the Great Council and Loredan wishing to keep it within the Ten. This important difference cannot be gleaned from Berlan's transcription, which places all three names before the two resolutions. However, the original records of the Ten clearly show the difference.

[146] DM, reg. 15, fol. 140r–v (22 October 1457); Berlan, 1852, 188–89. Again, Dolfin (448v) gets some of the particulars wrong when he says that they gave him just three days to vacate the Ducal Palace and offered him a yearly stipend of 2000 ducats.

[147] DM, reg. 15, fol. 140v (acts dated 22 October 1457); Berlan, 1852, 189–91.

[148] Dolfin, 448v; for the time of his renunciation, see Berlan, 1852, 167.

[149] Da Bisticci, 1997, 234.

[150] Muir, 1978, 147–48; Boholm, 1990, 76–80. Both discuss the destruction of the

151 Dolfin, 448v.

152 Ibid., 448v–449r.

153 DM, reg. 15, fol. 141r (26 October 1457); Berlan, 1852, 191–92.

154 MC, Deliberazioni, reg. 23 (Regina), fol. 20r (24 October 1457); Berlan, 1852, 167. It reads "non valentis propter senium illum exercere."

155 Mazzatinti, ed. 1903, 97. For examples of chroniclers repeating the official view that he was deposed on account of his age, see Da Soldo, 1938–42, 1:134; Soranzo, ed., 1915, 93–94; Gori, 1878–79; Da Gubbio, 1902, 67; Palmieri, 1906, 178.

156 Antoninus, 1913, 98.

157 Dolfin, 449v.

158 Dolfin, 449v.

159 ASM, Sforzesco, carteggio 344, letter from Marchese da Varese to Sforza dated 20 January 1457. It should be noted, however, that in May 1457 da Varese reported that Foscari had spoken with him concerning matters in Genoa: ibid., no. 115, letter from Marchese da Varese to Sforza dated 26 May 1457.

160 Romanin, 4:213, n. 69.

161 For Niccolò Bernardo as an opponent of Foscari, see Dolfin, 450r; for the Bernardo marriage tie to Foscari, see Gullino, 1997, 311.

162 Biondo, 1558, 176v, 177r. For the Loredans' naval service, see Stöckly, 1995, 304–08.

163 For Querini's career, see King, 1986, 419–21; for Querini as an intimate of Foscari, see Pertusi's introduction to his letters in Branca, ed., 1977, 167, n. 7.

164 The treatises, edited by Konrad Krautter, Paul Oskar Kristeller, and Helmut Roob, are in Branca, ed., 1977, 19–102.

165 As summarized in King, 1986, 118–24.

166 The treatise, edited and introduced by Carlo Seno and Giorgio Ravegnani, is in

Branca, 1977, 105–61; see also King, 1986, 126–27.

167 Branca, 1977, 88–89; I follow the translation in King, 1986, 122–23.

168 Branca, 1977, 124.

169 For Caldiera's career, see King, 1986, 344–45.

170 King, 1986, 112–16, quote on 116. For Foscari as under the protection of Respublica, see King, 1989, 42. King (1975, 538) suggests the work was written between 1447 and 1455 but "probably just prior to 1451."

171 King, 1986, 98–112, quotes on 109 and 111.

172 King, 1989, 35.

173 Copies of the will are found in NT, b. 1149, notary Paulus Benedicto, protocol, fols. 7v–8v and unbound testament no. 2. The will is dated 29 October 1457, but the paper copy contains a copy of a *grazia* passed by the Great Council on 4 June 1458 making this the official will. Hence the will was "published," as the protocol copy says on 7 June 1458.

174 D. Romano, 1996, 84. In contrast, one of Foscari's servants bequeathed items to two of his sons: ibid., 204.

175 The anonymous Veronese chronicler estimated Foscari's legacy to his grandsons at 150,000 ducats, 80,000 in cash. See Soranzo, ed., 1915, 97.

176 MC, Deliberazioni, reg. 23 (Ursa), fols. 22v–23v.

177 ASM, Sforzesco, carteggio 344, 30 October 1457; Archivio di Stato, Siena, Archivio del Concistoro, carteggio, filza 1991, no. 55 (30 October 1457); ASF, Signori, Responsive Copiari, reg. 1, fol. 52r (30 October 1457). I consulted the Sienese document via the Ilardi microfilm collection at Yale (reel 1470).

178 ASM, Sforzesco, carteggio 344, 8 November 1457; ibid., 19 November 1457. For reports to Sforza from Rome, Florence,

and Naples regarding events in Venice, ibid., carteggio 46, nos. 97, 101, 170 (6, 7, and 25 November 1457); carteggio 269, nos. 27 and 36 (30 October and 10 November 1457); carteggio 197, no. 211 (27 November 1457).

[179] ASM, Sforzesco, carteggio, 344, 5 November 1457, draft of letter from Sforza to Malipiero from Cremona.

[180] Dolfin, 449v.

[181] Dolfin, 449v; Sanudo, 1999, 534.

[182] Dolfin, 449v, a passage that is difficult to translate. The original reads: "Audita tal nova tutti se guardono lun laltro, dicendo non potevano indusiar .10. zorni de piu a far tal novita, et non bolar questa citade de inconstantia a questo modo. A tutti parse miraculo et stupino di tanta cosa, che si presto lui fosse expirato et dispia queli molto, della privation di tanto principe, Al qual mai fu ne sara in terra el simile."

[183] Ibid., 449v–450r.

[184] Dolfin, 450r; Sanudo, 1999, 534–35. Sanudo says, speaking of the Frari, "dove fo sepolto e posto in un deposito." The anonymous Veronese chronicler says that Foscari "bequeathed his body to his parish," and that after the funeral his body "fosse [. . .] a la sua parochia portato e sepulto" (Soranzo, 1915, 97). For a general analysis of ducal funerals, see Muir, 1981, 263–77; Boholm, 1990, 70–115.

[185] McManamon, 1989, 20.

[186] Muir (1981, 274–75) argues that in the early sixteenth century members of the Signoria avoided ducal funerals as a way of signifying that the government "lived on." However, it seems that Doge Malipiero (and perhaps other members of the Signoria) attended Foscari's funeral since Bernardo Giustinian addressed Malipiero directly in his oration (Giustiniano, 1798, 33).

[187] The words are those of Patricia Labalme, whose analysis of the oration I

follow in this paragraph: Labalme, 1969, 114–25, quote on 123.

[188] Giustiniano, 1798, 53–54.

[189] Ibid., 27, 46, 47, 53.

[190] Ibid., 21, 57. Why the epitaph of Foscari's successor, Pasquale Malipiero, refers to Foscari is a mystery that remains to be solved. Seemingly, it would have been more expedient to ignore entirely the events that brought Malipiero to the ducal throne. For Malipiero's epitaph, see Palazzi, 1696, 161.

[191] Giustiniano, 1798, 57.

[192] Ibid., 54.

[193] Ibid., 21 ("parentis potius quam principis curam pietatemque praestitit").

[194] Ibid., 33, 57.

[195] Ibid., 22.

[196] Ibid., 28–29. In his *Itinerario per la terraferma veneziana*, written in 1483, Sanudo went against his usual anti-Foscari bias and also used the term *Pater Patriae* to describe the doge. Sanuto, 1847, 116.

[197] McManamon, 1989, 45–53.

[198] Giustiniano, 1798, 23.

[199] Ibid., 25.

[200] Ibid., 58–59.

[201] Ibid., 22, 37, 46, 56.

[202] Dolfin, 449r–v.

[203] DM, reg. 15, fol. 202v (undated); see also Berlan, 1852, 178. Berlan also was unable to identify the exact circumstances which led to the compilation of this list.

[204] DM, reg. 15, fols. 141v–142r (acts dated 26 November 1457); Berlan, 1852, 192–94. Berlan does not include the first couple of decisions in his transcription regarding whether or not Girolamo Donato and Leonardo and Davide Contarini could participate.

[205] SS, reg. 20, fols. 140v–141r (30 December 1457). This particular bill concerned international diplomacy.

[206] DM, reg. 15, fol. 163r (23 October 1458); Berlan, 1852, 194–95.

[207] DM, reg. 15, fol. 163r (acts dated 25 October 1458); Berlan, 1852, 195–96.

[208] DM, reg. 15, fol. 163v (26 October 1458); Berlan, 1852, 196–98. In an obvious typographical error, Berlan's transcription incorrectly gives the date of this bill as 15 October.

[209] DM, reg. 15, fol. 163v (25 October 1457); Berlan, 1852, 198–99.

[210] MC, Deliberazioni, reg. 23 (Regina), fols. 82v–83r (18 September 1468); see also Maranini, 1974, 2:419, n. 1.

[211] Muraro, 1961a.

[212] On Marian devotion at the Frari, see Goffen, 1986.

[213] Sanudo, 1999, 168. It seems likely that his other sons were buried there as well.

[214] My description of the tomb follows A. M. Schulz, 1978a, 9–12; Pincus, 1976, 402–04.

[215] Much of it is summarized in Pincus, 1976, 408–12. See also A. M. Schulz, 1996; A. M. Schulz, 1999.

[216] A. M. Schulz, 1978a, 14.

[217] Pincus, 1976, 431.

[218] A. M. Schulz, 1978a, 12.

[219] Giustiniano, 1798, 57. For her discussion of two angels, see A. M. Schulz, 1978a, 11. I also disagree with her contention (A. M. Schulz, 1996, 156–57) that such an important sculptor as Bartolomeo Bon would have been "the least desirable" candidate to sculpt the tomb because of his close association with the Signoria. Such connections would have made him the perfect candidate to participate in the family's effort to reintegrate themselves into the inner circles of power.

[220] A. M. Schulz (1978a, 10) has argued, incorrectly I believe, that the inscription is a double dedication, which should be translated: "For his grandfather Francesco doge, and for his most pious brother Francesco, Niccolò son of Jacopo built this magnificent monument." The term "divus" was commonly used for Roman emperors after their deaths. Its use on Foscari's tomb again suggests the growing influence of the Roman empire on the Venetian imagination.

[221] Boys were registered at age eighteen. According to the Foscari family genealogy, Niccolò was registered in 1465 and Francesco in 1460. See Archivio Gradenigo, Rio Marin, b. 333, Pietro Gradenigo, "Lavoro storico," entries 64–65. The registration for Niccolò is found in AC, reg. 164, "Balla d'Oro," fol. 174r, dated 5 November 1465. Niccolò's mother Lucrezia presented the boy; the pledges were Filippo Foscari and Andrea Contarini.

[222] PSM, Misti, Commissarie, b. 125a, Commissaria of Michele Zon, notebook for the period 1449–60, acts dated 9 February 1457mv and 1 March 1458 and another act labeled "Debita soluta" on a badly deteriorated page also dated 1 March 1458.

[223] Collegio, Notatorio, reg. 10, fol. 34r, act 111, 26 June 1461. Di Pozzo would relinquish his salary for the time he would be out of the city. Jacopo's daughter Marina married nobleman Francesco Bragadin. See her will in CI, Notai, b. 99, notary Antonio de Grasellis, protocol, fols. 45r–46r, dated 2 June 1485. She wished to be buried at Santa Croce della Giudecca.

[224] Pincus, 1976, 431. There are also four shields in the surrounding fresco, but it is unclear whether these represented the Foscari arms or the arms of Venice.

[225] Archivio Gradenigo, Rio Marin, b. 333, Pietro Gradenigo, "Lavoro storico cronologico biografico sulla veneti famiglia Foscari, con prospetti, documenti e note", entry 64.

[226] Ibid., entries 71–74.

[227] Sartori, ed., 2001, 79–84.

[228] Giudici del Proprio, Vadimoni, reg. 4, fol. 16r. For background on this process, see Chojnacki, 2000, 97–98.

229 Giudici del Esaminador, Preces, reg. 33, fols. 41v–43v. I wish to thank Holly Hurlbut for this reference. Gullino (2005b, 111) claims that she retired to the convent of Sant'Andrea de Zirada but offers no citation.

230 MCC, Ms. Correr, 979, fasc. 10, act dated 10 March 1473. See also Sanudo, 1980, 194.

231 NT, b. 66, notary Priamo Businello, unbound testament 114.

232 A. M. Schulz, 1983, 45–46.

233 For the corrections to the *promissione*, see MC, Deliberazioni, reg. 23 (Regina), fols. 21v–22r (25 October 1457); they are also well summarized in Dolfin, 452r–453v. The five correctors were Paolo Tron, Cristoforo Moro, Orsato Giustinian, Michele Venier, and Niccolò Bernardo.

234 See, for example, the assessment of Pius II in Piccolomini, 1991, 26–30, and of Vespasiano da Bisticci in Da Bisticci, 1997, 231.

235 For a useful summary of the virtues, see Skinner, 2002, 61–92.

236 Piccolomini, 2003, 144; Antoninus, 1913, 98; Paltroni, 1966, 44. Giustinian, in his biography of his uncle Lorenzo, described Foscari as having a "natura vehementior" (Labalme, 1969, 115).

237 Finlay, 1980, 137–38.

CHAPTER 6   REMEMBERING FOSCARI, 1457 TO THE PRESENT

1 Byron, 1905, 145.

2 This survey is intended to be indicative rather than exhaustive. I have not included every history, tract, play, poem, or painting that includes Foscari or has him as its theme.

3 Muraro, 1961a; Muir, 1981, 265–68.

4 Rubinstein, 1974; Gleason, 2000.

5 Lane, 1973, 234.

6 For a brief summary of these events, ibid., 234–37, 241–49.

7 Lane, 1992, 253.

8 For some remarks on the "landward-looking" and "seaward-looking" parties, see Lane, 1973, 248–49.

9 Quoted in Cozzi, 1986, 85.

10 Ibid., 128; Gilbert, 1974, 274–75.

11 Quoted in Gilbert, 1974, 275.

12 Cozzi, 1970, 431–35.

13 Gaeta, 1980, 84. Of course, as described in chapter 1, the speeches are not an integrated part of Sanudo's life of Foscari as the Muratori edition makes them appear to be.

14 Ibid., 76–78. There was little direct defense of Foscari at this time, since his policy of mainland expansion and protection remained official policy. It would be interesting, however, to examine the new literature on villa life, with its evocation of the terraferma, as a defense of his policies.

15 For a discussion of Marc'Antonio Coccio Sabellico's view, ibid., 72–73.

16 Rubinstein, 1974.

17 Morosini, 1969, 107–08, 118–19; Finlay, 1980, 138–39.

18 Finlay, 1980, 223.

19 Vianoli, 1680–84, 1:645–46; Palazzi, 1696, 155. Loredan's unexpected death also led to suspicion that he had been poisoned by Visconti. See MCC, MS. Cicogna 3782, Girolamo Priuli, "Pretiosi frutti," fol. 159r. As mentioned above, the rumor that Foscari survived in his old age by drinking human milk was already in circulation in the fifteenth century: Soranzo, ed., 1915, 93.

20 For an introduction to Domenico Morosini and the text of his treatise, see Morosini, 1969.

21 Cozzi, 1974, 301–03; Finlay, 1980, 139.

22 Morosini, 1969, 109–16; Cozzi, 1970, 416.

23 Cozzi, 1970, 416.

24 Muir, 1979, 16–52; Brunetti, 1917, 351–55.

[25] The literature on the myth and anti-myth is large. For introductions, see Muir, 1981, 13–61; Grubb, 1986, 43–94.

[26] As discussed in Gaeta, 1980, 69.

[27] I have used the 1556 edition. Sabellico, 1556, 870.

[28] Sansovino [Bardi], 1587, 103. The work was first published in 1556. For background on Sansovino's work, see Gaeta, 1984, 459–62; and Doglio, 1983, 163–66. For Manfredi, 1598, I consulted the copy in BNM, Rari 124. See also Wilson, 2005, 192.

[29] Egnazio, 1554.

[30] Ibid., 41, 120, 167–68.

[31] Ibid., 79, 88–89, 107.

[32] Ibid., 178, 224.

[33] Ibid., 114, 188.

[34] I have used the edition of the *Discorsi politici di Paruta, 18.u. an 377*

[35] See the excellent summary of Paruta's thought in Gaeta, 1984, 454–59; and Baiocchi, 1975–76, 157–233.

[36] Paruta, 1852, 232.

[37] Ibid., 214–18.

[38] The material in the paragraph is based on Muir, 1981, 29–30, 46–47, 49–50.

[39] As discussed in Haitsma Mulier, 1980, 77–119, esp. 113.

[40] Bouwsma, 1974, 459.

[41] Ibid., 456. He meant the words as a compliment to the patricians' willingness to serve the regime. For Amelot de la Houssaye, see Gaeta, 1984, 491–93; and the more positive assessment in Del Negro, 1984, 420–21.

[42] Vianoli, 1680–84, 1:518–650, esp. 643–50.

[43] J. C. Davis, 1962.

[44] Palazzi, 1696, 155.

[45] Dean, 1997, 29.

[46] BNM, It. Cl.VII, 779 (7287), "Raccolta di memorie," fol. 57r–v. Dean (1997, 34) notes that in Mediterranean societies one finds "the conceptualization and remembrance of injury as debt, and of vengeance as repayment."

[47] MCC, MS. Correr 1098, "Miscellanea." The item bears the title "Iscrizioni sotto dei Quadri representanti ritratti esistenti alla Malcontenta." For this practice, which was followed by many Venetian noble families, and the phrase "a continuum of outstanding men," see J. C. Davis, 1975, 2–8; see also Brown, 2004, 16–19, 71, 73.

[48] It is worth noting that the current scion of the family, Antonio Foscari, has chosen the word "abdication" to describe the doge's action: Foscari, 2001, xxvi.

[49] Like many noble houses, it appears that the Foscari also owned histories of their family, which often included apocryphal events such as the supposed Egyptian prophecy to Foscari's father Niccolò. See Archivio Gradenigo, Rio Marin, b. 333, Pietro Gradenigo, "Lavoro storico cronologico biografico sulla veneta famiglia Foscari, con prospetti, documenti e note," 31. Gradenigo states that this event "Trovase ciò rifferito da Papa Pio II, o meglio si dirà un manoscritto di casa Foscari."

[50] Ibid., 114–15, entry 138. Gradenigo states that Alvise died in 1715; however the inscription on the plaque gives the date 1720. See also Pincus, 1976, 404–05; Gullino, 1997, 296. I have been unable to locate his will.

[51] Feldman, 2000, 217–60.

[52] For a full discussion of what he calls "Leontoclastia Giacobina" (Jacobin Lionoclasm), see Rizzi, 2001, 1:87–96; and for the Porta della Carta doge and lion group in particular, ibid., 2:18. See also Antonelli, 1979, 23.

[53] I have used a later edition: Daru, 1828, 24 vols.

[54] Ibid., 8:95.

[55] Ibid.

[56] Ibid., 8:98.

[57] Ibid., 8:99–100.

[58] Ibid., 8:108–114, quotes on 114. For Daru and the capitulary, see Povolo, 2000, 491–99.

[59] Sismonde de Sismondi, 1807–18, 10:36–46.

[60] All page references in the text are to Byron's *Three Plays: Sardanapalus; The Two Foscari; Cain*, reprint of London 1821 edition (Oxford and New York: Woodstock Books, 1990).

[61] For a brief summary, see Graham, 1998, 1–9.

[62] Plant, 2002, 89–95.

[63] The play was, however, performed at the Drury Lane Theatre in 1838. See Byron, 1905, 114. See also Franklin, 2000, 82–84.

[64] Byron, 1905, 115.

[65] John Ruskin was also strongly influenced by Daru's history. According to Ruskin (1860, 1:4–5), Venice's decline began in 1418, but took its "visible" form with the death of Mocenigo. And, according to Ruskin, the establishment of the State Inquisitors in 1454 marked the date at which the "government takes the perfidious and mysterious form under which it is usually conceived." *The Stones of Venice* was first published in 1851–53.

[66] As Peter W. Graham notes, "If the Aristotelian fatal flaw in the former play [*Marino Faliero*] is violent resistance to the state's injustice, the cause of tragedy in the latter [*The Two Foscari*] is passive obedience, which brings both the doge and his son to their death" (Graham, 1998, 111).

[67] Ibid., 108–09.

[68] O'Connor, 2003, 1:539.

[69] Other versions of the story in dramatic form include: John Blake White's *Foscari, or, the Venetian Exile* (1806); and Giacinto Battaglia's *La famiglia Foscari: Dramma storico in cinque atti* (Milan, 1844). For the play by White (an American), see D. Romano, 2003.

Foscari was also the subject of poems (Samuel Rogers, *Poems*, 1852, 2:93) and an anonymous novel entitled *Foscari: A Venetian Tale, Founded on Facts*, which was published in London in 1790. I wish to thank Dierdre Lynch for this last reference.

[70] Pavanello and Romanelli, eds., 1983, 146–79; *Romanticismo storico*, 1974, 69–73, 192–99, 283–86, 361–65.

[71] O'Connor, 2003, 1:545–46.

[72] Abbiati, 1959, 1:513.

[73] For the letter of 14 May 1844 from Verdi to Piave, ibid., 1:514.

[74] Ibid., 1:515. The *copialettere* dates this letter 22 May.

[75] Ibid., 1:516.

[76] Conati, 1983, 58–59. But he incorrectly dates the letter 1843 rather than 1844.

[77] Ibid., 59 (again listed as 1843).

[78] Ibid., 62–63 (again listed as 1843).

[79] Rosselli, 1984, 84.

[80] Ginsborg, 1979, 32.

[81] As cited in the brief introduction by Dorle J. Soria to the libretto for *I due Foscari*: Verdi and Piave, 1968, iii.

[82] Conati, 1983, 149–52, and 257, n. 13; Girardi and Rossi, 1989, cat. nos. 515, 587.

[83] Soria does not translate Piave's final comment about the changes he had to make to the story. See instead the libretto, Piave and Verdi, 1910, 3–4.

[84] Ibid., 8.

[85] Verdi and Piave, 1968, 27. As Abbiati (1959, 1:526) says: "Là, e soltanto là, il musicista si erge in un impeto di rigenerata gagliardia, il drammaturgo si scopre alla luce improvvisa di un contatto spirituale invano cercato negli atti precedenti."

[86] Abbiati, 1959, 1:527.

[87] For a selective list of these works, see the exhibition catalogue *Romanticismo storico*, 1974, 72–73.

[88] For Francesco Hayez's connections to the world of opera, see Mazzocca, 1994, 55–60.

[89] Pavanello and Romanelli, eds., 1983, 155.

[90] Mazzocca, 1982, 41–44.

[91] Ibid., 132.

[92] Ibid., 132; Pavanello and Romanelli, eds., 1983, 154.

[93] Mazzocca, 1997, 255.

[94] Mazzocca, 1982, 116–17; Pavanello and Romanelli, eds., 1983, 152–53; Plant, 2002, 103, 124.

[95] Pavanello and Romanelli, eds., 1983, 154.

[96] Johnson, 2001, 116–17.

[97] Ibid., 112.

[98] Joannides, 2001, 134.

[99] Mazzocca, 1997, 254.

[100] Pavanello and Romanelli, eds., 1983, 153.

[101] Lazzarini, 1963, 294.

[102] Cornelio, 1758, 85–201. Corner also published an account of Andrea Donato. For more on Corner, see Preto, 1983, 191–93.

[103] Benzoni, 1990, 45–57.

[104] For some background on Romanin's place in Venetian historiography, see Manfroni, 1908.

[105] Romanin, 4:7–8, n. 1.

[106] Ibid., 4:98, n. 36; 4:157, n. 26.

[107] Ibid., 4:120, n. 52. Manzoni drew heavily on Sismondi. See Lonardi, 1976, 33.

[108] Romanin, 4:156, n. 25.

[109] Ibid., 4:196, n. 8. The references are to Léon Galibert, *Histoire de la République de Venise* (Paris, 1847), and Marc Antoine Laugier, *Histoire de la République de Venise depuis sa fondation jusqu'à présent* (Paris, 1759–68).

[110] Romanin, 4:84.

[111] Romanin, 4:211, n. 59. Romanin states that Loredan's consolation of Foscari appears in Dolfin, but I have been unable to locate such a passage in the chronicle.

[112] Ibid., 4:213, n. 69.

[113] Ibid., 4:215–19.

[114] Povolo, 2000, 499, 503.

[115] Romanin, 4:83, n. 60, 194, n. 1.

[116] Berlan, 1852.

[117] Ibid., 1–2.

[118] Ibid., 62.

[119] Ibid., 140.

[120] For background on Berlan, see Craveri, 1967, 112–14; and Cecchetti, 1886.

[121] Berlan, 1852, 47.

[122] Ibid., 181.

[123] For further analysis of Romanin and Berlan, see Canella, 1976, esp. 90–100. Sentiments similar to Berlan can be found in Ignazio Neumann de' Rizzi's essay on Foscari (Neumann de' Rizzi, 1862).

[124] Antonelli, 1979, 23–29; Rizzi, 2001, 1:375–76.

[125] Cappello and Bernardi, 1898, including the remark that under Foscari's reign Venice reached "the apogee of its glory" (p 3). For the identity of Cesare and Elisabeta, see Pietro Gradenigo's history of the family: Archivio Gradenigo, Rio Marin, b. 333, Pietro Gradenigo, "Lavoro storico crono-logico biografico sulla veneta famiglia Foscari, con prospetti, documenti e note," 67, entry 170 (Cesare Foscari).

[126] Morosini and Morosini, eds., 1897; Barozzi et al., eds., 1897.

[127] Archivio Gradenigo, Rio Marin, b. 333, Pietro Gradenigo, "Lavoro storico cronologico biografico sulla veneta famiglia Foscari, con prospetti, documenti e note." It includes information on family members up to 1896.

[128] Vecchiato, 1898.

[129] Symonds (1888, 215, n. 1) says that "the Council of Ten subjected him [Foscari] and his son Jacopo to the most frightfully protracted martyrdom that a relentless oligarchy has ever inflicted;" see also ibid., 219, 234, n. 1. In his history of Venice, Horatio Brown viewed the "whole episode of the private life of the Foscari family" as a lesson in the

"internal history of Venice," specifically in the increasing power of the Council of Ten, which he interpreted as the price the Venetians paid for their "terror lest their State should suffer the doom of all its Italian neighbours, and pass under the dominion of a single ruler" (Brown, 1893, 305–06).

130 Wiel, 1891.

131 Ibid., 107, n. 1.

132 Ibid., 43. Wiel attributes Foscari's dethronement to his incapacity, although she contends that Loredan's opposition to Jacopo and his father "was the result, there can be little doubt, of personal hatred and rancour" (ibid., 108). In a brief essay, the distinguished numismatist Nicolò Papadopoli argued that the deposition was motivated by "cruel reason of state or by other motives which are difficult, after centuries, to evaluate" (Papadopoli, 1892, 4).

133 Lane, 1973, 229–30, 267.

134 Trevor-Roper, 1965, 110; Mallett, 1984, 172.

135 Chambers, 1970, 89; Babinger, 1957, 68. The characterization of Foscari as ambitious continues. See Brown, 1996, 104; Casini, 1996, 198 (who speaks of Foscari's "hard to control personality"); Marconato, 2002, 229 (who describes Foscari as "dominated by a great ambition"); Gullino, 2005b, 12.

136 Maranini, 1974, 2:280 (especially n. 2), 418.

137 Trevor-Roper, 1965, 115, 121.

138 Tenenti, 1996, 333. Tenenti, Italian by birth, spent his academic career in France.

139 Lane, 1973, 267.

140 Finlay, 1980, 191.

141 Crouzet-Pavan, 2002, 200.

142 Trevor-Roper, 1965, 112.

143 Finlay, 1980, 117.

144 Cessi, 1981, 398–401, quote on 398.

145 Cozzi, 1986, 30; for a fascinating interpretation of the events of this period as an effort by the Venetian elite to maintain their city-state regime in the "henceforth irreversible context of the territorial state," see Cracco, 1979, esp. 90.

146 Da Mosto, 1983, 162; Gullino, 1996c, 345.

147 The three works, all invaluable to this study, are: Sanudo, 1999; Sartori, 2001; Girgensohn, 2004.

148 Gullino, 2005b, 149–75, esp. 171, 174.

149 I wish to thank Carlo Montanaro for identifying these films and their directors for me and for making available the publicity photo from the Fulchignoni version.

150 Ojetti, 1923, 229–33. The chapter is entitled "La Forca in Piazza San Marco" (The Gallows in Piazza San Marco).

151 Ibid., 232.

BIBLIOGRAPHY

ARCHIVAL SOURCES

Florence, Archivio di Stato [ASF]
  Mediceo avanti il principato [MAP].
  Signori, Responsive Copiari, reg. 1.

Florence, Biblioteca Nazionale [BN]
  Fondo Tordi 1, "Copialettere del
  Doge di Venezia Francesco Foscari
  – 1443–1455."
  Nuovi acquisti 445, Porcellio Pandoni,
  "Commentariorum secundi anni
  de gestis Scipionis Picinini exercitus Venetorum imperatoris in Hannibalem Sforciam Mediolanensium
  ducem."

London, British Library
  MS. Add. 15586, "Historia de l'origine
  di Venetia, e delle valorosissime
  imprese fatte sino l'anno 1460."

Milan, Archivio di Stato [ASM]
  Sforzesco. Carteggii 46, 197, 269,
  342–44.

Siena, Archivio di Stato
  Archivio del Concistoro, carteggio,
  filza 1991 [Yale University, Ilardi
  microfilm collection, reel 1470].

Syracuse, New York. Syracuse University Library
  Ranke MS. 41. "Historia venetiana di
  Agostino Agostini dal principio
  della fondazione di Venetia sino
  all'anno 1570."

Vatican City, Archivio Apostolico
  Vaticano [AAVa]
  Arm. XXXIX, vol. 6. "Breviarum."

Vatican City, Biblioteca Apostolica Vaticana [BAV]
Vat. Lat. 6085, "Cronica di Venetia."
Vat. Lat. 3194, Letters of Lauro Querini.

Venice, Archivio di Stato [incl. AC, CI, DM, MC, PSM, SM, SMar, SS, ST]
Archivio Gradenigo, Rio Marin, b. 333, 340.
Archivio Notarile, Testamenti, b. 66, 858, 1149, 1155, 1255.
Avogaria di Comun, b. 162, 164, "Balla d'Oro."
Avogaria di Comun, b. 106, "Liber nuptiarum."
Avogaria di Comun, Raspe, reg. 3646, 3647, 3648, 3649, 3650.
Cancelleria Inferiore, Notai, b. 96, 99, 103, 170, 191, 193, 228.
Collegio, Notatorio, reg. 4–10.
Consiglio dei Dieci, Deliberazioni, reg. 8–15.
Giudici del Esaminador, Preces, reg. 33.
Giudici di Petizion, Sentenze e interdetti, reg. 8.
Giudici del Proprio, Vadimoni, reg. 4.
Libri commemoriali, reg. 14.
Maggior Consiglio, Deliberazioni, reg. 22–23.
Procuratori di San Marco de citra, b. 27, 53, 87, 93, 96, 98, 126, 127, 206, 272.
Procuratori di San Marco, de supra, Serie Chiesa, b. 79.
Procuratori di San Marco, Misti, b. 12, 52, 125a.
Provveditori al sal, b. 6, reg. 3.
San Cristoforo della Pace, b. 3, 11.
Sant'Elena in Isola, b. 1.

Scuola di Santa Maria del Rosario, Commissaria Girardi, b. 28–29.
Segretario alle Voci, reg. 4.
Senato, Deliberazioni Misti, reg. 46–60.
Senato, Deliberazioni Secreti, reg. 1–20.
Senato, Mar, Deliberazioni, reg. 1–5.
Senato, Terra, Deliberazioni, reg. 1–4.

Venice, Biblioteca Nazionale Marciana [BNM]
It. Cl. VII, 95 (8610), "Cronica di Donato Contarini."
It. Cl. VII, 125 (7460), "Cronica Sanuda."
It. Cl. VII, 380 (7471), Marco Barbaro, "Procuratori di San Marco."
It. Cl. VII, 779 (7287), "Raccolta di memorie."
It. Cl. VII, 794 (8503), Zorzi (Giorgio) Dolfin, "Cronica."
It. Cl. VII, 800 (7151), Marino Sanudo, "Vite dei dogi."
It. Cl. VII, 2048–49 (8332.1–2), Antonio Morosini, "Cronica."

Venice, Biblioteca del Seminario Patriarchale
MS. 950, Jacopo d'Albizzotto Guidi, "El sommo della condizione e stato e principio della citta di Vinegia."

Venice, Museo Civico Correr [MCC]
MS. Cicogna 1645, Pietro Dolfin, "Cronica Dolfina," 3 (1405–22).
MS. Cicogna 3234/III/29, fasc. "S. Cristoforo della Pace."
MS. Cicogna 3782, Girolamo Priuli, "Pretiosi frutti."

MS. Correr 979, fasc. 10, "Miscellanea."

MS. Correr 1098, "Miscellanea."

MS. Gradenigo 199, "Dogi."

MS. Gradenigo-Dolfin 65/I–III, Jan [Giovanni] Grevembroch, "Varie venete curiosità sacre e profane."

MS. Gradenigo-Dolfin 288/I–III, Jan [Giovanni] Grevembroch, "Monumenta veneta ex antiquis ruderibus templorum."

MS. Gradenigo-Dolfin 229, Jan (Giovanni) Grevembroch, "Saggi di familiari magnificenze preservate tra le moderne nelli chiostri e palaggi di Venezia."

Prov. Div. 2362/II, "Promissione ducale di Francesco Foscari."

Mariegola 124.

Stampe Gherro 290, Marco Sebastiano Giampiccoli, "Monumenta del Doge Francesco Foscari esistente eretto" (1777).

PRINTED SOURCES

Abbiati, Franco. 1959. *Giuseppe Verdi.* 4 vols. Milan: Ricordi.

Aikema, Bernard. 2000. "La capella d'oro di San Zaccaria: Arte, religione e politica nella Venezia del doge Foscari." *Arte veneta* 57:23–41.

Alexandrescu-Dersca Bulgaru, Marie-Mathilde. 1974. "L'action diplomatique et militaire de Venise pour la défense de Constantinople (1452–1453)." *Revue Roumaine d'Histoire* 12:247–67.

Antonelli, Vincenzo. 1979. "I restauri della Porta della Carta dal 1797." In *La Porta della Carta: I restauri*, edited by Serena Romano, 23–29. Venice: Tipo-Litografia Armena.

Antonini, Federico. 1930. "La pace di Lodi ed i segretti maneggi che la prepararono." *Archivio storico lombardo* 6th ser., 72:233–96.

Antoninus, Saint [Antonio Pierozzi]. 1913. *Chroniques de Saint Antonin: Fragments originaux du titre xxii (1378–1459).* Edited by L'Abbé Raoul Morçay. Paris: Librairie Gabalda.

Arslan, Edoardo. 1965. "Bastiani, Lazzaro." *DBI* 7:167–69.

Arslan, Edoardo. 1971. *Gothic Architecture in Venice.* Translated by Anne Engel. London: Phaidon Press.

Ashtor, Eliyahu. 1983. *Levant Trade in the Later Middle Ages.* Princeton: Princeton University Press.

Babinger, Franz. 1957. "Le vicende veneziane nella lotta contro i Turchi durante il secolo XV." In *La civiltà veneziana del Quattrocento*, 49–73. Florence: Sansoni.

Babinger, Franz. 1978. *Mehmed the Conqueror and his Time.* Translated by Ralph Manheim. Princeton: Princeton University Press.

Baiocchi, Angelo. 1975–76. "Paolo Paruta: Ideologia e politica nel Cinquecento veneziano." *Studi veneziani* 17–18:157–233.

Baldrighi, Aldo. 1977. "La battaglia navale sul Po del 1431." *Archivio storico lombardo* 10th ser., 3:331–36.

Barbaro, Francesco. 1991–99. *Epistolario.* Edited by Claudio Griggio. 2 vols. Florence: Leo S. Olschki Editore.

Barbaro, Nicolò. 1856. *Giornale dell'assedio di Costantinopoli, 1453.* Edited by

Enrico Cornet. Vienna: Libreria Tendler and Comp.

Barbaro, Nicolò. 1976. "Giornale dell' assedio di Costantinopoli." In *La caduta di Constantinopoli: Le testimonianze dei contemporanei*, edited by Agostino Pertusi, 5–38, 345–71. Milan: Arnoldo Mondadori Editore.

Barbiani, Wilma. 1927. *La dominazione veneta a Ravenna*. Ravenna: Arti Grafiche.

Bardi, Girolamo. See Sansovino, Francesco.

Barker, John W. *Manuel II Palaeologus (1391–1425): A Study in Late Byzantine Statemanship*. New Brunswick: Rutgers University Press, 1969.

Baron, Hans. 1955. *Humanistic and Political Literature in Florence and Venice at the Beginning of the Quattrocento: Studies in Criticism and Chronology*. Cambridge, MA: Harvard University Press.

Barozzi, Nicolò, et al., eds. 1897. *Gli ultimi due anni del dogado di Francesco Foscari (Dalle Vite dei dogi di Marino Sanuto). (Nozze Widmann-Rezzonico/Foscari)*. Venice: Tipografia Emiliana.

Battistella, Antonio. 1889. *Il conte Carmagnola: Studio storico con documenti inediti*. Genoa: Stabilimento Tip. e Lit. dell'Annuario Generale d'Italia.

Bellavitis, Giorgio. 2005. "'Venetiarum universitas in domo Foscari': Tradizione e rinnovamento, storia e progetto, nel nostro lavoro a Cà Foscari." In *Cà Foscari: Storia e restauro del palazzo dell'Università di Venezia*, edited by Giuseppe Maria Pilo, Laura de Rosso, Domizia Alessandri, and

Flavio Zuanier, 90–101. Venice: Marsilio.

Belting, Hans. 1994. *Likeness and Presence: A History of the Image before the Era of Art*. Translated by Edmund Jephcott. Chicago and London: University of Chicago Press.

Beltrami, Luca. 1906. *La Cà del Duca sul Canal Grande ed altre reminiscenze sforzesche in Venezia*. Milan: Tipografia di Umberto Allegretti.

Benzoni, Gino. 1990. "Ranke's Favorite Source: The Venetian *Relazioni*: Impressions with Allusions to Later Historiography." In *Leopold von Ranke and the Shaping of the Historical Discipline*, edited by Georg G. Iggers and James M. Powell, 45–57. Syracuse: Syracuse University Press.

Berlan, Francesco. 1852. *I due Foscari*. Turin: Tipografia G. Favale.

Bertalot, Ludwig. 1975. "Iacobi Zeni Descriptio Coniurationis Patavine (das Ende des letzten Carraresen 1435)." In *Studien zum Italienischen und Deutschen Humanismus*, 2:103–29. Rome: Edizioni di Storia e Letteratura.

Berti, Marcello. 2001. *Il leone di San Marco e il gallo di Romagna: Venezia e Romagna: Da sudditanza a signoria*. Lugo di Romagna: Walter Berti Editore.

Besta, Enrico. 1899. *Il senato veneziano (origine, costituzione, attribuzioni e riti)*. Miscellanea di storia veneta. 2nd ser., vol. 5. Venice: Tip. Visentini Cav. Federico.

Besta, Fabio. 1912. *Bilanci generali della repubblica di Venezia*. vol. 1, tome 1. Venice: Stab. Grafico Visentini Cav. Federico.

Bianchi, Alessandro. 1994. "L'architettura civile." In *Storia di Venezia: Temi: L'arte*, edited by Rodolfo Pallucchini, 1:147–83. Rome: Istituto della Enciclopedia Italiana.

Biondo, Flavio. 1558. *Roma ristaurata, et Italia illustrata di Biondo da Forli. Tradotte in buona lingua volgare per Lucio Fauno*. Venice: Domenico Giglio.

Bistort, Giulio. 1969. *Il magistrato alle pompe nella Republica di Venezia: Studio storico*. Reprint of 1912 edition. Bologna: Forni Editore.

Boerio, Giuseppe. 1973. *Dizionario del dialetto veneziano*. Reprint of 1856 edition. Venice: Filippi Editore.

Boholm, Åsa. 1990. *The Doge of Venice: The Symbolism of State Power in the Renaissance*. Gothenburg: Institute for Advanced Studies in Social Anthropology.

Bouwsma, William J. 1974. "Venice and the Political Education of Europe." In *Renaissance Venice*, edited by J. R. Hale, 445–66. London: Faber and Faber.

Branca, Vittore, ed. 1977. *Lauro Quirini umanista*. Florence: Leo S. Olschki Editore.

Brown, Horatio F. 1893. *Venice: An Historical Sketch of the Republic*. London: Percival and Co.

Brown, Patricia Fortini. 1988. *Venetian Narrative Painting in the Age of Carpaccio*. New Haven and London: Yale University Press.

Brown, Patricia Fortini. 1990. "Measured Friendship, Calculated Pomp: The Ceremonial Welcomes of the Venetian Republic." In *"All the World's a Stage . . ." Art and Pageantry in the Renaissance and Baroque, Part I, Triumphal Celebrations and the Rituals of Statecraft*, edited by Barbara Wisch and Susan Scott Munshower, 136–86. University Park: Pennsylvania State University Press.

Brown, Patricia Fortini. 1996. *Venice and Antiquity: The Venetian Sense of the Past*. New Haven and London: Yale University Press.

Brown, Patricia Fortini. 2004. *Private Lives in Renaissance Venice: Art, Architecture and the Family*. New Haven and London: Yale University Press.

Brunetti, Mario. 1917. "Il doge non è 'segno di taverna'." *Nuovo archivio veneto* n.s. 33:351–55.

Bruni, Leonardo. 1741. *Epistolarum libri VIII*. Edited by Lorenzo Mehus. 2 vols. Florence: Typographia Bernardi Paperini.

Bueno de Mesquita, D. M. 1972. "Bussone, Francesco, detto il Carmagnola." *DBI* 15:582–87.

Byron, Lord. 1905. *The Works of Lord Byron: Poetry. Vol. V*. Edited by Ernest Hartley Coleridge. London: John Murray; and New York: Charles Scribner's Sons.

Byron, Lord. 1990. *Three Plays: Sardanapalus; The Two Foscari; Cain*. Reprint of London 1821 edition. Oxford and New York: Woodstock Books.

Caferro, William. 1998. *Mercenary Companies and the Decline of Siena*. Baltimore and London: Johns Hopkins University Press.

Canella, Massimo. 1976. "Appunti e spunti sulla storiografia veneziana dell'Ottocento." *Archivio veneto* 5th ser., 106:73–116.

Canetta, Carlo. 1885. "La pace di Lodi (9 Aprile 1454)." *Rivista storica italiana* 2:516–64.

Cappello, Michelangelo, and Giovanni Bernardi. 1898. *L'elezione a doge di Francesco Foscari. (Nozze Foscari/ Barozzi).* Venice: Stab. C. Ferrari.

Carile, A. 1977. "Caresini, Rafaino." *DBI* 20:80–83.

Carile, A. 1991. "Dolfin, Giorgio (Zorzi)." *DBI* 40:498–99.

Casini, Matteo. 1996. *I gesti del principe: La festa politica a Firenze e Venezia in età rinascimentale.* Venice: Marsilio.

Catalano, Franco. 1956. "Capitolo I: La pace di lodi e la lega italica." In *Storia di Milano*, vol. 7: *L'eta sforzesca dal 1450 al 1500*, 3–81. Milan: Fondazione Treccani degli Alfieri.

Cecchetti, Bartolomeo. 1886. "Francesco prof. Berlan." *Archivio veneto* n.s. 32:259–63.

Cerioni, Lydia. 1970. *La diplomazia sforzesca nella seconda metà del Quattrocento e i suoi cifrari segreti.* 2 vols. Rome: Il Centro di Ricerca Editore.

Cessi, Roberto. 1916. "Venezia alla Pace di Ferrara del 1428." *Nuovo archivio veneto* n.s. 31:321–71.

Cessi, Roberto, ed. 1970. *Deliberazioni del Maggior Consiglio di Venezia.* Reprint of 1931–50 edition. 3 vols. Bologna: Forni.

Cessi, Roberto. 1981. *Storia della Repubblica di Venezia.* Reprint of 1968 edition. Florence: Giunti-Martello. First published in 1944–46, 2 vols.

Cessi, Roberto, and Annibale Alberti. 1934. *Rialto: L'isola, il ponte, il mercato.* Bologna: N. Zanichelli.

Chambers, D. S. 1970. *The Imperial Age of Venice, 1380–1580.* London: Thames and Hudson.

Chambers, D. S. 1971. *Patrons and Artists in the Italian Renaissance.* Columbia, SC: University of South Carolina Press.

Chambers, D. S. 1997. "Merit and Money: The Procurators of St Mark and their *Commissioni*, 1443–1605." *Journal of the Warburg and Courtauld Institutes* 60:23–88.

Chittolini, Giorgio. 2005. "Guerre, guerricciole e riassetti territoriali in una provincia Lombarda di confine: Parma e il parmense, agosto 1447–febbraio 1449." *Società e storia* 108: 221–49.

Chojnacki, Stanley. 1974. "In Search of the Venetian Patriciate: Families and Factions in the Fourteenth Century." In *Renaissance Venice*, edited by J. R. Hale, 47–90. London: Faber and Faber.

Chojnacki, Stanley. 2000. *Women and Men in Renaissance Venice: Twelve Essays on Patrician Society.* Baltimore and London: Johns Hopkins University Press.

Cicogna, Emmanuele Antonio. 1969–70. *Delle inscrizioni veneziane.* Reprint of 1824–53 edition. 6 vols. Bologna: Forni Editore.

Cognasso, Francesco. 1955. Parts I and I: "Il ducato visconteo da Gian Galeazzo a Filippo Maria;" and "La Repubblica di S. Ambrogio." In *Storia di Milano*, vol. 6: *Il Ducato Visconteo e la Repubblica Ambrosiana (1392–1450)*, 3–448. Milan: Fondazione Treccani degli Alfieri.

Colombo, Elia. 1894. "Re Renato: Alleato del duca Francesco Sforza contro i veneziani." *Archivio storico lombardo* 3rd ser., 1:79–136, 361–98.

Conati, Marcello. 1983. *La bottega della musica: Verdi e la Fenice*. Milan: Il Saggiatore.

Concina, Ennio. 2006. *Tempo novo: Venezia e il Quattrocento*. Venice: Marsilio.

Cornelio [Corner], Flaminio. 1749. *Ecclesiae venetae antiquis monumentis nunc etiam primum editis illustratae ac in decades distributae.* 13 vols. Venice: Jo. Baptistae Pasquali.

Cornelio [Corner], Flaminio. 1758. *Opuscula quatuor quibus illustrantur gesta B. Francisci Quirini Patriarchae Gradensis, Francisci Foscari ducis venetiarum, Joannis de Benedictis Episcopi Tarvisini, Andreae Donati equitis accedit opusculum quintum de cultu S. Simonis pueri Tridentini martyris apud venetos.* Venice: Apud Marcum Carnioni.

Corner, Flaminio. 1990. *Notizie storiche delle chiese e monasteri di Venezia e di Torcello.* Reprint of 1758 edition. Bologna: Arnaldo Forni Editore.

Coronelli, Vincenzo. 1697. *Le singolarità di Venezia.* 3 vols. Venice.

Covini, N. 1997. "Cabrino Fondulo." *DBI* 48:586–89.

Cozzi, Gaetano. 1958. *Il doge Nicolò Contarini: Ricerche sul patriziato veneziano agli inizi del Seicento.* Venice and Rome: Istituto per la Collaborazione Culturale.

Cozzi, Gaetano. 1970. "Domenico Morosini e il 'De bene istituta re publica'." *Studi veneziani* 12:405–58.

Cozzi, Gaetano. 1974. "Authority and Law in Renaissance Venice." In *Renaissance Venice*, edited by J. R. Hale, 293–345. London: Faber and Faber.

Cozzi, Gaetano. 1986. "Politica, società, istituzioni." In Gaetano Cozzi and Michael Knapton, *Storia della Repubblica di Venezia: Dalla guerra di Chioggia alla riconquista della terraferma*, 1–271. Turin: UTET.

Cozzi, Gaetano. 1992–93. "Giuspatronato del doge e prerogative del primicerio sulla Cappella Ducale di San Marco (secoli xvi–xviii). Controversie con i procuratori di San Marco de supra e i patriarchi di Venezia." In *Atti dell'istituto veneto di scienze, lettere ed arti: Classe di scienze morali, lettere ed arti, 151.1 70.*

Cracco, Giorgio. 1979. "Patriziato e oligarchia a Venezia nel Tre-Quattrocento." In *Florence and Venice: Comparisons and Relations*, vol. 1: *Quattrocento*, edited by Sergio Bertelli, Nicolai Rubinstein, and Craig Hugh Smyth, 71–98. Florence: La Nuova Italia Editrice.

Craveri, Piero. 1967. "Berlan, Francesco." *DBI* 9:112–14.

Crouzet-Pavan, Elisabeth. 1992. *"Sopra le acque salse:" Espaces, pouvoir, et société à Venise à la fin du Moyen Age.* 2 vols. Rome: École Française de Rome.

Crouzet-Pavan, Elisabeth. 1995. *La mort lente de Torcello: Histoire d'une cité disparue.* Librairie Arthème Fayard.

Crouzet-Pavan, Elisabeth. 2002. *Venice Triumphant: The Horizons of a Myth.* Translated by Lydia G. Cochrane. Baltimore and London: Johns Hopkins University Press. French original 1999.

Cumming, Julie E. 1992. "Music for the Doge in Early Renaissance Venice." *Speculum* 67:324–64.

Da Bisticci, Vespasiano. 1997. *The Vespasiano Memoirs: Lives of Illustrious Men of the XVth Century.* Trans. William George and Emily Waters. Reprint of 1963 edition. Toronto: University of Toronto Press.

Da Gubbio, Ser Guerriero. 1902. *Cronaca di Ser Guerriero da Gubbio.* Edited by Giuseppe Mazzatinti. Rerum Italicarum Scriptores. 2nd ser., tome 21, pt. 4. Città di Castello: S. Lapi.

Da Mosto, Andrea. 1937–40. *L'Archivio di Stato di Venezia: Indice generale, storico, descrittivo ed analitico.* 2 vols. Rome: Biblioteca d'Arte.

Da Mosto, Andrea. 1983. *I dogi di Venezia nella vita pubblica e privata.* Revision of 1977 edition. Florence: Giunti-Martello.

Daru, Pierre Antoine Noël. 1828. *Histoire de la République de Venise.* 24 vols. Stuttgart: Charles Hoffmann.

Da Soldo, Cristoforo. 1938–42. *La cronaca di Cristoforo da Soldo.* Edited by Giuseppe Brizzolara. Rerum Italicarum Scriptores. 2nd ser., tome 21, pt. 3 (in 3 fascicles). Bologna: Nicola Zanichelli.

Davis, James C. 1962. *The Decline of the Venetian Nobility as a Ruling Class.* Baltimore: Johns Hopkins University Press.

Davis, James C. 1975. *A Venetian Family and its Fortune 1500–1900: The Donà and the Conservation of their Wealth.* Philadelphia: American Philosophical Society.

Davis, Robert C. 1991. *Shipbuilders of the Venetian Arsenal: Workers and Workplace in the Preindustrial City.* Baltimore: Johns Hopkins University Press.

Dean, Trevor. 1997. "Marriage and Mutilation: Vendetta in Late Medieval Italy." *Past and Present* 157:3–36.

Dean, Trevor. 2000. *The Towns of Italy in the Later Middle Ages.* Manchester and New York: Manchester University Press.

Dean, Trevor, and Kate Lowe. 1998. "Introduction: Issues in the History of Marriage." In *Marriage in Italy, 1300–1600,* edited by Trevor Dean and K. J. P. Lowe, 1–21. Cambridge: Cambridge University Press.

De Peppo, P. 1991. "Donà (Donato, Donado), Ermolao." *DBI* 40:722–24.

Del Negro, Pietro. 1984. "Forme e istituzioni del discorso politico veneziano." In *Storia della cultura veneta* pt. 4, vol. 2: *Dalla controriforma alla fine della repubblica,* edited by Girolamo Arnaldi and Manlio Pastore Stocchi, 407–36. Vicenza: Neri Pozza.

Del Torre, Giuseppe. 1992–93. "Stato regionale e benefici ecclesiastici: Vescovadi e canonicati nella terraferma veneziana all'inizio dell'età moderna." In *Atti dell'istituto veneto di scienze, lettere ed arti: Classe di scienze morali, lettere ed arti* 151 (IV): 1171–1236.

Del Torre, Giuseppe. 1997a. "'Dalli preti è nata la servitù di quella repubblica'. Ecclesiastici e segreti di stato nella Venezia del '400,'" 131–58. In *Itinerari per la storia della città,* edited by S. Gasparri, G. Levi, and A. Moro. Bologna: Società Editrice il Mulino.

Del Torre, Giuseppe. 1997b. "Foscari, Polidoro." *DBI* 49:347–50.

Demus, Otto. 1960. *The Church of San Marco in Venice: History, Architecture, Sculpture*. Dumbarton Oaks Studies VI. Washington: Dumbarton Oaks.

Di Chio, Leonardo. 1976. "Epistola [. . .] de urbis Constantinopoleos captivitate." In *La caduta di Costantinopoli: Le testimonianze dei contemporanei*, edited by Agostino Pertusi, 120–71, 390–407. Milan: Arnoldo Mondadori Editore.

Doglio, Maria Luisa. 1983. "La letteratura ufficiale e l'oratoria celebrativa." In *Storia della cultura veneta* pt. 4, vol. 1: *Dalla controriforma alla fine della repubblica*, edited by Girolamo Arnaldi and Manlio Pastore Stocchi, 163–87. Vicenza: Neri Pozza.

Donzelli, Carlo, and Giuseppe Maria Pilo. 1967. *I pittori del Seicento veneto*. Florence: Edizioni Remo Sandron.

Dursteler, Eric. 2006. *Venetians in Constantinople: Nation, Identity and Coexistence in the Early Modern Mediterranean*. Baltimore: Johns Hopkins University Press.

Eglin, John. *Venice Transfigured: The Myth of Venice in British Culture, 1660–1797*. New York: Palgrave, 2001.

Egnazio, Giovanni Battista. 1554. *De exemplis illustrium virorum venetae civitatis atque aliarum gentium*. Venice: Nicolaus Tridentinus.

Eisler, Colin. 1989. *The Genius of Jacopo Bellini: The Complete Paintings and Drawings*. New York: Harry N. Abrams, Inc.

Epstein, Steven A. *Genoa and the Genoese, 958–1528*. Chapel Hill and London: University of North Carolina Press, 1996.

Eroli, Giovanni. 1879. *Erasmo Gattamelata da Narni: Suoi monumenti e sua famiglia*. Rome: Coi Tipi del Salviucci.

Feldman, Martha. 2000. "Opera, Festivity, and Spectacle in 'Revolutionary' Venice: Phantasms of Time and History." In *Venice Reconsidered: The History and Civilization of an Italian City-State, 1297–1797*, edited by John Martin and Dennis Romano, 217–60. Baltimore and London: Johns Hopkins University Press.

Fine, John V. A. Jr. 1987. *The Late Medieval Balkans: A Critical Survey from the Late Twelfth Century to the Ottoman Conquest*. Ann Arbor: University of Michigan Press.

Finlay, Robert. 1980. *Politics in Renaissance Venice*. New Brunswick: Rutgers University Press.

Fletcher, Stella R. 1996. "The Making of a Fifteenth-Century Venetian Cardinal." *Studi veneziani* n.s. 31:27–49.

Foscari, Antonio. 1993. "Introduzione a una ricerca sulla costruzione della libreria medicea nel convento di San Giorgio Maggiore a Venezia." In *Studi per Pietro Zampetti*, edited by Ranieri Varese, 226–36. Ancona: Il Lavoro Editoriale.

Foscari, Antonio. 2001. "*Magnanimi monumenta ducis domus inclyta salve*: Un'ode sulla costruzione di Cà Foscari." In *La casa grande dei Foscari in volta de canal: Documenti*, edited by Fabiola Sartori, ix–xxxiv. Venice: La Malcontenta.

Foscari, Antonio. 2005a. "Il doge e la costruzione della sua 'casa granda'." In

Cà Foscari: Storia e restauro del palazzo dell'Università di Venezia, edited by Giuseppe Maria Pilo, Laura de Rossi, Domizia Alessandri, and Flavio Zuanier, 52–67. Venice: Marsilio.

Foscari, Antonio. 2005b. "Prima di Cà Foscari: La 'casa delle due torri' e il doge." In *Cà Foscari: Storia e restauro del palazzo dell'Università di Venezia,* edited by Giuseppe Maria Pilo, Laura de Rossi, Domizia Alessandri, and Flavio Zuanier, 22–37. Venice: Marsilio.

Fossati, Felice. 1957. "Francesco Sforza e la pace di Lodi." *Archivio veneto* 5th ser., 60–61:15–34.

Francastel, Galienne. 1965. "Une peinture anti-hérétique à Venise?" *Annales E.S.C.* 20:1–17.

Franklin, Caroline. 2000. *Byron: A Literary Life.* Basingstoke, Hampshire: Macmillan Press Ltd.

Frazier, Alison Knowles. 2004. *Possible Lives: Authors and Saints in Renaissance Italy.* New York: Columbia University Press.

Frick, Carole Collier. 2002. *Dressing Renaissance Florence: Families, Fortunes, and Fine Clothing.* Baltimore and London: Johns Hopkins University Press.

Fubini, Riccardo. 1982. "Appunti sui rapporti diplomatici fra il dominio sforzesco e Firenze medicea." In *Gli Sforza a Milano e in Lombardia e i loro rapporti con gli stati italiani ed europei (1450–1535),* 291–334. Milan: Cisalpino-Goliardica.

Gaeta, Franco. 1980. "Storiografia, coscienza nazionale e politica culturale nella Venezia del Rinascimento."

In *Storia della cultura veneta,* pt. 3, vol. 1: *Dal primo Quattrocento al Concilio di Trento,* edited by Girolamo Arnaldi and Manlio Pastore Stocchi, 1–91. Vicenza: Neri Pozza.

Gaeta, Franco. 1984. "Venezia da 'stato misto' ad aristocrazia 'esemplare'." In *Storia della cultura veneta,* pt. 4, vol. 2: *Dalla controriforma alla fine della repubblica,* edited by Girolamo Arnaldi and Manlio Pastore Stocchi, 437–94. Vicenza: Neri Pozza.

Galli, Alessandro. 1997. Catalogue entry "Cristoforo Cortese, 1422, Promissione del doge Francesco Foscari." In *Miniature a Brera, 1100–1422: Manoscritti dalla Biblioteca Nazionale Braidense e da collezioni private,* edited by Miklós Boskovits et al., 238–43. Milan: Federico Motta Editore.

Gallo, Donato. 1994. "Il primo secolo veneziano (1405–1509)." In *Monselice: Storia, cultura e arte di un centro "minore" del Veneto,* edited by Antonio Rigon, 191–209. Canova: 1994.

Gallo, Rodolfo. 1967. *Il tesoro di S. Marco e la sua storia.* Venice and Rome: Istituto per la Collaborazione Culturale.

Gatari, Galeazzo, and Bartolomeo Gatari. 1909–32. *Cronaca carrarese.* Edited by A. Medin and G. Tolomei. Rerum Italicarum Scriptores, 2nd ser., tome 17, pt. 1. Bologna: Zanichelli.

Ghezzo, Michele Pietro, John R. Melville-Jones, and Andrea Rizzi, eds. 1999. *The Morosini Codex,* vol. 1: *To the Death of Andrea Dandolo (1354).* Padua: Unipress.

Gilbert, Felix. 1974. "Venice in the Crisis of the League of Cambrai." In

Renaissance Venice, edited by J. R. Hale, 274–92. London: Faber and Faber.

Gill, Joseph S. J. 1961a. *The Council of Florence.* Cambridge: Cambridge University Press.

Gill, Joseph S. J. 1961b. *Eugenius IV: Pope of Christian Union.* Westminster, MD: Newman Press.

Ginsborg, Paul. 1979. *Daniele Manin and the Venetian Revolution of 1848–49.* Cambridge: Cambridge University Press.

Girardi, Michele, and Franco Rossi. 1989. *Il teatro la Fenice: Cronologia degli spettacoli, 1792–1936.* Venice: Albrizzi Editore.

Girgensohn, Dieter. 1996. *Kirche, Politik und adelige Regierung in der Republik Venedig zu Beginn des 15. Jahrhunderts.* 2 vols. Göttingen: Vandenhoeck & Ruprecht.

Girgensohn, Dieter, ed. 2004. *Francesco Foscari: Promissione ducale, 1423.* Venice: La Malcontenta.

Girgensohn, Dieter. 2005. "In primis omnium rectum dimitto decimum: Kirchenzehnt und Legate pro anima in Venedig während des hohen und späteren Mittelalters." *Zeitschrift der Savigny-Stiftung für Rechtsgeschichte* 122:237–98.

Giustiniano, Bernardo. 1798. *Orazione recitata da Bernardo Giustiniano nell'esequie del doge Francesco Foscari.* In *Orazioni, elogi e vite scritte da letterati veneti patrizi in lode di dogi, ed altri illustri soggetti.* Edited by Girolamo Ascanio Molin, 2:21–59. 2nd edition. 2 vols. Venice: Tipografia di Antonio Curti.

Gleason, Elisabeth G. 1993. *Gasparo Contarini: Venice, Rome, and Reform.* Berkeley, Los Angeles, and Oxford: University of California Press.

Gleason, Elisabeth G. 2000. "Confronting New Realities: Venice and the Peace of Bologna, 1530." In *Venice Reconsidered: The History and Civilization of an Italian City-State, 1297–1797,* edited by John Martin and Dennis Romano, 168–84. Baltimore and London: Johns Hopkins University Press.

Goffen, Rona. 1986. *Piety and Patronage in Renaissance Venice: Bellini, Titian, and the Franciscans.* New Haven and London: Yale University Press.

Gori, Fabio. 1878–79. "Una memoria contemporanea del Doge Foscari." *Archivio storico artistico archeologico e letterario della città e provincia di Roma* 3:211.

Gothein, Percy. 1932. *Francesco Barbaro: Früh-humanismus und Staatskunst in Venedig.* Berlin: Verlag die Runde.

Goy, Richard J. 1992. *The House of Gold: Building a Palace in Medieval Venice.* Cambridge: Cambridge University Press.

Graham, Peter W. 1998. *Lord Byron.* New York: Twayne Publishers.

Graziato, Gisella, ed. 1986. *Le promissioni del doge di Venezia: Dalle origini alla fine del Duecento.* Venice: Il Commitato Editore.

Grendler, Paul F. 1989. *Schooling in Renaissance Italy: Literacy and Learning, 1300–1600.* Baltimore and London: Johns Hopkins University Press.

Greppi, Crescentino. 1913. "Le case degli Sforza a Venezia e Fra Simeone da Camerino." *Nuovo archivio veneto* n.s. 26:324–58.

Grubb, James S. 1986. "When Myths Lose Power: Four Decades of Venetian Historiography." *Journal of Modern History* 58:43–94.

Grubb, James S. 1988. *Firstborn of Venice: Vicenza in the Early Renaissance State*. Baltimore and London: Johns Hopkins University Press.

Grubb, James S. 2000. "Elite Citizens." In *Venice Reconsidered: The History and Civilization of an Italian City-State, 1297–1797*, edited by John Martin and Dennis Romano, 339–64. Baltimore and London: Johns Hopkins University Press.

Guerrini, Paolo. 1933. "Il monumento della vittoria di Maclodio." *Archivio storico lombardo* 60:338–50.

Guidi, Jacopo d'Albizzotto. 1995. *El sommo della condizione di Vinegia*. Edited by Marta Ceci. Rome: Zauli Arti Grafiche.

Guilland, Rodolphe. 1959. *Études Byzantines*. Paris: Presses Universitaires de France.

Gullino, Giuseppe. 1982. "Cocco, Cristoforo." *DBI* 26:516–18.

Gullino, Giuseppe. 1991. "Donà (Donati, Donato), Andrea." *DBI* 40:706–09.

Gullino, Giuseppe. 1996a. "Le frontiere navali." in *Storia di Venezia*, vol. 4: *Il Rinascimento: Politica e cultura*, edited by Alberto Tenenti and Ugo Tucci, 13–111. Rome: Istituto della Enciclopedia Italiana.

Gullino, Giuseppe. 1996b. "Il patriziato." in *Storia di Venezia*, vol. 4, *Il Rinascimento: Politica e cultura*, edited by Alberto Tenenti and Ugo Tucci,

379–413. Rome: Istituto della Enciclopedia Italiana.

Gullino, Giuseppe. 1996c. "L'evoluzione costituzionale." In *Storia di Venezia*, vol. 4: *Il Rinascimento: Politica e cultura*, edited by Alberto Tenenti and Ugo Tucci, 345–78. Rome: Istituto della Enciclopedia Italiana.

Gullino, Giuseppe. 1997. "Foscari, Alvise" (296), "Foscari, Filippo" (303–04), "Foscari, Francesco (detto Franzi)" (304–06), "Foscari, Francesco" (306–14), "Foscari, Jacopo" (323–25); "Foscari, Marco" (325–28), and "Foscari Niccolò" (333–35). *DBI* 49.

Gullino, Giuseppe. 2005a. "Loredan, Giacomo" (754–58), "Loredan, Pietro" (775–79). *DBI* 65.

Gullino, Giuseppe. 2005b. *La saga dei Foscari: Storia di un enigma*. Verona: Cierre Edizioni.

Gundersheimer, Werner L. 1973. *Ferrara: The Style of a Renaissance Despotism*. Princeton: Princeton University Press.

Gutkind, Kurt Sigmar. 1938. *Cosimo de' Medici: Pater Patriae, 1389–1464*. Oxford: Clarendon Press.

Haitsma Mulier, Eco O. G. 1980. *The Myth of Venice in Dutch Republican Thought in the Seventeenth Century*. Translated by Gerard T. Moran. Assen: Van Gorcum.

Hatfield, Rab. 1965. "Five Early Renaissance Portraits." *Art Bulletin* 47:315–34.

Hazlitt, W. Carew. 1966. *The Venetian Republic: Its Rise, its Growth, and its Fall, A.D. 409–1797*. Reprint of 1915 edition. 2 vols. New York: AMS Press, Inc.

Heinemann, Fritz. 1962–91. *Giovanni Bellini e i Belliniani*. 3 vols. Venice: Neri Pozza Editore (vols. 1–2) and Hildesheim: Georg Olms Verlag (vol. 3).

Hempel, Giulia and Kenneth Hempel. 1979. "Il degrado e le fasi del restauro." In *La Porta della Carta: I restauri*, edited by Serena Romano, 30–33. Venice: Tipo-Litografia Armena.

Hersey, George. L. 1973. *The Aragonese Arch at Naples, 1443–1475*. New Haven and London: Yale University Press.

Holgate, Ian. 2002. "Paduan Culture in Venetian Care: The Patronage of Bishop Pietro Donato (Padua 1428–47)." *Renaissance Studies* 16:1–23.

Hopkins, Andrew. 1998. "Architecture and *Infirmitas*: Doge Andrea Gritti and the Chancel of San Marco." *Journal of the Society of Architectural Historians* 57:182–97.

Howard, Deborah. 1975. *Jacopo Sansovino: Architecture and Patronage in Renaissance Venice*. New Haven and London: Yale University Press.

Howard, Deborah. 2000. *Venice and the East: The Impact of the Islamic World on Venetian Architecture 1100–1500*. New Haven and London: Yale University Press.

Hubala, Erich. 1965. "Venezia-Venedig." In *Oberitalien Ost*, 606–1004. Stuttgart: Philipp Reclam Jun.

Hurlburt, Holly S. 2006. *The Dogaressa of Venice, 1200–1500: Wife and Icon*. New York: Palgrave Macmillan.

Ilardi, Vincent. 1959. "The Italian League, Francesco Sforza, and Charles VII (1454–1461)." *Studies in the Renaissance* 6:129–66.

Jacoff, Michael. 1993. *The Horses of San Marco and the Quadriga of the Lord*. Princeton: Princeton University Press.

Joannides, Paul. 2001. "Delacroix and Modern Literature." In *The Cambridge Companion to Delacroix*, edited by Beth S. Wright, 130–53. Cambridge: Cambridge University Press.

Johnson, Dorothy. 2001. "Delacroix's Dialogue with the French Classical Tradition." In *The Cambridge Companion to Delacroix*, edited by Beth S. Wright, 108–29. Cambridge: Cambridge University Press.

Kent, Dale. 1978. *The Rise of the Medici: Faction in Florence, 1426–1434*. Oxford: Oxford University Press.

Kent, Dale. 2000. *Cosimo de' Medici and the Florentine Renaissance: The Patron's Oeuvre*. New Haven and London: Yale University Press.

Kent, F. W. 1995. "Individuals and Families as Patrons of Culture in Quattrocento Florence." In *Languages and Images of Renaissance Italy*, edited by Alison Brown, 171–92. Oxford: Clarendon Press.

Kent, F. W. 2004. *Lorenzo de' Medici and the Art of Magnificence*. Baltimore and London: Johns Hopkins University Press.

Kent, D. V., and F. W. Kent. 1982. *Neighbours and Neighbourhood in Renaissance Florence: The District of the Red Lion in the Fifteenth Century*. Locust Valley, NY: J. J. Augustin.

King, Margaret L. 1975. "Personal, Domestic, and Republican Values in the Moral Philosophy of Giovanni Caldiera." *Renaissance Quarterly* 28: 535–74.

King, Margaret L. 1986. *Venetian Humanism in an Age of Patrician Dominance*. Princeton: Princeton University Press.

King, Margaret L. 1989. "Umanesimo cristiano nella Venezia del Quattrocento." In *La chiesa di Venezia tra medioevo ed età moderna*, edited by Giovanni Vian, 15–45. Venice: Edizione per lo Studium Cattolico Veneziano.

King, Margaret L. 1994. *The Death of the Child Valerio Marcello*. Chicago and London: University of Chicago Press.

Klapisch-Zuber, Christiane. 1987. *Women, Family, and Ritual in Renaissance Italy*. Translated by Lydia C. Cochrane. Chicago and London: University of Chicago Press.

Knapton, Michael. 1986. "Guerra e finanza (1381–1508)." In Gaetano Cozzi and Michael Knapton, *Storia della Repubblica di Venezia: Dalla guerra di Chioggia alla riconquista della terraferma*, 273–353. Turin: UTET.

Knapton, Michael. 1998. "'Nobiltà e popolo' e un trentennio di storiografia veneta." *Nuova rivista storica* 82:167–92.

Kohl, Benjamin G. 1998. *Padua under the Carrara, 1318–1405*. Baltimore and London: Johns Hopkins University Press.

Labalme, Patricia H. 1969. *Bernardo Giustiniani: A Venetian of the Quattrocento*. Rome: Edizioni di Storia e Letteratura.

Lafontaine-Dosogne, Jacqueline. 1996. "Le rappresentazioni della vita della vergine e dell'infanzia di Cristo nelle sculture e nei mosaici di San Marco." In *San Marco: Aspetti storici e agiografici: Atti del convegno internazionale di studi. Venezia, 26–29 aprile 1994*, edited by Antonio Niero, 343–69. Venice: Marsilio.

Lane, Frederic C. 1944. *Andrea Barbarigo: Merchant of Venice, 1418–1449*. Baltimore: Johns Hopkins Press.

Lane, Frederic C. 1966. *Venice and History: The Collected Papers of Frederic C. Lane*. Baltimore: Johns Hopkins Press.

Lane, Frederic C. 1971. "The Enlargement of the Great Council of Venice." In *Florilegium Historiale: Essays Presented to Wallace K. Ferguson*, edited by J. G. Rowe and W. H. Stockdale, 236–74. Toronto: University of Toronto Press.

Lane, Frederic C. 1973. *Venice: A Maritime Republic*. Baltimore and London: Johns Hopkins University Press.

Lane, Frederic C. 1992. *Venetian Ships and Shipbuilders of the Renaissance*. Reprint of 1934 edition. Baltimore and London: Johns Hopkins University Press.

Law, John E. 2000. *Venice and the Veneto in the Early Renaissance*. Aldershot: Ashgate.

Lazzarini, Vittorio. 1895. *I Foscari: Conti e signori feudali*. Padua: Tipografia del Seminario.

Lazzarini, Vittorio. 1963. *Marino Faliero: Avanti il dogado, la congiura, appendici*. Florence: G. C. Sansoni.

Lightbown, Ronald. 1986. *Mantegna: With a Complete Catalogue of the Paintings, Drawings, and Prints*. Berkeley and Los Angeles: University of California Press.

Lonardi, Gilberto. 1976. "Il *Carmagnola*, Venezia e il 'potere inguisto'." In *Manzoni, Venezia e il Veneto*, edited by Vittore Branca, Ettore Caccia, and Cesare Galimberti, 19–41. Florence: Olschki.

Lorenzetti, Giulio. 1975. *Venice and its Lagoon: Historical-Artistic Guide*. Translated by John Guthrie. Trieste: Edizioni Lint.

Lorenzi, Giambattista. 1868. *Monumenti per servire alla storia del palazzo ducale di Venezia ovvero serie di atti pubblici dal 1253 al 1797*, pt I: *Dal 1253 al 1600*. Venice: Tipografia Marco Visentini.

Lowe, Kate. 2001. "Elections of Abbesses and Notions of Identity in Fifteenth- and Sixteenth Century Italy, with Special Reference to Venice." *Renaissance Quarterly* 54:389–429.

Luzzatto, Gino, ed. 1929. *I prestiti della repubblica di Venezia (sec. xiii–xv): Introduzione storica e documenti*. Padua: Libreria Editrice A. Draghi.

Luzzatto, Gino. 1954. "Sull'attendibilità di alcune statistiche economiche medioevali." In his *Studi di storia economica veneziana*, 271–84. Padua: Cedam.

Luzzatto, Gino. 1961. *Storia economica di Venezia dall'xi al xvi secolo*. Venice: Centro Internazionale delle Arti e del Costume.

Madden, Thomas F. 2003. *Enrico Dandolo and the Rise of Venice*. Baltimore and London: Johns Hopkins University Press.

Mallett, Michael E. 1967. *The Florentine Galleys in the Fifteenth Century*. Oxford: Clarendon Press.

Mallett, Michael E. 1974. "Venice and its Condottieri, 1404–54." In *Renaissance Venice*, edited by J. R. Hale, 121–45. London: Faber and Faber.

Mallett, Michael E. 1984. "The Military Organization of a Renaissance State, Part I: c. 1400 to 1508." In Michael E. Mallett and John R. Hale, *The Military Organization of a Renaissance State: Venice c. 1400 to 1617*, 1–210. Cambridge: Cambridge University Press.

Mallett, Michael E. 1996a. "La conquista della terraferma." In *Storia di Venezia*, vol. 4: *Il Rinascimento: Politica e cultura*, edited by Alberto Tenenti and Ugo Tucci, 181–244. Rome: Istituto della Enciclopedia Italiana.

Mallett, Michael E. 1996b. "Venezia e la politica italiana: 1454–1530." In *Storia di Venezia*, vol. 4: *Il Rinascimento: Politica e cultura*, edited by Alberto Tenenti and Ugo Tucci, 245–310. Rome: Istituto della Enciclopedia Italiana.

Manfredi, Fulgenzio. 1598. *Dodici tavole intagliate in rame nelle quali si dà la pianta della città di Venezia e sue isolette, si espone l'origine [. . .] coi ritratti e gli stemmi dei dogi*. Venice: G. B. Mazza and Gaetano Uccelli.

Manfroni, Camillo. 1908. "Gli studi storici in Venezia dal Romanin ad oggi." *Nuovo archivio veneto* 16:352–72.

Maranini, Giuseppe. 1974. *La costituzione di Venezia*. 2 vols. Reprint of 1927–31 edition. Florence: La Nuova Editrice.

Marcon, Susy. 2004. "Bellini, Leonardo." In *Dizionario biografico dei miniatori italiani, secoli ix–xvi*, edited by Milvia Bollati, 76–78. Milan: Edizioni Sylvestre Bonnard.

Marconato, Ruggiero. 2002. *Antonio Baratella (1385–1448): Vita, opera e cultura di un umanista padovano.* Cittadella: Biblioteca Cominiana.

Margaroli, Paolo. 1992. *Diplomazia e stati rinascimentali: Le ambascerie sforzesche fino alla conclusione della lega italica (1450–1455).* Florence: La Nuova Italia Editrice.

Martindale, Andrew. 1993. "The Venetian Sala del Gran Consilio and its Fourteenth-Century Decoration." *Antiquaries Journal* 73:76–124.

Marx, Barbara. 1978. "Venezia-Altera Roma? Ipotesi sull'umanesimo veneziano." *Quaderni del centro tedesco di studi veneziani* 10:3–18.

Mathews, Thomas F. 1993. *The Clash of Gods: A Reinterpretation of Early Christian Art.* Princeton: Princeton University Press.

Mattingly, Garrett. 1955. *Renaissance Diplomacy.* Boston: Houghton Mifflin Company.

Mazzatinti, Giuseppe, ed. 1903. *Annales Forolivienses ab origine urbis usque ad annum MCCCCLXXIII.* Rerum Italicarum Scriptores. 2nd ser., tome 22, pt. 2. Città di Castello: S. Lapi.

Mazzocca, Fernando, 1982. *Invito a Francesco Hayez.* Milan: Rusconi Libri.

Mazzocca, Fernando. 1994. "Pittura storica e melodramma: Il caso di Hayez." In *Scritti in onore di Nicola Mangini,* 55–60. Rome: Viella.

Mazzocca, Fernando. 1997. "The Renaissance Repertoire in the History Painting of Nineteenth-Century Italy." In *Reviving the Renaissance: The Use and Abuse of the Past in Nineteenth-Century Italian Art and Decoration,* edited by Rosanna Pavoni,

239–67. Cambridge: Cambridge University Press.

McManamon, John M. 1989. *Funeral Oratory and the Cultural Ideals of Italian Humanism.* Chapel Hill and London: University of North Carolina Press.

Menniti Ippolito, A. 1993. "Erasmo da Narni, detto il Gattamelata." *DBI* 43:46–52.

Merkel, Ettore. 1973. "Un problema di metodo: la 'Dormitio Virginis' dei Mascoli." *Arte veneta* 27:65–80.

Molà, Luca. 2000. *The Silk Industry of Renaissance Venice.* Baltimore and London: Johns Hopkins University Press.

Molho, Anthony. 1979. "Cosimo de' Medici: Pater Patriae or Padrino?" *Stanford Italian Review* 1:5–33.

Montobbio, Luigi. 1989. *Splendore e utopia nella Padova dei Carraresi.* Noventa Padovana: Corbo e Fiore Editori.

Morosini, Domenico. 1969. *De bene istituta re publica.* Edited by Claudio Finzi. Milan: Giuffré Editore.

Morosini, Domenico, and Ottaviano Morosini., eds. 1897. *Eletion del dose Francesco Foscari, 1423. (Nozze Widmann-Rezzonico/Foscari).* Conegliano: Tipo-Litografia Francesco Cagnani.

Mueller, Reinhold C. 1971. "The Procurators of San Marco in the Thirteenth and Fourteenth Centuries: A Study of the Office as a Financial and Trust Institution." *Studi veneziani* 13:105–220.

Mueller, Reinhold C. 1979a. "Catalogo: Dalla reazione alla prevenzione." In

Venezia e la peste: 1348/1797, 77–92. Venice: Marsilio.

Mueller, Reinhold C. 1979b. "Peste e demografia: Medioevo e Rinascimento." In *Venezia e la peste: 1348/1797*, 93–95. Venice: Marsilio.

Mueller, Reinhold C. 1997. *The Venetian Money Market: Banks, Panics, and the Public Debt 1200–1500*, Baltimore and London: Johns Hopkins University Press.

Muir, Edward. 1978. "The Doge as *primus inter pares*: Interregnum Rites in Early Sixteenth-Century Venice." In *Essays Presented to Myron P. Gilmore*, vol. 1: *History*, edited by Sergio Bertelli and Gloria Ramakus, 145–60. Florence: Nuova Italia Editrice.

Muir, Edward. 1979. "Images of Power: Art and Pageantry in Renaissance Venice." *American Historical Review* 84:16–52.

Muir, Edward. 1981. *Civic Ritual in Renaissance Venice*. Princeton: Princeton University Press.

Muraro, Michelangelo. 1961a. "La scala senza giganti." In *De artibus opuscula XL: Essays in Honor of Erwin Panofsky*, edited by Millard Meiss, 1:350–70. New York: New York University Press.

Muraro, Michelangelo. 1961b. "The Statutes of the Venetian *Arti* and the Mosaics of the Mascoli Chapel." *Art Bulletin* 43:263–74.

Musatti, Eugenio. 1888. *Storia della promissione ducale*. Padua: Tipografia del Seminario.

Neumann de' Rizzi, Ignazio. 1862. *Il palazzo del doge Francesco Foscari*

(Nozze Morosini-Costantini). Venice: Tip. del Commercio.

Nicol, Donald M. 1988. *Byzantium and Venice: A Study in Diplomatic and Cultural Relations*. Cambridge: Cambridge University Press.

Nogarola, Isotta. 1886. *Isotae Nogarolae veronensis opera quae supersunt omnia accedunt Angelae et Zeneverae Nogarolae epistolae et carmina*. Edited by Eugenius Abel. 2 vols. Budapest: Apud Gerold et Socios.

Nogarola, Isotta. 2004. *Complete Writings: Letterbook, Dialogue on Adam and Eve, Orations*. Edited and translated by Margaret L. King and Diana Robin. Chicago and London: University of Chicago Press.

O'Connell, Monique. 2004. "The Venetian Patriciate in the Mediterranean: Legal Identity and Lineage in Fifteenth-Century Crete." *Renaissance Quarterly* 57:466–93.

O'Connor, Robert H. 2003. "George Gordon, Lord Byron." In *Critical Survey of Drama*. 1:535–47. 2nd revised edition, updated by Gregory W. Lanier. 8 vols. Pasadena: Salem Press.

Ojetti, Ugo. 1923. *Cose viste*. Milan: Fratelli Treves.

Olivieri, A. 1982. "Condulmer, Francesco." *DBI* 27:761–65.

Ongania, Ferdinando. 1886. *Documenti per la storia dell'augusta ducale basilica di San Marco in Venezia dal nono secolo sino alla fine del decimo ottavo*. Venice: Tipografia Emiliana.

Palazzi, Giovanni. 1696. *Fasti ducales ab Anafesto I ad Silvestrum Valerium venetorum ducem cum eorum iconibus, insignibus, nummismatibus publicis, et privatis aere sculptis: inscriptionibus ex Aula M. Consilii, ac sepulchralibus.* Venice: Hieronymi Albrizzi.

Palmer, Richard J. 1979. "L'azione della Repubblica di Venezia nel controllo della peste." In *Venezia e la peste: 1348/1797*, 103–10. Venice: Marsilio.

Palmieri, Matteo. 1906. *Annales (AA. 1429–1474)*. Edited by Gino Scaramella. Rerum Italicarum Scriptores. 2nd ser., tome 26, pt. 1. Città di Castello: S. Lapi.

Paltroni, Pierantonio. 1966. *Commentari della vita et gesti dell'illustrissimo Federico Duca d'Urbino*. Edited by Walter Tommasoli. Urbino: Accademia Raffaello.

Paoletti, John, and Gary M. Radke. 2002. *Art in Renaissance Italy*. 2nd edition. Upper Saddle River, NJ: Prentice Hall, Inc., and Harry N. Abrams Publishers.

Paoletti, Pietro. 1893–97. *L'architettura e la scultura del Rinascimento in Venezia: Ricerche storico-artistiche*. 2 pts in 3 vols. Venice: Ongania-Naya Editori.

Paoletti, Pietro. 1929. *La scuola grande di San Marco*. Venice: Libreria Emiliana Editrice.

Papadopoli, Nicolò. 1892. *Francesco Foscari e le sue monete (1423–1457)*. Milan: Tipografia Editrice L. F. Cogliati.

Paruta, Paolo. 1852. *Opere politiche di Paolo Paruta*. Edited by C. Monzani. 2 vols. Florence: Felice Le Monnier.

Pavanello, Giuseppe, and Giandomenico Romanelli, eds. 1983. *Venezia nell'Ottocento: Immagini e mito*. Milan: Electa.

Pertusi, Agostino. 1965. "Quedam regalia insignia: Ricerche sulle insegne del potere ducale a Venezia durante il medioevo." *Studi veneziani* 7:3–123.

Pertusi, Agostino. 1970. "Gli inizi della storiografia umanistica nel Quattrocento." In *La storiografia veneziana fino al secolo xvi: Aspetti e problemi*, edited by Agostino Pertusi, 269–332. Florence: Leo S. Olschki Editore.

Pezzolo, Luciano. 1996. "La finanza pubblica: Dal prestito all'imposta." In *Storia di Venezia dalle origini alla caduta della Serenissima*, vol 5: *Il Rinascimento: Società ed economia*, edited by Alberto Tenenti and Ugo Tucci, 503–51. Rome: Istituto della Enciclopedia Italiana.

Piave, Francesco Maria, and Giuseppe Verdi. 1910. *I due Foscari: Tragedia lirica*. Sesto S. Giovanni: Casa Editrice Madella.

Piccolomini, Aeneas Silvius. 1991. *De viris illustribus*. Edited by Andrianus Van Heck. Vatican City: Biblioteca Apostolica Vaticana.

Piccolomini, Aeneas Silvius. 2001. *De Europa*. Edited by Adrianus Van Heck. Vatican City: Biblioteca Apostolica Vaticana.

Piccolomini, Aeneas Silvius [Pius II]. 2003. *Commentaries:* Vol. I, *Books I–II*. Edited by Margaret Meserve and Marcello Simonetta. Cambridge, MA, and London: Harvard University Press.

Picotti, G. B. 1908. "Dei 'Commentari del secondo anno' di Porcellio Pandoni e di un codice marciano che li contiene." *Archivio muratoriano* 1/6: 291–305.

Pillinini, Giovanni. 1963. "L'umanista veneziano Francesco Barbaro e l'origine della politica di equilibrio." *Archivio veneto* 5th ser., 72:23–27.

Pillinini, Giovanni. 1970. *Il sistema degli stati italiani, 1454–1494*. Venice: Libreria Universitaria Editrice.

Pincus, Debra. 1976. *The Arco Foscari: The Building of a Triumphal Gateway in Fifteenth-Century Venice*. New York and London: Garland Publishing, Inc.

Pincus, Debra. 2000a. *The Tombs of the Doges of Venice*. Cambridge: Cambridge University Press.

Pincus, Debra. 2000b. "Hard Times and Ducal Radiance: Andrea Dandolo and the Construction of the Ruler in Fourteenth-Century Venice." In *Venice Reconsidered: The History and Civilization of an Italian City-State*, edited by John Martin and Dennis Romano, 89–136. Baltimore and London: Johns Hopkins University Press.

Plant, Margaret. 2002. *Venice: Fragile City, 1979–1997*. New Haven and London: Yale University Press.

Poppi, Mario. 1972–73. "Un'orazione del cronista Lorenzo de Monacis per il millenario di Venezia (1421)." *Atti dell'istituto veneto di scienze, lettere ed arti: Classe di scienze morali, lettere ed arti* 131:463–97.

Povolo, Claudio. 2000. "The Creation of Venetian Historiography." In *Venice Reconsidered: The History and Civilization of an Italian City-State, 1297–1797*, edited by John Martin and Dennis Romano, 491–519. Baltimore and London: Johns Hopkins University Press.

Predelli, R., et al. 1876–1914. *I libri commemoriali della Republica di Venezia: Regesti*. Monumenti storici publicati dalla R. deputazione veneta di storia patria. 1st ser., Documenti. 8 vols. Venice: Tipografia Visentini.

Preto, Paolo. 1983. "Corner, Flaminio." *DBI* 29:191–93.

Preyer, Brenda. 1990. "L'archittetura del palazzo mediceo." In *Il Palazzo Medici Riccardi di Firenze*, edited by Giovanni Cherubini and Giovanni Fanelli, 58–75. Florence: Giunti.

Priuli, Girolamo. 1912–40. *I diarii di Girolamo Priuli*. Edited by Arturo Segre et al. Rerum Italicarum Scriptores. 2nd ser., tome 24, pt. 3, 4 vols. Bologna: Nicola Zanichelli.

Pullan, Brian. 1971. *Rich and Poor in Renaissance Venice: The Social Institutions of a Catholic State, to 1620*. Cambridge, MA: Harvard University Press.

Queller, Donald E. 1986. *The Venetian Patriciate: Reality versus Myth*. Urbana and Chicago: University of Illinois Press.

Radke, Gary M. 2001. "Nuns and their Art: The Case of San Zaccaria in Renaissance Venice." *Renaissance Quarterly* 54:430–59.

Raulich, Italo. 1888. "La prima guerra fra i veneziani e Filippo Maria Visconti." *Rivista storica italiana* 5:441–68, 661–96.

Raulich, Italo. 1890. *La caduta dei Carraresi signori di Padova con documenti*. Padua. Drucker & Senigalia.

Ravegnani, G. 1997. "Foscari, Giovanni" (320–21) and "Foscari, Paolo" (336–38). *DBI* 49.

Righetti, Marilia. 1993. *Il santuario di S. Maria di Monteortone*. Padua: Editoriale Programma.

Rizzi, Alberto. 1987. *Scultura esterna a Venezia: Corpus delle sculture erratiche all'aperto di Venezia e della sua laguna*. Venice: Stamperia di Venezia Editrice.

Rizzi, Alberto. 2001. *I leoni di San Marco: Il simbolo della Repubblica veneta nella scultura e nella pittura*. 2 vols. Venice: Arsenale Editrice.

Rollo-Koster, Joëlle. 2003. "The Politics of Body Parts: Contested Topographies in Late-Medieval Avignon." *Speculum* 78:66–98.

Romanin, Samuele. 1972–75. *Storia documentata di Venezia*. 3rd edition. 10 vols. Venice: Filippi Editore.

Romano, Dennis. 1984. "Charity and Community in Early Renaissance Venice." *Journal of Urban History* 11:63–82.

Romano, Dennis. 1987a. "The Aftermath of the Querini-Tiepolo Conspiracy in Venice." *Stanford Italian Review* 7:147–59.

Romano, Dennis. 1987b. *Patricians and Popolani: The Social Foundations of the Venetian Renaissance State*. Baltimore: Johns Hopkins University Press.

Romano, Dennis. 1996. *Housecraft and Statecraft: Domestic Service in Renaissance Venice, 1400–1600*. Baltimore: Johns Hopkins University Press.

Romano, Dennis. 1998. "'Molto ben sepe guidar la optima constelation sua': Francesco Foscari as Procurator of San Marco." *Studi veneziani* n.s. 36:37–55.

Romano, Dennis. 2003. "Doge Francesco Foscari in America." *Studi veneziani* n.s. 46:407–15.

Romano, Dennis. 2005. "Vecchi, poveri, e impotenti: The Elderly in Renaissance Venice." In *At the Margins: Minority Groups in Premodern Italy*, edited by Stephen J. Milner, 249–71. Minneapolis and London: University of Minnesota Press.

Romano, Giacinto. 1890. "Filippo Maria Visconti e i Turchi." *Archivio storico lombardo* 2nd ser., 7:585–618.

Romano, Serena, ed. 1979. *La porta della carta: I restauri*. Venice: Tipo-Litografia Armena.

Romanticismo storico: Firenze, La Meridiana di Palazzo Pitti: Dicembre 1973/Febbraio 1974. 1974. Florence: Centro di Edizioni.

Rondinini, Gigliola Soldi. 1982. "Milano, il regno di Napoli e gli aragonesi (secoli xiv–xv)." In *Gli Sforza a Milano e in Lombardia e i loro rapporti con gli stati italiani ed europei (1450–1535)*, 229–90. Milan: Cisalpino-Goliardica.

Rosand, David. 1984. "*Venetia figurata*: The Iconography of a Myth." In *Interpretazioni veneziane: Studi di storia dell'arte in onore di Michelangelo Muraro*, edited by David Rosand, 177–96. Venice: Arsenale Editrice.

Rosand, David. 2001. *Myths of Venice: The Figuration of a State*. Chapel Hill and London: University of North Carolina Press.

Rosselli, John. 1984. *The Opera Industry in Italy from Cimarosa to Verdi: The Role of the Impresario*. Cambridge: Cambridge University Press.

Rossi, Vittorio. 1893. "Jacopo d'Albizzotto Guidi e il suo inedito poema su Venezia." *Nuovo archivio veneto* 5:397–451.

Rubieri, Ermolao. 1879. *Francesco Primo Sforza: Narrazione storica.* 2 vols. Florence: Successori le Monnier.

Rubinstein, Nicolai. 1974. "Italian Reactions to Terraferma Expansion in the Fifteenth Century." In *Renaissance Venice,* edited by J. R. Hale, 197–217. London: Faber and Faber.

Runciman, Steven. 1965. *The Fall of Constantinople, 1453.* Cambridge: Cambridge University Press.

Ruskin, John. 1860. *The Stones of Venice.* 3 vols. New York: J. Wiley. First published 1851–53.

Ryder, Alan. 1990. *Alfonso the Magnanimous: King of Aragon, Naples and Sicily, 1396–1458.* Oxford: Clarendon Press.

Sabbadini, Remigio. 1896. "Guarino Veronese e la polemica sul Carmagnola." *Nuovo archivio veneto* 11:327–61.

Sabellico, Marco Antonio. 1556. *Historiae rerum Venetarum ab urbe condita, libri xxxiii.* Basel: Nic. Episcopium Iuniorem.

Sagredo, Agostino. 1839. *San Cristoforo della Pace.* Venice: Tipografia di Alvisopoli.

Sansovino, Francesco [Girolamo Bardi fiorentino]. 1587. *Delle cose notabili della città di Venetia, libri II.* Venice: Felice Valgrisio. First published 1556.

Sansovino, Francesco. 1968. *Venetia città nobilissima et singolare con le aggiunte di Giustiniano Martinioni.* Additions by Martinioni, 1663, to edition of 1581. Reprint. Venice: Filippi Editore.

[Sanudo] Sanuto, Marino. 1733. *Vitae ducum venetorum italice scriptae ab origine urbis, sive ab anno CCCCXXI. usque ad annum MCCCCXCIII.* Rerum Italicarum Scriptores. Edited by L. A. Muratori, 1st ser., tome 22. Milan: Ex Typographia Societatis Palatinae.

[Sanudo] Sanuto, Marin. 1847. *Itinerario di Marin Sanuto per la terraferma veneziana nell'anno MCCCCLXXXIII.* Edited by Rawdon Brown. Padua: Tipografia del Seminario.

Sanudo, Marin il Giovane. 1980. *De origine, situ et magistribus urbis Venetae ovvero la città di Venetia (1493–1530).* Edited by Angela Caracciolo Aricò. Milan: Cisalpino-La Goliardica.

Sanudo, Marin il Giovane. 1989. *Le vite dei dogi (1474–1494).* Edited by Angela Caracciolo Aricò. Padua: Editrice Antenore.

Sanudo, Marin il Giovane. 1999. *Le vite dei dogi: 1423–1474: I tomo (1423–1457).* Edited by Angela Caracciolo Aricò. Transcription by Chiara Frison. Venice: La Malcontenta.

Sardella, Pierre. 1948. *Nouvelles et spéculations a Venise au début du xvie siècle.* Paris: Librairie Armand Colin.

Sarnelli, Mauro. 2004. "Premesse per la delineazione di figure protagonistiche nella storiografia dell' umanesimo: il rex/princeps/dux belli (e pacis)." *Studi veneziani* n.s. 48:15–39.

Sartori, Fabiola, ed. 2001. *La casa grande dei Foscari in volta de canal: Documenti.* Venice: La Malcontenta.

Saxl, F. 1957. *Lectures.* 2 vols. London: Warburg Institute.

Scher, Stephen K. 1994. *The Currency of Fame: Portrait Medals of the Renaissance.* New York: Harry N. Abrams, Inc.

Schulz, Anne Markham. 1978a. *Niccolò di Giovanni Fiorentino and Venetian*

Sculpture of the Early Renaissance. New York: New York University Press.

Schulz, Anne Markham. 1978b. *The Sculpture of Giovanni and Bartolomeo Bon and their Workshop*. Transactions of the American Philosophical Society. Vol. 68, pt. 3. Philadelphia: American Philosophical Society.

Schulz, Anne Markham. 1983. *Antonio Rizzo: Sculptor and Architect*. Princeton: Princeton University Press.

Schulz, Anne Markham. 1996. "Further Thoughts on Niccolò di Giovanni Fiorentino in Dalmatia and Italy." In *Quattrocento Adriatico: Fifteenth-Century Art of the Adriatic Rim*, edited by Charles Dempsey, 143–62. Bologna: Nuova Alfa Editoriale.

Schulz, Anne Markham. 1999. "Niccolò di Giovanni Fiorentino in Venice: The Documentary Evidence." *Burlington Magazine* 141:749–52.

Schulz, Juergen. 1991. "Urbanism in Medieval Venice." In *City States in Classical Antiquity and Medieval Italy*, edited by Anthony Molho, Kurt Raaflaub, and Julie Emlen, 419–45. Stuttgart: Franz Steiner Verlag.

Schulz, Juergen. 2004. *The New Palaces of Medieval Venice*. University Park, PA: Pennsylvania State University Press.

Segarizzi, A. 1903. "Antonio Carabello: Umanista bergamasco del secolo xv." *Archivio storico lombardo* 3rd ser., 30: 470–83.

Segarizzi, A. 1904. "Lauro Quirini umanista veneziano del secolo xv." *Memorie della R. accademia delle scienze di Torino*, 2nd ser., 54:1–28.

Segarizzi, A. 1916. "Contributo alla storia delle congiure padovane." *Nuovo archivio veneto* n.s. 31:48–78.

Seneca, Federico. 1959. *Il doge Leonardo Donà: La sua vita e la sua preparazione politica prima del dogado*. Padua: Antenore.

Senatore, Francesco. 1998. *"Uno Mundo de Carta": Forme e strutture della diplomazia sforzesca*. Naples: Liguori Editore.

Setton, Kenneth M. 1978. *The Papacy and the Levant (1204–1571)*, vol. 2: *The Fifteenth Century*. Philadelphia: American Philosophical Society.

Shaw, Christine. 2005. "Principles and Practice in the Civic Government of Fifteenth-Century Genoa." *Renaissance Quarterly* 58:45–90.

Sinding-Larsen, Staale, 1974. *Christ in the Council Hall: Studies in the Religious Iconography of the Venetian Republic*. Istitutum Romanum Norvegiae, Acta ad Archaeologiam et Artium Historiam Pertinentia 5. Rome: "L'erma" di Bretschneider.

Sismonde de Sismondi, J. C. L. 1807–18. *Histoire des Républiques Italiennes du Moyen Age*. 16 vols. Paris: Treuttel and Würtz.

Skinner, Quentin. 2002. *Visions of Politics*, vol. 2: *Renaissance Virtues*. Cambridge: Cambridge University Press.

Soranzo, Giovanni, ed. 1915. *Cronaca di anonimo veronese, 1446–1488*. Monumenti storici pubblicati dalla R. deputazione veneta di storia patria. 3rd ser. (Cronache e Diarii), vol. 4. Venice: A spese della società.

Soranzo, Giovanni. 1924. *La lega italica (1454–1455)*. Milan: Società Editrice "Vita e pensiero."

Soranzo, G. 1957. "L'ultima campagna del Gattamelata al servizio della Repubblica veneta (luglio 1438-gennaio 1440)." *Archivio veneto* 5th ser., 60–61:79–114.

Sphrantzes, George [Phrantzes, Georgios]. 1980. *The Fall of Constantinople: A Chronicle by George Sphrantzes, 1401–1477.* Translated by Marios Philippides. Amherst: University of Massachusetts Press.

Stahl, Alan M. 1995. "The Deathbed Oration of Doge Mocenigo and the Venetian Mint." *Mediterranean Historical Review* 10:284–301.

Stahl, Alan M. 2000. *Zecca: The Mint of Venice in the Middle Ages.* Baltimore and London: Johns Hopkins University Press.

Stahl, Alan M. 2001. "Numismatic Portraiture in Renaissance Venice." *Quaderni ticinesi: Numismatica e antichità classiche* 30:305–12.

Stöckly, Doris. 1995. *Le système de l'incanto des galées du marché à Venise (fin xiiie-milieu xve siècle).* Leiden: E. J. Brill.

Symonds, John Addington. 1888. *Renaissance in Italy: The Age of the Despots.* New York: Henry Holt and Company.

Syropoulos, Sylvestre. 1971. *Les "Mémoires" du Grand Ecclésiarque de l'Église de Constantinople Sylvestre Syropoulos sur le concile de Florence (1439–1439).* Edited by V. Laurent. Paris: Éditions du Centre National de la Recherche Scientifique.

Tafuri, Manfredo, ed. 1984. *"Renovatio urbis": Venezia nell'età di Andrea Gritti (1523–1538).* Rome: Officina Edizioni.

Tarducci, Francesco. 1899. "L'alleanza Visconti-Gonzaga del 1438 contro la Republica di Venezia." *Archivio storico lombardo* 3rd ser., 11:265–329.

Tassini, Giuseppe. 1970. *Curiosità veneziane ovvero origini delle denominazioni stradali di Venezia.* 8th edition. Venice: Filippi Editore.

Tenenti, Alberto. 1996. "Il senso dello stato." In *Storia di Venezia dalle origini alla caduta della Serenissima,* vol. 4: *Il Rinascimento: Politica e cultura,* edited by Alberto Tenenti and Ugo Tucci, 311–44. Rome: Istituto della Enciclopedia Italiana.

Thiriet, F. ed. 1958–61. *Régestes des délibérations du sénat de Venise concernant la Romanie.* 3 vols. Paris: Mouton.

Thomas, George Martin, ed. 1969. *Diplomatarium Veneto-Levantinum sive acta et diplomata res venetas graecas atque levantis.* 2 vols. Reprint of 1880–89 edition. New York: Burt Franklin.

Tomasino, Giacomo Filippo. 1644. *Historia della B. Vergine di Monte Ortone [. . .] e la vita di Fr. Simone da Camerino fondatore di essa.* Padua: Giovanni Battista Pasquali.

Trevor-Roper, Hugh. 1965. "Doge Francesco Foscari." In *Renaissance Profiles,* edited by J. H. Plumb, 107–21. New York: Harper and Row.

Trexler, Richard C. 1978. *The Libro Cerimoniale of the Florentine Republic by Francesco Filarete and Angelo Manfidi: Introduction and Text.* Geneva: Librarie Droz S. A.

Trexler, Richard C. 1980. *Public Life in Renaissance Florence.* New York: Academic Press.

Troilo, Sigfrido. 1932. *Andrea Giuliano: Politico e letterato veneziano del Quattrocento*. Geneva and Florence: Leo S. Olschki.

Vast, Henri. 1977. *Le Cardinal Bessarion, 1403–1472: Étude sur la Chrétienté et la Renaissance vers le milieu du xve siècle*. Reprint of 1878 edition. Geneva: Slatkine-Megariotis Reprints.

Vecchiato, Edoardo. 1898. *I Foscari ed i Loredano*. Padua.

Venezia e la peste: 1348/1797. 1979. Venice: Marsilio.

Verdi, Giuseppe, and Francesco Maria Piave. 1968. *I due Foscari: Opera in Three Acts*. Translated by Dorle J. Soria. New York: Franco Colombo.

Vianoli, Alessandro Maria. 1680–84. *Historia veneta*. 2 vols. Venice: Gio. Giacomo Hertz.

Walsh, Katherine. 1979. "Cazzuli, Agostino." *DBI* 23:182–84.

Walsh, Katherine. 1989. "La congregazione riformata di Monte Ortone nel veneto." *Rivista di storia della chiesa in Italia* 43:80–100.

Weber, Annette. 1993. *Venezianische Dogensporträts des 16. Jahrhunderts*. Sigmaringen: Jan Thorbecke Verlag.

Wiel, Alethea, 1891. *Two Doges of Venice; being a slight sketch of the lives and times of Tomaso Mocenigo and Francesco Foscari*. London: Chiswick Press.

Wills, Garry. 2001. *Venice: Lion City: The Religion of Empire*. New York: Simon and Schuster.

Wilson, Bronwen. 2005. *The World in Venice: Print, the City, and Early Modern Identity*. Toronto: University of Toronto Press.

Wirobisz, André. 1965. "L'attività edilizia a Venezia nel xiv e xv secolo." *Studi veneziani* 7:307–43.

Wolters, Wolfgang. 1976. *La scultura gotica veneziana (1300–1460)*. 2 vols. Venice: Alfieri Edizioni d'Arte.

Wolters, Wolfgang. 1994. "L'architettura civile." In *Storia di Venezia: Temi: L'arte*, edited by Rodolfo Pallucchini, 305–41. Rome: Istituto della Enciclopedia Italiana.

Woods-Marsden, Joanna. 2001. "Portrait of the Lady, 1430–1520." In *Virtue and Beauty: Leonardo's Ginevra de'Benci and Renaissance Portraits of Women*, edited by David Alan Brown, 63–87. Princeton: Princeton University Press.

Zaccaria, R. 1991. "Dolfin, Pietro." *DBI* 40:562–65.

Zamperetti, Sergio. 1991 *I piccoli principi: Signorie locali, feudi e comunità soggette nello stato regionale veneto dall'espansione territoriale ai primi decenni del '600*. Treviso: Il Cardo.

Zanetti, Ginevra. 1961. "Il dominio Visconteo dall'avvento di Gian Galeazzo alla caduta di Pandolfo Malatesta." In *Storia di Brescia*, vol. 1: *Dalle origini alla caduta della signoria Viscontea (1426)*, edited by Giovanni Treccani degli Alfieri, 856–76. Brescia: Morcelliana Editrice.

Zannini, Andrea. 1996. "L'impiego pubblico." In *Storia di Venezia dalle origini alla caduta della Serenissima*, vol. 4: *Il Rinascimento: Politica e cultura*, edited by Alberto Tenenti and Ugo Tucci, 415–63. Rome: Istituto della Enciclopedia Italiana.

Zannoni, Maria. 1941–42. "Giorgio Dolfin, cronista veneziano del sec.

xv." *Memorie della R. Accademia di scienze, lettere ed arti in Padova* 58:5–23.

Zannoni, Maria. 1942. "Il dramma dei Foscari nella cronaca di Giorgio Dolfin." *Nuova rivista storica* 26:201–15.

Zoccoletto, Giorgio. 1999. *La contea dei Foscari a Zelarino*. Mestre: Tipolitografia F.lli Liberalato.

Zorzi, Marino, ed. 1988. *Biblioteca Marciana, Venezia*. Florence: Nardini Editore.

INDEX